Accounting Theory

TEXT AND READINGS

ACCOUNTING TEXTBOOKS FROM JOHN WILEY & SONS

Accounting Theory

TEXT AND READINGS

Third Edition

Richard G. Schroeder
The University of Texas at El Paso

Levis D. McCullers
Hagyard-Davidson-McGee DVM

Myrtle Clark
The University of Kentucky

John Wiley and Sons

New York Chichester Brisbane Toronto Singapore

Material from the Uniform CPA Examination
Questions and Unofficial Answers, Copyright ©
1972–1986 by the American Institute of Certified
Public Accountants, Inc., is reprinted with permission.

Library of Congress Cataloging in Publication Data:

Accounting theory.

  Includes index.
  1. Accounting. 2. Accounting—Problems, exercises,
etc. I. Schroeder, Richard G. II. McCullers, Levis D.,
1936–   . III. Clark, Myrtle.
HF5625.A25 1987   657   86-15966
ISBN 0-471-81891-7

Printed in the United States of America

10 9 8 7 6 5 4 3 2

Preface

As the literature of financial accounting theory is expanding at an ever increasing rate, today's accounting student has the monumental task of attempting to assimilate and evaluate readings from various sources. While the point of general agreement on a theory of accounting has yet to be reached, there are certain concepts and principles that have general acceptance. The objective of this book is to provide the student with a framework within which to operate by discussing various financial accounting topics and expanding upon these topics by including readings directly connected with each of the chapters.

The text part of the book is primarily a descriptive interpretation of the Opinions and Standards issued by the Accounting Principles Board (APB) and the Financial Accounting Standards Board (FASB). The readings at the end of each chapter were selected either to provide additional discussion of complex material or a dissenting opinion from current generally accepted accounting principles (GAAP). Additionally, each chapter contains several multiple-choice and essay questions related to the text material. Adapted from recent Uniform CPA Examinations, these questions provide exposure to the types of issues the Board of Examiners has stressed in recent years.

This book is designed to be used by undergraduate accounting students as well as graduate students and those wishing to review for the theory section of the Uniform CPA Examination. The hope is that this work will provide students with a broader view of accounting theory than can be provided by using only techniques and procedures.

This book may be used in several ways: (1) It may be used by itself in a course that is descriptive of existing accounting theory while critically examining alternatives to current practice through the use of the articles contained at the end of each chapter. (2) It may be used in a course designed to explore existing accounting theory in depth. In such a course, the text material could be used in conjunction with Commerce Clearing House Accounting Principles—Current Edition. (3) It may be used in a normative accounting theory course in which the text is supplemented by the use of the discussion memoranda that preceded the issuance of APB Opinion and FASB Statements. (4) It may used in a course designed to evaluate the conclusion reached by the APB and FASB through the use of the research articles contained at the end of each chapter and the supplemental readings.

We are indebted to many colleagues whose comments and criticisms contributed to the third edition and we single out for special thanks to Professor J. David Fred of Indiana University at South Bend, Professor Joseph Hilmy of George Washington University, Professor Janet Omundson of the University of Texas at El Paso, Professor Deborah Pavelka of the University of Texas at El Paso, Professor Karl Putnam of the University of Texas at El Paso, Professor Mary Stevens of the Univeristy of Texas at El Paso, and Professor Lynn Thomas of Kansas State University. We are also indebted to our research assistants, Abelardo Munoz and Tammy Vasilatos; their contributions were invaluable, as was the assistance provided by our typist, Guadalupe Talavera. Appreciation is also extended to our editorial and production staff including Lucille Sutton, Ann Meader and Elizabeth Meder. Finally, we thank the American Institute of Certified Public Accountants for permission to use materials adapted from the Uniform CPA Examinations.

Richard G. Schroeder
Levis D. McCullers
Myrtle Clark

Contents

1

SOURCE
AND
METHODOLOGY
OF
ACCOUNTING
PRINCIPLES

Accounting records dating back several thousand years have been found in various parts of the world. These records indicate that at all levels of development people desire information about their efforts and accomplishments. For example, the Zenon papyri, which were discovered in 1915, contain information about the construction projects, agricultural activities, and business operations of the private estate of Apollonius for a period of about thirty years during the third century B.C.

According to Hain, "The Zenon papyri give evidence of a surprisingly elaborate accounting system which had been used in Greece since the fifth century B.C. and which, in the wake of Greek trade or conquest, gradually spread throughout the Eastern Mediterranean and Middle East."[1] The accounting system used by Zenon contained provisions for responsibility accounting, a written record of all transactions, a personal account for wages paid to employees, inventory records, and a record of asset acquisitions and disposals. In addition, there is evidence that all of the accounts were audited.[2]

Although the Zenon papyri and other records indicate accounting *practice* has a long history, most organized efforts at developing accounting *theory* have occurred since 1930. Individual writers such as Sprague, Hatfield, Kester, and Paton made significant contributions before that time (in the early 1900s), but those contributions did not receive widespread acceptance and did not have the influence of the more organized efforts of recent years.

[1]H. P. Hain, "Accounting Control in the Zenon Papyri," *The Accounting Review* (October 1966), p. 699.
[2]Ibid., pp. 700–701.

1

One of the first attempts at improving accounting began shortly after the Great Depression with a series of meetings between representatives of the New York Stock Exchange (NYSE) and the American Institute of Accountants (now American Institute of Certified Public Accountants or AICPA). The purpose of these meetings was to discuss problems pertaining to the interests of investors, the NYSE, and accountants in the preparation of external financial statements.

Similarly, in 1935 the American Association of University Instructors in Accounting changed its name to the American Accounting Association (AAA) and announced its intention to expand its activities in the research and development of accounting principles and standards. The first result of these expanded activities was the publication, in 1936, of a brief report cautiously titled ''A Tentative Statement of Accounting Principles Underlying Corporate Financial Statements.'' The four-and-one-half-page document summarized the significant concepts underlying financial statements at that time.

These activities are cited simply to illustrate that the history of accounting theory is relatively short. Thus, when accounting is compared to professions that have had a theoretical base for hundreds of years, it is readily apparent why so much remains to be done in developing a coherent and consistent theoretical basis for the practice of accounting.

One result of the meetings between the AICPA and members of the NYSE was a revision in the wording of the certificate issued by CPAs. The opinion paragraph formerly said something to the effect that the financial statements had been examined and were accurate. The terminology was changed to say that the statements are ''fairly presented in accordance with generally accepted accounting principles.'' This expression is now interpreted as encompassing the conventions, rules, and procedures that are necessary to explain accepted accounting practice at a given time. Therefore, financial statements are fair only to the extent that the principles are fair and the statements comply with the principles.

The expression *generally accepted accounting principles* (GAAP) has thus come to play a significant role in the accounting profession. The precise meaning of the term, however, has evolved rather slowly. In addition to official pronouncements promulgated by authoritative organizations, another method of developing principles is to determine whether other accountants are actually following the particular practice in question. There is no need for complete uniformity; rather, when faced with a particular transaction, the accountant is to review the literature and current practice to determine if a treatment similar to the one proposed is being used. For example, if many accountants are using sum-of-years-digits (S-Y-D) depreciation for assets, this method becomes a GAAP. In the theoretical sense, depreciation may not even be a principle; however, according to accounting theory formation, if many accountants are using S-Y-D, it becomes a GAAP.

Another example of the approach to establishing GAAP is illustrated by the last in, first out (Lifo) inventory method. The use of Lifo inventory was originally sanctioned by the Internal Revenue Service under a particular set of circumstances. Because Lifo inventory will result in lower income taxes during periods of rising prices, more and more people begin searching for those special circumstances in order to use Lifo. Over time many firms began using Lifo, and Lifo acquired the status of a GAAP; therefore, anyone could use Lifo and the CPA could attest that the statements were prepared in accordance with GAAP.

According to the Accounting Principles Board (APB), generally accepted accounting principles

> *incorporate the consensus at any time as to which economic resources and obligations should be recorded as assets and liabilities, which changes in them should be recorded, when these changes should be recorded, how the recorded assets and liabilities and changes in them should be measured, what information should be disclosed and how it should be disclosed, and which financial statements should be prepared.*[3]

This statement does not mean that a GAAP is based on what is most appropriate or reasonable in a given situation but simply that the practice represents a consensus. However, even this definition lacks clarity, since a variety of practices may exist despite a consensus in favor of one or the other. For example, such variation occurs in inventory and depreciation methods.

In 1975 the Auditing Standards Executive Committee of the AICPA issued its Statement on Auditing Standards (SAS) No. 5 with the purpose of explaining the meaning of the phrase "present fairly . . . in conformity with generally accepted accounting principles" as used in the report of independent auditors. According to the committee, the auditor's opinion on the fairness of an entity's financial statements in conformity with GAAP should be based upon his judgment as to whether

> *(a) the accounting principles selected and applied have general acceptance; (b) the accounting principles are appropriate in the circumstances; (c) the financial statements, including the related notes, are informative of matters that may affect their use, understanding, and interpretation; (d) the information presented in the financial statements is classified and summarized in a reasonable manner, that is, neither too detailed nor too condensed; and (e) the financial statements reflect the underlying events and transactions in a manner that presents the financial position, results of operations, and changes in financial position stated within a range of acceptable limits, that*

[3]Accounting Principles Board Statement No. 4, "Basic Concepts and Accounting Principles Underlying Financial Statements of Business Enterprises" (New York: American Institute of Certified Public Accountants, 1970), par. 27.

is, limits that are reasonable and practicable to attain in financial statements.[4]

A GAAP thus serves to provide the auditor with a framework for making judgments about the fairness of financial statements on the basis of some uniform standard.

The most precise criterion that has been set forth for determining whether a practice has gained the stature of a GAAP was set forth by the AICPA and NYSE committee. Those principles having "substantial authoritative support" were to be classified as GAAP. The meaning of the term was not specifically defined at that time, and no single source exists for all established accounting principles. However, Rule 203 of the AICPA Code of Professional Ethics requires compliance with accounting principles promulgated by the body designated by the Council of the Institute to establish such principles, except in unusual circumstances. (Currently that body is the Financial Accounting Standards Board [FASB].)

Later, SAS No. 5 was amended by SAS No. 43. This amendment classified the order of priority that an auditor should follow in determining whether an accounting principle is generally accepted. Also, it added to the sources of established accounting principles certain types of pronouncements that did not exist when SAS No. 5 was issued. This release noted that the determination that a particular accounting principle is generally accepted may be difficult because no single source exists for all such principles. The sources of generally accepted accounting principles were identified as

1. Pronouncements of an authoritative body designated by the AICPA Council to establish accounting principles, pursuant to Rule 203 of the AICPA Code of Professional Ethics (FASB Statements, FASB Interpretations, APB Opinions, Accounting Research Bulletins).
2. Pronouncements of bodies composed of expert accountants that follow a due process procedure, including broad distribution of proposed accounting principles for public comment, for the intended purpose of establishing accounting principles or describing existing practices that are generally accepted (AICPA Industry Audit Guides).
3. Practices or pronouncements that are widely recognized as being generally accepted because they represent prevalent practice in a particular industry or the knowledgeable application to specific circumstances of pronouncements that are generally accepted (FASB Technical Bulletins).
4. Other accounting literature.[5]

[4]Statement on Auditing Standards No. 5, "The Meaning of 'Present Fairly in Conformity with Generally Accepted Accounting Principles' in the Independent Auditor's Report" (New York: American Institute of Certified Public Accountants, 1975), par. 4.
[5]Statement on Auditing Standards No. 43, "Omnibus Statement on Auditing Standards" (New York: American Institute of Certified Public Accountants, 1982), par. 5–7.

These recommendations have evolved from the sources identified by the Accounting Principles Board in 1964 for determining whether an accounting practice had substantial authoritative support. Those sources were

1. Published opinions by committees of the AICPA.
2. Published opinions by committees of the AAA.
3. Affirmative opinions of practicing and academic certified public accountants.
4. Regulations and opinions issued by the Securities and Exchange Commission (SEC).
5. Pronouncements by other regulatory agencies about the accounting to be employed in reporting to the agency.
6. Practices commonly found in business.
7. Writings and opinions of individual accountants found in textbooks and articles.

In this chapter and throughout much of the book, special attention will be given to the pronouncements referred to in Rule 203 of the AICPA Code of Professional Ethics. The reason for this special attention is apparent: Practicing CPAs have an ethical obligation to consider such pronouncements as the primary source of generally accepted accounting principles in their exercise of judgment as to the fairness of financial statements. Opposing views as well as alternative treatments will be considered in the text narrative and in the selected articles; however, the reader should keep in mind the significance of the primary source in current practice.

THE AICPA AND ACCOUNTING PRINCIPLES

The American Institute of Certified Public Accountants established several committees and boards to deal with the need for further development of accounting principles. Among these were the Committee on Accounting Procedure (CAP), the Accounting Principles Board (APB), and the Financial Accounting Standards Board (FASB). Each of these bodies has issued pronouncements on accounting issues as discussed later. In each case the pronouncements are intended to apply to current and future financial statements and are not intended to be applied retroactively unless the pronouncement makes retroactive presentation mandatory.

COMMITTEE ON ACCOUNTING PROCEDURE

Professional accountants became more actively involved in the development of accounting principles following the meetings between members of the New York Stock Exchange and the AICPA. In 1938 the AICPA's Committee on Accounting Procedure was formed. This committee had the authority to issue pronouncements on matters of accounting practice and procedure in order to establish generally accepted practices. The works of the committee were published in the form of Accounting Research Bulletins (ARBs); however, such pronouncements did not dictate mandatory practice and received authority only from their general acceptance.

These publications were consolidated in 1953 into Accounting Terminology Bulletin No. 1, "Review and Resume,"[6] and Accounting Research Bulletin No. 43.[7] From 1953 until 1959 Accounting Research Bulletins No. 44 through No. 51 were published. The recommendations of these bulletins, which have not been superseded, are contained throughout this text where the specific topics covered by the ARBs are discussed.

ACCOUNTING PRINCIPLES BOARD

By 1959 the methods of formulating accounting principles were being criticized, and wider representation in the formation of accounting principles was sought by accountants and financial statement users. The AICPA reacted by forming the Accounting Principles Board. This body had as its objectives the advancement of the written expression of generally accepted accounting principles, the narrowing of areas of difference in appropriate practice, and the discussion of unsettled and controversial issues. The APB was comprised of between 17 and 21 members who were selected primarily from the accounting profession but also included individuals from industry, government, and academia.

Initially, the pronouncements of the APB which were termed "Opinions" were not mandatory practice; however, the issuance of APB Opinion No. 2[8] and subsequent partial retractions contained in APB Opinion No. 4[9] highlighted the need for more authority. This controversy was due to differences in accounting for the investment tax credit. In 1961 the investment tax credit was passed by Congress. This legislation provided for a direct tax reduction based upon a percentage of the cost of a qualified investment. The APB, after a review of the accounting requirements of this legislation, issued Opinion No. 2, which stated that this tax deduction amounted to a cost reduction, and the effects of this cost reduction should be amortized over the useful life of the asset acquired. Nevertheless, several large public accounting firms decided to report the results of the investment credit only in the period in which it occurred. The APB was thus faced with a serious threat to its authority.

---

[6]Accounting Terminology Bulletin No. 1, "Review and Resume" (New York: American Institute of Certified Public Accountants, 1953).

[7]Accounting Research Bulletin No. 43, "Restatement and Revision of Accounting Research Bulletins" (New York: American Institute of Certified Public Accountants, 1953).

[8]Accounting Principles Board Opinion No. 2, "Accounting for the 'Investment Credit'" (New York: American Institute of Certified Public Accountants, 1962).

[9]Accounting Principles Board Opinion No. 4, "Accounting for the 'Investment Credit'" (New York: American Institute of Certified Public Accountants, 1964).

Due to the lack of general acceptance of its Opinion No. 2, the APB partially retreated from its previous position. Though reaffirming its previous decision as being the proper and most appropriate treatment, Opinion No. 4 approved the use of either of the two methods.

The lack of support for its pronouncements, and concern over the formulation and acceptance of "generally accepted accounting principles" caused the Council of the American Institute of Certified Public Accountants to adopt Rule 203 of the Code of Professional Ethics. This rule required departures from accounting principles published in APB Opinions or Accounting Research Bulletins to be disclosed in footnotes to financial statements or in independent auditors' reports when the effects of such departures were material. This action had the effect of requiring companies and public accountants who deviated from APB Opinions and Accounting Research Bulletins to justify such departures.

Rule 203

In addition to the difficulties associated with the passage of APB Opinions No. 2 and No. 4, the Accounting Principles Board encountered other problems. The members of the APB were, in effect, volunteers. These individuals had full-time responsibilities to their employers; therefore, the performance of their duties on the APB became secondary. By the late 1960s criticism of the development of accounting principles again arose. This criticism centered on the following factors

1. The independence of the members of the Accounting Principles Board members. The individuals serving on the board had full-time responsibilities elsewhere that might have an impact upon their views of certain issues.
2. The structure of the board. The largest eight public accounting firms were automatically awarded one member and there were usually five or six other public accountants on the APB.
3. Response time. The emerging accounting problems were not being investigated and solved quickly enough by the part-time members.

THE FINANCIAL ACCOUNTING STANDARDS BOARD

As a result of the growing criticism of the Accounting Principles Board, the board of directors of the American Institute of Certified Public Accountants appointed two committees in 1971. The Wheat Committee, named after its chairman, Francis Wheat, was to study how financial accounting principles should be established. The Trueblood Committee, named after its chairman, Robert Trueblood, was to determine the objectives of financial statements.

The Wheat Committee issued its report in 1972 with a recommendation that the Accounting Principles Board be abolished and the Financial Accounting Standards Board (FASB) be created. This new board was to be composed of representatives from various organizations, in contrast to the APB, whose members were all from the AICPA. The members of the FASB were also to be paid and were to work full-time, unlike the APB members, who served part-time and were not paid.

The Trueblood Committee, formally known as the Study Group on Objectives of Financial Statements, issued its report in 1973 after substantial debate and with considerably more tentativeness in its recommendations about objectives than the Wheat Committee had with respect to the establishment of principles. The study group requested that its report be regarded as an initial step in developing objectives and that significant efforts should be made to continue progress on the refinement and improvement of accounting standards and practices. The objectives enumerated by the Trueblood Committee came largely from the standards and guidelines provided by APB Statement No. 4. These objectives later became the basis for Statement of Financial Accounting Concepts No. 1 (discussed later in the chapter).

The AICPA quickly adopted the Wheat Committee recommendations, and the FASB became the official body charged with issuing accounting standards. The structure of the FASB is as follows. A panel of electors from nine organizations that support the activities of the FASB is selected. (The nine organizations selecting the electors are representative of the breadth of support for the activities of the FASB in the business community. They are the AICPA, the Financial Executives Institute, the National Association of Accountants, the Financial Analysts Federation, the American Accounting Association, the Security Industry Association, and three not-for-profit organizations.) The electors appoint the board of trustees that govern the Financial Accounting Foundation. The 10 trustees are elected to three-year terms and are chosen as follows

1. Four members are CPAs in public practice, nominated by the AICPA.
2. Two members are financial executives, nominated by the Financial Executives Institute.
3. One member is nominated by the National Association of Accountants.
4. One member is nominated by the Financial Analysts Federation.
5. One member is nominated by the American Accounting Association.
6. One member is nominated by the Security Industry Association.
7. The remaining member is the senior elected officer of the AICPA, not an employee of that organization.

The FAF appoints the Financial Accounting Standards Advisory Council, which advises the FASB on major policy issues, the selection of task forces, and the agenda of topics. The FAF is also responsible for appointing the seven members of the FASB and raising the funds to operate the FASB. The FAF currently collects in excess of $11 million a year to support the activities of the FASB.

Figure 1.1 on page 9 illustrates the current structures of the FASB.

Both the FAF and the FASB have a broader representation of the total profes-

Figure 1.1   Structure of the FASB.

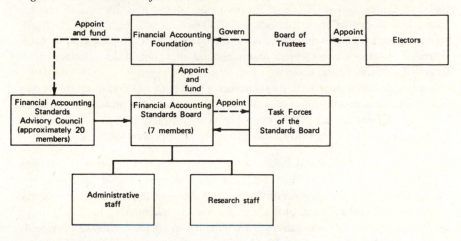

sion than did the APB; however, the majority of members are still CPAs from public practice. This membership structure raises the question of how different the FASB is from the APB. No matter what the answer, however, the FASB is now the body officially designated by the AICPA as having the authority to issue standards for financial accounting. Thus, throughout this book pronouncements of the FASB and APB will be presented as generally accepted accounting principles. (One of the first acts of the FASB was to sanction all actions of the APB until such time as they could be reviewed or revised. The APB had done likewise for actions of the Committee on Accounting Procedures. Thus, at this point, the FASB has accepted all currently outstanding pronouncements of both the CAP and the APB.) In this book there will be frequent references to the APB, since much of what will be presented originated with that group; however, the reader should keep in mind that the FASB has adopted those pronouncements.

Originally the FASB issued two types of pronouncements, *Statements* and *Interpretations.* Subsequently, the Financial Accounting Standards Board established two new series of releases entitled (1) Statements of Financial Accounting Concepts and (2) Technical Bulletins. Statements of Financial Accounting Concepts are intended to establish the objectives and concepts that the FASB will use in developing standards of financial accounting and reporting. To date, the FASB has issued six Statements of Financial Concepts as discussed later in this chapter.

Statements of Financial Accounting Concepts differ from Statements of Financial Accounting Standards in that they do not establish generally accepted accounting principles. Likewise, they are not intended to invoke Rule 203 of the

Rules of Conduct of the Code of Professional Ethics. It is anticipated that the major beneficiary of these Statements of Concepts will be the FASB itself. However, knowledge of the objectives and concepts the board uses should enable financial statement users better to understand the content and limitations of financial accounting information.

Technical Bulletins are strictly interpretive in nature and do not establish new standards or amend existing standards. They are intended to provide guidance on financial accounting and reporting problems on a timely basis.

In summary, the FASB now issues four types of pronouncements.

1. *Statements of Financial Accounting Concepts*—releases designed to establish the fundamentals upon which financial accounting standards are based.
2. *Statements of Financial Accounting Standards*—releases indicating required accounting methods and procedures for specific accounting issues.
3. *Interpretations*—modifications or extensions of issues related to previously issued FASB Statements, APB Opinions or Accounting Research Bulletins. They require the support of a majority of the members of the FASB.
4. *Technical Bulletins*—guidance on accounting and reporting problems issued by the staff of the FASB.

EMERGING ISSUES

The FASB has been criticized recently for failing to provide timely guidance on emerging implementation and practice problems. During 1984 the FASB attempted to respond to this criticism by (1) establishing a task force to assist in identifying issues and problems that might require action, the Emerging Issues Task Force, and (2) expanding the scope of the FASB Technical Bulletins in an effort to offer quicker guidance on a wider variety of issues.

Emerging issues arise because of new types of transactions, variations in accounting for existing types of transactions, new types of securities, and new products and services. They frequently involve the company's desire to achieve "off balance sheet" financing or "off income statement" accounting.

The Emerging Issues Task Force was formed to assist the FASB in issuing timely guidance on these emerging issues. That is, the task force's responsibility is to identify emerging issues as they develop, investigate and review them, and finally to advise the board whether the issue merits its attention.

The members of the task force all occupy positions that make them aware of emerging issues. The current members include the directors of accounting and auditing from 11 public accounting firms (including all of the "Big Eight"), two representatives from the Financial Executives Institute, one from the National Association of Accountants and the Business Roundtable, and the FASB's top staff member, who serves as chairman. It is also expected that the chief accountant of the SEC will attend the meetings of the task force.

STANDARDS OVERLOAD

In recent years, the Financial Accounting Standards Board, the Securities and Exchange Commission, and the American Institute of Certified Public Accountants have been criticized for imposing too many accounting standards on the business community. This *standards overload* problem has been particularly burdensome on small businesses that do not have the necessary economic resources to research and apply all of the pronouncements issued by these sources. Those who contend that there is a standards overload problem base their arguments on two allegations.

1. Not all GAAP requirements are relevant to small business financial reporting needs.
2. Even when they are relevant, they frequently violate the pervasive cost-benefit constraint (discussed later in the chapter).

Critics of the standard-setting process for small businesses also assert that GAAP were developed primarily to serve the needs of the securities market. Many small businesses do not raise capital in these markets; therefore, it is contended that GAAP were not developed with small business needs in mind.

Some of the consequences of the standards overload problem to small business are as follows.

1. If a small business omits a GAAP requirement from audited financial statements, a qualified or adverse opinion may be rendered.
2. The cost of complying with GAAP requirements may cause a small business to forgo the development of other, more relevant information.
3. Small CPA firms that audit smaller companies must keep up to date on all of the same requirements as large international firms, but cannot afford the specialists that are available on a centralized basis in the large firms.

Many accountants have argued for differential disclosure standards as a solution to the standards overload problem. That is, standards might be divided into two groups. One group would apply to businesses regardless of size. The second group would be applied selectively only to large businesses, small businesses, or particular industries. For example, the disclosure of significant accounting policies would pertain to all businesses, whereas a differential disclosure such as earnings per share would be applicable only to large businesses.

The FASB and various other organizations have been studying this issue for several years, but a complete agreement has not yet been reached. A special committee of the AICPA favored differential measurement.[10] However, the FASB has generally taken the position that finaicial-statement users might be confused by two measures used to describe or disclose the same economic event. Additionally, bankers (a major source of capital for small businesses) and financial analysts have fairly consistently criticized differential measurement as a solution to the standards overload problem.[11]

AUTHORITY

Neither the AICPA nor any of its committees or boards has any legal authority. In order to be a member of the AICPA it is necessary to be a certified public accountant, but it is not necessary to be a member in order to be a CPA. The designation CPA and the license to practice are both granted by the individual states. Therefore, a CPA can become a member of the AICPA if he or she so chooses and, in fact, a majority of practicing CPAs are members.

Under these circumstances, when official statements are issued, those CPAs who are not members of the AICPA can simply choose to ignore the position taken in the statements. Those who are members can also assert that they are following other substantial authoritative support, and the AICPA can do little in the way of penalty. The individual state boards of accountancy, on the other hand, may suspend a CPA's license for a variety of reasons, and that is indeed a significant penalty. The state boards, however, have played virtually no part in developing or establishing accounting principles.

The fact that acceptance and compliance by CPAs with the pronouncements of the APB and the Financial Accounting Standards Board is voluntary, not legally mandatory, is most important to an understanding of the structure of accounting principles that will be presented in this text, since the text draws primarily upon those pronouncements. In contrast to the APB and FASB pronouncements, the numerous legal requirements issued by the Securities and Exchange Commission (SEC) *must* be complied with by those companies that report to the SEC.

THE SECURITIES AND EXCHANGE COMMISSION

The Securities and Exchange Commission was created to administer various securities acts, and under powers provided by Congress, the SEC has the authority to prescribe accounting principles and reporting practices. Although this au-

---

[10]Special Committee on Accounting Standards Overload, *Report on the Special Committee on Accounting Standards Overload* (New York: American Institute of Certified Public Accountants, 1983).
[11]"The FASB's Second Decade," *Journal of Accountancy* (November 1983), p. 95.

thority has seldom been used, the SEC has exerted pressure on the accounting profession and has been especially interested in narrowing areas of difference in accounting practice.

Generally speaking, the SEC has approved APB Opinions and FASB Statements before their issuance. It has also played a more direct role in formulating accounting practice through the publication of Accounting Series Releases and Financial Reporting Releases. Thus, while the SEC has the authority to decide arbitrarily what constitutes "generally accepted accounting principles," this authority has usually been exercised in the form of persuasion rather than edict. Further evidence of the commission's position can be found in Accounting Series Release No. 4, which stated that the commission would only accept financial statements prepared in accordance with generally accepted accounting principles, or rules, regulations, or official pronouncements of the SEC or its chief accountant. In this same release, the commission also endorsed the concept of "substantial authoritative support" by asserting that when financial statements are "prepared in accordance with accounting principles for which there is no substantial authoritative support, such financial statements will be presumed to be misleading or inaccurate."

ACCOUNTING PRINCIPLES BOARD STATEMENT NO. 4

The Accounting Principles Board utilized a research division whose responsibility was to broaden the scope of research into generally accepted accounting principles and to rely more heavily upon the deductive method in the development of such principles. This division commissioned research studies to specific individuals as a means of obtaining information about a specific topic. These studies were intended to stimulate discussion and provide the background for the reasoning leading to the issuance of the various Opinions.

Two early research studies created a furor within the profession. Accounting Research Studies No. 1, "The Basic Postulates of Accounting,"[12] and No. 3, "A Tentative Set of Broad Accounting Principles for Business Enterprises,"[13] were attacked as being radically different from current accounting practice, and were rejected by the APB. Almost immediately the board commissioned a new study which ultimately resulted in the publication of Accounting Research Study No. 7, "Inventory of Generally Accepted Accounting Principles for Business

---

[12]Maurice Moonitz, "The Basic Postulates of Accounting," Accounting Research Study No. 1 (New York: American Institute of Certified Public Accountants, 1961).

[13]Robert T. Sprouse and Maurice Moonitz, "A Tentative Set of Broad Accounting Principles for Business Enterprises," Accounting Research Study No. 3 (New York: American Institute of Certified Public Accountants, 1962).

Enterprises."[14] By October 1970 the Accounting Principles Board had reviewed these publications and issued Statement No. 4, "Basic Concepts and Accounting Principles Underlying Financial Statements of Business Enterprises." The board asserted that the statement had two broad purposes, one educational and the other developmental. The board also used the term "descriptive" to describe the nature of the statement. According to the board, most of Statement No. 4 is descriptive of current practice rather than developmental or prescriptive. Furthermore, "The description of present generally accepted accounting principles is based primarily on observation of accounting practice. Present generally accepted accounting principles have not been formally derived from the environment, objectives, and basic features of financial accounting."[15]

In the context of a discussion about the objectives of financial accounting and financial statements, the board was somewhat more prescriptive than suggested in the preceding comments. The board asserted that "The basic purpose of financial accounting and financial statements is to provide financial information about individual business enterprises that is useful in making economic decisions."[16] This statement of purpose thus provides a description of present accounting and a basic premise, or prescription, for future developments.

The board further noted that the qualities of "relevance, understandability, verifiability, neutrality, timeliness, comparability, and completeness"[17] make financial information useful; therefore, financial accounting should provide information that has these qualities.

These criteria for accounting information were intended to guide future research efforts as well as give insight into current practice. They did not indicate precisely what should be done, but they suggested, that if a particular activity is not relevant, it probably should not be included as accounting information. For example, the criterion of relevance is frequently cited as the basis for adopting current value accounting. Many people consider historical cost to be almost totally irrelevant; therefore, financial statements prepared on the basis of historical cost are not relevant. Current values are considered to be highly relevant; however, such values are extremely difficult to verify. Historical costs, to the contrary, are easily verifiable. Thus, we have a conflict between the two criteria which suggests that some compromise is necessary. Many of the qualities discussed in Statement No. 4 were also embraced by the FASB.

[14]Paul Grady, "Inventory of Generally Accepted Accounting Principles for Business Enterprises," Accounting Research Study No. 7 (New York: American Institute of Certified Public Accountants, 1965).
[15]APB Statement No. 4, op. cit.
[16]Ibid., par. 21.
[17]Ibid., par. 23.

THE CONCEPTUAL FRAMEWORK PROJECT

The Conceptual Framework Project is an attempt by the FASB to develop concepts useful in guiding the board in establishing standards and in providing a frame of reference for resolving accounting issues. Over the years this project first attempted to develop principles or broad qualitative standards to permit the making of systematic rational choices among alternative methods of financial reporting. Subsequently the project focused on how these overall objectives could be achieved. The FASB has stated that it intends the Conceptual Framework Project to be viewed not as a package of solutions to problems but rather as a common basis for identifying and discussing issues, for asking relevant questions, and for suggesting avenues for research. The Conceptual Framework Project has resulted in the issuance of five statements of Financial Accounting Concepts that impact upon financial accounting: No. 1—Objectives of Financial Reporting by Business Enterprises; No. 2—Qualitative Characteristics of Accounting Information; No. 3—Elements of Financial Statements of Business Enterprises; and No. 5—Recognition and Measurement in Financial Statements of Business Enterprises Statement No. 6—Elements of Financial Statements.

Statements of Concepts No. 1 and No. 2 are reviewed in the following paragraphs. Statements of Concepts Nos. 3 and 6 are discussed in Chapters 3 and 4. Statement of Concepts No. 5 is discussed in Chapter 2.

STATEMENT OF CONCEPTS NO. 1: OBJECTIVES OF FINANCIAL REPORTING BY BUSINESS ENTERPRISES

This release points out that external financial reporting by business enterprises is not an end in itself. That is, it is a source of useful information furnished by management to financial-statement users who can obtain this information in no other way. The objective of financial reporting is to give users a basis for choosing among alternative uses of scarce resources. Effective financial reporting must meet several broad objectives. It must enable current and potential investors, creditors, and other users to

1. Make investment and credit decisions.
2. Assess cash flow prospects.
3. Report enterprise resources, claims to those resources, and changes in them.
4. Report economic resources, obligations, and owners equity.
5. Report enterprise performance and earnings.
6. Evaluate liquidity, solvency, and flow of funds.
7. Evaluate management stewardship and performance.
8. Explain and interpret financial information.

The FASB intends that these objectives will act as guidelines for providing information for investment and credit decisions by financial-statement users. This goal will help facilitate the efficient use of scarce resources and the operation of capital markets.

STATEMENT OF CONCEPTS NO. 2: QUALITATIVE CHARACTERISTICS OF ACCOUNTING INFORMATION

This statement bridges the gap between Statement of Concepts No. 1 and other statements, issued later, covering the elements of financial statements and their recognition, measurement, and disclosure. It addresses the question: What are the characteristics of accounting information that make it useful? Later statements are then intended to be concerned with how the purposes of financial accounting are to be attained.

Statement of Concepts No. 2 notes that accounting choices are made on at least two levels. First, the FASB or other agencies have the power to require businesses to report in some particular way or to prohibit a method that might be considered undesirable. Second, accounting choices between alternatives are made by the reporting enterprise. SFAC No. 2 attempts to identify and define the qualities that make accounting information useful by developing a number of generalizations or guidelines for making accounting choices on both levels.

The statement goes on to say that the primary criterion of choice between two alternative accounting methods involves asking which method produces the better, that is, the more useful, information. If the answer to that question is clear, it then becomes necessary to ask whether the value of the better information significantly exceeds that of the inferior information to justify any extra cost (cost-benefit analysis). If a satisfactory answer is given, the choice between alternatives should be clear. The qualities that distinguish better (or more useful) information from inferior (less useful) are primarily the qualities of relevance and reliability (discussed later).

Figure 1.2 illustrates the Hierarchy of Accounting Qualities discussed by SFAC No. 2 in reviewing the characteristics of accounting information.

From Figure 1.2 we can see that the characteristics of information that make it a desirable commodity are viewed as a hierarchy of qualities, with usefulness for decision making being the most important quality. However, a limitation of the hierarchy is that it does not distinguish between the primary qualities and other qualities, nor does it assign priority among qualities. In the following paragraphs we discuss each of the hierarchical levels in detail.

Decision Makers and Their Characteristics

Each decision maker judges what accounting information is useful, and that judgment is influenced by such factors as the decision to be made, the methods of

FASC #2 *Understand & Know*

Figure 1.2 A hierarchy of accounting qualities.

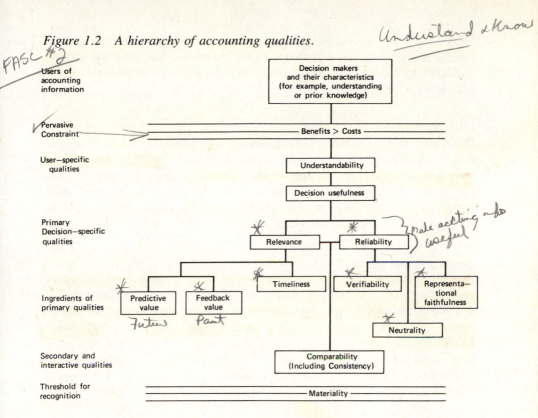

decision making to be used, the information already possessed or obtained from other sources, and the decision maker's capacity to process the information. These characteristics indicate that generally managers and owners of small or closely held enterprises may find some external financial reporting information less useful to them than it is to stockholders of large publicly held enterprises.[18]

Cost-Benefit Constraint
Unless the benefits to be desired from a commodity or service exceed the costs associated with it, it will not be sought after. However, financial information differs from other commodities in that the costs of providing financial information fall initially on preparers while the benefits accrue to both preparers and

[18]This conclusion is expanded on in the FASB's Exposure Draft, ''Financial Statements and Other Means of Financial Reporting.'' This release examines the issues of what information should be provided, who should provide it, and where it should be presented. Additionally, it examines the question, Should GAAP be the same for all companies regardless of size? As noted earlier, the FASB has not issued a final statement that addresses this question.

users. Ultimately, a standard-setting body must do its best to meet the needs of society as a whole when it promulgates a standard that sacrifices one of those qualities for the other, and it must constantly be aware of the relationship of costs and benefits.

Understandability

Understandability of information is governed by a combination of user characteristics and characteristics inherent in the information. It serves as a "link" between decision makers and accounting information. Understandability can be classified as relating to particular decision makers (Does the decision maker speak that language?) or relating to classes of decision makers (Is the disclosure intelligible to the audience for which it is intended?).

Decision Usefulness

Relevance and reliability are the two primary qualities that make accounting information useful for decision making. Subject to constraints imposed by cost and materiality, increased relevance and increased reliability are the characteristics that make information a more desirable commodity—that is, one useful in making decisions. If either of those qualities is completely missing, the information will not be useful. Although, ideally, the choice of an accounting alternative should produce information that is both more reliable and more relevant, it may be necessary to sacrifice some of one quality for a gain in another.

Relevance

Relevant accounting information is capable of making a difference in a decision by helping users to form predictions about the outcomes of past, present, and future events or to confirm or correct prior expectations. Information can make a difference to decisions by improving decision makers' capacities to predict or by providing feedback on earlier expectations. Usually, information does both at once, because knowledge about the outcomes of actions already taken will generally improve decision makers' abilities to predict the results of similar future actions. Without a knowledge of the past, the basis for a prediction will usually be lacking. Without an interest in the future, knowledge of the past is sterile.

Predictive Value and Feedback Value

Information can make a difference to decisions by improving decision makers' capacities to predict or by confirming or correcting their earlier expectations. Usually, information does both at once, because knowledge about the outcome of actions already taken will generally improve decision makers' abilities to predict the results of similar future actions.

Timeliness

Having information available to decision makers before it loses its capacity to influence decisions is an ancillary aspect of relevance. If information is not available when it is needed or becomes available so long after the reported events that it has no value for future action, it lacks relevance and is of little or no use. Timeliness alone cannot make information relevant, but a lack of timeliness can rob information of relevance it might otherwise have had.

Reliability

The reliability of a measure rests on the faithfulness with which it represents what it purports to represent, coupled with an assurance for the user that it has that representational quality. To be useful, information must be reliable as well as relevant. Degrees of reliability must be recognized. It is hardly ever a question of black or white, but rather of more reliability or less. Reliability rests on the extent to which the accounting description or measurement is verifiable and representationally faithful. Neutrality of information also interacts with those two components of reliability to affect the usefulness of the information.

Verifiability

Verifiability is a quality that may be demonstrated by securing a high degree of consensus among independent measurers using the same measurement methods. Representational faithfulness, on the other hand, refers to the correspondence or agreement between the accounting numbers and the resources or events those numbers purport to represent. A high degree of correspondence, however, does not guarantee that an accounting measurement will be relevant to the user's needs if the resources or events represented by the measurement are inappropriate to the purpose at hand.

Representational Faithfulness → likely to happen in preparing schedules

This quality is the correspondence or agreement between a measure and the phenomenon it purports to represent. Sometimes information may be unreliable because of simple misrepresentation. For example, receivables may misrepresent large sums as collectible that are actually uncollectible. Social scientists have defined this concept as validity.

Sure can rely cuz sure they used proper techniques

Neutrality

must be appropriate technique

In formulating or implementing standards, the primary concern should be the relevance and reliability of the information that results, not the effect that the new rule may have on a particular interest. A neutral choice between accounting alternatives is free from bias towards a predetermined result. The objectives of financial reporting serve many different information users who have diverse interests, and no one predetermined result is likely to suit all interests.

NOT Biased

Comparability and Consistency

Information about a particular enterprise increases greatly in usefulness if it can be compared with similar information about other enterprises and with similar information about the same enterprise for some other period or some other point in time. Comparability between enterprises and consistency in the application of methods over time increases the informational value of comparisons of relative economic opportunities or performance. The significance of information, especially quantitative information, depends to a great extent on the user's ability to relate it to some benchmark.

Materiality Constraint

Materiality is a pervasive concept that relates to the qualitative characteristics, especially relevance and reliability. Materiality and relevance are both defined in terms of what influences or makes a difference to a decision maker, but the two terms can be distinguished. A decision not to disclose certain information may be made, say, because investors have no need for that kind of information (it is not relevant) or because the amounts involved are too small to make a difference (they are not material). Magnitude by itself, without regard to the nature of the item and the circumstances in which the judgment has to be made, will not generally be a sufficient basis for a materiality judgment. The FASB's present position is that no general standards of materiality can be formulated to take into account all the considerations that enter into an experienced human judgment. Quantitative materiality criteria may be given by the board in specific standards in the future, as in the past, as appropriate. See Chapter 2 for a further discussion of materiality.

RESEARCH METHODOLOGY

Accounting theory can be developed by using several research methodologies. Among the more commonly identified methodologies are (1) the deductive approach, (2) the inductive approach, (3) the pragmatic approach, (4) the ethical approach, (5) the behavioral approach, (6) the sociological approach, and (7) the communication theory approach. This section will briefly describe each of these approaches, with emphasis on the pragmatic approach. In addition, the scientific method of inquiry, which is essentially a combination of deductive and inductive reasoning, will be presented as a guide to research in accounting theory development.

DEDUCTIVE APPROACH

The deductive approach to the development of accounting theory begins with establishing the objectives of accounting. Once the objectives have been identified, certain key definitions and assumptions must be stated. The researcher must then develop a logical structure for accomplishing the objectives, based upon the definitions and assumptions. This methodology is often described as "going from the general to the specific," because the researcher is developing a structure that includes the objectives of accounting, the environment in which accounting is operating, the definitions and assumptions of the system, and the procedures and practices, all of which follow a logical pattern.

This method is essentially a mental or "armchair" type of research. Therefore, the validity of any theory developed through this process is highly dependent upon the ability of the researcher to identify correctly and relate the various components of the accounting process in a logical manner. To the extent that the researcher is in error as to the objectives, the environment, or the ability of the procedures to accomplish the objectives, the conclusions reached will also be in error. More will be said about this weakness in the deductive approach in the discussion of the scientific method.

INDUCTIVE APPROACH

The inductive approach to research emphasizes making observations and drawing conclusions from those observations. Thus, this method is described as "going from the specific to the general," because the researcher generalizes about the universe on the basis of limited observations of specific situations.

Accounting Principles Board Statement No. 4, which was previously discussed, serves as a good example of primarily inductive research. The board clearly stated that the "generally accepted accounting principles" which were described in the statement were based primarily on observation of current practice. In addition, the board acknowledged that the current principles have not been derived from the environment, objectives, and basic features of financial accounting. Thus, the study was essentially inductive in approach. This approach has certain limitations, which will be discussed in the section on the scientific method.

PRAGMATIC APPROACH

At present generally accepted accounting principles are primarily the result of the pragmatic approach. This approach to accounting theory development is based upon the concept of utility or usefulness. Once the problem has been identified, the researcher attempts to find a utilitarian solution, that is, one that will resolve the problem. This does not suggest that the optimum solution has been found, or that the solution will accomplish some stated objective. (Actually, the only objective may be to find a "workable" solution to a problem.) Thus, any answers obtained through the pragmatic approach should be viewed as tentative solutions to problems.

Unfortunately in accounting, most of the present principles and practices have resulted from the pragmatic approach, and the solutions have been adopted as "generally accepted accounting principles," rather than as an expedient resolution to a problem. Accounting Principles Board Statement No. 4 provided rather clear evidence of this situation when it stated that the principles presented were descriptions of present practice but were not formally derived from the environment, objectives, and basic features of financial accounting. As a result, the accounting profession must frequently admit that a certain practice is followed merely because "that is the way we have always done it." That is a most unsatisfactory reason, particularly when such questions arise in legal suits.

SCIENTIFIC METHOD OF INQUIRY

The scientific method of inquiry, as the name suggests, was developed for the natural and physical sciences and not specifically for social sciences such as accounting. There are some clear limitations on the application of this research methodology to accounting; for example, the influence of people and the economic environment makes it impossible to hold the variables constant. Nevertheless, the method can indicate how research should be conducted. The researcher and the user of the findings should keep the limitations in mind so that no one places undue reliance on the results.

Conducting research by the scientific method involves five major steps, which may also have several substeps.

1. Identify and state the problem to be studied.
2. State the hypotheses to be tested.
3. Collect the data that seem necessary for testing the hypotheses.
4. Analyze and evaluate the data in relation to the hypotheses.
5. Draw a tentative conclusion.

Although the steps are listed sequentially, there is considerable back-and-forth movement between the steps. For example, at the point of stating the hypotheses, it may be necessary to go back to step 1 and state the problem more precisely. Again, when collecting data, it may be necessary to clarify the problem or the hypotheses, or both. This back-and-forth motion continues all through the process and is a major factor in the strength of the scientific method.

The back-and-forth movement involved in the scientific method also suggests why it is impossible to do purely deductive or inductive research. Once the problem has been identified, the statement of hypotheses is primarily a deductive process, but the researcher must have previously made some observations in order to formulate expectations. The collection of data is primarily an inductive process, but determining what to observe and which data to collect will be influenced by the hypotheses. Thus, the researcher may, at any given moment, emphasize induction or deduction, but each is influenced by the other and the emphasis is continually shifting so that the two approaches are coordinate aspects of one method.

Unfortunately, the scientific method of inquiry has received only limited attention in accounting research. Those procedures found to have "utility" have become generally accepted irrespective of whether they were tested for any relevance to a particular hypothesis. stop

OTHER RESEARCH APPROACHES

Various writers have at times discussed the ethical, behavioral, and communication theory approaches to research as being applicable to the development of accounting principles. Others view these approaches as supportive rather than as specific methods for research; that is, they can, and should, influence the attitude of the researcher but cannot by themselves lead to tightly reasoned conclusions.

The ethical approach, which is attributed to DR Scott,[19] places emphasis upon the concepts of truth, justice, and fairness. No one would argue with these concepts as guides to actions by the researcher, but there is always the question of fair to whom, for what purpose, and under what circumstances? Because of questions such as these, this approach is operationally limited when applied to accounting theory.

The behavioral approach is based upon research activities in the behavioral sciences. It emphasizes the way individuals and groups react to accounting information. Since the purpose of accounting is to provide information for decision makers, it is certainly appropriate to be concerned with how the users react to different information. However, this approach covers only one aspect of the research necessary under the scientific method of inquiry and thus cannot be the complete approach for accounting developments.

The communication theory approach is similar to the behavioral approach in that both emphasize reactions of the user. When applied to accounting, this method strives to determine whether the user of accounting information perceives the same message from the data as the accountant intends. Again, this approach should be an inherent part of research in accounting, but it cannot be the total research methodology.

[19]DR Scott, "The Basis for Accounting Principles," *The Acounting Review* (December 1941), pp. 341–349.

SUMMARY

Accounting activities have been conducted for many hundreds of years, but formal accounting theory is still in the development stage. Although some work in accounting theory occurred in the early 1900s, it was the 1929 depression that gave impetus to the improvement of accounting practice. The AICPA and its various subgroups continue to be active in the development of accounting principles. In addition, the practices of the accounting profession, the actions of the Securities and Exchange Commission, and the opinions of the academic community influence the development of accounting principles and theory.

The term "generally accepted accounting principles" has become significant in accounting practice, although it does not have a single authoritative definition. In general, the term refers to a consensus within the profession that a given principle is generally accepted as being appropriate to the circumstances in which it is used. Although there are several possible sources for statements of accounting principles, the most authoritative is the Financial Accounting Standards Board and its predecessors, the Accounting Principles Board and the Committee on Accounting Procedures.

The theoretical framework of accounting has been studied by both the Accounting Principles Board and The Financial Accounting Standards Board. The APB's conclusions are outlined in its Statement no. 4; whereas; the FASB's conclusions are contained in the conceptual framework project.

Of the several methodologies for research into the development of accounting theory, the scientific method of inquiry seems to hold the most promise. This approach is particularly strong because it incorporates both inductive and deductive reasoning, and because it emphasizes testing hypotheses and proposed solutions. In addition, ethical, behavioral, and communication theory approaches have a subordinate contribution to make to accounting theory. Unfortunately, most current accounting practice is based on the pragmatic approach, which emphasizes finding a utilitarian solution to a problem, not necessarily the best solution.

In the following readings, the development of the accounting profession is examined further. Stephen Zeff discusses the economic impact of FASB pronouncements. Robert Sterling contrasts education and practice in the accounting profession with that of other professions. He suggests that accounting lags behind other professions because accounting theory is not being effectively taught and thus ultimately incorporated into practice. Finally, William R. Kinney introduces an approach to designing research in accounting. This article may also be useful in evaluating the research design of other articles contained in this text.

important)

THE RISE OF "ECONOMIC CONSEQUENCES"

STEPHEN A. ZEFF

Since the 1960s, the American accounting profession has been aware of the increasing influence of "outside forces" in the standard-setting process. Two parallel developments have marked this trend. First, individuals and groups that had rarely shown any interest in the setting of accounting standards began to intervene actively and powerfully in the process. Second, these parties began to invoke arguments other than those which have traditionally been employed in accounting discussions. The term "economic consequences" has been used to describe these novel kinds of arguments.

By "economic consequences" is meant the impact of accounting reports on the decision-making behavior of business, government, unions, investigators and creditors. It is argued that the resulting behavior of these individuals and groups could be detrimental to the interests of other affected parties. And, the argument goes, accounting standard setters must take into consideration these allegedly detrimental consequences when deciding on accounting questions. The recent debates involving foreign currency translation and the accounting for unsuccessful exploration activity in the petroleum industry have relied heavily on economic consequences arguments, and the Financial Accounting Standards Board and the Securities and Exchange Commission have become extremely sensitive to the issue.[1]

The economic consequences argument represents a veritable revolution in accounting thought. Until recently, accounting policy making was either assumed to be neutral in its effects or, if not neutral, it was not held out to the public as being responsible for those effects. Today, these assumptions are being severely questioned, and the subject of social and economic consequences "has become *the* central contemporary issue in accounting."[2] That the FASB has commissioned research papers on the economic consequences of selected standards and has held a conference devoted entirely to the subject[3] underscores the current importance of this issue.

Accounting policy makers have been aware since at least the 1960s of the third-party intervention issue,[4] while the issue of

---

[1]Several articles have been written on "economic consequences." See, e.g., Alfred Rapaport, "Economic Impact of Accounting Standards—Implications for the FASB," JofA May77, pp. 89–98; Arthur R. Wyatt, "The Economic Impact of Financial Accounting Standards," JofA, Oct.77, pp. 92–94; and Robert J. Swieringa, "Consequences of Financial Accounting Standards," *Accounting Forum*, May 1977, pp. 25–39.

[2]*Report of the Committee on the Social Consequences of Accounting Information* (Sarasota, Fla.: American Accounting Association, 1978), p. 4.

[3]*Conference on the Economic Consequences of Financial Accounting Standards* (Stamford, Conn.: FASB, 1978).

[4]In this article, I am chiefly concerned with third-party intervention in the standard setting for unregulated industries. Accounting policy makers in this country have been alive for several decades to the accounting implications of the rules and regulations of ratemaking in the energy, transportation and communication indus-

economic consequences has surfaced only in the 1970s. Indeed, much of the history of the Accounting Principles Board during the 1960s was one of endeavoring to understand and cope with the third-party forces which were intervening in the standard-setting process. In the end, the inability of the APB to deal effectively with these forces led to its demise and the establishment in 1973 of the FASB.

The true preoccupations of the intervening third parties have not always been made clear. When trying to understand the third-party arguments, one must remember that before the 1970s the accounting model employed by the American Institute of CPAs committee on accounting procedure (CAP) and the APB was, formally at least, confined to technical accounting considerations (sometimes called "accounting principles" or "conceptual questions") such as the measurement of assets, liabilities and income and the "fair presentation" of financial position and operations. The policy makers' sole concern was with the communication of financial information to actual and potential investors, for, indeed, their charter had been "granted" by the SEC, which itself had been charged by Congress to assure "full and fair disclosure" in reports to investors. Third-party intervenors, therefore, would have had an obvious incentive to appeal to the accounting model used by policy makers rather than raise the specter of an economic consequences model preferred by the third parties.

When corporate management began intervening in the standard-setting process to an increasing degree, therefore, its true position was probably disguised. An examination of management arguments suggests the following range of tactical rhetoric. Arguments were couched in terms of

1. The traditional accounting model, where management was genuinely concerned about unbiased and "theoretically sound" accounting measurements.
2. The traditional accounting model, where management was really seeking to advance its self-interest in the economic consequences of the contents of published reports.
3. The economic consequences in which management was self-interested.

If one accepts Johnson's dictum that it requires a "lively imagination" to believe that management is genuinely concerned with fair presentation when choosing between alternatives,[5] it could be concluded that the first argument has seldom been employed in third-party interventions. In recent years, particularly since the early 1970s, management has become more candid in its dialogues with the FASB, insistently advancing the third argument and thus bringing economic consequences to the fore.

Two factors tend to explain why economic consequences did not become a substantive issue before the 1970s. First, management and other interested parties predominantly used the second argument cited above, encouraging the standard-setting bodies to confine themselves to the traditional accounting model. Second, the CAP and APB, with few exceptions, were

---

tries. See, e.g., George O. May, *Financial Accounting: A Distillation of Experience* (New York: The Macmillan Company, 1943), chs. 7–8, and William A. Paton, "Accounting Policies of the Federal Power Commission—A Critique," JofA, June44, pp. 432–460.

[5]Charles E. Johnson, "Management's Role in External Accounting Measurements," in Robert K. Jaedicke, Yuji Ijiri and Oswald Nielsen (editors), *Research in Accounting Measurement* ([n.p.], AAA, 1966), p. 91.

determined to resolve, or appear to resolve, standard-setting controversies in the context of traditional accounting.

EARLY USES OF ECONOMIC CONSEQUENCES ARGUMENTS

Perhaps the first evidence of economic consequences reasoning in the pronouncements of American policy makers occurred as long ago as 1941. In Accounting Research Bulletin no. 11, *Corporate Accounting for Ordinary Stock Dividends,* the CAP, in accordance with "proper accounting and corporate policy," required that fair market value be used to record the issuance of stock dividends where such market value was substantially in excess of book value.[6]

Evidently, both the New York Stock Exchange and a majority of the CAP regarded periodic stock dividends as "objectionable,"[7] and the CAP acted to make it more difficult for corporations to sustain a series of such stock dividends out of their accumulated earnings. As far as this author is aware, the U.S. is still the only country in which an accounting pronouncement requires that stock dividends be capitalized at the fair market value of the issued shares,[8] and this position was originally adopted in this country, at least in part, in order to produce an impact on the stock dividend policies of corporations.

A second evidence of economic conse-

quences' entering into the debates surrounding the establishment of accounting standards, this time involving management representations, occurred in 1947–48. It was the height of the postwar inflation, and several corporations had adopted replacement cost depreciation in their published financial statements.[9] Among the arguments employed in the debate involving the CAP were the possible implications for tax reform, the possible impact on wage bargaining and the need to counteract criticisms of profiteering by big business. Despite the pressures for accounting reform, the CAP reaffirmed its support of historical cost accounting for depreciation in ARB no. 33, *Depreciation and High Costs,* and in a letter issued in October 1948.

A clear use of the economic consequences argument occurred in 1958, when three subsidiaries of American Electric Power Company sued in the federal courts to enjoin the AICPA from allowing the CAP to issue a letter saying that the deferred tax credit account, as employed in the then-recently issued ARB no. 44 (Revised), *Declining-Balance Depreciation,* should be classified as a liability.[10] The three public utility companies were concerned that the SEC, under authority granted by the Public Utility Holding Company Act, would not permit them to issue debt securities in view of the unfavorable debt-to-equity ratios which the proposed reclassification would produce. The case reached the U.S. Supreme Court, where certiorari was denied. In the end, the clarifying letter was issued. Nonetheless, the

[6]Accounting Research Bulletin no. 11, *Corporate Accounting for Ordinary Stock Dividends* (New York: American Institute of Accountants, 1941), pp. 102–103.
[7]George O. May, letter to J. S. Seidman, dated July 14, 1941 (deposited in the national office library of Price Waterhouse & Co. in New York), p. 1.
[8]Price Waterhouse International, *A Survey in 46 Countries: Accounting Principles and Reporting Practices* ([n.p.], PWI, 1975), table 145.

[9]*Depreciation Policy When Price Levels Change* (New York: Controllership Foundation, Inc., 1948), ch. 14.
[10]*The AICPA Injunction Case—Re: ARB[No.] 44 (Revised),* Cases in Public Accounting Practice [no. 1] (Chicago, Ill.: Arthur Andersen & Co., 1960).

SEC accommodated the public utility companies by consenting to exclude the deferred tax credit from both liabilities and stockholders' equity for purposes of decisions taken under the Public Utility Holding Company Act.[11]

Shortly after the creation of the APB, the accounting treatment of the investment tax credit exploded on the scene. The three confrontations between the APB and the combined forces of industry and the administrations of Presidents Kennedy, Johnson and Nixon have already been amply discussed in the literature.[12] The government's argument was not that the accounting deferral of the investment tax credit was bad accounting but that it diluted the incentive effect of an instrument of fiscal policy.

In 1965, the subject of segmental reporting emerged from a hearing of the Senate Subcommittee on Antitrust and Monopoly on the economic effects of conglomerate mergers. The aim of the senatorial inquiry was not to promote better accounting practices for investor use but to provide the sub-committee and other government policy makers with accounting data that would facilitate their assessment of the economic efficacy of conglomerate mergers. Company managements naturally looked on such disclosures as potentially detrimental

to their merger ambitions. Pressure applied by this powerful sub-committee eventually forced the hand of the SEC to call for product-line disclosures in published financial reports. The repercussions of this intiative, which had its origin in a Senate hearing room, are still being felt.[13]

In 1967–69, the APB responded to an anguished objection by the startled Investment Bankers Association of America (today known as the Securities Industry Association) to a provision, once thought to be innocuous, in APB Opinion no. 10, *Omnibus Opinion–1966*, which imputed a debt discount to convertible debt and debt issued with stock warrants. The IBA was concerned about the impact of the accounting procedure on the market for such securities. In Opinion no. 14, *Accounting for Convertible Debt and Debt Issued With Stock Purchase Warrants*, the APB rescinded its action in regard to convertible debt while retaining the rest.[14]

From 1968 through 1971, the banking industry opposed the inclusion of bad-debt provisions and losses on the sales of securities in the net income of commercial banks. Bankers believed that the new measure would reflect unfavorably on the performance of banks. Eventually, through a concerted effort by the APB, the SEC and the bank regulatory agencies, generally accepted accounting principles were made applicable to banks.[15]

From 1968 through 1970, the APB

[11]*SEC Administrative Policy Re: Balance-Sheet Treatment of Deferred Income-Tax Credits*, Cases in Public Accounting Practice [nos. 5 and 6] (Chicago, Ill.: Arthur Andersen & Co., 1961), pp. 35–59.

[12]See Maurice Moonitz, "Some Reflections on the Investment Credit Experience," *Journal of Accounting Research*, Spring 1966, pp. 47–61; John L. Carey, *The Rise of the Accounting Profession: To Responsibility and Authority 1937–1969* (New York: AICPA, 1970), pp. 98–104; and Stephen A. Zeff, *Forging Accounting Principles in Five Countries: A History and an Analysis of Trends* (Champaign, Ill.: Stipes Publishing Company, 1972), pp. 178–80, 201–202, 219–221 and 326–327.

[13]Charles W. Plum and Daniel W. Collins, "Business Segment Reporting," in James Don Edwards and Homer A. Black (editors), *The Modern Accountant's Handbook* (Homewood, Ill.: Dow Jones-Irwin, Inc., 1976), pp. 469–511.

[14]Zeff, pp. 202, 211.

[15]Carey, p. 134; Maurice Moonitz, *Obtaining Agreement on Standards in the Accounting Profession*, Studies in Accounting Research no. 8 (Sarasota, Fla.: AAA, 1974), pp. 38–39; Zeff, pp. 210–211.

struggled with the accounting for business combinations. It was flanked on the one side by the Federal Trade Commission and the Department of Justice, which favored the elimination of pooling-of-interests accounting in order to produce a slowing effect on the merger movement and on the other by merger-minded corporations that were fervent supporters of pooling-of-interests accounting. The APB, appearing almost as a pawn in a game of political chess, disenchanted many of its supporters as it abandoned positions of principle in favor of an embarrassing series of pressure-induced compromises.[16]

In 1971, the APB held public hearings on accounting for marketable equity securities, leases and the exploration and drilling costs of companies in the petroleum industry. In all three areas, powerful industry pressures thwarted the board from acting. The insurance industry was intensely concerned about the possible effects on its companies' stock prices of including the unrealized gains and losses on portfolio holdings in their income statements.[17] The leasing initiative was squelched after senators, representatives and even the secretary of transportation responded to a letter-writing campaign by making pointed inquiries of the SEC and APB. The letter writers raised the specter of injury that the board's proposed action would supposedly cause to consumers and to the viability of companies in several key industries.[18] The petroleum industry was unable to unite on a solution to the contro-versy over full costing versus successful efforts costing, as it was alleged that a general imposition of the latter would adversely affect the fortunes of the small, independent exploration companies.[19] Using its considerable political might, the industry succeeded in persuading the board to postpone consideration of the sensitive subject.[20]

On each of the occasions enumerated above, outside parties intervened in the standard-setting process by an appeal to criteria that transcended the traditional questions of accounting measurement and fair presentation. They were concerned instead with the economic consequences of the accounting pronouncements.

"Economic consequences" have been invoked with even greater intensity in the short life of the FASB. Such questions as accounting for research and development costs, self-insurance and catastrophe reserves, development stage companies, foreign currency fluctuations, leases, the restructuring of troubled debt,[21] domestic

---

[16]Robert Chatov, *Corporate Financial Reporting: Public or Private Control?* (New York: The Free Press, 1975), pp. 212–222; and Zeff, pp. 212–216.
[17]Charles T. Horngren, "The Marketing of Accounting Standards," JofA, Oct. 73, pp. 63–64.
[18]Leonard M. Savoie, "Accounting Attitudes," in Robert R. Sterling (editor), *Institutional Issues in Public Accounting* (Lawrence, Kan.: Scholars Book Co., 1974), p. 326.

[19]See the testimony and submissions in *APB Public Hearing on Accounting and Reporting Practices in the Petroleum Industry,* Cases in Public Accounting Practice [no.] 10 (Chicago, Ill.: Arthur Andersen & Co., 1972).
[20]Savoie, p. 326.
[21]At the FASB's public hearing, some bankers warned of the dire economic consequences of requiring banks to write down their receivables following restructurings. Walter Wriston, chairman of Citicorp, asserted that the restructuring of New York City's obligations might just not have occurred if the banks would have been required to write down the carrying value of their receivables. Walter B. Wriston, *Transcript of Public Hearings* on FASB discussion memorandum, *Accounting by Debtors and Creditors When Debt Is Restructured* (1977–vol. 1–part 2), pp. 69–70. Yet the FASB, in its lengthy "Basis for Conclusions" in Statement no. 15, *Accounting by Debtors and Creditors for Troubled Debt Restructurings* (in which the feared write-downs were not required), did not refer to bankers' claims about the economic consequences of re-

inflation and relative price changes, and the exploration and drilling costs of companies in the petroleum industry have provoked widespread debate over their economic consequences.[22] The list is both extensive and impressive, and accounting academics are busily investigating the empirical validity of claims that these and other accounting standards may be linked with the specified economic consequences.

THE STANDARD-SETTING BODIES RESPOND

What have been the reactions of the standard-setting bodies to the intervention by

---

quiring significant write-downs. Does that omission imply that the FASB paid no attention to those assertions? Did the FASB conduct any empirical research (as it did concerning the economic consequences claims raised in connections with Statement no. 7, *Accounting and Reporting by Development Stage Enterprises*) to determine whether there was adequate ground to sustain such claims?

[22]See, e.g., Joseph M. Burns, *Accounting Standards and International Finance: With Special Reference to Multinationals* (Washington, D.C.: American Enterprise Institute for Public Policy Research, 1976); Committee on the Social Consequences of Accounting Information, pp. 9–12; Rappaport, pp. 90, 92; FASB, *Conference on the Economic Consequences of Financial Accounting Standards;* U.S. Department of Energy, comments before the Securities and Exchange Commission, "Accounting Practices—Oil and Gas Producers—Financial Accounting Standards," unpublished memorandum, dated April 3, 1978.

Evidence attesting to the attention given by the FASB to economic consequences issues may be found in the "Basis for Conclusions" sections of the applicable statements. In addition to companies and industry groups, government departments (such as the Department of Commerce, in Statement no. 7, and the Departments of Energy and Justice, in Statement no. 19, *Financial Accounting and Reporting by Oil and Gas Producing Companies*) were actively involved in the discussion of economic consequences.

outside parties and the claim that accounting standards should or should not be changed in order to avoid unhealthy economic or social consequences? In the 1940s and 1950s, the CAP enhanced its liaison with interested third parties through a wider circulation of exposure drafts and subcommittee reports. From 1958 to 1971, through appointments to key committees, joint discussions and symposiums, mass mailings of exposure drafts and formal public hearings, the Institute and the APB acted to bring interested organizations more closely into the standard-setting process. The hope was, one supposes, that these organizations would be satisfied that their views were given full consideration before the final issuance of opinions. These accommodations were, however, of a procedural sort, although it is possible that these outside views did have an impact on the substantive content of some of the resulting opinions. It would appear that the APB was at least somewhat influenced by economic consequences in its prolonged deliberations leading to the issuance of Opinions no. 16, *Business Combinations,* and no. 17, *Intangible Assets.*[23] During the public hearings in 1971 on marketable equity securities and the accounting practices of companies in the petroleum industry, management representatives on several occasions asserted economic consequences as relevant considerations. Yet members of the APB's subject-area committees neither asked for proof of those assertions nor, indeed, questioned their relevance to the setting of accounting standards.[24]

---

[23]Wyatt, pp. 92–93.

[24]*Proceedings* of Hearing on Accounting for Equity Securities, Accounting Principles Board (New York: AICPA, 1971), section A Transcript; and *APB Public Hearing on Accounting and Reporting Practices in the Petroleum Industry.*

Since it was the APB's inability to cope with the pressures brought by outside organizations that hastened its demise, it is worth noting that the FASB includes the Financial Executives Institute (FEI) among its co-sponsors. In my opinion, the incorporation of the FEI in the formal structure of the Financial Accounting Foundation (FAF, the FASB's parent) is one of the most significant advantages which the FASB possesses in relation to its predecessor.[25]

The procedural machinery established for the FASB is even more elaborate than that which existed in the final years of the APB. The object of these additional procedures has been to expand and intensify the interaction between the board and interested outside parties, notably companies, industry associations and government departments and agencies. A task force drawn from a broad spectrum of interested groups is appointed prior to the preparation of each discussion memorandum. The DM itself is much bulkier than the modest document the APB had issued before its public hearings; it contains a neutral discussion of the entire gamut of policy issues that bear on the resolution of the controversy before the board. A Financial Accounting Standards Advisory Council (FASAC), composed of representatives of a wide array of interested groups, was appointed to be a sounding board for the FASB. The board itself has been composed of members drawn from accounting practice, the universities, companies and government—again, so that it would be re-sponsive, and would appear to be responsive, to the concerns of those "constituencies." In an effort to persuade skeptics of the merit of its recommendations, the board includes in its statements a lengthy explanation of the criteria, arguments and empirical considerations it used to fashion the recommended standards.

Following criticism from within the profession of the board's operations and procedures, the FAF conducted a study in 1977 of the entire FASB operation. Among the FAF's many recommendations were proposals that the board expand its formal and informal contacts with interested groups and that it include an economic impact analysis in important exposure drafts. On this latter point the FAF's structure committee concluded: "The Board need not be unduly influenced by the possibility of an economic impact, but it should consider both the possible costs and the expected benefits of a proposal."[26] In addition, the structure committee recommended actions that would strengthen the roles of the task forces and the FASAC.[27] In 1978, under pressure from Congress, the board began to conduct virtually all its formal meetings (including those of the FASAC) "in the sunshine."

The history of the APB and the FASB is one of a succession of procedural steps taken to bring the boards' deliberations into closer proximity to the opinions and concerns of interested third parties. As in the case of the APB, it is possible that an effect of these more elaborate procedures has been a change in the substance of the FASB's conclusions and recommendations.

By the middle 1970s, however, it was

[25]The inclusion of the FEI could arguably become the undoing of the FASB. If the FEI were to lose confidence in the board, it is possible that many of the companies which now contribute to the Financial Accounting Foundation might decline to continue doing so, provoking a financial crisis that could threaten the board's viability.

[26]Financial Accounting Foundation structure committee, *The Structure of Establishing Financial Accounting Standards* (Stamford, Conn.: FAF, 1977), p. 51.
[27]Ibid., pp. 23–25.

decided that the FASB should add economic (and social) consequences to the substantive issues it normally addresses. The inclusion of "probable economic or social impact" among the other "qualities of useful information" in the board's conceptual framework DM,[28] the board's announcement of its interest in empirical studies of economic consequences[29] and the recommendation of the FAF structure committee that the board inform itself adequately on the "various impacts its pronouncements might have"[30] collectively confirm this new direction. The issue of economic consequences has, therefore, changed from one having only procedural implications for the standard-setting process to one which is now firmly a part of the standard setters' substantive policy framework.

ECONOMIC CONSEQUENCES AS A SUBSTANTVE ISSUE

Economic consequences have finally become accepted as a valid substantive policy issue for a number of reasons:

- The tenor of the times. The decade of the 1970s is clearly one in which American society is holding its institutions responsible for the social, environmental and economic consequences of their actions, and the crystallized public opinion on this subject eventually became evident (and relevant) to those interested in the accounting standard-setting activity.
- The sheer intractability of the accounting

problems being addressed. Since the mid-1960s, the APB and the FASB have been taking up difficult accounting questions on which industry positions have been well entrenched. To some degree, companies that are sensitive to the way their performances are evaluated through the medium of reported earnings have permitted their decision-making behavior to be influenced by their perceptions of how such behavior will be seen through the prism of accounting earnings. Still other such companies have tailored their accounting practices to reflect their economic performances in the best light— and the managers are evidently loathe to change their decision-making behavior in order to accommodate newly imposed accounting standards. This would also be a concern to managers who are being paid under incentive compensation plans.[31]

- The enormity of the impact. Several of the issues facing the APB and the FASB in recent years have portended such a high degree of impact on either the volatility or level of earnings and other key financial figures and ratios that the FASB can no longer discuss the proposed accounting treatments without encountering incessant arguments over the probable economic consequences. Particularly apt examples are accounting for foreign exchange fluctuations, domestic inflation and relative price changes and the exploration and drilling costs of companies in the petroleum industry.
- The growth in the information economics-social choice, behavioral, income smoothing and decision usefulness literature in accounting. Recent writings in

[28]Financial Accounting Standards Board discussion memorandum, *Conceptual Framework for Financial Accounting and Reporting: Elements of Financial Statements and Their Measurement* (Stamford, Conn.: FASB, 1976), par. 367.
[29]Financial Accounting Standards Board, *Status Report,* no. 45, February 7, 1977.
[30]Structure committee, p. 31.

[31]Alfred Rappaport, "Executive Incentives vs. Corporate Growth," *Harvard Business Review,* July–August 1978, pp. 81–88.

the information economics-social choice literature have provided a broad analytical framework within which the problems of economic consequences may be conceptualized. Beginning with Stedry,[32] the literature on the behavioral implications of accounting numbers has grown significantly, drawing the attention of researchers and policy makers to the importance of considering the effects of accounting information. The literature on income smoothing has suggested the presence of a managerial motive for influencing the measurement of earnings trends. Finally, the decision usefulness literature, although it is confined to the direct users of accounting information, has served to lessen the inclination of accountants to argue over the inherent ''truth'' of different accounting incomes and, instead, to focus on the use of information by those who receive accounting reports.[33]

- The insufficiency of the procedural reforms adopted by the APB and the FASB. Despite the succession of procedural steps which both boards have taken to provide outside parties with a forum for expressing their views, the claims of economic consequences—and the resulting criticisms of the boards' pronouncements—have continued unabated. The conclusion has evidently been reached that procedural remedies alone will not meet the problem.
- The Moss and Metcalf investigations. By the middle of 1976, it was known that Congressman John E. Moss (D—Calif.)

and the late Senator Lee Metcalf (D—Mont.) were conducting investigations of the performance of the accounting profession, including its standard-setting activities, and it could reasonably have been inferred that the responsiveness of the standard-setting bodies to the economic and social effects of their decisions would be an issue.

- The increasing importance to corporate managers of the earnings figure in capital-market transactions. Especially in the 1960s, when capital markets were intensely competitive and the merger movement was fast paced, the earnings figure came to be viewed as an important element of managerial strategy and tactics. This factor is of importance in today's markets, as the pace of merger activity has once again quickened.
- Accounting figures came to be viewed as an instrument of social control. The social control of American enterprise has been well known in the rate-regulated energy, transportation and communications fields, but in recent years the earnings figure has, to an increasing degree, been employed as a control device on a broader scale.[34] Examples are fiscal incentives (such as the investment tax credit and redefinitions of taxable income that diverge from accounting income) that have an influence on debates surrounding financial resporting,[35] the price-control mechanism of Phase II in 1972–73[36] and

[32]Andrew C. Stedry, *Budget Control and Cost Behavior* (Englewood Cliffs, N.J.: Prentice-Hall, Inc., 1960).
[33]Committee on concepts and standards for external financial reports, *Statement on Accounting Theory and Theory Acceptance* (Sarasota, Fla.: AAA, 1977), pp. 5–29.

[34]DR Scott, though writing in a different context, nonetheless was prophetic in his prediction that accounting would increasingly be used as a means of social control. DR Scott, *Cultural Significance of Accounts* (New York: Henry Holt and Co., 1931), esp. ch. 14.
[35]The ''required tax conformity'' issue of the early 1970s (see Zeff, pp. 218–19) is another instance.
[36]Robert F. Lanzillotti, Mary T. Hamilton and R. Blaine Roberts, *Phase II in Review; the Price*

the data base contemplated by the Energy Policy and Conservation Act of 1975.

- The realization that outsiders could influence the outcome of accounting debates. Before the 1960s, accounting controversies were rarely reported in the financial press, and it was widely believed that accounting was a constant, if not a fixed parameter, in the management of business operations. With the publicity given to the accounting for the investment credit in 1962–63, to the fractious dialogue within the AICPA in 1963–64 over the authority of the APB and to other accounting disagreements involving the APB, managers and other outside parties have come to realize that accounting may be a variable after all—that the rules of accounting are not unyielding or even unbending.

- The growing use of the third argument, advanced earlier in the article, in accounting debates. Mostly for the reasons enumerated above, outside parties began to discard the pretense that their objections to proposed changes in accounting standards were solely, or even primarily, a function of differences over the proper interpretation of accounting principles. True reasons came out into the open, and accounting policy makers could no longer ignore their implications.

It is significant that economic consequences have become an important issue at a time when accounting and finance academics have been arguing that the U.S. capital markets are efficient with respect to publicly available information and, moreover, that the market cannot be "fooled"

by the use of different accounting methods to reflect the same economic reality.[37]

THE DILEMMA FACING THE FASB

What are the implications of the economic consequences movement for the FASB? It has become clear that political agencies (such as government departments and congressional committees) expect accounting standard setters to take explicitly into consideration the possible adverse consequences of proposed accounting standards. This expectation appears to be strongest where the consequences are thought to be significant and widespread—and especially where they might impinge on economic and social policies being pursued by the government. In these instances, the FASB must show that it has studied the possible consequences but that the benefits from implementing the standards outweigh the possible adverse consequences. Where the claimed consequences have implications for economic or social policies of national importance, the FASB should not be surprised if a political resolution is imposed by outside forces.

To what degree should the FASB have regard for economic consequences? To say that any significant economic consequences should be studied by the board does not imply that accounting principles and fair presentation should be dismissed as the principal guiding factor in the board's determination. The FASB is respected as a body of accounting experts, and it should focus its attention where its expertise will be acknowledged. While some observers might opt for determining

Commission Experience (Washington, D.C.: Brookings Institution, 1975), pp. 73–77; and C. Jackson Grayson, Jr., and Louis Neeb, *Confessions of a Price Controller* (Homewood, Ill.: Dow Jones-Irwin, Inc., 1974), pp. 71–76.

[37]See, e.g., William H. Beaver, "What Should Be the FASB's Objectives?" JofA, Aug. 73, pp. 49–56.

accounting standards only with regard to their consequences for economic and social welfare, the FASB would surely preside over its own demise if it were to adopt this course and make decisions primarily on other than accounting grounds.

The board is thus faced with a dilemma which requires a delicate balancing of accounting and nonaccounting variables. Although its decisions should rest—and be seen to rest—chiefly on accounting considerations, it must also study—and be seen to study—the possible adverse economic and social consequences of its proposed actions. In order to deal adequately with this latter function, the board may find it convenient to develop a staff of competent analysts from allied disciplines, notably economics.

Economic consequences bids fair to be the most challenging accounting issue of the 1970s. What is abundantly clear is that we have entered an era in which economic and social consequences may no longer be ignored as a substantive issue in the setting of accounting standards. The profession must respond to the changing tenor of the times while continuing to perform its essential role in the areas in which it possesses undoubted expertise.

ACCOUNTING RESEARCH, EDUCATION AND PRACTICE

ROBERT R. STERLING

Any practitioner or teacher in the field of accounting would find it difficult to assert that there is a congruence between research in his field and actual education and professional practice. Can this absence of harmony be termed a conflict? I have been searching for conflicts, and this search has led me to some conclusions I want to share. In looking for instances of conflict I systematically compared research findings (i.e., articles in research journals) with education (i.e., contents of textbooks) and with practice (i.e., Accounting Principles Board pronouncements and *Accounting Trends and Techniques*). This comparison

resulted in a rather lengthy list of differences.

My first inclination was to classify these differences as conflicts. Two things bothered me about this classification. First, I noticed that some of these differences had existed for over 30 years and both sides had been unwilling to compromise. How could this be? In political science we would expect such a situation to lead to open warfare. The absence of open warfare between research and education-practice caused me to hesitate in classifying the differences as conflicts.

Second, I noticed that these differences did not seem to concern my friends and colleagues. This lack of concern was vividly illustrated when, while visiting another university, I sat in a friend's class. I heard him vigorously defend a position that was contrary to a position that he had earlier taken in the literature. When queried about this apparent conflict, he replied that he was preparing his students for practice, not research. Had it been a Ph.D. seminar, he said, he would have taken the contrary position.

In searching for an explanation for this behavior, schizophrenia occurred to me. However, that seemed overly harsh, as well as not providing an explanation for the prolonged presence of uncompromised differences without open warfare. Finally another explanation occurred to me; it is drawn from the field of political science and requires an initial digression. Consider the model in Figure 1 in terms of conflict and isolation.

The solid lines indicate the transportation capabilities of three countries in the 12th century. The transportation curves of England and France indicate the capability of each country for transporting troops and supplies (or diplomats and goods for exchange) to the other. There was a potential for conflict between these two countries *for this reason*. There was also the potential for compromise and complementarity. At various times in history all three occurred: wars, diplomatic arrangements, reciprocal trade and defense agreements.

There was a complete absence of conflict between Japan and England in the 12th century. The reason was isolation, not harmony. There were vast differences in the interests and cultures of the two countries, but since the curves did not intersect, these differences did not, in fact could not, result in conflict. For the same reason there was

Figure 2.

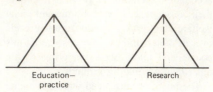

Education–
practice

Research

no need, in fact no possibility, for compromise. Similarly, there was no possibility of complementary relations.

In short, contact is a necessary condition for the occurrence of conflicts, compromises or complementarities. Isolation prohibits all three relations.

In our own field, this isolation attaches to research. Figure 2 sets forth the situation as I visualize it. Just as the isolation of 12th century Japan and England precluded conflicts despite different interests and cultures, so does the isolation of accounting research and education-practice preclude conflicts despite vast differences between them. There is no relationship. They are isolated.

There are indeed a few textbooks that present research results, but usually only to dismiss them with some offhand comments about being contrary to acceptable practice. There is even less contact between research and practice. Consider, for example, the vast amount of research time and effort devoted to price levels. This research resulted in the APB's permitting supplementary statements adjusted for price level change, but the 1971 *Accounting Trends and Techniques* reports that "none of the survey companies presented financial statements adjusted to a common dollar basis."[1] In short, although I recognize the

Figure 1.

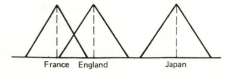

France   England   Japan

[1]Woolsey Carmalt, ed., *Accounting Trends and Techniques: Annual Survey of Accounting Practices Followed in 600 Stockholders' Reports* (New York: AICPA, 1971), p. 49.

existence of some contact, it is my judgment that this contact is so nebulous that it can be disregarded.

THE RELATION OF EDUCATION TO PRACTICE

On the other hand, the absence of conflicts between education and practice is due to harmony, not isolation. This also explains the lack of compromises, for two subjects with harmonious interests do not need to make any.

This complementary relation is due mainly to educators' predilection to prepare students for practice; we educators teach our students acceptable practices so that they can get jobs. Practice complements education in that it provides educators with information on what are the acceptable practices and practitioners practice what educators teach them. The process is summarized in Figure 3.

Strictly interpreted, Figure 3 would prohibit change. Since changes do, in fact, occur, we know that there are exogenous inputs to the circle. The source of these inputs is practice, not education or research. That is, practitioners add to (they rarely subtract from) their store of accepted practices and then educators observe, codify and teach these additional accepted practices.

AN EXAMPLE

The conclusions presented above can be illustrated, albeit not proved, by an example, the problem of valuing marketable securities. I selected this because (1) the APB has been considering the problem and issuing exposure drafts, (2) the problems encountered in accounting for marketable securities are more tractable than those encountered in accounting for other kinds of assets and (3) there is some clear evidence that there are nonaccounting forces at work on this problem.

RESEARCH

The research on marketable securities per se has been sparse. The index to the *Accounting Review* magazine does not contain a subject matter classification for "marketable securities" or for "investments" or for any cognate. Despite the paucity of specific articles on the subject, a number of authors have discussed marketable securities as an illustrative problem or as a subcategory of their main topic.

Going only as far back as 1939, I find that Kenneth MacNeal was concerned with the valuation problem in general but that he used marketable securities as one easily understandable example. One of the fables with which he begins his book, *Truth in Accounting*, concerns investment trusts holding marketable securities. MacNeal explains how the managements of these trusts could manipulate income by the timing of their sales. One of the trusts reported a large net income in Year 1 by selling its securities, thereby "realizing" a profit, and then it reinvested the cash in the same securities. The other trust did not sell any securities and, therefore, did not "realize"

Figure 3.

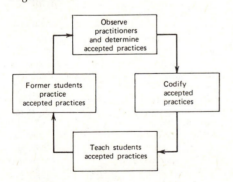

a profit. In this way the reported income of the two trusts went up and down at the discretion of the management. MacNeal showed how unscrupulous managements could bilk the shareholders by this device. He also showed that valuing marketable securities at their current market value both eliminated the possibility of such manipulations and gave investors and potential investors relevant information.

In the subsequent literature there were sporadic comments about the desirability of valuing marketable securities at current market price. However, most of the postwar literature was concerned with price levels, as opposed to price relatives, and these two issues became confused. The beginning of the 1960s saw a renewed interest in the formulation of accounting principles and in looking specifically at the valuation problem. It was then that Moonitz (Accounting Research Study No. 1) and Sprouse and Moonitz (ARS No. 3) appeared. The postulates contained in the former were criticized as being "self-evident observations" by Spacek; the general attitude seemed to be that Moonitz had simply made a collection of truisms and labeled them postulates of accounting. Utilizing these truisms as postulates or premises, Sprouse and Moonitz drew some conclusions, one of which was that marketable securities "should be measured by their current market price." In addition to the deduction, they pointed out that this practice would reveal good and bad decisions of the management in respect to holding these securities as well as eliminate the anomaly of valuing identical and interchangeable securities at different magnitudes. Shortly thereafter Sprouse's "Historical Costs of Current Assets—Traditional and Treacherous"[2] expanded upon the

conclusion that he and Moonitz had reached in ARS No. 3. With admirable patience and good humor, he once again explained the absurdities that could result if marketable securities were valued at historical cost (including an actual case, à la MacNeal, in which the management had manipulated its income by timing its sales of marketable securities) and the advantages that would result if marketable securities were valued at market price.

Insofar as I know, no one has challenged Sprouse and Moonitz's conclusion. In my opinion their logic was flawless. We noted above that their postulates were criticized for being truistic. This is a logician's Valhalla. To have unchallenged, truistic postulates and unchallenged, flawless logic is a state to which all logicians aspire but few achieve. In such a situation the conclusions are not only valid (because of the flawless logic) but they are also likely to be sound (because of the true premises).

Several other research reports have appeared, such as Edwards and Bell, and Chambers.[3] Although there have been some criticisms of the general valuation schemes of these authors, I have not seen any criticisms in regard to marketable securities in particular. I also wrote a book which used a trader in securities as a vehicle for discussion,[4] hoping that by narrowing the discussion we could reach agreement on a particular issue even if we couldn't solve the global problems of ac-

---

[2]Robert T. Sprouse, "Historical Costs of Current Assets—Traditional and Treacherous," *Accounting Review,* October 1963, pp. 687–695.
[3]E. O. Edwards and P. W. Bell, *The Theory of Measurement of Business Income* (Berkeley: University of California Press, 1964); R. J. Chambers, *Accounting Evaluation and Economic Behavior* (Englewood Cliffs, N.J.: Prentice-Hall, 1966).
[4]R. Sterling, *The Theory of the Measurement of Enterprise Income* (Lawrence: The University Press of Kansas, 1970).

counting. My work received some critical comments by Mattessich,[5] but he did not disagree with my conclusion: Marketable securities ought to be valued at market.

The last research report to which I will refer is contained in a recent article by Beaver. Utilizing the findings of empirical research on stock prices, he concludes as follows:

> *A constant lament in accounting is that we do not have sufficient evidence upon which to base policy decisions regarding appropriate reporting rules for financial statement preparation. The area of the valuation of marketable securities is rare in the sense that extensive evidence exists, supporting the current market value rule with remarkable consistency.*[6]

Note that this statement comes from considerations different from those of, say, Sprouse and Moonitz. Beaver utilizes concepts and evidence from finance in order to arrive at his conclusion. It is not simply a reiteration of what has gone before but comes from an entirely new direction. This being so, we should have even more confidence in the validity and soundness of that conclusion.

PRACTICE

The 1971 edition of *Accounting Trends and Techniques* reveals that for marketable securities in the current asset section the most frequently reported valuation method is unqualified "cost." Adding the qualifications "plus accrued interest" and "amor-

Table 1. Marketable Securities Valuation, Current Asset Section

Cost	75%	
Cost plus accrued interest	14	
Amortized cost	3	
Total cost		92%
Lower of cost or market		5
Market		2
Other		1
Total reporting valuation method		100%

Source: Accounting Trends and Techniques, 1971, Table 2–4, p.53.

tized" runs the total of cost valuations up to 92%. The breakdown of those companies reporting their valuation method is given in Table 1, above.

As expected, almost all (97%) of practice is on the basis of cost and lower of cost or market. Securities were valued at market in only 2% of the cases. Identical findings are reported in Sterling, Tollefson and Flaherty.[7] A random sample of 168 CPAs revealed that only 2% of the respondents would value marketable securities at market in the absence of an exchange.

EDUCATION

Naturally, textbooks furnished the main source of my evidence in regard to education. I restricted my examination of these to the respective "intermediate theory" volume in the popular elementary-intermediate-advanced series. The reason for this restriction, as supported by publishers' representatives and my personal observations, is that the intermediate theory vol-

[5]Richard Mattessich, "The Market Value Method According to Sterling: A Review Article," *Abacus,* December 1971, pp. 176–193.
[6]William H. Beaver, "Reporting Rules for Marketable Equity Securities," JofA, October 1971, p. 61.

[7]Robert R. Sterling, John O. Tollefson and Richard E. Flaherty, "Exchange Valuation: An Empirical Test," *Accounting Review,* October 1972, pp. 709–721.

ume is the only book containing theory that is widely used in undergraduate curriculums. Since over 95% of accounting students do not go past the baccalaureate degree, these intermediate texts are the sole source of theory education in perhaps 90% of the cases. (This figure is a guess. I tried to get a better estimate by asking various publishers' representatives to state their share of the market as a percentage. Unfortunately, the various individual estimates summed to 183%. On this basis I should conclude that 183% of our students use these intermediate texts.)

In regard to marketable securities held as temporary investments, the typical intermediate text presents the valuation of marketable securities as a question and then answers that question by referring to accepted practice. After considering the question of the "informative quality" of different valuation methods, Finney and Miller conclude: ". . . because such an alternative [market value] method could result in writing up an asset above cost, it is not generally accepted."[8] Another popular text says, "Whether realization should be limited to the period of sale when applied to marketable securities is a question worth considering" and after a half a page of consideration it concludes: "The question which must be answered is, 'What event in the life of the enterprise gives rise to the recognition of gains and losses from holding securities in lieu of cash?' Practicing accountants have generally applied the lower of cost or market rule to the valuation of marketable securities."[9]

A text published last year listed market valuation as a possible accounting method. However, the authors' reason for the listing was that "The APB is drafting an Opinion that would require fair value accounting for marketable securities."[10] In other words, the basis of this listing in the *authors' prediction of future accepted practice*, not research results. It has turned out, as we shall see later, that their prediction was wrong.

My secondary source of information was our former students. In the previous section, I stated that *Accounting Trends and Techniques* reported how our former students value marketable securities in practice. In addition, in connection with another activity, I recently asked 246 seniors in public practice to indicate the valuation method for marketable securities held as temporary investments, that is (a) in accordance with GAAP and (b) theoretically correct. Of the usable 239 responses, 229 (96%) checked "cost" or "lower of cost or market" as the answer to (a) and 220 (92%) checked the same answers to (b). Ten (4%) checked "net realizable value" or "market value" as the answer to (a), and 19 (8%) checked the same answers to (b).

In another test Sterling, Tollefson and Flaherty found that 82% of a random sample of CPAs agreed with the cost method of valuing marketable securities even though the market value was 3750% of the cost.

CONCLUSIONS FROM THE EXAMPLE

In research different people from different schools of thought using different postulates and different research methods have

[8]H. A. Finney and Herbert E. Miller, *Principles of Accounting Intermediate,* 6th ed., Prentice-Hall Accounting Series (Englewood Cliffs, N.J.: Prentice-Hall, 1965), p. 256.
[9]Walter B. Meigs, Charles E. Johnson and Thomas F. Keller, *Intermediate Accounting* (New York: McGraw-Hill Book Co., 1963), pp. 221–222.

[10]Glenn A. Welsch, Charles T. Zlatkovich and John A. White, *Intermediate Accounting,* 3d ed., Williard J. Graham Series in Accounting (Homewood, Ill.: Richard D. Irwin, 1972), p. 240.

drawn the same conclusion: Marketable securities ought to be valued at market. That conclusion has not been challenged in the research literature.

In practice the predominant method of valuation is cost, with lower of cost or market a distant second. Combined, the two valuation methods amount to about 97% of practice.

In education the intermediate texts raise the question of valuing marketable securities, but they "answer" this question by stating the accepted practice. These texts do not present the results of the research that has been done in this area. Over 80% of our former students believe that the present accepted practice is the theoretically correct method. Students tend to identify theoretically correct with accepted practice. I would conjecture that the manner of presentation in the texts (and in the lectures) is the reason for this identification.

Thus, the research results regarding marketable securities are contradicted in education and practice. Education and practice seem to be complementary in that educators teach accepted practice and practitioners accept and practice what they are taught. This complementary relationship excludes research from the chain of events that determine what is taught and what is practiced. Research is an isolated activity in accounting, as shown in Figure 2.

NORMATIVE RELATIONSHIPS

Turning from the *is* to the *ought*, I now consider the prescribing of relationships, the normative function of research in the educational process.

In the first half of the 19th century research as an organized activity was an unknown and alien notion. At that time universities concentrated on the teaching function, under the assumption that there was nothing new to discover. It was thought that the function of a university was to pass along the received dogma. In the second half of the 19th century British universities began to think of research as an activity complementary to teaching. Along about 1875 the relationship of the three activities became

1. $R(x) \rightarrow E(x) \rightarrow P(x)$—that is, if researchers found that x is the case, then students were taught that x is the case and then, upon graduation, students implemented x in practice.

The chain in (1) is now common to almost all disciplines. In medicine, for example, researchers discovered that phenoxymethylpenicillin has a powerful bacteriostatic effect against pneumococci and certain other malevolent bacteria. Subsequent to this discovery they educated their students in terms of this discovery.

They also educated their former students to this effect by publishing less technical articles in practitioners' magazines and inserting entries in the *Physician's Handbook* and *Physician's Desk Reference* that say, in effect, "If your patient has pneumonia, give him a shot of penicillin." The reader is invited to examine the various accounting and auditing handbooks and compare their pronouncements on marketable securities to the research results presented earlier.

By contrast, the chain in accounting is

2. $P(x) \rightarrow E(X) \rightarrow P(x)$—that is, if x is practiced, then students are taught that x is practiced and then, upon graduation, students implement x in practice. Note what would have happened in medicine had this procedure been followed. A survey of practicing physicians would have revealed that the accepted practice for treating pneumonia was the administration of sulfa drugs. Then medical professors would have taught their students to administer sulfa drugs in pneumonia cases. Upon graduation, their students would have implemented that treatment in practice. Then the teachers would have surveyed their former students and repeated the process. As is immediately apparent, the problem with (2) is that it prohibits progress. Had medical teachers adopted this procedure in the 18th century, they would still be teaching their students how to let blood between haircuts.

The solution is also immediately apparent: adopt chain (1), i.e., teach research results. I know that that is a revoluationary idea in accounting and that we accountants tend to be conservative. However, since that idea was adopted by all other disciplines in 1875, perhaps it is safe for us to adopt it in 1975. Except for some theologies, I don't know of any other discipline that perceives its duty to be the passing along of accepted practices. Many accountants have complained about the lack of respect accorded our discipline. You will recall that Hatfield complains about the "contempt of our colleagues."[11] Some, including Hatfield, have offered a defense of accounting. Perhaps it would be more productive to change accounting than to complain about the lack of respect. Perhaps if we changed we wouldn't need to defend our discipline.

The objection to teaching research results is that students need jobs, and, in order to get jobs, they need to know accepted practices, not research results. This is true, but to teach accepted practices to the exclusion of research results creates more problems than it solves. Perhaps we can teach both. In my undergraduate theory class I try to teach both by distinguishing

[11]Henry Rand Hatsfield, "An Historical Defense of Bookkeeping," *Significant Accounting Essays*, Maurice Moonitz and A. C. Littleton, ed. (Englewood Cliffs, N.J.: Prentice-Hall, 1965), p. 4.

between theory and GAAP. The theory part is taught like other theory courses in economics, management science, etc. The GAAP part is taught like a law or tax course. In regard to marketable securities, for example, a typical problem assignment would require (1) valuation in accordance with research results and (2) valuation in accordance with GAAP. For the GAAP part of the assignment the students are required to cite "substantial authoritative support" for the method that they use. Thus, in the same way that the students must find and follow the tax laws and precedents in order to determine taxable income, they must find and follow the APB laws and precedents in order to determine GAAP income. As far as I am concerned, the analogy is perfect. The fact that it is the law doesn't necessarily mean that it is right. It simply means that it is the law and one must know what the law is in order to obey it.

I believe the careful drawing of this distinction is vital to the progress of accounting. We educators have not been making this distinction clear in the past. The result is a rather subtle but particularly nefarious effect on our students.

The typical text collects accepted practices and tries to rationalize them by fitting them into a theory. Since the practices are inconsistent, the texts necessarily contain contradictions. For example, they characterize market values as indeterminable and too subjective to be used in one place, and in another they present the lower of cost or market rule which requires that market values be determined and used. Our students learn these contradictions: worse, it appears that they learn to reason by contradiction. Consider the following bit of evidence.

The questionnaire mentioned earlier (administered to the 246 seniors) included the following questions:

1. Application of the current market price method of valuing inventories can best be described as (check one word on each line)
   —feasible   —infeasible
             and
   —objective   —subjective
2. Application of the lower cost or market rule to inventories when market is below cost can best be described as (check one word on each line).
   —feasible   —infeasible
             and
   —objective   —subjective

(The two questions were separated by a number of other questions on the questionnaire.) The results were: 3% checked "feasible" and 6% checked "objective" in answer to question 1. In answer to question 2, 99% checked "feasible" and 62% checked "objective."

I was startled and dismayed by these results: some variation in the answers to the two questions was to be expected, but certainly not a difference of 96% and 52%. Although I don't have a control group, I don't believe that a group of nonaccountants would contradict themselves to this extent. I think we have to *teach* our students to make such contradictions. I also think that such teaching is dysfunctional.

If we teach research results, there will be a complementary relationship between research and education. If this course is adopted, conflict is inevitable, but it is preferable to isolation. I opt for conflict for two reasons.

First, I have faith in research. It provides the best chance for us to solve our problems. Admittedly, it does not provide us with a guarantee that the problems will be solved. Recently many accountants, particularly practitioners, have become disenchanted with it. They point out that research has failed to find the answer in many instances. I agree that research often fails us and I, too, sometimes become discouraged. But what is the alternative?

In medicine, research has failed to provide a cure for cancer despite the expenditure of more than a billion dollars. This is discouraging. However, the only two recognized alternatives in medicine are to (1) give up or (2) continue the research. In accounting, research has also failed to find the answer to our problems. But then we have spent practically no money on it: The whole American Accounting Association research budget is less than that for undergraduate research in a single science department at a typical university. As in medicine, we can either (1) give up on the problem or (2) continue to do research.

If we choose to continue research, then we must connect it to education and practice. To find the solution to a problem and then fail to teach it or practice it is to fail to solve the problem. Certainly, we would not consider cancer to be cured if a cure was found that was never taught or practiced. A problem is "solved" only after the solution is implemented. This requires that research be in contact with education and practice. If the outcome is conflict, then so be it.

Second, the conflicts that come out of this contact may be beneficial. Political scientists, particularly those influenced by Hegel, argue that one should expose conflicts or, if there is an embryonic conflict, then one should "exacerbate the cleavage," so that a new and better theory can spring from the conflicting theories. The crisis theory of democracy, with the conflicts that attend crisis, is a similar idea.

Consider another medical analogy. A physician at an accident scene without sterile instruments may be faced with an accident victim in need of a tracheotomy. Medical theory specifies (1) a tracheotomy and (2) sterile techniques. The exigencies of practice force the physician to make a choice. Hence, a conflict arises. The physician recognizes the conflict because he has been taught that he *ought* to use sterile instruments. As a direct result of this kind of conflict, researchers have developed packaging techniques that permit sterile instruments to be portable. In this way practice and research reinforce one another. New research was initiated because of conflicts between the necessary and the possible, and progress was the result.

Contrast an accountant on the job. The exigencies of practice (for example, current generally accepted accounting principles) may require that he account for marketable securities at cost. If he has been taught only accepted practices, and especially if he identifies accepted practices with theoretically correct practices, then he will not recognize a conflict. In the absence of such conflicts research and practice will not reinforce one another and no progress will be made. Therefore, I opt for conflict. Students should be taught what ought to be done even when it conflicts with accepted practice, nay, *especially* when it conflicts with accepted practice.

THE RELATION OF MANAGEMENT TO ACCOUNTING PRACTICE

The influence of management upon accounting practices is too important to be neglected in this discussion. We noted above that practitioners add to their store of practices but that they rarely subtract from that store. If we inquire into the reasons for this, we will find that managements desire additional practices and that managements have the power to get what they want.

Moonitz,[12] in an important but unfortunately neglected article, has compared problems encountered in the establishment of auditing standards to those encountered in the establishment of accounting principles. He finds one major difference: managements. It seems that managements are vitally interested in accounting principles. They would like to have a set of alternative practices from which to select. Further, they have sufficient power to implement their desires,[13] and they are the source of the exogenous inputs to the circle shown in Figure 3.

3. $M(x) \rightarrow P(x) \rightarrow E(x)$—that is, if managements desire x to be an accepted practice, then x will become an accepted practice and educators will teach that x is an accepted practice.

Chain (3) is illustrated by the recent history of the proposed marketable securities Opinion. The Accounting Principles Board issued a draft of an Opinion dated September 1, 1971, which required the valuation of marketable securities at market and the inclusion of the value differences in income. Managements disagreed.[14]

A somewhat weakened draft of the Opinion was issued January 10, 1972. Managements disagreed with that draft also. In fact, "somebody" started a mail campaign to Congress and the SEC. A review of all the possibilities was issued on March 29, 1972, which said, "The Board has not, however, reached a conclusion on the most appropriate recommendation." A recent report from the APB stated that they were going to "start all over" on the ques-

---

[12]Maurice Moonitz, "Why Is It So Difficult to Agree Upon a Set of Accounting Principles?"

The Australian Accountant, November 1968, pp. 621–631.
[13]See Robert R. Sterling, "Accounting Power," JofA, January 1973, pp. 61–67.
[14]For an example of this disagreement, see "APB Committee Considers Views on Equity Security Reporting," JofA, July 1971, p. 10.

tion of marketable securities. It now appears that no Opinion will be issued.

In short, the APB wanted to issue an Opinion that was in accord with the research results presented above. Managements resisted. The Board did not have the power to overcome managements' resistance and so it backed off and finally capitulated.

There are two things to note about this case. First, if you think that managements' defense of historical cost is based on the belief that it more fairly or accurately presents, you have a livelier imagination than I. It seems to me to be quite clear that managements desire "flexibility." In this case they want enough flexibility to be able to realize and report the amount of income that suits their purposes. Thus some, if not most, accepted practices spring from managements' desire to serve their own ends. For this reason, some accepted practices are bad practices. I would hope that you would agree that it is not the duty of educators to codify and teach bad practices.

Of course, the long-run solution is to give the APB (or the Financial Accounting Standards Board) the power to resist managements' self-serving wishes and to implement research results. The ability of the APB to institute reforms against managements' wishes would have been enhanced if there were agreement among public accountants.

The second thing to note about this case is this very lack of agreement. In addition to managements' resistance, the APB was faced with the resistance of a large number of public accountants. Evidence for this resistance is that the APB felt it necessary to include in their drafts those tired, invalid arguments for historical cost that were demolished by MacNeal in 1939 and by many other scholars since then. The problem is that many of our former students believe in those tired, invalid arguments and, there-

fore, they joined managements in resisting the APB's Opinion. Had there been solidarity among accountants, we would have had a better chance of issuing the Opinion. Had educators taught research results instead of accepted practices, perhaps we would have had more agreement among accountants and, hence, more solidarity.

SUMMARY

My argument is:

1. Research is isolated from education-practice.
2. Education and practice are complementary in that educators teach accepted practices and practitioners practice what they are taught.
3. Accepted practices are inconsistent and, therefore, the "theory" of accepted practice is contradictory.
4. Students taught the "theory" of accepted practices tend to identify "theoretically correct" with "accepted in practice." Students taught a contradictory theory tend to reason by contradiction. Students taught only accepted practices tend to resist attempts to reform practices by the APB.
5. Managements tend to resist accounting reforms that threaten to inhibit their own flexibility.
6. The resistance by management and by former students (practitioners) has been a major cause of our inability to reform practice.

My suggestion is that educators teach research results as *the desired state* and teach accepted practices as *the current state*. Adoption of this suggestion ought to lessen the resistance to reform within the profession and lessen the tendency to reason by contradiction. It may even endow accounting with sufficient prestige so that we will no longer need to apologize or defend its methods. Obviously, adoption of the suggestion won't solve the problem of managements' resistance to reform practice, but it ought to allow us to present a more solid front and, therefore, to enhance our chances of instituting reforms.

EMPIRICAL ACCOUNTING RESEARCH DESIGN FOR PH.D. STUDENTS

WILLIAM R. KINNEY, JR.

A frequently encountered problem in accounting Ph.D. programs is that first-year students do not have background in empirical research in accounting. Few B.B.A., M.B.A. or M.Acc. programs include courses in empirical research and many students have not seriously considered its nature. Yet, such an introduction is necessary if Ph.D students are to efficiently relate other courses to substantive problems in accounting and be able to take full advantage of accounting workshops.

The purpose of this paper is to show how a basic framework for evaluating empirical research in accounting can be obtained in a short introduction. This can be done at the start of the first term course and provides a context for further work in philosophy of science and statistical design as well as substantive areas of accounting. The approach is generic—it is not tied to an area of accounting and doesn't depend on prior knowledge of a particular paradigm.[1]

The generic approach focuses attention on the essence of scientific inquiry in accounting. Many of the problems faced by accounting experimenters who can manipulate some (but not all) of the levels of variables to be studied are similar to those faced by "passive observers" of the levels of all variables as set by Nature.[2] Thus, the generic approach may help to avoid premature specialization [Boulding, 1956, p. 199].

Section I presents a definition of empirical accounting research and theory, hypothesis, and fact. It also defines "dependent," "independent," and prior and contemporaneous influence variables. Section II discusses alternative means for separating the effects of prior and contemporaneous influence variables from the independent variable(s), and in Section III the interrelationships among significance, power, and research design are explored. Section IV gives a summary and conclusions.

[1]Illustrations and extensions from applied areas of accounting are also helpful. Good sources for financial accounting are Ball and Foster [1982], Lev and Ohlson [1982], and Abdel-khalik and Ajinkya [1979]. Good sources for behavioral work are Ashton [1982] and Libby [1981].

[2]The problems are not identical. For example, while experimenters have the advantage of being able to specify the values of some variables, they also face the risk of choosing values that are too close together (or too far apart) to allow precise estimates of treatment effects or to allow generalization of conclusions to the real world.

I. A FRAMEWORK FOR EMPIRICAL RESEARCH IN ACCOUNTING

Research is a purposive activity and its purpose is to allow us to understand, predict, or control some aspect of the environment. Research will be defined here as *the development and testing of new theories of 'how the world works' or refutation of widely held existing theories*. For accounting research, the theories concern how the world works with respect to accounting practices. Watts and Zimmerman [1984, p. 1], state: "The objective of accounting theory is to explain and predict accounting practice." This positive, how-the-world-is approach is in contrast with the more traditional normative view that accounting "theory" is concerned with what accounting practices *ought to be*.

Empirical accounting research (broadly considered) addresses the question: "Does how we as a firm or as a society account for things make a difference?"[3] Clearly, the accounting for items affecting tax payments makes a difference in our individual and collective lives. But does the accounting for, say, depreciation in internal or external reports affect decisions within a business firm or affect stock prices? If it does, then the size of the effect and why it occurs are important follow-up questions. Additionally, the accounting researcher must separate the underlying economic event (or state) from the accounting *report* of the event. Thus, while a finance researcher may be concerned only with firm characteristics, the accounting researcher must also be concerned with the costs and benefits of alternative accounting reports of those characteristics.[4]

In essence, empirical research involves *theory, hypothesis,* and *fact*. "Facts" are states or events that are observable in the real world. A "theory" offers a tentative explanation of the relationship between or among groups of facts in general. "Hypotheses" are predictions (or assertions) about the "facts" that will occur in a particular instance assuming that the theory is valid. Finally, observing "facts" consistent with the prediction or assertion made in the hypothesis lends credibility to the theory.

Ordinarily, research begins with a real-world problem or question. One thinks about or studies the problem, reads about seemingly similar problems in other areas or disciplines such as economics, psychology, organizational behavior, or political science. By immersing himself or herself in the problem, the researcher may, either by genius or by adapting a solution from another area, develop a general theory to explain relationships among facts [Simon, 1976, Chapter 7 and Boulding, 1956]. From this statement of the general relationship among facts, hypotheses about what should be observed in a particular situation can be derived. An experiment or passive observation study then can be designed to support or deny the hypotheses.

For example, suppose it is observed that

Note in text one

---

[3]Within this definition, relevant questions for auditing include, "Does how precisely we audit and report the state of a firm make a difference?" and, "How can audits of a given precision be conducted efficiently?" The first auditing question is related to the accounting question through the concept of materiality. Parallel questions involving the design of accounting systems also could be developed.

[4]Accounting professors may conduct research in finance, economics, behavioral science, or statistics. If the accounting question is not addressed, however, the accounting professor may face the disadvantage of being undertrained relative to other researchers. Also, he or she ignores a comparative advantage in the knowledge of accounting institutions and the sometimes subtle role of information.

a stock price increase usually follows the announcement that a firm has changed from straight-line to accelerated depreciation. Why should a mere bookkeeping change seem to lead to an increase in firms' values? An explanation might be that market participants believe that events leading to such an accounting change also typically lead to better prospects for the firm in the future. With development and elaboration of such a theory, the researcher might develop a passive observation study of past changes or an experiment to test hypotheses based on the proposed explanation.

Theories are usually stated in terms of theoretical variables or "principals" while empirical measurement requires observable variables. The difference between the principal and real-world observable variables presents difficulties for accounting researchers since accounting measurements may be either *surrogates* for some underlying principal of interest or may be the *principal* itself. For example, if firm "performance" is the theoretical principal and earnings is chosen as the surrogate measure of firm performance, then straight-line depreciation is a component of the surrogate.

As a surrogate, straight-line depreciation contains two sources of potential error that may require consideration by the researcher. One is the surrogation error due to the fact that straight-line depreciation does not "correctly" reflect the relevant performance of the firm for the purpose at hand. The other is application error due to mistakes or imprecision in applying straight-line depreciation.

On the other hand, in evaluating possible determinants of managerial behavior, audited earnings using straight-line depreciation may be specified in a contract and may serve as a principal. For example, if a manager is to receive a bonus or profit share of one percent of audited earnings, then audited earnings is the principal. Surrogation error, and any application error not detected and corrected by the auditor, is *ignored* for contract purposes. The same number used as a measure of firm performance will likely contain both surrogation and application error.[5]

To add credibility to a theory, one must not only be able to show hypothesis test results that are consistent with the theory's predictions, but also have a basis to rule out alternative explanations of the observed facts. This requires consideration of a reasonably comprehensive list of alternative explanations. Again, knowledge of related disciplines is useful in generating alternative explanations for accounting-related "facts." Some possible explanations can, of course, easily be ruled out as being of likely negligible effect, but others will require attention.

To be more specific, let Y denote the "dependent" variable to be understood, explained, or predicted. Variables causing Y (or at least related to Y) can be classified into three broad groups as follows:

X = the "independent" variable that the proposed theory states should effect Y,

Vs = prior-influence (prior-to-study period) factors that may affect Y, and

Zs = contemporaneous factors (other than X) that may affect Y.[6]

That is, $Y = f(X, V_1, V_2, \ldots, Z_1, Z_2, \ldots)$.

---

[5]Accounting systems designers and financial accounting standards setters can control the first type of measurement error, while auditors and auditing standards setters can control the second. Problems relating to the interaction of accounting and auditing standards setters, users, and auditors is, of course, a matter for accounting research.

[6]Some Zs may be expectations, at the time of the study, of still future values of X, Y, V, and other Zs.

A common Y for addressing an accounting question is the change in a firm's stock price. Others are a manager's act or decision. A common X is a change or difference in accounting method, whether by management's choice or by a regulatory directive. Prevalent Vs are the firm's prior period state variables such as profitability, leverage, liquidity, and size. For tests of theories about decision-making behavior of particular human subjects, relevant Vs often include the subject's personality traits, mathematical ability, education, training, age, firm association, and experience.

The most common Z factor in accounting research studies involving stock prices is the market return (Rm). Another common group of Zs for external reporting and managerial performance studies is the unexpected portion of contemporaneous accounting measures for other firms or other divisions. Finally, since the accounting researcher is concerned with the effect of accounting reports, Zs may be underlying characteristics of the "true state" of the firm at the time of the study as measured by contemporaneous nonaccounting reports about the firm.

DISENTANGLING THE EFFECTS FROM VS AND ZS FROM THE EFFECT OF X

For simplicity, assume that X is measured at only two levels. Either the observed Y is from the "control" group that receives no "treatment" or from the treatment group that receives the treatment. Alternatively, the two groups could simply be different on some relevant dimension (e.g., to test theories about accelerated depreciation, the control group might be defined as those firms that use straight-line and the treatment group as those that use accelerated).

Also for simplicity, assume that there is a single prior-influence factor V that effects Y and V has the same effect on Y whether the subject is from the control or treatment group. Furthermore, there are no contemporaneous Zs that affect Y and the model determining Y is:

$$(1) \quad Y_{ij} = B_0 + B_1 X_i + B_2 V_{ij} + e_{ij},$$

where Y_{ij} is the value of the dependent variable for the "j"th subject in the "i"th treatment, B_0 is the intercept for the control group, X_i is an indicator variable (zero for the control group and one for treatment), $B_0 + B_1$ is the intercept for the treatment group (that is, B_1 is the effect of treatment), B_2 is the regression coefficient relating V to Y, and e_{ij} is a random error term. The e_{ij} term will include the effects of other Vs and Zs that are here assumed to be negligible and randomly distributed between the two groups, and e_{ij} is assumed to have expectation zero and be uncorrelated with either X or V.

For the simple model of equation 1, a plot of the expected values of Y given V for both groups will be parallel lines with possibly different intercepts. The difference in intercepts is the effect of the treatment (B_1). Figure 1 shows the components of equation 1 along with ellipses that approximate the locus of members of the two groups.

An experimenter may ignore V and may randomly assign subjects to groups. On average, the groups will be equivalent on V. For small samples, however, there is nontrivial risk that such a procedure may assign to the treatment group, say, those with high values of V and to the control group those with low V. In analyzing results, the effect of the high V values (i.e., $B_2 V_{ij}$) will be mixed with the treatment effect. An experimenter may rule out the possible effect of V by random assignment of subjects measured on V between groups.

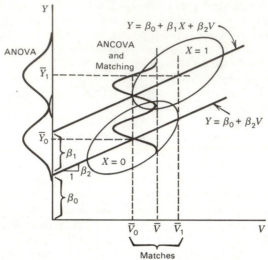

The sample subjects are measured on V, matched into pairs according to their V values, and one from each pair is randomly assigned to treatment. Thus, even for small samples the two groups will be approximately equivalent on V.

The passive observer has no opportunity to randomly assign sample subjects to treatment. Even experimenters may have difficulty developing a satisfactory randomized design due to having too many potentially important Vs and Zs that must be simultaneously matched. Thus, in general, researchers face the problem of treatment groups that are not equivalent with respect to V.

For nonequivalent groups, there are three basic ways in which the researcher can mitigate the possible effects of the V factor in the model of equation 1. These are:

1. ignoring V (i.e., assuming or hoping that V is randomized with respect to X),
2. matching on V ex post (i.e., matching after X has been chosen by the subject or assigned by Nature), and
3. using covariance analysis to statistically estimate and remove the effect of V.

The first approach ignores V, and results can be analyzed with a single-factor analysis of variance (ANOVA). The second approach physically equates the treatment groups with respect to V, and results can be analyzed using a randomized block design. The third approach "statistically" equates the groups, and results can be analyzed using analysis of covariance (ANCOVA).

Each of these approaches is discussed in turn, along with some of the advantages and limitations of each for experimenters and passive observers.

IGNORING V

As discussed above, ignoring a potential V is generally inadvisable due to the unknown effect of V. A negligible effect is the *hoped for* result for any unmatched, unmeasured, or unknown Vs or Zs. However, most real-world events have multiple causes and a negligible overall effect is unlikely. Furthermore, larger samples will not help in research designs that ignore systematic effects of V.

While *ex post* matching and covariance analysis can't account for all possible Vs and Zs, they can reduce the risk that some potentially important Vs and Zs disguise the true effect of X. Figure 1 shows the relevant sampling distributions for the three approaches applied to the example. As shown in the relatively flat distributions on the left margin, ANOVA is based on the marginal distribution of Y with no consideration of V.

EX POST MATCHING

In many situations, the researcher selects a sample after the phenomenon of interest has taken place. Often, the researcher selects a sample of subjects from the treatment group and then selects a subject from the control group with V equal or similar to V for each treatment subject. This *ex post* matching on V is probably the most commonly used design for passive observational studies in accounting.

For *ex post* matching, the model assumed to determine Y is:

$$(2) \quad Y_{ij} = B_0 + B_1 X_i + \sum_{j=2}^{m} B_j M_j + e_{ij},$$

where B_0 is the overall mean of Y plus the effect of (arbitrarily designated) match 1, B_j (for $j > 1$) is the differential effect of match j compared to match 1, M_j is an indicator variable (equal to one if the sample subject is a member of match j and zero otherwise), and m is the number of matches.[7]

[7]The matches may be by individual subject ("precision" or "caliper" matching) as dis-

For passive observational studies, it is impossible to randomly assign subjects to treatments since by definition the subjects have already either "self-selected" into treatment groups, or have been so selected by Nature. It is possible that there will be few or even *no* matches. For example, all the firms using straight-line depreciation may be small firms and all firms using accelerated depreciation may be large. A firm's choice of accounting method (or decision to change methods) may merely reflect its V value. Figure 1 illustrates such a possibility in that only the bottom half of group 1 can be matched with a member of group 0 due to the difference in V for the groups.

Even experimenters using *ex ante* matching with random assignment of subjects often face the lack-of-matches problem for at least some Vs and Zs. Suppose, for example, that a researcher believes that an auditor's response in a professional task experiment may be related to the auditor's professional training (X) after accounting for his or her mathematical abilities (V). It may be difficult to match subjects from different firms based on mathematical abilities. This is because firms may hire and thus train (or students may choose firms and be trained) on the basis of mathematical ability.[8]

As will be discussed below, the efficiency of matching may be less than that for covariance analysis. However, *ex post* matching is likely to be superior to

cussed above, or by frequency distribution (e.g., equal mean and variance with respect to V for both groups). A test of equality on V is often used as a justification for ignoring V in the statistical analysis.
[8]An alternative design is to limit all subjects in an experiment to a fixed level of V. This equalizes the effect of V but greatly reduces the generalizability of results over the range of reasonable V values that might occur.

covariance analysis when the functional form of the $Y|V$ relationship is nonlinear or unknown. Given that the treatment effect is not correlated with V, matching can be used for any functional form of Y and V (known or not) and analyzed using a blocked design.

COVARIANCE ANALYSIS

A researcher using analysis of covariance (ANCOVA) statistically estimates the effect of V on Y and removes it. ANCOVA can be viewed as the result of projecting observed Y values along the regression line to a common point on the V axis, such as $\bar{V}$, to yield the conditional distributions as shown in Figure 1.[9]

Figure 1 shows that part of the difference between the marginal distributions of $\bar{Y}_0$ and $\bar{Y}_1$ (as estimated using ANOVA) is due to a larger $\bar{V}$ for the treatment group. Matching (equation 2) accounts for the difference by subtracting $\hat{B}_0 + \Sigma \hat{B}_j M_j$ from Y for each subject, and ANCOVA accounts for the difference by subtracting $\hat{B}_0 + \hat{B}_2 V_{ij}$ from Y for each subject. Thus, both matching and ANCOVA are seen to mitigate the differential effect of V. Figure 1 also shows that control group subjects with relatively high V for the control group are matched to subjects with relatively low V for the treatment group. For matched designs, all other potential sample subjects must be omitted due to lack of matches.

Matching and ANCOVA yield more efficient (more precise) estimates of the treatment effect than does ANOVA. In general, however, it is unclear which of the two will be more precise. This is due to the fact that

while the difference in $\bar{V}_0$ and $\bar{V}_1$ reduces the precision of ANCOVA, the reduction in sample size due to lack of matches reduces precision for matching. It is often difficult to predict which will be the greater problem.[10]

Equation 1 and Figure 1 present a very simple situation even for a single V. For example, the $Y|V$ relationship may differ depending on whether X is at level zero or one. Furthermore, the occurrence of a given level of V at time t-1 may have a direct effect on Y at time t but may also affect the level of X at time t which, in turn, affects Y at t. Thus, there may be two paths by which V affects Y. A complete approach would include a model of the "selection" process by which V affects X as well as the direct effects of X and V on Y.[11]

III. ALPHA, BETA, SAMPLE SIZE AND RESEARCH DESIGN

Planning research to disentangle X, Vs, and Zs involves four related factors. These are alpha (α), beta (β), sample size, and what will be called the "research design" factor (denoted D). In a given situation, setting any three of them sets the fourth. The statistical factors of α (the probability of a type I error or incorrectly rejecting a true

---

[9]The sampling distributions for matching and ANCOVA are shown as the same in Figure 1 since the expectations of estimates of the treatment effects are the same for both. As discussed, however, their standard errors will differ.

[10]ANCOVA will usually be less biased, however (see Cook and Campbell [1979, pp. 177–182], and Cochran [1983, pp. 127–128]).

[11]See Cochran's comments on R. A. Fisher's advice to "Make your theories elaborate." According to Cochran, Fisher meant that when "constructing a causal hypothesis one should envisage as many different consequences of its truth as possible, and plan observational studies to discover whether each of these consequences is found to hold" [Rosenbaum, 1984, p. 43]. This advice is consistent with Boulding's exhortation to develop and test theories that are at the level of the real world.

null hypothesis of no treatment effect), β (the probability of a type II error or not rejecting the null hypothesis when, in fact, there is a treatment effect), and sample size are well known. The research design factor is the ratio of two subfactors. Its numerator is the hypothesized magnitude of the (X) treatment effect (denoted δ), and its denominator is the standard deviation of the residuals in the equation used to estimate B_1 (denoted σ). Thus, $D = \delta/\sigma$. The numerator depends on the researcher's theory, and the denominator depends on how the researcher disentangles the Vs and Zs and the inherent variability in the phenomenon under examination.

The required sample size is a decreasing function of α, β, δ and an increasing function of σ. Therefore, for a given α and β, the required sample size will be small if the proposed theory implies a larger effect on Y and/or the researcher is clever in designing a plan to disentangle the effects of the Vs and Zs. For example, using ANOVA (no matching) in a single test with target $\alpha = .05$, $\beta = .1$, and $D=\delta/\sigma=.5$, the required sample size is 70 for each of the two groups.[12] If the researcher has a theory yielding a larger δ that would decrease D to .75, then the sample would be 32 each, and if D is 1.0 then the sample size is 18 per group. Alternatively, for $D = .5$ and holding δ constant, if matching is used and the Y_0, Y_1 correlation is .25 then the required sample is approximately 57 pairs.[13] If the Y_0, Y_1 correlation is .5 (implying a

reduction in σ of about 18 percent), then the required sample is 36 pairs.

The four factors and their implications for accounting research will be discussed through two subtopics. These are: 1) power, and 2) prejudice against the null hypothesis.

POWER

Consider a researcher who has a theory that the treatment effect (B_1) is positive, and who therefore is interested in testing the (null) hypothesis that the true effect of treatment is less than or equal to zero against the alternative that the true effect is greater than zero. Assume that a sample of treatment subjects has been matched or "paired" on V with control subjects. Also, based on an assessment of the appropriate significance level for the issue at hand, the researcher has set α at .05, and the researcher has a research design in mind.

What the researcher may not consider at the planning stage is the magnitude of the hypothesized effect (i.e., a particular δ for the alternative hypothesis) and the allowable β for that δ.[14] A δ may not be considered since most theories suggest only the direction of an effect and not its magnitude, and β is not considered because no particular δ is specified. The researcher may proceed to testing with little consideration of whether the planned test has an adequate chance to reject the null hypothesis even if it is false.

To illustrate, consider the sampling dis-

[12]The required sample size is:

$$n = 2[(t_\alpha, 2_{n-2} + t_\beta, 2_{n-2}) (1/D)]^2$$

See Ostle [1963, p. 553] for a table.
[13]The required sample size is:

$$n = [(t_{\alpha,n-1} + t_{\beta,n-1}) (1/D)]^2$$

See Ostle [1963, p. 551] for a table.

[14]See Tversky and Kahneman [1971]. This is in contrast to classical or normal distribution theory-based audit sampling where, in addition to setting α to control the risk of incorrect rejection, the auditor sets β to control the risk of incorrect acceptance and sets δ based on "intolerable" error (materiality). The auditor then selects an estimator and calculates the minimum sample size subject to the target α, β, and δ.

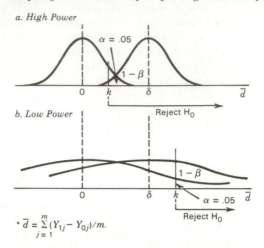

Figure 2   Sampling distributions of $\overline{d}*$ for high and low power tests

a. High Power

$\alpha = .05$

$1 - \beta$

0   k   δ $\overline{d}$

Reject H_0

b. Low Power

$1 - \beta$

0   δ   k $\alpha = .05$ $\overline{d}$

Reject H_0

$* \overline{d} = \sum_{j=1}^{m} (Y_{1j} - Y_{0j})/m.$

tributions in Figure 2. For both panels of Figure 2, the left-hand distribution is for the mean of the paired differences if the null hypothesis ($B_1 = 0$) is true, and the right-hand distribution applies if the particular alternative ($B_1 = \delta$) is true. Also for both panels, k is the point that yields $\alpha = .05$ or five percent of the area to the right of the point under the left-hand distribution (i.e., H_0). In panel a, the research design and sample size yield a sampling distribution with a large area ($1 - \beta$) to the right of k under the alternative hypothesis. Thus, there is high probability of rejecting H_0 when the alternative hypothesis is true. In other words, the power of the test ($1 - \beta$) is high.

In Figure 2, panel b, δ is the same as in panel a, but the sampling distributions are much flatter due either to small sample sizes or a large standard deviation due to remaining effects of Vs and Zs. Rather than the relatively high power test of panel a, the researcher faces a low power test. At $\alpha = .05$, β for the simple alternative hypothesis is greater than .5, and power is less than .5. Even if H_0 is false (i.e., $B_1 = \delta$),

and thus the researcher's theory of a positive treatment effect is correct, the researcher has a *less than even chance* of rejecting it!

Suppose that the researcher in panel b observes a test statistic that is almost significant, and the sample estimate of the treatment effect is equal to δ. He or she then decides to take a follow-up sample. The follow-up sample is also likely to indicate nonrejection due to its small size [Tversky and Kahneman, 1971, p. 107].

The real culprit, of course, is the low power of the test. If the low power is anticipated at the planning stage, an attempt can be made to mitigate its negative effects or else abort the project. In general, power can be increased by 1) increasing the sample size, or 2) increasing the design factor D by developing better theories (yielding larger δ) or by making better use of a given sample size and theory by careful attention to the Vs and Zs (yielding smaller σ).

As a practical matter, improved design is often the only alternative in accounting research since the size of samples in accounting frequently is effectively *fixed*. For experiments, the pool of available auditors, accountants, financial statement users, and even students is effectively limited to fairly small numbers. Subjects' time is not free, and the supply is not inexhaustible. For passive observation, the number of firms for which particular accounting and other required economic data are available may be relatively small. Thus, accounting researchers need to be aware of a variety of analytical techniques applicable to a variety of research problems.[15]

Furthermore, for a given research paradigm, the problem of low power is likely to become more difficult over time. Other things equal, as knowledge of the effects of accounting expands, the likely size of the effect of each new or more refined theory (B_1) will tend to have less additional explanatory power. As knowledge expands, the best potential Xs are investigated and become Vs or Zs. For example, early studies tested hypotheses about the degree of owner *versus* manager control as an X that affected accounting choices. Later studies have used the same variable as a V or Z. Absent developments that restructure the way a particular problem is addressed, future researchers will be faced with discovering new Xs that have less potential explanatory power.

In fact, it may be unreasonable to expect that a particular theory based on accounting methods will yield a true differential effect that is very large relative to the variance of Y. How things are accounted for simply can't be expected to explain a large portion of stock price variability or managerial or investor behavior. Under some conditions, the sample size required to yield reasonable

power exceeds the size of the known population!

A researcher can get some protection by making a tentative calculation of power before investing in expensive data collection or in experimentation. For example, passive observers of accounting changes and stock returns may be able to make reasonable estimates of the standard deviation of return residuals and might make power estimates for various levels of δ.[16] If the estimated power is inadequate even for the maximum δ that might reasonably exist, then the research can be redesigned or aborted. Experimenters are perhaps more familiar with prospective power calculations and frequently use a pilot sample to assist with the sample size and research design development.

PREJUDICE AGAINST THE NULL HYPOTHESIS

A theory usually specifies the direction of the treatment effect and a researcher generally sets out to reject hypotheses based on the assumption that the treatment effect is zero or in the opposite direction from what the theory predicts. The focus on rejecting the null hypothesis is the source of a number of "biases" against the null that may lead to dysfunctional consequences. Greenwald [1975] lists eight such consequences; four that seem most important for accounting researchers are discussed in order to be better able to avoid them.

1. A paper will not be submitted for publication consideration unless the results

---

[15]In debate on the preferability of parametric vs. nonparametric statistics in research, the ability of parametric methods to accommodate more Vs and Zs through covariance analysis is an often overlooked advantage.

[16]The choice of δ is somewhat arbitrary, but in planning it is useful to consider reasonable or plausible values for the true treatment effect of X. Alternatively, one might choose the smallest effect that informed persons would agree is empirically "important" and therefore worth knowing about if it exists, or the largest amount that one could reasonably expect.

against the null are "significant." Especially interesting or innovative results may be submitted on higher than .05 significance (or alternatively, the probability at which the results are significant are reported), but rarely does an editor see results with significance levels above .15. This prejudice need not exist if not rejecting the null gives reasonable credibility to the null.[17]

2. Ancillary hypotheses will be elevated in the exposition of results. Secondary hypotheses that are significant *ex post* will receive more attention than other secondary hypotheses and perhaps the primary hypotheses. Suggestions will be made that these results warrant further study, when in fact one would expect about one in ten nonsense relationships to be significant at the .10 level.

3. Alternative operationalization of variables or their functional form will be conducted only if "preliminary" results are insignificant. The extent to which this search activity is justified is open to debate since most theories don't imply a single measurement or functional form.

4. The search for errors will be asymmetric. Outliers that impede rejection of the null hypothesis will tend to receive more diligent attention than those that favor rejecting the null. If significant results are obtained on the first analysis of a problem, the neophyte researcher may not consider a search for outliers or for other violations of statistical assumptions underlying the analysis. Nonrejection may lead one to consider such explanations and to search for pro-

[17]In classical statistics, not rejecting the null is not equivalent to accepting the null. However, non-rejection by a reasonably powerful test or series of tests does increase one's subjective degree of belief in the null.

gramming errors and data coding errors.

V. SUMMARY AND CONCLUSIONS

In this paper we have stressed consideration of the planning for Vs and Zs to be able to isolate the effect of X as a potential explanation of differences in Y. This consideration may allow increased power in tests and may allow more to be learned from a given sample. Planning for Vs and Zs can reduce the risk of not rejecting the null hypothesis when it is false. Such planning may also allow a basis to argue that nonrejection of the null hypothesis may support *acceptance* of the null. That is, if the treatment has an important effect, then it should be revealed by the test. Thus, something may be learned whether results are statistically significant or not. This should increase the objectivity of the researcher, since the work is valuable whatever the empirical results.

There are at least two ways in which the approach discussed in this paper can be useful to Ph.D. students. One is in evaluating the research design of others, and the other is in planning the student's dissertation.[18] Students must evaluate the work of others whether in

[18]In planning research or evaluating the research of others, a useful practice is to give early attention to the *purpose* of the research through preparation of a three-short-paragraph abstract, synopsis, or working model of the research. The first paragraph answers the question "What is the problem?" The second asks, "Why is it an important problem?" and the third, "How will it be solved?" Alternatively, the questions might be: "What are you (or the researcher) trying to find out?", "Why?", and "How will it be done?" Note: In this reading the sections are not numbered in sequence.

published articles, working papers, or accounting research workshops. A student applying the approach to the work of others might try to answer the following questions: What is the Y and what is the X? What Vs and Zs are considered? Are there better ways to account for the effects of Vs and Zs? What are other Vs and Zs that might have important effects?

The same approach can be applied by the student to his or her own dissertation proposal. While the basic development of a research proposal is the responsibility of the student, there is much to warrant early faculty discussion of *planned* dissertation research. That is, the faculty can evaluate a proposal by considering the reasonableness of the theory and the adequacy of control of potential Vs and Zs.

The faculty should be asked: Is the magnitude of the hypothesized effect plausible? Are all important competing explanations listed and adequately dealt with in the plan? Will the proposed tests likely uncover evidence of a difference equal to δ if it exists? Will nonrejection lend credibility to the null?

Faculty approval of planned dissertation research reduces the student's risk by 1) ruling out potential topics that have little chance of successful completion, 2) gathering the right data on the first attempt, 3) eliminating outcome dependence (thus reducing moral hazard for the student), and 4) reducing the temptation of the student (and faculty) to pursue numerous tangents that may come to light as the research progresses.

REFERENCES

Abdel-khalik, A. R. and B. B. Ajinkya, *Empirical Research in Accounting: A Methodological Viewpoint,* Accounting Education Series No. 4 (American Accounting Association, 1979).

Ashton, R. H., *Human Information Processing in Accounting,* Accounting Research Study, No. 17 (American Accounting Association, 1982).

Ball, R. and G. Foster, "Corporate Financial Reporting: A Methodological Review of Financial Research," Studies in Current Research Methodologies in Accounting: A Critical Evaluation," *Journal of Accounting Research* (Supplement 1982), pp. 161–234.

Boulding, K. E., "General Systems Theory—The Skeleton of Science," *Management Science* (April 1956), pp. 197–208.

Cochran, W. G., *Planning and Analysis of Observational Studies,* edited by L. E. Moses and F. Mosteller (John Wiley & Sons, Inc. 1983).

Cook, T. D., and D. T. Campbell, *Quasi-Experimentation Design & Analysis Issues for Field Settings* (Houghton-Mifflin Company, 1979) especially chapters 3 and 4.

Greenwald, A. G., "Consequences of Prejudice Against the Null Hypothesis," *Psychological Bulletin* (January 1975), pp. 1–20.

Lev, B. and J. A. Ohlson, "Market-Based Empirical Research in Accounting: A Review, Interpretation, and Extension." "Studies in Current Research Methodologies in Accounting: A Critical Evaluation," *Journal of Accounting Research* (Supplement 1982), pp. 249–322.

Libby, R., *Accounting and Human Information Processing: Theory and Applications* (Prentice-Hall, Inc., 1981).

Ostle, B., *Statistics in Research,* 2nd Edition (The Iowa State University Press, 1963).

Rosenbaum, P. R., "From Association to Causation in Observational Studies: The Role of Tests of Strongly Ignorable Treatment Assignment," *Journal of the American Statistical Association* (March 1984), pp. 41–48.

Simon, J. L., *Basic Research Methods in Social Science: The Art of Empirical Investigation,* 2nd Edition (Random House, Inc., 1978) especially chapters 3, 7, and 11.

Tversky, A. and D. Kahneman, "Belief in the Law of Small Numbers," *Psychological Bulletin* (August 1971), pp. 105–110.

Watts, R. L. and J. L. Zimmerman, *Positive Accounting Theory* (Prentice-Hall, 1986).

QUESTIONS

1. Under Statement of Financial Accounting Concepts No. 2, feedback value is an ingredient of the primary quality of

	Relevance	*Reliability*
a.	No	No
b.	No	Yes
c.	Yes	Yes
d.	Yes	No

2. Under Statement of Financial Accounting Concepts No. 2, which of the following interacts with both relevance and reliability to contribute to the usefulness of information?
   a. Comparability
   b. Timeliness
   c. Neutrality
   d. Predictive value

3. As a general rule, Statements of the Financial Accounting Standards Board
   a. Represent the conclusions of all members of the board
   b. Are *not* intended to be retroactive
   c. May be departed from without disclosure in financial statements
   d. Should be applied to immaterial items
4. Which of the following research approaches emphasizes going from the specific to the general?
   a. Deductive
   b. Behavioral
   c. Inductive
   d. Pragmatic
5. The FASB has been functioning for several years. The best statement as to its current position with respect to generally accepted accounting principles is that
   a. Accounting Principles Board Opinions (issued by its predecessor) remain in effect if not specifically modified or rescinded
   b. Accounting Research Bulletins are no longer in effect
   c. Compliance with its pronouncements has become mandatory
   d. It has rendered Opinions covering all of the generally accepted accounting principles
6. Which of the following research approaches has most frequently been used by the APB and the FASB?
   a. Deductive
   b. Inductive
   c. Pragmatic
   d. Scientific method
7. According to Statement of Financial Accounting Concepts No. 2, an interim earnings report is expected to have which of the following?

	Predictive value	Feedback value
a.	No	No
b.	Yes	Yes
c.	Yes	No
d.	No	Yes

8. Which of the following bodies has the ultimate authority to issue accounting pronouncements for all publicly held corporations?
   a. Securities and Exchange Commission
   b. Financial Accounting Standards Board
   c. Internal Revenue Service
   d. Accounting Principles Board

9. Which of the following hierarchy of qualities did the FASB indicate as being the most important?
   a. Relevance
   b. Reliability
   c. Verifiability
   d. Decision usefulness
10. Which of the following types of pronouncements establishes generally accepted accounting principles?
   a. FASB Statement of Concepts
   b. APB Opinions
   c. APB Statements
   d. All of the above establish GAAP
11. Which of the following is considered a pervasive constraint by Statement of Financial Accounting Concepts No. 2?
   a. Benefits-costs
   b. Conservatism
   c. Timeliness
   d. Verifiability
12. Under Statement of Financial Accounting Concepts No. 2, which of the following is an ingredient of the primary quality of relevance?
   a. Predictive value
   b. Materiality
   c. Understandability
   d. Verifiability
13. Under Statement of Financial Accounting Concepts No. 2, which of the following is an ingredient of the primary quality of reliability?
   a. Understandability
   b. Verifiability
   c. Predictive value
   d. Materiality
14. Under Statement of Financial Accounting Concepts No. 2, the ability through consensus among measurers to ensure that information represents what it purports to represent is an example of the concept of
   a. Relevance
   b. Verifiability
   c. Comparability
   d. Feedback value
15. Under Statement of Financial Accounting Concepts No. 2, which of the following relates to both relevance and reliability?
   a. Timeliness
   b. Materiality

   c. Verifiability

   d. Neutrality

16. At the completion of the Darby Department Store audit, the president asks about the meaning of the phrase ''in conformity with generally accepted accounting principles'' that appears in your audit report on the management's financial statements. He observes that the meaning of the phrase must include more than what he thinks of as ''principles.''

   a. Explain the meaning of the term ''accounting principles'' as used in the audit report. (Do not discuss in this part the significance of ''generally accepted.'')

   b. The president wants to know how you determine whether or not an accounting principle is generally accepted. Discuss the sources of evidence for determining whether an accounting principle has substantial authoritative support. Do not merely list the titles of publications. [*handwritten:* Look at FASB publications]

   c. The president believes that diversity in accounting practice will always exist among independent entities despite continual improvements in comparability. Discuss the arguments that support his belief.

17. In the recent past the accounting profession has shown substantial interest in delineating the objectives and principles of accounting. An example of this is Statement of the Accounting Principles Board No. 4, ''Basic Concepts and Accounting Principles Underlying Financial Statements of Business Enterprises,'' that (1) discusses the nature of financial accounting, the environmental forces that influence it, and the potential and limitations of financial accounting in providing useful information; (2) sets forth the objectives of financial accounting and financial statements; and (3) presents a description of present generally accepted accounting principles.

Required: [*handwritten:* Should be useful to statement users, Assessing] Discuss the basic purpose of financial accounting and financial statements.

18. The following four statements have been taken directly or with some modification from the accounting literature. All of them are either taken out of context, involve circular reasoning, or contain one or more fallacies, halftruths, erroneous comments, conclusions, or inconsistencies (internally or with generally accepted principles or practices).

Statement 1

Accounting is a service activity. Its function is to provide qualitative financial information that is intended to be useful in making economic decisions about and for economic entities. Thus, the accounting function might be viewed primarily as being a tool or device for providing quantitative financial information to management to facilitate decision making.

Statement 2

Financial statements that were developed in accordance with generally accepted accounting principles that apply the conservatism convention can be free from bias (or can give a presentation that is fair with respect to continuing and prospective stockholders as well as to retiring stockholders).

Statement 3

When a company changes from the Lifo to the Fifo method of determining the cost of ending inventories and this change results in a $1 million increase both in income after taxes and in income taxes for the year of change, the increase would stem from the elimination of Lifo reserves established in prior years.

Statement 4

If the value of an enterprise were to be determined by the method that computes the sum of the present values of the marginal (or incremental) expected net receipts of individual tangible and intangible assets, the resulting valuation would tend to be less than if the value of the entire enterprise had been determined in another way, such as by computing the present value of total expected net receipts for the entire enterprise (i.e., the resulting valuation of parts would sum to an amount that was less than that for the whole). This would be true even if the same pattern of interest or discount rates was used for both valuations.

Evaluate each of the above numbered statements on separate appropriately numbered answer sheets as follows:

a. List the fallacies, half-truths, circular reasoning, erroneous comments or conclusions, and inconsistencies.

b. Explain by what authority or on what basis each item listed in (a) can be considered to be fallacious, circular, inconsistent, a half-truth, or an erroneous comment or conclusion. If the statement or a portion of it is merely out of context, indicate the context(s) in which the statement would be correct.

19. Rule 203 of the AICPA Code of Professional Ethics requires compliance with accounting principles, and Statement of Auditing Standards No. 43 classified the order of priority an auditor should follow in determining *answer at* whether an accounting principle is generally accepted.

Required: List and discuss the sources of generally accepted accounting principles.

20. The Financial Accounting Standards Board (FASB) is the official body charged with issuing accounting standards.

Required:
a. Discuss the structure of the FASB.
b. How are the members of the Financial Accounting Foundation nominated?
c. Discuss the types of pronouncements issued by the FASB.

21. During the past several years, The Financial Accounting Standard Board has attempted to strengthen the theoretical foundation for the development of accounting principles. Two of the most important results of this attempt are the Conceptual Framework Project and the Emerging Issues Task Force. During this same period the FASB has been criticized for imposing too many standards on the financial reporting process, the so-called standards overload problem.

Required:
Discuss the goals and objectives of
a. The Conceptual Framework Project
b. The Emerging Issues Task Force

BIBLIOGRAPHY

Abdel-khalik, A. Rashad, and Thomas F. Keller, eds. *The Impact of Accounting Research on Practice and Disclosure.* Durham, N.C.: Duke University Press, 1978.

American Accounting Association Committee to Prepare a Statement of Basic Accounting Theory. *A Statement of Basic Accounting Theory.* Sarasota, Fla.: American Accounting Association, 1966.

American Accounting Association, Committee on Concepts and Standards for External Financial Reports. *Statement on Accounting Theory and Theory Acceptance,* 1977.

Arnett, Harold E. "What Does 'Objectivity' Mean to Accountants?" *Journal of Accountancy* (May 1961), pp. 63–68.

Barlev, Benzion. "On the Measurement of Materiality." *Accounting and Business Research* (Summer 1972), pp. 194–197.

Beaver, William H. "What Should be the FASB's Objectives." *Journal of Accountancy* (August 1963), pp. 49–56.

Beaver, William H., and Joel S. Demski. "The Nature of Financial Accounting Objectives: A Summary and Synthesis." *Studies on Financial Accounting*

Objectives: 1974. Supplement to Vol. 12 of the *Journal of Accounting Research,* pp. 170–187.

Bedford, Norton, and Toshio Iino. "Consistency Reexamined." *The Accounting Review* (July 1968), pp. 453–458.

Bernstein, Leopold A. "The Concept of Materiality." *The Accounting Review,* Vol. 42 (January 1967), pp. 86–95.

Blough, Carman. "Development of Accounting Principles in the United States." Berkeley Symposium on the Foundations of Financial Accounting. Berkeley: Schools of Business Administration, University of California, 1967, pp. 1–14.

Burns, Thomas J., ed. *Accounting in Transition: Oral Histories of Recent U.S. Experience.* Columbus, Ohio: College of Administrative Science of The Ohio State University, 1974.

Burton, John C. "Some General and Specific Thoughts on the Accounting Environment." *Journal of Accountancy* (October 1973), pp. 40–46.

Carey, John L. *The Rise of the Accounting Profession,* Vol. 1. New York: American Institute of Certified Public Accountants, 1969.

Carey, John L. *The Rise of the Accounting Profession,* Vol. 2. New York: American Institute of Certified Public Accountants, 1970.

Carter, Clairmont P., Michael L. Fetters, Paul A. Janell, and Robert H. Strawser. "Materiality and Accounting Principles." *The Ohio CPA* (Spring 1977).

Chambers, Raymond J. "Accounting Principles or Accounting Policies?" *Journal of Accountancy* (May 1973), pp. 48–53.

Chatfield, Michael, *A History of Accounting Thought,* rev. ed. Huntington, N.Y.: Robert E. Krieger Publishing Co. Inc., 1977.

Chazem, Charles. "Accounting and Auditing Pronouncements: Their Source and Authority." *Practical Accountant* (September 1979), pp. 54–60.

Committee for the Collection of Historical Materials, *American Accounting Association, Fiftieth Anniversary 1916–1966.* AAA, 1966.

Cyert, Richard M., and Yuji Ijiri. "Problems of Implementing the Trueblood Objectives Report." *Studies on Financial Accounting Objectives: 1974.* Supplement to Vol. 12 of the *Journal of Accounting Research,* pp. 29–42.

Daniels, Mortimer B. *Corporation Financial Statements.* Ann Arbor: University of Michigan, 1934.

Defliese, Philip L. "The Search for a New Conceptual Framework of Accounting." *Journal of Accountancy* (July 1977), pp. 59–67.

Deinzer, Harvey T. "The American Accounting Association–Sponsored Statements of Standards for Corporate Financial Reports—A Perspective.'' Gainesville: College of Business Administration, University of Florida, 1964.

Deinzer, Harvey T. *Development of Accounting Thought*. New York: Holt, Rinehart and Winston, Inc. 1965, Chapter 8 and 9.

De Roover, Raymond. "New Perspectives on the History of Accounting." *The Accounting Review,* Vol. 30 (July 1955), pp. 405–420.

Dewhirst, John F. "Dealing with Uncertainty." *Canadian Chartered Accountant* (August 1971), pp. 139–146.

Fremgren, James M. "The Going Concern Assumption: A Critical Appraisal." *The Accounting Review,* Vol. 43 (October 1968), pp. 649–656.

Frishkoff, Paul. "An Empirical Investigation of the Concept of Materiality in Accounting." *Empirical Research in Accounting: Selected Studies* (1970), pp. 116–129.

Frishkoff, Paul. "Consistency in Auditing and APB Opinion No. 20." *Journal of Accountancy* (August 1972), pp. 64–70.

Gellein, Oscar S. "Good Financial Reporting." *The CPA Journal* (November 1983), pp. 39–45.

Gonedes, Nicholas J. "Perception Estimation and Verifiability." *International Journal of Accounting Education and Research* (Spring 1969), pp. 63–73.

Hagerman, Robert L., Thomas F. Keller, and Russell J. Peterson. "Accounting Research and Accounting Principles." *Journal of Accountancy* (March 1973), pp. 51–55.

Hatfield, Henry Rand. "An Historical Defense of Bookkeeping." *Journal of Accountancy* (April 1924), pp. 241–253.

Hertz, Ronald S. "Standards Overload—a Euphemism." *The CPA Journal* (October 1983), pp. 24–33.

Hickok, Richard S. "Looking to the Future: A Key to Success." *Journal of Accountancy* (March 1984), pp. 77–82.

Horngren, Charles T. "Accounting Principles: Private or Public Sector?" *Journal of Accountancy* (May 1972), pp. 37–41.

Ijiri, Yugi. *Theory of Accounting Measurement*. Sarasota, Fla.: American Accounting Association, 1975.

Kapnick, Harvey. "Accounting Principles—Concern or Crisis?" *Financial Executive* (October 1974), pp. 23–25, 64.

Lambert, Samuel Joseph, III. "Basic Assumptions in Accounting Theory Construction." *Journal of Accountancy* (February 1974), pp. 41–48.

Langenderfer, Harold Q. "A Conceptual Framework for Financial Reporting." *Journal of Accountancy* (July 1973), pp. 43–55.

Larson, Rholan E., and Thomas P. Kelley. "Differential Measurement in Accounting Standards: The Concept Makes Sense." *Journal of Accountancy* (November, 1984), pp. 78–86.

Lee, Bernard Z., Rholan E. Larson, and Philip B. Chenok. "Issues Confronting the Accounting Profession." *Journal of Accountancy* (November, 1983), pp. 78–85.

Lee, T. A. "Utility and Relevance—the Search for Reliable Financial Accounting Information." *Accounting and Business Research* (Summer 1971), pp. 242–249.

Mautz, Robert K. "Accounting Principles—How Can They Be Made More Authoritative?" *The CPA Journal* (March 1973), pp. 185–192.

Mautz, R. K. "The Place of Postulates in Accounting." *Journal of Accountancy* (January 1965), pp. 46–49.

Mautz, R. K., and Jack Gray. "Some Thoughts on Research Needs in Accounting." *Journal of Accountancy* (September 1970), pp. 54–62.

May, Robert G., and Gary L. Sundem. "Research for Accounting Policy: An Overview." *The Accounting Review* (October 1976), pp. 747–763.

Metcalf, Richard W. "The Basic Postulates in Perspective." *The Accounting Review*, Vol. 39 (January 1964), pp. 16–21.

Meyer, Philip E. "The APB's Independence and Its Implications for the FASB." *Journal of Accounting Research* (Spring 1974), pp. 188–196.

Meyer, Philip E. "A Framework for Understanding 'Substance Over Form' in Accounting." *The Accounting Review* (January 1976), pp. 80–89.

Miller, Paul B. W. "A New View of Comparability." *Journal of Accountancy* (August 1978), pp. 70–78.

Moe, Palmer. "How to Research an Accounting or Auditing Problem." *Practical Accountant* (June 1979), pp. 60–67.

Moore, Michael L. "Conservatism." *The Texas CPA* (October 1972), pp. 41–47.

Mortimer, Terry. "Reporting Earnings: A New Approach." *Financial Analysts Journal* (November–December 1979), pp. 67–71.

Mosso, David. "Standards Overload—No Simple Solution." *The CPA Journal* (October 1983), pp. 12–22.

Norby, William C., and Frances G. Stone. "Objectives of Financial Accounting and Reporting from the Viewpoint of the Financial Analyst." *Financial Analysts Journal* (July–August 1972), pp. 39–41, 76–81.

Paton, William Andrew. *Accounting Theory*. Houston: Scholars Book Co., 1972 (originally published, New York: The Ronald Press Company, 1922).

Paton, W. A., and A. C. Littleton. *An Introduction to Corporate Accounting Standards*. Sarasota, Fla.: American Accounting Association, 1940.

Pattillo, James W. *The Concept of Materiality in Financial Reporting*. New York: Financial Executives Research Foundation, 1976.

Pines, J. Arnold. "The Securities and Exchange Commission and Accounting Principles." *Law and Contemporary Problems* (Autumn 1965), pp. 727–751.

Popoff, Boris. "Postulates, Principles and Rules." *Accounting and Business Research* (Summer 1972), pp. 182–193.

Previts, Gary John. "The SEC and Its Chief Accountants: Historical Impressions." *Journal of Accountancy* (August 1978), pp. 83–91.

Raiborn, Mitchell H., and D. D. Raiborn. "Defining the Boundaries of GAAP." *The CPA Journal* (July 1984), pp. 10–22.

Rappaport, Donald. "Materiality." *Price Waterhouse Review* (Summer 1963), pp. 26–33.

Revsine, Lawrence. "Towards Greater Comparability in Accounting Reports." *Financial Analysts Journal* (January–February 1975), pp. 45–51.

Rice, C. D., H. C. Ford, R. J. Williams, and G. W. Silverman. *The Businessman's View of the Purposes of Financial Reporting*. New York: Financial Executives Research Foundation, 1973.

Ronen, Joshua, and Michael Schiff. "The Setting of Financial Accounting Standards—Private or Public?" *Journal of Accountancy* (January 1978), 66–73.

Rose, J., W. Beaver, S. Becker, and G. Sorter. "Toward an Empirical Measure of Materiality." *Empirical Research in Accounting: Selected Studies* (1970), pp. 138–153.

Rosenfield, Paul. "Stewardship." In *Objectives of Financial Statements—Selected Papers*, Vol. 2. New York: American Institute of Certified Public Accountants, 1974, pp. 123–140.

Schuetze, Walter P. "The Early Days of FASB." *World* (Summer 1979), pp. 34–39.

Seidler, Lee J. "Chaos in Accounting: Will It Continue?" *Financial Analysts Journal* (March–April 1972), pp. 88–91.

Shwayder, Keith. "Relevance." *Journal of Accounting Research*, Vol. 6 (Spring 1968), pp. 86–97.

Simmons, John K. "A Concept of Comparability in Financial Reporting." *The Accounting Review*, Vol. 42 (October 1967), pp. 680–692.

Skousen, K. Fred. *An Introduction to the SEC*. Cincinnati: South-Western Publishing Co., 1976.

Solomons, David. "The Politicization of Accounting." *Journal of Accountancy* (January 1978), pp. 65–72.

Sorter, George H., and Martin S. Gans. "Opportunities and Implications of the Report on Objectives of Financial Statements." *Studies on Financial Accounting Objectives: 1974*. Supplement to Vol. 12 of the *Journal of Accounting Research*, pp. 1–12.

Spacek, Leonard. "The Need for an Accounting Court." *The Accounting Review* (July 1958), pp. 368–379.

Sprouse, Robert T. "The Importance of Earnings in the Conceptual Framework." *Journal of Accountancy* (January 1978), pp. 64–71.

Sprouse, Robert T. "Prospects for Progress in Financial Reporting." *Financial Analysts Journal* (September–October 1979), pp. 56–60.

Stanga, Keith G., and Jan R. Williams. "The FASB's Objectives of Financial Reporting." *The CPA Journal* (May 1979), pp. 30–34.

Staubus, George J. "An Induced Theory of Accounting Measurement." *The Accounting Review* (Janaury 1985), pp. 53–75.

Sterling, Robert R. "Conservatism: The Fundamental Principle of Valuation in Traditional Accounting." *Abacus* (December 1967), pp. 109–132.

Sterling, Robert R. "Decision Oriented Financial Accounting." *Accounting and Business Research* (Summer 1972), pp. 198–208.

Sterling, Robert R. "The Going Concern: An Examination." *The Accounting Review* (July 1968), pp. 481–502.

Sterling, Robert R. "A Test of the Uniformity Hypothesis." *Abacus* (September 1969), pp. 37–47.

Sterling, Robert R. "On Theory Construction and Verification." *The Accounting Review* (July 1970), pp. 444–457.

Storey, Reed K. *The Search for Accounting Principles—Today's Problems in Perspective*. New York: American Institute of Certified Public Accountants, Inc., 1964.

Tippet, M. "The Axioms of Accounting Measurement." *Accounting and Business Research* (Autumn 1978), pp. 266–278.

Vatter, William J. "Obstacles to the Specification of Accounting Principles." In *Research in Accounting Measurement*, Robert K. Jaedicke, Yuji Ijiri, and Oswald Nielson, eds. Sarasota, Fla.: American Accounting Association, 1966, pp. 71–87.

Williams, Jan Robert. "Differing Opinions on Accounting Objectives." *The CPA Journal* (August 1973), pp. 651–656.

Williams, Thomas H., and Charles H. Griffin. "On the Nature of Empirical Verification in Accounting." *Abacus* (December 1969), pp. 143–178.

Yu, S. C. *The Structure of Accounting Theory*. Gainesville, Fla.: University of Florida Press, 1976.

Zeff, Stephen A. "Some Junctures in the Evolution of the Process of Establishing Accounting Principles in the U.S.A.: 1917–1972." *The Accounting Review* (July 1984), pp. 447–468.

2
INCOME
CONCEPTS

8/31/88

The emergence of income reporting as the primary source for individual decision making has been well documented,[1] and income reporting serves to aid our economic society in a variety of ways. For example, the Study Group on Business Income documented the need for the income concept in society, and Alexander noted the following uses of income in this work.

1. Income is used as the basis of one of the principal forms of taxation.
2. Income is used in public reports as a measure of the success of a corporation's operations.
3. Income is used as a criterion for the determination of the availability of dividends.
4. Income is used by rate-regulating authorities for investigating whether those rates are fair and reasonable.
5. Income is used as a guide to trustees charged with distributing income to a life tenant while preserving the principal for a remainderman.
6. Income is used as a guide to management of an enterprise in the conduct of its affairs.[2]

Despite the wide use of the income concept, there is a general lack of agreement as to the proper definition of income. This disagreement is most noticeable

[1]Clifford D. Brown, "The Emergence of Income Reporting: An Historical Study," M.S.U. Business Studies (East Lansing, Michigan: Division of Research, Graduate School of Business Administration, Michigan State University, 1971).
[2]Sidney S. Alexander, "Income Measurement in a Dynamic Economy," *Five Monographs on Business Income*, report by Study Group on Business Income (New York, 1950), p. 6.

when the prevailing definitions used in the disciplines of economics and accounting are analyzed. Although there is a general consensus that economics and accounting are related sciences and that both are concerned with the activities of business firms and deal with similar variables, there has been a lack of agreement between the two disciplines regarding the proper timing and measurement of income. In order to reconcile these differences the following questions must be answered.

1. What is the nature of income?
2. When should income be reported?
3. Who are the recipients of income?

THE NATURE OF INCOME

Income may take various forms; for example, Bedford noted that three basic concepts of income are usually discussed in the literature.

1. *Psychic income,* which refers to the satisfaction of human wants.
2. *Real income,* which refers to increases in economic wealth.
3. *Money income,* which refers to increases in the monetary valuation of resources.[3] Does Not take care of inflation + Deflation

These three concepts are all important yet there are advantages and disadvantages associated with each. The measurement of psychic income is difficult because human wants are not quantifiable and are satisfied on various levels as an individual gains real income.[4] Moreover, money income is easily measured, but does not take into consideration changes in the value of the monetary unit. Economists generally agree that the objective of measuring income is to determine how much better off an entity has become during some period of time. Hence economists have focused upon the determination of real income. The definition of the economic concept of income is usually credited to the economist J. R. Hicks, who stated:

> The purpose of income calculation in practical affairs is to give people an indication of the amount which they can consume without impoverishing themselves. Following out this idea it would seem that we ought to define a man's income as the maximum value which he can consume during a week, and still expect to be as well off at the end of the week as he was at the beginning.[5]

[3]Norton M. Bedford, *Income Determination Theory: An Accounting Framework* (Reading, Mass.: Addison-Wesley Publishing Co., 1965), p. 20.
[4]See, for example, Abraham H. Maslow, *Motivation and Personality* (New York: Harper & Brothers, 1954), Chapter 5.
[5]J. R. Hicks, *Value and Capital* (Oxford: Clarendon Press, 1946), p. 172.

The preceding Hicksian definition places emphasis on individual income; however, the concept can also be used as the basis for determining business income by changing the word *consume* to *distribute*. In so doing, a business entity would be required to measure its net assets at the beginning of a period and at the end of the same period, exclusive of capital and dividend transactions. Income would then be the result of the change in net asset values over the measurement period. This method of income determination is termed the *capital maintenance* concept by accountants. Initially, the application of the capital maintenance concept may appear to be a simple measurement of the change in net worth exclusive of capital and dividend transactions; however, strict adherence to it entails a much more complex measure of "well-offness" and net worth than usually envisioned by accountants.

Specifically, it would be necessary to measure the *net present values* of enterprise assets and liabilities at the beginning and the end of a particular period and report the difference. Income in this instance would comprise two factors.

1. Increases or decreases in net assets that were the result of operations.
2. Increases or decreases in net assets that were caused by changes in their expected future values.

Although there can be little argument on the theoretical merit of the Hicksian definition, its critics do not believe that it has practical applicability because of two operational constraints. First, it is subjective because future inflows from assets and outflows from liabilities are not known with certainty. That is, how much cash will be received in the future because an enterprise holds land? Second, the appropriate discount factor is unknown and subject to future conditions. For these reasons accountants have generally not attempted to use the economic concept of real income and have delayed the timing of income reporting until more substantial evidence exists that income has been earned. These arguments are discussed more fully in Chapter 13, which deals with current value accounting.

INCOME RECOGNITION

In an attempt to overcome the subjective difficulties associated with the economic concept of income, accountants have traditionally taken the position that income should be reported when there is evidence of an outside exchange (or an "arms length transaction"). This *transactions* approach generally requires that reported income be the result of dealings with firms and individuals external to the reporting unit and gives rise to the realization principle. The realization principle holds that income should be recognized when the earnings process is complete, or virtually complete, and an exchange has taken place. The exchange transaction is the basis of accountability and determines both the time of revenue recognition and the amount of revenue to be recorded.

Income in an accounting sense contrasts with income in the economic sense in that the former is limited to the *recorded* changes in net asset values, exclusive of capital and dividend transactions, during a period. The accounting concept of income does not attempt to place an expected value on the firm or report on changes in the expected values of assets or liabilities. Because of these limitations, accounting has been criticized for not reporting all relevant information about the entity.

Those who favor a more liberal interpretation of the income concept argue that income should include all gains and losses in assets or liabilities held by an entity during a particular period. This broader measure of income was given its initial impetus by Edwards and Bell in their *Theory and Measurement of Business Income*[6] and Sprouse and Moonitz in Accounting Research Study No. 3, "A Tentative Set of Broad Accounting Principles for Business Enterprises."[7]

Edwards and Bell suggested that with only slight changes in present accounting procedures four types of income can be isolated. These income measures are defined as (1) current operating profit—the excess of sales revenues over the current cost of inputs used in production and sold; (2) realizable cost savings—the increases in the prices of assets held during the period; (3) realized cost savings—the difference between historical costs and the current purchase price of goods sold; and (4) realized capital gains—the excess of sales proceeds over historical costs on the disposal of long-term assets. Edwards and Bell contended that these measures are a better indication of well-offness and allow users more information in analyzing enterprise results.[8]

Sprouse, in elaborating on the findings of Accounting Research Study No. 3, discusses the concept somewhat more narrowly:

> *Because ownership interests are constantly changing hands, we must strive for timely recognition of measurable changes, and in so doing we must identify the nature of the changes. As currently reported, income may well be composed of three elements, each of which has considerably different economic significance. Is the gross margin truly the result of operations—the difference between current selling prices of products and current costs of producing products, both measured in today's dollars? How much of the company's income is not the result of its operations but is the result of*

---

[6]Edgar O. Edwards and Phillip W. Bell, *The Theory and Measurement of Business Income* (Berkeley and Los Angeles: University of California Press, 1961).

[7]Robert T. Sprouse and Maurice Moonitz, "A Tentative Set of Broad Accounting Principles for Business Enterprises," Accounting Research Study No. 3 (New York: AICPA, 1962).

[8]Edwards and Bell, op. cit., p. 111.

changes in the value of a significant asset, for example, a large supply of raw material, perhaps a warehouse full of sugar? Such changes are apt to be fortuitous and unpredictable and therefore need to be segregated, if financial statements are to be interpreted meaningfully and if rational investment decisions are to be based on income measurements. And how much of what is now reported as income is not income at all but is merely the spurious result of using a current unit of measurement for revenues and an obsolete unit of measurement for costs—particularly depreciation.[9]

The major change advocated by both Edwards and Bell and Accounting Research Study No. 3 is the reporting of gains or losses in the net assets of the entity during a period. These changes have been termed *holding gains and losses,* and proponents claim that the reporting of holding gains and losses would increase the information content of published financial statements. This argument focuses upon two points: (1) windfall gains and losses from holding specific assets and liabilities should be reported as they occur, and (2) changes in the measuring unit should be eliminated from the reporting process. (The discussion of the second point will be deferred until Chapter 13.)

The effect on income of the failure to record holding gains is illustrated by the following example. Suppose two individuals, A and B, both purchase 100 shares of corporation Z's common stock for $5 per share on January 1, 1987. Also assume that the value of the shares increased to $10 per share by December 31, 1987, and that A sells his shares on that date while B retains hers. Traditional accounting principles would allow A to recognize a gain of $500, whereas individual B would record no gain. This difference occurs even though the economic substance of both events is essentially the same. This example illustrates the general emphasis on the transactions approach to income determination.

COMPREHENSIVE INCOME

In Statement of Financial Accounting Concepts No. 3, the Financial Accounting Standards Board attempted to broaden the scope of the measurements of the operating results of business enterprises by introducing the definition of comprehensive income. According to this statement,

Comprehensive income is the change in equity (net assets) of an entity during a period from transactions and events and circumstances from non-owner

[9]Robert T. Sprouse, "The Radically Different Principles of Accounting Research Study No. 3," *Journal of Accountancy* (May 1964), p. 66.

CHAPTER 2: INCOME CONCEPTS

sources. It includes all changes in equity during a period except those result-
ing from investments by owners and distributions to owners.[10]

This approach represents an attempt by the Financial Accounting Standards Board to tie together the Hicksian capital maintenance approach and the traditional accounting transaction approach to income measurement. As such, net income is defined as the maximum amount of a firm's resources that can be distributed to owners during a given period of time (exclusive of new owner investments) and yet still leave the business enterprise as well off at the end of that period as it was in the beginning. However, the FASB attempted to allay fears that the concept of comprehensive income might imply radical changes in reported income by stating that most assets and liabilities in current practice would continue to qualify as such. The board further emphasized that the definitions included in SFAC No. 3 would not require upheavals in present practice; rather, they were expected to lead to some evolutionary changes.

As discussed in Chapter 1, Statements of Financial Accounting Concepts are ultimately intended to be a framework for the analysis of accounting practice. This framework has not yet been fully established and two general modifications to the transaction approach continue to have an impact on financial reporting. These modifications are conservatism and materiality.

CONSERVATISM

Sterling called *conservatism* the most influential principle of valuation in accounting.[11] This doctrine can be summarized as: when in doubt choose the accounting alternative that will be least likely to overstate assets and income.

The principle of conservatism gained prominence as a partial offset to the eternal optimism of management and the tendency to overstate financial statements that characterized the first three decades of the twentieth century. Conservatism was seen as overriding the holding gains argument because many accountants believed that by placing the least favorable alternative valuation on the firm, the users of financial accounting information were less likely to be misled.

However, in recent years the pressures for more realistic and relevant information have reduced the influence of this concept. Conservative financial statements are usually unfair to present stockholders and biased in favor of prospective stockholders because the net valuation of the firm does not fully include

In favor of new owners not present owners

---

[10]Statement of Financial Accounting Concepts No. 3, "Elements of Financial Statements of Business Enterprises" (Stamford, Conn.: Financial Accounting Standards Board, 1980), pp. xi–xii.
[11]Robert R. Sterling, *Theory of the Measurement of Enterprise Income* (Lawrence, Kan.: University of Kansas Press, 1970), p. 256.

future expectations. That is, the company's common stock will be priced at a relatively lower value in the marketplace.

MATERIALITY

The concept of *materiality* has had a pervasive influence upon all accounting activities despite the fact that no all-encompassing definition of the concept exists. Although materiality affects the measurement and disclosure of all information presented on the financial statements, it has its greatest impact on items of revenue and expense.

The concept has both qualitative and quantitative aspects, as can be seen by the pronouncements of various legal and quasi-legal bodies. Accounting Research Study No. 7 stated,

A statement, fact or item is material, if giving full consideration to the surrounding circumstances, as they exist at the time, it is of such a nature that its disclosure, or the method of treating it, would be likely to influence or to "make a difference" in the judgment and conduct of a reasonable person.[12]

Quantitative requirements have been established by authoritative bodies in their pronouncements. For example, in Accounting Principles Board Opinion No. 18, an investment of 20 percent or more in the voting stock of an investee is considered material. And in APB No. 15, a reduction of less than 3 percent in the aggregate of earnings per share is not considered material. The FASB defined a reportable segment as one that constitutes 10 percent of revenues, operating profits, or assets. Additionally, most FASB Statements contain the following: "The provisions of this Statement need not be applied to immaterial items."[13]

In Statement of Financial Accounting Concepts No. 2, the FASB made the following statement regarding materiality.

Those who make accounting decisions and those who make judgments as auditors continually confront the need to make judgments about materiality. Materiality judgments are primarily quantitative in nature. They pose the question: Is this item large enough for users of the information to be influenced by it? However, the answer to that question will usually be affected by the nature of the item; items too small to be thought material if they result

[12]Paul Grady, Accounting Research Study No. 7, "Inventory of Generally Accepted Accounting Principles for Business Enterprises" (New York: American Institute of Certified Public Accountants, 1965), p. 40.
[13]See, for example, Statement of Financial Accounting Standards No. 42, "Determining Materiality for Capitalization of Interest Cost" (Stamford, Conn.: FASB, November 1980), p. 3.

from routine transactions may be considered material if they arise in abnormal circumstances.[14]

This statement then went on to define materiality judgments as "screens" or thresholds. That is, is an item (error or omission) large enough to pass through the threshold that separates material from immaterial items? The more important the item the finer the screen that will exist.

The following items are cited.

1. An accounting change in circumstances that puts an enterprise in danger of being in breach of covenant regarding its financial condition may justify a lower materiality threshold than if its position were stronger.
2. A failure to disclose separately a nonrecurrent item of revenue may be material at a lower threshold than would be the case if the revenue turns a loss into a profit or reverses the trend of earnings from a downward to an upward trend.
3. A misclassification of assets that would not be material in amount if it affected two categories of plant or equipment might be material if it changed the classification between a noncurrent and a current asset category.
4. Amounts too small to warrant disclosure or correction in normal circumstances may be considered material if they arise from abnormal or unusual transactions or events.[15]

The American Accounting Association has provided both quantitative and qualitative guidelines.

Materiality, as used in accounting, may be described as a state of relative importance. Materiality is not, however, entirely dependent upon relative size. Importance may depend on either quantitative or qualitative characteristics, often upon a combination of both. Factors indicative of materiality may be classified as follows:

1. Characteristics having primarily quantitative significance:
   a. the magnitude of the item (either smaller or larger) relative to normal expectation
   b. the magnitude of the item relative to similar or related items (relative to total of its class, earnings for the period, etc.)
2. Characteristics having primarily qualitative significance:
   a. the inherent importance of the action, activity, or condition reflected

[14]Statement of Financial Accounting Concepts No. 2, "Qualitative Characteristics of Accounting Information" (Stamford, Conn.: FASB, May 1980), par. 123.
[15]Ibid., par. 128.

(unusual, unexpected, improper, in violation of contract or stature, etc.)

b. *the inherent importance of the item as an indicator of the probable course of future events (suggestive of a change in business practices, etc.)*[16]

The Securities and Exchange Commission (SEC) states in Rule 1.02 of Regulation S-X,

The term "material" when used to qualify a requirement for the furnishing of information as to any subject limits the information required to those matters about which an average prudent investor ought reasonably to be informed.[17]

The SEC also provides many quantitative guidelines as to how revenues and expenses should be reported and has also introduced percentage guidelines. Although the specific guidelines are too numerous to present, 10 percent is becoming a popular figure in the SEC literature.

The Cost Accounting Standards Board (CASB) considered materiality at some length. In its *Statement of Operating Policies, Procedures, and Objectives,* the CASB said,

The Board believes that the administration of its rules, regulations, and Cost Accounting Standards should be reasonable and not seek to deal with insignificant amounts of cost.[18]

Furthermore, the statement goes on to list the following criteria for determining materiality.

1. *The absolute dollar amount involved. . . .*
2. *The amount of the total contract cost compared with the amount under consideration. . . .*
3. *The relationship between a cost item and cost objective. . . .*
4. *The impact on government funding. . . .*
5. *The relationship to price. . . .*
6. *The cumulative effect of individually immaterial items. . . .*

---

[16]American Accounting Association, Committee on Concepts and Standards Underlying Corporate Financial Statements, *Accounting and Reporting Standards for Corporate Financial Statements and Preceding Statements and Supplements,* "Standards of Disclosure for Published Financial Reports: Supplementary Statement No. 8" (Columbus, Ohio: American Accounting Association, 1957), p. 49.

[17]Securities and Exchange Commission Regulation S-X Rule 1.02.

[18]*Cost Accounting Standards Board Statement of Operating Policies, Procedures, and Objectives* (Washington, D.C.: Cost Accounting Standards Board, 1973), p. 4.

CHAPTER 2: INCOME CONCEPTS

These criteria should be considered together; no one criterion is wholly determinative of immateriality. In particular Standards, the Board will give consideration to defining materiality in specific dollar amounts and/or specific percentages of impact on operations covered by the entire Standard or any provision thereof whenever it appears feasible and desirable to do so.[19]

The CASB was progressive in its approach for determining materiality. Note, for instance, the CASB's delineation of criteria and also its statement that in certain instances specific dollars or percentages will be specified.

Finally, significant judicial decisions have concerned themselves with materiality. In the Bar Chris case, the judge stated,

The average prudent investor is not concerned with minor inaccuracies or with errors as to matters which are of no interest to him. The facts which tend to deter him from purchasing a security are facts which have an important bearing upon the nature or conditions of the issuing corporation or its business.[20]

The concept of materiality was expanded in the case of *SEC* v. *Texas Gulf Sulphur Company*, where the decision stated,

Material facts include not only information disclosing the earnings and distributions of a company but also those facts which affect the probable future of the company and those which may affect the desire of investors to buy, sell, or hold the company's securities.[21]

In *Hertzfeld* v. *Laventhal, Krekstein, Horwath and Horwath* the judicial concept of materiality takes somewhat the same form as the current accounting definition, as can be seen from Judge MacMahon's statement referring to an earlier decision.

In this context, material facts are those which a reasonable investor would deem important in making his decision to buy . . . securities. . . . Materiality, therefore, depends on whether a reasonable man . . . "might well have acted otherwise than to purchase" if informed of the crucial facts.[22]

These definitions leave much to be desired, and the elusiveness of the concept of materiality is a topic of continuing interest to the Financial Accounting Stan-

[19]Ibid., pp. 4–5.
[20]*Escott et al.* v. *Bar Chris Construction Corporation et al.*, 283 Fed. Supp. (District Court S.D., New York), p. 681.
[21]*Securities and Exchange Commission* v. *Texas Gulf Sulphur Company*, 401 Fed. 2d(2d cir. 1968), p. 848.
[22]*Hertzfeld* v. *Laventhal, Krekstein, Horwath and Horwath*, Fed. See Law Reports (District Court S.D., New York, 1974), pp. 995–998.

dards Board. Hopefully, new guidelines will be established that narrow the concept and render it operational.

MEASUREMENT

The reporting of business income assumes that items of revenue and expense are capable of being measured. One requirement of measurement is that the object or event is capable of being ordered or ranked in respect to some property. Measurement is the assigning of numbers to objects or events according to rules. It is also a process of comparison in order to obtain more precise information to distinguish one alternative from another in a decision situation.

The measuring unit in the United States is the dollar; however, the instability of the measuring unit causes a major problem. For example, consider the room you are now in. If you were to measure its width in feet and inches today, next week, and next year, accurate measurements would give the same result each time. In contrast, the accounting measurement of sales revenue will undoubtedly differ each year even if exactly the same number of units are sold. Much of this difference will be the result of changes in the value of the dollar.

Another factor that complicates accounting measurement is that arbitrary decisions must be made for periodic reporting purposes. Depreciation, depletion, and amortization are all examples of arbitrary and inexact measurement techniques that complicate the measurement process. Although changes in the measurement unit and arbitrary measurements caused by the necessity of periodic presentation are not likely to disappear in the near future, the users of accounting information should recognize the inherent limitations in the use of measurement techniques in accounting.

REALIZATION

There has been a great deal of confusion in accounting literature over the precise meaning of the term *realization*. In general, realization refers to the formal recognition of revenue in the computation of net income. However, there have been arguments over the proper timing of revenue recognition. Critics of the accounting process favor the economic concept of real income, whereby revenue is earned continuously over time. For accountants, however, it would not be practical to record revenues on a continuous basis. Rather, the accountant must choose an appropriate point in time on which to record the occurrence of revenues.

In 1964, the American Accounting Association Committee on Realization recommended that the concept of realization could be improved if the following criteria were applied: (1) revenue must be capable of measurement, (2) the measurement must be verified by an external market transaction, and (3) the

80

crucial event must have occurred.[23] The key element in these recommendations is the third criterion. The crucial-event test states that revenue should be realized upon the completion of the most crucial task in the earning process. This test results in the recognition of revenue at various times for different business organizations.

The use of the crucial-event test and the transactions approach has resulted in accounting income that measures the difference between sales of the company's product (revenue) and costs incurred in the production and sale of that product (expenses). Revenue has been defined by the Financial Accounting Standards Board as "inflows or other enhancements of assets of an entity or settlements of its liabilities (or a combination of both) during a period from delivering or producing goods, rendering services or other activities that constitute the entity's ongoing operations."[24]

The use of the realization convention usually results in revenue being recognized at the point of sale; however, the timing of recognition may be advanced or delayed by the nature of the specific transaction.

Revenue Recognized During the Production Process "Futures"
When production of the company's product carries over into two or more periods, the allocation of revenue to the various accounting periods is considered essential for proper reporting. In such cases a method of revenue recognition termed *percentage of completion* may be used. This method allocates revenue on the basis of the percentage of the expected total costs that were incurred in a particular accounting period. The method requires a known selling price and the ability to estimate reasonably the total costs of the product. It is used in accounting for long-term construction contracts such as roads, shipbuilding, and dams.

Revenue Recognized at the Completion of Production
When the company's product is to be sold at a determinable price on an organized market, revenue may be realized when the goods are ready for sale. The gold market formerly was an example of this method, in that all gold mined was required to be sold to the government at a fixed price. Some farm products and commodities also meet these conditions.

Revenue Recognized as Services Are Performed
There are three steps involved in service contracts: (1) order taking, (2) performance of services, and (3) collection of cash. These steps may all be performed

[23]American Accounting Association 1964 Concepts and Standards Research Study Committee: The Matching Concept, "The Matching Concept," *The Accounting Review*, Vol. 40 (April 1965), p. 318.
[24]Statement of Financial Accounting Concepts No. 3, op cit., par. 63.

in one accounting period or divided between periods. In service contracts, realization should generally be connected with the performance of services, and revenue should be recorded in relation to the degree of services performed. Realization should be tied to services performed because it is the most crucial decision. The signing of the contract results in a partially executory contract, and the collection of cash may precede or follow the performance of services.

Revenue Recognized as Cash is Received
In certain circumstances, where the ultimate collectibility of the revenue is in doubt, recognition is delayed until cash payment is received. The installment method and the cash recovery method are examples of delaying revenue recognition until the receipt of cash. However, the Accounting Principles Board has stated that revenue recognition should not be delayed unless ultimate collectibility is so seriously doubted that an appropriate allowance for the uncollectible amount cannot be estimated.

Revenue Recognized upon the Occurrence of Some Event
In some instances, where binding contracts do not exist or rights to cancel are in evidence, revenue recognition may be delayed until the point of ratification or the passage of time. For example, some states have passed laws that allow door-to-door sales contracts to be voided within certain periods of time. In such cases recognition should be delayed until that period has passed.

Special Recognition Circumstances
The FASB specifically addressed revenue recognition criteria for franchisors and in situations where the right of return exists in two separate SFASs. In Statement No. 45, "Accounting for Franchise Fee Revenue," the board stated that franchise fee revenue (net of an appropriate provision for uncollectible accounts) should be recognized when all material services have been substantially performed by the franchisor. In most cases the earliest point at which revenue may be recognized by franchisors will be the start of operation by the franchisee. Additionally, the installment method may only be used when revenue is collected over an extended period of time and there is no reasonable basis for estimating its ultimate collectibility.

In Statement No. 48, "Revenue Recognition When Right of Return Exists," the board stated that a seller should recognize revenue at the point of sale when a return privilege exists only when all of the following conditions are met.

1. The selling price is fixed or determinable at the date of sale.
2. The buyer has paid or is obligated to pay the seller.
3. The buyer bears the risk of loss from theft or damage.
4. The buyer has economic substance apart from the seller.

5. The seller has no major obligations for future performance involving the resale of the product.
6. Future returns are reasonably estimable.

In the event these conditions are not met and revenue recognition is deferred, revenue should be recognized at the first point at which the return privilege has expired or any conditions are satisfied.

The preceding discussion illustrates that the timing of revenue recognition may differ substantially. Unfortunately, there is no specific criterion by which the accountants can make judgments as to the most appropriate moments of recognition. Thus, over the years, various precedents and conventions have provided support for the recognition of revenues at different times, and the realization convention has taken on the meaning of a set of criteria to be used when certain circumstances are in evidence.

STATEMENT OF FINANCIAL ACCOUNTING CONCEPTS NO. 5

In 1984 the FASB released its Statement of Financial Accounting Concepts No. 5, "Recognition and Measurement in Financial Statements of Business Enterprises." This document does not suggest major changes in the current structure and context of financial statements. However, it does suggest that a statement of cash flows should replace the current statement of changes in financial position.

In general, SFAC No. 5 attempted to set forth recognition criteria and guidance on what information should be incorporated into financial statements, and when this information should be reported. According to this Statement, a full set of financial statements for a period should show

1. Financial position at the end of the period. _< Balance Sheet_
2. Earnings for the period. _Earnings Statement_
3. Comprehensive income for the period. _Income Statement. This is evolutionary say FASB_
4. Cash flows during the period. _Change in Financial Statement (cash flow)_
5. Investments by and distributions to owners during the period. _owners Equity Statement_

The statement of financial position should provide information about an entity's assets, liabilities, and equity and their relationship to each other at a moment in time. It should also delineate the entity's resource structure—major classes and amounts of assets—and its financing structure—major classes and amounts of liabilities and equity. The statement of financial position is not intended to show the value of a business, but it should provide information to users wishing to make their own estimates of the enterprise's value.

Earnings is a measure of entity performance during a period. It measures the extent to which asset inflows (revenues and gains) exceed asset outflows. The concept of earning provided in SFAC No. 5 is similar to net income for a period in current practice. However, it excludes certain adjustments from earlier periods now recognized in the current period. It is expected that the concept of earnings will continue to be subject to the process of gradual change that has characterized its development.

Comprehensive income is defined as a broad measure of the effects of transactions and other events on an entity. It comprises all recognized changes in equity of the entity during a period from transactions except those resulting from investments by owners and distributions to owners.

The relationship between earnings and comprehensive income is illustrated as follows.

Revenues	Earnings
Less: Expenses	Plus or minus cumulative accounting adjustments
Plus: Gains	Plus or minus other nonowner changes in equity
Less: Losses	
= Earnings	= Comprehensive income

The statement of cash flows should directly or indirectly reflect an entity's cash receipts classified by major source and its cash payments classified by major uses during a period. The statement should include cash flow information about its operating, financing, and investing activities.

A statement of investments by and distributions to owners reflects an entity's capital transactions during a period, that is, the extent to which and in what ways the equity of the entity increased or decreased from transactions with owners.

The scope of SFAC No. 5 and its relationship to other methods of reporting is illustrated in Figure 2.1.

SFAC No. 5 also addresses certain measurement issues that are closely related to recognition. That is, an item and information about it should meet four recognition criteria and should be recognized at the time these criteria are met (subject to the cost-benefit and materiality constraints).

1. **Definitions**—the item meets the definition of an element contained in SFAC No. 3.
2. **Measurability**—it has a relevant attribute measurable with sufficient reliability.
3. **Relevance**—the information about the item is capable of making a difference in user decisions.
4. **Reliability**—the information is representationally faithful, verifiable and, neutral.

These recognition criteria are consistent with and in fact drawn from Statements of Financial Accounting Concepts Nos. 1, 2, and 3. SFAC No. 5 goes on to provide guidance in applying the recognition criteria when enterprise earnings are affected by the recognition decision. This guidance is consistent with the

Figure 2.1 Relationship of SFAC No. 5 to other methods of reporting.

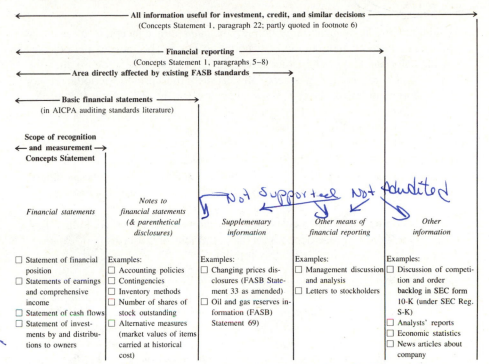

←————— **All information useful for investment, credit, and similar decisions** —————→
(Concepts Statement 1, paragraph 22; partly quoted in footnote 6)

←————— **Financial reporting** —————→
(Concepts Statement 1, paragraphs 5–8)
←——— **Area directly affected by existing FASB standards** ———→

←——— **Basic financial statements** ———→
(in AICPA auditing standards literature)

Scope of recognition
←— **and measurement** —→
Concepts Statement

Financial statements	*Notes to financial statements (& parenthetical disclosures)*	*Supplementary information*	*Other means of financial reporting*	*Other information*
☐ Statement of financial position	Examples:	Examples:	Examples:	Examples:
☐ Statements of earnings and comprehensive income	☐ Accounting policies	☐ Changing prices dis-	☐ Management discussion	☐ Discussion of competi-
	☐ Contingencies	closures (FASB State-	and analysis	tion and order
	☐ Inventory methods	ment 33 as amended)	☐ Letters to stockholders	backlog in SEC form
☐ Statement of cash flows	☐ Number of shares of	☐ Oil and gas reserves in-		10-K (under SEC Reg.
☐ Statement of invest-	stock outstanding	formation (FASB)		S-K)
ments by and distribu-	☐ Alternative measures	Statement 69)		☐ Analysts' reports
tions to owners	(market values of items			☐ Economic statistics
	carried at historical			☐ News articles about
	cost)			company

Not Supported Not Audited

Source: Statement of Financial Accounting Concepts No. 5, ''Recognition and Measurement in Financial Statements of Business Enterprises'' (Stamford Conn.: FASB, 1985), par. 8.

doctrine of conservatism. That is, recognition of revenues and gains is based upon the additional tests of their (1) being realized or realizable and (2) being earned before recognized as income. Guidance for recognizing expenses and losses is dependent upon either consumption of benefit or loss of future benefit.

SFAC No. 5 will undoubtedly create a controversy because it does not resolve the current value/historical cost debate. This failure is apparently due to the board's position of accepting *decision usefulness* as the overriding objective of financial reporting.

This document will also be disappointing to those who had hoped it would have provided a formula or set of formulas from which solutions to specific accounting problems could be derived. That is, some accountants and financial-statement users would prefer a document that provides answers to questions about when, if at all, a specific event should be recognized and what amount best measures that event.

In addition to the realization principle, the *matching* concept is of primary importance in the determination of accounting income because of periodic reporting. Normal accounting procedures are based upon the premise that the business enterprise is a going concern and, as such, must provide periodic reports to investors in order for them to assess their investment. Therefore, it is necessary for accountants to establish certain rules as to which revenue and expense items will be included in a periodic report.

Paton and Littleton described the matching concept as the association of effort and accomplishment.[25] Similarly, an American Accounting Association Committee investigating the matching concept recommended that costs should be related to revenues realized within a specific period on the basis of some correlation of these costs with the recognized revenues.[26]

The determination of when costs are of no future benefit and should therefore be charged against revenue depends on the definitions of the terms *cost, expense,* and *loss*. These terms are defined as follows:

Cost—the amount given in consideration of goods received or to be received. Costs can be classified as unexpired (assets), which are applicable to the production of future revenues, and expired, those not applicable to the production of future revenues and thus deducted from revenues or retained earnings in the current period.[27]

Expense—outflows or other using up of assets or incurrences of liabilities (or a combination of both) during a period from delivering or producing goods, rendering services, or carrying out other activities that constitute the entity's ongoing major or central operations.[28]

Loss—decreases in equity (net assets) from peripheral or incidental transactions of an entity and from all other transactions and other events and circumstances affecting the entity during a period except those that result from expenses or distributions to owners.[29]

In other words, expenses are revenue-producing cost expirations while losses are non-revenue-producing cost expirations.

---

[25]W. A. Paton and A. C. Littleton, *An Introduction to Corporate Accounting Standards,* American Accounting Association Monograph No. 3 (AAA, 1940).

[26]American Accounting Association 1964 Concepts and Standards Research Study Committee, op. cit., pp. 368–372.

[27]Committee on Terminology, American Institute of Certified Public Accountants, "Review and Resume," Accounting Terminology Bulletin No. 4 (New York, 1953).

[28]FASB Statement of Concepts No. 3, op. cit., par. 64.

[29]Ibid., par. 68.

CHAPTER 2: INCOME CONCEPTS

These definitions are illustrated as follows:

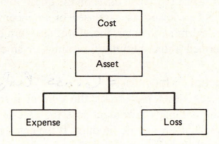

Thus, the accountant must determine the costs that have expired during the current period and whether or not such costs are revenue-producing or non-revenue-producing cost expirations. This determination is aided by differentiating expenses into product costs and period costs. Product costs are those cost expirations that can be directly associated with the company's product, such as direct material, direct labor, and direct factory overhead. Additionally, it is common practice arbitrarily to assign some costs, such as indirect overhead, to the product even though a direct measure of association may be lacking. Product costs are released to expense on the basis of the number of products sold. Period costs are those cost expirations that are more closely related to a period of time than to a product, such as administrative salaries. Period costs are released to expense on the basis of the period of benefit. All losses were written off in the period in which their lack of future benefit is determined.

In reviewing the preceding requirements, it can be seen that income in the accounting sense is the result of the ability to measure inflows (revenues) and associated outflows (expenses). Where inflows or outflows are not measurable, the timing of income recognition is deferred. Income in this sense is closely tied to past and present operations, and the traditional income statement indicates little in the way of future expectations. Accountants have generally taken the position that the best indicator of the future is past performance and that reporting anticipated gains involves an element of subjectivity in the calculation that could impair the usefulness of financial statements.

INCOME RECIPIENTS

In addition to the questions concerning the nature and reporting of income, there is the corollary query, Who are the recipients of income? This question involves determining the proper recipients of income and the proper reporting procedures to incorporate under each of the various alternatives. Hendriksen has suggested that net income may be presented under the following concepts: value added, enterprise net income, net income to investors, net income to stockholders, and net income to residual equity holders.[30] The determination of the net income figure to be reported in each instance turns on the question of whether deductions from revenue are to be viewed as expenses or as income distributions. The question of income determination can, therefore, also turn on whether a particular distribution is termed a distribution of earnings or an external expense.

Value-Added Concept of Income = Gross Profit

The economic concept views income as the current market price (including holding gains) of the company's product less the external cost of goods and services associated with acquiring the product. If the enterprise is thus viewed in the broad social sense, individuals other than owners or creditors may have claims against this income. For example, employees and the government may also be viewed as the recipients of income.

The value-added concept of income may be defined as the net amount of the increase in the market price of a product attributable to each enterprise. It indicates the total amount of income that can be divided among the various interested parties. In recent years this income concept has attained additional attention because of an alternative method of taxation termed the value-added tax.   M.K. value - cost = value of business plus

Enterprise Net Income   -   Owners (Ded Income tax +   )

The modern corporation generally has two main activities: operations and financing. Enterprise net income is determined from the operations aspect only, and all financing activities and other payments necessitated by operations are regarded as return on investment rather than as expenses. Thus, stockholders, bondholders, and the government are viewed as the recipients of income. Under this concept, revenue less all expenses, exclusive of interest and income taxes, provides the net income figure. A major criticism of this concept is the inclusion of the government as an income recipient while excluding employees.

exclude   interest + expenses

Net Income to Investors - creditors

The concept of net income to investors is based upon the entity view of the accounting equation which states that assets equal equities. (See chapter 11 for a further discussion of the entity concept) According to this concept, both long-term debtholders and stockholders are viewed as investors in the firm, and income would be reported as revenue less all expenses except interest. The difference between the enterprise and net income to investors concepts is the treatment of taxes. Under the net income to investors concept the government is

Eliminate - interest

[30]Eldon S. Hendriksen, *Accounting Theory*, 4th ed. (Homewood, Ill.: Richard D. Irwin, 1982), pp. 163–167.

not viewed as an income recipient and taxes are treated as expenses. The major premise of this concept of income is that the method of obtaining investment funds should not have an impact upon income determination.

Net Income to Shareholders— *Lenders*

The owners of the enterprise are usually viewed as the proper recipients of income. Accordingly, the net income to shareholders concept is based upon the proprietary view of the accounting equation that states assets equal liabilities plus proprietorship. This view sees income as accruing to both preferred and common stockholders and net income is determined by subtracting all expenses from revenue. *isolate the lenders*

Net Income to Residual Equity Holders

The recent emphasis on earnings per share computations is an outgrowth of the concept of net income to residual equity holders. The income available to common stockholders is viewed as the single most important figure under this concept and, in addition to all expenses, preferred dividends are deducted from revenue in arriving at a net income figure. *Subtract Preferred Stock*

Figure 2.2 summarizes the nature of income under each of the preceding assumptions.

Figure 2.2 Summary of various net income concepts.

Current market price of the product

Less:	Cost of goods produced and other external expenses
	= *Value-added Income*
	Less: Unrealized holding gains and payments to employees
	= *Enterprise net income*
	Less: Income taxes
	= *Net income to investors*
	Less: Interest charges
	= *Net income to shareholders*
	Less: Preferred dividends
	= *Net income to residual equity holders*

Although net income to shareholders is the income concept used in published financial reports, it should be noted that each of these income figures has usefulness in certain instances. The value-added concept is used in determining the gross national product; the enterprise net income and net income to investors concepts are useful in determining the profitability of a firm exclusive of financing activities; and the residual equity concept forms the basis of earnings per share computations. The income concept that is most useful will be determined by the goals of the various groups of users.

SUMMARY

Although the concept of income is constantly used, there is no clear-cut agreement as to its definition. To clarify the way in which the concept is being used, three questions must be answered: What is the nature of income? When should income be reported? Who are the recipients of income?

We have viewed income as the result of two factors: (1) the sale of the company's product (*realized income*) and (2) increases or decreases in retained net assets (*realizable income,* that is, holding gains). Thus, complete reporting of income would require that both of these factors be included in income, but limitations in techniques and objective evidence constrain the reporting process.

Deciding when to report income has been largely controlled by the accounting convention of *realization.* This convention generally requires that a transaction with an outsider take place, or that there be evidence that such a transaction will soon take place, before income is recognized. Nevertheless, the timing of revenue recognition may vary with different types of transactions. Accountants have also placed emphasis on the proper matching of cost expiration with the revenue recognized during a particular accounting period.

Still another variation in the income concept is that different groups can be viewed as income recipients. The expenses deducted from revenue in reporting income vary with these different assumptions as to the income recipients. There is no one "correct" view of income recipients. Rather, the various assumptions are used by different segments of the economy for different purposes.

The readings for this chapter explore some of these concepts more thoroughly. In "A Comparison of Accounting and Economic Concepts of Business Income," Bert Mitchell focuses on how differences in the concept of income as defined by economists and accountants affect several well-known principles of accounting. The second article, "The Realization Concept," presents the American Accounting Association's committee report on realization in full. Finally, Tiller and Williams discuss revenue recognition under some new FASB pronouncements.

A COMPARISON OF ACCOUNTING AND ECONOMIC CONCEPTS OF BUSINESS INCOME

BERT N. MITCHELL, CPA

The determination of annual business income is, for accountants, a major area of research, study and discussion. Economists, too, are intrigued with this determination. However, the concept of income held by the two groups, broadly, is radically different, as will be evident from the ensuing exposition.

Accountants and economists have been unable to come to terms in developing a uniform concept of income. Indeed, there exists within each profession many different concepts of income. Both professions have agreed that income determination is one of their most important concerns. Irving Fisher, a celebrated American economist, pointed out the prominent role of the income concept to the economists when he stated that:

> *I believe that the concept of income is, without exception, the most vital concept in economic science . . .*[1]

The accountant too, has placed paramount importance on the income statement—it is the most important accounting report in today's business world.

So it is, that both accountants and economists have ascribed a most important role to the income concept. But, further examination shows that the two disciplines have different objectives in their conceptual approach to it.

The economist is concerned primarily with the income of persons, groups of persons and of society as a whole. The accountant, on the other hand, is concerned primarily with income as it arises in transactions of business enterprises.

The economist's approach to income is therefore much broader than that of the accountant; but the domain of the accountant is also covered by the economist. Since the economist is concerned with income of society as a whole, then of necessity he must be concerned with income of business enterprises which is an integral part of total income. Therefore, income concepts as they apply to business enterprises are common grounds to both economists and accountants. Despite the common interest, each discipline views business income from a different vantage point and consequently sees it in a different light—which is the point of this article.

WHAT IS BUSINESS INCOME?

In accounting, business income is generally conceived as the residual from matching revenue realized against costs consumed.

The economist uses different concepts of income. The Hicksian concept is probably the most generally accepted by economists. Hicks stated that:

> *It would seem that we ought to define a man's income as the maximum value*

[1]Morton Backer, American Economic, XIV. *Modern Accounting Theory* (Englewood Cliffs, N.J.: Prentice-Hall, Inc., 1966), p. 72.

which he can consume during a week and still expect to be as well off at the end of the week as he was at the beginning.[2]

This approach to being as "well off" at the end of a period as the beginning has been used by the economist to determine business income. Consequently, the economic income of a business for a given period, may be described as:

> . . . the amount of wealth that can be distributed to the owner during the period without diminishing the entity's future prospects below those that prevailed at the start of the period.[3]

If a business has residual value of its revenue over its related costs, then it has earned income and consequently increased its net worth. Similarly, if the business is better off at the end of a period than it was at the beginning, then it has also increased its net worth. Consequently, we see that both the economist and the accountant agree that income is an increase in net worth, but each has a different concept of net worth; and therein lies the major difference between the concepts of business income by the accountant and the economist.

The accountant determines net worth on an historical cost basis by the formula of "assets − liabilities = net worth": whereas the economists's determination is "current value of tangible assets ÷ discounted value of future net receipts − liabilities." The following oversimplified example will serve to illustrate the accounting as well as the economic method of computing net worth and consequently the determination of income.

[2]John R. Hicks, *Value and Capital* (Oxford, England: The Clarendon Press, 1946), p. 172.
[3]Backer, op. cit., p. 100.

ILLUSTRATION OF NET WORTH DETERMINATION

On January 1, 1967 a corporation was organized with a capital of $100,000 with which it purchased a new building. The building is on land leased for a period of forty years, at the end of which time, it is assumed, the building will have no value. The corporation then leased the building for a period of forty years at an annual rental of $20,000. The expected operating cost, including depreciation, would be $15,000 per annum, leaving a net profit of $5,000, disregarding income tax. The determination of the corporation's net worth as of January 1, 1967, and December 31, 1967, computed by the accountant and economist would be as follows: Assume the appropriate rate of interest to be 5%.

	Jan. 1 1967	Dec. 31 1967
Net Worth—per CPA		
Assets	$100,000	$105,000
Liabilities	0	0
Net Worth	$100,000	$105,000
Net Worth— per Economist		
Tangible assets	$100,000	$105,000*
Goodwill†	85,795	85,085
Net Worth	$185,795	$190,085

†Represents the discounted value of future net receipts, present value of $5,000 per annum at 5%, for 40 and 39 years respectively.
*No change in market value of building.

ILLUSTRATION OF INCOME DETERMINATION

In order to arrive at net income for the year 1967, the accountant would merely determine the excess of revenue realized over cost consumed or $20,000 − $15,000 = $5,000. The same result would be arrived at by obtaining the difference between the net worth at the beginning and end of the period, giving the appropriate recognition to capital additions or withdrawals and dividend distribution, if any. The economist uses only the change-in-net worth method in arriving at net income. His net income would thus be $4,290 ($190,085 − $185,795).

VARIATION IN CONDITIONS AT END OF YEAR

An extention of the economist's concept of income determination is illustrated by the introduction of two factors, both ignored by the accountant but meaningful to the economist. These factors are (1) a rise in the general price index at the end of 1967 to 110% of the base period (January 1, 1967), and (2) an increase in the market value of the building, which then had a depreciated basis of $97,500, to $120,000.

Under the above conditions the accounting income would remain at $5,000, as computed earlier, but the economic income would be $7,464, computed as shown in the table on the following page.

Net Worth—Dec. 31, 1967	
Building, at market	$120,000
Other assets	7,500
Discounted value of future receipt	$85,085
Less, losses due to price level changes	19,326*
	65,759
Net Worth	193,259
Net Worth—Jan. 1, 1967	
Per prior computation	185,795
Net Income for the Year	7,464

*Computed at 110% of base at Jan. 1, 1967.

This computation reflects some of the basic differences between the accountants' and the economists' concepts of income determination. The accountant does not consider the price level changes or the holding gains resulting from the appreciation of fixed assets.

The differences between these two concepts of increase in net worth, economic income and accounting income may be reconciled by starting with accounting income and arriving at economic income as follows:

Accounting Income
±Unrealized changes in the value of tangible assets which took place during the period, over and above value changes recognized as depreciation of fixed assets and inventory mark-downs.
−amounts realized this period in respect of value changes in tangible assets which took place in previous periods and were not recognized in these periods.
+changes in the value of intangible assets during the period (which may be considered as changes in the value of goodwill)
=economic income.

THE UNDERLYING ASSUMPTION OF THE INCOME CONCEPTS

- The going concern.
- Objectivity.
- Realization of revenues.
- Stable monetary unit.

In the succeeding paragraphs, an attempt will be made to bring out the economist's view of the above concepts.

THE GOING CONCERN CONCEPT

Accountants have accepted the presumption that:

> . . . in the absence of evidence to the contrary, the productive life of the enterprise may be deemed to be indefinitely long.[4]

As a result of this postulate, all costs of the enterprise are deferred until such time as they have been consumed by a revenue producing process or have expired because of the passing of time.

When fixed assets are purchased they are recorded at cost which generally represents market price at the time of acquisition. Later change in market value is not recorded, except in the case of a reorganization, appreciation as the asset is a deferred cost chargeable against future revenues in a rational and systematic manner. This line of reasoning is justified by the accountant on the assumption that the life of the entity is indefinitely long and the cost of the asset will eventually be completely written off.

Another case in point is the valuation of accounts receivable. From an accounting standpoint, accounts receivable at any given time are valued at the full expected amount to be collected in future periods, on the presumption that on a going concern basis, there is no need to decrease the asset to its present value. However, the economist, in order to arrive at his current net worth would consider accounts receivable only at the discounted present value.

The economist rejects the thesis of the going concern as a basis for income determination for the reason that he "values" the company annually. Since he must first determine net worth to compute net income, then each year's balance sheet is equivalent to a terminal determination, except for no provision for liquidation.

OBJECTIVITY

The accountant, because of his intention to utilize accuracy in accounting procedures, has come to regard objectivity as a major guidepost. Thus, the accountant endeavors to measure the effects of business transaction on verifiable evidence, whereas the economist generally makes his measurements on the basis of expectations.

Professor Moonitz, in outlining "The Basic Postulates of Accounting," wrote:

> Changes in assets and liabilities and related effects (if any) on revenues, expenses, and retained earnings and the like, should not be given formal recognition in the accounts earlier than the point of time at which they can be measured in objective terms.[5]

The accountant's concept of income, therefore, is well supported by his reliance on objectivity. The process of matching cost against current revenue could not be properly carried out without the full employment and the objective approach. Paton and Little stated that:

> The fundamental problem of accounting . . . is the division of the stream of cost incurred between the present and the future in the process of measuring periodic income.[6]

[4]The Study Group on Business Income, "The Changing Concept of Business Income" (New York: The Macmillan Company, 1952), p. 19.

[5]Maurice Moonitz, "The Basic Postulate of Accounting" (New York: American Institute of CPA's, 1961), p. 50.

[6]W. A. Paton and A. C. Littleton, "Introduction to Corporate Accounting Standards" (American Accounting Association, 1960), p. 67.

However, the economist does not adhere to the principle of objectivity in developing his concept of income. There is heavy reliance on subjectivity and individual judgment by the economist in his determination of income. This is so because the economist, before he can arrive at current net income, must first determine the ability of the enterprise to earn future income. He must estimate what the total future income might be (by computing its discounted value), and then arrive at the current net worth of the enterprise. Therefore, since the economist is called upon to predict the future events of the enterprise, in order to arrive at current net worth and net income, then his net income is based upon less objectively verifiable evidence than that of the accountant. Of course, the accountant also estimates future events of the enterprise, such as the useful life of depreciable assets, but in this respect he merely reviews management's determinations. But by and large, the accountant is concerned with what has been, or what is, rather than what might be.

REALIZATION OF REVENUES

Accountants take the conservative view in determining the point at which income should be recognized. It has become the general practice to record income at the point of realization, indeed at the point of sale. W. A. Paton said:

The process of exchanging product for cash or definite claim to cash, constitutes realization and justifies the description of revenue measured by sale as realized revenues.[7]

[7]W. A. Paton and W. A. Paton, Jr. "Corporation Accounts and Statements" (New York: The Macmillan Company, 1955), p. 278.

The point of sale is chosen as the time of realization because it offers an objective measurement of the value of the product being exchanged. Further, the disposal of the product is the final fulfillment of the contribution such product can ultimately make to the enterprise. Finally, this position is a conservative one, which is a popular and creditable stance.

If the contribution to be made to the well-being of an enterprise by the assets it owns is anticipated before the actual realization of such contribution, then the entire income for the life of the enterprise could be determined at the time the enterprise is capitalized. But this would be inconsistent with other accounting concepts because

• accounting presumes the business to be a going concern, and
• such measurement could not be made objectively.

On the other hand, the economist conceives that the enterprise at any given time should recognize the income it expects its assets will ultimately contribute in the future. This is done by making an estimate of the value of such future income, and capitalizing it as goodwill (as was done with the expected rental income from the leased building in our prior discussion). If the estimate made by the economist is correct, then all the income of an enterprise would be recognized at the time of its inception except for interest to be earned, if any, since it represents the difference between the future and present values.

In addition, the economist will currently reflect income representing holding gains and monetary fluctuations. In the holding gains, he includes increases in the current market value of assets. For example, appreciation in real estate is recognized as income is determined. The accountant, however, in accordance with generally accepted accounting principles which rest on the realization concept, will not recognize this appreciation until it has actually been realized.

STABLE MONETARY UNIT[8]

The accountant still adheres to the concept of the stable monetary unit. One of the postulates of accounting states:

Fluctuation in value of the monetary unit which is the accounting symbol may properly be ignored.[9]

The economist is diametrically opposed to this presumption and takes an adamant position that all changes in price levels must be reflected in income during the period of such changes. By so doing, the economist adjusts for variable monetary values from one period to another in order to reflect a constant base and thus maintain the "real" monetary value.

The accountant's approach to price-level changes in income determination is to completely ignore the effects of such changes. Here again, the reasoning is based on the interlocking of other basic concepts in accounting. Firstly, income should be reported only when realized and a mere change in the purchasing power of the monetary unit is not a realization of income or loss. Secondly, the life of the enterprise is deemed to be indefinitely long, and therefore, barring a liquidation of the enterprise, the effects of the money fluctuation might never be realized.

[8]For a comprehensive treatment of Price-Level Changes, see Accounting Research Study No. 6.
[9]"The Changing Concept of Business Income," op. c.f.—p. 19.

CONCLUSION

The economist and the accountant have different objectives in the determination of income, as well as different concepts of income. The accountant measures income independently, and the balance sheet, in effect, is the residue of prepaid and deferred items. The economist, on the other hand, uses successive balance sheets as real value determinants and the annual increases or decreases represent real economic income. The accountant, on the whole, is interested in what is or what has been, whereas the economist is interested in what might be. Income of an enterprise from the accountants' point of view must be realized and objectively quantified. But the economist's point of view is that income can accrue only after proper provision has been made to keep capital intact. This is done by capitalizing all expected future net receipts as goodwill. Therefore, economic income is the sum of the future net receipts plus interest earned on capital plus other unexpected gains such as appreciation of fixed assets and monetary fluctuations. The economist deals with certainties and uncertainties. If his estimate of the uncertainties turns out to be accurate, then in the long run he would have arrived at the same point of cumulative income as the accountant.

The underlying assumptions on which the economic concepts of income are based bear heavily on subjective judgments while the accounting assumptions are objective in nature. Nevertheless, there is a great deal of inter-relationship of the framework of the two disciplines. As Professor K. E.

Boulding wrote in his article, "Economics and Accounting, the Uncongenial Twins:"[10]

. . . many of the basic concepts of economics are, in fact, derived from

[10]Boulding, K. E. "Economics and Accounting: The Uncongenial Twins." In W. T. Baxter and Sidney Davidson, eds., *Studies In Accounting Theory* (Homewood, Illinois: Richard D. Irwin, Inc., 1962), p. 44.

accounting practice and many accounting practices have been devised in an attempt to answer what are essentially economic questions.

Notwithstanding whatever degree of inter-relationship there is between the development of the theories of accounting and economics, there remain some differences in the conceptual view of business income between the two disciplines.

THE REALIZATION CONCEPT

AMERICAN ACCOUNTING ASSOCIATION'S 1964 CONCEPTS AND STANDARDS RESEARCH STUDY COMMITTEE—THE REALIZATION CONCEPT, AMERICAN ACCOUNTING ASSOCIATION, *THE ACCOUNTING REVIEW.*

This committee report is designed to expand substantially and to amend in part the statement on realization in *Accounting and Reporting Standards for Corporate Financial Statements*—1957 Revision. That statement says "the essential meaning of realization is that a change in any asset or liability has become sufficiently definite and objective to warrant recognition in the accounts." In considering this statement, and realization principles generally, attention will be focused on the problems of (1) asset recognition and valuation and (2) revenue recognition.

The committee concurs with the statement of the 1957 Revision that primary emphasis should be given to "the use by investors of published financial statements in making investment decisions and in exercising control over management. . . ." In the analysis that follows, the realization concept will be studied in terms of its effect on the data used by present and potential

investors and those interested in evaluating management.

A great variety of economic events determine the financial position (and change in position) of every business unity. Two crucial decisions that must be reached in accounting are (1) which of the economic events should be recorded in the accounts and (2) how the recorded events should be reported on in the financial statements. On the first decision, the committee unanimously recommends that the effect of changes in value of all assets, other than goodwill, that can be supported by adequate evidence be recorded in the accounts. For the second question, a majority of the committee recommends that "unrealized" changes in the value of assets should not be included in the computation of reported net income, but should be shown on the income statement below the net income line; on the position statement, the cumulative unrealized changes in value would be shown as a separate item in the retained earnings section. Two members of the committee (Davidson and Gray) disagree; they feel that the effect of all value changes should be included in the calculation of net income although one of them (Davidson) would report "unrealized" value changes as a separate component of net income.

The committee recognizes the difficulty of developing a definition of realization that will have general applicability. Nevertheless, four of the committee members feel there is sufficient significance in the difference between realized and unrealized changes in value to justify making the distinction. They would, however, refine the meaning of realization and supplement the reporting of realized events by a reporting of unrealized changes in asset values. The fifth committee member (Gray) holds that reporting a distinction between realized and unrealized changes impugns the recognition of unrealized value changes and is therefore undesirable. He suggests that if the evidence is strong enough to justify recording value changes in the accounts, no further gradation of income recognition is appropriate with present measurement techniques.

Problems with regard to realization arise mainly from two types of events.

1. Transactions associated with the exchange of goods and services between the accounting entity and some independent, external group. These are referred to hereafter as *revenue transactions*.
2. Changes in the value of resources during the time they are held by the firm. These are referred to hereafter as *holding gains and losses*[1]

[1]These terms have been widely used in the accounting literature since the publication of *The Theory and Measurement of Business Income* by

In the report that follows, the major recording and reporting questions for each of these two types of events will be analyzed after a brief consideration of the historical origin and current meaning of the term "realization."

DEVELOPMENT OF THE REALIZATION CONCEPT

The concept of realization is an integral part of the process of income measurement. Most economic views consider income to be an enhancement in wealth. With this view and with a focus on the private business firm, income of a period can be described as the amount of wealth that can be distributed to the owners during the period without diminishing the entity's future prospects below those that prevailed at the start of the period. To make such a concept operational it would be necessary to have well defined rules for measuring the firm's prospects (wealth) at the start and close of the period. This requires a measure of the discounted value of the entity's anticipated net cash inflows. Such a measure would be highly subjective, depending on the measurer's current prognosis of the likely amount and timing of future inflows and on the appropriate discount rates to employ.

A more restricted definition would equate wealth with the sum of the values of individual tangible assets, rather than the worth of the firm as a whole. With this definition of wealth, income would be determined by intertemporal differences in the sum of individual asset values (adjusted

E. O. Edwards and P. W. Bell (Universtiy of California Press, 1961). They define (p. 36) holding gains as resulting from events "that yield a gain because the prices of assets rise (or prices of liabilities fall) while such assets (or liabilities) are in possession of the firm."

for changes in liabilities and capital contributions and withdrawals). This view of income was widely accepted in accounting until about the middle or end of the first decade of the twentieth century. Paton, in the preface to *Accounting Theory* said, "The liberal view that, ideally, all bona fide value changes in either direction, from whatever cause, should be reflected in the accounts has been adopted without argument. . . . This logical position is the proper one for the professional accountant, at least as a starting point."[2] Similarly, George O. May stated that "A review of accounting, legal and economic writing suggests that the realization postulate was not accepted prior to the First World War. In 1913 leading authorities in all these fields in England and America seemed to agree on the 'increase in net worth' concept of income. . . ."[3]

This view of income was gradually supplanted by one that emphasized the disposition of assets, their "separation" from the firm. Great increases in the significance of specialized long-lived assets that were difficult to value contributed to this change as did the adoption of a graduated income tax in the United Kingdom in 1909 and the Sixteenth (income tax) Amendment to the Constitution and related legislation in the United States. In the landmark *Eisner* v. *Macomber* case in 1920, Charles Evans Hughes, later to become Chief Justice, summed up in his brief to the court the view that was becoming dominant: "It is of the essence of income that it should be realized. . . . Income necessarily implies separation and realization. . . . The increase in the value of lands due to growth and prosperity of the community is not income until it is realized."[4] The Court accepted the view and defined income "as not a *growth* or *increment* of value *in* the investment, but a gain, a profit, something of exchangeable value *proceeding from* the property, severed from the capital. . . ."[5] This view of income remains the dominant one in accounting today.

Even though the realization or separation test for recognition of income was almost universally accepted, there continued to be sporadic recording of changes in values of assets, matched by credits to appraisal surplus. The disastrous experience with appraisal valuations in the 1930's discredited this approach, and today it is virtually impossible to find a listed American corporation that records upward changes in the value of assets in its formal accounting records.

In the next two sections, consideration will be given to the criteria to be employed in evaluating revenue transactions to determine whether they meet the realization test and to the question of whether changes in value which have occurred while assets have been held (holding gains and losses) should be recorded in the accounts and recognized as income. In that analysis, no specific consideration will be given to problems raised by changes in the value of the monetary unit, i.e. changes in the general price level. Once an appropriate basis for recognition of changes in value of specific assets is developed, those gains or losses can, if desired, be divided into "real" and "nominal" portions by the application of a suitable index of the general price level.

[2]W. A. Paton, *Accounting Theory*, Ronald Press, 1922 (republished by Accounting Studies Press, 1962), p. vii. Although originally published in 1922, the volume is an adaptation of Paton's doctoral dissertation completed in 1917.
[3]George O. May, "Business Income," *The Accountant*, September 30, 1950, p. 316.

[4]*Eisner* v. *Macomber*, 25 U.S. 188, 195 (1920).
[5]Ibid., at 207. Emphasis in the original.

REVENUE TRANSACTIONS AND REALIZATION

When should realization be considered to have been achieved in a revenue transaction? Three factors have generally been considered significant in answering this question:

1. The nature of the asset received.
2. The presence of a market transaction.
3. The extent to which services have been performed.

It is difficult to be precise about what is the current prevailing practice, but it appears that presently accepted tests for realization require receipt of a current (or liquid) asset capable of objective measurement in a market transaction for services rendered.

NATURE OF ASSET RECEIVED

The two attributes of assets received in revenue transactions that affect realization are liquidity and measurability. The two factors go hand in hand in many cases. This is obviously the situation in the receipt of cash. Second, short-term accounts receivable meet both tests so well it is difficult to explain the persistence of the "cash method of recognizing revenue" by doctors, lawyers and accountants except in terms of income-tax advantage and an unwillingness to maintain separate income-tax and financial reporting records.

When the asset received in a revenue transaction does not have its valuation indicated explicitly on its face,[6] liquidity and measurability characteristics may be of dif-

ferent quality. Marketable securities rank high in both liquidity and measurability, and their receipt is considered acceptable for realization by most groups. As we move down the asset side of a typical balance sheet, there seems to be increasing skepticism about the realization of revenue. Receipt of even relatively marketable inventories in exchange for products or services is usually not considered sufficient to meet the realization test. Acquisition of plant assets in sales transactions is even more rarely viewed as realization. Where cash "boot" is received in such transactions, it presents a difficult problem. In income-tax accounting, and probably financial reporting as well, there is a willingness to recognize revenue (income) in the amount of the value of the noncash asset acquired.

The significance of the liquidity attribute of assets received as a test of realization is called into question by some generally accepted accounting practices. For example, it is customary to treat earnings of a sinking fund or accumulation of discount on purchased bonds as realized revenue. This suggests that objective measurability of the asset received rather than its liquidity may be the crucial factor in the recording of realized revenue.

The committee recommends continued adherence to a policy of requiring objective evidence of the valuation of the asset received before recognizing realized revenue. However, it feels that present tests of measurability may be too stringent in many cases. Objective valuations can usually be secured for merchandise and other inventories acquired in exchange for products and services; if so, realized revenue should be recognized at the time of the barter transaction. The committee would stress measurability, and not liquidity, as the essential attribute required for recognition of realized revenue.

---

[6]Par or stated values of stocks and bonds received in revenue transactions are not considered to be valuations in this context; instead they are viewed as nominal amounts marked on the instruments without relation to their value.

PRESENCE OF A MARKET TRANSACTION

There is general acceptance of the view that a market transaction is necessary for revenue to be realized. The committee concurs in this requirement. However, there is an intriguing question of whether the firm whose records are being kept has to be one of the parties directly engaged in the market transaction. Take a situation where the product held (and being sold in the market) is homogeneous (all of the various units in inventory are essentially identical), there is a large market (the firm's holdings are small relative to the normal number of units sold in the market), and there is little or no selling effort associated with making the sale. This is a situation where there is close to 100% probability of the firm's being able to sell its holdings at the market price.

In such a situation (typified by the holding of 100 shares of General Motors stock) one member of the committee (Bierman) believes that the gain may be viewed as being realized without the firm's actually engaging in a market transaction.

A majority of the committee feels that a market transaction involving the firm is required for realization; the change in value of the securities would be handled by labeling it an unrealized holding gain. It would be treated in the same way as other unrealized holding gains (see next section). The majority position emphasizes the market transaction aspect of realization. If unrealized holding gains were not also to be recorded and reported, several members of the committee would favor weakening this test of realization in the direction suggested by Bierman.

EXTENT OF SERVICE PERFORMED

The third, and in many ways the most complex, criterion for realization relates to the extent of service performed by the accounting entity. The several steps involved in performing of service are order taking, production of the goods ordered, delivery of the goods, and collection of cash for them. Occasionally there may be an additional step involving guarantees or warranties. The steps need not be taken in the order listed.

Three types of service situations should be distinguished. These are:

1. All of the service, including receipt of cash, is performed in one accounting period.
2. Cash is received in connection with a revenue transaction, but all of service has not been performed by the end of the period.
3. All (or a substantial part) of the service other than the receipt of cash is performed in one period, but the cash associated with the transaction will be received in a subsequent period or periods.

The simplest realization situation occurs where there is a sale for cash of services, inventory or other property, with no accompanying warranty, guarantee or future commitment of any kind. All of the service has been performed; the other tests of asset quality and market transaction have been met, and revenue in the full amount of the cash receipt is realized.

In the situation where cash is received but performance of the service has not been completed by the end of the accounting period, a cash advance has been made by the customer. Since not all of the service has been performed, it would be inappropriate to treat the entire amount of the cash received as realized revenue. The revenue is joint to the periods of cash receipt and performance of other services. The problem of assignment of this joint revenue is analogous to the assignment of joint cost. There is no completely logical solution; instead, accounting relies on subjective, conventional procedures.

Traditionally, in establishing a realization test, accountants have considered the degree to which the seller has furnished the services being purchased. The committee is suggesting that another factor is more relevant, namely, whether the seller has performed an action which is the crucial event in the process of earning revenue.[7] This crucial event may be something distinct from the rendering of services to the customer.

Assume a situation where a magazine subscription is sold to a customer for cash. This is a crucial event from the point of view of the seller and he should recognize some of the revenue at the time of the subscription and cash collection. Additional revenue will be recognized when the magazines are published and mailed in the next accounting period. This is a situation where the revenue is joint to several time periods and two economic functions (selling and filling subscriptions).

Where the costs of filling the obligation to the customer can be accurately predicted, as with the magazine subscription, a significant percentage of the revenue would be realized during the time period of the order and cash collection. Where it is very difficult to estimate the costs (say with a new product), it may not be appropriate to recognize any of the income during the period in which the cash is advanced and the contract is signed. In any event, there is no necessary reason for assuming that each dollar of cost incurred earns an equal amount of profit.

The minimum revenue to be deferred as

[7]This approach was first suggested by John H. Myers in ''The Critical Event and Recognition of Net Profit,'' *The Accounting Review*, October 1959, p. 528.

being unrealized (and to be considered a liability) is the present value of the costs expected to be incurred in connection with performing the remainder of the service under the contract. If the actual expenses equalled the expectations, the entire profit associated with the contract, except for the interest factor, would be recorded in the initial period. This would not be a reasonable timing of profit except in the special situation where the present value of the future expenses was known with virtual certainty. The method (except for the present-value factor) is followed presently in connection with guarantees and warranties.

Normally the expenses of completing the remainder of the services of a partially fulfilled contract will be uncertain. They will be affected by such factors as changes in the price of factors of production to be purchased and variations in efficiency of their usage. With this uncertainty, how much of the expected income should be considered to be realized at the time of the signing of the contract? There is no single correct answer to this question; however, assuming the presence of a contract which can be expected to be honored by both parties, a significantly large percentage of the total income should usually be recorded as being realized in the period of the cash advance. The percentage should vary with the confidence of the estimate of future costs, and inversely with the length of time until they are incurred. Development of operational rules in this area is sorely needed. Until they can be developed, accounting is likely to rely on the assumption that each dollar of cost incurred earns equal profit, even though the assumption is conceptually unsatisfactory.

In the third basic situation, most of the service has been performed or the product has been shipped, but the cash associated with the transaction has not yet been received. A distinction between two classes

CHAPTER 2: INCOME CONCEPTS

of sales in this general category can be made. If the time period until the expected collection is relatively short, the transaction can be described as a conventional sale on account; if the collection period is expected to be long, the situation can be designated as sale on special terms. Sales on special terms frequently, but not always, provide for installment payments.

In conventional sales on account it is customary and reasonable to record the revenue as being realized when the sale is made despite the absence of cash collection. The likelihood of collection is so high in the normal business situation and collection so routine that complete realization of revenue may be assumed. The small possibility of not collecting is taken into consideration by adjustments for estimated uncollectible accounts. The collection period is usually short enough so that discounting to present value would not materially alter the measure. Where the probability of collection is highly uncertain, valuation of the receivables from account sales becomes a major problem. If the receivables are salable without recourse, a satisfactory valuation may be provided. In extreme cases, it may be necessary to tie the recording of realization to the receipt of cash.

Sales on special terms generally have more risk than conventional sales on account since the payments are spread over a longer time period and transactions are frequently between a business firm and individuals rather than between two business firms. In addition, the individuals making purchases on special terms may normally be expected to be persons short of cash, adding another reason why such transactions on the average have a higher degree of risk than the conventional sales on account. The collection process is now not routine but rather a major part of the profit-earning operation. Again there is a joint revenue situation. The revenue (and the

profit) of a transaction of this type should be assigned to the several types of operations and several time periods. There is no single logically correct method of allocation. Since there is not the same degree of confidence of collection as with a conventional sale, it is not appropriate to recognize all of the revenues as being realized at the moment of sale. Relating amounts of realization to dollars collected is a convenient, but not necessarily logical, method of allocating joint revenues. Where the long-term receivables have a market value, this may provide an appropriate measurement criterion; the market value will normally reflect outsiders' estimates of future collection costs and the possibility of uncollectibility.

In summary on revenue transactions, the committee suggests several changes in the way present criteria for recognizing realization are applied. It recommends that measurability, rather than liquidity, should be the prime consideration in judging the quality of the asset received in a revenue transaction. It feels (with one dissent) that the accounting entity should be a party to the market transaction before realized revenue is recognized. The committee recommends that the test of rendering services to customers be supplemented by one of first recognizing realized revenue when the crucial event in the revenue process has occurred. The suggested changes would tend to advance in time the recognition of realized revenue. Before the changes can be fully implemented, there is need for work in the development of operational rules in the specific areas.

HOLDING GAINS AND LOSSES

Holding gains and losses represent changes, over a time period of values of assets and liabilities held during that period. This definition implies that a base figure for the asset or liability in question, commonly acquisition cost (or valuation at the start of the period), can be compared with an adjusted valuation at the end of the period or at the date of disposal during the period to give a measure of the change in value of the item. If the time period is long, the change in value is likely to be caused by a variety of factors—changes in the general price level, in technology, and in demand—that are difficult to separate.

The identification of holding gains and losses necessitates the selection of a yardstick to measure changes in value over time. Cost is the usual basis of valuation at acquisition. In the relatively infrequent cases of non-cash acquisitions, market value at acquisition is used as a substitute for acquisition cost.[8] The subsequent valuation to be compared with acquisition cost in the determination of holding gains or losses is some measure of current economic significance. There are many possibilities, e.g., replacement cost, opportunity cost, and net realizable value.

In dealing with holding gains and losses, the basic questions are whether the gains and losses should be recognized in the accounts, how such gains and losses should be measured, and whether they should be included in the determination of net income.

The reports of activity of the firm can be broken down into two parts, namely, operating and holding.[9] Operating results stem from the sale of goods or services. In most endeavors the primary object of the business is to sell a product or a service and to make a profit while doing so. Coincident with these operations that are largely shaped by management, there are events transpiring that are not directly influenced by managerial decisions, but nevertheless modify the fortunes of the business. These are, as examples, changes in value resulting from technological advances, movements in the general price level, changes in tastes that affect demand for the firm's product, and alterations in various factors relating to the supply of items held by a company.

PRESENT PROCEDURE IN RECOGNIZING HOLDING GAINS AND LOSSES

The accounting profession follows the practice of recognizing gains only to the extent that they are realized in market transactions, but losses are sometimes anticipated by writing down asset values before disposition. Gains were occasionally recorded on the basis of appraisals in the past, but this practice has almost completely come to an end in the last quarter of a century.

Informal processes have been followed in accounting to apprise the statement reader of changes in values. These have included footnoting, parenthetical notation, and disclosure by general comment in the annual report or in the president's letter. Whenever these means are employed, there is an implicit acknowledgement of change in value without a formal recording of such an event. The advocates of recognition of holding gains and losses wish such changes in value to be recorded in the accounts and in the statements.

It has become customary to report gains and losses from the sales of fixed assets

---

[8]In a corporate acquisition that is treated as a pooling of interests, acquisition costs as shown on the books of the acquired company are carried forward on the books of the acquiring company; if the transaction were not treated as a pooling, current market values would serve as the basis for valuing the assets of the acquired company.

[9]This follows the usual meaning of Edwards and Bell, op. cit., p. 36.

and investments in a different manner from ordinary sales of product or service. These former gains and losses, if material, are usually separately reported in the income statement, or in the reconciliation of retained earnings, depending on whether an all-inclusive or current operating income statement is being prepared. One reason for this different reporting is that these gains may be nonrecurring. Another reason is that the gains realized and reported this period may incorporate value changes that occurred in a prior period or periods. The same possibility exists in connection with sales of regular product, but is likely to be less dramatic because of more rapid turnover. Under present procedures, holding gains and losses associated with long-lived assets are frequently incorporated in realized income, but not necessarily in the period when the increase or decrease in value occurs.

RECORDING OF HOLDING GAINS AND LOSSES RECOMMENDED

This committee unanimously recommends that holding gains and losses be recognized and recorded in the accounts. By recognizing these value changes three related objectives would be secured:

1. Expenses would be stated on a current cost basis.
2. Gains and losses from price changes would be recognized in the period when the change in value occurs, rather than in the period when the asset is sold.
3. On the balance sheet, assets would be valued at amounts representing their current economic significance.[10]

[10]These three objectives are similar to those cited in *Accounting and Reporting Standards for Corporate Financial Statements*, 1957 Revision, p. 6. The objectives were presented there in connection with cost of goods sold. This committee feels that they have a more general applicability.

The 1963 Committee on Concepts and Standards—Long-Lived Assets summarized the rationale and significance of a current cost measurement of income from operations, saying:

Measurement of . . . income from ordinary operations can be accomplished only if the expiration of service potential is measured in terms of current cost. That is, in order to continue operations without contracting the level of operating capacity, exhausted services must be restored; the relevant cost of expired services is the current cost of restoration. . . .

Income from ordinary operations is important to investors in making investment decisions. This amount, when compared with cash dividends, is relevant to an appraisal of the intent of the management to contract or expand the operating capacity of the firm. Secondly, it facilitates predictions of future income from ordinary operations, assuming that costs other than depreciation are also stated in current terms. Third, inter-firm income comparability is improved by universal measurement of depreciation [and other expenses] on the basis of current cost.[11]

Recognition of holding gains and losses would make possible a timely acknowledgement of changes in values of assets. At present, especially in the case of long-lived assets, there is no specific recognition of gain or loss from increments or decrements of value in the period when the change occurs. Instead, the gain is recognized in the period or periods when the asset is utilized

[11]Committee on Concepts and Standards—Long Lived Assets, "Accounting for Land, Building and Equipment," *The Accounting Review*, July 1964, p. 696.

or in the period when the asset is disposed of, which may be a period in which there is no value change at all. For merchandise or raw materials, value change and asset disposition are more likely to occur in the same period, but the value changes are lumped with income from operations in a single net income figure. Since income from operations and holding gains or losses result from different causes, they can be expected to have different patterns of recurrence. Effective prediction of future income is facilitated by reporting them separately.

Current-cost valuations on the balance sheet attempt to measure the economically relevant quantity of resources being employed by management and for which it is responsible. In calculating periodic rates of return, more meaningful results can be secured if the resources employed are valued in current terms rather than in terms of acquisition costs, which may lack current significance.

MEASURING HOLDINGS GAINS AND LOSSES

Reliable measurement of holding gains and losses is most easily secured in the case of marketable securities traded on a national stock exchange. Objective estimates of net realizable value can be secured easily in most cases. Where security holdings are so large that their disposition would affect market prices or where the market is chaotic and ability to sell at the market price is questionable, acceptance of quoted market figures may not be appropriate. In most other cases, however, current market quotations give a reliable and objective measurement, comparable in quality to that provided by data reflecting acquisition cost of the securities.

The problem of measuring inventory values for the determination of holding gains and losses is more complex. In general, a choice must be made between valuations based on net realizable values and those that seek to reflect replacement costs. In considering this question, the 1963 Committee on Concepts and Standards—Inventory Measurement said:

A net realizable value method is generally impractical and is therefore not recommended for general use. The major disadvantage of using a net realizable value method is the problem of measurement. Many subjective estimates are required in its implementation: expected revenue, expected expenses, and allocations of margins between acquisition and distribution functions. Furthermore, if selling prices fluctuate in harmony with replacement costs, the replacement cost method generally will yield a reliable approximation of net realizable value less normal operating income. Therefore, replacement cost can generally meet conceptual and practical criteria more easily than some version of net realizable value.[12]

The committee elaborated on replacement cost problems by stating:

There are practical problems of implementing a replacement cost concept. Estimation and sampling processes may simplify the problem of measurement. Although in most situations the determination of replacement cost can be accomplished with a high degree of objectivity, difficult problems may arise, particularly in manufacturing situations. In the case of a merchandising

[12]Committee on Concepts and Standards—Inventory Measurement, "A Discussion of the Various Approaches to Inventory Measurement." *The Accounting Review*, July 1964, p. 708.

106

enterprise, the determination of replacement cost should be easier, because extensive reliance can be placed on recent invoice prices. Sometimes it will be necessary to obtain quotations from suppliers as of the inventory pricing date. These quotations should be compatible with the company's usual purchasing procedures for the particular item in regard to quantities, discount terms, and method of shipment. A similar situation should prevail in the case of the raw material inventory of a manufacturing concern.

Calculation of the replacement cost of the finished product or work in process inventory of a manufacturer will not be such a simple process. It will be necessary to determine the current (replacement) cost of each element of the total cost of the inventory units. In many cases the current cost of raw materials and labor should be determinable with tolerable precision by employing current wage rates and material costs multiplied by the actual (or standard) quantity of labor or material related to the partially or fully completed product. In the case of indirect manufacturing costs, adjustment of historical cost to current cost by the use of index numbers which give effect to changes in the price level of indirect cost factors may be the best available procedure.

As a practical matter, currently attainable standard costs of manufactured goods should suffice in many instances. In most other situations the divergence of replacement cost from acquisition cost will largely be traceable to volatile prices for raw material components rather than to significant changes in direct labor or factory overhead.[13]

The Realization Concepts Committee concurs in the preference expressed by the Inventory Measurement Committee for replacement-cost valuation of inventories.

Measurement problems in connection with holding gains or losses on long-lived assets are probably more difficult than those in any other category. The Committee on Concepts and Standards—Long-lived Assets summed up its recommendations on this subject thus:

> The current cost of obtaining the same or equivalent services should be the basis for valuation of assets subsequent to acquisition, as well as at the date of acquisition. Were there is an established market for assets of like kind and condition, quoted prices may provide the most objective evidence of current cost. Such prices may be readily available for land, buildings, and certain types of standard equipment. Where there is no established market for assets of like kind and condition, current costs may be estimated by reference to the purchase price of assets which provide equivalent service capacity. The purchase price of such substitute assets should be adjusted for differences in operating characteristics such as cost, capacity, and quality.
>
> In other cases, adjustment of historical cost by the use of specific price indexes may provide acceptable approximations of current cost. Appraisals are acceptable only if they are based on the above methods of estimating current cost. Whenever there is no objective method of determining the current cost of obtaining the same or equivalent services, depreciated acquisition cost should continue as the basis of valuation.[14]

[14]Committee on Concepts and Standards—Long-lived Assets, op. cit., p. 695.

[13]Ibid., p. 710.

The Realization Concepts Committee accepts the recommendation of the Long-lived Assets Committee for use of current-cost valuations for plant assets.

REPORTING OF HOLDING GAINS AND LOSSES

A majority of the committee (Bierman, Black, and Sapienza) recommends that only realized holding gains be included in reported net income. They recommend an income statement form that would show operating income and realized holding gains or losses separately. The sum of these two would be designated as net income (and would be the amount carried to the statement of retained earnings). To this figure for net income would be added the increase in unrealized holding gains or the decrease in unrealized holding losses (an increase in unrealized holding losses or a decrease in unrealized holding gains would be subtracted) to give an amount that would be labeled net income plus holding gains and losses. The stockholders' equity section of the balance sheet would include separate items for realized retained earnings and unrealized holding gains and losses. Assets would be shown at current values.

Operating income would reflect the result of revenue transactions with expenses stated on a current cost basis. Realized holding gains or losses would be that portion of holding gains or losses recognized in this or earlier periods that have been validated by sales to customers or by charges to expense this period. For example, the excess of current cost depreciation over depreciation on an acquisition cost basis would be a realized holding gain of the period and a decrease in unrealized holding gains.

The majority feels that the process of recognizing all holding gains and losses, but only including realized items in net income, provides full disclosure of relevant information but at the same time retains a net income test that gives a meaningful distinction between significantly different economic events. They argue that there is a difference in the quality of evidence generated by a market transaction involving goods sold and the securing of estimates of replacement cost or current cost of assets held and that this difference should be the basis of the net income test.

One member of the committee (Davidson) recommends the use of an income statement form similar to that recommended by the majority except that he would label the sum of operating income and realized holding gains as realized income; the sum of realized income and the net increase in unrealized holding gains would be designated as total net income. He would carry the entire total net income amount to the retained earnings account.

Davidson holds that income is the enhancement of wealth. It comes about by changes in value of assets, whether the assets are disposed of this period or not. He recognizes the force of the traditional realization distinction, however, and would use it to subdivide net income rather than to determine it.

One committee member (Gray) favors dropping the distinction between realized and unrealized holding gains. He recommends an income statement form that would report operating income and holding gains separately and would add the two to obtain the net income figure. When our measurement techniques reach the point that we can attach probability estimates that various streams of revenue will actually generate cash inflows, Gray would recommend the reporting of the separate revenue streams and the associated probability measures. The distinction between realized and unrealized income is so crude a measure of uncertainty that it is meaningless and could lead the statement user to make incorrect assessments of the probability that reported items will lead to an ultimate cash inflow. At present, he feels that if the evidence is sufficient to recognize a holding gain, any further distinction is unnecessary.

Statements of the Concepts and Standards Research Study Committee—The Realization Concept represent the reasoned judgment of at least two thirds of the committee members and are approved for publication by the Director of Research. They *are not official pronouncements of the American Accounting Association or of its Executive Committee.*

1964 Concepts and Standards Research Study Committee—The Realization Concept:

HAROLD BIERMAN, JR.
HOMER A. BLACK
JACK GRAY
SAMUEL R. SAPIENZA
SIDNEY DAVIDSON, Chairman

REVENUE RECOGNITION UNDER NEW FASB STATEMENTS

MIKEL G. TILLER, DBA
JAN R. WILLIAMS, CPA, Ph.D.

The timing of revenue recognition is an important consideration in financial reporting. Determining precisely when to recognize revenue has never been as simple as it might appear. As a practical matter, revenue is usually recognized at the point of sale.

The recognition of revenue in the determination of income should parallel the "earning" of that revenue. While this idea is conceptually appealing, the presence of objective evidence establishing the earning process is sometimes difficult to discern. Thus, revenue is conventionally recognized at the point in the earning process when assets are sold or services rendered. At this point, two primary elements necessary for revenue recognition become evident:

- The earning process is complete or virtually complete;
- An exchange has taken place.[1]

The sales transaction establishes that an exchange has taken place and usually identifies a monetary value for the items exchanged. This is considered to represent the virutal completion of the earning process since, at this point, the seller has completed most of its responsibilities to earn the revenue. The cost of incomplete responsibilities can usually be estimated at this point. Expenses can then be "matched" with revenues to provide a meaningful measure of income.

The number and importance of exceptions to this apparently simple approach suggest that the underlying concepts of revenue recognition are not so simple. For ex-

[1]APB Statement 4, Basic Concepts and Accounting Principles Underlying Financial Statements of Business Enterprises (AICPA, 1970).

ample, consider revenue recognition practices related to long-term contracts, installment sales, sale-leaseback arrangements and made-to-order products. For a variety of reasons, each of these situations may demand revenue recognition other than at the point of sale.

Three recent FASB Statements deal with problems of revenue recognition. Two deal with the timing of revenue recognition in situations involving franchises (SFAS 45) and right of return (SFAS 48). The other (SFAS 49) deals with identifying whether a sales transaction has actually taken place where product financing is an issue. In the following sections, we will review each of these new pronouncements briefly, relating each statement to the general concepts of revenue recognition. In the opinion of the authors, these pronouncements represent refinements of general revenue recognition concepts in specialized situations rather than changes in those concepts.

FASB 45—ACCOUNTING FOR FRANCHISE FEE REVENUE

A franchise is a written business agreement which meets the following criteria:

1. The agreement is in force for a specified time, confirming the rights and responsibilities of both the franchisor and franchisee;
2. The purpose of the agreement is the distribution of a product or service or an entire business concept within a particular market area;
3. Both the franchisor and the franchisee contribute resources for establishing and maintaining the franchise;
4. The following are specified in the agreement: marketing practices to be followed, contributions of each party, and operating procedures;
5. The establishment of the franchised outlet creates a business entity that will, in most cases, require and support the full-time business activity of the franchisee;
6. Both the franchisee and the franchisor have a common public identity (e.g., trademark or trade name).

SFAS 45 addresses a number of different aspects of accounting for franchise agreements by the franchisor. In the following paragraphs, several of the most pervasive of these are reviewed, with particular emphasis on the timing of revenue recognition. This pronouncement was previously issued as an AICPA Industry Accounting Guide.

FRANCHISE FEES

Initial franchise fee revenue is recognized when all material services and conditions relating to the sale have been substantially performed or satisfied by the franchisor. Substantial performance means that the franchisor has no remaining obligations or intent to refund any cash received or forgive any unpaid notes or receivables; substantially all the initial services of the franchisor required by the franchise agreement have been performed; and no other material obligations related to the determination of substantial performance exist. In general, the earliest point at which substantial performance has occurred is when the franchisee begins operations.

In this simplest of all possible situations, the franchisor would recognize revenue at the "point of sale" and make an appropriate provision for estimated uncollectibles associated with the initial franchise fee.

If the franchisor is required by the agreement to provide continuing services for which there is no subsequent fee charged to the franchisee, or such continuing franchise fees are small in relation to the required services, then a portion of the initial franchise fee should be deferred and amortized in those periods in which the services are provided. The amount of deferred revenue plus any continuing franchise fees should be sufficient to cover the estimated costs of the required future services and provide a reasonable profit on these services.

Continuing franchise fees are recognized as revenue as the fees are earned and become receivable from the franchisee. Even though a portion of the continuing fee may be designated for a particular purpose, such as an advertising program, it is not recognized as revenue until the fee is earned and is receivable from the franchisee.[2] Any costs which are related to continuing franchise fees are expensed as incurred.

FRANCHISING COSTS

Costs related directly to franchise sales for which revenue has not yet been recognized are deferred until the related revenue is recognized. Costs deferred in this manner, however, would not exceed anticipated revenue less estimated additional related costs. Indirect costs of a regular and recurring nature which are incurred regardless of the level of sales—such as general, selling and administrative costs—are expensed as incurred. Costs yet to be incurred are accrued and charged against income no later than the period in which the related revenue is recognized.

DISCLOSURE REQUIREMENTS

The following statements summarize information that should be disclosed in the financial statements or related notes:

- The nature of all significant commitments and obligations resulting from franchise agreements;
- The details of any franchise fees that

[2]An exception to the recognition of a franchise fee specified for a particular purpose exists if the franchise constitutes an agency relationship wherein a designated portion of the continuing fee is required to be segregated and used for a specified purpose. In this case, the designated amount is recorded as a liability against which the specified costs would be charged.

have been deferred, including an identification of the accounting method being used;
- The separation of initial franchise fees from other franchise fee revenues if they are significant;
- Revenues and costs related to franchise-owned outlets shall be distinguished from revenues and costs related to franchised outlets when practicable.

In addition to the above areas of concern in virtually all franchises, several other matters are covered by SFAS 45. These are not discussed here, but some are identified briefly below:

Area franchise sales—An agreement that transfers franchise rights within a geographic area permitting the opening of a number of franchised outlets.

Relationships between franchisor and franchisee—Arrangements where the franchisor and franchisee have other relationships, such as guaranteed borrowings or affiliated operations.

Commingled revenue—A franchise where a portion of the fee covers tangible property, such as signs, equipment, inventory, land and buildings.

Continuing product sales—A stipulation in a franchise where the franchisee is able to acquire equipment or supplies from the franchisor, frequently at a bargain purchase price.

Agency sales—Franchises where the franchisor is an agent for the franchisee by placing orders for inventory and equipment and selling to franchisees at no profit.

Repossessed franchises—Situations where the franchisor may recover franchise rights through repossession if a franchisee does not open an outlet.

Business combinations—Situations where a franchisor acquires the business of an operating franchise which ordinarily should be treated as a business combination in accordance with APB Opinion 16.

SFAS 45 includes brief descriptions of appropriate accounting procedures to be followed in each of the above situations. SFAS 45 is effective for financial statements for fiscal years beginning after June 15, 1981. Earlier application is encouraged. The provisions of the statement shall be applied retroactively.

FASB 48—REVENUE RECOGNITION WHEN RIGHT OF RETURN EXISTS

The problem of right of return is important in the proper recognition of revenue, since the return effectively cancels the sale which had previously taken place.

Right of return problems vary from situation to situation. For example, in industries such as newspapers and perishable foods, returns follow quickly after the sales transaction, due to the nature of the products involved. In other industries, such as book publishing and equipment manufacturing, returns may occur long after the original sales transaction. Reasons underlying sales returns also vary from situation to situation. Where goods are sold to ultimate consumers, goods may be returned because the buyers are simply not satisifed with the items. Where goods are acquired for resale, returns may come about because of the inability of the buyer to subsequently resell the goods.

SFAS 48 was formerly published as AICPA SOP 75-1. When this statement was issued, at least three practices were being used to account for sales where the right of return existed. At the one extreme, sales were recorded with no recognition being given to the possibility of returns cancelling the sales. Under this approach, returns were accounted for when they actually occurred. At the other extreme was the deferral of the recognition of the sales transaction until all uncertainty concerning the right of return was resolved. In some cases this approach resulted in the deferral of the recognition of revenue from one accounting period until some future period. Between these two approaches was the method of recognizing the sales transaction in income determination when the sale took place and allowing for returns by estimation based on past trends. This third approach is required by FASB Statement 48, but only if certain conditions are met.

CONDITIONS NECESSARY FOR REVENUE RECOGNITION

The FASB addresses the problem of revenue recognition when the right of return exists by identifying conditions which must be met before revenue can be recognized. Specifically, where the buyer or another party has the right of return, revenue should be recognized on the original sale only when *all* of the following conditions are met:

1. The price of the product is substantially fixed or determinable at the exchange date;
2. The buyer has paid or is obligated to pay the seller. Payment is not contingent on the resale of the product by the buyer;
3. The buyer's obligation to pay the seller is not changed if the products are damaged, destroyed or stolen;
4. The buyer has economic substance apart from that provided by the seller;
5. The seller does not have significant obligations for future performance to assist the buyer in the resale of the products;
6. The amount of future returns can be estimated with reasonable objectivity.

112

The fourth condition states that the buyer has economic substance apart from that provided by the seller. This condition is included to eliminate the practice of sellers' establishing entities specifically for purposes of transfers of products in which the seller recognizes revenue. In these situations, the "buyers" frequently had no physical substance, i.e., no physical facilities and no employees.

SFAS 48 provides guidance concerning condition six listed above. In estimating the amount of returns to be expected, exchanges by ultimate consumers of one item for another item of the same kind, quality and price are not considered returns. Several factors are cited which may impair an enterprise's ability to estimate the amount of future returns:

1. The susceptibility of the product to significant external factors which might influence the amount of returns, such as technological obsolescence or changes in demand;
2. Relatively long periods of time during which the product may be returned;
3. Absence of historical experience with sales of similar products or the inability to apply past experience in a particular situation because of changed circumstances;
4. Absence of a large volume of relatively similar transactions.

SFAS 48 points out that the right of return may exist either from a formal contractual relationship between the parties or simply as a result of existing practice. If the right of return exists for either reason, and the conditions required for revenue recognition are *not* met, *sales and related cost of sales* are not recognized in the period of the initial sales transaction. Instead, both sales and cost of sales on those trans-actions expected to result in returns are deferred.

Where sales revenue is recognized because the conditions for recognition reviewed above are met, any costs or losses that are expected in connection with returns should be recognized in accordance with FASB Statement 5, *Accounting for Contingencies*. Sales with the right of return represent loss contingencies because of the likelihood of reversal of the sales transaction and the related reduction in assets (receivables) or incurrence of a liability (payable for amounts already paid by customers). Sales and cost of sales reported in the income statement should exclude amounts for those sales expected to be returned.

SFAS 48 does *not* apply to accounting for revenue in the service industries if part or all of the service revenue may be returned under cancellation privileges granted by the buyer. It is *not* applicable to transactions involving real estate and does *not* apply to sales transactions in which the customer may return defective goods, such as under warranty provisions.

DISCLOSURE REQUIREMENTS

The Statement is effective for fiscal years beginning after June 15, 1981. Earlier application is encouraged. Changes in accounting policy required to apply SFAS 48 should be applied retroactively. The financial statements for the fiscal year in which the statement is first applied should disclose the nature of the restatement, the effect on sales, income before extraordinary items, net income and related per share amounts for each year restated. If retroactive application to all years presented is not possible, the cumulative effect of applying the statement should be included in the year in which the statement is first applied.

FASB 49—ACCOUNTING FOR PRODUCT FINANCING ARRANGEMENTS

A product financing arrangement is an agreement involving the transfer or sponsored acquisition of inventory which, although it sometimes resembles a sale of inventory, is in substance a means of financing inventory through a second party. For example, if a company transfers inventory to another company in an apparent sale, and in a related transaction agrees to repurchase the inventory at a later date, the arrangement may be a product financing arrangement rather than a sale and subsequent purchase of inventory. Product financing arrangements include agreements in which a sponsor:[3]

- Sells a product to another party, and in a related transaction, agrees to repurchase the product at a specified price, or controls the disposition of the product;
- Arranges for another entity to acquire a product on the sponsor's behalf, and in a related transaction, agrees to purchase the product at a specified price, or controls the disposition of the product.

SFAS 49 provides criteria for determining when certain arrangements involving inventory transactions are product financing arrangements, and sets forth the appropriate accounting treatment for such arrangements. This pronouncement was previously issued as AICPA SOP 78-8.

SITUATIONS WHICH ARE PRODUCT FINANCING ARRANGEMENTS

If a sponsor transfers inventory to a purchaser, and in a related transaction agrees to repurchase the product at a specified price, or guarantees some specified resale price for sales of the product to outside parties, the arrangement is a product financing arrangement. On transfer of the inventory to the purchaser, the sponsor records a liability to the extent that the product is covered by the financing arrangement. No sale is recorded by the sponsor, and the inventory covered by the product financing arrangement remains on the sponsor's books.

Other situations which require recognition as product financing arrangements involve the sponsored purchase of inventory by another entity on behalf of the sponsor. If the sponsor arranges for another entity to purchase inventory, and in a related transaction agrees to purchase the inventory at a specified price, or guarantees some specified resale price for products sold to outside parties, the arrangement is a product financing arrangement. As such, when the other party purchases the inventory on behalf of the sponsor, the sponsor records the inventory purchase and related liability to the extent that the product is covered by the financing arrangement.

In all of these possible situations, SFAS 49 requires that any subsequent financing and holding costs (for example, insurance, warehousing and interest costs) incurred by the other entity be accounted for by the *sponsor* in accordance with the sponsor's accounting policies for these costs, to the extent that they are covered by the product financing arrangement. Financing and holding costs do not, however, include further inventoriable processing costs incurred by the other entity.

In all of these product financing arrangements, the product which is repurchased or

---

[3]The term "sponsor" is used in Statement 49 to identify the party which ultimately bears the risks and rewards of ownership associated with inventory.

guaranteed by the sponsor may be the same physical product which was originally transferred or acquired. In addition, it may be a substantially identical product, or processed goods of which the product is a component. SFAS 49 is *not* applicable to certain products. Unmined or unharvested natural resources and financial instruments are specifically excluded.

To provide assistance in the identification of agreements which are product financing arrangements, SFAS 49 identifies four conditions which are typical for product financing arrangements:

- The purchaser is created for the purpose of acquiring and financing the inventory, or is an existing trust, nonbusiness organization, or credit grantor;
- The product involved in the agreement is used or sold by the sponsor;
- The product is physically stored by the sponsor;
- The purchaser's debt associated with the inventory is guaranteed by the sponsor.

Finally, for an agreement to be a product financing arrangement, the specified prices (repurchase prices or guaranteed resale prices) must cover substantially all of the purchase price and financing and holding costs incurred by the purchaser, plus any related fee charged by the purchaser. These specified prices may take the following forms:

1. Resale price guarantees where the sponsor agrees to make up the difference between the guaranteed price and the actual resale price if the product is sold to outside parties;
2. An option, on the part of the sponsor, to purchase the product from the purchaser where the economic effect of the option is such that the sponsor is compelled to purchase the product at a predetermined price;

3. An option, on the part of the purchaser, to require the sponsor to purchase the product at a predetermined price.

It is also important that the specified prices in a product financing arrangement cannot be subject to change *except for* fluctuations due to changing financing and holding costs.

SFAS 49 is to be applied prospectively to product financing arrangements entered into after June 15, 1981.

CONCLUSION

Generally revenue is recognized when the earning process is complete or virtually complete and an exchange has taken place. Accounting for revenue recognition in FASB Statements 45, 48 and 49 represents a further refinement of this general principle.

An important point of SFAS 45 deals with the timing of revenue recognition from initial franchise fees. As described earlier, the accounting for initial franchise fees requires the deferral of recognition of revenue from initial franchise fees to those periods in which otherwise uncompensated continuing services are expected to be provided. The existence of these continuing services beyond the time at which initial franchise fees are received (i.e., the exchange) indicates that the earning process is not yet complete. When these services are provided, expenses are incurred and revenue is moved forward in time to the periods in which the earning process is continuing. Thus, revenue recognition, as applied to initial franchise fees, must be focused on the earning process if it extends beyond the exchange.

The revenue recognition problem addressed in SFAS 48 relates primarily to the timing or certainty of the exchange, rather than to the completion of the earning process. Because a product return effectively cancels a sale, any sales transaction which includes the right to return the product certainly raises questions about whether such a transaction constitutes an exchange. Five of the six criteria which are required to be met in order to recognize revenue when the right of return exists deal with some uncertainty related to the sales transaction. If any of these criteria is not met when the right of return exists, then both the revenue and related cost of sales are not recognized at the point of sale. Rather, sales and cost of sales are deferred until the right of return has substantially expired or those criteria which were not met at the point of sale are subsequently met, whichever occurs first. So, the problem of uncertainty surrounding an exchange where the right of return exists is a significant consideration in revenue recognition.

Unlike SFAS 45 and 48, which deal largely with the *timing* of revenue recognition, SFAS 49 addresses the issue of whether revenue has been earned. The statement requires, in line with the notion of "substance over form" than an apparent sale and repurchase of inventory be treated as a *borrowing and repayment*. In terms of revenue recognition, this treatment is appropriate, because at the time of the initial inventory transfer ("sale") by the sponsor, the earning process is not yet complete. Although an exchange has taken place, the earning process continues inasmuch as the risks of ownership remain with the sponsor.

These new pronouncements represent refinements of general revenue recognition concepts in current standard setting efforts rather than changes in those concepts.

QUESTIONS

1. One concept of income measurement suggests that income be measured by determining the net change over time in the present discounted value of net cash flow expected to be received by the firm. Under this concept of income, which of the following, ignoring income taxes, would not affect the amount of income for a particular period?
   a. Providing services to outsiders and investment of the funds received
   b. Production of goods or services not yet sold or delivered to customers or clients
   c. Windfall gains and losses due to external causes
   d. The method used to depreciate property, plant, and equipment

2. The term *revenue recognition* conventionally refers to
   a. The process of identifying transactions to be recorded as revenue in an accounting period
   b. The process of measuring and relating revenue and expenses of an enterprise for an accounting period
   c. The earning process that gives rise to revenue realization

d. The process of identifying those transactions that result in an inflow of assets from customers

3. In the transactions approach to income determination, income is measured by subtracting the expenses resulting from specific transactions during the period from revenues of the period also resulting from transactions. Under a strict transactions approach to income measurement, which of the following would not be considered a transaction?
   a. Sale of goods on account at 20 percent markup
   b. Exchange of inventory at a regular selling price for equipment
   c. Adjustment of inventory in lower of cost or market inventory valuations when market is below cost
   d. Payment of salaries

4. Conventionally accountants measure income
   a. By applying a value-added concept
   b. By using a transactions approach
   c. As a change in the value of owners' equity
   d. As a change in the purchasing power of owners' equity.

5. Arid Lands, Inc., is engaged in extensive exploration for water in the Caprock Desert. If upon discovery of water the corporation does not recognize any revenue from water sales until the sales exceed the costs of exploration, the basis of revenue recognition being employed is the
   a. Production basis
   b. Cash (or collection) basis
   c. Sales (or accrual) basis
   d. Sunk cost (or cost recovery) basis

6. The installment method of recognizing revenue is not acceptable for financial reporting if
   a. The collectibility of the sales price is reasonably assured
   b. The installment period is less than 12 months
   c. The method is applied to only a portion of the total
   d. Collection expenses can be reasonably predicted

7. The principal disadvantage of using the percentage-of-completion method of recognizing revenue from long-term contracts is that it
   a. Is unacceptable for income tax purposes
   b. May require that interperiod tax allocation procedures be used
   c. Gives results based upon estimates that may be subject to considerable uncertainty
   d. Is likely to assign a small amount of revenue to a period during which much revenue was actually earned

8. One of the basic features of financial accounting is the
   a. Direct measurement of economic resources and obligations and changes in them in terms of money and sociological and psychological impact

    b. Direct measurement of economic resources and obligations and changes in them in terms of money

    c. Direct measurement of economic resources and obligations and changes in them in terms of money and sociological impact

    d. Direct measurement of economic resources and obligations and changes in them in terms of money and psychological impact

9. Uncertainty and risks inherent in business situations should be adequately considered in financial reporting. This statement is an example of the concept of *(CIN recognize future losses only immediately)*

    a. Conservatism

    b. Completeness

    c. Neutrality

    d. Representational faithfulness

10. Determining periodic earnings and financial position depends on measuring economic resources and obligations and changes in them as these changes occur. This explanation pertains to

    a. Disclosure

    b. Accrual accounting

    c. Materiality

    d. The matching concept

11. Under what condition is it proper to recognize revenues prior to the sale of the merchandise?

    a. When the ultimate sale of the goods is at an assured sales price

    b. When the revenue is to be reported as an intallment sale

    c. When the concept of internal consistency (of amounts of revenue) must be complied with

    d. When management has a long-established policy to do so

12. Bonanza Trading Stamps, Inc., was formed early this year to sell trading stamps throughout the Southwest to retailers who distribute the stamps gratuitously to their customers. Books for accumulating the stamps and catalogs illustrating the merchandise for which the stamps may be exchanged are given free to retailers for distribution to stamp recipients. Centers with inventories of merchandise premiums have been established for redemption of the stamps. Retailers may not return unused stamps to Bonanza.

    The following schedule expresses Bonanza's expectations as to the percentages of a normal month's activity that will be attained. For this purpose, a *normal month's activity* is defined as the level of operations expected when expansion of activities ceases or tapers off to a stable rate. The company expects that this level will be attained in the third year and that sales of stamps will average $2,000,000 per month throughout the third year.

Expense = is an expired cost

Month	Actual Stamp Sales Percentage	Merchandise Premium Purchases Percentage	Stamp Redemptions Percentage
6	30%	40%	10%
12	60	60	45
18	80	80	70
24	90	90	80
30	100	100	95

Required:

a. Discuss the factors to be considered in determining when revenue should be recognized in measuring the income of a business enterprise.

b. Discuss the accounting alternatives that should be considered by Bonanza Trading Stamps, Inc., for the recognition of its revenues and related expenses.

c. For each accounting alternative discussed in (b) above, give balance sheet accounts that should be used and indicate how each should be classified.

13. You were requested to deliver your auditor's report personally to the board of directors of Sebal Manufacturing Corporation and answer questions posed about the financial statements. While reading the statements, one director asked, "What are the precise meanings of the terms cost, expense, and loss? These terms sometimes seem to identify similar items and other times seem to identify dissimilar items."

Required:

a. Explain the meanings of the terms (1) *cost,* (2) *expense,* and (3) *loss* as used for financial reporting in conformity with generally accepted accounting principles. In your explanation discuss the distinguishing characteristics of the terms and their similarities and interrelationships.

b. Classify each of the following items as a cost, expense, loss, or other category, and explain how the classification of each item may change:

  i. Cost of goods sold ― Expense
  ii. Bad debts expense = expense
  iii. Depreciation expense for plant machinery = Cost
  iv. Organization costs = Cost
  v. Spoiled goods = cost If it is abnormal spoilage, then it is a loss

c. The terms *period cost* and *product cost* are sometimes used to describe certain items in financial statements. Define these terms and distinguish between them. To what types of items do each apply?

14. Revenue is usually recognized at the point of sale. Under special circum-

119

stances, however, bases other than the point of sale are used for the timing of revenue recognition.

Required:

a. Why is the point of sale usually used as the basis for the timing of revenue recognition?

b. Disregarding the special circumstances when bases other than the point of sale are used, discuss the merits of each of the following objections to the sales basis of revenue recognition:

    i. It is too conservative because revenue is earned throughout the entire process of production.

    ii. It is not conservative enough because accounts receiveable do not represent disposable funds, sales returns and allowances may be made, and collection and bad debt expenses may be incurred in a later period.

c. Revenue may also be recognized (1) during production and (2) when cash is received. For each of these two bases of timing revenue recognition, give an example of the circumstances in which it is properly used and discuss the accounting merits of its use in lieu of the sales basis.

15. The earning of revenue by a business enterprise is recognized for accounting purposes when the transaction is recorded. In some situations, revenue is recognized approximately as it is earned in the economic sense. In other situations, accountants have developed guidelines for recognizing revenue by other criteria, for example, at the point of sale.

a. Required (ignore income taxes):

    i. Explain and justify why revenue is often recognized as earned at the time of sale.

    ii. Explain in what situations it would be appropriate to recognize revenue as the productive activity takes place.

    iii. At what times, other than those included in (1) and (2), may it be appropriate to recognize revenue? Explain.

    iv. Income measurements can be divided into different income concepts classified by income recipients. The income concepts in the following table are tailored to the listed categories of income recipients.

b. Required:

For each of the concepts listed in the table, explain in separately numbered paragraphs what major categories of revenue, expense, and other items would be included in the determination of income.

16. The Financial Accounting Standards Board recently issued its Statement of Financial Accounting Concepts No. 5, "Recognition and Measurement in Financial Statements of Business Enterprises." In general, this Statement

Income Concepts	Income Recipients
1. Net income to residual equity holders	Common stockholders
2. Net income to investors	Stockholders and long-term debt holders
3. Value-added income	All employees, stockholders, governments, and some creditors

attempts to set recognition criteria and guidance on what information should be incorporated into financial statements and when this information should be reported.

Required:

According to SFAC No. 5, five general categories of information should be provided by a full set of financial statements. List and discuss these five categories of information.

① Balance, Income Comprehensive Cash Flow
Income

Pg 83

BIBLIOGRAPHY

Accounting for Extraordinary Gains and Losses. New York: Ronald Press Co., 1967, particularly Chapters 1, 2, and 3, and Appendix B.

Alexander, Sidney S. "Income Measurement in a Dynamic Economy." Revised by David Solomons and reprinted in W. T. Baxter and Sidney Davidson, *Studies in Accounting Theory,* Homewood, Ill.: Richard D. Irwin, Inc., 1962, pp. 126–200.

Amenta, Michael J. "Unsettled Issues and Misapplications of APB Opinion No. 19 [*sic*] as to Treatment of Extraordinary Items." *The CPA Journal* (August 1972), pp. 640–643, 664.

American Accounting Association, Committee on External Reporting. "An Evaluation of External Reporting Practices." *The Accounting Review*. Supplement to Vol. 44 (1969), pp. 79–122.

American Accounting Association 1964 Concepts and Standards Research Study Committee. "The Realization Concept." *The Accounting Review* (April 1965), pp. 312–322.

American Accounting Association 1964 Concepts and Standards Research Committee. "The Matching Concept." *The Accounting Review* (April 1965), pp. 368–372.

American Accounting Association 1972–73 Committee on Concepts and Standards-External Reporting. *The Accounting Review*. Supplement to Vol. 49 (1974), pp. 203–222.

Amey, L. R. *The Efficiency of Business Enterprises*. New York: Augustus M. Kelley Publishers, 1970.

Anderson, James A. *A Comparative Analysis of Selected Income Measurement Theories in Financial Accounting*. Sarasota, Fla.: American Accounting Association, 1976.

Barlev, Benzion, and Haim Levy. "On the Variability of Accounting Income Numbers." *Journal of Accounting Research* (Autumn 1979), pp. 305–315.

Barton, A. D. "Expectations and Achievements in Income Theory." *The Accounting Review* (October 1974), pp. 664–681.

Beams, Floyd A. "Income Reporting: Continuity with Change." *Management Accounting* (August 1972), pp. 23–27.

Beaver, William H., and Joel S. Demski. "The Nature of Income Measurement." *The Accounting Review* (January 1979), pp. 38–46.

Bedford, Norton M. "Income Concept Complex: Expansion or Decline." In

CHAPTER 2: INCOME CONCEPTS

Robert R. Sterling, *Asset Valuation and Income Determination*. Lawrence, Kans.: Scholars Book Co., 1971, pp. 135–144.

Bedford, Norton M. *Income Determination Theory: Accounting Framework*. Reading, Mass.: Addison-Wesley Publishing Co., Inc., 1965.

Benis, Martin, and Robert Johnson. "Case of Premature Income Recognition." *The CPA Journal* (October 1973), pp. 863–867.

Bernstein, Leopold A. "Extraordinary Gains and Losses—Their Significance to the Financial Analyst." *Financial Analyst Journal* (November–December 1972), pp. 49–52, 88–90.

Boulding, K. E. "Economics and Accounting: The Uncongenial Twins." In W. T. Baxter and Sidney Davidson, eds., *Studies in Accounting Theory*. Homewood, Ill.: Richard D. Irwin, Inc., 1962, pp. 44–45.

Bowers, Russell. "Tests of Income Realization." *The Accounting Review* (June 1941), pp. 139–155.

Calhoun, Charles H., III. "Accounting for Initial Franchise Fees: Is it a Dead Issue?" *Journal of Accountancy* (February 1975), pp. 60–67.

Chambers, Raymond J. *Accounting, Evaluation and Economic Behavior*. Englewood Cliffs, N.J.: Prentice-Hall, Inc., 1966.

Devine, Carl Thomas. "Loss Recognition." In Sidney Davidson, David Green, Jr., Charles T. Horngren, and George H. Sorter, eds., *An Income Approach to Accounting Theory*. Englewood Cliffs, N.J.: Prentice-Hall, Inc., 1964, pp. 162–172 (originally published in *Accounting Research* [October 1955], pp. 310–320).

Edwards, Edgar O., and Phillip W. Bell. *The Theory and Measurement of Business Income*. Berkeley and Los Angeles: University of California Press, 1961.

Enthoven, Adolf J. H. *Accountancy and Economic Development Policy*. New York: American Elsevier Publishing, 1973.

FASB Discussion Memorandum. Criteria for Determining Materiality. Stamford, Conn.: Financial Accounting Standards Board, 1975.

Fess, Philip E., and William L. Ferrara, "The Period Cost Concept for Income Measurement—Can it be Defended?" *The Accounting Review* (October 1961), pp. 598–602.

Graese, Clifford E., and Joseph R. Demario. "Revenue Recognition for Long Term Contracts." *Journal of Accountancy* (December 1976), pp. 53–59.

Heilman, E. A. "Realized Income." *The Accounting Review* (June 1929), pp. 80–87.

Hepworth, Samuel R. "Smoothing Periodic Income." *The Accounting Review* (January 1953), pp. 32–39.

Horngren, Charles T. "How Should We Interpret the Realization Concept?" *The Accounting Review* (April 1965), pp. 323–333.

Hylton, Delmer P. "On Matching Revenue with Expense." *The Accounting Review* (October 1965), pp. 824–828.

Jarrett, Jeffrey F. "Principle of Matching and Realization as Estimation Problems." *Journal of Accounting Research* (Autumn 1971), pp. 378–382.

Lee, T. A. "A Case for Cash Flow Reporting." *Journal of Business Finance* (Summer 1972), pp. 27–36.

Mobley, Sybil C. "The Concept of Realization: A Useful Device." *The Accounting Review* (April 1966), pp. 292–296.

Mueller, Gerhard G. "Accounting Within a Macroeconomic Framework." In *International Accounting*. New York: Macmillan, 1967, Chap. 1.

Paton, William A. "Premature Revenue Recognition." *Journal of Accountancy* (October 1953), pp. 432–437.

Petri, Enrico. "Income Reporting and APB Opinion No. 18." *Management Accounting* (December 1974), pp. 49–52.

Schwayder, Keith. "The Capital Maintenance Rule and the Net Asset Valuation Rule." *The Accounting Review* (April 1969), pp. 304–316.

Schwayder, Keith. "A Critique of Economic Income as an Accounting Concept." *Abacus* (August 1967), pp. 23–35.

Solomons, David. "Economic and Accounting Concepts of Income." *The Accounting Review* (July 1961), pp. 374–383.

Spiller, Earl A., Jr. "The Revenue Postulate—Recognition or Realization." *N.A.A. Bulletin* (February 1962), pp. 41–47.

Sprouse, Robert T. "The Importance of Earnings in the Conceptual Framework." *Journal of Accountancy* (January 1978), pp. 64–71.

Sterling, Robert R. *Theory of the Measurement of Enterprise Income.* Lawrence, Kans.: The University Press of Kansas, 1970.

Storey, Reed K. "Revenue Realization, Going Concern and Measurement of Income." *The Accounting Review* (April 1959), pp. 232–238.

Storey, Reed K. "Cash Movements and Periodic Income Determination." *The Accounting Review* (July 1960), pp. 449–454.

Thomas, Arthur L. *Revenue Recognition.* Michigan Business Reports No. 49. Ann Arbor: Bureau of Business Research, Graduate School of Business Administration, University of Michigan, 1966.

CHAPTER 2: INCOME CONCEPTS

Tucker, Marvin W. "Probabilistic Aspects of Revenue Recognition, Convertional and Innovational." *Australian Accountant* (May 1973), pp. 198–202, 205.

Walker, Lauren M., Gerhard G. Mueller, and Fauzi G. Dimian. "Significant Events in the Development of the Realization Concept in the U.S." *Accountants Magazine* [Scotland] (August 1970), pp. 357–360.

Windal, Floyd W. "The Accounting Concept of Realization." *The Accounting Review* (April 1961), pp. 249–258.

3

FINANCIAL STATEMENTS I: THE INCOME STATEMENT

The emphasis upon corporate income reporting has caused a continuing dialogue among accountants about the proper identification of revenues, gains, expenses, and losses. These financial-statement elements were originally defined in Statement of Financial Accounting Concepts No. 3 as follows.

Revenues—inflows or other enhancements of assets of an entity or settlement of its liabilities (or a combination of both) during a period from delivering or producing goods, rendering services, or other activities that constitute the entity's ongoing major or central operations.

Gains—increases in net assets from peripheral or incidental transactions of an entity and from all other transactions and other events and circumstances affecting the entity during a period except those that result from revenues or investments by owners.

Expenses—outflows or other using up of assets or incurrences of liabilities (or a combination or both) during a period from delivering or producing goods, rendering services, or carrying out other activities that constitute the entity's ongoing major or central operations.

Losses—decreases in net assets from peripheral or incidental transactions of an entity and from all other transactions and other events and circumstances affecting the entity during a period except from expenses or distributions to owners.[1]

---

[1]Financial Accounting Standards Board Statement of Concepts No. 3, "Elements of Financial Statements of Business Enterprises" (Stamford, Conn.: FASB, 1980) pars. 63–73. These definitions were reaffirmed in Statement of Financial Accounting Concepts No. 6, "Elements of Financial Statements," (Stamford Conn.: FASB, 1985) pars. 79–88.

The important distinction between revenues and gains and expenses and losses is whether or not they are associated with ongoing operations. Over the years, this distinction has generated questions concerning the nature of income reporting desired by various financial-statement users. Historically, two viewpoints have dominated this dialogue and have been termed the *current operating performance concept* and the *all-inclusive concept* of income reporting. These viewpoints are reviewed in the following paragraphs.

STATEMENT FORMAT

The proponents of the *current operating performance* concept base their arguments on the belief that normal and recurring items should constitute the principal measure of enterprise performance. That is, net income should reflect the day-to-day, profit-directed activities of the enterprise, and the inclusion of other items of profit or loss distort the meaning of the term *net income*.

On the other hand, the advocates of the *all-inclusive* view believe that net income should reflect all items that affected the net increase or decrease in stockholders' equity during the period, with the exception of capital transactions. Specifically, these individuals believe that the total net income for the life of an enterprise should be determinable by summing the periodic net income figures.

The underlying assumption behind this controversy is that the method of presentation of financial information is important. That is, both viewpoints agree on the information to be presented but disagree on where to disclose different types of revenue, expenses, gains, and losses. Research has tended to indicate that investors are not influenced by the format of financial statements if the statements disclose the same information (see the Chapter 14 section on the efficient market hypothesis for a discussion of this research). So, perhaps, this concern over statement format is unwarranted.

APB OPINION NO. 9

One of the first problems the Accounting Principles Board studied was the question of the proper financial statement elements to include under the term *net income*. An APB study revealed that business managers were exercising a great deal of discretion in determining which revenues and expenses to include on the income statement or on the retained earnings statements. The lack of formal guidelines concerning adjustments to retained earnings resulted in the placement of most items of revenue or gains on the income statement; whereas many expense and loss items that were only remotely related to previous periods were treated as adjustments to retained earnings.

The APB's study of these reporting abuses and its general review of the overall nature of income resulted in Opinion No. 9, "Reporting the Results of Operations.'' This opinion took a middle position between the current operating performance and all-inclusive concepts by stating that net income should reflect all items of profit and loss recognized during the period, with the exception of prior period adjustments. Additionally, the prescribed statement format included two income figures: net income from operations and net income from operations plus extraordinary items. This pronouncement required business managers and accountants to determine whether revenues and expenses, and gains and losses, were properly classified as normal recurring items, extraordinary items, or prior period adjustments according to established criteria. In general, the provisions of APB No. 9 specified that all items were to be considered normal and recurring unless they met the stated requirements for classification as either extraordinary items or prior period adjustments.

The division of the income statement into net income from operations and net income after extraordinary items allowed for the disclosure of most items of revenue and expense, or gains and losses, on the income statement during any period. Additionally, it allowed financial-statement users to evaluate the results of normal operations or total income according to their needs. In later opinions the board further divided the income statement to provide for the separate disclosure of disposal of a business segment and accounting changes (discussed later). Figure 3.1 (on page 140) provides an illustration of how the income statement might look for a company that disclosed all of the components of income defined by the APB and FASB in various Opinions and Statements.

EXTRAORDINARY ITEMS

Extraordinary items were originally defined in APB No. 9 as events and transactions of material effect that would not be expected to recur frequently and that would not be considered as recurring factors in any evaluation of the ordinary operating processes of the business.[2] This release provided the following examples of such items: gains or losses from the sale or abandonment of a plant or a significant segment of the business; gains or losses from the sale of an investment not held for resale, the write-off of goodwill owing to unusual events during the period, the condemnation or expropriation of properties, and major devaluations of currencies in a foreign country in which the company was opearting.

Subsequently, the usefulness of the prevailing definition of extraordinary items came under review in 1973, and the Accounting Principles Board concluded that similar items of revenues and expenses were not being classified in the same manner across the spectrum of business enterprises. The board also concluded that business enterprises were not interpreting Opinion No. 9 in similar manner and decided that more specific criteria were needed to ensure a more

[2]Ibid.

uniform interpretation of its provisions. In APB Opinion No. 30, "Reporting the Results of Operations," extraordinary items were defined as events and transactions that are distinguished by both their unusual nature and infrequency of occurrence. These characteristics were described as follows.

Unusual nature—the event or transaction should possess a high degree of abnormality and be unrelated or only incidentally related to ordinary activities.
Infrequency of occurrence—the event or transaction would not reasonably be expected to recur in the foreseeable future.[3]

In Opinion No. 30 several types of transactions were defined as not meeting these criteria. These included write-downs and write-offs of receivables, inventories, equipment leased to others, deferred research and development costs, or other intangible assets; gains or losses in foreign currency transactions or devaluations; gains or losses on disposals of segments of a business; other gains or losses on the sale or abandonment of property, plant, and equipment used in business; effects of strikes; and adjustments of accruals on long-term contracts. The position expressed by the Accounting Principles Board in APB Opinion No. 30 was therefore somewhat of a reversal in philosophy; some items previously defined as extraordinary in APB Opinion No. 9 were now specifically excluded from that classification. The result of APB Opinion No. 30 was the retention of the extraordinary item classification on the income statement; however, the revenues and expenses allowed to be reported as extraordinary items were significantly reduced.

In the latter years of its existence, the Accounting Principles Board was particularly concerned with the number of alternative methods available to account for similar transactions. Where evidence existed that several alternatives were available, the board was apparently more concerned with narrowing of alternatives than in developing an overall theory of accounting or income reporting. The issuance of Opinion No. 30 may have accomplished this objective, but whether or not it better satisfies user needs is subject to question.

PRIOR PERIOD ADJUSTMENTS

The test for the classification of an item as a prior period adjustment was made quite rigid in APB Opinion No. 9. In order for events and transactions to be classified as prior period adjustments, they must have been

(a) specifically identified and directly related to the business activities of particular prior periods, (b) not attributable to economic events occurring subsequent to the date of the financial statements for the prior period, (c)

---

[3] Accounting Principles Board Opinion No. 30, "Reporting the Results of Operations" (New York: American Institute of Certified Public Accountants, 1973), par. 20.

dependent primarily on determination by persons other than management, (d) not susceptible of reasonable estimation prior to such determination.[4]

At the time Opinion No. 9 was issued, the Accounting Principles Board took the position that prior period adjustments, that are disclosed as increases or decreases in the beginning retained earnings balance, should have been related to events of previous periods that were not susceptible to reasonable estimation at the time they occurred. Additionally, since these amounts were material by definition, it would be expected that the auditor's opinion would be at least qualified on the financial statements issued when the event or transaction took place. Examples of such items were settlements of income tax cases or other litigations. The category of errors was later added to this classification. Errors would, of course, not result in an opinion qualification because they would be unknown when the financial statements were released.

On June 8, 1976 the Securities and Exchange Commission released *Staff Accounting Bulletin No. 8,* which concluded that litigation is inevitably an economic event and that settlements of litigation constitute economic events of the period in which they occur. This conclusion created a discrepancy between generally accepted accounting principles and reporting for companies listed with the SEC. Prior to the release of *Staff Accounting Bulletin No. 8,* the FASB had undertaken a study of prior period adjustment reporting of 600 companies and also concluded that a clarification of the criteria outlined in APB Opinion No. 9 was required.

Subsequently, the FASB issued its Statement No. 16, "Prior Period Adjustments." This release concluded that the only items of profit and loss that should properly be reported as prior period adjustments are

a. *Correction of an error in the financial statements of a prior period.*
b. *Adjustments that result from the realization of income tax benefits of preacquisition operating loss carry-forwards of purchased subsidiaries.*[5]

This release put the FASB on the side of the all-inclusive concept of income and, when considered in conjunction with APB Opinion No. 30, ensures that almost all items of profit and loss are reported as a part of normal recurring operations.

EARNINGS PER SHARE

The use of the income statement as the primary source of information by decision makers has resulted in a need to disclose the amount of earnings that accrue to different classes of investors. The amount of earnings accruing to holders of debt and preferred stock (termed senior securities) is usually fixed, so that the income

[4]APB Opinion No. 9, op. cit., par. 23.
[5]Statement of Financial Accounting Standards No. 16, "Prior Period Adjustments" (Stamford, Conn.: Financial Accounting Standards Board, 1977), par. 11.

remaining after the distribution of interest and preferred dividends is available to common stockholders. This residual amount is reported on the income statement on a per share basis.

The basic calculation of earnings per share is relatively easy. The net income available to common stockholders after deducting required payments to senior security holders is divided by the weighted average number of common shares outstanding. However, this method of calculating earnings per share is frequently not appropriate because of the wide variety of securities now being issued by corporations. Many companies have issued stock options, stock warrants, and convertible securities that can be converted into common stock at the opinion of the holder of the securities. In the event these securities are exchanged for common stock, they have the effect of reducing (diluting) the earnings of previous stockholders. Additionally, increases in reported earnings could cause the holders of options, warrants or convertibles to exchange their securities for common stock. The effect of increases in earnings then might be a decrease in reported earnings per share. (That is, the increase in common shares outstanding might be proportionately greater than the increase in net income.)

The Accounting Principles Board first discussed the ramifications of these issues in Opinion No. 9 and developed the residual security and senior security concepts. This release stated

> When more than one class of common stock is outstanding, or when an outstanding security has participation dividend rights, or when an outstanding security clearly derives a major portion of its value from its conversion rights or its common stock characteristics, such securities should be considered "residual securities" and not "senior securities" for purposes of computing earnings per share.[6]

This provision of Opinion No. 9 was only "strongly recommended" and not made mandatory, but the development of the concept formed the framework for Opinion No. 15, "Earnings Per Share."[7] The latter opinion noted the importance placed upon per share computation by investors and the marketplace and concluded that a consistent method of computation was needed to make such amounts comparable across all segments of the business environment.

Opinion No. 15 made mandatory the presentation of earnings per share figures for net income before extraordinary items and total net income, and also recommended that per share amounts for extraordinary items be disclosed when they were reported.[8]

---

[6]APB Opinion No. 9, op. cit., par. 23.
[7]Accounting Principles Board Opinion No. 15, "Earnings Per Share" (New York: American Institute of Certified Public Accountants, 1969).
[8]In Statement of Financial Accounting Standards No. 2, the FASB suspended the reporting requirements of APB No. 15 for nonpublic companies. Nevertheless, if nonpublic companies choose to report earnings per share, they must comply with the provisions of APB No. 15.

When common stock is the only residual security, the company is said to have a *simple capital structure*. In such cases, only one set of earnings per share amounts is presented. On the other hand, if a company has convertible securities, options, warrants, or other rights that upon conversion or exercise could (in the aggregate) dilute earnings per share by 3 percent or more, the board defined the enterprise as having a *complex capital structure*.

Two earnings per share computations are required for a company having a complex capital structure: (1) primary earnings per share and (2) fully diluted earnings per share. The numerator to use in computing primary earnings per share is determined by summing net income and the net of tax earnings accruing to securities properly classified as common stock equivalents. The denominator consists of the weighted average number of common shares outstanding during the period plus the weighted average number of shares that would be issued if all securities classified as common stock equivalents were assumed to have been exchanged at the beginning of the period or when they become exchangeable during the period. The fully diluted computation adds all contingent issuances of shares available during the period to the denominator and adds the earnings (net of tax) that accrue to these additional securities to the numerator. These computations can be expressed as

Primary earnings per share $=$ $\dfrac{\text{net income after taxes} - \text{preferred dividends (if declared or on cumulative preferred if not declared for nonconvertible preferred stock or convertible preferred stock that is not a common stock equivalent)} + \text{interest and dividends (net of tax effect) on securities considered to be common stock equivalents}}{\text{weighted average of common shares outstanding} + \text{shares issuable from common stock equivalents}}$

Fully diluted earnings per share $=$ $\dfrac{\text{the numerator for primary EPS} + \text{interest and dividends (net of tax effect) on securities assumed converted for fully diluted purposes}}{\text{the denominator for primary EPS} + \text{all other contingently issuable shares}}$

The calculation of the primary and fully diluted earnings per share denominator amounts is heavily influenced by the concept of common stock equivalents. *Common stock equivalents* are defined as securities that are not in form common stock but that contain provisions that enable the holders of such securities to become common stockholders and to participate in any value appreciation of the common stock. Examples of such securities are stock warrants and options, participating securities, and convertible securities subject to the 66 ⅔ percent Aa bond rating test.[9]

According to this definition, stock options and stock warrants are always assumed to be common stock equivalents. On the other hand, the establishment of the Aa rate test for including convertible securities as common stock equivalents was apparently the result of some disagreement among the board members. Whenever convertible securities are issued, there is always the question of the effect of the conversion feature on the securities' marketability. In some cases, investors may be purchasing these securities for their dividends or interest, while in others, investors may be purchasing them mainly for their conversion rights. The 66 ⅔ percent test was apparently the result of a compromise and now sets the point of major emphasis on convertibility at 66 ⅔ percent of the Aa bond interest rate. That is, when a convertible security has an effective yield to maturity of less than 66 ⅔ percent of the Aa bond rate at the date of issuance, it is assumed to be purchased for its conversion feature and, therefore, defined as a common stock equivalent. All other convertible securities that fail the 66 ⅔ test are assumed to be purchased for their return on investment and only included in the fully diluted earnings per share computation.

At the time of the release of Opinion No. 15 the APB was also faced with the issue of how to handle stock options and warrants. Most stock options and warrants require that their exchange for common stock be accompanied by the payment of a sum of money. Thus, if these securities are exchanged for common stock, the business entity would have an additional sum of money available. The problems the APB faced dealt with how to disclose the effects of this assumed exchange when calculating earnings per share and how to accrue an earnings rate on the additional assets created by an assumed conversion. The board settled upon what was termed the *treasury stock method.* (As a practical matter the APB recommended that the assumption of exercise of options and warrants should not be reflected in earnings per share data until the market price exceeds the exercise price for substantially all of three consecutive months ending with the last month of the fiscal period.)

[9]APB Opinion No. 15 originally specified the prime interest rate for this test. Due to the volatility of the prime rate in recent years, the FASB substituted the interest rate on Aa bonds instead of the prime rate for this test. Later, in 1985, the FASB amended this test from cash yield to effective yield to maturity. This amendment was largely due to the emergence of zero coupon bonds (discussed in Chapter 8).

In calculating the primary earnings per share effect for options and warrants, the net positive difference between the number of shares that might be issued if all options and warrants were exercised and the number of shares that could be purchased on the open market at the average market price of the common stock with the proceeds obtained from the exchange must be calculated. That is, the net difference between the shares that could be exchanged and those assumed repurchased as treasury shares is added to the denominator. For fully diluted purposes, the average market price of the common stock is also used unless the end-of-the-year price is more than the average price. The application of the treasury stock method is subject to the limitation that the number of common shares deemed repurchased cannot exceed 20 percent of the common shares outstanding at the end of the period. Any excess in such cases should be applied first as if used to reduce any short-term or long-term borrowings, and second as if invested in U.S. government securities or commercial paper with the appropriate income tax effects.

The following steps illustrate the calculation of the shares to be added for outstanding options and warrants for primary earnings per share.

Step 1. Determine the number of shares that would be issued if all options and warrants were redeemed.

Step 2. Determine the proceeds accompanying conversion.

Step 3. Determine the average market price of the common stock.

Step 4. Determine the number of treasury shares that could be repurchased with the proceeds for redemption (the results of step 2 divided by the results of step 3).

Step 5. Determine the number of shares to be added to the earnings per share denominator for primary purposes (the results of step 1 minus the results of step 4). *Note that this number is only added if it is positive.*

An Example

Assume Company C has 100,000 shares of common stock outstanding and 25,000 options outstanding that allow the holders of these securities to purchase 25,000 common shares at $20 per share. During the year the average market price of the common stock was $25 and the end of year price was $23 per share. The steps listed above would be carried out as follows.

Step 1. Number of shares to be issued	25,000
Step 2. Proceeds (25,000 × $20)	$500,000
Step 3. Average market price	$25.00
Step 4. Treasury shares ($500,000 ÷ $25)	20,000
Step 5. Additional shares (25,000 − 20,000)	5,000

In this example, the denominator for both primary and fully diluted earnings per share purposes would be 105,000 shares since the end-of-the-year market price of the common stock was less than the average price.

In contrast to the Aa bond rating test, which is made only at the time of issuance of convertible securities, the treasury stock computation must be made each period because the average market price of its common stock will be different each year for most companies. As noted earlier, where this computation results in more shares being repurchased than would be issued upon the exchange of options and warrants for common stock (where the average market price is less than the exchange price), such computations are deemed to be *antidilutive* and, therefore, are not included in the computation of earnings per share. If more than one type of potentially dilutive securities is present, each calculation is made separately from the most to least dilutive. Those that have an antidilutive effect are excluded from the computation of earnings per share. Antidilution in effect means an increase in earnings per share or a decrease in the loss per share.

Once the number of shares to be included in calculating primary earnings per share is determined, it is necessary to consider whether other contingent issuances may be possible in order to calculate fully diluted earnings per share. The fully diluted figure is intended to show the maximum possible dilution of earnings if all additional issuances of common stock had taken place at the beginning of the period or at the time they became issuable during the period. Examples of securities to be included under this computation are convertible securities that did not meet the common stock equivalent test and shares that are issuable upon the happening of some event. These shares are also only included if they have a dilutive effect upon earnings per share (fully diluted earnings per share must be less than or equal to primary earnings per share).

After all dilutive securities have been included in the calculation of earning per share, a materiality test is undertaken. Opinion No. 15 provides that any reduction in earnings per share due to dilutive convertible securities may be ignored if it is less than 3 percent in the aggregate. This materiality test may be expressed as follows. If the total dilution from all dilutive securities is less than 3 percent, the company need only disclose simple earning per share. If fully diluted earnings per share is less than or equal to 97 percent of primary earnings per share, both primary and fully diluted earnings per share must be disclosed.

The overall objective of earnings per share data is to provide investors with an indication of (1) the value of the firm and (2) expected future dividends. A major theoretical issue surrounding the presentation of earnings per share data is whether this information should be based upon historical or forecasted information. Authoritative accounting bodies have generally taken the position that financial information should be based only upon historical data, and the views expressed by the APB in Opinion No. 15 followed this trend. However, investors' needs might be better satisfied with measures that predict future cash flows (such as current or pro forma dividends per share). Hopefully, the FASB's conceptual framework project will review "value of the firm" measures and achieve a balance between the desire for objective information and predictive information to satisfy investors' needs.

USEFULNESS OF EARNINGS PER SHARE

Earnings per share has been termed a *summary indicator,* that is, a single item that communicates considerable information about an enterprise's performance or financial position. The continuing trend toward complexity in financial reporting has caused many financial statement users to utilize summary indicators. EPS is particularly popular because it is thought to contain information useful in making predictions about future dividends and stock prices. Nevertheless, the use of *summary indicators* such as EPS is discouraged by many accountants. These individuals maintain that an understanding of a company's performance requires a more comprehensive analysis than is provided by a single ratio.

ACCOUNTING CHANGES

The accounting standard of consistency implies that similar transactions should be recorded and reported in the same manner each year. That is, management should choose the set of accounting practices that best satisfies the needs of the reporting unit and continue to use these practices each year. However, individual entities may occasionally find that reporting is improved by changing the methods and procedures previously used or changes in reporting may be dictated by the Financial Accounting Standards Board or the Securities and Exchange Commission. In such cases the comparability of financial statements between periods is impaired, and the accounting standard of disclosure dictates that such changes must be reported in the year of the change. The major question surrounding changes in accounting practices is the proper method to use in disclosing them. That is, should previously issued financial statements be changed to reflect the new method or procedure?

The Accounting Principles Board studied this problem and issued its findings in Opinion No. 20, "Accounting Changes." This release identified three types of accounting changes, discussed the general question of errors in the preparation of financial statements, and defined these changes and errors as follows.

1. Change in an accounting principle. *This type of change occurs when an entity adopts a generally accepted accounting principle that differs from one previously used for reporting purposes. Examples of such changes are a change from Lifo to Fifo inventory pricing or a change in depreciation methods.*
2. Change in an accounting estimate. *These changes result from the necessary consequences of periodic presentation. That is, financial statement presentation requires estimation of future events, and such estimates are subject to*

periodic review. Examples of such changes are the life of depreciable assets and the estimated collectibility of receivables.

3. Change in a reporting entity. *Changes of this type are caused by changes in reporting units, which may be the result of consolidations, changes in specific subsidiaries, or a change in the number of companies consolidated.*

4. Errors. *Errors are not viewed as accounting changes; rather they are the result of mistakes or oversights such as the use of incorrect accounting methods or mathematical miscalculations.*[10]

The board then went on to specify the accounting treatment required to satisfy disclosure requirements in each instance. As noted, the basic question was the advisability of retroactive presentation. The following paragraphs summarize the board's recommendations.

CHANGE IN AN ACCOUNTING PRINCIPLE

When an accounting principle is changed, it should be treated currently. That is, the corporation should present its previously issued financial statements as they were before the change occurred, with the cumulative prior effects of the change shown as a component of net income for the period in which the change occurred. This requirement necessitates determining the yearly changes in net income of all prior periods attributable to the changed principle. For example, if a company changed from straight line to sum-of-the-years-digits depreciation, what was the total annual effect of this change on all years prior to the change? This total amount of change in income (net of tax) is then disclosed as a separate figure between extraordinary items and net income. In addition, per share data for all comparative statements should include the results of the change as if the change had been consistently applied. This requirement results in additional pro forma per share figures being disclosed for each period presented in which the change affected net income. The general conclusion of APB Opinion No. 20 was that previously issued financial statements need not be revised for changes in accounting principles. Exceptions were noted for situations deemed to be of such importance that they required retroactive presentation in the financial statements of all prior periods presented. Specifically retroactive changes are: (1) a change from Lifo inventory valuation to any other method, (2) any change in the method of accounting for long-term construction contracts, and (3) a change to or from the full-cost method in the extractive industries. In each of these cases the previous income statements must be recast to reflect the adoption of the new principle, and no additional pro forma figures need to be disclosed.

Additionally, since it is typically not practicable to compute the cumulative effect of a change to Lifo, changes to Lifo from any other inventory method

---

[10]Accounting Principles Board Opinion No. 20, ''Accounting Changes'' (New York: American Institute of Certified Public Accountants, 1971).

should be treated prospectively. That is, no restatement of previous financial statements is made and no cumulative effect is reported. In these cases, the ending inventory costed under the old method becomes the beginning Lifo inventory.

CHANGE IN ESTIMATES

Estimate changes are handled prospectively. They require no adjustments to previously issued financial statements. These changes should be accounted for in the period of the change, or in the period of the change and in the future if more than one period is affected. For example, assume that a company originally estimated an asset to have a useful service life of 10 years, and after 3 years of service its total service life was estimated to be only 8 years. The book value of the asset should then be depreciated over the remaining useful life of 5 years. The effects of changes in estimates on operating income, extraordinary items, and the related per share amounts should also be disclosed in the year they occur.

CHANGE IN REPORTING ENTITIES

Changes in reporting entities must be declared retroactively by restating all financial statements presented as if the new reporting unit had been in existence at the time these statements were first prepared. That is, previously issued statements are recast to reflect the results of a change in reporting entity. The financial statements should also indicate the nature of the change and the reason for the change. Additionally, the effect of the change on operating income, net income, and the related per share amounts should be disclosed for all comparative statements presented.

ERRORS — disclose and reflect corrected

Errors were defined as prior period adjustments in APB No. 20. In the period the error is discovered, the nature of the error and its effect on operating income, net income, and the related per share amounts should be disclosed. In the event the prior period affected is reported for comparative purposes, the corrected information should be disclosed for the period in which it occurred.

SPECIAL PROBLEMS IN INCOME STATEMENT PRESENTATION

DISPOSAL OF A SEGMENT OF A BUSINESS

As indicated earlier, the study of the results of the application of Opinion No. 9 by various entities disclosed some reporting abuses. For example, some companies were reporting the results of the disposal of segment assets as extraordinary while including the revenue from these segments during the disposal period

138

as ordinary income. In Opinion No. 30, the APB concluded that additional criteria were necessary to identify disposed segments of businesses. The APB required the separate presentation of the results of operations and gain or loss on the sale of assets for disposed segments. This information was seen as necessary to users in order to evaluate the past and expected future operations of a particular business entity. The total gain or loss is determined by *summing any gains or losses on disposal of segment assets and gains or losses incurred by the operations of the disposed segment* during the period of disposal. The following definitions were provided by the APB to aid in determining when and how to report a disposal of a segment of a business.

Segment of a business—a component of an entity whose activities represent a separate major line of business or class of customers. A segment may be a division, department, or joint venture providing its operations can be clearly distinguished physically and operationally. If the component is truly a segment, it should be possible to recast the financial statements to segregate its operations. If its operations cannot be segregated, the presumption is that the component is not a segment.

Measurement date—the date on which management commits itself to a formal plan of disposal. This plan should include identification of the assets, the method of disposal, the period of disposal, the estimated results of operations from the measurement date to the disposal date, and the estimated proceeds from disposal.

Disposal date—the date of sale or the date operations cease.

The accounting treatment for the disposal of a segment of a business is influenced by whether a gain or a loss is anticipated on the measurement date. The expected total gain or loss is determined by comparing the expected net realizable value of the segment assets to the book value of those same assets, less the expenses connected with disposal. Any expected gains or losses on operations of the segment during the period of disposal are then added or subtracted to arrive at the expected total gain or loss. If a loss is expected, the loss is recorded on the measurement date, whereas gains are recognized when realized (ordinarily this will be the disposal date). This accounting treatment is in accordance with the general principle of conservatism discussed earlier in Chapter 2.

Figure 3.1 on page 140 is an illustrative financial statement for Company X showing the manner in which an income statement might be presented if an entity had normal, extraordinary, and discontinued operations, and a cumulative effect change in accounting principle.

INTERIM FINANCIAL STATEMENTS

Many companies issue financial statements for periods of less than a year and also release information on their periodic performance through various news

Figure 3.1
Company X
Statement of Income
For the Year Ended December 31, 1988

Net sales		$900,000
Cost of goods sold		(400,000)
Gross profit		$500,000
Operating expenses		(200,000)
Operating income		$300,000
Other revenue and expense		
Gain on sale of equipment	$5,000	
Interest expense	(30,000)	(25,000)
Pretax income from continuing operations		$275,000
Income tax expense		(125,000)
Income from continuing operations		$150,000
Discontinued operations (Note 1)		
Gain on Disposal of		
Division Assets	$25,000	
Less applicable taxes	12,000	$13,000
Loss from Discontinued Division A	$(20,000)	
Less applicable tax reduction	9,000	(11,000) 2,000
Extraordinary items net of tax of $29,000		
(Note 2)		31,000
Cumulative effect of change in accounting		
principle (S-Y-D depreciation to S-L)		5,000
Net income		$188,000

Earnings Per Share (Note 3)

	Primary	Fully Diluted
Income from continuing operations	1.76	1.70
Discontinued operations	.02	.02
Extraordinary items	.36	.35
Cumulative effect of accounting changes	.06	.06
Net Income	2.20	2.13

Note 1.   During 1988 the comany disposed of one of its plants at a net gain of $13,000 after an applicable income tax reduction of $12,000. Net operating losses of the plant during the period of disposal amounted to $11,000 after an applicable tax reduction of $9,000.

Note 2.   In 1988 X sold its 2% investment in Company ABC at a gain of $60,000 less applicable taxes of $29,000.

Note 3.   Assuming the appropriate conditions for primary and fully diluted earnings per share calculations, and full compliance with FASB requirements and recommendations for full disclosure.

media. These statements' major value is their timeliness. That is, investors need to be aware of any changes in the financial position of the company as soon as possible. In addition, much of the information disclosed in interim financial statements enters into the analytical data used by the government to develop information on the state of the economy, the need for monetary controls, or the need for modifications in the tax laws. Moreover, there is also evidence that interim reporting has an impact on stock prices, indicating that investors do use interim financial information. It is therefore important that interim information be as reliable as possible.

A wide variety of practices have existed with regard to the methods of reporting in these so-called interim periods. Thus such things as seasonal fluctuations in revenues and the application of fixed costs to the various periods had a significant impact on the reported results for interim periods.

In 1973 the Accounting Principles Board studied this problem and issued the results in Opinion No. 28, "Interim Financial Reporting." In discussing the general question, the board noted that two views existed as to the principal objective of interim financial report.

1. *One view held that each interim period was a separate accounting period and that income should be determined in the same manner as for the annual period, thus revenues and expenses should be reported as they occur.*
2. *The other view held that interim periods were an integral part of the annual period, thus revenues and expenses might be allocated to various interim periods even though they occurred only in one period.*[11]

In Opinion No. 28 the board noted that interim financial information was essential to provide timely data on the progress of the enterprise, and that the usefulness of the data rested on its relationship to annual reports. Accordingly, it was determined that interim periods should be viewed as integral parts of the annual period and that the principles and practices followed in the annual period should be followed in the interim period. However, certain modifications were deemed necessary in order to provide a better relationship to the annual period. That is, the following modifications will enable users of interim financial statements to tie the results into the annual report and allow for more informative disclosure.

1. *Revenue should be recognized on the same basis as in the annual period.*
2. *Costs directly associated with products should be recognized as the revenue from those products is recognized.*
3. *Inventories should be costed on the same flow assumptions as in the annual period except that:*

[11]Accounting Principles Board Opinion No. 28, "Interim Financial Reporting" (New York: American Institute of Certified Public Accountants, 1973), par. 5.

a. The gross profit method is acceptable for an interim period but must be disclosed.

b. The liquidation of base period inventories under the Lifo method may not be appropriate if they are expected to be replaced; in such cases the replacement value of the liquidated base may be used.

c. Losses from the application of the lower of cost or market rule should be recognized during the interim period in which they occur and recoveries of such losses should also be recognized when they occur. However, temporary losses need not be recorded.

d. If standard costs are used, variances not expected to reverse in subsequent periods should be expensed.

4. *All other costs should be expensed on the basis of direct expenditures made, accruals for estimated expenditures, or amortization of multiperiod expenses. Costs not associated with products should be expensed as incurred or allocated on the basis of the expiration of time or period of benefit.*

5. *Businesses with material seasonal variations should disclose this fact so that interim reports are not misleading.*

6. *Income tax allocation should be based on the tax rate expected to be applicable to the sum of interim periods' net income.*

7. *Extraordinary items and gains or losses from the disposal of a segment of a business should be reported as they occur and not prorated over the year.*

8. *Changes in accounting principles from comparable or previous interim periods or a prior annual period should be reported according to the provisions of APB No. 20.*[12]

Additionally, it was stated that the publicly traded companies that provided summary information for financial analysis should provide, as a minimum, certain information for the interim period in question and the same interim period for the previous year: These guidelines were provided to offset partially the reduction in detail from interim reports.

1. Sales or gross revenues, extraordinary items, the cumulative effect of a change in accounting principle or practice, and net income.
2. Primary and fully diluted earnings per share.
3. Seasonal revenue.
4. Significant changes in income tax provisions or estimates.
5. Disposal of a segment of a business and extraordinary items.
6. Contingencies.
7. Changes in accounting principles.
8. Significant changes in financial position.

[12]Ibid., pars. 11–15.

Subsequent to the issuance of APB No. 28 problems in reporting certain types of events became evident. These problems were mainly concerned with the reporting of the cumulative effect of an accounting change for changes in accounting principles during interim periods, and the reporting of accounting changes during the fourth quarter of a fiscal year by a company whose securities are publicly traded.

With respect to the cumulative adjustments required for interim changes in accounting principles, APB No. 28 stated,

> A change in accounting principle or practice adopted in an interim period that requires an adjustment for the cumulative effect of the change to the beginning of the current fiscal year should be reported in the interim period in a manner similar to that found in the annual report. . . . The effect of the change from the beginning of the annual period to the period of change should be reported as a determinant of net income in the interim period in which the change is made.[13]

Because of this requirement, the cumulative effect of the change on retained earnings at the beginning of the fiscal year was presented as a component of net income in the interim period in which the change was adopted. However, problems arose because reissued interim period balance sheets did not reflect the cumulative effect of the change on retained earnings, whereas reissued interim period income statements did reflect this effect.

Upon becoming aware of this inconsistency, the FASB reviewed the provisions of APB No. 28 and issued Statement of Financial Accounting Standards No. 3, "Reporting Accounting Changes in Interim Financial Statements."[14] The provisions of this statement were to apply separately to changes other than changes to the Lifo inventory pricing method and fourth quarter accounting changes made by publicly traded companies.

For all cumulative effect changes other than changes to Lifo, an accounting change made during the first interim period of the fiscal year should reflect the cumulative effect of the change on retained earnings in the net income of the first interim period. For changes in other than the first interim period, no cumulative effect of the change should be included in net income in the period of change. Rather, the new principle should be retroactively applied to all prior interim periods, and the cumulative effect of the change on retained earnings at the beginning of the year should be included in the net income for the first interim period. The statement also specifies certain disclosures as to the nature and

[13]Ibid., par. 27.
[14]Statement of Financial Accounting Standards No. 3. "Reporting Accounting Changes in Interim Financial Statements" (Stamford, Conn.: Financial Accounting Standards Board, 1974).

justification for the change and its effect on continuing operations, net income, and per share amounts.

Where changes to the Lifo method of inventory pricing have occurred, the cumulative effect of the change cannot ordinarily be calculated. Therefore, SFAS No. 3 requires a paragraph explaining the reasons for omitting accounting for a cumulative effect and disclosure of the pro forma amounts for prior years.

With respect to fourth quarter changes by publicly held companies, some of these organizations are required by the provisions of APB No. 28 to disclose certain fourth quarter information in footnotes. Information concerning the effects of an accounting change made during the fourth quarter was not explicitly identified as a part of this requirement. SFAS No. 3 amended APB No. 28 to require such disclosures.

SUMMARY

There has been a great deal of discussion among accountants about the proper concept of income to use and the need for comparability among entities because various financial-statement users have relied on the corporate net income figure. Since 1966 several pronouncements have had a major impact upon the preparation of the income statement. These pronouncements affect the presentation of income from normal operations and other sources, earnings per share computations, changes in methods of presenting information, disposal of parts of the entity, and interim financial reports. In each case the number of alternatives is narrowed in an attempt to improve comparability.

The extent to which these pronouncements have improved the understandability of corporate financial reports is not readily determinable. Only the most sophisticated users of financial statements are likely to be able to understand the differences between normal and abnormal events, the effects of accounting changes, or the relative merits of any number of earnings per share figures. Accounting is often criticized as being too simplistic in the establishment of its assumptions about the behavior of revenue and costs; however, attempting to provide comparability while still maintaining some degree of flexibility to accommodate the reporting needs of various entities may lead to more confusion.

In the following readings, Patricia Boyer and Charles Gibson examine the concept of earnings per share in more detail, D. Jacque Grinnell and Corine T. Norgaard suggest some new methods of reporting accounting changes, and Henry Jaenicke and Joseph Rascoff discuss the problems of overhead allocation and balance sheet presentation of assets for a disposal of a segment of a business.

HOW ABOUT EARNINGS PER SHARE?

PATRICIA A. BOYER, CPA, CMA
CHARLES H. GIBSON, CPA

Financial analysts and investors emphasize a particular type of income figure, earnings per share. Trend analysis of earnings on a per share basis is a frequently used measure of performance, which may form a basis for valuation of securities. This extensive utilization requires that the earnings per share data be meaningful and useful.

OBJECTIVE

The objective of this article is to study the usefulness of earnings per share data. This will be accomplished by reviewing the development of the current earnings per share computations, by examining the reporting of earnings per share data by the financial services, and by a survey of the comprehension of earnings per share by finance oriented users of accounting information.

DEVELOPMENT OF EARNINGS PER SHARE COMPUTATIONS

APB OPINION #9

APB Opinion #9 was issued in 1966. In this Opinion the Board strongly recommended that earnings per share be furnished in conjunction with the statement of income. While some companies complied with this request, others did not. If the computation posed difficulties, as often occurred, the figure could simply be omitted. Further, the Board recommended that two

presentations of earnings per share be given:

1. The amount of earnings applicable to each share of common stock or other residual security outstanding; and
2. If potential dilution is material, pro forma computations of earnings per share should be furnished, showing what the earnings would be if the conversions or contingent issuances took place.

Prior to this statement, earnings per share had been computed on the basis of outstanding common stock only, with no consideration for potential dilution and with no concern for common stock equivalents. However, the wording in APB Opinion #9 was vague and caused varying methods of application. "Residual securities" were defined as those deriving a major portion of their value from their conversion rights or common stock characteristics. These "residual securities," as distinguished from "senior securities" such as nonconvertible preferred stock, were to be considered as common stock in the calculation of earnings per share. For example, if a convertible bond selling at $1,000 was convertible into 20 shares of common, selling at $30, then it was considered to be a bond and was classified as a senior security. If the stock price rose to $60, and the bond price to $1,200, then it derived its value from the conversion feature and was to be considered a "residual security." The difficulty is that the classification of convertible securities could change with fluctuations in the stock market, leading to periodic revisions. Further, no designation was specified for stock warrants and options.

While APB Opinion #9 furnished guidelines so that some degree of consistency was obtained and assured that in many cases the data would be subject to examination by auditors, its imprecision posed problems in application. Further, during this period of merger activity a large number of "complex securities" were issued. These were exactly the kind of securities which caused difficulties in the interpretation of Opinion #9, and for these reasons, APB Opinion #15 was developed.

APB OPINION #15, PRESENTATION OF PRIMARY AND FULLY DILUTED EARNINGS

This pronouncement on earnings per share issued in 1969 distinguishes between primary and fully diluted earnings per share. Primary earnings per share is computed by dividing earnings after preferred dividends by the weighted average number of shares of common stock and common stock equivalents outstanding. Stock options and warrants are always treated as common stock equivalents. Convertible debt and convertible preferred stocks are determined to be common stock equivalents if, at time of issue, the cash yield was less than two-thirds of the prime interest rate. This determination is made at time of issue and does not change thereafter. If a security is considered a common stock equivalent, then any effects of dilution related to that security are included in the calculation of primary earnings per share. Fully diluted earnings per share represent the earnings that would occur if all potential dilution occurred; options and warrants are assumed to have been exercised and convertibles exchanged for common stock. A cor-

poration that has potential dilution of less than 3 percent of earnings per common share outstanding is considered to have a simple capital structure. In this case, the dual presentation is ignored and only a single earnings per share computation is presented. This earnings per share concept ignores all dilutive securities.

THE PROBLEMS OF APB OPINION #15

This Opinion took two years to develop and while it apparently solved some of the deficiencies of Opinion #9, it received considerable criticism, including three dissents and five assents with qualifications to the Opinion itself. The advantages and difficulties will be discussed in turn.

First, the Opinion required that earnings per share be shown on the face of the income statement. Next it established a uniform, consistent method of claculating earnings per share, primarily by a strict definition of common stock equivalents. Warrants and options are always considered common stock equivalents. The classification of a security as a common stock equivalent is established at the time of its issue, depending on the cash yield. Primary earnings per share take into account dilution from common stock equivalents; fully diluted earnings per share represents the results of maximum potential dilution. Uniform computations and reporting on the income statement are achieved.

A *Wall Street Journal* editorial[1] praised the Opinion which tightened the rules on reporting earnings per share. It expressed the opinion that the methods of business acquisitions involving warrants and other complex securities might become less widespread due to this reporting of poten-

[1]*Wall Street Journal*, May 19, 1969, p. 22.

tial dilution. As termed "funny money," these complex securities would no longer mislead the public.

The theoretical justification of APB Opinion #15 was not universally accepted and questions were raised concerning the ultimate usefulness of the data.

A number of arguments were raised by the Board members, including the following:

1. Common stock equivalents are based on assumptions that may change or may never occur.
2. The cash yield basis for determining equivalency was arbitrary and did not seriously consider the valuation method.
3. Options and warrants may not be exercised and the treasury stock method may be unrealistic.
4. The "if converted" approach to common stock equivalent convertibles is inappropriate in primary earnings per share.
5. Common stock equivalents, such as convertible bonds, should be so classified in the financial statements.

Coupled with these was the argument that the new figures might not be as useful as expected. *Financial Executive* published the results of a questionnaire sent to its members concerning the proposed opinion.[2]

This survey indicated that a large number of respondents, 74 percent, did not agree with the residual security (common stock equivalent) concept. Those who disagreed preferred a single earnings per share presentation based on actual common stock outstanding, supplemented by a pro forma figure based on full potential dilution assuming conversion of all outstanding convertible securities to be presented in a foot-

[2]*Financial Executive*, March 1969, p. 12.

note. Second choice was dual presentation, on the face of the statement, of these same two figures.

FINANCIAL SERVICES REPORTING OF EARNINGS PER SHARE

The financial services' reporting of earnings per share of Witco Chemical for 1975 was used to determine how the financial services report this information. Witco, a producer of chemical and petroleum products, had the following earnings in 1975: Primary—2.46, Fully Diluted—2.28.

In that year, the difference between primary and fully diluted earnings per share was 7.3 percent, certainly a material amount.

Exhibit 1 summarizes the findings of a survey to determine which earnings per share figures were being published by selected financial services.

Most commonly, primary earnings per share was the only number presented. If the fully diluted amount was shown, it was usually in footnote format. This indicates that primary earnings per share figures are the principal subject of financial service reporting.

EMPIRICAL SURVEY OF FINANCE-ORIENTED USERS

A mail survey was made of members of the Eastern Finance Association, whose membership is comprised of academicians and practitioners in finance and closely related fields such as economics and accounting. Its purpose was to determine if a group of professional users would exhibit a clear understanding of the computations and implications contained in Opinion #15. Further, its purpose was to determine whether these users were content with the current

		Earnings Per Share	
		Primary	Fully Diluted
Witco Chemical (1975)		$2.46	$2.28*
Financial Service			
Barron's		Yes	No
Business Week		Yes	No
Moody's Handbook	Graph	Yes	No
	Statistics	Yes	No
	Interim Earnings	Yes	No
Moody's Industrials		Yes	Yes(footnote)
Standard and Poor's			
Industry Surveys	Annual	Yes	No
	Interim	Yes	No
Standard and Poor's Stock			
Reports	Quarterly	Yes	No
	Statistics	Yes	Yes(footnote)
	Text	Yes	Yes
Value Line	Statistics	Yes	No
	Quarterly	Yes	No
Wall Street Journal		Yes	Yes

*Represents a dilution of 7.3 percent from primary earnings.

dual presentation of data or the format of presentation.

Nine hundred and ninety-eight (998) questionnaires were mailed. One hundred and fifty-five (155) or 15.5 percent were returned. One hundred and fifty-four or 15.4 percent were usable. Approximately, 80 percent of the respondents were academicians: the remainder were practitioners. These responses were considered sufficient to give meaningful results.

WHAT ARE EARNINGS PER SHARE?

The computations of earnings per share are sometimes difficult: the underlying theory is complex. Several questions were asked to determine whether these implications were understood by this group of users. Some of the types of questions follow.

CONVERTIBLES

Company A issued a material amount of convertible debentures with a stated interest rate of 5 percent at a time when the prime rate was 8 percent. If converted, there will be a dilutive effect on earnings. Which earnings per share figure(s) will reflect this potential dilution? (See Table 1.)

A convertible bond or preferred stock is considered a common stock equivalent if, at the time of issuance, the cash yield is less than two-thirds of the prime interest rate. If a convertible meets this test, then both the primary and fully diluted earnings per share are based on the assumption that conversion had occurred at the beginning of the year or date of issuance, whichever is later.

The correct answer to this question is "both." Only 33.1 percent of the re-

Table 1

	Number of Responses	%
Primary	15	9.7
Fully Diluted	74	48.1
Both	51	33.1
Neither	9	5.8
No response	5	3.2
	154	100.0

spondents had this correct answer. The largest number of respondents' conclusion was that only the fully diluted figure included the "if converted" assumption. Clearly, there is limited understanding of the common stock equivalency concept of convertibles, which influences primary earnings per share.

OPTIONS AND WARRANTS

Company *B* has outstanding a large number of stock options, which, if exercised, will have a dilutive effect on earnings. Which earnings per share figure(s) will reflect this potential dilution? (See Table 2.)

Options and warrants are regarded as common stock equivalents at all times. Primary and fully diluted earnings per share reflect the dilution that would result from the exercise of these securities and the use of the funds obtained. Therefore, the correct answer is "both." Only 30.5 percent of the respondents indicated the correct answer. Again, the most common answer was fully diluted, an indication that the common stock equivalency of options and warrants is not well understood.

Only 24.2 percent of the respondents had the correct response to both of these questions. There were no significant differences between academicians and practitioners as to the percentage responding correctly.

DILUTION IN PRIMARY EARNINGS PER SHARE

Another question was designed to determine the awareness of dilution in primary earnings per share.

Assuming that a firm has securities which offer potential dilution, is any potential dilution ever reflected in primary earnings per share? (See Table 3.)

These percentages indicate that a slight majority of the respondents realize there may be dilution in primary earnings per share. Given the large number of incorrect responses to the two principal types of dilutive securities that were questioned, it is clear that more respondents are aware that a potential dilution can exist in primary earnings per share than those who can correctly identify the proper use of dilutive securities in the computations.

Table 2

	Number of Responses	%
Primary	16	10.4
Fully Diluted	69	44.8
Both	47	30.5
Neither	19	12.3
No response	3	1.9
	154	100.0

Table 3

	Number of Responses	%
Yes	81	52.6
No	69	44.8
No Response	4	2.6
	154	100.0

PRESENTATION BY FINANCIAL SERVICES

The respondents were asked to describe their observation of how the financial services presented earnings per share. Over fifty-one percent (51.3 percent) felt that the figure primary supplemented by the fully diluted would be most common; over twenty-two percent (22.7 percent) felt that both would be presented. About twelve percent (12.3) indicated that primary would be presented alone, which is the most typical case.

FAVORED PRESENTATION

Three types of earnings per share computations were described for the respondents as shown in Table 4:

For each earnings per share figure, the respondents were asked to indicate whether they felt the presentation of that figure useful, and if so, whether the presentation should be on the face of the statement or in supplementary form.

The results in Exhibit 2 show that the

Table 4 Methods of Computing Earnings Per Share

Actual earnings per share is computed by dividing the actual earnings applicable to the common shares by the weighted average number of shares outstanding.

Primary earnings per share is computed by dividing the earnings applicable to the common shares by the weighted average number of shares of common stock and common stock equivalents (convertibles meeting a yield test plus warrants and stock options).

Fully diluted earnings per share gives the earnings that would occur if all potential dilution resulted.

---

fully diluted information is most strongly favored. However, both actual and primary appear to have strong support with actual having more support than primary. Based on the responses favoring each method, the presentation of actual earnings per share is most favored for the face of statement pre-

Exhibit 2

Type of Earnings Per Share	Should It be Presented			Method of Presentation		
Actual	Yes	119	77.3%	Face of Statement	103	88.6%
	No	31	20.1%	Supplementary	14	11.8%
	No Response	4	2.6%	No Response	2	1.7%
		154	100.0%		119	100.0%
Primary	Yes	111	72.1%	Face of Statement	83	74.8%
	No	39	25.3%	Supplementary	27	24.3%
	No Response	4	2.6%	No Response	1	9%
		154	100.0%		111	100.0%
Fully Diluted	Yes	131	85.1%	Face of Statement	85	64.9%
	No	19	12.3%	Supplementary	46	35.1%
	No Response	4	2.6%	No Response	0	0.0%
		154	100.0%		131	100.0%

CHAPTER 3: FINANCIAL STATEMENTS I: THE INCOME STATEMENT

Exhibit 3 Combinations of Earnings Per Share Data Deemed Useful

	Number of Responses	%
Actual only	3	1.9%
Primary only	4	2.6
Fully diluted only	2	1.3
Actual and primary	11	7.1
Actual and fully diluted	33	21.4
Primary and fully diluted	24	15.6
Actual, primary and fully diluted	72	46.8
None of these	1	.6
No response	4	2.6
	154	100.0%

sentation. However, there is a good majority favoring face of statement presentation for all three figures.

Responses concerning these earnings per share figures were then cross tabulated to determine the interrelationships between the responses. The results are shown in Exhibit 3.

There is a distinct preference for having all three earnings per share figures presented. The distant second choice is the combination of actual and fully diluted earnings

Table 5 Methods of Presenting Earnings Per Share

Face of Statement—	Earnings per share figure disclosed on the face of the income statment.
Supplementary as Footnote	Earnings per share figure disclosed in a footnote to the income statement.

per share. The requirements of APB Opinion #15 is third, with 15.6 percent of the respondents favoring this presentation. Clearly, a combination including actual earnings per share, eliminating the effects of common stock equivalents, is favored.

CONCLUSION

Current generally accepted accounting principles require that both primary and fully diluted earnings per share be shown on the face of the Income Statement. Both of these earning per share figures are considered necessary for adequate financial reporting.

The survey of financial services reporting of earnings per share indicates that, most commonly, primary earnings per share was the only number presented. If fully diluted earnings per share was shown, it was usually in footnote format.

This survey of users of earnings per share figures indicates there is considerable misunderstanding of the effects of common stock equivalents in primary earnings per share. Specifically, it is commonly assumed that dilution from convertibles, options and warrants is evident only in fully diluted earnings per share.

Given a choice of earnings per share computations, presentation of actual, primary and fully diluted earnings per share is clearly favored over the primary and fully diluted figures currently required. There is also a preference that earnings per share data be presented on the face of the income statement, which is currently the case.

Since only four respondents indicated that reporting primary earnings only would be most useful, it appears that the financial services could im-prove their services by reporting both primary and fully diluted earnings per share.

These conclusions indicate that finance oriented users find difficulty in interpreting the current earnings per share figures. Further, financial reporting only increases the magnitude of this problem. The Financial Accounting Standards Board should reevaluate the requirements of earnings per share accounting and reporting and the financial services should reevaluate their reporting of this information.

REPORTING CHANGES IN ACCOUNTING PRINCIPLES—TIME FOR A CHANGE?

D. JACQUE GRINNELL
CORINE T. NORGAARD

A change in an accounting principle used by a reporting entity may significantly affect financial statement measurements and other related accounting data. Proper interpretation of financial data may be difficult, and the comparability of such data diminished, without adequate accounting and disclosure of the effects of such a change. The objective of reporting the effects of a change in an accounting principle should be to enhance understanding and interpretation of the change.

The adequacy of the current system of reporting the effects of changes in accounting principles has been questioned by the accounting standards executive committee of the American Institute of CPAs. In a

letter to the Financial Accounting Standards Board, AcSEC called for a reconsideration of those provisions of Accounting Principles Board Opinion No. 20, *Accounting Changes*.[1] The purpose of this article is to analyze and evaluate the current reporting requirements for accounting principle changes in order to determine whether alternative practices should be adopted.

BACKGROUND

Current treatment of a change in accounting principle is governed by whether the

[1]Letter from Raymond C. Lauver, chairman, accounting standards executive committee, to Marshall S. Armstrong, chairman, Financial Accounting Standards Board, March 25, 1977.

change is voluntary (made at the discretion of management) or mandatory (necessitated by a pronouncement of an authoritative body). In the first case, the manner in which the change is reported is governed by APB Opinion No. 20.[2] In the second case, the appropriate treatment is prescribed by each specific pronouncement.

VOLUNTARY CHANGES

Opinion No. 20 requires that, in general, the change's cumulative effect on retained earnings for years prior to the year of change be computed and reported as part of the change year's income. Pro forma income calculations, together with related earnings per share data, must be disclosed for all periods presented as if the newly adopted accounting principle had been applied retroactively. Disclosure of the new principle's effect on the change year's income and earnings per share must also be made.

Opinion No. 20 cited three specific exceptions to the general cumulative effect treatment, and it requires, for these cases, retroactive application of the new principle through restatement of the financial statements of prior periods.[3] The APB justified these exceptions to the general cumulative effect treatment by stating that certain changes in accounting principles are such that the advantages of retroactive application outweigh the disadvantages. In these cases, the effect of the new principle on income and earnings per share of the change year and of all prior years for which income statements are presented must be disclosed.

In addition, Opinion No. 20 recognized that, in some cases, the cumulative effect may not be determinable, and it cited, as an example, the change in inventory costing from the Fifo to the Lifo method. The prescribed treatment of changes of this type is to disclose the effect of the change on income and earnings per share of the change year and to explain the reasons for omitting the cumulative income effect and pro forma income and per share data for prior years.

In still other cases, while the total cumulative effect on prior years' income is determinable, the identification of the effect with specific prior years may not be possible due to lack of adequate information. An example cited in Opinion No. 20 concerns changing from the completed contract to the percentage-of-completion method of accounting for long-term contracts. In such cases, the reasons for not showing pro forma information for prior years should be disclosed.

MANDATORY CHANGES

APB Opinions

The accounting and reporting requirements of Opinion No. 20 do not extend to certain accounting principle changes made to implement recommendations of specialized industry pronouncements of the AICPA or to mandatory accounting principle changes made to conform with APB opinions and FASB statements of financial accounting standards.

When APB Opinion No. 20 was issued in 1971, it permitted AICPA industry audit guides, which dealt with auditing pro-

[2]Accounting Principles Board Opinion no. 20. *Accounting Changes* (New York: AICPA, 1971).
[3]The three cases cited are (1) a change from Lifo to another inventory costing method, (2) a change in accounting for long term construction projects and (3) a change to or from the "full cost" method used by extractive industries. See APB Opinion no. 20, par. 27.
[4]Ibid., par. 4.

cedures and accounting practices for specialized industries, to prescribe methods of reporting the effects of changing to recommended principles applicable to these specialized industries.[4] Subsequently, the AICPA issued a new series of specialized industry accounting guides, with each guide specifying the manner of reporting the effects of accounting principle changes to conform with its recommendations. The industry accounting guide series has now been replaced by statements of position concerning specialized industry accounting practices. The FASB has issued Interpretation No. 20, *Reporting Accounting Changes Under AICPA Statements of Position,* which states

"For purposes of applying *APB Opinion No. 20,* an enterprise making a change in accounting principle to conform with the recommendations of an AICPA statement of position shall report the change as specified in the statement. If an AICPA statement of position does not specify the manner of reporting a change in accounting principle to conform with its recommendations, an enterprise making a change in accounting principles to conform with the recommendations of the statement shall report the change as specified by Opinion No. 20."[5]

The general policy of the APB was that its opinions, unless otherwise stated, were intended to be applied prospectively, not retroactively. This general policy did not necessarily rule out retroactive application at the election of the accounting entity. For example, Opinion No. 11, *Accounting for Income Taxes,* stated that "the Board recognizes that companies may apply this Opinion retroactively to periods prior to the

effective date to obtain comparability in financial presentations for the current and future periods."[6]

In other instances, the APB did rule out retroactive application by provision in the specific opinion. For example, Opinion No. 8, *Accounting for the Cost of Pension Plans,* stated that "the effect of any changes in accounting methods made as a result of the issuance of this Opinion should be applied prospectively . . . and not retroactively by an adjustment of retained earnings or otherwise."[7] Similar prohibitions of retroactive application are provided in several other opinions.

In still other cases, the APB prohibited the prospective approach by specifically calling for retroactive applications. Examples include APB Opinion No. 18, *The Equity Method of Accounting for Investments in Common Stock,* and two related opinions, Nos. 23 and 24, dealing with income tax considerations. In Opinion No. 23, as well as No. 24, the APB stated that "the conclusions of the Board . . . represent a clarification of current practice" and "accordingly, this Opinion should be applied retroactively. . . ."[8] In elaborating, the board stated further that "adjustment resulting from a change in accounting method to comply with this Opinion should be treated as an adjustment of prior periods, and financial statements presented for the periods affected should be restated."[9]

In short, all the APB opinions call for

---

[5]FASB Interpretation no. 20, *Reporting Accounting Changes Under AICPA Statements of Position* (Stamford, Conn.: FASB, 1977), par. 5.

[6]Accounting Principles Board Opinion no. 11, *Accounting for Income Taxes* (New York: AICPA, 1967), par. 67.

[7]Accounting Principles Board Opinion no. 8, *Accounting for the Cost of Pension Plans* (New York: AICPA, 1966), par. 49.

[8]Accounting Principles Board Opinion no. 23, *Accounting for Income Taxes—Special Areas* (New York: AICPA, 1972), par. 32.

[9]Ibid.

either prospective or retroactive application of the provisions, or permit either. In no case, either with respect to opinions issued prior or subsequent to Opinion No. 20, did the APB stipulate the use of the cumulative effect method for implementing a mandated accounting principle change.

FASB Statements

The method of transition to conform with new requirements is prescribed by each specific statement. The statements selected for comparison in this article are those which are concerned with financial statement measurement alternatives as opposed to mere disclosure of information or statement classification. In cases where changes in accounting measurement principles are mandated, three basic transition methods exist as potential choices for implementing the changes: retroactive application through prior period restatement; prospective application; and the cumulative effect method in accordance with APB Opinion No. 20. All three transition methods have been selected at various times, although retroactive application has been the dominant choice. Further, the choice of transition method has frequently been changed between exposure draft and final statement.

Only once, in the case of Statement No. 5, *Accounting for Contingencies,* was the cumulative effect method prescribed in a final statement as the basis for implementing a mandated accounting principle change. However, in Statement No. 11, *Accounting for Contingencies—Transition Method,* the FASB reversed its position and displaced the cumulative effect method by requiring a modified retroactive application approach for implementing Statement No. 5. The FASB stated that the decision to change the transition method was reached after a "reconsideration of all the circum-

stances."[10] However, the change was brought about primarily, it would appear, because of inconsistencies in the transition method originally required for Statement No. 5 versus that for Statement No. 8, *Accounting for the Translation of Foreign Currency Transactions and Foreign Currency Financial Statements.* Statements Nos. 8 and 11 recognized a hybrid approach that combines prior period restatement with the cumulative effect method. "Information presented shall be restated for as many consecutive periods . . . as is practicable, and the cumulative effect . . . on the retained earnings at the beginning of the earliest period restated . . . shall be included on determining net income of that period."[11]

A further modification of the hybrid approach taken in Statements Nos. 8 and 11 is associated with Statement No. 13, *Accounting for Leases.* In implementing the provisions of Statement No. 13, only prospective application is initially required. Retroactive application is required after 1980, although earlier adjustment is encouraged. After retroactive application is accomplished, post-1976 income statements and balance sheets as of year-end 1976 and thereafter must be restated when presented. Earlier financial statements, when presented, must also be retroactively adjusted to the extent practicable with the cumulative effect on retained earnings at the beginning of the earliest period restated included in the net income of that period.

In Statement No. 9, *Accounting for Income Taxes—Oil and Gas Producing Companies,* the FASB added an additional shade of gray to the accounting for its man-

[10]Statement of Financial Accounting Standards no. 11, *Accounting for Contingencies—Transition Method* (Stamford, Conn.: FASB, 1975), par. 6.
[11]Ibid., par. 10.

dated accounting principle changes by "permitting" as opposed to "requiring" retroactive application in certain specified situations. If the reporting entity does not choose to restate, it must prospectively apply the new provisions; the cumulative effect method is not permitted as an alternative to retroactive application.

JUSTIFICATION FOR TRANSITION METHODS ADOPTED

VOLUNTARY CHANGES

When it issued Opinion No. 20, the APB clearly was concerned with abuses developing from a switch in accounting principle when circumstances did not warrant such a switch. The APB stated

"The Board concludes that in the preparation of financial statements there is a presumption that an accounting principle once adopted should not be changed in accounting for events and transactions of a similar type. Consistent use of accounting principles from one accounting period to another enhances the utility of financial statements to users by facilitating analysis and understanding of comparative accounting data.[12]

"The presumption that an entity should not change an accounting principle may be overcome only if the enterprise justifies the use of an alternative acceptable accounting principle on the basis that it is preferable."[13]

Accordingly, Opinion No. 20 requires that the justification for a principle change be disclosed in the financial statements in terms of "why the newly adopted accounting principle is preferable."[14]

Since the cumulative effect method

highlights, as a special item in the income statement, the retroactive impact on income of an accounting principle change, it may be reasoned that the method was adopted as a punitive measure to inhibit arbitrary or inappropriate principle changes. In fact, three members of the APB dissented to the issuance of the opinion on the basis of their belief that this method was adopted as a disciplinary measure rather than as a way of enhancing the usefulness of financial statements.

MANDATORY CHANGES

While the expressed policy of the APB was that its opinions, unless otherwise stated, were intended to be applied prospectively and not retroactively, the board apparently was not disposed to provide reasons for adopting this policy. It might be presumed that fear of dilution of public confidence in previously reported financial statements was a prime factor militating against retroactive application. As noted earlier, there were some exceptions to this general approach, such as in the case of Opinion No. 11 where the board did permit retroactive application to obtain comparability in financial presentations.

Although no stated policy on transition methods has been adopted by the FASB, there appears to be a growing propensity to select the retroactive application approach unless special circumstances dictate otherwise. The selection of the retroactive application method has been made on the basis that it will provide the most useful information for comparing financial data for periods after the effective date of a particular statement with data presented for earlier periods. This presumption that retroactive restatement through prior period adjustment provides the most useful information is clearly acknowledged in several final statements (including Nos. 2, 7,

[12]APB Opinion no. 20, par. 15.
[13]Ibid., par. 16.
[14]Ibid., par. 17.

8, 11, 13 and 19). This view also was acknowledged as the basis for selecting the retroactive application method in the exposure drafts for Statements Nos. 5 and 12, although the choice of method was later altered in the final statements.

Departures from the retroactive application approach generally have been made on the basis of extenuating circumstances. In Statement No. 5, the cumulative effect method was selected, in part because there might be "significant difficulties involved in determining the degree of probability and estimability that had existed in prior periods."[15] The amendment of that statement by Statement No. 11, as noted earlier, was justified by the FASB on the basis of a "reconsideration of all circumstances," but primarily on the basis of inconsistencies with the treatment required by Statement No. 8. In Statement No. 8, the FASB required the use of retroactive application to the extent practicable since "restatement requires the availability of records or information that an enterprise may no longer have or that its past procedures did not require."[16]

Again in Statement No. 13, based on similar reasoning, retroactive application is required to the extent practicable, but is coupled with a four-year transition period before full implementation is necessitated. The purpose of this four-year grace period is to give companies time to resolve problems of data accumulation and issues relating to restrictive covenants in loan agreements.

In case of applying Statement No. 12, *Accounting for Certain Marketable Securities,* retroactive application was initially proposed in the exposure draft, but prospective application was ultimately selected in the final statement. The prospective approach was justified as follows:

"The Board has obtained information . . . that a number of companies have in past years made substantial reclassifications of marketable equity securities as between current and noncurrent assets. With the Board's decision to provide for separate portfolios of current and noncurrent marketable equity securities with different accounting for changes in carrying value of the two portfolios, the number of and seemingly divergent bases for reclassifications that have occurred in recent years would, in the case of retroactive restatement, result in less rather than more comparability."[17]

The FASB also required prospective application of Statement no. 15, *Accounting by Debtors and Creditors for Troubled Debt Restructurings,* on the basis that comparability would not be greatly enhanced by prior period restatement and of the difficulty in generating the information required for restatement.

In summary, a marked contrast in transition methods for implementing voluntary and mandatory accounting principle changes is apparent. While the cumulative effect method serves as the general approach for implementing voluntary changes, this method has not been considered appropriate for implementing mandatory changes. Failure to adopt the cumulative effect method for implementing

[15]Statement of Financial Accounting Standards no. 5, *Accounting for Contingencies* (Stamford, Conn.: FASB, 1975), par. 104.

[16]Statement of Financial Accounting Standards no. 8, *Accounting for the Translation of Foreign Currency Transactions and Foreign Currency Financial Statements* (Stamford, Conn.: FASB, 1975), par. 241.

[17]Statement of Financial Accounting Standards no. 12, *Accounting for Certain Marketable Securities* (Stamford, Conn.: FASB, 1975), par. 41.

mandatory changes adds additional credibility to the view that the method was intended as a punitively oriented way of treating voluntary accounting principle changes.

Further, a marked difference in attitude toward implementing mandatory changes exists between the APB and the FASB. The general approach of the APB was one of prospective application whereas the FASB tends to prefer the use of the retroactive approach to the extent practicable.

MANDATORY VERSUS VOLUNTARY ACCOUNTING CHANGES

In determining if it is appropriate to change the existing system for implementing accounting changes, a basic question that must be answered is that of whether we should distinguish between voluntary changes and mandatory changes. The AICPA accounting standards executive committee has pointed out three factors in support of more congruence in implementing voluntary and mandatory accounting principle changes: the financial accounting and reporting environment has changed substantially since the issuance of Opinion No. 20; inconsistencies result under the current system; and management may be reluctant to voluntarily adopt different accounting principles considered by it to be preferable.[18]

There can be little doubt as to the validity of the first factor. Since Opinion No. 20 was issued, the range of acceptable accounting and reporting alternatives has significantly narrowed and continues to diminish through the issuance of pronouncements by authoritative bodies. For example, the range of permitted practices

has been reduced in the important and controversial areas of research and development costs, leases and investments.

Further, another inhibitor to inappropriate changes in accounting principles has been established by the Securities and Exchange Commission. Accounting Series Release no. 177, *Notice of Adoption of Amendments to Form 10-Q and Regulation S-X Regarding Interim Financial Reporting,* requires the independent accountant to state whether or not a voluntary principle change by a client in certain SEC filings is to an alternative which in the accountant's judgment is preferable under the circumstances.[19] The SEC holds that the justification of a voluntary principle change by management is inadequate unless it is sufficient to persuade an independent accountant that the new principle results in better measurement of business operations in the particular circumstances.[20] In addition, SEC requirements concerning the reporting of client disagreements with auditors when there is a change in auditors may help to curb abuses brought about by undesirable principle changes.[21]

[18]Letter from AcSEC to FASB.

[19]Securities and Exchange Commission, Accounting Series Release no. 177, *Notice of Adoption of Amendments to form 10-Q and Regulation S-X Regarding Interim Financial Reporting,* September 10, 1975; also see Securities and Exchange Commission, Staff Accounting Bulletin no. 6, *Interpretations of ASR No. 177, Relating to Interim Financial Reporting,* March 1, 1976, and Staff Accounting Bulletin no. 14, *Amended Interpretations Relating to Reporting Requirements for Accounting Changes,* February 3, 1977.

[20]For an excellent discussion of the preferability issue see Lawrence Revsine, "The Preferability Dilemma," JofA, Sept. 77, pp. 80–89.

[21]Securities and Exchange Commission, Accounting Series Release no. 165, *Notice of Amendments to Require Increased Disclosure of Relationships Between Registrants and Their Independent Public Accountants,* December 20, 1974.

The contention that inconsistencies arise because of current reporting requirements also is legitimate. For example, if a company adopts a change voluntarily, it may have to account for the results of the change using the cumulative effect method. On the other hand, if another company made the same change, but did so at a later date as the result of an FASB statement, the change would undoubtedly be accounted for in a manner other than that based on the cumulative effect method. Under these circumstances, it appears logical that the manner of implementing accounting principle changes should provide the same result irrespective of whether such changes are voluntary or imposed through an authoritative pronouncement.

A third argument concerns the behavioral effect of the cumulative effect method on management decisions. A company that is considering the voluntary adoption of a different accounting principle could well be penalized by having to absorb a lump-sum charge to income in the year of change. As a result, management may be reluctant to adopt a new principle which it genuinely considers to be preferable. Conversely, management might be motivated to adopt a less desirable accounting principle, if such adoption was to result in a lump-sum credit to income in the year of change.

In summary, one can hardly take issue with the position that voluntary accounting principle changes which endanger the credibility of financial accounting and reporting and facilitate manipulation should be discouraged. However, the objective of restraining inappropriate accounting principle changes should not be accomplished through the imposition of transition rules which seemingly are intended as disciplinary measures, but which may well have a dysfunctional effect. Accounting rules for implementing accounting principle changes should serve to improve, rather than impair, the quality of financial measurements. The professional judgment and expertise of the independent auditor must be relied on as the basis for monitoring the validity of accounting principle changes. Since the issuance of APB Opinion No. 20, the range of available accounting principle alternatives has been reduced and new safeguards have been built into the system to restrain the adoption of inappropriate accounting principle changes. Consequently, little support can be found for the view that voluntary and mandatory accounting principle changes should be accounted for differently.

ESTABLISHING TRANSITION METHOD GUIDELINES

Questions of merit aside, APB Opinion No. 20 does provide a general frame of reference for implementing voluntary accounting principle changes. No similar basic framework exists for implementing mandatory accounting principle changes; rather, transition approaches are established on a case-by-case basis without reference to an established policy. To provide more consistency between voluntary and mandatory changes, and to ensure consistency within the context of mandatory changes, the need exists for replacing that portion of APB Opinion No. 20 concerning accounting principle changes with new guidelines for implementing all accounting principle changes.

CUMULATIVE EFFECT AND PROSPECTIVE APPLICATION METHODS

In developing policy guidelines for implementing accounting principle changes, a preference for one of the three basic transition methods must be established. The cumulative effect method has little theoretical support as a general implementation approach. The primary deficiency of the cumulative effect method concerns its failure to maintain comparability of financial measurements over time. This lack of comparability is particularly acute over the three-year period spanning the change year. Income for the year preceding the change year would be based on the old principle: income for the change year would be based on the new principle and also would include the cumulative effect of the change; and income for the year subsequent to the change year would be based on the new principle.

A related criticism of the method concerns that of distortion of the results of current year's operations through inclusion in the change year's income, as a current period item, of the "catch-up" adjustment which is applicable to prior years. The distortion of the change year's income could be avoided, and comparability of income of the change year with that of subsequent years obtained, by including the cumulative effect as an adjustment to the beginning balance of retained earnings for the change year. However, noncomparability with income of years prior to the change year would remain.

Although prospective application avoids the problems of determining and reporting a cumulative effect adjustment, it also is subject to criticism on the basis of noncomparability of results of the change year and subsequent years with those of the years preceding the change year. In addition, the measurement of operating results for the change year, and for a number of years following, are based on a combined use of the old and new principles.

RETROACTIVE APPLICATION

While practical problems of estimating and reconstructing past data may exist, the retroactive approach to implementation of accounting principle changes has a conceptual advantage over the other approaches. The retroactive application method is the only approach which provides complete comparability of financial statements generated over time by a company. The FASB has frequently stressed the benefits of retroactive application in terms of providing more meaningful and comparable financial statements. The APB also acknowledged the merits of retroactive application. It stated in APB Opinion No. 9

"A change in the application of accounting principles may create a situation in which retroactive application is appropriate. In such situations, these changes should receive the same treatment as that for prior period adjustments."[22]

While recognizing a difference between accounting principle changes and prior period adjustments, the APB also acknowledged that the same accounting treatment was applicable to both, namely, retroactive application. Subsequently, this Opinion No. 9 position was altered by Opinion No. 20 with the following comment:

"Paragraph 25 of APB Opinion No. 9 is superseded. Although the conclusion of the paragraph is not modified, this Opinion deals more completely with accounting changes."[23]

It is also interesting to note that the APB in the original exposure draft of Opinion No. 20 stated

"The Board concludes that where changes in accounting methods are appropriate, consistency of treatment is overriding and that accounting changes, except in

[22]Accounting Principles Board Opinion no. 9, *Reporting the Results of Operations* (New York: AICPA, 1968), par. 25.
[23]APB Opinion no. 20, par. 5.

the instances explained hereinafter, should be computed and applied retroactively by restating financial statements presented for any period affected by the change."[24]

This position was subsequently changed in a second exposure draft leading to the final opinion.

A major criticism of the retroactive application approach is that it might lead to erosion of public confidence in the independent auditor who reported on the original statements and in financial reporting in general. Conversely, one may argue that, without retroactive application, financial presentations lead to investor confusion and make comparisons difficult or impossible. This, in turn, might lead to greater dilution of public confidence.

While past decisions by users of financial statements were made on the basis of the old numbers which the auditors approved, this does not justify prohibiting retroactive restatement for changes to preferable accounting principles. Financial statements should be viewed as tentative and subject to revision if judgments and subjective assessments are subsequently altered in light of further information and the development of improved accounting methods. Although not directly related to accounting principle changes, there is a precedent for revision in another area of accounting, namely, the audit function. Because of new information or changed circumstances, the auditor, in updating his report on previously issued financial statements, may express an opinion different from that expressed in an earlier report.[25]

Past decisions by users of financial statements cannot be altered. It is current and future decisions which are relevant. These new decisions should be based on the best possible information available which includes measurements based on the application of different, if preferable, accounting principles. Ideally, for current decision-making purposes, comparative financial statements should be presented on a consistent basis using that set of accounting principles considered to be the best under the existing circumstances. Of course, a full and complete disclosure of the impact of a principle change on the current and previously issued financial statements is appropriate. If firms and their auditors, relative to voluntary changes, and the FASB and other authoritative bodies, relative to mandatory changes, genuinely believe that a different principle improves the quality of financial measurements, then it should, in most cases, improve the measurement of past as well as current and future results.

In the final analysis, the comparability of financial data which results through retroactive application and restatement is a compelling argument in support of this transition method for implementing accounting principle changes. Having a set of internally consistent statements and related statistics based on a common set of accounting principles is a strong reason for the adoption of this method as the general mode for implementing accounting principle changes.

While the authors believe that retroactive application represents the best ap-

[24]Accounting Principles Board Exposure Draft, *Proposed APB Opinion: Changes in Accounting Methods and Estimates* (New York: AICPA, February 16, 1970), par. 11.
[25]Statement on Auditing Standards no. 15, *Reports on Comparative Financial Statements*

(New York: AICPA, 1976), par. 6–7. Also found in *AICPA Professional Standards,* "Report With an Updated Opinion Different From a Previous Opinion" (Chicago, Ill.: Commerce Clearing House, 1977), AC sec. 505.06.07.

proach for implementing accounting principle changes under normal circumstances, it is not practicable to prescribe a single approach for implementing all changes. However, exceptions to retroactive application should be made only when special circumstances exist to justify modification or which preclude its use. For example, the lack of information relating to prior periods or other problems of data accumulation may preclude strict retroactive application: in such cases, a modified or hybrid approach might be in order, possibly along the lines taken in Statements Nos. 8 and 11, or No. 13. In other rare situations, determining the impact of a principle change on prior years' statements may require arbitrary assumptions, for example, when adopting the Lifo method of inventory costing; prospective application would appear necessary under these circumstances.

Although this discussion has been concerned exclusively with accounting principle changes which influence financial statement measurements, many pronouncements of authoritative bodies deal with information disclosure and statement classification. In these situations, implementation by retroactive application might also serve as the ideal norm, with limited retroactive application or prospective application or prospective application justified in particular circumstances.

SUMMARY AND CONCLUSIONS

There appears to be little theoretical justification for maintaining the existing framework for implementing voluntary accounting principle changes in a manner different from those which are mandated by authoritative bodies. From a practical viewpoint, the continuing development of new standards by authoritative bodies which tend to reduce the range of acceptable accounting alternatives, and the development of new safeguards by the SEC, serve to restrain alleged abuses stemming from inappropriate accounting principle changes.

The need exists to develop new guidelines for implementing voluntary and mandatory accounting principle changes in a consistent and logical manner. Based on the importance and utility of statement comparability and trend analysis, the retroactive application and restatement approach should serve as the general means of implementing principle changes, with special circumstances dictating departures from this norm.

SEGMENT DISPOSITION: IMPLEMENTING APB OPINION NO. 30

HENRY R. JAENICKE
JOSEPH RASCOFF

Since the publication of APB Opinion No. 9, "Reporting the Results of Operations," in 1966, the accounting literature has been replete with critiques both of the Opinion itself and the manner in which the Opinion has been interpreted and applied. That Opinion specified the criteria to be used in determining which items recognized during the current period were to be considered extraordinary items. In Opinion No. 30, also entitled "Reporting the Results of Operations," issued in 1973, the Accounting Principles Board acknowledged that there had been difficulty in interpreting the criteria for extraordinary items and that significant differences of opinion existed as to certain parts of Opinion No. 9.

While accountants may suggest many ways in which Opinion No. 9 raised the level of income reporting, critics of the earlier Opinion most often cited abuses in accounting for events and transactions which in Opinion No. 30 are referred to as disposals of a segment of a business. This is also the principal concern of this article. Disposals of segments of businesses will continue to be the subject of frequent management decisions, and the new Opinion provides accounting guides for some, but not all, of the transactions inherent in those decisions.

ACCOUNTING FOR SEGMENT DISPOSITIONS

In Opinion No. 30, the Board has identified four income figures, namely, income from continuing operations, income before extraordinary items and before the cumulative effect of changes in accounting principles, and net income.[1] These four income concepts are necessary because the Board concluded "that the results of con-

tinuing operations should be reported separately from discontinued operations and that any gain or loss from disposal of a segment of a business should be reported in conjunction with the related results of discontinued operations and not as an extraordinary item." The segregation of extraordinary items as prescribed in Opinion No. 9 is continued in the new Opinion.[2]

The term "discontinued operations" refers to the operations of a segment of a business that has been or will be disposed of or otherwise eliminated. The Board has attempted to remove much uncertainty from the application of the Opinion by listing the characteristics of a segment of a business, by setting strict rules for the calculation of gain or loss from disposal of a segment of a business, by defining the measurement date for determining the gain or loss and by authorizing an accounting interpretation amplifying those guidelines. However, the Opinion does not cover certain other problem areas related to accounting for and reporting of a disposal of a segment of a business. Several of these issues will be discussed below.

The Opinion defines a segment of a business as "a component of an entity whose activities represent a separate major line of business or class of customer. A segment may be in the form of a subsidiary, a division or a department, and in some cases a joint venture or other nonsubsidiary investee, provided that its assets, results of operations and activities can be clearly distinguished, physically and oper-

[1]A note to the Opinion, keyed to the captions "income from continuing operations before income taxes" and "income from continuing operations," states that "these captions should be modified appropriately when an entity reports an extraordinary item or the cumulative effect of a change in accounting principle."

[2]A significant, though perhaps inadvertent, blessing resulting from Opinion No. 30 is that there now exists a caption to describe that thing that was never described in Opinion No. 9, income from continuing operations. After Opinion No. 9, one often felt that it was a major endeavor to describe an item of "ordinary" revenue or expense since that Opinion never used the title "income from ordinary operations."

ationally and for financial reporting purposes, from the other assets, results of operations, and activities of the entity." Paragraph 13 of the Opinion explains the characteristics that distinguish a segment of a business and (as has been suggested above) an accounting interpretation further refines the concept.

The Opinion distinguishes the measurement date of a disposal of a segment from the actual disposal date. The measurement date is the date on which management "commits itself to a formal plan to dispose of a segment of the business, whether by sale or abandonment." The disposal date "is the date of closing the sale if the disposal is by sale or the date that operations cease if the disposal is by abandonment." The distinction between the two dates is a significant one, for an anticipated loss from the disposal should be recognized at the measurement date, but an anticipated gain should be recognized only when realized, which is ordinarily the disposal date.

The gain or loss on disposition includes three items: (1) the difference between the book value and realizable value of the segment, (2) estimated costs directly associated with the disposal and (3) estimated income or loss from operations during a period, not to exceed one year, from the measurement date to the disposal date. Several problems may be faced when computing the gain or loss on disposal. One of these relates to the proscription in the Opinion against including in the gain or loss from disposal any "adjustments, costs, and expenses associated with normal business activities that should have been recognized on a going-concern basis up to the measurement date." Examples of such adjustments include writedown of receivables, inventory and deferred research and development costs. While these adjustments must be included in income from continuing operations, the Opinion does not specify whether the amounts should be shown as a single figure or as part of cost of sales, bad debts expense, etc. The authors believe that writedowns on a going-concern basis should not be shown as a single figure because that treatment would not ordinarily be appropriate in the absence of a disposal of a segment of the business.

In addition to amounts disclosed in the statement of income, there are additional disclosure requirements relating to a disposal of a segment of a business. These call for disclosure of the identity of the segment of the business that has been or will be discontinued, the expected disposal date if known, the expected manner of disposition and a description of the remaining assets and liabilities of the segment at the balance sheet date. With regard to the income statement, further disclosure is required of the income or loss from operations and any proceeds from disposition of the segment during the period from the measurement date to the date of the balance sheet. Disclosure of carrying values of the net assets of the discontinued segment is suggested but is not required. A later section of this article covers the alternatives regarding disclosure in the balance sheet.

UNRESOLVED ISSUES

ALLOCATION OF CORPORATE OVERHEAD

A major problem of implementation is that of determining the amount of general corporate overhead to be allocated to the segment of a business which is being disposed of. That allocation will affect the following income statement items in the period of recognition of a gain or loss on a disposal of a segment of a business: (a) income from continuing operations, (b) income from operations of the discontinued segment and (c) the provision for operating losses or gains during the phase-out period that is part of the calculation of the gain or loss on disposal.

The Opinion does not provide guidance as to either the method of overhead allocation to determine income from continuing operations *or* the interpretation which the reader of the financial statements should give to that figure. These two ideas are clearly related.

The issue is essentially whether a portion of the general corporate overhead should be allocated to the discontinued segment. The authors believe that only those costs that will *not* continue upon disposition should be assigned to the discontinued segment. The figure for income from continuing operations should not be thought of as a predictor of the level of income in a future period when the disposition is complete and the proceeds from the disposition of the segment may have been reinvested.

Accounting is essentially a historical process. It presents "what was," not "what might have been" or "what will be." As such, there should be as few assumptions as possible regarding future events. The figure for income from continuing operations should reveal what the income was, exclusive of the discontinued segment, not what income would have been had some future event occurred (such as the reinvestment of the proceeds from the disposition).

It could be argued that in instances where the income statement is detailed by line of business, an allocation of general corporate overhead should be made to the discontinued segment. In this way, it is argued, intertemporal comparisons of the contribution to net income of the separate continuing segments could be made both before and after a particular segment has been discontinued or a new segment added. However, the accounting profession has not been able to resolve the issue of expense allocation where data are presented by line of business, and segmented income statements usually are not presented beyond some level of segment contribution to overhead and profit. Unless a particular company presents line-of-business data for the entire income statement, down to the final net income figure, the argument for allocation of general corporate overhead *away* from the continuing operations and *to* the discontinued segment does not appear valid. If the company either does not present any line-of-business disclosure of revenue and expense, or presents such disclosures only as far as some intermediate income figure, then the company will not have allocated corporate overhead in the *absence* of the disposal of a segment of the business and should not do so in the *presence* of the disposal of a segment.[3]

BALANCE SHEET

Opinion No. 30, as noted earlier, gives some guidance to the income statement presentation of a segment disposition. Little guidance, however, is offered with respect to balance sheet treatment. Let us assume that a company anticipates a loss from the proposed sale of a segment and accordingly recognizes the estimated loss in the income statement at the measurement date. Where does the offsetting credit

[3]Closely related to the problem of determining a proper basis for the allocation of corporate overhead is the problem of determining appropriate pricing policies for intersegment raw material or product transfers. Different transfer pricing policies between segments will result in different amount of income for each segment. This, too, is an unresolved issue with regard to segment reporting generally.

Exhibit 1

A Company Balance Sheet
December 31, 197X

Cash		$100	Accounts payable		$150
Accounts receivable		200	Accrued expenses		50
		200	Total current liabilities		200
Total current assets		500	Long-term debt		300
Fixed assets	$400		Stockholder's equity		
Less accumulated			Capital stock	$100	
depreciation	(150)	250	Retained earnings	150	250
		$750			$750

appear? Also, how should the net assets to be sold be disclosed?

There appear to be at least four basic alternatives for balance sheet treatment if a loss on disposition is recognized[4]:

1. Establish a deferred credit for the total estimated loss on disposition of the segment (including costs and expenses directly associated with the decision to dispose, such as severance pay, employee relocation expenses, etc.).

2. Establish a deferred credit for the estimated loss on disposition of the net assets to be sold with the portion of the loss representing costs and expenses of disposal shown as an accrued liability.

3. Establish allowances for anticipated losses which offset each appropriate balance sheet asset caption. In addition, show the portion of the loss representing costs and expenses of disposal as a current liability.

4. Segregate in the balance sheet the net assets and liabilities (current and noncurrent) to be sold and establish a deferred credit for the anticipated loss on

[4]There were, to be sure, certain other alternative balance sheet treatments. However, the authors believe that careful analysis of such treatments will show that they are variations of the four basic alternatives cited herein.

disposition of such net assets. In addition, show the portion of the loss representing costs and expenses of disposal as a current liability.[5]

Exhibit 1 illustrates the four alternatives described. Assume a simplified balance sheet.

On December 31, 197X, management is committed to selling a segment of the busi-

[5]A question arises as to the balance sheet location of the deferred credit suggested by Alternatives 1, 2 and 4. Certainly the anticipated cost directly associated with the decision to dispose is a current liability. Also, it can be argued that the excess of book value of assets expected to be sold over their anticipated realizable value that relates to current assets should be reported as a current liability. (The reasoning here is similar to that employed in APB Opinion No. 11, "Accounting for Income Taxes," with regard to the balance sheet treatment of the deferred tax account.) Therefore, an appropriate modification of Alternatives 1, 2 and 4 would be to divide the deferred credit as to its current and noncurrent portions. The authors believe, however, that showing the account as an unallocated, noncurrent, deferred credit is also acceptable, primarily as a result of the precedent established by the reporting of other deferred credits which may include a portion either related to current assets or subject to realization within a year. Included in this category, for example, would be the excess of net assets acquired in a purchase transaction (which has not been allocated to noncurrent assets) over their cost.

Exhibit 2

	Book Value	Anticipated Loss	Anticipated Realizable Value
Accounts receivable	$ 25	$ 5	$ 20
Inventories	75	15	60
Fixed assets	$100		
Less accumulated depreciation	(30) 70	10	60
	$170	30	$140
Estimated expenses and costs directly related to disposal		5	
		$35	

ness. The plan of disposition is shown in Exhibit 2.

Under the four alternative presentations cited, the balance sheets, after giving effect at the measurement date to the loss on disposition, would appear as shown in Exhibits 3–6.

EVALUATION OF THE ALTERNATIVES

Paragraph 18(d) of Opinion No. 30 calls for disclosure in notes to the financial statements of "a *description* of the remaining assets and liabilities of the segment at the balance sheet date" (emphasis supplied). Compliance with this requirement does not appear to necessitate disclosure of the *amounts*—either at book value or realizable value of the net assets to be sold. If such amounts are disclosed together with the anticipated loss on disposition, strategic information regarding the company's bargaining position with respect to the sale might be revealed.

A footnote to paragraph 18(d) notes that "consideration should be given to disclosing this information by segregation *in the balance sheet* of the net assets and liabilities (current and noncurrent) of the discontinued segment" (emphasis supplied). However, such disclosure might "tip the hand" of the company's bargaining position, since disclosing both the book value

Exhibit 3. Alternative 1: Deferred Credit for Total Loss

A Company Balance Sheet 1
December 31, 197X

Cash		$100	Accounts payable		$150
Accounts receivable		200	Accrued expenses		50
Inventories		200	Total current liabilities		200
Total current assets		500	Long-term debt		300
Fixed assets	$400		Estimated loss on antici-		
Less accumulated			pated sale of segment		35
depreciation	(150)	250	Stockholders' equity:		
			Capital stock	$100	
			Retained earnings	115	215
		$750			$750

Exhibit 4. Alternative 2: Deferred Credit for Loss on Net Assets Only

A Company Balance Sheet 2
December 31, 197X

Cash		$100	Accounts payable		$150
Accounts receivable		200	Accrued expenses, including		
Inventories		200	estimated costs of disposing		
Total current assets		500	of segment		55
Fixed assets	$400		Total current liabilities		205
Less accumulated			Long term-debt		300
depreciation	(150)	250	Excess of book value of assets		
			expected to be sold over		
			anticipated realizable value		30
			Stockholders equity:		
			Capital stock	$100	
			Retained earnings	115	215
		$750			$750

of the assets to be sold (either on the face of the balance sheet or by footnote) and the anticipated loss on disposition of these assets is tantamount to disclosing the anticipated proceeds. Since such disclosures are likely to be inimical to the interests of the company and its shareholders in achieving the best possible sale price, the authors believe that disclosure of these amounts will rarely be made. Accordingly, Alternative 4, which incorporates the disclosures suggested in the Opinion, will probably not be followed in practice. This is not to say, however, that this approach is without mer-

Exhibit 5. Alternative 3: Allowance Method

A Company Balance Sheet 3
December 31, 197X

Cash		$100	Accounts payable		$150
Accounts receivable	200		Accrued expenses, including		
Less allowance for			estimated cost of		
anticipated loss on			disposing of segment		55
sale	(5)	195	Total current liabilites		205
Inventories	200		Long-term debt		
Less allowance for			Stockholders' equity:		
anticipated loss on			Capital stock	$100	
sale	(15)	185	Retained earnings	115	215
Total current assets		480			$720
Fixed assets	400				
Less accumulated					
depreciation	$150				
Allowance for					
anticipated loss on					
sales	10 (160)	240			
		$720			

Exhibit 6. Alternative 4: Segregation of Net Assets

A Company Balance Sheet 4
December 31, 197X

Cash	$100	Accounts payable	$150
Accounts receivable	175	Accrued expenses, including	
Inventories	125	estimated costs of	
Book value of current assets		disposing of segment	55
expected to be sold	100	Total current liabilities	205
Total current assets	500	Long-term debt	300
Fixed assets	$300	Excess of book value of as-	
Less accumulated depreciation (120)	180	sets expected to be sold	
Book value of fixed assets		over anticipated realizable	
expected to be sold	70	value	30
		Stockholders' equity:	
		Capital stock $100	
		Retained earnings 115	215
	$750		$750

---

it. Alternative 4 alone enables the preparation by analysts of a pro forma balance sheet after disposition of the segment and also permits the calculation of meaningful data on return on investment from continuing operations. Therefore, in those cases where "tipping the hand" is of no consequence, such as when agreement with a buyer of the segment has been reached, Alternative 4, although cumbersome, might well be preferable. It should be noted that disclosure by footnote rather than in the balance sheet would also meet the spirit of this suggested solution and might well be less cumbersome.

In comparison, Alternative 1 is extremely easy to apply. Although simple, however, the disclosure is hardly full and adequate. The reader of the financial statements is not told (a) the book value by category of the assets being disposed of or (b) how much of the loss on the anticipated sale of the segment represents expected costs of disposal as opposed to the difference between realizable value and book value of assets to be sold. That information is important for meaningful analysis. Ac-

cordingly, the authors believe that although Alternative 1, coupled with the appropriately descriptive footnote disclosure as prescribed by paragraph 18(d), satisfies the minimum literal requirements of Opinion No. 30, the standard of informative disclosure calls for a more expansive balance sheet treatment. Showing the estimated loss as an unallocated deferred credit in the balance sheet gives the reader merely the same information that is available from an examination of the income statement—namely, the amount of the loss itself.

Alternative 2 has not much more to commend it. To its credit, it does provide for an estimate of the nonrecurring costs of disposal to be shown separately from the anticipated loss on the sale of the assets and liabilities of the segment. In addition, it in no way reveals the book values of the assets to be disposed of, and hence cannot be deleterious to the company's bargaining position. However, Alternative 2 does not provide for segregation of the anticipated loss by category of asset and/liability. Thus, while the reader can expect that the company will lose $30 on the sale of the segment's net assets, he needs to know for analytical purposes the type of net assets, by balance sheet category, that will be disposed of and therefore excluded from assets used in the continuing operations. To the extent that the balance sheet is a useful tool for financial analysis, these disclosures are important to the user of that statement. These additional disclosures lead to Alternative 3.

Alternative 3 provides the reader with informative data with which an intelligent investment decision can be made and, at the same time, does not compromise the company's bargaining position in seeking the most advantageous sales price for the discontinued segment. Thus, the reader is given the following information:

1. A description of the assets and liabilities of the segment to be sold.
2. An estimate of the nonrecurring costs associated with the sale of the segment such as severance pay, pension adjustments, relocation costs, etc.
3. An estimate of the amount by which the anticipated sales price exceeds the book value of the respective assets and liabilities to be sold.

It is to be noted that in Alternative 3 the reader is not given the book value of the assets of the discontinued segment, as he is in Alternative 4. There is no doubt that this disclosure is more informative than is the mere assignment of the losses to specific balance sheet captions, as proposed in Alternative 3. But, as was suggested earlier, the cost of disclosing the additional data called for by Alternative 4 may be too great in terms of hindering the seller from attaining the best price for the segment. Thus, Alternative 3 is probably the most informative balance sheet treatment that can ordinarily be expected.

It should be further noted that in Alternative 3, a portion ($20) of the allowance for anticipated losses on the sale of the segment's assets appears contra to the current asset section of the balance sheet. In Alternatives 1, 2 and 4, the same amount appears as an unallocated deferred credit. The treatment in Alternative 3 recognizes the nature of the assets to be sold; certain of these assets are current, whereas others are not. Thus, Alternative 3 affords the further advantage of ascribing the estimated loss on disposition to the nature of the asset to be sold. A further advantage of this approach is that it, and it alone, recognizes that conceptually the excess of book value over selling price of the segment to be disposed of is not a liability at all, but rather a reduction in the carrying value of the particular assets. It is the only method which includes the assets of the discontinued segment in the balance sheet at not more than their net realizable value. As a result, the accountant is removed from the position of creating another questionable category of deferred credits whose existence on a statement of assets and equities has long been a source of discontent to accounting theorists.

CONCLUSION

There is little doubt that the determination of whether a particular event or transaction is ordinary, extraordinary or a disposal of a segment will be the major source of problems in implementing the Opinion. However, the authors believe that some of the issues in accounting for the disposal of a segment of a business, such as the allocation of corporate overhead and balance sheet presentation, are matters which must be definitively resolved. The authors hope that their views on these two particular matters will be helpful to accountants and therefore will aid the profession in achieving uniform reporting practices for these issues.

QUESTIONS

1. An example of the correction of an error in previously issued financial statements is a change
   a. From the completed-contract to the percentage-of-completion method of accounting for long-term construction-type contracts *GAAP*
   b. In the depletion rate, based on new engineering studies of recoverable mineral resources
   c. From the sum-of-years-digits to the straight-line method of depreciation for all plant assets
   d. From the installment basis of recording sales to the accrual basis, when collection of the sales price has been and continues to be reasonably assured *GAAP, yes*

   Not GAAP

2. Which of the following is characteristic of a change in an accounting estimate?
   a. It usually need not be disclosed
   b. It does not affect the financial statements of prior periods
   c. It should be reported through the restatement of the financial statements
   d. It makes necessary the reporting of pro forma amounts for prior periods

   Pg 138

3. Which of the following items, if material in amount, would normally be considered an extraordinary item for reporting results of operations?
   a. Utilization of a net operating loss carryforward
   b. Gains or losses on disposal of a segment of a business
   c. Adjustments of accruals on long-term contracts
   d. Gains or losses from a fire

4. Which of the following is an example of an extraordinary item in reporting results of operations?
   a. A loss incurred because of a strike by employees
   b. The write-off of deferred research and development costs believed to have no future benefit
   c. A gain resulting from the devaluation of the U.S. dollar
   d. A gain resulting from the state exercising its right of eminent domain on a piece of land used as a parking lot

5. A company changed its method of inventory pricing from last-in, first-out to first-in, first-out during the current year. Generally accepted accounting principles require that this change in accounting method be reported by:
   a. Disclosing the reason for the change in the current year's footnotes along with pro forma effects on future earnings for the succeeding five years
   b. Showing the cumulative effect of the change in the current year's financial statements and pro forma effects on prior year's financial statements in an appropriate footnote
   c. Disclosing the reason for the change in the "significant accounting policies" footnote for the current year but not restating prior year financial statements

In this case, it has to be shown at the botom of Income statement as cummulative.

d. Applying retroactively the new method in restatements of prior years and appropriate footnote disclosures

6. In computing earnings per share, a convertible debt security is classified as a common stock equivalent at the time of issuance if
   a. Its cash yield is less than the effective interest rate on similar nonconvertible debt
   b. Its yield to maturity is more than 66 ⅔ percent of its stated rate
   c. Its yield to maturity is less than 66 ⅔ percent of the bond rate
   d. It is issued at a price above its face value.

7. A transaction that is material in amount, unusual in nature, but *not* infrequent in occurrence should be presented separately as a (an)
   a. Component of income from continuing operations, but *not* net of applicable income taxes
   b. Component of income from continuing operations, net of applicable income taxes
   c. Extraordinary item, net of applicable income taxes
   d. Prior period adjustment, but *not* net of applicable income taxes

8. An extraordinary item should be reported separately as a component of income
   a. Before cumulative effect of accounting changes and after discontinued operations of a segment of a business
   b. Before cumulative effect of accounting changes and before discontinued operations of a segment of a business
   c. After cumulative effect of accounting changes and after discontinued operations of a segment of a business
   d. After cumulative effect of accounting changes and before discontinued operations of a segment of a business → Net income.

9. The correction of an error in the financial statements of a prior period should be reflected, net of applicable income taxes, in the current
   a. Income statement after income from continuing operations and before extraordinary items
   b. Income statement after income from continuing operations and after extraordinary items
   c. Retained earnings statement as an adjustment of the opening balance
   d. Retained earnings statement after net income but before dividends

10. In a primary earnings per share computation, the treasury stock method is used for options and warrants to reflect assumed reacquisition of common stock at the average market price during the period. If the exercise price of the options or warrants exceeds the average market price, the computation would
    a. Fairly present primary earnings per share on a prospective basis
    b. Fairly present the maximum potential dilution of primary earnings per share on a prospective basis

c. Reflect the excess of the number of shares assumed issued over the number of shares assumed reacquired as the potential dilution of earnings per share

d. Be antidilutive → *If this is used, it would increase the Earning per shares.*

11. A loss from the disposal of a segment of a business enterprise should be reported separately as a component of income

a. After cumulative effect of accounting changes and before extraordinary items

b. Before cumulative effect of accounting changes and after extraordinary items

c. After extraordinary items and cumulative effect of accounting changes

d. Before extraordinary items and cumulative effect of accounting changes

12. A prior period adjustment should be reflected, net of applicable income taxes, in the financial statements of a business entity in the

a. Retained earnings statement after net income but before dividends

b. Retained earnings statement as an adjustment of the opening balance

c. Income statement after income from continuing operations

d. Income statement as part of income from continuing operations

13. Antidilutive common stock equivalents would generally be used in the calculation of

	Primary earnings per share	Fully diluted earnings per share
a.	Yes	Yes
b.	No	Yes
c.	No	No
d.	Yes	No

Pg 135

14. A change in the salvage value of an asset depreciated on a straight-line basis and arising because additional information has been obtained is

a. An accounting change that should be reported in the period of change and future periods if the change affects both → *This is called Prospective type.*

b. An accounting change that should be reported by restating the financial statements of all prior periods presented

c. A correction of an error

d. Not an accounting change

15. A loss should be presented separately as a component of income from continuing operations when it is unusual in nature and which of the following?

	Material in amount	Infrequent in occurrence
a.	No	Yes
b.	No	No
c.	Yes	No
d.	Yes	Yes

only unusual and frequent

16. In determining earnings per share, interest expense, net of applicable income taxes, on convertible debt which is both a common stock equivalent and dilutive should be
    a. Added back to net income for both primary earnings per share and fully diluted earnings
    b. Added back to net income for primary earnings per share, and ignored for fully diluted earnings per share
    c. Deducted from net income for both primary earnings per share and fully diluted earnings per share
    d. Deducted from net income for primary earnings per share, and ignored for fully diluted earnings per share

17. When a segment of a business has been discontinued during the year, this segment's operating losses of the current period up to the measurement date should be included in the
    a. Income statement as part of the income (loss) from operations of the discontinued segment
    b. Income statement as part of the loss on disposal of the discontinued segment
    c. Income statement as part of the income (loss) from continuing operations
    d. Retained earnings statement as a direct decrease in retained earnings

18. For interim financial reporting, an inventory loss from a temporary market decline in the first quarter which can reasonably be expected to be restored in the fourth quarter
    a. Should be recognized as a loss proportionately in each of the first, second, third, and fourth quarters
    b. Should be recognized as a loss proportionately in each of the first, second, and third quarters
    c. Need *not* be recognized as a loss in the first quarter
    d. Should be recognized as a loss in the first quarter

19. An inventory loss from a market decline occurred in the first quarter that was not expected to be restored in the fiscal year. For interim financial reporting purposes, how would the dollar amount of inventory in the balance sheet be affected in the first and fourth quarters?

	First quarter	Fourth quarter
a.	Decrease	No effect
b.	Decrease	Increase
c.	No effect	Decrease
d.	No effect	No effect

20. Over the years, two types of income statements based upon differing views of the concept of income have been advocated by accountants. These types have been termed the *current operating performance* and *all-inclusive* concepts of income.

174   CHAPTER 3: FINANCIAL STATEMENTS I: THE INCOME STATEMENT

Required:

a. Discuss the general nature of these two concepts of income.

b. How would the following items be handled under each concept?
- i. Cost of goods sold
- ii. Selling expenses
- iii. Extraordinary items
- iv. Prior period adjustments

21. It is important in accounting theory to be able to distinguish the types of accounting changes.

Required:

a. If a public company desires to change from the sum-of-the-years-digits depreciation method to the straight-line method for its fixed assets, what type of accounting change would this be? Discuss the permissibility of this change.

b. When pro forma disclosure is required for an accounting change, how are these pro forma amounts determined?

c. If a public company obtained additional information about the service lives of some of its fixed assets which showed that the service lives previously used should be shortened, what type of accounting change would this be? Include in your discussion how the change should be reported in the income statement of the year of the change, and what disclosures should be made in the financial statements or notes.

d. Changing specific subsidiaries comprising the group of companies for which consolidated financial statements are presented is an example of what type of accounting change, and what effect does it have on the consolidated income statements?

22. Progresso Corporation, a new audit client of yours, has not reported earnings per share data in its annual reports to stockholders in the past. The president requested that you furnish information about the reporting of earnings per share data in the current year's annual report in accordance with generally accepted accounting principles.

Required:

a. Define the term *earnings per share* as it applies to a corporation with a capitalization structure composed of only one class of common stock and explain how earnings per share should be computed and how the information should be disclosed in the corporation's financial statements.

b. Explain the meanings of the terms *senior securities* and *residual securities,* which are often used in discussing earnings per share, and give examples of the types of items that each term includes

c. Discuss the treatment, if any, that should be given to each of the following items in computing earnings per share of common stock for financial statement reporting.

  i. The declaration of current dividends on cumulative preferred stock.
 ii. The acquisition of some of the corporation's outstanding common stock during the current fiscal year. The stock was classified as treasury stock.
iii. A two-for-one stock split of common stock during the current fiscal year.
 iv. A provision created out of retained earnings for a contingent liability from a possible lawsuit.
  v. Outstanding preferred stock issued at a premium with a par value liquidation right.
 vi. The exercise at a price below market value but above book value of a common stock option issued during the current fiscal year to officers of the corporation.
vii. The replacement of a machine immediately before the close of the current fiscal year at a cost 20 percent above the original cost of the replaced machine. The new machine will perform the same function as the old machine, which was sold for its book value.

23. The unaudited quarterly statements of income issued by many corporations to their stockholders are usually prepared on the same basis as annual statements, the statement for each quarter reflecting the transactions of that quarter.

Required:
a. Why do problems arise in using such quarterly statements to predict the income (before extraordinary items) for the year? Explain.
b. Discuss the ways in which quarterly income can be affected by the behavior of the costs recorded in a *repairs and maintenance of factory machinery* account.
c. Do such quarterly statements give management opportunities to manipulate the results of operations for a quarter? If so, explain or give an example.

24. The controller of Navar Corporation wants to issue to stockholders quarterly income statements that will be predictive of expected annual results. He proposes to allocate all fixed costs for the year among quarters in proportion to the number of units expected to be sold in each quarter, stating that the annual income can then be predicted through use of the following equation:

$$\text{annual income} =$$

$$\frac{\text{quarterly} \times \quad 100\%}{\text{income} \quad \text{percentage of unit sales}}$$
$$\text{applicable to quarter}$$

Navar expects the following activity for the year.

	Units	Average per Unit	Total (in $1,000s)
Sales revenue:			
First quarter	500,000	$2.00	$1,000
Second quarter	100,000	1.50	150
Third quarter	200,000	2.00	400
Fourth quarter	200,000	2.00	400
	1,000,000		
Costs to be incurred:			
Variable:			
Manufacturing		$0.70	700
Selling and administration		0.25	250
		$0.95	950
Fixed:			
Manufacturing			380
Selling and administrative			220
			600
Income before income taxes			$ 400

Required:

Ignore income taxes in answering the following questions.

a. Assuming that Navar's activities do not vary from expectations, will the controller's plan achieve his objective? If not, how can it be modified to do so? Explain and give illustrative computations.

b. How should the effect of variations of actual activity from expected activity be treated in Navar's quarterly income statements?

c. What assumption has the controller made in regard to inventories? Discuss.

25. Accounting Principles Board Opinion No. 20 is concerned with accounting changes.

Required:

a. Define, discuss, and illustrate each of the following in such a way that one can be distinguished from the other:

   i. An accounting change

   ii. A correction of an error in previously issued financial statements

b. Discuss the justification for a change in accounting principle.

c. Discuss the reporting (as required by Accounting Principles Board Opinion No. 20) of a change from the Lifo method to another method of inventory pricing.

26. Sometimes a business entity may change its method of accounting for certain items. The change may be classified as a change in accounting principle, a change in accounting estimate, or a change in reporting entity.

Listed below are three independent, unrelated sets of facts relating to accounting changes.

Situation I

A company determined that the depreciable lives of its fixed assets are presently too long to fairly match the cost of the fixed assets with the revenue produced. The company decided at the beginning of the current year to reduce the depreciable lives of all of its existing fixed assets by five years.

Situation II

On December 31, 1976, Gary Company owned 51 percent of Allen Company, at which time Gary reported its investment using the cost method due to political uncertainties in the country in which Allen was located. On January 2, 1977, the management of Gary Company was satisfied that the political uncertainties were resolved and the assets of the company were in no danger of nationalization. Accordingly, Gary will prepare consolidated financial statements for Gary and Allen for the year ended December 31, 1977.

Situation III

A company decides in January 1977 to adopt the straight-line method of depreciation for plant equipment. The straight-line method will be used for new acquisitions as well as for previously acquired plant equipment for which depreciation had been provided on an accelerated basis.

Required:

For each of the preceding situations, provide the information indicated below. Complete your discussion of each situation before going on to the next situation.

a. Type of accounting change

b. Manner of reporting the change under current generally accepted accounting principles, including a discussion, where applicable, of how amounts are computed

c. Effects of the change on the statement of financial position and earnings statement

d. Footnote disclosures that would be necessary

27. Morgan Company grows various crops and then processes them for sale to retailers. Morgan has changed its depreciation method for its processing equipment from the double-declining balance method to the straight-line method effective January 1 of this year. This change has been determined to be preferable.

In the latter part of this year, Morgan had a large portion of its crops destroyed by a hailstorm. Morgan has incurred substantial costs in raising the crops destroyed by the hailstorm. Severe damage from hailstorms in the locality where the crops are grown is rare.

Required:
  a. How should Morgan report and calculate the effect of this change in accounting principle relative to the depreciation method in this year's income statement? Do not discuss earnings per share requirements.
  b. Where should Morgan report the effects of the hail storm in its income statement? Why?
  c. How does the classification in the income statement of an extraordinary item differ from that of an operating item? Why? Do not discuss earnings per share requirements.

28. David Company's statements of income for the year ended December 31, 1981, and December 31, 1980, are presented below.

Additional facts are as follows:

David Company
STATEMENTS OF INCOME

	Year ended December 31,	
	1981	1980
	(000 omitted)	
Net sales	$900,000	$750,000
Costs and expenses:		
Cost of goods sold	720,000	600,000
Selling, general and administrative expenses	112,000	90,000
Other, net	11,000	9,000
Total costs and expenses	843,000	699,000
Income from continuing operations before income taxes	57,000	51,000
Income taxes	23,000	24,000
Income from continuing operations	34,000	27,000
Loss on disposal of Dex Division, including provision of $1,500,000 for operating losses during phase-out period, less applicable income taxes of $8,000,000	8,000	—

Cumulative effect on prior years of change in depreciation method, less applicable income taxes of $1,500,000	—	3,000
Net income	$ 26,000	$ 30,000
Earnings per share of common stock:		
Income before cumulative effect of change in depreciation method	$ 2.60	$ 2.70
Cumulative effect on prior years of change in depreciation method, less applicable income taxes	—	.30
Net income	$ 2.60	$ 3.00

- On January 1, 1980, David Company changed its depreciation method for previously recorded plant machinery from the double-declining-balance method to the straight-line method. The effect of applying the straight-line method for the year of and the year after the change is included in David Company's statements of income for the year ended December 31, 1981, and December 31, 1980, in "cost of goods sold."
- The loss from operations of the discontinued Dex Division from January 1, 1981, to September 30, 1981 (the portion of the year prior to the measurement date), and from January 1, 1980, to December 31, 1980, is included in David Company's statements of income for the year ended December 31, 1981, and December 31, 1980, respectively, in "other, net."
- David Company has a simple capital structure with only common stock outstanding, and the net income per share of common stock was based on the weighted average number of common shares outstanding during each year.
- David Company common stock is listed on the New York Stock Exchange and closed at $13 per share on December 31, 1981, and $15 per share on December 31, 1980.

Required:

Determine from the preceding additional facts whether the presentation of those facts in David Company's statements of income is appropriate. If the presentation is appropriate, discuss the theoretical rationale for the presentation. If the presentation is not appropriate, specify the appropriate presentation and discuss its theoretical rationale.

Do not discuss disclosure requirements for the notes to the financial statements.

BIBLIOGRAPHY

Barton, M. Frank, William B. Carper, and Thomas S. O'Conner. "Chartered Financial Analysts Speak Out in the Need and Information Content of Interim Financial Reports." *The Ohio CPA* (Winter 1979), pp. 28–32.

Beresford, Dennis R. "Understanding the New Rules for Interim Financial Reporting." *The Ohio CPA* (Winter 1975), pp. 27–35.

Beresford, Dennis R., and Earl J. Elbert. "Reporting Discontinued Operations." *The Ohio CPA* (Spring 1974), pp. 56–65.

Berstein, Leopold A. "Reporting the Results of Operations—A Reassessment of APB Opinion No. 9." *Journal of Accountancy* (July 1970), pp. 57–61.

Bows, Albert J. Jr., and Arthur R. Wyatt. "Improving Interim Financial Reporting." *Journal of Accountancy* (October 1973), pp. 54–59.

Brown, Lawrence D. "Accounting Changes and the Accuracy of Analysts' Earnings Forecasts." *Journal of Accounting Research* (Autumn 1983), pp. 432–443.

Curry, Dudley W. "Opinion 15 vs. a Comprehensive Financial Reporting Method for Convertible Debt." *The Accounting Review* (July 1971), pp. 495–503.

Cushing, Barry E. "Accounting Changes: The Impact of APB Opinion No. 20." *Journal of Accountancy* (November 1974), pp. 54–62.

Deming, John R. "New Guidelines for Extraordinary Items." *The CPA Journal* (February 1974), pp. 21–26.

Dudley, Lola Woodard. "A Critical Look at EPS." *Journal of Accountancy* (August 1985), pp. 102–111.

Eisenman, Seymour, Murray S. Akresh, and Charles Snow. "Reporting Unusual Events in Income Statements." *The CPA Journal* (June 1979), pp. 23–27.

Gibson, Charles H., and John Daniel Williams. "Should Common Stock Equivalents Be Considered in Earnings per Share?" *The CPA Journal* (March 1973), pp. 209–213.

Greipel, Rudolph C. "Review of APB Opinion No. 20—Accounting Changes." *The CPA Journal* (January 1972), pp. 17–24.

Hopwood, William S., and James C. McKeown. "The Incremental Informational Content of Interim Expenses over Interim Sales." *Journal of Accounting Research* (Spring 1985), pp. 161–174.

Knutson, Peter H. "Income Distribution: The Key to Earnings per Share." *The Accounting Review* (January 1970), pp. 55–58.

Koons, Robert L. "Changes in Interim Reports Are Coming." *Financial Executive* (July 1978), pp. 48–54.

Lambert, Richard A. "Income Smoothing as Rational Equilibrium Behavior." *The Accounting Review* (October 1984), pp. 604–618.

Matulich, Serge, Loren A. Nikolai, and Steven K. Olson. "Earnings Per Share: A Flowchart Approach to Teaching Concepts and Procedures." *The Accounting Review* (January 1977), pp. 233–247.

Miller, Jerry D. "Accounting for Warrants and Convertible Bonds." *Management Accounting* (January 1973), pp. 26–28.

Miller, Rene A. "Interim Financial Accounting and Reporting—Review of APB Opinion No. 28." *The CPA Journal* (September 1973), pp. 755–761.

Nichols, Donald R. "The Never-to-Recur Unusual Item—A Critique of APB Opinion No. 30." *The CPA Journal* (March 1974), pp. 45–48.

Pacter, Paul A. "APB Opinion No. 15: Some Basic Examples." *The New York Certified Public Accountant* (August 1970), pp. 638–646.

Rhodes, Lola, and H. J. Snavely. "Convertible Bonds and Earnings Per Share." *The CPA Journal* (December 1973), pp. 1116–1119.

Ricks, William E., and John S. Hughes. "Market Reactions to a Non-Discretionary Accounting Change: The Case of Long-Term Investments." *The Accounting Review* (January 1985), pp. 33–52.

Savage, Linda, and Joel Siegel. "Disposal of a Segment of a Business." *The CPA Journal* (September 1978), pp. 32–37.

Schiff, Michael. "Accounting Reporting Problems—Interim Financial Statement." New York: Financial Executives Research Foundation, 1978.

Werner, G. Frank, and Jerry J. Weygandt. "Convertible Debt and Earnings Per Share: Pragmatism vs. Good Theory." *The Accounting Review* (April 1970), pp. 280–289.

4

FINANCIAL STATEMENTS II: THE BALANCE SHEET AND THE STATEMENT OF CHANGES IN FINANCIAL POSITION

Financial reports can be divided into two categories. The first category discloses the results of the flow of resources over time and includes the income statement, the statement of retained earnings, and the statement of changes in financial position. The second category, which is reported on the balance sheet, summarizes the status of resources at a particular point in time.

These two categories also suggest an important distinction in measurement emphasis between so-called *flows* and *stocks*. Flows may be defined as productive services that must be measured over some period of time, while stocks are resources that are measured at a particular point in time. The emphasis upon the income statement in recent years is based upon the assumption that flows are more important than stocks and results in the measurement of stocks at residual values. On the other hand, a measurement technique that emphasized the balance sheet would suggest that flows should be measured only when the characteristics of specific assets and liabilities have changed.

Accounting may be described as the means by which management reports to various users of financial information, and the evaluation of the financial position of a business enterprise is an important factor for creditors, stockholders, management, the government, and other interested parties. Management attempts to satisfy this need by presenting information on resources, obligations, and equities of the firm at period intervals.

The usefulness of financial information as currently prepared has been criticized, and much of this criticism deals with the lack of research into the decision processes of various user groups. For example, Ross has stated,

> *It is surprising how little the decision-making processes of the investor appear to have been studied by accountants. It is often insisted that a balance sheet and income statement must appear in every prospectus for the protection of the investor . . . yet it is difficult to imagine how the statements will lead him toward a reliable conclusion if they do not even attempt to place a valuation on the concern.*[1]

In this chapter we will discuss the measurement techniques currently in use rather than deal extensively with the criticism posed. In so doing, there is no presumption on our part that current stock measurement techniques provide enough relevant information; instead, we believe a thorough examination of the techniques will in itself disclose their inherent limitations.

THE BALANCE SHEET

The Financial Accounting Standards Board Statement of Concepts No. 3 defined the components of the balance sheet as:

Assets—Assets are probable future economic benefits obtained or controlled by a particular entity as a result of past transactions or events. An asset has three essential characteristics: (1) it embodies a probable future benefit that involves a capacity, singly or in combination with other assets, to contribute directly or indirectly to future net cash inflows; (2) a particular enterprise can obtain the benefit and control others' access to it; and (3) the transaction or other event giving rise to the enterprise's right to or control of the benefit has already occurred.

Liabilities—Liabilities are probable future sacrifices of economic benefits arising from present obligations of a particular entity to transfer assets or provide services to other entities in the future as a result of past transactions or events. A liability has three essential characteristics: (1) it embodies a present duty or responsibility to one or more other entities that entails settlement by probable future transfer or use of assets at a specified or determinable date, on occurrence of a specified event, or on demand; (2) the duty or responsibility obligates a particular enterprise, leaving it little or no discretion to avoid the future sacrifice; and (3) the transaction or other event obligating the enterprise has already happened.

Equity—Equity is the residual interest in the assets of an entity that remains after

[1]Howard Ross, *The Elusive Art of Accounting* (New York: The Ronald Press, 1966), p. 177.

184   CHAPTER 4: FINANCIAL STATEMENTS II: THE BALANCE SHEET

deducting its liabilities. In a business enterprise, the equity is the ownership interest. Equity in a business enterprise stems from ownership rights (or the equivalent). It involves a relation between an enterprise and its owners *as owners* rather than as employees, supplier, customers, lenders, or in some other nonowner role.[2]

The preceding definitions should be carefully examined; they assert that assets are economic resources of an enterprise and that liabilities are economic obligations of an enterprise. These statements probably correspond to most users' understanding of the terms *assets* and *liabilities* and, therefore, they are not likely to be misunderstood. However, in order properly to understand the numbers presented on a balance sheet, the user must be aware of the recognition and measurement processes associated with generally accepted accounting principles.

In addition to the basic components, it has been considered more informative to provide subclassifications for each of these balance sheet components. This classification scheme makes information more easily attainable to the various interested user groups and allows for more rapid identification of specific types of information for decision making. In general, the following classification scheme may be viewed as representative of the typical balance sheet presentation.

Assets
    Current assets
    Investments
    Plant and equipment
    Intangible assets
    Other assets
Liabilities
    Current liabilities
    Long-term liabilities
    Other liabilities
Stockholders' Equity
    Capital stock
    Additional paid-in capital
    Retained earnings

In the following paragraphs we examine each of the components of the balance sheet and discuss the accounting principles used in measuring these components.

---

[2]Financial Accounting Standards Board Statement of Concepts No. 3, "Elements of Financial Statements of Business Enterprises" (Stamford, Conn.: FASB, 1980), pars. 19, 20, 28, 29, 43, and 44 (later reaffirmed in SFAC No. 6, pars. 25, 26, 35, 36, and 49).

Current Assets

The most commonly encountered definition of current assets was supplied by the Committee on Accounting Procedure. This definition may be summarized as follows: current assets are those assets that may *reasonably be expected* to be realized in cash or sold or consumed during the normal operating cycle of the business or one year, whichever is longer. The operating cycle is defined as the average time it takes to acquire materials, produce the product, sell the product, and collect the proceeds from customers.[3]

Current assets are presented on the balance sheet in order of their liquidity and generally include the following items: cash, marketable securities, receivables, inventories, and prepaid expenses. Nevertheless, special problems are connected with the valuation procedure for each of these items. Monetary current assets (cash, securities, and receivables) are generally recorded at an amount that approximates the expected present value of those items, since they are to be consumed in a short period of time. Generally accepted accounting principles dictate that items should not be valued at an amount in excess of their current realizable value. Thus, it is considered appropriate to value securities at market value when market is below cost, and receivables are valued at their recorded amount less an amount deemed to be uncollectible, or their *expected net realizable value*.

Inventories and prepaid expenses also present some valuation problems. With the emphasis upon net income reporting, the inventory valuation process has become secondary to the matching of expired inventory costs to sales. The use of any of the acceptable inventory flow assumption techniques (e.g., Lifo, Fifo, weighted average discussed in Chapter 5) prescribes the amount that remains on the balance sheet, and it is likely that each of these flow assumptions will result in different inventory valuations in fluctuating market conditions. Additionally, the accounting convention of conservatism requires the lower of cost or market rule also to be applied to inventories. In any case, the financial-statement user should interpret the inventory figure as being less than its estimated selling price.

Prepaid items are valued at historical cost with an appropriate amount being charged to expense each year until they are consumed. The general agreement among accountants that prepaid expenses are included as current assets might, if taken to its logical conclusion, cause other items to be reclassified. Prepaid expenses are included under the current asset section because it is argued that if these items had not been paid in advance, they would require the use of current funds. However, the same argument might be made for other assets, and the fact

---

[3]Accounting Research Bulletin No. 43, "Restatement and Revision of Accounting Research Bulletins" (New York: American Institute of Certified Public Accountants, 1953), Chapter 3, par. 5.

that the lives of many prepaid items encompass several accounting periods does not add to the logic of the argument. It should also be noted that prepaid items are not usually material, and perhaps that is where the argument loses its significance.

As can be seen from the previous discussion, two problems arise in attempting to classify an asset as current: (1) the period of time over which it is to be consumed and (2) the proper valuation technique. In many cases it is likely that precedent rather than accounting principles may dictate the inclusion of items as current. The valuation procedures associated with each of the items may in themselves be appropriate, but when all items are summed to arrive at a figure termed total current assets, it is difficult to interpret the result. This total usually approximates the minimum amount of cash that will be collected during the next fiscal period, but leaves to the imagination of the user the actual amount expected to be realized. The issues associated with the valuation of current assets and current liabilities (i.e., working capital) are explored more fully in the next chapter.

Investments

Investments may be divided into three categories.

1. Securities acquired for specific purposes, such as the use of idle funds for long periods or to exercise influence upon operations of another company.
2. Assets not currently in use by the business organization, such as land held for a future building site.
3. Special funds to be used for specific purposes in the future, such as sinking funds.

The primary factor used in deciding which items to include under the investments caption is *managerial intent*. That is, an organization may own two identical blocks of common stock in another company, but one block may be classified as current because it is anticipated that these shares will be disposed of in the current period, whereas the other block may be classified as an investment because the intention is to retain it for a longer period.

The valuation procedures required for each type of investment depend on the specific nature of the individual assets. When shares of stock are classified as an investment, any of three valuation procedures—the lower of cost or market, the equity method, or the market value method—may be appropriate depending on the percentage of ownership and the type of business. Therefore, the resulting asset value may be either historical cost adjusted for changes in the market value of the securities, or historical cost plus or minus the net changes in investee retained earnings since acquisition. (For a more detailed discussion of these methods see Chapter 7.)

Investments in bonds or notes are disclosed on the balance sheet at their original cost adjusted for the amortization of any purchase premium or discount.

Land and other assets held as investments are properly valued at cost unless there is reason to believe that a material and permanent decline in this cost has occurred.

As with current assets, the valuation of investments depends on the type of asset and the surrounding circumstances. In the case of bonds, the investments are not adjusted for short-term fluctuations in market conditions, since they were acquired for long-term purposes; however, as noted earlier, investments in stock may be valued at an amount above or below cost, reflecting the use of one of the three available methods.

Plant and Equipment—Intangibles

Although plant and equipment and intangibles are physically dissimilar assets, the valuation procedures associated with them are similar. Except for land, the cost of these assets is allocated to the various accounting periods benefiting from their use. In the case of plant and equipment, the carrying value is disclosed as the difference between cost and accumulated depreciation. However, intangible assets are generally carried at the net amount of their cost less amortization.

These valuation procedures are again the result of the emphasis upon income reporting. Various methods of depreciation and amortization are available, but there is no attempt to show the current value of long-term assets on the statements. The emphasis rather is upon a proper matching of revenues and expenses, with asset valuation being the residual effect of this process.

Other Assets

The preceding asset category captions usually will allow for the disclosure of all assets, but some corporations include a final category termed "other assets." Items such as fixed assets held for resale or long-term receivables may be included under this category. The valuation of these items is generally their carrying value at the time they were originally recorded in the other assets category. Since the amounts associated with these items are usually immaterial, it is unlikely that any alternative valuation procedure would result in a significantly different carrying value.

Asset Valuation

From the preceding discussion it can be seen that many different measurement techniques are used when valuing assets on the typical balance sheet. Under almost any measurement scheme devised, it is common practice to add and subtract only like items measured in the same manner. However, the measurement of assets on the balance sheet takes an unusual form when we consider that sums are derived for subclassifications as well as total assets.

Consider the following measurement bases that are included in a typical balance sheet presentation of assets:

Asset	Measurement Base
Cash	Current value
Accounts receivable	Expected realizable value
Marketable securities	Lower of cost or market
Inventory	Lower of cost or market
Investments	Lower of cost or market, or historical cost
Plant and equipment	Historical cost minus accumulated depreciation

Summing these items is much like adding apples and oranges. If assets are truly economic resources of the firm, it seems plausible to conclude that the totals on the statements should reflect somewhat more than values arrived at by convention. Presentation of information on the expected future benefits to be derived from holding these items would seem to be more appropriate.

As mentioned earlier, most numbers presented on the balance sheet are residual in nature. That is, they result from an emphasis on flows rather than stocks. For example, net plant assets on the balance sheet represent unexpired costs—those costs that have not yet flowed through the income statement as expenses. At the same time, other items on the balance sheet result from the valuation of stocks. Marketable equity securities are valued at the lower of cost or market. Any change therein is reported on the income statement as a gain or loss.

LIABILITIES

Current Liabilities

Current liabilities have been defined as "obligations whose liquidation is reasonably expected to require the use of existing resources properly classified as current assets or the creation of other current liabilities."[4] Notice that, although the operating cycle is not explicitly discussed in this definition, it is implied because the definition of current liabilities depends upon the definition of current assets. Examples of current liabilities are short-term payables, the current maturity portion of long-term debt, and accrued liabilities.

Current liabilities are usually measured at liquidation value because their period of existence is relatively short and the satisfaction of these obligations generally involves the payment of cash. Since current liabilities usually require the use of current funds, it might be considered justifiable to offset them against current assets; however, the principle of disclosure requires that they be shown separately unless a specific right of offset exists. APB Opinion No. 10 emphasized this point in stating: "It is a general principle of accounting that offsetting

[4]Ibid., Chapter 3, par. 7.

of assets and liabilities in the balance sheet is improper except where a right of offset exists."[5]

Long-Term and Other Liabilities

Long-term liabilities are those obligations that will not require the use of current assets within the current year or operating cycle. In general, these obligations take the form of bonds, notes, and mortgages and are originally valued at the amount of consideration received by the entity incurring the obligation. A problem exists, however, when this consideration is different from the amount to be repaid. Generally accepted accounting principles dictate that premiums or discounts on long-term obligations should be written off over the life of the obligation to properly reflect the effective interest rate on the debt. In such cases it is the conventions of realization and matching that dictate the balance sheet presentation of long-term liabilities.

The long-term liability section also may include long-term prepayments on contracts, deferred income taxes, minority interests in consolidations, and, in some cases, contingent liabilities, each of which has an associated measurement problem. Deferred revenues and deferred taxes are measured at their historical cost and retained at such amounts until the situation that caused them to be recorded has reversed. Those reversals are dictated by the conventions of realization and matching. Minority interests are recorded at the unowned percentage of equity book value in a specific subsidiary and are adjusted according to the realization convention. Contingent liabilities, when they are actually recorded on the books, are measured as the best approximation of a future loss that the entity believes is forthcoming on the basis of the convention of conservatism.

Other Liability Measurement Issues

During the past several years, some additional measurement issues relating to liabilities have arisen. Among the most important of these are accrued liabilities for compensated absences and the disclosure of "off–balance sheet" financing arrangements.

Compensated absences occur due to paid vacations, paid holidays and sick leaves. An accrued liability for compensated absences must be recorded when

1. The right to receive compensation is attributable to services previously rendered.
2. The right vests or accumulates.
3. The payment of the compensation is probable.
4. The amount of the payment can be reasonably estimated.

[5]Accounting Principles Board Opinion No. 10, "Omnibus Opinion—1966" (New York: American Institute of Certified Public Accountants, 1966).

The proportion of debt in a firm's capital structure is often perceived as an indicator of the level of risk associated with investing in that company. Recently, some innovative financing arrangements have been structured by corporations in such a manner that they do not satisfy liability recognition criteria. These arrangements have been termed *off–balance sheet* financing. The principal goal of these arrangements is to keep debt off the balance sheet. For example, several oil companies may form a joint venture to drill for offshore oil, and agree to make payments to support the venture over time. In such cases, neither their share of the assets or the future liability will appear on the balance sheet. It seems probable that the evolving concept of liability recognition will ultimately result in the recording of most off–balance sheet financing arrangements, but current practice still frequently allows for nonrecognition or footnote disclosure.

Liability Valuation

As with assets, liabilities are measured by a number of different procedures. Most current liabilities are measured by the amount of resources that it will ultimately take to cancel the obligation, and they ignore the time value of money. Long-term liabilities, on the other hand, are frequently measured by the present value of future payments discounted at the yield rate at the date of issue. In all cases, liability valuations are not changed to reflect current changes in the market rates of interest. The failure to consider the current market interest rates may cause the financial statements to be biased in favor of current creditors, particularly when many obligations are of a long-term nature.

EQUITY

State laws and corporate articles of incorporation make generalizations about the equity section of the balance sheet somewhat difficult. However, certain practices have become widespread enough to discuss several standards of reporting.

Common Stock

Initially, most corporations value their stock at a par or stated value and as each share of common stock is sold, an amount equal to the par or stated value is reported in the common stock section of the balance sheet. Any differences between selling price and par value are then reported under the caption "additional paid-in capital." These captions have no particular accounting significance except perhaps to determine an average issue price of common stock if such a computation seems meaningful.

Preferred Stock

Many companies also issue other classes of stock termed "preferred." These shares generally have preference as to dividends and a stated amount of dividends must be paid to preferred shareholders before any dividends can be paid to the common stockholders. The measurement basis of preferred stock is similar to that of common stock, with amounts divided between the par value of the shares and additional paid-in capital.

Retained Earnings

Ownership interest in a corporation may be defined as the residual interest in the company's assets after the liabilities have been deducted. The recorded amount of retained earnings is clearly associated with the measurement techniques used in recording specific assets and liabilities; however, this amount should not be confused with any attempt to measure the owners' current value interest in the firm.

Most states require that dividends not exceed the balance of retained earnings, and stockholders may wish to have extra dividends distributed when the retained earnings balance becomes relatively large. However, individual entities may have various long-range plans and commitments that do not allow for current distribution of dividends, and firms may provide for the dissemination of this information through an appropriation of retained earnings. This appropriation is termed a *reserve* and is measured by the sum of retained earnings set aside for the stated purpose. It should be emphasized that this appropriation does not provide the cash to finance such projects and is only presented to show managerial intent. This intent might just as easily be disclosed through a footnote.

The measurement of equity can be said to be based primarily upon the measurement of specific assets and liabilities. The transfer of assets to expense and the cancellation of liabilities determines the measurement of changes in equity. As such, equity does not have a measurement criterion other than a residual valuation.

THE STATEMENT OF CHANGES IN FINANCIAL POSITION

Prior to 1971, the income statement and the balance sheet were the only financial statements required by generally accepted accounting principles even though many large firms were including additional financial statements to disclose relevant information needed to make economic decisions. However, investors, creditors, and others voiced the desire to receive information on the financing and investing activities of business organizations. In response to this need, a statement titled the *funds statement* began to appear in the financial reports. This statement reported on the resources provided and the uses to which these resources were put during the reporting period.

Funds statements were not uniformly prepared initially and the method of reporting sources and application of resources depended on the concept of funds preferred by the reporting entity. In general, the concepts of funds uses can be categorized as cash, working capital, and all financial resources, although other concepts of funds such as quick assets or net monetary assets may also be encountered.

Statements using the cash concept of funds summarize all material changes in the cash balance. Therefore, the funds statement becomes, in effect, a statement of cash receipts and disbursements, and the impact of these receipts and disbursements on all other accounts is reported.

Under the working capital definition of funds, all material transactions that result in a change in working capital are reported (working capital being defined as current assets minus current liabilities). When using this concept, *funds* is defined as the amount of increases or decreases in cash, receivables, payables, inventories, and other current items. Many accountants believe that the basic purpose of the funds statement is to account for changes in working capital during the period covered by the statement.

Finally, if the all-financial-resources concept is used, the entity reports on the effect of all transactions with outsiders. This concept of funds must be used in conjunction with another concept of funds (e.g., cash, working capital) and includes all items that affect the financing and investing activities of the enterprise. An example of an all-financial-resources transaction that would not appear on a traditional statement prepared using cash or working capital basis is the purchase of assets by issuing stock. The advantage of this concept is its inclusion of all transactions that are important items in the financial administration of the entity.

APB OPINIONS NO. 3 AND NO. 19

In 1963 the Accounting Principles Board noted the increased attention that had been given to flow of funds analysis and issues Opinion No. 3. This release suggested that funds statements should be presented as supplemental information in financial reports but did not make such disclosures mandatory.[6] In Opinion No. 3 the board also suggested that the title of the statement be as descriptive as possible.

By 1971, the Accounting Principles Board had noted that regulatory agencies were requiring the preparation of funds statements and that a number of companies were voluntarily disclosing funds statements in their annual reports. As a result, the board issued APB Opinion No. 19. This release stated that information usually contained on the funds statement was essential to financial-statement users and that such a statement should be presented each time a balance sheet and

---

[6]Accounting Principles Board Opinion No. 3, "The Statement of Source and Application of Funds" (New York: American Institute of Certified Public Accountants, 1963).

an income statement were prepared. Additionally, the board stated that funds statements should be prepared in accordance with the all-financial-resources concept and that the statement should be titled "Statement of Changes in Financial Position."[7]

The board went on to prescribe the format of the statement as follows.

1. The statement may be prepared in such a manner as to express the financial position in terms of cash, cash and temporary assets, quick assets, or working capital so long as it utilizes the all-financial-resources concept and gives the most useful portrayal of the financing and investing activities of the entity.
2. In each case the statement should disclose the net change in the cash, cash and temporary investments, quick assets or working capital, depending upon the form of presentation.
3. The statement should disclose outlays for long-term assets, net proceeds from the sale of long-term assets, conversion of long-term debt or preferred stock to common stocks, issuances and repayments of debts, issuances or repurchases of capital stock and dividends.[8]

The statement of changes in financial position should enable financial statement users to answer such questions as

1. Where did the profits go?
2. Why weren't dividends larger?
3. How was it possible to distribute dividends in the presence of a loss?
4. Why are current assets down when there was a profit?
5. Why is extra financing required?
6. How was the expansion financed?
7. Where did the funds from the sale of securities go?
8. How was the debt retirement accomplished?
9. How was the increase in working capital financed?

Although definitive answers to these questions are not readily obtainable from a casual inspection of the funds statement, usual practice is to elaborate on the presentation in the footnotes. Additionally, comparative analyses covering several years of operations enable the user to obtain useful information on past methods and practices and the contribution of funds derived from operations to the growth of the company.

The statement of changes in financial position is designed to report on the financial operations of the company and should disclose the results of the company's financial management policies. It should also improve the predictive

[7]Accounting Principles Board Opinion No. 19, "Reporting Changes in Financial Position" (New York: American Institute of Certified Public Accountants, 1971).
[8]Ibid.

decision-making ability of users. When the statement is used in conjunction with the balance sheet and income statement, user information needs are better satisfied, and predictions about future cash flows and changes in resource allocations are more easily determined.

Cash Flow Information

The cash inflows and outflows of a business are of primary importance to investors and creditors. The presentation of cash flow information by a business enterprise should enable investors to (1) predict the amount of cash that is likely to be distributed as dividends or interest in the future and (2) evaluate the potential risk of a given investment.

The FASB has emphasized the importance of cash flow information in its deliberations. Statement of Financial Accounting Concepts No. 1 states that effective financial reporting must enable investors, creditors, and other users to (1) assess cash flow prospects and (2) evaluate liquidity, solvency, and flow of funds. In addition, the FASB recently proposed that a statement of cash flows should replace the current statement of changes in financial position.

The presentation of cash flow data is necessary to evaluate a firm's liquidity, solvency, and financial flexibility. *Liquidity* is the firm's ability to convert an asset to cash or to pay a current liability. It is referred to as the "nearness to cash" of an entity's economic resources and obligations. Liquidity information is important to users in evaluating the timing of future cash flows; it is also necessary to evaluate solvency and financial flexibility.

Solvency refers to a firm's ability to obtain cash for business operations. Specifically, it refers to a firm's ability to pay its debts as they become due. Solvency is necessary for a firm to be considered a "going concern." Insolvency may result in liquidation and losses to owners and creditors. Additionally, the threat of insolvency may cause the capital markets to react by increasing the cost of capital in the future; that is, the amount of risk is increased.

Financial flexibility is the ability of a firm to use its financial resources to adapt to change. It is the ability of a firm to take advantage of new investment opportunities or to react quickly to a "crisis" situation. Financial flexibility comes in part from quick access to the company's liquid assets. However, liquidity is only one part of financial flexibility. Financial flexibility also stems from a firm's ability to generate cash from its operations, contributed capital, or the sale of economic resources without disrupting continuing operations.

The presentation of cash flow data is intended to enable investors to make rational decisions by providing them with useful information. The FASB in Statement of Financial Concepts No. 2 has identified *relevance* and *reliability* as the primary ingredients that make accounting information useful. A statement of cash flows will undoubtedly allow for the presentation of more useful information to investors and creditors because it will enable users better to predict the probability of future returns and to evaluate risk.

DEVELOPMENT STAGE ENTERPRISES

A company in the development stage is a new organization attempting to become a going concern. As such, some of the expenditures it makes may be considered investments in the future, and some of the principles of reporting and recording may be altered during the development period. Many companies in the development stage are faced with financing problems, and the use of generally accepted accounting principles may in themselves compound these financing problems. That is, reporting all start-up costs as expenses during the first years of operations will cause reported income to be reduced and thereby make it more difficult for the company to obtain investment funds.

The proper reporting procedures to use in accounting for development stage enterprises have been discussed for many years. The basic question in these discussions has been: Should generally accepted accounting principles differ for an organization just beginning operations? In 1975 the Financial Accounting Standards Board undertook a study of this question and issued its Statement No. 7, ''Accounting and Reporting by Development Stage Enterprises.''[9] This release specifies guidelines for the identification of a development stage enterprise and for the procedures to be used to record and report on the activities of these types of organizations.

The board noted that the activities of a development stage enterprise typically would be devoted to financial planning, raising capital, exploring for natural resources, developing natural resources, research and development, acquiring assets, recruiting and training personnel, developing markets, and beginning production. Thus, the FASB defined development stage enterprises as those devoting substantially all of their efforts to establishing a new business, and required that either of the following conditions be met.

1. Planned principal operations have not commenced.
2. Planned principal operations have commenced, but no significant revenue has been received.[10]

The FASB reached the conclusion that generally accepted accounting principles should apply to development stage enterprises, and that GAAP should govern the recognition of revenue and the determination of whether a cost should be charged to expense or capitalized. That is, reporting on the activities of a

[9]Statement of Financial Accounting Standards No. 7, ''Accounting and Reporting by Development Stage Enterprises'' (Stamford, Conn.: Financial Accounting Standards Board, 1975).
[10]Ibid., par. 8.

development stage enterprise should not differ from any other type of organization. However, the FASB did state that certain additional information should be disclosed for development stage enterprises.

a. A balance sheet, including any cumulative net losses reported with a descriptive caption such as "deficit accumulated during the development stage" in the stockholders' equity section.

b. An income statement, showing amounts of revenue and expenses for each period covered by the income statement and, in addition, cumulative amounts from the enterprise's inception.

c. A statement of changes in financial position, showing the sources and uses of financial resources for each period for which an income statement is presented and, in addition, cumulative amounts from the enterprise's inception.

d. A statement of stockholders' equity showing from the enterprise's inception:

   1. For each issuance, the date and number of shares of stock, warrants, rights or other equity securities issued for cash and for other consideration.

   2. For each issuance, the dollar amounts (per share or other equity unit in total) assigned to the consideration received for shares of stock, warrants, rights, or other equity securities. Dollar amounts shall be assigned to any noncash consideration received.

   3. For each issuance involving noncash consideration, the nature of the noncash consideration and the basis for assigning amounts.[11]

The conclusions reached in SFAS No. 7 indicate that the board believed that additional standards of disclosure for development stage enterprises would alleviate the accounting and reporting problems faced by these companies. This release tended to indicate that the FASB was retaining the emphasis on interfirm comparability initiated by the APB, that is, similar situations should be reported similarly by all companies. It also provided additional evidence that the FASB believed that GAAP should be the same for all business organizations regardless of their special needs or particular environment.

SUMMARY

The measurement techniques currently being used for assigning values to balance sheet items have been criticized for failing to give enough relevant information to financial-statement users. A review of balance sheet valuation procedures shows that most of them are the result of the residual effect of the emphasis on net

[11]Ibid., par. 11.

income reporting. As such, they make little contribution to the users' ability to predict the future.

Partially in response to this need, the statement of changes in financial position has become the third major financial statement. In 1971, the Accounting Principles Board (1) stated that a funds statement should be prepared, (2) designated its title, and (3) prescribed its format. The disclosure of the information available on this statement should enable users to make more accurate predictions.

Standards of accounting and reporting for development stage enterprises are also discussed in this chapter. In its Statement No. 7, the FASB set out guidelines for defining development stage enterprises and for reporting on their activities. The FASB retained the view that GAAP should be the same for all organizations, but did allow the reporting of additional information for development stage organizations.

In the readings for this chapter, Harold Bierman discusses the concept of measurement in relation to accounting, and Edward Swanson and Richard Vangermeersch suggest changes in the statement of changes in financial position to make it more informative.

MEASUREMENT AND ACCOUNTING

HAROLD BIERMAN, JR.

The business of pinning numbers on things—which is what we mean by measurement—has become a pandemic activity in modern science and human affairs. The attitude seems to be: if it exists, measure it. Impelled by this spirit, we have taken the measure of many things formerly considered to lie beyond the bounds of quantification. In the process we have scandalized the conservatives, created occasional chaos, and stirred a ferment that holds rich promise for the better ordering of knowledge. Restrictive definitions of measurement have toppled as the practice of measurement, outrunning legis- *lation, has forced us to broaden and generalize our conceptions.*[1]

Accounting is the art of measuring and communicating financial information.[2] This statement is not shocking or even surprising, yet the acknowledgement that accounting is concerned with measurement is the first necessary step towards a long awaited revolution in accounting. This revolution is not restricted to accounting; it has already taken place in other disciplines

[1]S. S. Stevens, "Measurements, Psychophysics, and Utility," in [1], p. 18.
[2]The reader is also encouraged to read R. H. Homburger, "Measurement in Accounting," *The Accounting Review*, January, 1961, pp. 94–99. The point of view of Homburger's article is related to that presented in this article.

where measurement is crucial. For example, the classical concepts of measurement in physics and psychology have already undergone drastic changes.[3] It is time for restrictive definitions of measurement in accounting to topple.

In the distant past man used numbers in a simple manner. For example, he counted the number of sheep in the field and possibly added the number of sheep in one pasture to the number of sheep in another pasture to find the total number of sheep. But now numbers are used in a much more complex manner. For example, psychophysicists use numbers to express measures of loudness and physicists measure the mass of the sun or the velocity of an electron. These measures are expressed in terms of numbers, but they are assigned using different rules than are used by the peasant counting sheep. As S. S. Stevens has written:

". . . the fact that numerals can be assigned under different rules leads to different kinds of scales and different kinds of measurement, not all of equal power and usefulness.

. . . There is no requirement that measurement remain confined to the simpler problems of counting which first gave rise to it."[4]

Stevens suggests the use of four types of measurement scales:

Scales	Examples
Nominal	Numbering of football players
Ordinal	Hardness of minerals
Interval	Temperature
Ratio	Density

[3]For example, see J. L. McKnight, "The Quantum Theoretical Concept of Measurement," in [1], pp. 192–203.
[4]S. S. Stevens, op. cit., p. 19.

Going from top to bottom each scale is more descriptive than the previous scale. Thus the nominal scale is used to tell us whether water is frozen or liquid, and an ordinal scale whether it is cold or colder, and the interval scale is used to measure the temperature. It is important for the accountant to recognize that different descriptions or measurements may be used for different purposes.

The "true" or exactly correct measurement in the physical sciences is seldom attainable. There is a likelihood of a measurement coinciding with the true state of nature, but it is more correct to speak of a probability distribution about the measure. We can measure a table and say it is six feet long, but a more exact measure (or a measurement with a different tool) may indicate 6.1 feet, or 6.15, or 6.158, etc. Any of these measurements (or an average of several measures) could be interpreted as a mean of a distribution with the unknown true measure falling within a given interval.

The accountant uses the unit "dollars" to measure financial position at a moment in time and income for a period of time. It is not possible for the accountant (in any except an artificially simple situation) to measure either of these items exactly. It is possible to know when we are moving closer to the true measure or away from it. Assume the true measure of total assets is A and that we are attempting to estimate A. It is possible to be able to measure a component of A in several ways and be reasonably certain that one measure will lead to a less biased measure of A than the other measures. For example, we can count cash and consider that sum to be a component part of A, or we can take the sum of cash and subtract $1 million for purposes of conservatism. The second procedure introduces a bias, and on the average moves the estimate of total assets away from a true estimate of A. Thus, while it is conceded that the accountant cannot be expected to find the true measures of income and financial position (in fact these terms are not defined in this paper) he can tend to move closer to the true measures instead of allowing known biases to exist.

The misconception held by some, that accountants should be able to present the one true measure, has hindered progress in the reporting of financial information. If accounting limited itself to presenting the amount of cash in the bank, a true measurement might be attainable, but when the scope of accounting is broadened from the limited objective of measuring cash, the possibility of finding a true measure falls out of reach. The goal of the accountant should be to present useful financial information arrived at in a fair or reasonable manner. Instead of fair we could say "objective" if objective is not interpreted in the conventional sense of the accountant. The following statement by Guilford is closer to the sense in which I am using the word:

> Objectivity is one of the major goals of science. According to a convenient, operational definition, "objectivity" means interpersonal agreement. Where many persons reach agreement as to observations and conclusions, the descriptions of nature are more likely to be free from the biases of particular individuals. They form the body of knowledge that is taken to be "true." Furthermore, the descriptions are in a form that can be communicated to others. Science is a social institution. One of its chief values is that observations and conclusions of some individuals can be passed on meaningfully to others.[5]

[5]From [2], p. 1.

You could substitute accounting for science in the above quotation and have a very meaningful statement. But while it is reasonable to be objective, i.e., attempt to remove the biases of individuals and to reach interpersonal agreement, this agreement should be in the form of what a reasonable man would conclude based on the evidence. It should not mean that all reasonable men would arrive at the estimate, but rather that the average estimate of a group of reasonable men would be reasonable close to the measure given.[6]

The practicing accountant has preempted the use of the term "objective" for a more narrow meaning than that suggested in this paper. Thus, while I would prefer to use objective in the sense described above (i.e., unbiased estimates by reasonable men), I will shift to the use of the word subjective. The word is being used here not to describe a procedure for incorporating personal bias, but rather for bringing personal knowledge and experience into the measure.

Perhaps we can narrow the potential areas of disagreement by defining some of the general choices of reporting that are available to the accounting profession.

a. Measure cash only.
b. Restrict inputs to objective evidence (with no interpretation).
c. Continue use of conventional accounting practices.
d. Use subjective measures.

[6]I presented similar arguments to those presented here, from a slightly different point of view, in a previous paper. See H. Bierman, Jr., "Probability, Statistical Decision Theory and Accounting," *Accounting Review*, July, 1962, pp. 400–405. The link between the two papers is that statistical decision theory and measurement theory are both being changed by the same developments; for example, the theory of invariant measure, utility theory, and a shift from point measures to probability distributions.

MEASURE CASH

The closest the accountant can come to reporting exact information is for him to measure the amount of cash on hand. Unfortunately, while the amount of cash on hand is important information, it is not sufficient information. The business manager or investment analyst wants to know more than the amount of cash or changes in the amount of cash. If the accountant restricted his efforts to measuring cash he would increase his accuracy but would decrease his usefulness. We shall see that there is an exchange of accuracy and reliability for usefulness as we go down the list of possible procedures, but the type of accuracy given up does not constitute a high cost.

OBJECTIVE EVIDENCE

Let us assume that before recording a transaction the accountant required objective evidence in a strict sense, but less strict a sense than the accountant only willing to measure cash would require. Receivables and liabilities can now be recorded and there is a double entry accounting system. All assets would be recorded at cost, and expiration or write-off of the assets would take place only on their departure from the firm. There would be no depreciation accounting since this measure is not objective. Each transaction would be recorded as objectively as possible, but there are difficulties which were not present when we recorded only the changes in cash. There would be difficulties in finding objective measures of values for receivables and liabilities because of risk and time discounting. Purchased inventories would be difficult to value because of the necessity of using a cost flow assumption, and manufactured inventories have many measurement difficulties even though only objective evidence is being used. And what

would be the treatment of research and development expenditures under a strict adherence to objective evidence? There is no answer to this query since the expenditure and its results are naturally of a subjective nature and the recording must be subjective.

In fact it becomes clear that it is impossible to have a strict interpretation of objective evidence unless we limit the accounting to measuring cash. Conventional accounting is an improvement over objective accounting since it recognizes the necessity for and allows some use of subjective evidence in order to obtain more useful information.

CONVENTIONAL ACCOUNTING

There is no need to describe in detail the present conventional accounting practices. However, I will list a few items which make clear why this classification is not merged with the objective evidence classification:

a. Long-lived assets are depreciated.
b. Uncollectable accounts receivable are estimated and revenue is recognized on an accrual basis.
c. Liability accounts are created even though the exact amount is uncertain.
d. Market valuations are used for inventories (when the market is less than cost).

Despite the above list of subjective measures, it is fair to characterize objective evidence as a foundation of present accounting practice. The requirement that gains be realized before they are recognized is one facet of requiring a high degree of objectivity. The recording of changes in the price level is rejected to some extent because of the lack of objective measures of the changes, and the resulting financial information would not be objective.

SUBJECTIVE MEASURES

Conventional accounting stops short of recording transaction where there is strong evidence that an economic change has taken place, but the change is not complete (i.e., the gain is unrealized). The desire for accuracy causes the accountant to fail to communicate the full potential of the information at his disposal. But his prized accuracy which he strives to attain is somewhat of a fiction. How does he measure accuracy? A statement concerning accuracy implies two measures:

a. the true measure
b. the estimated measure

To say that the present measures are more accurate than other possible measures implies that the difference between the estimate and the true is being minimized in some sense. If the accountant wants to minimize the difference between a true measure and an estimate, he should restrict his estimate to a counting of cash since he will be able to come very close to measuring the actual cash. But as soon as the accountant moves from the measure of cash, by the very nature of the financial world, he is dealing with subjective factors which are not subject to attainable "true" measures. The true measure exists, but only nature knows the amount since the true measure is dependent on the outcomes of future events. The best the accountant can do is attempt to minimize the difference between the unknown true state of the world and his estimate. It seems reasonable that he should attempt to present useful information, even if it is imperfect information.

But accounting information is going to be of limited use as long as the accountant thinks it is possible to find true measures, for then he restricts himself to objective evidence produced by pulling invoices and listing unpaid bills. If there was an attainable true measure then this would be the way to find it, for the true measure could not be found by allowing accountants to use their judgment. When accountants read an invoice there is one answer: when they use judgment there may be more than one answer obtained. It becomes obvious that a "true" answer cannot be attained if we allow subjective estimates. It has not been obvious that "true" measures are not attainable if we stick to objective evidence. It is time to admit a "true" measure is not attainable.

It is necessary for the accountant to realize that his measures of income or financial position are actually probability distributions. At best he is presenting the most likely figures, but the true values (forever unknown to man) may be different. The physicist is willing to estimate the distances to stars in terms of thousands of light years. There is no reason why accountants cannot apply the same sort of reasoned judgment to financial affairs.

Today the accountant presents his information and the knowledgeable reader knows the reports are prepared in accordance with certain principles. These principles restrict the differences that would be obtained if another accountant had been hired, thus the dispersion of possible outcome arising from hiring different accountants is relatively small (though by no means close to zero). However, there is another distribution of interest, namely the dispersion of the estimate prepared under conventional accounting about the unknown true measure. This dispersion is larger than it has to be. The estimate of the income or financial position prepared following conventional accounting may be far removed from a fair or reasonable measure of income or financial position. This is because the accountant is not making effective attempts to approach the unknown true measures. Rather he is presenting reliable information, where the term reliable refers to a comparison of the measures of other accountants applying the same principles. An accountant applying different principles might obtain results that are considerably different.

Thus the choice comes down to:

a. Conventional procedures which result in measures which will be independent of the accountant who is applying them, but which are not necessarily close to true measures of financial position or income.

b. Suggested procedures which attempt to come close to the unknown true measures of financial position or income, but which open up the possibility of wider differences among accountants since more judgment is being applied.

How would the suggested procedures specifically differ from conventional accounting? They would insist on the introduction of independent expert judgment in valuing assets, and would incorporate these asset changes in the report of income since they would affect the stockholders' equity. Where reasonable measures of market value are available these would be used in the presentation of financial position. Where the market values are not readily available, then cost (or amortized cost) would be used as an approximate measure of value. This does not preclude adjusting cost for the measurable changes in the price level. Specifically, the types of items which would be affected are the recording of the estimated value of:

1. Oil which is in reserve rather than costs of drilling for oil.

2. Timber which is on the land leased or owned by the firm rather than the cost of the seedlings planted a large number of years prior.

3. Current investment of nonconsolidated subsidiaries rather than the initial cost of the investment.

4. Long-lived assets adjusted for changes in the price level.

5. Marketable securities and inventories at market rather than cost or market (especially removing the distortion caused by Lifo accounting for inventories).

6. Research and development expenditures to take note that an asset is initially created, rather than expensing all expenditures in the year of the expenditure.

It is not suggested that following the above procedures will necessarily lead to true measures. It has already been conceded that the goal is beyond our reach. On the other hand, by incorporating the available information of the types listed, thus breaking down the barriers against this type of information into financial reports, the reports will be made more useful and will move closer to the true measures.

If we leave behind the restriction that original cost is the basis of accounting measures, then the accountant is faced with a variety of choices. He might use any or all of the following: cost adjusted for changes in the price level by the use of price indexes, the net present value of expected future cash flows, the net present value of expected future cash flows with adjustments for risk, and liquidation values. The accountant's task would be much more complex, the results more interesting.[7]

The above suggestions could lead to manipulation of the reports. There would be increased burden on public accountants and

[7]This paragraph was added at the suggestion of Professor William Stewart of the University of New South Wales who also made other helpful suggestions.

government bodies such as the SEC since there would be more latitude in the reporting of the information. Currently the oil company accountant can record as an asset only the expenditures incurred to find oil. Practice ranges from recording nothing to recording the entire amount which was expended by the company throughout the world during that year. The suggested theory would change the basis of the entry from how much was spent to the amount of oil in the ground and its economic value (i.e., the net present value of the future cash flows, which may be less than the conventional cost). Under either procedure there is judgment, but with the suggested approach we are recording a figure which is related to the present value of the asset, rather than the historical accident of how much it cost to find the oil (also, it is impossible to determine the cost).

The following comments, made in a letter by Mr. Leonard Spacek, effectively expand the thoughts of this section.

. . . the readers should not assume, for instance, that measuring oil reserves in a field is just a matter of an accountant multiplying numbers based on certain geological data and arriving at his own idea as to what the reserves are. There are geological experts who do measure oil reserves on which major transactions are based, such as the purchase and sale of whole companies. Therefore, this information is used in making decisions now on financial matters. Since this is the most useful information available, and recognizing that it may not be accurate, it is used as the basis for transactions. Why shouldn't that information be used by the man on the street as well as the business executive, who deals in much bigger figures, who makes the same decision as the man on the street, with the only difference being the size of the figures. Relatively, as to its effect on the individual, the man on the street may be making a more important decision with respect to his entire life than the businessman.

. . . The most appropriate methods of measurement could be adopted by the accountants and these would become standard practices or standard principles of measurement that would be followed in all cases unless judgment dictated otherwise. This would be a big step toward making accounting much more worthwhile.

CONCLUSIONS

Henry Morgeneau has written:

The trouble with the idea of measurement is its seeming clarity, its obviousness, its implicit claim to finality in any investigative discourse. Its status in philosophy of science is taken to be utterly primitive; hence the difficulties it embodies, if any, tend to escape detection and scrutiny. Yet it cannot be primitive in the sense of being exempt from analysis; for if it were, every measurement would require to be simply accepted as a protocol of truth, and one should never ask which of two conflicting measurements is correct, or preferable. Such questions are continually being asked, and their propriety in science indicates that even measurement, with its implications of simplicity and adroitness, points beyond itself to other matters of importance on which it relies for validation.[8]

[8]Henry Morgeneau, ''Philosophical Problems Concerning the Meaning of Measurement on Physics,'' in [1], p. 163.

The accounting profession cannot consider the basic questions of measurement to be exempt from analysis. Certainly, present accounting practices of measurement are not "protocols of truth." Accountants must understand the nature and problems of measurement for the practice of accounting to realize its full potential in the area of reporting financial information.[9]

[9]This article has focused attention on the relevance of measurement theory to financial accounting. Measurement is equally important to accounting for management and managerial decisions, but that is another topic.

SELECTED BIBLIOGRAPHY

1. Churchman, C. W. and Ratoosh, P. (Eds.) *Measurement Definitions and Theories* (New York, Wiley, 1959).

2. Guilford, J. P. *Psychometric Methods,* 2d ed. (New York: McGraw-Hill, 1957).

3. Gulliksen, H. and Messick, S. (Eds.) *Psychological Scaling* (New York: Wiley, 1960).

4. Homburger, R. H., "Measurement in Accounting," *The Accounting Review,* January, 1961, pp. 94–99.

5. Thrall, R. M., Coombs, C. H., and Davis, R. L. (Eds.) *Decision Process* (New York: Wiley, 1954).

6. Thurstone, L. L. *The Measurement of Values* (Chicago: University of Chicago Press, 1959).

7. Torgerson, W. S. *Theory and Methods of Scaling* (New York: Wiley, 1958).

STATEMENT OF FINANCING AND INVESTING ACTIVITIES

EDWARD P. SWANSON, CPA, PH.D.
RICHARD VANGERMEERSCH, CPA, PH.D., CMA

Loyd C. Heath, in both his award-winning book and three closely-related journal articles, has called for important changes in financial reporting.[1] One of Heath's most controversial suggestions is that the statement of changes in financial position

Reprinted with permission of *The CPA Journal* November 1981, Vol LI/No. 11 Copyright 1981, The New York State Society of Certified Public Accountants.

[1]Loyd C. Heath, *Financial Reporting and the Evaluation of Solven:* (AICPA 1978), Loyd C. Heath, "Let's Scrap the 'Funds' Statement," *Journal of Accountancy* (October 1978), pp. 94–

should be discontinued and replaced with three new statements. Many of Heath's criticisms of the "funds statement" are valid. If accountants were to scrap the funds statement, however, they would be guilty of the age-old maxim of "throwing out the baby with the bath water." The purpose of this article is to propose a revised version of the present-day funds statement, retitled the "Statement of Financing and Investing Activities" (SFIA), instead of Heath's three new statements. This single, new statement overcomes the most important of Heath's criticisms. In addition, the SFIA incorporates important new subtotals which may be useful in predicting future cash flows.

CONCEPTS UNDERLYING TRANSACTIONS REPORTED

One general criticism of the funds statement is that confusion exists concerning the purpose of the statement. As Heath discusses, one reason for this confusion is that the present funds statement represents a compromise between two objectives. One objective is to explain change in a pool of liquid resources; changes in this "pool" measure changes in the entity's solvency. A second objective is to explain changes in the balance sheet items. This latter objective has probably evolved from years past when analysts prepared a form of funds statement as a tool to analyze changes in the balance sheet.

APB Opinions 3 and 19 are compro-

mises that accept both objectives to some extent. Concerning the first objective, both opinions require a measure of changes in liquid resources; however, the most appropriate measure of liquid resources is not specified. Both opinions accept statements prepared using several concepts of funds (i.e., measures of the pool of liquid resources): cash, cash plus marketable securities, quick assets, or working capital. And this situation has not been resolved by the widespread acceptance in practice of the working capital measure of funds since the definition of working capital is seriously flawed, as so well described by Heath. Furthermore, Heath argues that there is no useful purpose in revising the definition in an attempt to remove the flaws.

Concerning the second objective, the two APB Opinions require that changes in balance sheet items should be recorded. Opinion 3 proposed a vaguely defined concept requiring disclosure of changes in "all financial resources" and Opinion 19 was even more vague when concluding "the statement . . . should be based on a broad concept embracing all changes in financial position" (i.e., Which broad concept?). In summary, a revised statement must take a clear stance concerning which concept of funds should be required and which balance sheet changes could be recorded.

Both Heath's proposal and the SFIA are based on the cash concept of funds. Heath proposes a "Statement of Cash Receipts and Payments" as one of the three new statements replacing the funds statement. In addition, Heath proposes two additional statements (see Appendices 1 and 2) to disclose all changes in balance sheet items, including noncash "direct exchanges" (e.g., issuance of a long-term note payable to acquire equipment). The SFIA also requires disclosure of all changes caused by cash exchanges. However, disclosure of all

103; Loyd C. Heath and Paul Rosenfield, "Solvency: The Forgotten Half of Financial Reporting," *Journal of Accountancy* (January 1979), pp. 48–54; and Loyd C. Heath, "Is Working Capital Really Working?" *Journal of Accountancy* (August 1980), pp. 55–62.

financing and investing activities is given priority over recording only cash exchanges, as evidenced by inclusion of noncash "direct exchanges" on the SFIA. (A description of all noncash "direct exchanges" on the SFIA should be provided in the footnotes.) The SFIA discloses all changes in balance sheet items except for the changes in retained earnings and the carrying amount of assets and liabilities disposed of. The former changes are already disclosed in a statement of retained earnings. The later changes are omitted because the cash exchanged is disclosed when assets and liabilities are disposed of.

NEED FOR SEPARATE DISCLOSURE OF SEPARATE TYPES OF ACTIVITY

In addition to criticizing APB Opinion 19 for accepting several concepts of funds and for vaguely defining the changes in balance sheet items to be included, Heath criticizes the two explicit objectives of Opinion 19 as unclear and unattainable. However, he approves of the implicit objectives, and each of Heath's three statements (see Appendices 1 & 2) is designed to meet one of the three implicit objectives. In the conclusion to Chapter 6, he discusses the three implicit objectives as follows:

1. Changes in debt paying ability are of such obvious interest to creditors and investors that the matter hardly requires comment; the only issue is which measure of debt paying ability is likely to be most useful.
2. Changes in the size and composition of a company's capital structure are also of interest. One of the most widely used financial ratios in credit analysis is the ratio of debt to equity. That ratio would obviously be affected by changes in the composition of a company's capital

structure, such as the conversion of debentures into common stock and various kinds of refinancing operations. The nature of those activities and a report of how they affect a company's capital structure would, therefore, also be of interest.
3. Changes in the amount of composition or long-term assets are likely to signal changes in a company's future profits and future cash needs, so that they, too, are likely to be of interest to investors and creditors.

Heath, therefore, concludes that the problem is not that the information presented on the funds statement is not useful, but that too many different types of information are included in the same statement, with the result that the statement is confusing and does not communicate any information clearly. He then proposes three separate statements, presenting the following rationale: "The solution to the problem of the unsatisfactory funds statement is obvious; different statements are needed to report the different types of information now crammed into a single statement." However, a different solution is even more obvious: The information presented on the funds statement should be rearranged into four sections to present separately the four different types of information currently spread throughout the statement. (The writers have added a dividends section as the fourth section, so that users can better analyze dividend policy.)

For two reasons, one statement with four sections is preferable to three statements. The four types of activities—changes in debt-paying ability, capital structure, asset composition and dividends—are interrelated, and this interrelationship can be presented best in one statement. For example, cash from operations is not only the key measure of debt-paying ability, it is also important to capital structure changes since cash from operations represents internal, as opposed to external, financing. A second reason for requiring only one statement is purely practical. Our experience has been that many practicing accountants, both public accountants and financial executives, react with disbelief at the thought of three new statements. They believe that the addition of so many statements might actually impair many users' understanding of cash flows.

APPENDIX 1

Example Inc.
Statement of Financing and Investing Activities
For Year Ending December 31, 1977

Internal Financing From Operations:

Net Income	$17,541
Add (deduct) revenues and expenses not requiring an exchange of cash within a year:	
Depreciation	30,580
Amortization	2,264
Change in the long-term deferred income tax account	2,059
Loss (gain) on sale of property, plant and equipment	(1,188)
Cash collected and collectible from continuing operations:	$51,256
(Increase) decrease in operating receivables	(3,800)
Increase (decrease) in operating payables	2,204
(Increase) decrease in inventories	(19,181)
(Increase) decrease in prepayments	(2,942)
Cash from continuing operations and from other internal financing operations	$27,537

External Financing

	Increases 1977	Decreases 1977	
Common stock	$37,495		$37,495
Preferred stock		$30,000	(30,000)
Notes payable	50,000	18,908	31,092
			$38,587

CHAPTER 4: FINANCIAL STATEMENTS II: THE BALANCE SHEET

Cash from internal and external financing		$66,124

Investments:

Property, plant and equipment		$62,119
Cash received or collectible from disposition of property, plant and equipment		(12,793)
Marketable securities		(3,062)
Total cash investments		$46,264

Dividends:

Common		$10,558
Preferred		3,000
Total cash dividends		$13,558
Total cash investments and cash dividends		$59,822
Change in cash		$ 6,302

APPENDIX 2

Example, Inc.
Statement of Cash Receipts and Payments
For Year Ending December 31, 1977

Cash balance 12/31/76		$ 15,666
Sources of cash:		
Cash provided by operations (Schedule 1)	$ 27,537	
Sale of marketable securities	3,062	
Sale of land, buildings and equipment	12,793	
Net amount borrowed	31,902	
Received from issuance of common stock	7,495	81,979
Cash available		97,645
Uses of cash:		
Purchase of land, buildings and equipment	62,119	
Payment of dividends	13,558	75,677
Cash balance 12/31/77		$ 21,968

From Heath, "Financial Reporting and Evaluation of Solvency," p. 126.

Schedule 1
Cash Provided by Operations

Cash collected from customers		$783,545
Interest and dividends received		1,417
Total cash receipts from operations		784,962
Cash disbursements:		
For merchandise inventories	$457,681	
For administrative and selling expenses	264,577	
For interest	6,941	
For other expenses	14,953	
For taxes	13,273	757,425
Cash provided by operations		$ 27,537

Ibid.

Example, Inc.
Statement of Financing Activities
For 1977

	Increase or (decrease)
Debt Financing	
Notes payable to banks:	
Borrowed	$ 50,000
Repaid	(16,908)
Net amount borrowed	33,092
Amounts paid on mortgage payable	(2,000)
Net increase in debt financing	$ 31,902
Equity Financing	
Convertible preferred	
Conversion of 300 shares $100 par value 5 percent convertible preferred for 1,500 shares $10 par value common stock	$(30,000)
Common stock and capital in excess of par value:	
Issued 1,500 shares on conversion of 300 shares 5 percent convertible preferred	30,000
Issued 500 shares for $7,495 case	7,495
Retained earnings	
Net increase	3,983
Net increase in equity financing	$ 11,478

Ibid., p. 133.

CHAPTER 4: FINANCIAL STATEMENTS II: THE BALANCE SHEET

Example, Inc.
Statement of Investing Activities
For Year Ending December 31, 1977

Properties

Land, buildings and equipment, 12/31/76	$319,101
Plus: Purchases	62,119
	381,220
Less: Cost of properties disposed of	31,595
Land, buildings and equipment, 12/31/77	$349,625

Ibid., p. 135.

THE STATEMENT OF FINANCING AND INVESTING ACTIVITIES

The format of the SFIA is presented in Exhibit 1.[2] In addition, the Appendices contain both the example Heath used to illustrate the three statements he proposes and a SFIA constructed from the same data. The major features of the SFIA should be mandatory, although minor variations are probably necessary to accommodate industry differences. A mandatory format will increase comparability between entities. This will facilitate understanding by the moderately sophisticated and less sophisticated users of financial statements. The costs incurred by sophisticated users in adjusting the information to a comparable basis are also likely to decline. In addition, the accuracy of information stored in central databases, such as Compustat and Valueline, should be improved.

[2]The classification of financial statement items into short-term and long-term is incorporated in this exhibit to be in accord with present practice. However, the authors agree with Heath that the distinction between short-term and long-term should be eliminated.

ADVANTAGES OF THE NEW FORMAT

There are several additional advantages to the format presented in Exhibit 1; the remainder of this section will explain these advantages. First, the SFIA represents an improvement over the conventional Statement of Changes in Financial Position, because information on internal financing through operations, external financing, investing and dividends is presented in four separate sections. This serves to emphasize financing, investing and dividend paying activities and their interrelationships. In contrast, the conventional funds statement emphasizes "sources" and "applications." Sources can have little in common except for the existence of a transaction resulting in an inflow of funds; for instance, sources often include dissimilar items such as receipts from external financing (i.e., the issuance of debt or equity) and proceeds from disinvestments (i.e., receipts from the sale of non-inventory assets). Similarly, applications typically include any repayments of external financing (such as the repurchase of debt or equity), as well as investments in non-inventory assets. Not surprisingly, many users do not

EXHIBIT 1
Statement of Financing and Investing Activities
For Years of 19×1 and 19×0

Internal Financing From Operations:

	19×1	19×0
Net income from continuing operations	$ xx	$ xx
Add (deduct) revenues and expenses not requiring an exchange of cash within a year:		
Depreciation	xx	xx
Amortization	xx	xx
Change in the long-term deferred income tax account	xx	xx
Change in the long-term pension account	xx	xx
Difference between dividends received and income (or loss) of an equity method investee	xx	xx
Foreign currency translation gain or loss	xx	xx
Loss (gain) on sale of property, plant and equipment	xx	xx
Other items	xx	xx
Cash collected and collectible from continuing operations	$ xx	$ xx
Cash collected and collectible from nonrecurring items	xx	xx
Cash collected and collectible from operations:	$ xx	$ xx
(Increase) decrease in operating receivables	xx	xx
Increase (decrease) in operating payables	xx	xx
(Increase) decrease in inventories	xx	xx
(Increase) decrease in prepayments	xx	xx
Cash change from operations and from other internal financing operations	$ xx	$ xx

External Financing:

	Increases		Decreases			
	19×1	19×0	19×1	19×0		
Common stock	$xx	$xx	$xx	$xx	$ xx	$ xx
Preferred stock	xx	xx	xx	xx	xx	xx
Bonds	xx	xx	xx	xx	xx	xx
Short-term non-opt. notes payable	xx	xx	xx	xx	xx	xx
Long-term notes payable	xx	xx	xx	xx	xx	xx
External financing changes	xx	xx	xx	xx	$ xx	$ xx
Less external financing accomplished in a noncash transaction not offset within this section					xx	xx
Cash from external financing					$ xx	$ xx
Cash from internal and external financing					$ xx	$ xx

Investments:

	19×1	19×0
Property, plant and equipment:	$ xx	$ xx
Acquisitions for replacement	xx	xx
Acquisitions for expansion	xx	xx

212   CHAPTER 4: FINANCIAL STATEMENTS II: THE BALANCE SHEET

Acquisitions for pollution control/government regulations	xx	xx
Cash received from sale of plant, property or equipment	(xx)	(xx)
Short-term securities increase (decrease)	xx	xx
Long-term securities increase (decrease)	xx	xx
Other long-term assets increase (decrease)	xx	xx
Total investments	$ xx	$ xx
Less investments accomplished in a noncash transaction not offset in this section	xx	xx
Total cash investments	$ xx	$ xx
Dividends:		
Common stock	$ xx	$ xx
Preferred stock	xx	xx
Total dividends	$ xx	$ xx
Less dividends declared but not paid	xx	xx
Total cash dividends	$ xx	$ xx
Total cash investments and cash dividends	$ xx	$ xx
Change in cash	$ xx	$ xx

know what to do with a listing of sources and applications.[3] This proposed new mandatory format focusing on financing, investing and dividend activities should increase user understanding of the usefulness of funds statement information.

The mandatory format requires the indirect, rather than the direct approach of calculating cash from operations. The direct approach begins with cash receipts and deducts cash payments, individually listing each revenue and expense after converting each to a cash basis. The indirect approach begins with net income before extraordinary items and adds (or deducts) noncash components of income. The indirect approach highlights the differences between income and cash flows. These differences

may be important in improving predictions of future cash flows.

The indirect approach also clearly identifies many allocations whose treatment as revenues and expenses are often criticized. (These revenue and expense items are often said to affect the "quality" of income.) For example, depreciation and amortization, which, by definition, are not based on events occurring during the year, are added back to income. In addition, gains or losses from the sale of long-term assets, which represent the results of events usually occurring several years apart, are removed from the current period's income. Furthermore, two other items affecting income, yet not necessarily resulting in an inflow or outflow of cash, are removed: Excluded are income recognized on long-term investments accounted for on the equity method and the change in long-term deferred income taxes which is ordinarily due primarily to the use of straight-line depreciation for reporting but accelerated depreciation for taxes. Similarly, foreign exchange gains or losses arising from translation or from debt maturing in a period beyond one

[3]Part of the confusion is due to the ordinarily poor discussion of the uses of the funds statement in accounting textbooks. The chapter on preparing a funds statement typically refers to the statement's value in evaluating financing and investing decisions, with no discussion of how to conduct such an evaluation. And often the chapter on financial statement analysis never mentions the funds statement.

year are removed. Largely for these reasons, Harold Williams, recent Chairman of the SEC, has argued that cash flow from operations is a better measure of performance than earnings-per-share.

Removing the effects on income of these revenues and expenses, because they do not require an exchange of cash within a year, results in the useful subtotal, "Cash collected and collectible from continuing operations" (CCCCO). This subtotal is accrual-based and contributes to its potential to improve user predictions of cash flow from operations. FASB Concepts Statement No. 1, which identified the prediction of the amount, timing and uncertainty of net cash flows as the key objective of financial reporting, argues for the predictive usefulness of accrual accounting as follows: "Information about enterprise earnings based on accrual accounting generally provides a better indication of an enterprise's present and continuing ability to generate favorable cash flows than information limited to the financial effects of cash receipts and payments."

The prediction of cash flow would involve a two-step process. The first step would require the prediction for a future period of CCCCO based, at least as a starting point, on past period's amounts. The second step would be the estimate of cash flow for that future period based on the prediction of CCCCO for that same period. This two-step prediction process should provide more accurate predictions of cash flow than would be obtained from a similar two-step prediction process requiring the prediction of income as the first step. This should be the case since the "noise" effect of many of the noncash revenues and expenses whose treatment is widely criticized (discussed previously) is removed when the first step is based on CCCCO.

To predict *net* cash flow (which is the focus of Concepts Statement 1), an additional deduction from CCCCO is needed to provide for capital replacement. There are many ways in which an allowance for capital replacement can be calculated. In some cases, current cost depreciation is available and appropriate; in other cases, actual expenditures in this period may be used. To assist those users basing the capital allowance on actual expenditures, cash invested in property, plant and equipment (PPE) has been reported in three categories in the "Investments" section of the SFIA. While these totals are difficult to estimate if rapid technological change occurs, the writers have been told that some analysts seek this information by contacting management directly. Therefore, in the interests of reducing the potential value of this information as "insider information," it should be publicly disclosed. The total of PPE acquisitions for replacement, plus possibly pollution control expenditures for PPE on hand, is often a reasonable estimate of an allowance for capital replacement; therefore, this total can be deducted from CCCCO to obtain an improved figure for estimating net cash inflows. The third category of PPE investment, acquisitions for expansion, can be used to estimate net cash flows anticipated from new investments. The average rate of cash return anticipated on new investments could be multiplied by the dollar amount invested for expansion to estimate cash flows anticipated from new investments. These anticipated cash flows would be added to the estimate of cash flows based on direct extrapolation of past trends. There are several other possible adjustments—particularly for the impact of general and specific price level changes—that may further improve this rough outline of an approach to predict future net cash inflows from funds statement information. Experimentation with empirical data is needed to determine the ability of CCCCO to improve user predictions of the amount, timing and uncertainty of future net cash flows.

One other advantage of the format in Exhibit 1 should be discussed. Changes in operating receivables and payables and inventories are emphasized to a greater extent in the SFIA than in the customary funds statement. This emphasis is useful because an increase in operating receivables and payables and inventories that is not justified by volume increases is often a key indicator of impending liquidity problems. W. T. Grant is the classic case of an extreme increase in receivables that should have (but surprisingly had not), tipped off the stock market about the impending liquidity crisis.[4] Of course, large inventory increases are a more common indicator of impending liquidity problems.

It seems sufficient to comment only briefly on the ways in which the SFIA information can be used to formulate new types of ratios. One possibility is the ratio of cash generated from operations to cash from debt financing and/or from equity financing. These ratios could be used to evaluate the use of leverage (as a supplement to the debt to equity ratio). A related possibility is to calculate new debt and equity coverage ratios using CCCCO (after adding back interest) instead of net income. The possibilities for new types of ratio analysis are almost endless.

[4]For an interesting analysis of the W. T. Grant case, see James A. Largay and Clyde P. Stickney, "Cash Flows, Ratio Analysis and the W. T. Grant Company Bankruptcy," *Financial Analysts Journal* (July–August 1980), pp. 51–54.

CONCLUSION

The SFIA has several advantages as compared to the present funds statement:

1. A single concept of funds is required (cash);
2. The format is mandatory;
3. Information on internal financing through operations, external financing, investing and dividends is presented in four separate sections;
4. A new subtotal, "cash collected and collectible from continuing operations," which may be useful in predicting cash flows, is introduced;
5. Capital expenditures are separated into three subtotals to assist in predicting net cash flows;
6. Changes in operating receivables and payables and inventories—which may indicate impending liquidity problems—are highlighted.

In conclusion, accountants owe much to Heath's efforts in changing the direction of accounting thought, particularly in his attack on the misplaced emphasis on working capital and on the lack of clarity of the goals of the funds statement. The FASB is currently considering several changes in the reporting of funds flows. The SFIA deserves serious consideration by the FASB since it blends the best features of the present-day funds statement with the best features of Heath's proposal.

QUESTIONS

1. On a balance sheet, what is the preferable presentation of notes or accounts receivable from officers, employees, or affiliated companies?
   a. As trade notes and accounts receivable if they otherwise qualify as current assets
   b. As assets but separately from other receivables

QUESTIONS

215

    c. As offsets to capital

    d. By means of notes or footnotes

2. The basis for classifying assets as current or noncurrent is the period of time normally elapsed from the time the accounting entity expends cash to the time it converts

    a. Inventory back to cash or 12 months, whichever is shorter

    b. Receivables back into cash or 12 months, whichever is longer

    c. Tangible fixed assets back into cash or 12 months, whichever is longer

    d. Inventory back to cash or 12 months, whichever is longer

3. The valuation basis used in conventional financial statements is

    a. Replacement cost

    b. Market value

    c. Original cost

    d. A mixture of costs and values

4. A transaction that would appear as an application of funds on a conventional funds statement using the all-financial-resources concept, but not on a statement using the traditional working capital concept would be the

    a. Acquisition of property, plant, and equipment for cash

    b. Reacquisition of bonds issued by the reporting entity

    c. Acquisition of property, plant, and equipment with an issue of common stock

    d. Declaration and payment of dividends

5. There would probably be a major difference between a statement of source and application of working capital and a cash flow statement in the treatment of

    a. Dividends declared and paid

    b. Sales of noninventory assets for cash at a loss

    c. Payment of long-term debt

    d. A change during the period in the accounts payable balance

6. Which of the following concepts of *funds* is preferable for statements of sources and applications of funds prepared for presentation in annual reports?

    a. Current assets

    b. Net working capital

    c. Net income plus depreciation

    d. All financial resources

7. A basic objective of the statement of changes in financial position is to

    a. Supplant the income statement and balance sheet

    b. Disclose changes during the period in all asset and all liability accounts

    c. Disclose the change in working capital during the period

    d. Provide essential information for financial statement users in making economic decisions

8. A statement of changes in ~~financial position~~ should be issued by a profit-oriented business

a. As an alternative to the statement of income and retained earnings

b. Only if the business classifies its assets and liabilities as current and noncurrent

c. Only when two-year comparative balance sheets are not issued

d. Whenever a balance sheet and a statement of income and retained earnings are issued

9. When preparing a statement of changes in ~~financial position~~ using the cash basis for defining funds, an increase in ending inventory over beginning inventory will result in an adjustment to reported net earnings because

a. Funds were increased since inventory is a current asset

b. The net increase in inventory reduced cost of goods sold but represents an assumed use of cash

c. Inventory is an expense deducted in computing net earnings, but is not a use of funds

d. All changes in noncash accounts must be disclosed under the all financial resources concept

10. Which of the following should be presented in a statement of changes in ~~financial position~~ only because of the all-financial-resources concept?

a. Conversion of preferred stock to common stock

b. Purchase of treasury stock

c. Sale of common stock

d. Declaration of cash dividend

11. The retirement of long-term debt by the issuance of common stock should be presented in a statement of changes in ~~financial position~~ as a

	Source of funds	Use of funds
a.	No	No
b.	No	Yes
c.	Yes	No
d.	Yes	Yes

12. The working capital format is an acceptable format for presenting a statement of changes in ~~financial position~~. Which of the following formats is (are) also acceptable?

	Cash	Quick Assets
a.	Acceptable	Not acceptable
b.	Not acceptable	Not acceptable
c.	Not acceptable	Acceptable
d.	Acceptable	Acceptable

13. A gain on the sale of plant assets in the ordinary course of business should be presented in a statement of changes in ~~financial position~~ as a (an) *cash flow*
   a. Source and use of funds
   b. Use of funds
   c. Addition to income from continuing operations
   d. Deduction from income from continuing operations

14. Which of the following should be presented in a statement of ~~changes in~~ *cash flow* ~~financial position~~?

	Conversion of long-term debt to common stock	Conversion of preferred stock to common stock
a.	No	No
b.	No	Yes
c.	Yes	Yes
d.	Yes	No

15. In determining whether to accrue employee's compensation for future absences, among the conditions that must be met are that the obligation relates to rights that

The official answer Pg 190

	Accumulate	Vest	— entitled whether work or not
a.	No	No	
b.	No	Yes	
c.	Yes	No	The correct answer
d.	Yes	Yes ←	

16. Presenting information on cash flows has become an imporant part of financial reporting.

Required:
   a. What goals are attempted to be accomplished by the presentation of cash flow information to investors?
   b. Discuss the following terms as they relate to the presentation of cash flow information.
      i. Liquidity.
      ii. Solvency.
      iii. Financial flexibility.

Pg 195 important

17. The measurement of assets and liabilities on the balance sheet is frequently a secondary goal to income determination. As a result, various measurement techniques are used to disclose assets and liabilities.

Pg 189-191

Required:

Discuss the various measurement techniques used on the balance sheet to disclose assets and liabilities.

18. The financial statement on the next page was prepared by employees of your client, Linus Construction Company. The statement is unaccompanied by footnotes, but you have discovered the following:

a. The average completion period for the company's jobs is 18 months. The company's method of journalizing contract transactions is summarized in the following pro forma entries:

1. Materials, supplies, labor and overhead charged to construction $xxx,xxx

   Cash, various other assets, payables, depreciation and other accounts $xxx,xxx

   To record actual costs incurred on jobs

2. Materials, supplies, labor and overhead charged to construction $xxx,xxx

   Unearned revenue on work in progress $xxx,xxx

   To accrue but defer estimated profit earned on work in progress.

3. Accounts receivable $xxx,xxx

   Unearned revenue on work in progress $xxx,xxx

   To charge customers for costs incurred to date. (Most contracts provide that customers shall be billed for costs as incurred at the end of each month and that while jobs are in progress 95 percent of amounts billed shall be remitted within 15 days of billing. Upon job completion, the remainder of the contract price is billed and recorded in an entry [s] in which the profit or loss realized on the job is also recognized.)

4. Cash $xxx,xxx

   Accounts receivable $xxx,xxx

   To record collections.

5. Accounts receivable $xxx,xxx

   Unearned revenue on work in progress $xxx,xxx

   (Loss) Profit realized on completed jobs $xx,xxx or $xx,xxx

   Materials, supplies, labor and overhead charged to construction $xxx,xxx

   To record completion of job number.

b. Linus both owns and leases equipment used on construction jobs. Typically, its equipment lease contracts provide that Linus may return the equipment upon completion of a job or may apply all rentals in full toward purchase of the equipment. About 70 percent of lease rental payments made in the past have been applied to the purchase of equipment. While leased equipment is in use, rents are charged to the account *payments made on leased equipment* (except for $1 balance) and are charged to jobs on which the equipment has been used. In the event of purchase the balance in the *payments made on leased equipment* account is transferred to the *machinery and equipment* account and the depreciation and other related accounts are corrected.

c. Management is unable to develop dependable estimates of costs to complete contracts in progress.

LINUS CONSTRUCTION COMPANY
Statement of Financial Position
October 31, 1970

Current assets:			
Cash		$ 182,200	
Accounts receivable (less allowance of $15,000 for doubtful accounts)		220,700	
Materials, supplies, labor and overhead charged to construction		2,026,000	
Materials and supplies not charged to construction		288,000	
Deposits made to secure performance of contracts		360,000	$3,076,900
Less Current Liabilities:			
Accounts payable to subcontractors		$ 141,100	
Payable for materials and supplies		65,300	
Accrued payroll		8,260	
Accrued interest on mortgage note		12,000	
Estimated taxes payable		66,000	292,660
Net working capital			$2,784,240

Property Plant and Equipment (at cost):

	Cost	Depreciation	Value
Land and buildings	$ 983,300	$310,000	$ 673,300
Machinery and equipment	905,000	338,000	567,000
Payments made on leased equipment	230,700	230,699	1
	$2,119,000	$878,699	$1,240,301

Deferred charges:		
Prepaid taxes and other expenses	$ 11,700	
Points charged on mortgage note	10,800	22,500
Total net working capital and noncurrent assets		4,047,041

Less Deferred Liabilities:		
Mortgage note payable	$ 300,000	
Unearned revenue on work in progress	1,898,000	2,198,000
Total Net Assets		$1,849,041
Stockholders' Equity:		
6% preferred stock at par value	$ 400,000	
Common stock at par value	800,000	
Paid-in surplus	210,000	
Retained earnings	483,641	
Treasury stock at cost (370 shares)	(44,600)	
Total Stockholders' Equity		$1,849,041

Required:
  i. Identify the weaknesses in the financial statement.
  ii. For each item identified in part (a), indicate the preferable treatment and explain why the treatment is preferable.

19. The following statement of source and application of funds was prepared by the controller of the Clovis Company. (See page 222.) The controller indicated that this statement was prepared under the all-financial-resources concept of funds, which is the broadest concept of funds and includes all transactions providing or requiring funds.

Required:
  i. Why is it considered desirable to present a statement of source and application of funds in financial reports?
  ii. Define and discuss the relative merits of the following three concepts used in funds flow analysis in terms of their measurement accuracy and freedom from manipulation (window dressing) in one accounting period:
    (a) cash concept of funds
    (b) net monetary assets (quick assets) concept of funds
    (c) working capital concept of funds
  iii. Identify and discuss the weaknesses in presentation and disclosure in the statement of source and application of funds for Clovis Company. Your discussion should explain why you consider them to be

CLOVIS COMPANY
Statement of Source and Application of Funds
December 31, 1968

Funds were provided by:	
Contribution of plant site by the City of Camden (Note a)	$115,000
Net income after extraordinary items per income statement (Note b)	75,000
Issuance of note payable—due 1972	60,000
Depreciation and amortization	50,000
Deferred income taxes relating to accelerated depreciation	10,000
Sale of equipment—book value (Note c)	5,000
Total funds provided	$315,000
Funds were applied to:	
Acquisition of future plant site (Note a)	$250,000
Increase in working capital	30,000
Cash dividends declared but not paid	20,000
Acquisition of equipment	15,000
Total funds applied	$315,000

weaknesses and what you consider the proper treatment of the items to be. Do not prepare a revised statement.

Notes to Statement of Source and Application of Funds:

a. The City of Camden donated a plant site to Clovis Company valued by the board of directors at $115,000. The company purchased adjoining property for $135,000.

b. Research and development expenditures of $25,000 incurred in 1968 were expensed. These expenses were considered abnormal.

c. Equipment with a book value of $5,000 was sold for $8,000. The gain was included as an extraordinary item on the income statement.

20. The statement of changes in financial position is normally a required basic financial statement for each period for which an earnings statement is presented. The reporting entity has flexibility in form, content, and terminology of this statement to meet the objectives of differing circumstances. For example, the concept of funds may be interpreted to mean, among other things, cash or working capital. However, the statement should be prepared based on the all-financial-resources concept.

Required:

a. What is the all-financial-resources concept?

b. What are two types of financial transactions that would be disclosed under the all-financial-resources concept that would not be disclosed without this concept?

c. What effect, if any, would each of the following seven items have upon the preparation of a statement of changes in financial position prepared in accordance with generally accepted accounting principles using the cash concept of funds?

    i. Accounts receivable—trade

   ii. Inventory

  iii. Depreciation

   iv. Deferred income tax credit from interperiod allocation

    v. Issuance of long-term debt in payment for a building

   vi. Payoff of current portion of debt

  vii. Sale of a fixed asset resulting in a loss

BIBLIOGRAPHY

American Accounting Association Committee on Accounting Valuation Bases. "Report of the Committee on Accounting Valuation Bases." *The Accounting Review,* Supplement to Vol. 47 (1972), pp. 535–573.

American Accounting Association. "Report of the Committee on Foundations of Accounting Measurement." *The Accounting Review.* Supplement to Vol. 46 (1979), pp. 36–45.

Anton, Hector R. *Accounting for the Flow of Funds.* Boston: Houghton Mifflin Co., 1962.

Ashton, Robert H. "Objectivity of Accounting Measures: A Multirule-Multimeasurer Approach." *The Accounting Review* (July 1977), pp. 567–575.

Beams, Floyd A., and Robert H. Strawser. "Preferences for Alternative Presentations of the Statement of Changes in Financial Position." *Massachusetts CPA Review* (November–December 1973), pp. 14–18.

Birnberg, Jacob G. "An Information Oriented Approach to the Presentation of Common Shareholders' Equity." *The Accounting Review* (October 1964), pp. 963–971.

Braiotta, Louis, Jr. "Cash Basis Statement of Changes." *The CPA Journal* (August 1984), pp. 34–40.

Buzby, Stephen L., and Haim Falk. "A New Approach to the Funds Statement." *Journal of Accountancy* (January 1974), pp. 55–61.

Coleman, Almand R. "Restructuring the Statement of Changes in Financial Position." *Financial Executive* (January 1979), pp. 34–42.

Crooch, G. Michael, and Bruce E. Collier. "Reporting Guidelines for Companies in a State of Development." *The CPA Journal* (July 1973), pp. 579–584.

Dun, L. C. "Working Capital—A Logical Concept," *Australian Accountant* (October 1969), pp. 461–464.

Fadel, Hisham, and John M. Parkinson. "Liquidity Evaluation by Means of Ration Analysis." *Accounting and Business Research* (Spring 1978), pp. 101–107.

Giese, J. W., and T. P. Klammer. "Achieving the Objectives of APB Opinion No. 19." *Journal of Accountancy* (March 1974), pp. 54–61.

Grinnell, D. Jacque, and Corine T. Norgaard. "Reporting Changes in Financial Position." *Management Accountant* (September 1972), pp. 15–22.

Heath, Loyd C. "Financial Reporting and the Evaluation of Solvency." New York: American Institute of Certified Public Accountants, 1978.

Heath, Loyd C. "Financial Reporting and the Evaluation of Solvency. Accounting Research Monograph No. 3. AICPA, 1978.

Heath, Loyd C. "Is Working Capital Really Working?" *Journal of Accountancy* (August 1980), pp. 55–62.

Heath, Loyd C. "Let's Scrap the 'Funds' Statement." *Journal of Accountancy* (October 1978), pp. 94–103.

Heath, Loyd C., and Paul Rosenfield. "Solvency: The Forgotten Half of Financial Reporting." *Journal of Accountancy* (January 1979), pp. 48–54.

Hunter, Robert D. "Concept of Working Capital." *Journal of Commercial Bank Lending* (March 1962), pp. 24–30.

Ijiri, Yuji. *The Foundations of Accounting Measurement*. Englewood Cliffs, N.J.: Prentice-Hall, 1967.

Jaedicke, Robert K., and Robert T. Sprouse. *Accounting Flows: Income, Funds, and Cash*. Englewood Cliffs, N.J.: Prentice-Hall, Inc., 1965.

Kafer, Karl, and V. K. Zimmerman. "Notes on the Evolution of the Statement of Source and Application of Funds." *International Journal of Accounting Education and Research* (Spring 1967), pp. 89–121.

Largay, James A., III, Edward P. Swanson, and Max Block. "The 'Funds' Statement: Should it Be Scrapped, Retained or Revitalized?" *Journal of Accountancy* (December 1979), pp. 88–97.

Lemke, Kenneth W. "The Evaluation of Liquidity: An analytical Study." *Journal of Accounting Research* (Spring 1970), pp. 47–77.

Mason, Perry. *Cash Flow Analysis and the Funds Statement*. New York: American Institute of Certified Public Accountants, 1961.

Merrill, Walter W. "The Statement of Changes in Financial Position Cash Format Is Far Easier to Understand." *Massachusetts CPA Review* (November–December 1973), pp. 23–26.

Moonitz, Maurice. "Reporting on the Flow of Funds." *The Accounting Review* (July 1956), pp. 378–385.

Nurnberg, Hugo. "APB Opinion No. 19—Pro and Con." *Financial Executive* (December 1972), pp. 58–60, 62, 64, 66, 68, 70.

Oliver, Joseph R. "The Statement of Changes in Financial Position." *National Public Accountant* (August 1972), pp. 20–24.

Rayburn, Frank R., and G. Michael Crooch. "Currency Translation and the Funds Statement: A New Approach." *Journal of Accountancy* (October 1983), pp. 51–62.

Rayman, R. A. "Extension of the System of Accounts: The Segregation of Funds and Value." *Journal of Accounting Research* (Spring 1969), pp. 53–89.

"Report of the Committee on Accounting Valuation Bases." *The Accounting Review,* Supplement to Vol. 47 (1972), esp. pp. 556–568.

"Report of the Committee on Foundations of Accounting Measurements." *The Accounting Review,* Supplement to Vol. 46 (1971), pp. 3–48.

Roberts, Aubrey, and David R. L. Gabhart. "Statement of Funds: A Glimpse of the Future?" *Journal of Accountancy* (April 1972), pp. 54–59.

Rosen, L. S., and Don T. DeCoster, " 'Funds' Statements: A Historical Perspective." *The Accounting Review,* Vol. 44 (January 1969), pp. 124–136.

Seed, Allen H., III. "Utilizing the Funds Statement." *Management Accounting.* (May 1976), pp. 15–18.

Spiller, Earl A., and Robert L. Virgil. "Effectiveness of APB #19 in Improving Funds Reporting." *Journal of Accounting Research* (Spring 1974), pp. 112–133.

Sprouse, Robert T. "Balance Sheet—Embodiment of the Most Fundamental Elements of Accounting Theory." *Foundations of Accounting Theory.* Gainesville, Fla.: University of Florida Press, 1971, pp. 90–104.

Staubus, George J. "Measurement of Assets and Liabilities." *Accounting and Business Research* (Autumn 1973), pp. 243–262.

Walker, R. G. "Asset Classification and Asset Valuation." *Accounting and Business Research* (Autumn 1974), pp. 286–296.

Yu, S. C. "A Flow of Resources Statement for Business Enterprises." *The Accounting Review* (July 1969), pp. 571–582.

5

WORKING CAPITAL

this dont have to be reported flow anymore

A company's *working capital* is the net short-term investment needed to carry on day-to-day activities. The measurement and disclosure of working capital on financial statements has been considered an appropriate accounting function for decades and the usefulness of this concept for financial analysis is accepted almost without question. However, there are some serious problems with the concept such as (1) inconsistencies in the measurements of the various components of working capital, (2) differences of opinion over what should be included as the elements of working capital, and (3) a lack of precision in the meaning of certain key terms involved in defining the elements of working capital, such as *liquidity* and *current*. This chapter (1) examines the foundation of the working capital concept, (2) reviews the concept and its components as currently understood, and (3) discusses how the concept might be modified to add to its usefulness.

DEVELOPMENT OF THE WORKING CAPITAL CONCEPT

The concept of working capital originated with the distinction between fixed and circulating capital at the beginning of the twentieth century. At this time accounting was in its adolescent stage and such concepts as asset, liability, income, and expense were not clearly understood.[1] The impetus for the fixed and circulating capital definitions came from court decisions on the legality of dividends in Great

---

[1] For a complete documentation of the history of the working capital concept, see William Huizingh, *Working Capital Classification* (Ann Arbor: Bureau of Business Research, Graduate School of Business Administration, University of Michigan, 1967).

226

Britain. As first defined, fixed capital was the money expended in purchasing that was sunk once and for all, while circulating capital was defined as such items as stock in trade, which are parted with and replaced by others in the ordinary course of business.

These definitions were not readily accepted by members of the accounting profession, some of whom feared that the general public would misinterpret the distinction. Soon thereafter British and American accountants began to examine the valuation bases of the various assets, and gave increased attention to a method of accounting termed the *double-account system*. The double-account system divided the balance sheet horizontally into two sections. The upper portion contained all of the long-lived assets, the capital, the debt, and a balancing figure that represented the difference between capital and long-term liabilities, and long-lived assets. The lower section contained all other assets, current liabilities, and the balancing figure from the top section.

During this same period the notion of *liquidity* was becoming established as a basis for the classification of assets on the financial statements. Liquidity classification schemes were intended to report on the short-run solvency of the enterprise; however, criticisms arose which suggested that such schemes were in conflict with the going-concern concept. Nevertheless, the liquidity concept continued to gain acceptance among accountants and financial statement users and was included by Paton in his distinction between fixed and current assets.[2] Additionally, Paton noted that length of life, rate of use, and method of consumption were also important distinctions. He described the distinction between fixed and current assets as follows: a fixed asset will remain in the enterprise two or more periods, while current assets will be used more rapidly; fixed assets may be charged to expense over many periods, while current assets are used more quickly; and fixed assets are used entirely to furnish a series of similar services, whereas current assets are consumed.[3]

During the first three decades of the twentieth century, the balance sheet was viewed as the principal financial statement by most users in the United States. As such, financial statements were prepared on the basis of their usefulness to creditors, and investors were left to make their decisions on whatever basis they felt applicable. In 1936, the American Institute of Certified Public Accountants attempted to modify this viewpoint when it acknowledged the different points of view of the creditor and the investor as follows.

As a rule a creditor is more particularly interested in the liquidity of a business enterprise and the nature and adequancy of its working capital; hence the details of the current assets and current liabilities are to him of

---

[2]William A. Paton, *Accounting Theory* (New York: Ronald Press, 1922).
[3]Ibid., pp. 215–216.

relatively more importance than details of long-term assets and liabilities. He also has a real interest in the earnings, because the ability to repay a loan may be dependent upon the profits of the enterprise. From an investor's point of view, it is generally recognized that earning capacity is of vital importance and that the income account is at least as important as the balance sheet.[4]

This release also led to a clearer understanding of the distinction between current and noncurrent items. By the 1940s the concept of working capital as a basis for determining liquidity had become well established, even though there was some disagreement as to its exact meaning. The confusion centered on how properly to classify current assets and whether this classification should be based on those items that *will be* converted into cash in the short run or those that *could be* converted into cash. At this time the one-year rule was fairly well established as the dividing point between current and noncurrent assets. But Anson Herrick, who was an active member of the American Institute of Certified Public Accountants, began to point out some of the fallacies of the one-year rule.

Herrick focused upon the differences in preparing statements for credit and investment purposes and noted some inconsistencies in current practice, such as including inventories under the current classification when their turnover might take more than a year while excluding trade receivables due more than a year after the balance sheet date.[5] His thoughts are summarized in the following statement.

It is not logical to adopt a practice which may result in substantial difference between the reported amount of net current assets . . . and the amount which would be shown if the statement were to be prepared a few days earlier or later.[6]

In lieu of the one-year rule, Herrick proposed the *operating cycle* as the basis for classifying assets as current. This distinction was based upon the contrast of the assets' economic substance as either *fixed* or *circulating* capital.[7]

In 1947, while Herrick was a committee member, the Committee on Accounting Procedure issued Accounting Research Bulletin No. 30. This release defined current assets as "cash or other resources commonly identified as those which are reasonably expected to be realized in cash or sold or consumed during the normal operating cycle of the business." Current liabilities were defined as "debts or obligations, the liquidation or payment of which is reasonably ex-

[4]*Examination of Financial Statements by Independent Public Accountants* (New York: American Institute of Certified Public Accountants, 1936), p. 4.

[5]Anson Herrick, "Current Assets and Current Liabilities," *Journal of Accountancy,* (January 1944), pp. 48–55.

[6]Ibid., p. 49.

[7]Ibid., p. 50.

228

pected to require the use of existing resources properly classifiable as current assets or the creation of other current liabilities."[8] The operating cycle was then defined as "the average time intervening between the acquisition of materials or services . . . and the final cash realization." The committee also established one year as the basis for classification when the operating cycle was shorter than one year.[9] Although this distinction was slightly modified by Accounting Research Bulletin No. 43, it has stood essentially intact since that time.

CURRENT USAGE

It is usually argued that the working capital concept provides useful information by giving an indication of an entity's liquidity and the degree of protection given to short-term creditors. The concept gained increased prominence after the issuance of Accounting Principles Board Opinion No. 19, which made the presentation of a statement of changes in financial position mandatory. Specifically, the presentation of working capital can be said to add to the flow of information to financial-statement users by (1) indicating the amount of margin or buffer available to meet current obligations, (2) presenting the flow of current assets and current liabilities from past periods, and (3) presenting information upon which to base predictions of future inflows and outflows. In the following sections we examine the measurement of the items included under working capital.

COMPONENTS OF WORKING CAPITAL

The Accounting Research Bulletin definitions of current assets and current liabilities include examples of each classification as follows.

Current Assets:

a. cash available for current operations and items which are the equivalent of cash
b. inventories of merchandise, raw materials, goods in process, finished goods, operating supplies, and ordinary maintenance materials and parts
c. trade accounts, notes, and acceptances receivable
d. receivables from officers, employees, affiliates, and others if collectible in the ordinary course of business within a year
e. installment of deferred accounts and notes receivable if they conform generally to normal trade practices and terms within the business
f. marketable securities representing the investment of cash available for current operations

[8]Accounting Research Bulletin No. 30, pp. 248–249.
[9]Ibid., pp. 247, 249.

g. prepaid expenses, such as insurance, interest, rents, taxes, unused royalties, current paid advertising service not yet received and operating supplies[10]

Current Liabilities:

a. obligations for items which have entered into the opening cycle, such as payables incurred in the acquisition of materials and supplies to be used in the production of goods or in providing services to be offered for sale

b. collections received in advance of the delivery of goods or performance of services

c. debts which arise from operations directly related to the operating cycle, such as accruals for wages, salaries and commission, rentals, royalties, and income and other taxes

d. other liabilities whose regular and ordinary liquidation is expected to occur within a relatively short period of time, usually twelve months, are also intended for inclusion, such as short-term debts arising from the acquisition of capital assets, serial maturities of long-term obligations, amounts required to be expended within one year under sinking fund provisions and agency obligations arising from the collection or acceptance of cash or other assets for the account of third persons[11]

These items will now be examined in more detail.

CURRENT ASSETS

Cash

The accurate measurement of cash is important not only because it represents the amount of resources available to meet emergency situations, but also because most accounting measurements are based on actual or expected cash inflows and outflows. The prediction of future cash flows is essential to investors, creditors, and management to enable these groups to determine (1) the availability of cash to meet maturing obligations, (2) the availability of cash to pay dividends, and (3) the amount of idle cash that can safely be invested for future use. Measuring cash normally includes counting not only the cash on hand and in banks but also formal negotiable paper, such as personal checks, cashier's checks, and bank drafts.

The amount of cash disclosed as a current asset must be available for current use and not subject to any restrictions. For example, sinking fund cash should not be reported as a current asset because it is intended to be used to purchase long-term investments.

---

[10]Accounting Research Bulletin No. 43, "Restatement and Revision of Accounting Research Bulletins" (New York: American Institute of Certified Public Accountants, 1953), pars. 6010–11.
[11] Ibid., par. 6011.

It has also become commonplace for banks to require a portion of amounts borrowed to remain on deposit during the period of the loan. These deposits are called *compensating balances*. This type of agreement has two main effects: (1) It reduces the amount of cash available for current use and (2) it increases the effective interest rate on the loan. In 1973, the SEC issued Accounting Series Release No. 148, which recommended that compensating balances against short-term loans should be shown separately in the current assets section of the balance sheet. Compensating balances on long-term loans should be classified as either investments or other assets.[12]

Temporary Investments

In the event that cash balances are larger than necessary to provide for current operations, it is advisable to invest idle funds until the use of these funds becomes necessary. In order for these investments to be classified as current assets, they must be readily marketable and intended to be converted into cash within the operating cycle or a year, whichever is longer.

In theory, the procedures used to report the value of temporary investments on the balance sheet should provide investors with an indication of the resources that will be available for use in the future. That is, the amount of cash that will be generated from the future disposal of these securities. Temporary investments are unlike most other assets in that an objectively determined measurement of their value is available in the securities market on a day-to-day basis. Therefore, accountants are divided over the proper methods to use to value temporary investments. Three alternative methods for reporting temporary investments have been debated by accountants: **historical cost, market value,** and the **lower of cost or market.**

The *historical cost* method reports temporary investments at their acquisition cost until disposal. The advocates of historical cost believe an objectively verified purchase price provides the most relevant information about investments to decision makers. They also argue that current market prices do not provide any better information on future prices than does original cost, and that only realized gains and losses should be reported on the income statement.

Investments reported at *market value* are adjusted to reflect both upward and downward changes in value, and these changes are reported as either gains or losses on the income statement. Advocates of the market value method state that current amounts represent the current resources that would be needed to acquire the same securities now and also the amount that would be received from the sale of the securities. Additionally, they note that market value is as objectively

---

[12]"Amendments to Regulation S-X and Related Interpretations and Guidelines Regarding the Disclosure of Compensating Balances and Short-Term Borrowing Agreements." *Accounting Series Release No. 148* (Washington D.C.: SEC, November 13, 1973).

determined as historical cost for most investments, and it also presents more timely information on the effect of holding investments.

The *lower of cost or market* method, as originally defined, reports only downward adjustments in the value of temporary investments. The proponents of this method believe that it provides users with more conservative balance sheet and income statement valuations. They argue that conservative valuations are necessary in order not to mislead investors.

According to current practice, temporary investments should initially be valued at cost, with an appropriate discount factor where there are uncertainties of collection, unless the market value falls below cost. Accounting for temporary investments when their value falls below cost was studied by the Financial Accounting Standards Board in response to stock market conditions in 1973 and 1974. During this period the stock market declined substantially from previous levels and then made a partial recovery. The general movement in stock prices during this period had two main effects upon financial reporting for investments:

1. Some companies did not write their investments down to reflect market prices and were therefore carrying their portfolios of investments at amounts above current market prices.
2. Some companies wrote their investments down to current prices when the stock market reached its lowest level. The partial recovery experienced by the stock market then could not be reflected on these companies' financial statements, which resulted in the companies carrying their investments at an amount below both cost and current market.

Subsequently, the FASB issued Statement No. 12, "Accounting for Certain Marketable Securities," which attempted to alleviate this problem.[13]

According to the provisions of FASB Statement No. 12, marketable equity securities are to be valued at their aggregate cost or market value, whichever is lower on each balance sheet date. This determination is to be made by comparing the total cost of the entire portfolio of temporary investments in equity securities against its total market value. Losses in market value are to be accounted for as charges against income and reported on the balance sheet by way of a valuation account offset against the temporary investment account.

The requirement is not substantially different from previous practice. However, the FASB did provide for one major difference. If losses have previously been recorded, and a valuation account is in existence, recovery of market value is to be reported as income to the extent of previously recorded losses. The following example illustrates the provisions of this statement.

---

[13]Statement of Financial Accounting Standards No. 12, "Accounting for Certain Marketable Securities" (Stamford, Conn.: Financial Accounting Standards Board, 1975).

	Date	Portfolio Cost	Portfolio Market Value	Reported Increase/ (Decrease) of Income	Reported Increase/ (Decrease) of Valuation Account
Initial purchase	1/1/87	$18,000	$18,000	$0	$0
Balance sheet date	12/31/88	18,000	20,000	0	0
Balance sheet date	12/31/89	18,000	15,000	(3,000)	3,000
Balance sheet date	12/31/90	18,000	17,000	2,000	(2,000)
Balance sheet date	12/31/91	18,000	21,000	1,000	(1,000)

If all or any part of the portfolio is sold, a gain or loss to be recognized by comparing the original cost of the investment securities sold and the proceeds from the sale without giving effect to any valuation allowance. Changes in the valuation allowance are to be recorded at the balance sheet date by comparing the cost of any remaining securities with their market value. If no equity securities remain, the entire valuation account should be eliminated.

The provisions of FASB Statement No. 12 have the impact of allowing investors to evaluate the management of the temporary investment portfolio. For example, it may be possible to compare the yearly change in the market value of the portfolio to the overall trend in the stock market to assess the effect of management's temporary investment strategy.

FASB Statement No. 12 refers only to marketable equity securities and does not alter the accounting treatment required for bonds. (Although it should be noted that some accountants contend that FASB Statement No. 12 also applies to temporary investments in bonds. Those holding this view believe that the transactions are similar enough to require the same treatment.) Under traditional GAAP, temporary investments in bonds may be reported by using either the cost or the lower of cost or market methods. However, if the lower of cost or market method is used, losses should only be recorded when there has been a permanent impairment in value and no recoveries in the market value of bonds are ever recorded.

Additionally, when temporary investments in bonds are acquired at a price that is different from the face value of the securities, no amortization of the premium or discount is attempted. Since temporary investments, by their very nature, are not held long enough for such differences to be major factors in computing effective interest rates, any fluctuations in market values caused by unamortized premiums or discounts are recognized when the investment is sold.

Receivables

The term *receivables* encompasses a wide variety of claims held against others. These are generally classified into two categories for financial statement presentation: (1) trade receivables and (2) nontrade receivables.

The outstanding receivable balance constitutes a major source of cash inflows with which to meet maturing obligations and must be carefully evaluated so that financial statement users are not misled. In order for an item to be properly classified as a receivable both the amount to be received and the expected due date must be subject to reasonable estimation.

Ideally, each enterprise would make only cash sales; however, given the nature of our economic society, most firms must extend various types of credit. Businesses sell on credit to increase sales, but when credit is extended, losses from nonpayments invariably occur. Once a business decides to sell on credit, it may record bad debts by one of the following procedures.

1. Bad debts are recorded as the loss is discovered (the direct write-off method).
2. Bad debts are estimated in the year of the sale (the estimation method).

Under the *direct write-off* method, a loss is recorded when a specific customer account is determined to be uncollectible. Frequently this determination may not be made until a subsequent accounting period and, therefore, results in an improper matching of revenues and expenses. Additionally, FASB Statement No. 5 requires estimated losses to be accrued when it is probable that an asset has been impaired or a liability incurred, and the amount of the loss can be estimated. Since these conditions are usually satisfied for uncollectible accounts, most companies estimate bad debts.

Two methods are generally used to estimate expected losses from nonpayment of outstanding accounts receivable: (1) Losses are estimated on the basis of either current sales or (2) the estimated loss is based upon the outstanding accounts receivable balance. When the estimated losses are based upon sales, the matching process is enhanced because expenses are directly related to the revenues that caused the expenses. On the other hand, a more precise measure of anticipated losses can usually be made by reviewing the age and characteristics of the various accounts, and the resultant valuation of the asset account more closely resembles the expected amount to be collected in the future (*net realizable value*). With the increased emphasis on the income statement as the primary financial statement, most accountants now recommend estimating losses on the basis of sales; however, where sales and credit policies are relatively stable, it is unlikely that the use of either method will materially affect reported expenses.

Some accountants have also suggested that receivables should be carried at their present value by applying a discount factor. But this treatment is not usually considered necessary due to the relatively short collection (or discount) period involved for most accounts receivable.

234

Inventories

The term *inventory:*

> . . . designate[s] the aggregate of those items of tangible personal property which: (1) are held for sale in the ordinary course of business, (2) are in process of production for such sale, or (3) are to be currently consumed in the production of goods or services to be available for sale.[14]

The valuation of inventories is of major importance for two reasons. First, inventories generally constitute a major portion of current assets and, as such, have a significant impact on determining working capital and current position. Second, inventory valuation has a major and immediate impact on the reported amount of net profit and funds flow.

Inventory valuation procedures are different from those associated with cash, temporary investments, and receivables. The amounts disclosed for cash, temporary investments, and receivables approximate the amount of funds expected to be received from these assets. The amount of inventory disclosed on the financial statements does not represent the future cash receipts expected to be generated. Rather, this amount represents the acquisition value of a cost expected to generate future revenues.

The proper valuation of inventories rests upon answers to the following questions.

1. What amount of goods are on hand?
2. What flow assumption is most reasonable for the enterprise?
3. Has the market value of the inventory declined since its acquisition?

Inventory Quantity

The inventory quantity question posed above involves determining the amount of goods on hand by (1) an actual count, (2) perpetual records, or (3) estimating procedures.

Business enterprises that issue audited financial statements are usually required to *actually count* all items of inventory at least once a year unless other methods are able to provide reasonable assurance that the inventory figure is correct. When only this count is used, as in a *periodic inventory system,* to determine ending inventory, the expectation is that all goods not on hand were sold. However, other factors, such as spoilage and pilferage, must be taken into consideration.

When inventory quantity is determined by the *perpetual records method,* all items of inventory are tabulated as purchased and sold, and the amount of inventory on hand and the amount on the accounting records should be equal. However, it is necessary to verify the records by an actual count of inventory at

---

[14]"Restatement and Revision of Accounting Research Bulletins," *Accounting Research and Terminology Bulletins, Final Edition, No. 43* (New York: AICPA).

least once a year. Accounting control over inventories is increased by the use of a perpetual system. But a perpetual system should only be used when the benefits derived from maintaining the records are greater than the cost of keeping the records.

Two methods may be used to estimate inventories: (1) the gross profit method and (2) the retail method. The *gross profit* method computes the ending inventory on a dollar basis by subtracting the estimated cost of sales from the cost of goods available. This method is especially useful in estimating inventories for interim financial statements or in computing losses from casualties, such as fire or theft.

The *retail method* is used most frequently where merchandise is available for sale directly to customers, such as in department or discount stores. In this method, the retail value of inventory is computed by subtracting the retail price of goods sold from the retail price of goods available. Inventory at cost is then computed by applying the average markup percentage to the ending inventory at retail.

Both the gross profit and retail methods, although approximating balance sheet values, fail to provide management with all available information concerning the quantity and unit prices of specific items of inventory. For this reason it is necessary to also take an actual count of goods at least yearly.

Flow Assumptions

The matching of costs with associated revenue is the primary objective in inventory valuation. That is, balance sheet valuations are secondary to income determination. Each of the flow assumptions discussed later necessarily requires a trade-off between asset valuation and income calculation. Four general methods are available by which to account for the flow of goods from purchase to sale: (1) specific identification, (2) first in, first out, (3) last in, first out, and (4) averaging.

If an exact matching of expenses and revenues is the primary objective of inventory valuation, then *specific identification* of each item of merchandise sold may be the most appropriate method. On the other hand, this method may have low informational content to balance sheet readers because the valuation of inventories at original cost generally has little relation to future expectations. In using specific identification, the inventory cost is determined by keeping a separate record of each item acquired and totaling the cost of the items not sold at the end of each accounting period. Most companies find that the cost of the required record keeping outweighs any expected benefits associated with this procedure and turn to other methods. Specific identification is most feasible where the volume of sales is low and the cost of individual items is high, for example, jewelry, automobiles, and yachts.

The *first in, first out method* (Fifo) is based upon assumptions about the actual flow of merchandise throughout the enterprise; in effect, it is an approximation of specific identification. In most cases this assumption conforms to reality because the oldest items in the inventory are the items management wishes to sell first, and where perishables are involved, the oldest items must be sold quickly or they will spoil.

The Fifo flow assumption satisfies the historical cost and matching principles since the recorded amount for cost of goods sold is similar to the amount that would have been recorded under specific identification if the actual flow of goods is on a Fifo basis. Additionally, the valuation of inventory more closely resembles the replacement cost of the items on hand, and thereby allows financial-statement users to evaluate future working capital flows more accurately.

During the last decade, rising inflation rates have caused accountants to question the desirability of using Fifo. Using older and lower unit costs during a period of inflation causes an inflated net profit figure that may mislead financial statement users. Additionally, this inflated profit figure could result in the payment of additional income taxes. The *last in, first out method* (Lifo) of inventory valuation is based upon the assumption that current costs should be matched against current revenues. Most advocates of Lifo cite the matching principle as the basis for their stand and argue that the past three decades of almost uninterrupted inflation require that Lifo be used in order to approximate more closely actual net income. Such arguments are, of course, based upon the belief that price level changes should be eliminated from the statements, and Lifo is in effect a partial price level adjustment. (See Chapter 13 for a further discussion of price level adjustments.)

An added impetus to the use of Lifo in financial reports is the Internal Revenue Service's requirement that it must be used for reporting purposes when it is used for income tax purposes. (This requirement was amended to allow footnote or other supplemental information using Fifo or some other method. However, care must be exercised so as not to imply that another method might be a better measure of income.) Since Lifo can result in substantial tax savings, many companies that might not otherwise use it for reporting purposes do so because of tax considerations. This situation is an unfortunate example of tax accounting dictating financial reporting.

In addition to the advantage claimed by Lifo proponents of matching current costs and current revenues, this flow assumption may also eliminate inventory holding gains where the amount of inventory remains stable from year to year and may more clearly reflect cash flows available to meet current and future obligations. On the other hand, inventory valuations under Lifo are almost meaningless when attempting to assess the working capital position of the firm. And if inventory is depleted beyond the usual level, the cost of goods sold associated with these items may be very low, out of date, and result in additional tax payments when prices are rising.

The computation of inventory valuation under Lifo requires a great deal of bookkeeping because the physical quantity of each item of inventory must be recorded. Additionally, as technology changes, the raw materials necessary to manufacture a product may change. Strict application of Lifo would require a new Lifo inventory base for each item of inventory.

Dollar-value Lifo overcomes these disadvantages by using current costs and inventory pools. The general assumption of dollar-value Lifo is that the real increase or decrease in inventory can be estimated by eliminating the price change from the physical quantity of the ending inventory. This real increase or decrease is determined by comparing the beginning and ending inventory valuations at base-year costs.

The calculation of inventory under this method requires the use of index numbers (discussed later) measured at base-year prices and can be summarized as follows.

Step 1. Price the ending inventory at current cost.

Step 2. Restate the ending inventory by applying the base-year index to the current cost (year-end index/base-year index).

Step 3. Restate the beginning inventory by applying the base-year index to its current cost (beginning-of-the-year index/base-year index).

Step 4. Compare the ending inventory at base-year prices with the beginning inventory at base-year prices to determine if there was an increase or decrease in inventory at base year prices.

Step 5. (a) Increases—price the beginning inventory at the previous year's cost and add the additional inventory at current prices.

(b) Decreases—subtract the decrease at the base-year price from the latest items acquired at the base-year price. Price the remaining inventory items at the cost in existence when they were acquired.

For example, assume that the Newmann Company manufactures one product and adopted the dollar-value Lifo inventory method on December 31, 1986. The inventory on that date using the dollar-value Lifo inventory method was $200,000 and the index was 100. Table 5.1 shows the calculation of inventory for this example.

The preceding computation required the use of an index, and either a price index or a cost index may be used. A *price index* is a general index prepared by an external organization such as the U.S. Bureau of Labor Statistics. The Economic Recovery Act of 1981 made price indices more acceptable when it authorized their use for tax purposes. A *cost index* is internally generated and more specific to a company's inventory. Cost indices are generally prepared by using a

Table 5.1   Calculating Inventory by the Dollar-Value LIFO Method

Year	Inventory at Year-End Price	Price Index
1987	231,000	1.05
1988	299,000	1.15
1989	300,000	1.20

1987
Step 1 $231,000
Step 2 $231,000 ÷ (1.05/1.00) = $220,000
Step 3 $200,000 ÷ (1.00/1.00) = $200,000
Step 4 $220,000 − $200,000 = $20,000 *increase*
Step 5a $200,000 + (20,000 × 1.05) = $221,000

1988
Step 1 $299,000
Step 2 $299,000 ÷ (1.15/1.00) = $260,000
Step 3 $231,000 ÷ (1.05/1.00) = $220,000
Step 4 $260,000 − $220,000 = $40,000 *increase*
Step 5a $200,000 + ($20,000 × 1.05) + ($40,000 × 1.15) = $267,000

1989
Step 1 $300,000
Step 2 $300,000 ÷ (1.20/1.00) = $250,000
Step 3 $299,000 ÷ (1.15/1.00) = $260,000
Step 4 $260,000 − $250,000 = $10,000 *decrease*
Step 5b $200,000 + ($20,000 × 1.05) + ($30,000 × 1.15)* = $255,500

*$40,000 previous less $10,000 decrease in inventory during 1984.

sample of the total inventory. Two methods may be used to compute a cost index: (1) the double extension method and (2) the link-chain method.

In the *double extension* method, the ending inventory sample is priced at current-year costs and divided by the ending inventory at base-year costs to arrive at the cost index. Under the *link-chain* method, the cost index is found by computing the ratio of the current cost of the ending inventory to the beginning-of-the-year current cost of the ending inventory, and multiplying this ratio by the cost index for the previous year.

The major argument in favor of the use of dollar-value Lifo is expediency, and the procedure has little theoretical foundation. In addition to the disadvantages of

Lifo discussed previously, dollar-value Lifo may have an additional problem if the index number is based upon an economywide average. When such an average index number is applied against a particular inventory item, it is only an approximation of the change in the price associated with the inventory item and could further distort the amount disclosed on the financial statements.

Averaging techniques are, in effect, a compromise position between first in, first out and last in, first out. As such, each purchase affects both inventory valuation and cost of goods sold. Averaging does not result in either a good match of costs with revenues or a proper valuation of inventories in fluctuating market conditions. However, proponents of averaging base their arguments on the necessity of periodic presentation. That is, all of the transactions during a particular period are viewed as reflective of the period as a whole rather than as individual transactions, and they maintain that financial statements should reflect the operations of the entire period as a whole rather than as a series of transactions.

When the averaging method used is a weighted or moving weighted average, a claim can be made that the cost of goods sold is reflective of the total period's operations. However, the resulting inventory valuation is not representative of expected future cash flows unless prices remain stable. When the simple average method is used, the resulting valuations can result in completely distorted unit prices when lot sizes and prices are changing.

Market Fluctuations

Many accountants have advocated valuing inventories at market because they believe that current assets should reflect current values. Such procedures might add to the information content of the working capital computation, but to date the doctrine of conservatism has been seen as overriding the advantages claimed by current valuation advocates. Nevertheless, when inventories have declined in value, traditional accounting thought is that selling price will move in the same direction and anticipated future losses should be recorded in the same period as the inventory decline.

The AICPA has provided the following definitions to use in applying the lower of cost or market rule to inventories.

As used in the phrase lower of cost or market *the term* market *means current replacement cost (by purchase or reproduction, as the case may be) except that:*

1. market should not exceed the net realizable value (i.e., estimated selling price in the ordinary course of business less reasonably predictable costs of completion and disposal), and

240

2. *market should not be less than net realizable value reduced by an allowance for an approximately normal profit margin.*[15]

It should be noted that the application of the lower of cost or market rule results in inventory being recorded at an *expected utility* value and in the recording of a "normal profit" when the inventory is sold. Therefore, expenses are understated in the period of sale which may give rise to misinterpretations by external users.

The use of the lower of cost or market rule for inventories is consistent with the qualitative characteristics of accounting information contained in Statement of Financial Accounting Concepts No. 2, and the definitions of assets and losses contained in Statement of Financial Accounting Concepts No. 6. That is, when the cost of inventory exceeds its expected benefit, a reduction of the inventory to its market value is a better measure of its expected future benefit.

The major criticism of the lower of cost or market rule is that it is only applied for downward adjustments. Therefore, holding losses are recognized while holding gains are ignored. As noted earlier, this criticism has not been viewed as important as maintaining conservative financial statements, and the importance of the concept of conservatism was reaffirmed by the FASB in Statement of Financial Accounting Concepts No. 5.

Prepaids

Prepaid items result from recording expected future benefits from services to be rendered. They do not represent current assets in the sense that they will be converted into cash, but rather in the sense that they will require the use of current assets during the operating cycle if they were not in existence.

The measurement of prepaids is generally the residual result of the attempt to charge their expiration to expense, and little attention is given to balance sheet valuations. Two main cost expiration methods are used in the measurement of prepaids: (1) specific identification and (2) time. Specific identification is used where the items are consumed, as with office supplies, and time is used where no tangible asset is in existence and rights are in evidence over a certain period, such as with unexpired insurance or prepaid rent.

In most cases, the amortization method will be of little consequence because of the relative unimportance of these items. However, where substantial prepayments occur, care should be exercised to ensure that the allocation method is reasonable under the circumstances. *stop*

---

[15]Ibid., chap. 4 Para. 7

CURRENT LIABILITIES

Payables

The measurement of payables presents no particular difficulty, since the amount of the obligation is usually fixed by a transaction and involves a promise to pay at a subsequent date. As with receivables, discounts from face value are not considered necessary because the period of debt is generally short. However, where interest is not specifically stated on notes payable, Accounting Principles Board Opinion No. 21, "Interest on Receivables and Payables," requires that interest be calculated for certain types of notes.[16] (See Chapter 8.) In addition to notes and accounts payable, dividends and taxes represent payables that require the use of current funds.

It should be noted that liability recognition frequently results from the necessity to recognize an asset or an expense where the focus of attention is not on the liability. On the other hand, the recognition of short-term liabilities may have significant impact upon the working capital position of the enterprise.

Deferrals

Generally, deferrals are a special type of liability whose settlement requires the performance of services rather than the payment of money. Examples of deferrals include such items as subscriptions collected in advance or unearned rent. They are similar to prepaid expenses in that they are generally the residual result of the attempt to measure another amount. In this case the amount attempted to be measured is revenue, whereas it was an expense in the case of prepaids.

The placement of deferrals in the current liability section of the balance sheet has been criticized because they are not really liabilities in the general sense of the term in that there is no claimant; but unless they are unusually large, it is unlikely that the recording of deferrals as liabilities will have much impact upon financial statement presentation. Nevertheless, care should be taken to ensure that the company is not being overly cautious in reporting income as a deferral, and to determine that the deferral accounts are not being used as an additional allowance for uncollectible accounts.

Current Maturities

Unlike most assets, liabilities may be transferred from the long-term to the current classification due to the passage of time. Where the payment of long-term debt in the current period requires the use of current funds, proper accounting dictates that these amounts should be classified as current, but not all current maturities are classified as current liabilities. When the long-term liability is to

---

[16]Accounting Principles Board Opinion No. 21, "Interest on Receivables and Payables" (New York: American Institute of Certified Public Accountants, 1971).

242

be retired out of a special fund or by issuing additional long-term debt, the obligation should not be classified as current.

The proper classification of current maturities is of great importance because of the significance it can have on the working capital presentation. Where adequate provision has not previously been made to retire current maturities, a company may find itself in a weak working capital position and future capital sources may evaporate.

MODIFICATION OF THE WORKING CAPITAL CONCEPT

Earlier it was suggested that the working capital concept was useful to investors, creditors, and management in indicating the amount of buffer available to meet current obligations, presenting information about flows, and predicting future flows. However, current usage suggests that much of the foundation for the concept is based upon a moderate evolution of long-established customs and conventions. A historical examination of the development and current status of the working capital concept suggests that it is more closely associated with the notion of circulating capital than the fulfillment of various user needs concerning liquidity and flows.

Current practice is based upon the assumption that the items classified as current assets will be used to retire existing current liabilities and that the measurement procedures used in valuing these items are a valid indicator of the amount of cash expected to be realized or paid. A close examination of these assumptions discloses two fallacies: (1) all of the items are not measured in terms of their expected cash equivalent and (2) some of the items will never be received or paid in cash.

On the current asset side only cash, which is actual, and receivables, which are measured at expected net realizable value, show a high degree of correlation with the cash which will become available. In cases where the market price is lower than cost, temporary investments also indicate the current cash equivalent; but where market is higher than cost, this relationship no longer exists. Inventories are measured at cost, but the expectation is that they will be exchanged for amounts substantially above cost. Prepaid expenses have been included as current assets because if they had not been acquired, they would require the use of current assets in the normal operations of the business. However, prepaids will be used rather than exchanged for cash and, therefore, do not aid in predicting future cash flows. The valuation of current liabilities exposes similar problems. Payables and the current portion of long-term debt represent the amounts to be paid in cash to retire these obligations during the coming period, but deferred credits will be retired by the performance of services rather than the payment of monies.

If the working capital concept is to become truly operational, it would seem necessary to modify it in such a manner as to show the amount of actual buffer between maturing obligations and the resources expected to be used in retiring these obligations. Such presentation should include only the current cash equivalent of the assets to be used to pay the existing debts. It would therefore seem more reasonable to base the working capital presentation on the monetary–nonmonetary dichotomy used in price level accounting. (See Chapter 13). To review this concept briefly, monetary items are claims to or against specific amounts of money; all other assets and liabilities are nonmonetary.

The monetary working capital presentation would list as assets cash, temporary investments, and receivables and would list as liabilities current payables. Additionally, it is suggested that more meaningful information could be provided if temporary investments were measured in terms of current market price. This presentation would have the following advantages: (1) it would be a more representative measure of liquidity and buffer because it would only be concerned with future cash flows, (2) it would provide more information about actual flows because only items expected to be realized or retired by cash transactions would be included, and (3) it would give greater predictive ability because actual cash flows could be traced.

The concept of working capital is a valid and useful device for presenting information to financial-statement users, and yet its usefulness is impaired because much of the concept's foundation is based upon tradition rather than user needs. The implementation of new ideas into accounting theory is always a slow and tedious process, but the adoption of this new concept of working capital should more completely satisfy users' needs.

SUMMARY

A review of the concept and components of working capital from a historical point of view shows that the concept has its foundation in an earlier period, when the focus was upon the balance sheet and the ability to repay debts. Because of these factors, the presentation of working capital has not evolved fast enough to accommodate user needs.

An examination of the various measurement bases of current assets and current liabilities indicates that the measurement bases and methods of reporting the various accounts are dissimilar. We believe that user needs would be better satisfied if the working capital concept were modified to include only monetary items.

In the following readings, Andrew A. Haried and Ralph E. Smith discuss accounting for marketable securities in depth, and Caroline Strobel and Ollie Powers review some recent events that have resulted in new reporting requirements for inventories.

ACCOUNTING FOR MARKETABLE EQUITY SECURITIES

ANDREW A. HARIED
RALPH E. SMITH

Financial Accounting Standards Board Statement No. 12, "Accounting for Certain Marketable Securities,"[1] was issued in December 1975. The objectives of the Statement were to (1) eliminate some of the flexibility that has developed in reporting the carrying value of marketable securities and (2) provide authoritative support for some problems not previously covered. Specifically, the Board, in paragraph 3, addressed the following questions:

1. Under what circumstances should marketable equity securities that are carried on the cost basis be written down below cost?
2. Should marketable equity securities that have been written down be written back up based on market recoveries or other criteria?
3. If a parent company and one or more subsidiaries or investees follow different methods of accounting for marketable securities, should any adjustments be made to conform the subsidiaries' or investees' methods of accounting to that of the parent company in consolidated or parent company financial statements?

The Board viewed the project as being of limited scope to be completed in a limited time. The Board did not take a position on the issue of whether all marketable securities should be reported at market value and the related issue of reporting all unrealized gains and losses on the income statement.

Fluctuations in market values of equity securities create practical and theoretical reporting problems for management and accountants. Unfortunately, the authoritative literature provided little guidance in developing solutions to these problems. Accounting Research Bulletin No. 43 (chapter 3A, par. 9), issued in 1947, simply stated

> . . . *practice varies with respect to the carrying basis for current assets such as marketable securities and inventories. In the case of marketable securities where market value is less than cost by a substantial amount and it is evident that the decline in market value is not due to a mere temporary condition, the amount to be included as a current asset should not exceed the market value.*[2]

The ARB provided little guidance in accounting for marketable securities classified as noncurrent, but it is common prac-

[1]Financial Accounting Standards Board Statement No. 12, "Accounting for Certain Marketable Securities" (Stamford, Conn.: FASB, 1975).

[2]Committees on Accounting Procedure and on Terminology, *Accounting Research for Terminology Bulletins, Final Edition* (New York: AICPA, 1961).

tice to report noncurrent investments at cost unless a decline in market value was "evidently not a mere temporary condition."[3] Further, the literature leaves unclear what criteria should be applied in classifying a security as current or noncurrent.[4]

APPLYING STATEMENT NO. 12

According to paragraph 5, Statement No. 12 does not apply to

1. not-for-profit organizations
2. mutual life insurance companies
3. employee beneift plans

Investments accounted for under the equity method were considered beyond the scope of the Statement and such equity investments are accordingly excluded from the investment portfolio when computing aggregate cost and market values. The Statement does apply to mutual savings banks and other for-profit mutual enterprises.

The Statement classified accounting for marketable securities into two categories: companies in industries not having specialized accounting practices and companies in certain industries where special accounting practices are applied (e.g., investment companies, brokers and dealers in securities, stock life insurance companies and fire and casualty insurance com-

panies). The focus of this article is on the former category.

WHAT IS A MARKETABLE SECURITY?

The marketable equity securities covered by the Statement fall into three categories, which are defined in paragraph 7-a:

1. ownership shares—e.g., common, preferred and other capital stock
2. right to acquire ownership shares—e.g., warrants, rights and call options
3. right to dispose of ownership shares at a fixed or determinable price—e.g., put options

The term does not apply to 1) preferred stock that must be redeemed by the issuing firm or is redeemable at the option of the investor, 2) treasury stock and 3) convertible bonds. Also, to be marketable, a sales price or bid and ask price must be currently available on a national security exchange or in the over-the-counter market (Statement No. 12, par. 7-b).

WHEN SHOULD EQUITY SECURITIES BE WRITTEN DOWN?

Accounting for marketable equity securities by a firm that does not follow specialized practices is summarized as follows:

1. Classify marketable securities into two portfolios: current and noncurrent (in the case of an unclassified balance sheet, marketable equity securities are considered to be classified as noncurrent).
2. Determine aggregate cost and market value for each of the separate portfolios.
3. The carrying amount of each portfolio is the lower of its aggregate cost or market value.

---

[3]Accounting Principles Board Opinion No. 18, "The Equity Method of Accounting for Investments in Common Stock" (New York: AICPA, 1971), par. 5.

[4]Common criteria for classifying a security as current are (1) a security must be readily marketable and (2) it is the intention of management that the security is available to be converted into cash for use in normal operations. All other securities are classified as noncurrent. The problems associated with applying these two terms will be discussed later in this article.

4. The amount by which aggregate cost of each portfolio exceeds market value is accounted for as a valuation allowance.

To illustrate the provisions of the Statement specifically, a sample of stock included in the Dow-Jones Industrial Index was selected (see Table 1). It is assumed that 100 shares of each security were purchased and held during a two-year period in which Statement No. 12 was effective. To make the illustration realistic, recent year end prices for the securities selected are used.

At the end of year 1, the carrying amount for the current portfolio is the aggregate market value of the investments, which is less than the aggregate cost.

In this case an unrealized loss of $1,135 (difference between the aggregate market value and aggregate cost) is deducted in the determination of net income. The portfolio approach results in some unrealized gain ($300) being indirectly recognized to the extent that it can offset unrealized losses in market values of other securities in the portfolio. The loss of $2,020 on the decline in market value of the noncurrent investments is reported separately as a reduction in the equity section of the balance sheet.

Traditionally, it was considered appropriate accounting practice to recognize a decline in the market value below cost of an investment as a realized loss in the income statement if the decline was judged to be substantial and other than temporary. With the decision to report declines in market values of noncurrent investments as a reduction in stockholders' equity, a loss in value judged to be permanent would have been excluded from the income statement. Recognizing this possibility, paragraph 21 of Statement No. 12 requires that a decline in market value of a noncurrent investment that is judged to be other than temporary is

to be reported as a realized loss in the determination of income.

SUBSEQUENT RECOVERIES IN MARKET VALUES

In subsequent periods, recoveries in market value on securities still held are recognized to the extent that the resulting carrying amount of the portfolio does not exceed original cost. Such a reversal of the original writedown is not viewed as an unrealized gain but as a change in accounting estimate of a realized loss. In other words, the original writedown represented a reduction in realizable value of the asset and subsequent recovery reduces or eliminates the need for the allowance (Statement No. B, par. 29-c). Thus, in the case of the current and noncurrent accounts, an adjustment of the allowances to balances of $215 and $410, respectively, is required in year 2. The $920 change in the valuation account of the current asset is reported on the income statement. The $1,610 change in the noncurrent valuation account is reported in the equity section of the balance sheet (Statement No. 12, par. 11).

One exception to the above is the case of the reduction in market value below cost of a security classified as noncurrent being judged other than temporary. If, for example, the Allied Chemical writedown in the first year had been judged to be other than temporary, a loss of $2,060 would be reported on the income statement rather than combined with the unrealized gains and losses of the other noncurrent securities. Presumably, the writedown is made directly to the investment account (new cost basis is now $2,840), and since the investment is still part of the portfolio, any subsequent recovery above $2,840 is not recognized in the income statement but in the stockholders' equity section, and then only

Table 1   Portfolio of Marketable Equity Securities

	End of Year 1			End of Year 2		
	Cost	Market	Unrealized Gain (Loss)	Cost	Market	Unrealized Gain (Loss)
Current Assets:						
Security						
Esmark	$2,490	$2,790	$300	$2,490	$3,160	$670
International Harvester	2,575	1,975	(600)	2,575	2,240	(335)
Chrysler	1,560	725	(835)	1,560	1,010	(550)
Total	$6,625	$5,490	($1,135)	$6,625	$6,410	($215)
Noncurrent Assets:						
Security						
American Can	$2,625	$2,900	$275	$2,625	$3,140	$515
Goodyear	1,525	1,290	(235)	1,525	2,175	650
Allied Chemical	4,900	2,840	(2,060)	4,900	3,325	(1,575)
Total	$9,050	$7,030	($2,020)	$9,050	$8,640	($410)

to the extent it can offset unrealized losses of other noncurrent securities.

We fail to see the merit of this treatment. Surely a subsequent recovery of an unrealized loss previously judged as permanent can be viewed as a change in accounting estimate of an unrealized loss (since the loss was not actually realized after all) and a writeup permitted in the income statement to the extent of a previous writedown (see par. 2 of FASB statement No. 5 and par. 10 of APB Opinion No. 20). This requirement is inconsistent with the treatment of losses in the current portfolio where recoveries in what were judged to be imminent losses are recognized in the income statement.

SALE OF STOCK

A realized gain and loss from the sale of stock (both current and noncurrent) is to be reported on the income statement and is the difference between the net proceeds from the sale and its cost. If all securities classified as current are sold during the second year for $6,410 (market values), a realized gain of $670 and a realized loss of $885 are recognized. If no other securities are purchased, the valuation allowance is reduced to zero and a change in valuation allowance of $1,135 is reported on the income statement. The realized gains, realized losses and changes in the valuation allowance can be reported separately on the income statement or combined and disclosed separately in a footnote.

DISCLOSURE REQUIREMENTS

The following information is required, according to paragraph 12 of the Statement, either in the body of the financial statements or in accompanying notes:

As of the date of each balance sheet presented

1. aggregate cost—segregated between current and noncurrent when classified
2. aggregate market value—segregated between current and noncurrent when classified
3. identification as to which is the carrying amount

Date of latest classified balance sheet presented, segregated between current and noncurrent

1. gross unrealized gains
2. gross unrealized losses

For each period in which an income statement is presented

1. net realized gains or losses included in the determination of net income
2. basis on which cost is determined in computing gain or loss
3. change in valuation allowance that has been included in the equity section of the balance sheet during the period
4. when a classified balance sheet is presented, the amount of such change included in the determination of net income

CHANGE IN CLASSIFICATION

The Board recognized that reclassification of securities between current and noncurrent classifications occurs frequently in practice and that such reclassification could have a significant impact on net income. For example, if in year 1 the firm reclassified Chrysler to a noncurrent asset, the unrealized loss reported in the income statement would be reduced by $835 to $300. To reduce the opportunities for this possible manipulation, a change in classification is to be made at the lower of cost or market. If market is lower, the security is written down to a new cost basis and the difference is to be accounted for as realized loss in the determination of net income.

Presumably, any subsequent recovery in market value above this new basis would not be recognized except to the extent it could offset other declines in market value below cost of other securities in the portfolio.

There is still some possibility of manipulation by changing the classification of a security that has a market value greater than cost to reduce unrealized losses. For example, if in year 1 American Can was reclassified and included in the current portfolio, the amount of unrealized loss would be reduced by $275.

INCOME TAX EFFECTS

Tax effects on unrealized gains and losses that are recognized in net income or included in the equity section are to be accounted for in accordance with APB Opinion No. 11, "Accounting for Income Taxes," except that tax effects on unrealized capital losses shall be recognized only when there exists assurance beyond a reasonable doubt that the benefit will be realized by the offset of the loss against capital gains. Although consistent with APB Opinion No. 11, this exception presents a number of problems in application.

For example, whether or not a tax benefit is assured of realization depends on subjective evaluation of

1. management's intent regarding the timing of the disposal of securities
2. the probable proceeds from both gain and loss securities when they are disposed of
3. the amount of existing capital gains against which carryback losses may be utilized and anticipated capital gains that may be used to offset loss carryforwards

Furthermore, the appropriate tax rate to use in calculating tax effects is dependent on the nature of net capital gains and losses that may be used to offset loss carrybacks and carryforwards and management's intent as to the timing and composition of securities to be disposed of.

In addition, there are other complications that arise in the appropriate determination, recording and disclosure of tax effects. However, it is beyond the scope of this article to cover the rather complex tax issues and computations associated with accounting for marketable securities.

CONSOLIDATED VERSUS UNCONSOLIDATED SUBSIDIARIES

An interesting effect of the application of FASB Statement No. 12 explicitly recognized by the Board is that it may result in an exception to paragraph 19 of Opinion No. 18, which states that "an investor's net income for the period . . . [is] the same whether an investment in a subsidiary is accounted for under the equity method or the subsidiary is consolidated. . . ."

To illustrate, assume that the current portfolio of marketable securities of P Company and S Company are as shown below and the S Company is a 100 percent owned subsidiary of P Company.

If the subsidiary is consolidated, Statement No. 12 requires that the current portfolios of both companies be treated as a single consolidated portfolio for purposes of determining the amount of a consolidated valuation allowance and hence the amount of unrealized loss recognized in the income statement. In this example, aggregate cost is $8,000, aggregate market is $7,000, and consolidated income would be reduced by $1,000 of unrealized losses.

If the subsidiary is not consolidated, Statement No. 12 requires that the portfolios shall not be combined. As a result, income in this example will be reduced by $1,700, rather than $1,000 if the invest-

Table 2 Hypothetical Portfolio of Marketable Securities Classified as Current (end of year 1)

Security	Company P Cost*	Company P Market	Company S Cost*	Company S Market
A	$2,000	$2,500	0	0
B	1,000	1,200	0	0
C	0	0	$3,000	$1,800
D	0	0	2,000	1,500
Total	$3,000	$3,700	$5,000	$3,300

*Securities assumed to be acquired during year 1.

ment in S Company is reported under the equity basis rather than consolidated. This occurs because P Company must pick up 100 percent of the $1,700 unrealized loss reported in the income statement of S Company and cannot offset against that loss the $700 of unrealized gain in its portfolio.

The Board rejected recommendations that the portfolios of equity method subsidiaries be combined with the parent's because "to do so could produce illogical results either with respect to the carrying amount of marketable securities as reflected in the consolidated balance sheet, or the carrying amount of the equity method subsidiary as reflected in the same balance sheet" (par 35). For example, in this illustration either the parent's current marketable security portfolio or its investment in S Company would have to be written up by $700 to obtain the same income result as would be obtained by consolidating Company S.

EFFECTIVE DATE AND TRANSITION

It was the Board's opinion in the exposure draft[5] that application of the Statement by retroactively adjusting prior period financial statements would improve comparability. In addition, this would be consistent with the transition required in some other Statements. However, the Board concluded that with the substantial reclassifications of securities that have occurred, and with the new requirement that changes between portfolios be made at a lower of cost or market basis, retroactive adjustment would result in less comparability. Therefore, the effects on financial statements from the initial application of the Statement should be reported in the year that it is first applied in the case of industries not following specialized accounting practices.

IMPLEMENTATION PROBLEMS

DISTINCTION BETWEEN CURRENT AND NONCURRENT PORTFOLIOS OF MARKETABLE EQUITY SECURITIES

In the exposure draft, the Board proposed that all marketable securities, irrespective of balance sheet classification, should be treated as a single portfolio for the purpose

[5]Proposed Statement of Financial Accounting Standards, "Accounting for Certain Marketable Securities" (Stamford, Conn.: FASB, November 6, 1975).

of determining a valuation allowance and that all changes in the carrying amount of the marketable equity securities portfolio be reflected in income currently with no distinction between the current or noncurrent classifications of such securities.

The authors believe that the change from the single portfolio basis to the current, noncurrent portfolio classification basis constitutes a conceptual error and that it creates serious implementation problems that the Board failed to, but should have, addressed in making the change.

Conceptual Merit

The argument by some that to reflect fluctuations in the market value of long term investments in income would cause distortions that would not be understood by investors apparently weighed heavily on the Board when it retreated from the position taken in the exposure draft. The Board then justified its new position by stating in paragraph 30 that "present concepts of income require clarification with respect to the recognition of unrealized gains and losses on *long term assets*" and that such clarification was "beyond the scope of this Statement." (Emphasis added.)

Present concepts of income, however, also require clarification with respect to the recognition of unrealized gains and losses on current assets, e.g., investments, inventories, etc., as is evidenced by the need for Statement No. 12 itself. By requiring that changes in the carrying value of marketable equity securities classified as current be reflected in income and that similar changes in such securities classified as noncurrent be reflected directly in shareholders' equity, the Board has indeed dealt, at least temporarily, with the appropriate treatment of unrealized gains and losses associated with one category of both long term assets and current assets. What

the Board decided, in effect, is that unrealized losses, the realization of which is regarded as imminent, should be recognized in income determination, but, if the realization of such losses is not regarded as imminent, they should be reflected in the balance sheet only.

Unfortunately, however, the distinction between securities that will be sold in the near future and those that will not be is not necessarily the same as the present criteria for distinguishing between current and noncurrent investments including investments in marketable equity securities (see discussion following).

More to the point, it is the authors' contention that unrealized gains and losses which can be objectively identified should be measured and reported in income in the current period and that appropriate disclosure of the distinction between unrealized and realized gains and losses so recognized would not result in distortion and confusion but would add measurably to the information content of financial statements.

Inadequate Criteria

Assuming that the Board was correct in distinguishing between current and noncurrent portfolios of marketable equity securities and in determining that the method of recognizing unrealized gains and losses should be different based on such classification, we believe that it was incumbent upon the Board to authoritatively define operational criteria for classification of investments between current and noncurrent categories.

The Board itself recognized in the exposure draft that distinction between current and noncurrent classifications of marketable equity securities is "frequently a subjective judgement by management that is subject to change according to a number of variables" (exposure draft, par. 28).

There is no authoritative statement as to whether only marketable securities that management intends to convert to cash within the normal operation cycle should be included in the current portfolio or whether, in addition, securities that management does not intend to sell, but may sell at any time at their option, should also be included. Some authors propose that all marketable investments should be classified as current; others propose that all marketable securities except those that management definitely does not intend to dispose of for good business reasons (such as investment in suppliers and sinking fund investments) should be classified as current.

Recent quasiauthoritative literature on this question certainly fails to fully clarify this issue:

Whether marketable securities are properly classified depends to a large extent on management's intent. If management intends to dispose of the securities in the next fiscal year, the securities are classified as a current asset. Marketable securities that represent an excess of funds available for operations, but which management does not intend to dispose of, are often [but not necessarily?] classified as current assets since management can sell them at any time at their option.[6]

Since income determination is now dependent on the classification of marketable equity securities, we believe that it is now incumbent upon the Board to promulgate authoritative operational standards for appropriate classification of such securities

[6]Auditing Interpretation, "Evidential Matter for the Carrying Amount of Marketable Securities," JofA, April 1975, p. 69.

and that their failure to do so in this Statement was a serious omission.

It is interesting to note that only two of the four securities classified as current in 1974 in Appendix B to Statement No. 12 are disposed of in 1975 in the Board's illustration of the application of the provisions of the Statement.

With or without clarification in this area, the auditor now has the additional burden of obtaining more evidence as to appropriate classification of equity securities since appropriate classification now pervades the income statement as well as the balance sheet, and the effect on the balance sheet (unrealized losses in shareholders' equity) is now more pervasive than before.

OTHER THAN TEMPORARY DECLINES IN MARKETABLE SECURITIES CLASSIFIED AS NONCURRENT

Under the single portfolio approach proposed in the exposure draft, there would no longer be the need to make judgments as to whether or not the decline in the market value of a security was permanent or temporary. Losses, whether permanent or temporary, as measured by the market value of the portfolio would have been recognized as a charge to income in the year the decline occurred and, if the market value of the portfolio subsequently recovered, that fact would be reflected by a credit to income to the extent of the losses previously charged to income. In the exposure draft (par. 27), the Board recognized that "to recognize a loss only when the decline in market value is deemed other than temporary is to base accounting for these types of securities on the ability to predict future market value changes" and that "such judgments are subjective by nature, whereas market value for these securities, by definition, is readily verifiable." Hence, at that time the Board, in paragraph 28, "saw little merit in applying the lower of cost or market requirement only to those marketable equity securities classified as current assets, while *continuing to apply other less objective criteria* for determining permanent impairment of value of similar securities classified as noncurrent assets." (Emphasis added.)

The change to a dual portfolio approach, however, reintroduces the problem of identifying other than temporary declines in securities classified as long term. The problem arises because the Board now concludes that temporary declines should not be reflected in income, whereas permanent declines should.

Management and its auditors are again in a position where they must make judgment as to whether the decline in the market value of a security classified as noncurrent is likely to reverse. If the decline is judged to be other than temporary, the cost of the individual security must be written down to a new cost basis and the writedown accounted for as a realized loss. The cost basis shall not be changed for subsequent recoveries in market value.

Determining whether a decision is temporary is a subjective judgment indeed and one for which there is little competent supporting evidential matter. An auditing Interpretation provides some—but little—guidance to auditors and management in this area:

> When the market decline is attributable to specific adverse conditions for a particular security . . . a writedown in carrying amount is necessary unless persuasive evidence exists to support the carrying amount.
>
> The value of investments in marketable securities classified as noncurrent assets may decline because of general market conditions that reflect prospects of the economy as a whole or prospects of a particular industry. Such declines may or may not be indicative of the ability to ultimately recover the carrying amount of investments. The auditor should consider all available evidence to evaluate the carrying amount to the securities.[7]

In the authors' opinion, existing criteria and evidence for applying this provision of the Statement are so subjective and ambiguous that the provision will be largely ignored in practice.

The Interpretation recognizes that there will be instances (whether many or few is not indicated) where available information does not support a judgment as to eventual recovery or a contrary judgment that recovery will not occur, in which case a "subject to" qualification based on the uncertainty of the recoverability would be required in the auditor's report.

The single portfolio approach obviated the need for this type of subjective and nonverifiable judgment. Regrettably, the dual portfolio approach reintroduces the problem, and, in the authors' opinion, the problems of subjectivity reintroduced here along with the subjectivity in determining portfolio classification previously discussed far outweigh the reasons given by the Board for retreating from the single portfolio approach.

CONCLUSION

We cannot refrain from pointing out that, had the Board been in a position to consider favorably the alternative of market (whether higher or lower than cost) as a basis for valuation of marketable securities and income deter-

[7]Ibid., p. 70.

mination, the implementation problems of (1) current and noncurrent classification, (2) portfolio basis valuation, (3) other than temporary declines in noncurrent securities, (4) transfers between portfolios, (5) income tax effects and (6) equity basis investments could all be easily and consistently resolved. We also believe that, as the Board proceeds with its conceptual framework study, market as a basis for valuation of marketable securities and income determination will be even more strongly endorsed.

Given the implementation problems of the short run solution adopted in Statement No. 12, we conclude that it would have been better for the Board to defer action until it was in a position to consider all viable alternatives.

ACCOUNTING FOR INVENTORIES: WHERE WE STAND

CAROLINE D. STROBEL
OLLIE S. POWERS

Rapidly rising price levels in the United States have limited the usefulness of traditional historical cost based accounting measurement. Matching historical costs with current revenues is less likely to produce meaningful information when the price-level at the time the costs were incurred varies materially from the price-level at the time associated revenues are generated.

In periods of rising prices, historical cost accounting results in the inclusion of "inventory profits" in reported earnings. Inventory profit results from holding an inventory item during a period of rising prices and is measured by the difference between the historical cost of the item and its replacement cost at the time it is sold.

Although the degree to which inventory profit is included in earnings varies depending on the inventory accounting meth-

Reprinted with permission of *The CPA Journal* May, 1981, Vol. LI/No. 5 Copyright 1981, The New York State Society of Certified Public Accountants.

od selected, no method based on historical cost explicitly reports this profit. Since inventory profit is hidden in gross profit, this figure is not reflective of the economic earning activity of the business. Therefore, many have argued that, where "inventory profits" are material, disclosure is important in facilitating the reader's assessment of the quality of earnings.

Recognizing the significance of the inventory profit information, the SEC issued in 1974 ASR No. 151, which urged (but did not require) registrants to disclose inventory profit amounts. The SEC noted that various techniques might be used in arriving at this information and encouraged registrants to use any method or basis deemed appropriate, with a description of the method or basis used and the reasons for adopting it.

Companies are affected in varying degrees by price-level changes. Some firms operate in industries where the costs of goods purchased are more volatile than the selling prices of goods sold, and vice versa. Accordingly, the SEC in ASR No. 151

also urged registrants to discuss the relationship of costs and selling prices in the current year in connection with the recommended inventory profit disclosure. However, the disclosures were not made mandatory and few have been made.

LIFO AND CONFORMITY PROBLEMS

Another disclosure issue concerning inventory and rising prices arises from the widespread adoption of the LIFO inventory method by companies attempting to charge their most current inventory costs against current sales revenues. IRC Sec. 472 provides taxpayers with an election to account for inventories under the LIFO method. The code has traditionally required that, if LIFO is elected for tax purposes, another method of inventory valuation cannot be used for purposes of reporting income, profit or loss in credit statements, financial reports to shareholders, partners, other proprietors or beneficiaries. These conformity requirements have recently been amended by the issuance of new regulations.[1]

The new regulations list a number of situations where another method of inventory valuation can be used without violating the LIFO conformity requirements:

- As a supplement to or explanation of the primary presentation in statements of income for a taxable year;
- To ascertain the value of inventory of specified goods on hand for purposes of reporting such value on the balance sheet;
- For purposes of ascertaining information reported in internal management reports;
- For purposes of issuing reports or credit statements covering a single continuous

[1]Reg. 1.472-2 (e).

period of operations that is both less than the whole of a taxable year and less than 12 months.

In addition, market value may be used each year in lieu of the LIFO cost assigned to the items of inventory for federal income tax purposes, where market value is less than LIFO cost.

In defining what will be considered supplemental or explanatory information (and, therefore, allowed to be shown), the regulations provide that information reported on the face of the income statement will not be included. This eliminates all parenthetical information from being considered supplemental. The regulation does provide that footnotes to the statement are not a part of the face of the statement. Thus, another method of inventory valuation can be used and disclosed in a footnote, but cost of goods sold using the first-in, first-out method (FIFO) could not be disclosed parenthetically. The footnote disclosures should be issued with the income statement as part of a single report.

Appendices and supplements to primary financial statements for a taxable year will be considered a supplement to an explanation of the primary presentation if they are part of a single report with the income statement, and if they are clearly identified as such. Other reports, such as news releases, letters to shareholders, creditors, etc., will be considered a supplement to or explanation of primary presentation if they are clearly identified as such, and the item of information being supplemented or explained, such as cost of goods sold, net income, or earnings per share (ascertained using LIFO), is also reported in the news release, letter, or other report.

These regulations allow firms electing LIFO for tax purposes to meet the reporting requirements of FASB No. 33 as far as additional disclosures are concerned. The supplemental information to be footnoted or carried as a supplement to the primary financial statements will now be in conformity with the LIFO requirements under the IRC.

An additional requirement in the regulations provides that credit statements or financial reports that cover a one year period overlapping two taxable years are subject to the conformity requirement. Specifically, a series of such reports will be considered a single report if they are prepared using a single inventory method and, when added together, will present income for the year.

A number of revenue rulings have established that information reported to various governmental agencies need not meet the LIFO conformity requirements where it is not directly or indirectly available to shareholders, partners, proprietors, or beneficiaries of the taxpayer, or used for credit purposes.[2]

A recent Tax Court case[3] found that, where subsidiaries elected to use LIFO for tax and reporting purposes, the parent corporation could convert their inventories to the moving-average method for purposes of the consolidated annual report to shareholders. The conformity requirement of Sec. 472 was found to be satisfied as the financial report was not attributable to the subsidiaries. The right of the subsidiaries to use the LIFO inventory method in a consolidated tax return was preserved.

Several recent private letter rulings have further relaxed the LIFO conformity requirements. A company, having elected LIFO, requested permission to include a LIFO to FIFO comparison of inventory values in its financial statements and in a letter to be sent to its shareholders. The company also requested permission to include an analysis showing that the LIFO value of its inventory is the FIFO value reduced by the LIFO reserve for the year. The IRS held that the LIFO-FIFO comparison and disclosures of the FIFO inventory values will not violate the LIFO conformity requirement.[4]

In another ruling, the IRS held that a company wishing to change to LIFO could do so and still continue to use FIFO to compute employee bonuses under the company's incentive bonus plan.[5]

It is clear that there has been a relaxation by the IRS from the rigid stance traditionally taken in LIFO conformity requirements. As financial reporting requirements change to meet current economic reality, it appears that the IRS will continue to accommodate reporting requirements.

SEC REPORTING REQUIREMENTS FOR LIFO

ASR No. 150 requires a public company to include "Management's Discussion and Analysis of the Summary of Earnings" in filings with the SEC. In the case of a company which has changed to LIFO, an explanation of the change and its effect on earnings is called for by this Release. However, disclosure and discussion of the difference between earnings computed assuming LIFO and earnings computed under some other method (such as FIFO) appear to conflict with the book-tax conformity requirement. That is, in the past, disclosure of a FIFO earnings figure in the discussion would have been prohibited by the Regulations to the IRC.

ASR No. 169 discusses this financial

---

[2]Rev. Rul. 79-139, 1979-1 C.B. 190; Rev. Rul. 79-380, 1979-2 C.B. 222.
[3]Insilco Corp. v. Comm., 73 TC No. 43.

[4]Doc. 8037041.
[5]Doc. 8037040.

disclosure problem by confirming an agreement reached by the SEC and IRS regarding supplementary disclosure and the LIFO election. The LIFO election will not be terminated if the same language used in the financial statement footnote describing the effect of the change to LIFO is repeated in management's analysis of operations. This is true whether the analysis is included as a separate narrative or as part of the president's letter.

A typical example relating to the impact on earnings was provided in ASR No. 169 and reads as follows:

Footnote: The company has changed its method of accounting for inventories to Last-in, First-out (LIFO) method. This was done because the rapid increase in prices during the year would result in an overstatement of profits if use of the First-in, First-out (FIFO) method were continued since inventories sold were replaced at substantially higher prices. The effect on reported earnings for the year was a decrease of $XXX,XXX, or $X.XX per share.

Excerpt from Management's Analysis of Summary of Earnings:

In order not to overstate reported profits as a result of inflation during the year, the company changed its method of accounting for inventory from First-in, First-out to Last-in, First-out. This was necessary because of the rapid increase in prices in 197X which caused inventories sold to be replaced at substantially higher prices. The effect of the change was to decrease reported earnings by $XXX,XXX, or $X.XX per share.

A company that has changed to LIFO may make any disclosure required by Accounting Principles Board (APB) Opinion No. 20, "Accounting Changes," without causing the IRS to terminate the LIFO election. In addition, ASR No. 169 confirms that disclosures required by APB Opinion No. 28, "Interim Financial Reporting," and FASB Statement No. 3, "Reporting Accounting Changes in Interim Financial Statements," are permitted. The financial statement disclosures discussed herein may also be made in news releases in the year of the LIFO election. However, supplementary information on the face of the income statement (other than footnotes) is not acceptable and would violate the conformity requirement. For example, a two-column format, one for LIFO earnings and the other for FIFO, is unacceptable. The SEC is concerned with possible inferences that earnings information on a FIFO basis is more representative of actual performance than LIFO-based information. This is of special concern where a company has recently changed to LIFO under the presumption that LIFO is the preferable method for the determination of earnings.[6]

Since the IRS's LIFO conformity requirements now extend only to the face of the income statement, companies may add a footnote disclosure such as the following:

Many of the company's competitors use the FIFO method of inventory valuation. Had the company reported its LIFO inventories under the FIFO method, had a 44 percent tax rate been applied to changes in income resulting therefrom, and had no other assumptions been made as to changes in income, net income for 19X1 would have been $XXX,XXX ($X.XX per share) and for 19X2 $XXX,XXX ($X.XX per share).

[6]CCH, Accountants SEC Practice Manual, p. 3385.

CHAPTER 5: WORKING CAPITAL

Of special importance in a disclosure such as this one is the expression "and had no other assumptions been made as to changes in income." Because items other than income tax expense may change as a result of the difference in earnings using FIFO rather than LIFO, this qualification should be included. For example, profit sharing or executive bonus computations may be different if a company uses FIFO as opposed to LIFO. Supplementary disclosures should make reference to these possibilities.

SEC Regulation S-X requires that the disclosure made in the year of the change to LIFO be repeated any time the financial statements for that year are subsequently reported, such as in the five year summary of operations required to be included in the annual report to shareholders. Also, registrants using the LIFO method are required to disclose the excess of replacement or current cost overstated LIFO value, if material. These disclosures may be made without jeopardizing the LIFO election.

The SEC encourages (but does not require) companies to disclose on a pro forma basis the effect on earnings that LIFO would have had if it had been used in the year prior to the actual change to LIFO. This disclosure causes no conformity problems, since LIFO was not used for tax purposes in the year preceding its adoption.[7]

There is a growing sentiment in Congress for the repeal of the LIFO conformity requirement. If it is repealed, it is likely that many companies will elect to use FIFO for accounting purposes and LIFO for tax purposes. There is some concern that the SEC may not view this as appropriate, however. In a recent statement, Clarence Sampson, the Chief Accountant of the SEC, indicated that the SEC is not likely to take a position on changes from LIFO to FIFO for accounting purposes until some action to repeal the conformity requirement occurs.[8] Thus, the freedom of SEC registrants to make the change, should the tax law permit, is subject to question.

Apart from the LIFO conformity issue, LIFO involves another disclosure problem when a material amount of income is recognized as a result of a liquidation of LIFO quantities. The SEC calls for disclosure of the effect of the liquidation on income either on the face of the income statement or in a footnote.[9] The following disclosure would be appropriate:

During 19X2, inventory quantities were reduced. This resulted in a liquidation of LIFO inventory quantities carried at prior years' costs which were lower than the costs of 19X2 purchases. This liquidation had the effect of increasing net income by $XX,XXX, or $X.XX per share.

VALUING INVENTORY

Generally accepted accounting principles (GAAP) have for years called for a departure from the cost basis of inventory valuation when the utility of the goods is no longer as great as their cost. A decline in utility can be caused by physical deterioration, obsolescence or changes in the price level. When there is evidence that the utility of goods, in thier disposal in the ordinary course of business, will be less than cost, the loss should be charged against revenue of the current period by applying the rule of "lower of cost or market."

[7]ASR 169.

[8]"Tax Report," *The Wall Street Journal*, Nov. 12, 1980, p. 1.
[9]SAB No. 1 (Topic 10.H).

The lower of cost or market rule is intended to provide a practical means of measuring a decline in utility and, in turn, the residual usefulness of an inventory expenditure. The term "market" may be thought of as the equivalent expenditure which would have to be made on the inventory date to procure corresponding utility. Specifically, as used in this context, the term market means current replacement cost (by purchase or reproduction), except that:

1. Market should not exceed the net realizable value (i.e., estimated selling price in the ordinary course of business less reasonably predictable costs of completion and disposal); and
2. Market should not be less than net realizable value reduced by an allowance for an approximately normal profit margin.[10]

The general rule is that utility is indicated by the current cost of replacement. In applying this rule, however, judgment must be exercised so that no loss is recognized unless the evidence clearly indicates that a loss has been sustained. The constraints indicated above, which must be considered in determining "market," attempt to insure that no loss of utility is recognized unless it has actually been sustained.

Replacement cost would not be an appropriate measure of utility when net realizable value is lower. In such cases, net realizable value (the maximum or "ceiling," for market) more appropriately measures utility. Furthermore, when the evidence indicates that cost as well as a normal profit will be covered through sale in the normal course of business, an inventory item should not be carried at an amount less than net realizable value reduced by an allowance for a normal profit margin (the minimum, or "floor," for market). To value inventory at a lower amount would result in an excessive amount of loss of utility being recognized.

The most common practice is to apply the lower of cost or market rule individually to each item of inventory. However, if the inventory is comprised of only one category of items (such as a single product line), the utility of the inventory as a whole may have the greatest significance for accounting purposes. Similarly, when inventory is comprised of two or more categories, application of the lower of cost or market rule to each category as a whole may result in the most useful determination of income.

To the extent that stocks of particular materials or components are excessive in relation to others, the most widely recognized procedure is the application of lower of cost or market to the individual items comprising the excess. This is equally applicable to cases in which the items enter into the production of unrelated products or products having a material variation in the rate of turnover.[11]

These principles had been followed for many years by the profession. We may now want to rethink our position after a recent Supreme Court decision.

THOR POWER TOOL CO.

No recent court decision has had such impact on the tax treatment of inventories as Thor Power Tool Co.[12] Thor, following GAAP, had written down its "excess" inventory to net realizable value (generally

[10]ARB 43, Ch. 4.

[11]*Ibid.*

[12]*Thor Power Tool* v. *Comm.*, 439 U.S. 522 (1979), Ct. D. 1996, 1979-1 C.B. 167.

260

scrap value). This "excess" inventory consisted mostly of spare parts, which Thor continued to hold for sale at their original prices. Tax regulations provide that the valuation of inventories must conform: (1) as nearly as may be to the best accounting practice in the trade or business, and (2) must clearly reflect income.[13] The regulations identify the most common methods of inventory valuation as cost, or cost or market, whichever is lower. Market is defined as "the current bid price prevailing at the date of the inventory for the particular merchandise in the volume in which usually purchased by the taxpayer."[14] "Bid price" has been uniformly interpreted to mean replacement cost; that is, the price the taxpayer would have to pay on the open market to purchase or reproduce the inventory items.[15] Two situations are specified where a price below market price could be used: (1) where the taxpayer in the normal course of business has actually offered merchandise for sale at prices lower than replacement cost, and (2) where the merchandise is defective.[16]

While taxable income is to be determined under the accounting method used in keeping books, it must clearly reflect income. Acknowledging that Thor's financial statements could not have been given the desired unqualified auditor's opinion without writing down this "excess" inventory, the Court nevertheless found that the inventory valuation method used did not clearly reflect income, and, as required under Reg. 1.446-1, the Commission could prescribe the method which did. The Court

found that the regulations demand hard evidence of actual sales and actual dispositions to support a write-down. Well-educated guesses were used by management. This kind of subjective estimate in an area with well-known potential for tax avoidance required, in the Court's opinion, a high evidentiary standard before write-downs could be allowed.

The Court held that, even if GAAP were followed, the Commissioner, in the exercise of his discretion, may determine that a method does not clearly reflect income and may prescribe a different practice without having to rebut any presumption running against the Treasury. The Court further noted that GAAP provides for a range of reasonable treatments leaving the choice of alternatives to management, but such latitude would make the determination of tax liability not only inequitable but unenforceable. In this case, Thor had two alternatives: (1) scrap the parts, take the loss, and retool if future demand required more inventory; or (2) maintain the excess parts inventory judging that the marginal cost of unsellable inventory will be lower than the cost of retooling machinery should demand surpass expectations.

When a departure from cost to a lower inventory valuation is made, the regulations require that it be substantiated by objective evidence of actual offerings, sales or contract cancellations, and further that records of actual dispositions be kept.

The Service then applied the Thor Power Tool case to anyone taking prohibited inventory writedowns. In Rev. Rul. 80-5,[17] The Service waived the 180 day rule, and gave a blanket consent to taxpayers to change from a method of valuing "excess" inventory that is not in accordance with the "prescribed method to the pre-

[13]Reg. 1.471-2 (a).
[14]Reg. 1.471-4 (a).
[15]E.g., *D. Loveman & Export Corp.* v. *Comm.*, 34 T.C. 776, 796 (1960) aff'd. 296 F. 2d 732 (CA6 1961), cent. denied 369 U.S. 860 (1962) [A cg., 1961-2 C.B. 5].
[16]Reg. 1.471-2 (c).

[17]1980-a C.B. 15.

scribed method.'' The consent was granted for taxable years ending on or after December 25, 1979. The change was to be taken into account, including any necessary adjustment to income under Sec. 481. Rev. Rul. 80-60[18] stated that ''Taxpayers bear an obligation to file returns prepared in accordance with appropriate laws and regulations; income tax preparers are subject to a similar obligation in preparing returns.'' Therefore, if a taxpayer files a federal tax return not using the ''prescribed method'' of inventory valuation, the taxpayer will have filed a return not in accordance with the law. This is disturbing to accountants because, as preparers, they will be subject to a negligence penalty for preparation of a return not in accordance with the law, if these new inventory rules are not followed.

In the aftermath of this significant court decision and these Revenue Rulings, it is still not clear exactly where we are as far as lower of cost or market is concerned. The FASB may need to give some thought to the desirability of the continued use of lower of cost or market for accounting purposes. The use of varying inventory valuation principles for accounting versus income tax purposes creates another timing difference calling for deferred income tax recognition.

REPLACEMENT COST ACCOUNTING

The SEC made a significant move in a new direction in 1976 in requiring the disclosure of certain inventory (and fixed asset) information on a current replacement cost basis. ASR No. 190 requires registrants with inventories and gross property, plant and equipment aggregating more than

[18]1980-1 C.B. 5.

$100 million and comprising more than 10 percent of total assets to disclose in Form 10-K the estimated current replacement cost of inventories and productive capacity at the end of each fiscal year for which a balance sheet is required and the approximate cost of goods sold and depreciation based on replacement cost for each of the two most recent full fiscal years. The SEC was aware that it was calling for information that cannot be determined with precision and which must be estimated based upon a number of assumptions. Nevertheless, the information was thought to be important and useful to statement readers and should be reported, despite its lack of precision.

The SEC took the position that it was not preempting the role of the FASB in the development of GAAP. It did not believe that its replacement cost requirements would prejudge any positions taken by the FASB, including its impending ''Conceptual Framework Study.'' In fact, the replacement cost requirement was viewed as an experiment which might aid the FASB in drawing its conclusions regarding the basic accounting model, while providing meaningful supplementary information in the interim.

The FASB's pronouncement dealing with current cost came in September 1979, in the form of Statement No. 33, ''Financial Reporting and Changing Prices.'' The statement applies only to public enterprises that meet a specified size test. A public company is required to comply if, at the beginning of the fiscal year for which financial statements are being prepared, it had either (1) inventories and gross property, plant and equipment of $125 million or more, or (2) total assets of $1 billion or more. It requires these enterprises to disclose (in any published annual report that contains the primary financial statements) supplementary information about the effects of changing prices. This includes a measurement of income from continuing operations on the basis of "historical cost/constant dollar" accounting and on the basis of "current cost" accounting. The current cost disclosure also includes measurements of inventories and property, plant and equipment. Certain of the required items are to be reported for the current year only while some are to be reported for the most recent five years.

"Historical cost/constant dollar" inventory valuation involves adjusting the historical inventory costs for the effects of general inflation, that is, for changes in the value of the dollar. The historical dollars are adjusted using the Consumer Price Index for All Urban Consumers. Through use of this index, historical dollars may be inflated to represent the average purchasing power of the dollar for the current year. Inventories (and the related cost of goods sold) valued under such an approach reflect merely the effect of the changing value of the dollar on historical costs.

Current cost accounting is a method of measuring assets and related expenses at their current cost at the balance sheet date or the date they are sold or used. It focuses on specific price changes for individual assets rather than on price changes caused by general inflation. Current cost-basis cost of goods sold is the current cost of purchasing the goods concerned or the current cost of the resources required to produce the goods, whichever is applicable in the circumstances.

The FASB allows companies considerable flexibility in selecting methods of determining current cost, ranging from indexing historical costs with specific price indices to direct pricing techniques (e.g., invoices, unit pricing). Despite this flexibility, and the fact that most affected companies have been presenting the SEC's required replacement cost information, the

FASB realizes that some companies may encounter problems in developing the current cost disclosures.

As a result of uncertainties and anticipated problems, the FASB has taken a cautious and experimental approach in Statement No. 33. The Board has been more flexible than is customary, apparently to encourage experimentation that would help to develop techniques for accumulating, reporting and analyzing data on the effects of changing prices.

In response to FASB Statement No. 33, the SEC issued ASR No. 271 in October 1979, which deletes the Form 10-K replacement cost requirement for companies disclosing supplemental current cost information in accordance with Statement 33. In ASR No. 271 the SEC reiterates the position taken in ASR No. 190 that its replacement cost requirements would not result in any subsequent pronouncements of the FASB being prejudged. In fact, although there are a number of differences in the SEC's replacement cost rule and the current cost methodology prescribed by the FASB, the Commission concedes that, in all likelihood, it would have adopted many of the differences had it not been waiting for the FASB to complete its consideration of the issue.[19]

Recent changes in the Form 10-K reporting requirements require all registrants to discuss the impact of inflation on their financial statements. Those not subject to FASB Statement No. 33 need not report the numeric data called for by that statement but must include in "Management's Discussion and Analysis of Financial Condition and Results of Operations" a narrative discussion of the impact of inflation on revenues and income from continuing operations.[20]

[19]ASR 271.
[20]SEC Release No. 33-6231.

CONCLUSION

After considerable delay the FASB is beginning to take the initiative in prescribing accounting principles that are meaningful in today's economic environment. The positions taken by the SEC, and most recently the IRS, are forcing changes in the principles to be followed in accounting for inventories. Rulings of both these groups bring compliance because of their abilities to enforce their rules. The FASB needs to carefully review reporting requirements for inventories. Present problems should be addressed and speedily resolved. The Supreme Court decision in Thor Power Tool serves to emphasize the need for GAAP that will bring uniformity and thus better comparability between firms.

QUESTIONS

1. Of the following items, the one that should be classified as a current asset is
    a. Trade installment receivables normally collectible in 18 months
    b. Cash designated for the redemption of callable preferred stock
    c. Cash surrender value of a life insurance policy of which the company is beneficiary
    d. A deposit on machinery ordered, delivery of which will be made within six months

2. The advantage of relating a company's bad debt experience to its accounts receivable is that this approach
    a. Gives a reasonable correct statement of receivables in the balance sheet
    b. Relates bad debts expense to the period of sale
    c. Is the only generally accepted method for valuing accounts receivable
    d. Makes estimates of uncollectible accounts unnecessary

3. Assuming that the ideal measure of short-term receivables in the balance sheet is the discounted value of the cash to be received in the future, failure to follow this practice usually does not make the balance sheet misleading because
    a. Most short-term receivables are not interest bearing
    b. The allowance for uncollectible accounts includes a discount element
    c. The amount of the discount is not material
    d. Most receivables can be sold to a bank or factor

4. An account that would be classified as a current liability is
    a. Dividends payable in stock
    b. Accounts payable—debit balance
    c. Reserve for possible losses on purchase commitments
    d. Excess of replacement cost over Lifo cost of basic inventory temporarily liquidated

5. Which of the following statements is not valid as it applies to inventory costing methods?
    a. If inventory quantities are to be maintained, part of the earnings must be

invested (plowed back) in inventories when Fifo is used during a period of rising prices.

    b. Lifo tends to smooth out the net income pattern, since it matches current cost of goods sold with current revenue, when inventories remain at constant quantities.

    c. When a firm using the Lifo method fails to maintain its usual inventory position (reduces stock on hand below customary levels), there may be a matching of old costs with current revenue.

    d. The use of Fifo permits some control by management over the amount of net income for a period through controlled purchases, which is not true with Lifo.

6. Jamison Corporation's inventory cost on its statement of financial position was lower using first-in, first-out than last-in, first-out. Assuming no beginning inventory, what direction did the cost of purchases move during the period?

    a. Up

    b. Down

    c. Steady

    d. Cannot be determined

7. The carrying amount of a current marketable equity securities portfolio in the balance sheet of a company shall be the aggregate

    a. Cost of the portfolio, whether it is higher than or lower than the aggregate market value of the portfolio

    b. Cost of the portfolio, when it is higher than the aggregate market value of the portfolio

    c. Market value of the portfolio, whether it is higher than or lower than the aggregate cost of the portfolio

    d. Market value of the portfolio, when it is lower than the aggregate cost of the portfolio

8. If inventory levels are stable or increasing an argument that favors the Fifo method as compared to Lifo is

    a. Income taxes tend to be reduced in periods of rising prices

    b. Cost of goods sold tends to be stated at approximately current cost in the income statement

    c. Cost assignments typically parallel the physical flow of the goods

    d. Income tends to be smoothed as prices change over time

9. An inventory pricing procedure in which the oldest costs incurred rarely have an effect on the ending inventory valuation is

    a. Fifo

    b. Lifo

    c. Conventional retail

    d. Weighted average

10. When inventory declines in value below original (historical) cost, and this decline is considered other than temporary, what is the maximum amount that the inventory can be valued at?
    a. Sales price net of conversion costs
    b. Net realizable value
    c. Historical cost
    d. Net realizable value reduced by a normal profit margin

11. Which of the following conditions generally exists before market value can be used as the basis for valuation of a company's marketable equity securities?
    a. Market value must approximate historical cost
    b. Management's intention must be to dispose of the security within one year
    c. Market value must be less than cost for each security held in the company's marketable equity security portfolio
    d. The aggregate valuation of a company's marketable equity security portfolio must be less than the aggregate cost of the portfolio

12. Which of the following inventory cost flow methods involves computations based on broad inventory pools of similar items?
    a. Regular quantity of goods LIFO
    b. Dollar-value LIFO
    c. Weighted average
    d. Moving average

13. When the allowance method of recognizing bad debt expense is used, the entries at the time of collection of a small account previously written off would
    a. Increase net income
    b. Have no effect on total current assets
    c. Increase working capital
    d. Decrease total current liabilities

14. When the double extension approach to the dollar-value LIFO inventory cost flow method is used, the inventory layer added in the current year is multiplied by an index number. How would the following be used in the calculation of this index number?

	Ending inventory at a current year cost	Ending inventory at base-year cost
a.	Numerator	Denominator
b.	Numerator	Not used
c.	Denominator	Numerator
d.	Not used	Denominator

266

15. The original cost of an inventory item is above the replacement cost. The replacement cost is below the net realizable value less the normal profit margin. Under the lower cost or market method the inventory item should be priced at its *[handwritten: Example: Original cost $8.5]*

a. Original cost *[handwritten: Net Realizable 9+x]*

b. Replacement cost *[handwritten: Replacement cost 8]*

c. Net realizable value *[handwritten: NRV - Profit Margin 9 → market value]*

d. Net realizable value less the normal profit margin

16. Which of the following conditions generally exists before market value can be used as the basis for valuation of a company's marketable equity securities?

a. Management's intention must be to dispose of the securities within one year.

b. Market value must be less than cost for each security held in the company's marketable equity security portfolio.

c. Market value must approximate historical cost.

d. The aggregate market value of a company's marketable equity security portfolio must be less than the aggregate cost of the portfolio.

17. In order to effect an approximate matching of current costs with related sales revenue, the last-in, first-out (Lifo) method of pricing inventories has been developed

Required:

a. Describe the establishment of and subsequent pricing procedures for each of the following Lifo inventory methods:

    i. Lifo applied to units of product when the periodic inventory system is used

    ii. Application of the dollar-value method to a retail Lifo inventory or to Lifo units of product (these applications are similar)

b. Discuss the specific advantages and disadvantages of using the dollar-value Lifo applications. Ignore income tax considerations.

c. Discuss the general advantages and disadvantages claimed for Lifo methods. Ignore income tax considerations.

18. Cost for inventory purposes should be determined by the inventory cost flow method most clearly reflecting periodic income.

Required:

a. Describe the fundamental cost flow assumptions of the average cost, Fifo, and Lifo inventory cost flow methods.

b. Discuss the reasons for using Lifo in an inflationary economy.

c. Where there is evidence that the utility of goods, in their disposal in the ordinary course of business, will be less than cost, what is the proper accounting treatment and under what concept is that treatment justified?

19. Accountants generally follow the lower of cost or market basis of inventory valuations.

Required:
a. Define *cost* as applied to the valuation of inventories.
b. Define *market* as applied to the valuation of inventories.
c. Why are inventories valued at the lower of cost or market? Discuss.
d. List the arguments against the use of the lower of cost or market method of valuing inventories.

20. On December 31, 1981, Carme Company had significant amounts of accounts receivable as a result of credit sales to its customers. Carme Company uses the allowance method based on credit sales to estimate bad debts. Based on past experience, 1 percent of credit sales normally will not be collected. This pattern is expected to continue.

Required:
a. Discuss the rationale for using the allowance method based on credit sales to estimate bad debts. Contrast this method with the allowance method based on the balance in the trade receivables accounts.
b. How should Carme Company report the allowance for bad debts account on its balance sheet at December 31, 1981? Also, describe the alternatives, if any, for presentation of bad debt expense in Carme Company's 1981 income statement.

21. At the end of its first year of operations, Key Company had a current marketable equity securities portfolio with a cost of $500,000 and a market value of $550,000. At the end of its second year of operations, Key Company had a current marketable equity securities portfolio with a cost of $525,000 and a market value of $475,000. No securities were sold during the first year. One security with a cost of $80,000 and a market value of $70,000 at the end of the first year was sold for $100,000 during the second year.

Required:
How should Key Company report the preceding facts in its balance sheets and income statements for both years? Discuss the rationale for your answer.

22. Specific identification is sometimes said to be the ideal method for assigning cost to inventory and to cost of goods sold.

Required:
a. List the arguments for and against the foregoing statement.

268

b. First-in, first-out; weighted average; and last-in, first-out methods are often used instead of specific identification. Compare each of these methods with the specific identification method. Include in your discussion an analysis of the theoretical propriety of each method in the determination of income and asset valuation. (Do not define the methods or describe their technical accounting procedures.)

BIBLIOGRAPHY

Barden, Horace G. *The Accounting Basis of Inventories*. New York: American Institute of Certified Public Accountants, 1973.

Bastable, C. W., and Jacob D. Merriwether. "FIFO in an Inflationary Environment." *Journal of Accountancy* (March 1976), pp. 49–55.

Beresford, Dennis R., and Michael H. Sietta. "Short-Term Debt Agreements—Classification Issues." *The CPA Journal* (August 1983), pp. 32–37.

Blum, James D., and Herbert L. Jensen. "Accounting for Marketable Securities in Accordance with FASB Statement No. 12." *Management Accounting* (September 1978), pp. 33–41.

Bohan, Michael P., and Steven Rubin. "LIFO: What Should Be Disclosed." *Journal of Accountancy* (February 1985), pp. 72–77.

Buchman, Thomas A., and Larry A. Friedman. "Accounting for Certain Marketable Securities." *Management Accounting* (March 1977), pp. 42–44.

Buckley, John W., and James R. Goode. "Inventory Valuation and Income Measurement: An Improved System." *Abacus* (June 1976), pp. 34–48.

Copeland, Ronald M., Joseph F. Wojdak, and John K. Shank. "Use Lifo to Offset Inflation." *Harvard Business Review* (May–June 1971), pp. 91–100.

Cramer, Joe J. "Incompatibility of Bad Debt 'Expense' with Contemporary Accounting Theory." *The Accounting Review* (July 1972), pp. 596–598.

Dun, L. C. "Working Capital—A Logical Concept." *Australian Accountant* (October 1969), pp. 461–464.

Fess, Philip. "The Working Capital Concept." *The Accounting Review* (April 1966), pp. 266–270.

Fox, Harold F. "Exploring the Facts of Lifo." *National Public Accountant* (October 1971), pp. 22–25.

Gambling, Trevor E. "Lifo vs. Fifo under Conditions of 'Certainty.'" *The Accounting Review* (April 1968), pp. 387–389.

Grinnell, D. Jacque, and Corine T. Norgaard. "Reporting Rules for Marketable Equity Securities." *Financial Analysts Journal* (January–February 1980).

Hirschman, Robert W. "A Look at 'Current' Classifications." *Journal of Accountancy* (November 1967), pp. 54–58.

Hoffman, Raymond A., and Henry Gunders. *Inventories: Control, Costing and Effect upon Income and Taxes,* 2d ed. New York: Ronald Press, 1970.

Holmes, William. "Market Value of Inventories—Perils and Pitfalls." *Journal of Commercial Bank Lending* (April 1973), pp. 30–35.

Huizingh, William. *Working Capital Classification.* Ann Arbor: Bureau of Business Research, Graduate School of Business Administration, University of Michigan, 1967.

Hunter, Robert D. "Concept of Working Capital." *Journal of Commercial Bank Lending* (March 1972), pp. 24–30.

Johnson, Charles E. "Inventory Valuation—The Accountant's Achilles Heel." *The Accounting Review* (April 1954), pp. 15–26.

Lemke, Kenneth W. "The Evaluation of Liquidity: An Analytical Study." *Journal of Accounting Research* (Spring 1970), pp. 47–77.

McAnly, Herbert T. "How LIFO Began." *Management Accounting* (May 1975), pp. 24–26.

Moonitz, Maurice. "The Case against Lifo as an Inventory-Pricing Formula." *Journal of Accountancy* (June 1953), pp. 682–690.

Moonitz, Maurice. "Accounting for Investments in Debt Securities." In Stephen A. Zeff, Joel Demski, and Nicholas Dopuch, eds. *Essays in Honor of William A. Paton,* Ann Arbor, Mich.: The University of Michigan Graduate School of Business Administration Division of Research, 1979, pp. 57–72.

Morse, Dale, and Gordon Richardson. "The LIFO/FIFO Decision." *Journal of Accounting Research* (Spring 1983), pp. 106–127.

Munter, Paul, and Tommy Morse. "Transfers of Receivables with Recourse." *The CPA Journal* (July 1984), pp. 52–60.

O'Connor, Stephen J. "LIFO: Still a Valid Management Tool?" *Financial Executive* (September 1978), pp. 26–30.

Pantiack, Wayne G. "Last-In First-Out Accounting for Inventories." *The CPA Journal* (July 1985), pp. 42–48.

Skinner, R. C. "Combining LIFO and FIFO." *International Journal of Accounting, Education and Research* (Spring 1975), pp. 127–134.

Staubus, George J. "Testing Inventory Accounting." *The Accounting Review* (July 1968), pp. 413–424.

Storey, Reed K., and Maurice Moonitz. *Market Value Methods for Intercorporate Investments in Stock.* New York: American Institute of Certified Public Accountants, 1976.

Sunder, Shyam. "Optional Choice between FIFO and LIFO." *Journal of Accounting Research* (Autumn 1976), pp. 277–300.

6

LONG-TERM
ASSETS I —
PROPERTY, PLANT AND EQUIPMENT

The evolution of the circulating and noncirculating capital distinction into the working capital concept has been accompanied by the separate disclosure of long-term assets and their segregation into categories. In this chapter we shall examine one of the categories of long-term assets—property, plant and equipment. Long-term investments and intangibles will be discussed in Chapter 7.

PROPERTY, PLANT AND EQUIPMENT

The items of plant and equipment generally represent a major source of future service potential to the enterprise. As such, they are of primary interest to financial-statement users because they indicate the physical resources available to the firm and perhaps may give some clue as to future liquidity and cash flows. The objectives of plant and equipment accounting are

1. Accounting and reporting to investors on stewardship.
2. Accounting for the use and deterioration of plant and equipment.
3. Planning for new acquisitions, through budgeting.
4. Supplying information for taxing authorities.
5. Supplying rate-making information for regulated industries.

ACCOUNTING FOR COST

Accountants have placed a great deal of emphasis upon the principle of objective evidence to determine valuations, and nowhere is this emphasis more apparent than in accounting for the acquisition of property, plant and equipment. Accoun-

272

tants have favored cost as the valuation method for property, plant and equipment because cost is more easily identified and verified than any other method of valuation, and because it also represents the sacrifice of resources given up now to accomplish future objectives. There is also the general presumption among accountants that the agreed-upon purchase price represents the future service potential of the asset to the buyer in an arm's-length transaction.

The theoretically preferable method of accounting for items of property, plant and equipment is the discounted present value of all future earnings of these assets. That is, the amount and timing of all future earnings attributable to an asset would be calculated and the appropriate discount factor for the firm would then be applied to those earnings. The resulting measurement would indicate the value of the asset to the enterprise at any particular time.

If the purchase price does in fact reflect the future service potential of the asset, as measured by the present value of future earnings, then cost is not only objective and verifiable; it is also the theoretically correct value of the asset at the time of acquisition. However, if the purchase price of an item of plant and equipment is determined by discounting future earnings, the calculated amount may be incorrect because of errors in estimating the future earnings flow and discount rate (as discussed in Chapter 2).

Whether or not the management of a firm actually goes through a formal process of discounting future earnings in arriving at the purchase price of an asset, there seems to be tacit agreement that, at least intuitively, the process does occur. But for future financial reporting purposes, accountants generally take the position that cost should be viewed as objective and verifiable evidence of what was paid and not as a representation of future service potential. They argue that it is difficult, if not impossible, to measure future service potential because (1) neither the amount nor timing of future earnings is subject to reasonable estimation and (2) there is no generally accepted method of determining the appropriate discount factor to be used in the calculation.

Despite the objectivity and verifiability of the purchase price as the basis for initially recording property, plant and equipment, the assignment of cost to individual assets is not always as uncomplicated as might be expected. When assets are acquired in groups, when they are self-constructed, or when property contains assets that are to be removed, certain accounting problems arise. These problems are discussed in the following sections.

Group Purchases

When a group of assets is acquired for a lump-sum purchase price, such as the purchase of land, buildings, and equipment, an accounting problem arises. That is, the acquisition cost must be assigned to the individual assets so that this cost ultimately can be charged to expense as the service potential of the individual assets expires.

The most frequent, though arbitrary, solution to this problem has been to assign the acquisition cost to the various assets on the basis of the weighted average of their respective appraisal values. Where appraisal values are not available, the cost assignment may be based upon the relative carrying values on the seller's books. Since no evidence exists that either of these values is the relative value to the purchaser, their assignment would seem to be a violation of the objectivity principle, but the use of such methods is usually justified on the basis of expediency and the lack of acceptable alternative methods.

Self-Constructed Assets

Self-constructed assets give rise to questions about the proper components of cost. While it is generally agreed that all expenses directly associated with the construction process should be included in the recorded cost of the asset (material, direct labor, etc.), there are controversial issues regarding the assignment of fixed overhead and the capitalization of interest. The fixed-overhead problem has two aspects: (1) should any fixed overhead be allocated and, (2) if so, how much fixed overhead should be allocated? This problem has further ramifications. If a plant is operating at less than full capacity and fixed overhead is assigned to a self-constructed asset project, charging the project with a portion of the fixed overhead will cause the profit margin on all other products to increase during the period of construction (discussed further below). Three approaches are available to solve this problem.

1. Allocate no fixed overhead to the self-construction project.
2. Allocate only incremental fixed overhead to the project.
3. Allocate fixed overhead to the project on the same basis as it is allocated to other products.

Some accountants favor the first approach. They argue that the allocation of fixed overhead is arbitrary and therefore only direct costs should be considered. Nevertheless, the prevailing opinion is that the construction of the asset required the use of some amount of fixed overhead, and fixed overhead is a proper component of cost. If this problem is examined more closely, some additional issues arise.

When the production of other products has been discontinued to produce a self-constructed asset, allocation of the entire amount of fixed overhead to the remaining products will cause reported profits on these products to decrease. Under these circumstances the third approach seems most appropriate. On the other hand, it seems unlikely that an enterprise would discontinue operations of a unlikely that an enterprise would discontinue operations of a profitable product to construct productive facilities except in unusual circumstances.

When operations are at less than full capacity, it would seem that the second approach would be the most logical. The decision to build the asset was probably connected with the availability of idle facilities, and increasing the profit margin on existing products because of this decision does not seem to be reasonable reporting.

A corollary to the fixed overhead allocation question is the issue of the capitalization of interest charges during the period of the construction of the asset. During the construction period, extra financing for materials and supplies will undoubtedly be required, and these funds will normally be obtained from external sources. The central question is the advisability of capitalizing the cost of the use of such funds. Some accountants have argued that interest is a financing rather than an operating charge and, as such, should not be charged against the asset. Others have noted that if the asset were acquired from outsiders, interest charges would undoubtedly be part of the cost basis to the seller and therefore would be included in the sales price. Additionally, public utilities normally capitalize both actual and implicit interest (when their own funds are used) on construction projects because future rates are based upon the costs of services. Charging existing products for the expenses associated with a separate decision is not a reasonable solution. Therefore, a more logical approach is to capitalize incremental interest charges during the construction period. However, once the new asset is placed in service, interest should be charged to operations.

The application of this theory resulted in abuses and during the first part of the 1970s, many companies adopted the policy of capitalizing interest costs. However, in 1974 the SEC established a rule preventing this practice.[1] Later, in 1979, the FASB issued Statement No. 34, "Capitalization of Interest Costs."[2] In this release, the FASB took the position that interest should be capitalized only when an asset requires a period of time to be prepared for its intended use.

The primary objective of FASB No. 34 was to recognize interest cost as a significant part of the historical cost of acquiring an asset. The criteria for determining if an asset qualifies for interest capitalization are that the asset must not yet be ready for its intended purpose and must be undergoing activities necessary to get it ready. Qualified assets are defined as (1) assets that are constructed or otherwise produced for an enterprise's own use and (2) assets intended for sale or lease that are constructed or otherwise produced as discrete projects.[2] Additionally, the board excluded interest capitalization for inventories that are routinely manufactured or otherwise produced in large quantities on a repetitive basis. Assets that are currently in use or are not undergoing the activities necessary to get them ready for use are also excluded.

An additional issue addressed by FASB Statement No. 34 was the determination of the proper amount of interest to capitalize. The board decided that the amount of interest to be capitalized is the amount that could have been avoided if

---

[1]"Capitalization of Interest by Companies Other than Public Utilities," *SEC Accounting Series Release No. 163* (Washington, D.C.: SEC, 1974).

[2]FASB Statement No. 34, "Capitalization of Interest Costs" (Stamford, Conn.: FASB, 1979), par. 9.

the asset had not been constructed. The interest rate to be used is either the weighted average rate of interest charges during the period or the interest charge on a specific debt instrument issued to finance the project. The amount to be capitalized is determined by applying the appropriate interest rate to the average amount of accumulated expenditures for the asset during the construction period. Additionally, only actual interest costs on present obligations may be capitalized, not imputed interest on equity funds.

Removal of Existing Assets

When a firm acquires property containing existing structures that are to be removed, a question arises concerning the proper treatment of the cost of removing these structures. Current practice is to assign such costs less any proceeds to the land, since they are necessary to put the site in a state of readiness for construction.

ASSETS ACQUIRED IN NONCASH TRANSACTIONS

Many assets are acquired by trading equity securities, or one asset is exchanged in partial payment for another (trade-in). When equity securities are traded for assets, the cost principle dictates that the recorded value is the amount of consideration given, which is generally the market value of the securities exchanged. However, if the market value of the securities is not determinable, it is necessary to assign cost to the property on the basis of the market value of the property acquired. This last procedure is a departure from the cost principle and can be viewed as an example of the use of replacement cost in current practice.

When assets are exchanged, for example, in trade-ins, additional complications arise. Accountants have long argued the relative merits of using the fair market value versus the book value of the exchanged asset. In 1973 the Accounting Principles Board released its Opinion No. 29, "Accounting for Nonmonetary Transactions," which concluded that fair value should (*generally*) be used as the basis of accountability.[3] Therefore, the cost of an asset acquired in a straight exchange for another asset is the fair market value of the surrendered asset.

This general rule is subject to one exception. The APB stated that exchanges should be recorded at the book value of the asset given up when the exchange is not the culmination of the earning process. APB Opinion No. 29 gives two examples of exchanges that do not result in the culmination of the earning process:

1. Exchange of a *product or property held for sale* in the ordinary course of business (inventory) for a product or property to be sold in the same line of business to facilitate sales to customers other than parties to the exchange.

[3]Accounting Principles Board Opinion No. 29, "Accounting for Nonmonetary Transactions" (New York: American Institute of Certified Public Accountants, 1973).

276

2. Exchange of a *productive asset* not held for sale in the ordinary course of business for a *similar* productive asset or an equivalent interest in the same or similar productive asset.[4]

If the exchanged assets are of a dissimilar nature, the presumption is that the earning process is complete, and the acquired asset is recorded at the fair value of the asset exchanged including any gain or loss. This requirement exists for straight exchanges and for exchanges accompanied by cash payments (*boot*). For example, if Company G exchanges cash of $2,000, and an asset with a book value of $10,000 and a fair market value of $13,000, for a dissimilar asset, a gain of $3,000 should be recognized [$13,000 − $10,000], and the new asset should be recorded at $15,000.

On the other hand, accounting for the exchange of *similar productive assets* takes a somewhat different form. According to the provisions of APB No. 29, *losses* are always recognized in their entirety whether or not boot (cash) is involved; however, gains are never recognized unless boot is present, and only the recipient of boot may recognize a gain. The recipient of boot recognizes a gain in the ratio of the boot to the total consideration received. In effect, the receiver of boot is recognizing a proportionate sale and proportionate trade-in. For example, Company S acquires an asset with a fair market value of $10,000 and $5,000 cash in exchange for an asset with a book value of $12,000 and a fair market value of $15,000. A gain of $1,000 would be recognized. The recognized gain is calculated as follows.

$$\text{recorded gain} = \frac{\text{boot}}{\text{boot} + \text{fair market value of asset acquired}} \times \text{total gain } (\$15,000 - 12,000)$$

$$\frac{\$5,000}{\$5,000 + \$10,000} \times \$3,000 = \$1,000$$

The new asset should then be recorded at $8,000 ($10,000 − $2,000 gain not recognized).

DONATED AND DISCOVERY VALUES

Assets are sometimes acquired by corporations as gifts from municipalities, local citizens groups, or stockholders as inducements to locate facilities in certain areas. The cost principle holds that the recorded values of assets should be the consideration given in return, but strict adherence to this principle would result in a failure to record the assets at all, since no consideration was given in return. On

[4]Ibid., par. 21.

the other hand, failure to report values for these assets on the balance sheet would violate the disclosure principle.

Current practice suggests that donated assets should be recorded at their fair market values and that a similar amount should be placed in an equity account termed *donated capital*. Thereafter, as the service potential of these assets declines, depreciation should be charged to operations. Recording donated assets at fair market values can be defended on the grounds that if the donation had been in cash, the amount received would have been properly credited to donated capital. The cash could then have been used to purchase the asset at its fair market value.

Similarly, valuable natural resources may be discovered on property subsequent to its acquisition, and the original cost may not provide all relevant information about the nature of the property. In such cases, the cost principle may be modified to account for the appraisal increase in the property and this amount is also recorded in the stockholder equity section. An appropriate amount of depletion should then be recorded during each period these natural resources are extracted and sold.

CAPITAL AND REVENUE EXPENDITURES

The purchase and installation of plant and equipment does not eliminate the occurrence of costs associated with these assets. Almost all productive facilities require periodic maintenance that should be charged to current expense. The cost of the asset to the enterprise then properly includes the initial cost plus all costs associated with keeping the asset in working order. However, if additional expenditures give rise to an increase in future service potential, they should not be charged to current operations. Expenditures of this type should be added to the remaining unexpired cost of the asset and be released to expense over the estimated period of benefit.

In most cases the decision to expense or capitalize expenditures is fairly simple and is based upon whether the cost incurred is "ordinary and necessary" or "prolongs future life." But frequently this decision becomes more complicated and additional rules have been formulated that assist in determining whether an expenditure should be recorded as a capital improvement. If the asset's life is increased, the efficiency provided is increased, or output is increased, the cost of an expenditure should be capitalized and written off over the expected period of benefit. All other expenditures should be expensed when incurred.

ACCOUNTING FOR OIL AND GAS PROPERTIES

The assignment of cost to oil and gas properties has been a controversial subject for a number of years. These assets are unlike other long-term assets in that

278

relatively large expenditures are required to find them, and for every successful discovery there are frequently many "dry holes."

An important measure in evaluating an oil or gas property is the amount of attributable reserves, that is, the estimated amount of crude oil or natural gas recoverable under existing economic and operating conditions. Cooper et al. have noted that these estimates and revenue recognition from reserves are fraught with several elements of risk.

1. Quality of reserves. The economic value of reserves is significantly affected by attributes such as the British thermal unit (BTU) content, viscosity, sulfur content, and other "impurities."
2. Concentration of reserves. All else being equal, a small number of geographical locations with large reserves is preferable to the same amount of reserves scattered over numerous locations with relatively modest amounts at each site.
3. Accessibility/recoverability. Such characteristics as depth of reserves, ease of extraction and optimal recovery ratios also affect reserve value. (For example, two companies might have the "same" reserves, but the formations vary in such a way that one company could recover the reserves in a shorter period of time than the other could.)
4. Changes in technology. Depending on the technological method employed, reserve recovery can affect different companies in a variety of ways. Possibilities include recovery of heavy oil, coal gasification, and the ability of refiners to input crude with greater contaminates.
5. Political developments. Accessibility of reserves, production rates, taxes, costs, etc., may be greatly affected by political events. (For example, several years ago, reserves in Iran were probably viewed as relatively secure compared to other reserves in the Near East—an opinion probably not shared today.)
6. Changes in environmental standards. The value of reserves may be greatly altered by environmental and ecological constraints. (Compare, for example, the environmental and political hurdles of trying to develop and extract hydrocarbons in California with those in Texas.)
7. Location. The value of reserves is also affected by the location. This is most apparent in the case of reserves in remote and inaccessible areas, but such factors as the distance from existing pipelines and markets and water depth in the case of offshore reserves are also quite significant.[5]

Additionally, these factors may interact to affect further the expected timing, magnitude, and certainty of future cash flows from reserve recovery and sale.

[5]Kerry Cooper, Steven M. Flory, and Steven D. Grossman, "New Ballgame for Oil and Gas Accounting." *The CPA Journal* (January 1979), p. 72.

For a number of years there have been two major methods of accounting for the costs incurred in the development of and production of oil and gas properties. These methods are termed the successful-efforts and the full-cost methods. Under the *successful-efforts* method, costs that are directly identifiable with successful projects are capitalized and the costs of nonproducing efforts are expensed. The *full-cost* method capitalizes all of the costs incurred for exploration and drilling within a large geographic area (or cost center). These alternatives can yield significantly different asset valuations and net income figures.

The proponents of full costing maintain that oil companies undertake exploration and drilling activities knowing that only a small proportion of that activity will be fruitful. Therefore, unsuccessful activities must be viewed in the overall context of the entire exploration effort and all costs related to the overall effort must be matched with the production from the few successful wells. Opponents to full costing argue that exploration efforts in one geographical area often bear little resemblance or relationship to exploration efforts in another dissimilar geographical area and therefore it is theoretically incorrect to match the costs of unsuccessful wells with the revenue of successful wells discovered in other locations.

A second area of controversy concerns the relative financial effects of the full-cost and successful-efforts methods. One argument centers on the relative valuation of assets and measurement of net income under each method. Proponents of the full-cost method contend that the capitalization of all drilling costs results in a balance sheet measurement that is closer to the present value of proved reserves and further results in a higher net income. The larger assets and higher income enables small producers to attract the capital necessary to continue operations.

The proponents of the successful-efforts method counter by saying that there will not be a significant restriction on the inflow of capital to smaller producers solely due to the accounting method utilized. The evidence in the accounting literature shows that the stock market does not respond to changes in income that are caused by using alternative accounting principles.[6]

The Financial Accounting Standards Board undertook a study of these arguments and, in December 1977, issued FASB Statement No. 19, "Financial Accounting and Reporting by Oil and Gas Companies." In this release the board accepted the viewpoints advanced by the proponents of the successful-efforts method. The following is a summary of the rationale given for this decision.

1. Costs should be capitalized if they are expected to provide identifiable future benefits; otherwise they are considered to be an expense. Successful efforts is consistent with this concept while full cost is not.

---

[6]For a further discussion of these issues, see Steven M. Flory and Steven D. Grossman, "New Oil and Gas Accounting Requirements," *The CPA Journal* (May 1978), pp. 39–43.

2. Accounting focuses on individual assets. Aggregation (e.g., average cost methods for inventories) is considered acceptable only when its use is not expected to give results materially different from accounting for individual assets. With full cost, all acquisition, exploration, and development costs incurred in the broad cost centers (countries or continents) are aggregated and capitalized even if they relate to unsuccessful activities. Under successful efforts, only those costs relating directly to specific oil and gas reserves are capitalized.

3. Financial statements should report on the results of economic influences as they occur. If a firm's operations yield widely fluctuating earnings or only minor fluctuations, the financial statements should report them. If the statements do not show these differences that are perceived by investors and lenders as representing differences in risk, or if differences are shown that really do not exist, then capital may not be allocated equitably in the market. Full cost tends to obscure failure and risk by capitalizing both successful and unsuccessful activities; the successful-efforts method clearly depicts the risk involved by expensing unsuccessful operations.

4. Proponents of full cost argue that unsuccessful activities are unavoidable in the search for oil and gas, but there has been no direct cause-and-effect relationship demonstrated at the company level between total costs and reserves discovered. As with research-and-development costs, the absence of discernible future benefits at the time the costs are incurred indicates that these costs should not be capitalized.

5. Small companies have argued that their ability to raise capital will be impaired if full cost were used because their income statements would more likely report net losses and their balance sheets could report cumulative deficits in stockholders' equity. Studies on the effect of accounting methods on securities prices are not conclusive. The claim that full cost would inhibit a company's ability to obtain capital has not been demonstrated or refuted conclusively. In addition, accounting standards should not be designed to foster national economic goals, but instead should objectively report the results of operations.

Soon after the release of FASB Statement No. 19 many small oil and gas producers voiced objections and asked the U.S. Congress for relief from its provisions. This pressure ultimately resulted in three SEC Accounting Series Releases on oil and gas accounting. The result of these pronouncements was a posture of support for the overall efforts of the FASB but a rejection of the provisions of FASB Statement No. 19.

In reaction to Statement No. 19, the SEC asserted that both the full-cost and successful-efforts methods were so inadequate that it did not matter which was employed. As a substitute the SEC recommended a method termed *reserve recognition accounting* (RRA). This method is a current-value approach that is based upon the net present values of a company's oil and gas reserves.

The SEC's justification for RRA was based upon the contention that neither the full-cost nor the successful-efforts method discloses the most important event for oil and gas properties—the discovery of oil and gas reserves. Additionally, it argued that the earnings process for these companies is different from other companies in other industries. That is, the marketability of the product is relatively assured; therefore, a departure from point-of-sale revenue recognition is justified.

The end result of the SEC's position was a decision by the FASB to postpone indefinitely the implementation of Statement No. 19. However, in 1981, the SEC abandoned its support of RRA and returned jurisdiction of the issue to the FASB. This decision was based upon studies which indicated that reserve recognition accounting lacked the precision needed to be used as the basis for audited figures in annual reports.

Later, SFAS No's. 33 and 39 were issued by the FASB. These releases required large publicly held oil and gas companies to report the effects of changing prices on certain types of assets (see Chapter 13 for a further discussion of SFAS No. 33). At this time the board recognized that the accumulation of all of the required information was placing a significant burden upon oil-and-gas-producing companies. The usefulness of the required data was also questioned as was the failure to disclose other, seemingly more relevant information.

Thereafter, a task force comprised of individuals from the oil and gas industry and the financial and accounting community was formed to aid in the development of reporting standards for the oil and gas industry. The result of this review was the publication of Statement of Financial Accounting Standards No. 69, "Disclosures about Oil and Gas Producing Activities."

According to this release, publicly traded companies with significant oil and gas activities should disclose the following as supplementary information to their published financial statements.

1. Proved oil and gas reserve quantities.
2. Capitalized costs relating to oil-and-gas-producing activities.
3. Costs incurred in oil and gas property acquisition, exploration, and development activities.
4. Results of operations for oil-and-gas-producing activities.
5. A standardized measure of discounted future net cash flows relating to proved oil and gas reserve quantities.

DEPRECIATION — is the way of reducing cost

Once the appropriate cost of an asset has been determined, certain decisions must be made as to the exporation of that cost. One approach is to treat the entire cost as an expense of the period in which the asset was acquired. Another approach is to retain the entire cost on the books until disposal of the asset. However, neither of these approaches provides for a satisfactory measurement of periodic income. Thus, the concept of depreciation was devised in an effort to allocate the cost of property, plant and equipment over the periods that receive benefit from their use.

Financial-statement users' desire for periodic presentation of information on the results of operations necessitates allocating asset cost to the periods receiving benefit. All depreciation concepts are related to some view of income measurement. For example, if the economic concept of income is followed—the cost to be allocated as depreciation would be the change in real value of the fixed assets during the period.

Accountants view income as the end result of revenue recognition according to certain criteria coupled with the appropriate matching of expenses with those revenues. Thus, various depreciation methods emphasize the matching process and little attention is directed to balance sheet valuations. This point was emphasized by the Committee on Terminology of the American Institute of Certified Public Accountants as follows.

> Depreciation accounting is a system of accounting which aims to distribute the cost or other basic value of tangible capital assets, less salvage value (if any), over the estimated useful life of the unit (which may be a group of assets) in a systematic and rational manner. It is a process of allocation, not valuation.[7]

The AICPA's view of depreciation is particularly important to an understanding of the difference between accounting and economic concepts of income and also provides insight into the many misunderstandings about accounting depreciation. Economists see depreciation as the decline in real value of assets. Other individuals believe that depreciation charges, and the resulting accumulated depreciation, provide the source of funds for future replacement of assets. Still others have suggested that business investment decisions are influenced by the portion of the original asset cost that has been previously allocated; that is, new investments cannot be made because the old asset has not been fully depreciated. These views are not consistent with the stated objective of depreciation for accounting purposes. In the following section we examine the accounting concept of depreciation more closely.

ESTIMATION OF THE DEPRECIATION PROCESS

Estimating the depreciation process for long-term assets is based upon three separate factors.

---

[7]Accounting Terminology Bulletin No. 1, ''Review and Resume'' (New York: American Institute of Certified Public Accountants, 1953), p. 9513.

1. Establishing the proper depreciation base.
2. Estimating the useful service life.
3. Choosing the most applicable cost apportionment method.

Depreciation Base

The depreciation base is that portion of the cost of the asset that should be charged to expense over its expected useful service life. Although most businesses simply use cost as the depreciation base, proper accounting requires an estimation of the amount of disposal value to be received when the asset is retired. For example, rental car agencies normally acquire automobiles for only a short period of use, and the expected value of these automobiles at the time they are retired from service should be considered in establishing the depreciation base.

Useful Service Life

The useful service life of an asset is that period of time over which the asset is expected to function efficiently. An asset's useful service life may therefore be less than its physical life, and factors other than wear and tear need to be examined in establishing service life.

Various authors have suggested possible obsolescence, inadequacy, supersession, and changes in the social environment as factors to be considered in establishing the expected service life. For example, jet airplanes have replaced most of the propeller-driven planes on the airlines, and ecological factors have caused changes in manufacturing processes in the steel industry. Estimating such factors of course requires a certain amount of clairvoyance—a quality difficult to acquire.

Depreciation Methods

Most of the controversy in depreciation accounting revolves around the question of the proper method to use in allocating the depreciation base over its estimated service life. Theoretically, the expired cost of the asset should be related to the value received from the asset in each period; however, these measurements are extremely difficult.[8] Accountants have therefore attempted to estimate expired costs by other methods. These methods may be categorized as follows.

1. Straight line.
2. Accelerated.
3. Units of activity.

[8]See, for example, Arthur L. Thomas, "The Allocation Problem in Financial Accounting Theory," Studies in Accounting Research No. 3 (American Accounting Association, 1969).

4. Group and corporate.

5. Retirement and replacement.

6. Compound interest.

Straight Line

The straight-line method allocates an equal portion of depreciation to each period the asset is used. It is most often justified on the basis of the lack of evidence to support other methods. Since it is difficult to establish evidence that links the value received from an asset to any particular period, the advocates of straight-line depreciation accounting argue that other methods are arbitrary and therefore inappropriate. The use of the straight-line method implies that the asset is declining in service potential in equal amounts over its estimated service life.

Accelerated Depreciation

The-sum-of-the-year's-digits, fixed-percentage-of-declining-base, and the accelerated cost recovery system (ACRS)[9] are the most frequently encountered methods of accelerated depreciation. These methods result in larger charges to expense in the earlier years of asset use, although little evidence supports the notion that assets actually decline in service potential in the manner suggested by these methods. Accelerated depreciation methods probably give balance sheet valuations that are closer to the actual value of the assets in question, since most assets depreciate in value more rapidly in their earlier years of use. But since depreciation accounting is not intended to be a method of asset valuation, this factor should not be viewed as an advantage of using accelerated depreciation methods.

Units of Activity

Where assets, such as machinery, are used in the actual production process, it is sometimes possible to determine the total expected output to be obtained from these assets. Depreciation may then be based upon the number of units of output during an accounting period. The activity measures of depreciation assume that each product produced during the asset's existence receives the same amount of benefit from the asset, an assumption that may or may not be realistic. Additionally, care must be exercised in establishing a direct relationship between the measurement unit and the asset. For example, when direct labor hours are used as a measure of the units of output, a decline in productive efficiency in later

---

[9]ACRS depreciation has been adopted by the Internal Revenue Service as the only acceptable accelerated method for tax purposes for assets acquired since 1981. This method utilizes stated percentages and average life categories for various assets. Its acceptability for financial reporting purposes is highly debatable.

very close match between income and expense

years of the asset's use may cause the addition of more direct labor hours per product, which would result in charging more cost per unit.

Group and Composite Depreciation

Group and composite depreciation are similar methods that apply depreciation to more than one asset during each accounting period. The advantage claimed for both methods is that they simplify record keeping; however, they may also obscure gains and losses on the use of individual assets. Group depreciation is used for homogeneous assets that are expected to have similar service lives and residual values. Composite depreciation is used for dissimilar assets with varying service lives and residual values.

In either case, the total cost of the assets is capitalized in a single account and treated as if it were a single asset for depreciation purposes. The depreciation rate is based upon the average life of the assets, and periodic depreciation is calculated by multiplying this rate by the balance in the asset account. In the event an individual asset is taken out of service, no gain or loss is recognized, because the entire asset has not been retired. In an individual retirement, accumulated depreciation is charged for the difference between the original cost and the proceeds received. Any gain or loss is ultimately recorded when the entire asset has been taken out of service.

Retirement and Replacement Methods

Retirement and replacement methods have been advocated by some accountants as expedient alternatives to the other methods of depreciation previously discussed. Although retirement and replacement methods have not gained wide acceptance, they are used by public utilities. These methods recognize depreciation only at the time an asset reaches the end of its service life. Under the retirement method, depreciation is charged only when the asset is taken out of service, whereas the replacement method charges to depreciation only the cost of new assets while retaining the original cost of plant and equipment acquired as an asset. Where the number of assets in use is large and a similar number of replacements is occurring each year, such methods might be justified, but in general they completely distort the matching process. Another disadvantage inherent in the use of these methods is that the computation of net income may be significantly influenced and manipulated by management through advancing or postponing the replacement period.

Compound Interest Methods

Compound interest methods of depreciation have received attention because they focus on cost recovery and rate of return on investment. As discussed previously, assets may be viewed as future services to be received over their service lives,

286

and the cost of the asset may then be viewed as the present value of the periodic services discounted at a rate of interest that takes into consideration the risk of the investment. The two compound interest depreciation methods most often encountered are the annuity method and the sinking fund method. (See Chapter 8 for a more complete discussion of present-value computations.)

Under the *annuity method*, depreciation is based upon the theory that production should be charged not only with the depreciable cost of the property, but also with the unrecovered income that might have been earned if the funds had been invested in some other manner. Depreciation expense then is computed according to the following method.

$$\text{depreciation} = \frac{C - \dfrac{SV}{(1 + i)^n}}{\overline{c_n}i}$$

where
C = cost,
SV = scrap value,
i = interest rate,
n = useful life,
$\overline{c_n}i$ = present value of an annuity.

Consider the following example. An asset was purchased at a cost of $5,500. It had a scrap value of $500 and an estimated life of four years. The rate of interest for investments of this type is 10 percent. Depreciation would be computed as follows.

$$\frac{5,500 - \dfrac{500}{(1.10)^4}}{\overline{c_4}_{10}} = \frac{5,500 - \dfrac{500}{1.4641}}{3.170}$$

Table 6.1 illustrates the computation of depreciation for this example.

The major disadvantage to the use of the annuity method is its inclusion of interest in the periodic depreciation charge. Including interest as an element of the cost of the asset may be theoretically correct, but it is not a generally accepted accounting procedure.

The *sinking fund method* is based upon the assumption that an asset replacement fund is being established to replace the assets retired. The periodic addition to the fund then consists of both principle and interest and is computed on the following basis.

Table 6.1 Depreciation Table for the Annuity Method

Year	Depreciation[a]	Accumulated Depreciation[b]	Interest Income[c]	Asset Balance[d]
0	—	—	—	$5,500.00
1	$1,627.28	$1,077.28	$ 550.00	4,422.72
2	1,627.28	1,185.01	442.27	3,237.71
3	1,627.28	1,303.51	323.77	1,934.20
4	1,627.28	1,434.20	193.08	500.00
	$6,509.12	$5,000.00	$1,509.12	

[a]Based on formula.
[b]Depreciation minus interest income.
[c]Multiply 0.10 and previous asset balance.
[d]Previous asset balance minus accumulated depreciation.

$$\text{cash outlay} = \frac{C - SV}{S_{n|}i}$$

where C = cost,
SV = scrap value,
$S_{n|}i$ = amount of an annuity.

Using the previous example, depreciation would be calculated as follows.

$$\frac{\$5,500 - 500}{4.64} = \$1,077.35$$

Table 6.2 illustrates the computation of depreciation for this example.

The sinking fund method takes into consideration the time value of money and results in a constant rate of return on book value. This method has been criticized, however, because it yields an increasing charge to depreciation in each year of asset life, while accountants generally agree that the actual yearly decline in service potential decreases each year.

An important point to note about all of the depreciation methods is that no matter how simple or complex the calculations involved, the end result is an arbitrary cost allocation, and the asset amount disclosed on the balance sheet may not even approximate the current value of the asset. Since the avowed purpose of depreciation methods is to allocate cost, not determine value, the depreciation method selected should provide the most appropriate allocation of cost to the periods of benefit.

288

Table 6.2 Depreciation Table for the Sinking Fund Method

	Sinking Fund				Depreciation		
Year	Annual Deposit[a]	Interest	Fund	Fund Balance	Depr. Expense	Depr. Allow.	Asset Value
0	—	—	—			—	$5,500.00
1	$1,077.35	—	$1,077.35	$1,077.35	$1,077.35	$1,077.35	4,422.65
2	1,077.35	107.74[b]	1,185.09[c]	2,262.44[d]	1,185.09	1,185.09	3,237.56
3	1,077.35	226.24	1,303.59	3,566.03	1,303.59	1,303.59	1,933.97
4	1,077.35	356.67	1,433.98	5,000.00	1,433.97	1,433.97	500.00
	$4,309.40	$690.65	$5,000.00		$5,000.00	$5,000.00	

[a]From formula.
[b]$1,077.35 × 0.010.
[c]$1,077.35 + $107.74.
[d]$1,077.35 + $1,185.09.

DISCLOSURE OF SEC REPLACEMENT COST INFORMATION

In March of 1976 the Securities and Exchange Commission announced a requirement to disclose the cost of replacing inventories and plant for large publicly held companies. This requirement, which took effect December 25, 1976, had the goal of giving investors a better picture of the impact of inflation and was intended to show the effects of the use of replacement cost information on cost of sales and depreciation. The requirement applied to listed companies with inventories and gross plant totaling more than $100 million and amounting to more than 10 percent of total assets. This replacement cost information was to be disclosed in footnotes and can be separated into balance sheet information (the effect on assets) and income statement information (the effect on cost of sales and expenses) as follows.

Assets for the year in which the balance sheet is presented:

1. The current gross replacement cost of year-end inventories, and its excess, if any, over net realizable value.
2. The estimated current cost of replacing (new) the productive capacity together with the current replacement cost of depreciable, depletable, or amortizable assets net of accumulated depreciation so as to adjust for service potential used up in prior years.

Costs and expenses—for the two most recent fiscal years:

1. The approximate amount that cost of sales would have been if it had been calculated by estimating the current replacement cost of goods and services sold at the times when the sales were made.
2. The approximate amount of depreciation, depletion, and amortization that would have been recorded if it were estimated on the basis of average current replacement cost of productive capacity.[10]

These disclosure requirements of the SEC remained in effect until 1979, when the FASB issued Statement No. 33, "Financial Reporting and Changing Prices" (which is discussed in detail in Chapter 13). At that time the SEC, in a move that suggested considerable support for the FASB, rescinded its requirements in favor of those set forth in FASB No. 33.

---

[10]"Disclosure of Certain Replacement Cost Data," Accounting Series Release No. 190 (Washington: Securities and Exchange Commission, March 23, 1976).

SUMMARY

Property, plant and equipment are among the major long-term assets of a company. The overall objectives in accounting for these assets are to give management, investors, and government authorities accurate information about these assets and to plan for a new acquisition through realistic budgeting.

A number of problems arise in choosing methods for assigning costs for these assets. Generally acceptable accounting principles have been developed to handle most of these troublesome areas.

Assigning asset cost to the period of benefit remains the major problem in accounting for property, plant and equipment. There are a number of views as to the nature of depreciation as well as a number of alternative methods of calculating and assigning these costs.

In the readings for this chapter, Robert Reilly discusses "Capitalization Guidelines for Expenditures Subsequent to Asset Acquisition," and the rationale for the various methods of depreciation are discussed in greater detail in "Concepts of Depreciation—Business Enterprises," by John Pick.

CAPITALIZATION GUIDELINES FOR EXPENDITURES SUBSEQUENT TO ASSET ACQUISITION

ROBERT F. REILLY

IN THEORY . . .

Accounting theory distinguishes between expenditures incurred to produce income in the current accounting period and those incurred to produce income in future accounting periods. An expenditure incurred to generate income only in the current accounting period is called a revenue expenditure and is recorded as an expense. An expenditure incurred to generate income in future accounting periods is called a capital expenditure. A capital expenditure is recorded as an asset and is said to be capitalized. APB Statement No. 4, Chapter 6, defines the accounting treatment of expenses: "Expenses are the costs that are associated with the revenue of the period, often direct but, frequently indirectly through association with the period to which the revenue has been assigned."[1] In plain words, expenses are offset against current period revenues to arrive at current

Reprinted with permission from the *Ohio CPA Journal,* a publication of the Ohio Society of CPAs.

[1]APB Opinion No. 4, Chapter 6, Paragraph .19.

period earnings. This APB Statement continues to define the treatment of capital expenditures: "Costs to be associated with future revenue or otherwise to be associated with future accounting periods are deferred to future periods as assets."[2] In plain words, these costs are to be capitalized and changed to an asset account.

IN PRACTICE . . .

In theory, the above mentioned principles seem very straightforward. In practice, however, they are not always so easy to apply. In practice, the facts are not always as clear-cut as a textbook definition or APB general statement would make them appear.

APB Statement No. 4, Chapter 5, recognized that judgment would be called for in this, as well as many other, accounting decisions: "Financial accounting necessarily involves informed judgment."[3] Without decisive rules or quantitative guidelines, judgment calls will result in occasional errors. When a judgment call results in an error, the following accounting consequences can arise:

I. Capitalizing an item that should be expensed—
  (1) overstatement of earnings on income statement of current period
  (2) overstatement of assets and capital on balance sheet of current and future periods (this overstatement will be reduced in time due to depreciation or amortization)
  (3) understatement of earnings on income statement of future periods (due to recognition of depreciation or amortization expense)

II. Expensing an expenditure that should be capitalized—

[2]Ibid.
[3]Ibid., Chapter 5, Paragraph .12.

  (1) understatement of earnings on income statement of current period
  (2) understatement of assets and capital on balance sheet of current and future periods (this understatement will be relieved in time, since depreciation or amortization would have reduced the proper asset and capital balance over the years)
  (3) overstatement of earnings on income statement of future periods (due to the non-recognition of depreciation or amortization expense)

In practice, due to several pragmatic considerations, the management accountant will more likely lean towards expensing rather than capitalizing an expenditure that falls in the grey area. Among these pragmatic considerations are the following:

1. **bookkeeping and paper work convenience**—When an expenditure is expensed, one entry has to be made in one accounting period. Once the proper expense entry is made, the expenditure need never be reconsidered in the accounting records. When an expenditure is capitalized, the initial capitalization entry has to be made in the current accounting period. Next, usually, a complete record of the transaction must be posted to some kind of fixed asset sub-ledger. Next, a depreciation or amortization schedule must be generated (perhaps one schedule for book purposes and one schedule for tax purposes). A depreciation or amortization charge must be made in each accounting period until the entire cost is recognized; this may mean several years of periodic entries.

2. **uncertainty**—When an expenditure is expensed, little guesswork is involved. The total expenditure is usually known and recognized in the current period. When an expenditure is capitalized, es-

timates must be made of the asset's useful life, expected salvage value, etc.

3. **organizational convenience**—Most organizations have detailed a hierarchical approval procedure for capital expenditures. Economic analyses documents, approval documents, authorization documents, etc. may all be required. On the other hand, most organizations have approval procedures for expenses that are much simpler and less time-consuming.

4. **tax advantages**—Even though there is no absolute dollar advantage to deducting an expense in the current period as opposed to claiming depreciation expense over a period of several years, the time value of money argues strongly for the current tax savings as compared to a deferred tax savings. Although it is possible to expense an item for income tax purposes and capitalize it for book purposes, most accountants would prefer not to keep two sets of accounting records (book and tax) if they could avoid it. Also, these "timing differences" really stand out in a tax audit; and a much stronger case can usually be made for claiming the tax deduction on a grey area expenditure if it is expensed for book as well as tax purposes. Lastly, there are state and local personal property tax, insurance premiums, and other "hidden" costs related to a capitalized expenditure.

5. **conservatism**—When an expenditure falls legitimately in the grey area between capital and revenue expense, conservatism generally argues for expense versus capitalization. APB Opinion No. 4 asserts the conservatism argument: "Frequently, assets and liabilities are measured in the context of significant uncertainties. Historically, manager, investors, and accountants have generally preferred that possible errors in measurement be in the direction of understatement rather than overstatement of net income and net assets."[4]

AT HUFFY . . .

At Huffy Corporation, Dayton, Ohio, the issue of capitalization policy regarding expenditures subsequent to asset acquisition is current eliciting considerable interest. Capitalization policy regarding repair and maintenance (hereafter R & M) expenditures is of special interest.

The following are examples of the kinds of questions the operating division accounting managers must answer daily in a large manufacturing company:

1. How long should R & M work extend the useful life of an asset before the R & M expenditures should be capitalized? one year? two years? 20% of original useful life estimate?

2. A $200,000 (original cost) press has a useful life of ten years. Each two to three years, the $10,000 electric motor on the press must be replaced. Should the motor cost be capitalized each time it is replaced (it benefits more than one accounting period)? Should the cost be expensed (it is immaterial in relation to the $200,000 cost of the press)?

3. A shaft breaks on the same press; it costs $25,000 to replace the shaft. The new shaft (a critical part) may extend the useful life of the press five years. On the other hand, some other critical part could break tomorrow. Should the $25,000 expenditure be capitalized or expensed?

Each accounting manager will arrive at an answer to these questions based on "in-

[4]Ibid., Chapter 6, Paragraph .35.

formed judgment." However, different managers may arrive at different answers at different times. If the theoretically incorrect (but pragmatic) answer is arrived at, the error will be self correcting over a period of years, as explained above. Also, the impact of one wrong decision on the annual financial statements of an operating division will be immaterial. The impact on the annual consolidated financial statements of Huffy Corporation will certainly be immaterial. However, a $10,000 or $25,000 (as in the above example) charge to the R & M expense account of one maintenance supervisor at one plant may have a very material impact on his monthly budget. As his superiors start questioning his budget variance, he will start questioning the accounting manager. He will be expecting a cogent, coherent explanation why the expenditures were expensed and not capitalized.

A clear and decisive statement of capitalization guidelines for expenditures subsequent to asset acquisition will be developed, with the following objectives in mind:

1. consistency—Guidelines must be delineated so that different accounting managers confronting the same fact situation at different times will apply the capitalization policy consistently.
2. correctness—The guidelines must be in theoretical agreement with generally accepted accounting principles.
3. clarity—Guidelines must be understandable, logical, and provide as much practical direction as possible.

The discussion will assume the following general structure:

1. Current Huffy Corporation capitalization policy will be reviewed, in regard to the three above objectives.
2. The current text of generally accepted accounting principles will be reviewed, in search for more detailed guidelines.
3. Current Internal Revenue Service regulations and rulings in this area will be reviewed, for further clarification and detail.

HUFFY CORPORATION CAPITALIZATION POLICY

Company capitalization policy and procedures are delineated in the Huffy Corporation Fixed Asset Policy Manual. The basic policy is stated succinctly and with quantitative guidelines, as follows:

Individual assets with a value of $500.00 or more, and a useful life of at least 1 year will be capitalized.
Individual assets which have a value of less than $500.00, or that have a useful life of less than one year must be expensed.[5]

Huffy Corporation capitalization policy continues to specify the proper accounting treatment for expenditures subsequent to asset acquisition, as follows:

EXPENDITURES SUBSEQUENT TO OPERATIONAL USE

Ordinary repairs—Ordinary repairs and maintenance costs will be expensed as incurred; these expenditures should not be capitalized.

Maintenance costs are those costs, such as lubrication, cleaning, adjustment and painting, which are incurred to keep equipment in normal usable condition.

Ordinary repairs (as distinguished from major repairs) are outlays for parts, labor

[5]Huffy Corporation Fixed Asset Policy Manual, section 6.1.A.

CHAPTER 6: LONG-TERM ASSETS I

and other related costs which are necessary to keep the equipment in normal operating condition but do not add materially to the use value of the asset, nor prolong its life appreciably. Ordinary repairs are recurring and normally involve relatively small expenditures.

Extraordinary repairs—Extraordinary repairs will normally be capitalized. If the expenditure serves primarily to increase the use value of a fixed asset, the cost is debited to the related asset account. Extraordinary or major repairs involve relatively large amounts, are not recurring in nature, and tend to increase the use value or the service life of the asset beyond what it was originally.

Replacements and betterments—The cost of a replacement will normally be expensed if the replacement does not materially extend the useful life of the asset. Replacements involve the removal of a major part or component of plant or equipment and the substitution of a new part or component of essentially the same type and performance capabilities. Replacement may involve specific subunits or a number of major items.

Betterments normally are capitalized. Betterments, or improvements, constitute the removal of a major part or component of plant or equipment and the substitution of a different part or component having significantly improved and superior performance capabilities. The result of the improved substitute serves to increase the overall efficiency and tends to increase the useful life of the primary asset.[6]

The above policy statement is clear enough, except that it is strewn with the following adjectives and adverbs: ordinary, normal, materially, major, appreciably,

relatively small, relatively large, etc. These modifiers are vague and, without specific definitions, and do not serve well as decisive guidelines and quantitative rules.

CAPITALIZATION POLICY IN GENERALLY ACCEPTED ACCOUNTING PRINCIPLES

A review of the currently effective Accounting Principles Board Opinions, the Accounting Interpretations of the AICPA, and the Statements and Interpretations of the Financial Accounting Standards Board was made. Explicit guidelines regarding expenditures subsequent to asset acquisition (and especially R & M expenditures) were noticeably absent. Broad statements regarding materiality, consistency, measurement, etc. are abundant, but comprehensive guidelines regarding real life situations were not to be found.

APB Statement No. 4 generally defines "asset" and "expense" as follows:

Assets—economic resources of an enterprise that are recognized and measured in conformity with generally accepted accounting principles.[7]
Expenses—gross decreases in assets or gross increases in liabilities recognized and measured in conformity with generally accepted accounting principles that result from those types of profit-directed activities of an enterprise that can change owner's equity.[8]

APB Statement No. 4 includes these capitalization guidelines:

If an asset provides benefit for several periods, its cost is allocated to the peri-

---

[6]Ibid., section 6.4.F.

[7]APB Opinion No. 4, Chapter 5, Paragraph .19.
[8]Ibid., Paragraph .21.

ods in a systematic and rational manner in the absence of a more direct basis for associating cause and effect. The cost of an asset that provides benefits for only one period is recognized as an expense of that period (also a systematic and rational allocation). This form of expense recognition always involves assumptions about the pattern of benefits and the relationship between costs and benefits because neither of these two factors can be conclusively demonstrated.[9]

These definitions and guidelines, while useful theoretically, do not provide the exact functional criteria needed to make day-to-day capitalization decisions in practice.

Most introductory accounting texts present general capitalization rules that are not unlike the guidelines for the Huffy Corporation capitalization policy. The following examples are from *Accounting Principles* by Niswonger and Fess:

Expenditures for an addition to a plant asset clearly constitute capital expenditures.

It is equally clear that expenditures for maintenance and repairs of a recurring nature should be classified as revenue expenditures.

Expenditures that increase operating efficiency or capacity for the remaining useful life of an asset should be capitalized.

Expenditures that increase the useful life of an asset beyond the original estimate are also capital expenditures.

Expenditures that are minor in amount are usually treated as repair expense even though they may have the characteristics of capital expenditures.[10]

Unfortunately, real world situations are not always as black and white as the introductory textbook page. A popular intermediate accounting textbook states the dilemma this way:

Each expenditure requires careful analysis to determine whether it should be assigned to revenue of the current period, hence charged to an expense account, or whether it should be assigned to revenue of more than one period, which calls for a charge to an asset account or to an accumulated depreciation account. In many cases the answer may not be clear, and the procedures that are ultimately chosen may be a matter of judgement.[11]

Yet this same textbook proceeds to define such common expenditures subsequent to asset acquisition as maintenance, repairs, betterments, improvements, additions, and rearrangements with pat, textbook definitions and to state the capitalization rule for each situation as if it were cast in stone. These standard textbook definitions all seem to fall in line with the following:

Maintenance costs are those costs . . . which are incurred to keep equipment in normal useable condition. Ordinary repairs . . . are outlays . . . which are necessary to keep the equipment in normal operating condition but do not add materially to the use value of the asset, nor prolong its life appreciably.

Extraordinary repairs involve relatively

---

[9]Ibid., Chapter 6, Paragraph .23.
[10]Niswonger, C. Rollin and Fess, Philip E., *Ac-*

counting Principles, 12 Edition, South-Western Publishing Co., 1977, pages 245–246.
[11]Simons, Harry, *Intermediate Accounting,* fifth edition, South-Western Publishing Company, 1974, page 338.

large amounts, are not recurring in nature, and tend to increase the use value or the service life of the asset beyond what it was originally.

Replacements involve the removal of a major part or component of plant or equipment and the substitution of a new part or component of essentially the same type and performance capabilities. Betterments . . . constitute the removal of a major part or component . . . and the substitution of a different part or component having significantly improved and superior performance capabilities.[12]

Most advanced texts offer conceptual and qualitative arguments, though no quantitative guidelines. The Gordon and Shillinglaw text offers a unique conceptual solution:

The total productive capacity of a plant asset, or any complex of assets, is a joint function of the output per unit of time and the length of time over which satisfactory output is achieved (economic life), both of which factors are in turn more or less dependent upon the level of maintenance provided. At the time of acquisition, therefore, there is an expected lifetime capacity reflecting an intended maintenance policy. This fact provides a basis for the following rules governing the treatment of subsequent outlays: (1) any cost incurred to obtain the service initially expected is a maintenance cost; and (2) any cost incurred to increase lifetime productivity capacity by raising the output rate or by extending the economic life or by reduc-

ing operating cost is a capitalizable betterment.[13]

While the above is conceptually interesting, it does require the accountant to exercise considerable judgement. Its application to practical situations, therefore, is no less limited that the standard textbook definitions and rules for R & M expenditures.

IRS PRONOUNCEMENTS

The question of expenditures subsequent to asset acquisition has been the subject of numerous Internal Revenue Regulations and Revenue Rulings and of numerous Tax Court and other judicial proceedings. Basically, the primary question is likely to involve a determination of whether a particular expenditure is a capital item or a deductible repair. Capital expenditures are defined in Internal Revenue Code Section 263, and related Regulations. Deductible repair and maintenance expenditures are generally considered trade or business expenses. These expenses are treated in Code Section 162.

The general rule for capital expenditures defined in Code Section 263 is that: No deduction shall be allowed for—

1. Any amount paid out for new buildings or for permanent improvements or betterments made to increase the value of any property or estate.
2. Any amount expended in restoring property or in making good the exhaustion thereof for which an allowance is or has been made.

So, the taxpayer must capitalize (and recover the cost through depreciation allow-

---

[12]Welsh, Glenn A., Zlalkovich, Charles T., and White, John A., *Intermediate Accounting*, fourth edition, Richard D. Irwin, Inc., 1976, pages 516–518.

[13]Gordon, Myron J. and Shillinglaw, Gordon, *Accounting—A Management Approach*, fifth edition, Richard D. Irwin, Inc., 1974, page 343.

ances) expenditures incurred for the acquisition of assets having a more or less permanent value (i.e., more than one year). The same rule, then, applies to R & M expenditures that appreciably prolong the life, or enhance the value of, existing assets.

The general rule for R & M expenditures treated as trade or business expenses is defined in Code Section 162:

> There shall be allowed as a deduction all the ordinary and necessary expenses, paid or incurred during the taxable year in carrying on any trade or business.

Further definition of the requirements for deduction as a trade or business expense is provided by Regulation 1.162-1. Basically, three requirements determine whether an expenditure is deductible as a current period business expense:

1. it must be incurred in the taxpayer's trade or business
2. it must be "ordinary and necessary"
3. it cannot be a capital expenditure, as defined in Code Section 263

Expanding on the Section 162 general definitions of expense, Regulation 1.162-4 deals specifically with repair, maintenance, and replacement expenditures:

> —The cost of incidental repairs which neither materially add to the value of the property nor appreciably prolong its life, but keep it in an ordinary efficient operation condition, may be deducted as an expense, provided the cost of acquisition or production or the gain or loss basis of the taxpayer's plant, equipment, or other property, as the case may be, is not increased by the amount of such expenditures. Repairs in nature of replacements, to the extent that they arrest deterioration and appre-

ciably prolong the life of the property, shall either be capitalized and depreciated in accordance with section 167 or charged against the depreciation reserve if such an account is kept.

The court provided a more comprehensive definition of repair expenditures in Illinois Merchants Trust Co., Exr., 4 BTA 103, Dec. 1452.:

> —"To repair is to restore to a sound state or to mend, while a replacement connotes a substitution. A repair is an expenditure for the purpose of keeping the property in an ordinarily efficient operating condition. It does not add to the value of the property nor does it appreciably prolong its life. It merely keeps the property in an operating condition over its probable useful life for the uses for which it was acquired. Expenditures for that purpose are distinguishable from those for replacements, alterations, improvements or additions which prolong the life of the property, increase its value or make it adaptable to a different use. The one is a maintenance charge, while the others are additions to capital investment which should not be applied against current earnings."

The court used the rules that the expenditure (1) does not add to the value of the property and (2) does not appreciably prolong its life.

In Grand Rapids & I. Ry. Co. v. Doyle, (DC) 245 F. 792, the court ruled on the deductibility of maintenance expenditures as allowed under Regulation 1.162.4. The court used the rule that the expenditure (1) keeps the property in its ordinary efficient operation condition and (2) does not upgrade the efficiency or value of the property. In Grand Rapids, the court decided that:

Maintenance means the upkeep or preservation of the condition of the property to be operated, and does not mean additions to the equipment or property, or improvements of the former condition of the property.

In *Libby & Blouin, Ltd.*, 4BTA 910, Dec. 1637 (Acq.), the Tax Court rule on the definition and deductibility of replacement expenditures as allowed under Regulation 1.162.4. In Libby & Blouin, the Tax Court held that expenditures for small parts of a large machine, made in order to keep the machine in an efficient working condition, are ordinary and necessary expenses and not capital expenditures even though they may have a life of two or three years. The machine as a whole is only repaired by the replacements, which merely keep it in working condition. The decision that the cost of replacing short-lived parts of a machine (1) to keep it in its regularly efficient operating condition and (2) to not appreciably prolong its life are deductible current period expenses is reinforced in the following cases:

Covington Cotton Oil Co., 12 BTA 1015, Dec. 4174.
Berkley Machine Works, 36 TCM 733, Dec. 34,455 (M), TC Memo 1977-177.
Hawaiian Sugar Co., 13 BTA 683, Dec. 4389.
Marsh Fork Coal Co., 11 BTA 685, Dec. 3847 (Acq.).
Franklin Mills, 7 BTA 1290, Dec. 2775 (Acq.).
Chesapeake Corp. of Virginia, 17 TC 668, Dec. 18,578 (Acq.).

Code Section 167 deals with depreciation expense deductions. Regulation 1.167 describes much of the detail of the Asset Depreciation Range (ADR) System. Part of this Regulation, paragraph (a)-11, details the percentage repair allowance (RPA) procedures. For the taxpayer who elects the ADR System, the RPA rule (which is also an optional election) was designed to simplify the R & M expense vs. capital expenditure question. Under the RPA rule, the amount of the current period of R & M expense is considered an allowable deduction if it falls within a limit established by a mechanical computation of the RPA percentage (for each ADR category) times the basis in each ADR vintage account.

Since the RPA rule is an election, Regulation 1.167 also discusses the non-RPA treatment of R & M expenses vs. capital expenditures (and the accompanying depreciation expense). This regulation does expand somewhat the guidelines for determining if an expenditure should be capitalized. The rules for a capitalization are that the expenditure:

1. appreciably prolongs the life of the asset,
2. materially increases its value, or
3. adapts it to a different use

Paragraph (2)(i)(a) of this Regulation indicates that expenditures which do not meet these criteria may be deducted as an expense in the taxable year in which paid or incurred.

This section of the Regulation indicates that expenditures may appear to be R & M expenses but have characteristics of capital expenditures, as in the case of an "excluded addition." The term "excluded addition" is defined in paragraph (2)(vi) of this Regulation and means:

(a) *An expenditure, which substantially increases the productivity of an existing identifiable unit of property over its productivity when first acquired by the taxpayer;*

(b) *An expenditure which substantially increases the capacity of an existing identifiable unit of property over its capacity when first acquired by the taxpayer;*

(c) *An expenditure which modifies an existing identifiable unit of property for a substantially different use;*

(d) *An expenditure for an identifiable unit of property if (1) such expenditure is for an additional identifiable unit of property or (2) such expenditure (other than an expenditure described in (e) of this subdivision) is for replacement of an identifiable unit of property which was retired;*

(e) *An expenditure for replacement of a part in or a component or portion of an existing identifiable unit or property (whether or not such part, component or portion is also an identifiable unit or property) if such part, component or portion is for replacement of a part, component or portion which was retired in a retirement upon which gain or loss is recognized.*

(f) *In the case of a building or other structure (in addition to (b), (c), (d) and (e) of this subdivision which also apply to such property), an expenditure for additional cubic or linear space; and*

(g) *In the case of those units or property of pipelines, electric utilities, telephone companies, and telegraph companies consisting of lines, cables and poles (in addition to (a) through (e) of this subdivision which also apply to such property), an expenditure for replacement of a material portion of the unit of property.*

This section continues and specifies a materiality value of "excluded additions." An "excluded addition" does not include any expenditure for R & M, rehabilitation or improvement under $100 in cost. In addition, this section specifies quantitative guidelines for determining if an increase in capacity is substantial or if a replacement expenditure is material. The guidelines are [paragraph (2) (vi)]:

For the purposes of (a) and (b) of this subdivision, an increase in productivity or capacity is substantial only if the increase is more than 25 percent. *An expenditure which merely extends the productive life of an identifiable unit of property is not an increase in productivity within the meaning of (a) of this subdivision. Under (g) of this subdivision* a replacement is material only if the portion replaced exceeds 5 percent of the unit of property with respect to which the replacement is made. *For the purposes of this subdivision, a unit of property generally consists of each operating unit (that is, each separate machine or piece of equipment) which performs a discrete function and which the taxpayer customarily acquires for original installation and retires as a unit.*

These guidelines alleviate, to some extent, the confusion as to what qualifies as a current period R & M expense and what is a capital expenditure.

In summary, almost any renovation may constitute a repair (current period expense) in some cases and a capital expenditure (to be capitalized and depreciated) in others, depending upon the circumstances surrounding its occurrence. The general guidelines are that R & M expenditures qualify as current period expense deductions if they do not:

1. appreciably prolong the life of the asset
2. increase productivity or capacity by more than 25 percent
3. replace more than 5 percent of the original asset
4. materially enhance the value of the asset
5. adapt the asset for a substantially different use

Regulations 1.162 and 1.167 expand on these guidelines.

CONCLUSION

In conclusion, the Internal Revenue Code and Regulations, Revenue Rulings, and Tax Court and other judicial rulings give much more explicit guidelines for the treatment of expenditures subsequent to asset acquisition than does GAAP. In many cases, quantitative guidelines and explicit discrepancies help determine what expenditures qualify as R & M current period expense and what qualify as capital expenditures. There are still numerous grey areas to be sure. But, these are less numerous than would be if the more generalized GAAP rules were applied.

For the examples of the three subsequent expenditure decisions discussed earlier, IRS Regulation guidelines help provide substantive answers. The first question was how long R & M work can prolong asset life before the expenditures should be capitalized. Since pro-

longing asset life presumably increases its productivity (in total over the life of the asset), the 25 percent rule of Regulation 1.167 would appear to apply.

The second question related to repeated replacement of an electric motor on a piece of heavy machinery. Since these electric motors simply maintain the machine in its original efficient working condition, *Libby & Blouin, Ltd.* (and related Tax Court decisions) would seem to indicate that this would be a current period expense. The third question had to do with the infrequent replacement of a critical part. Regulation 1.167 would seem to indicate that the replacement part could be expensed and deducted if it were less than 5 percent of the original asset.

In practice, decisions related to expenditures subsequent to asset acquisition are never as simple as accounting theory would have us believe. Generally accepted accounting principles offer several qualitative guidelines related to accounting for these expenditures. The Internal Revenue Code, Regulations, and Revenue Rulings (and related judicial decisions) offer additional qualitative and some quantitative guidelines. Nonetheless, there are still grey areas. Decisions related to the accounting treatment of expenditures subsequent to asset acquisition must be made by the accountant based on informed judgement of the facts and circumstances in each instance.

CONCEPTS OF DEPRECIATION—BUSINESS ENTERPRISES

JOHN PICK, CPA

American accounting theory began to deal with depreciation in the nineteenth century and, at the century's end, treated it mainly as an acknowledgment of the deterioration of business assets due to wear and tear.[1] In that early concept, the recognition of depreciation was at times an alternative to that of repair and maintenance expenses. Today, the depreciation charge has the independent status of an accounting principle.

Unfortunately, the financial community sometimes seems inclined to treat depreciation as something "unreal"[2] and to give primary consideration to income without depreciation, the so-called "cash-flow." That is due to several factors, such as the insufficiency of information furnished in public financial reports with respect to depreciation, the ambiguity of the concept itself and the multiplicity of procedures. One source of ambiguity is the indiscriminate, simultaneous listing of financial and managerial accounting aspects of depreciation in the professional literature. This article will deal only with external reporting aspects, unless a phase of managerial accounting evidently bears upon the problem at hand. Depreciation for internal reporting can vary widely.

TERMINOLOGY

Kohler defines the term "concept" as "any abstract idea serving a systematizing function."[3] In Webster, a concept is ". . . a theoretical construct. . . ."[4] Accordingly, the nature of depreciation should be obtained inductively from accounting practices and/or deductively from accounting theory. Either procedure is impeded by the involvement of terms each of which has several meanings. These terms are: value, asset, capital, and income.

VALUE

"Value" in the popular sense denotes value in use or value in exchange. The former is the value to the owner; the latter is the market value. Value is also used in the sense of serviceability. However, that engineering term indicates only one of the factors influencing the value to the owner and/or the market value. A fourth meaning of value appears in the accountancy's book value. Here the word is used in a neutral sense.[5]

[1]P. D. Woodward, "Depreciation—Development of an Accounting Concept," *Accounting Review,* Vol 31 (January 1956), pp. 71–76.
[2]Benjamin Graham, David L. Dodd and Sidney Cottle, *Security Analysis* (4th ed., New York: McGraw-Hill Book Co., 1962), p. 151.

[3]Eric L. Kohler, *A Dictionary for Accountants* (3rd ed.: Englewood Cliffs, N.J.: Prentice-Hall, 1963), p. 114.
[4]*Webster's Third International Dictionary* (Springfield, Mass.: G. & C. Merriam Company, 1961).
[5]Joseph D. Coughlan and William K. Strand, *Depreciation Accounting, Taxes and Business Decisions* (New York: Ronald Press Company, 1969), p. 17.

ASSET

In present accounting practice, the book value of a fixed asset denotes an unexpired prepayment for service benefits. The prepayment and the service potentials embodied in an asset are not necessarily equivalent monetarily and often are differently emphasized conceptually. Two quotations illustrate the conceptual divergence. The American Institute of Certified Public Accountants (AICPA) stresses the prepayment view: "[an asset may be defined as] something represented by a debit balance . . . on the basis that it represents . . . an expenditure made which . . . is properly applicable to the future."[6] The American Accounting Association (AAA) emphasizes the economic utility aspect: "assets are . . . aggregates of service potentials available for or beneficial to expected operations."[7]

CAPITAL

Both net assets and the equity in them are frequently referred to as capital. Accordingly, capital may mean the monetary amounts appearing as balances in proprietorship accounts, or real capital in the sense of the actual service potentials of the business, its purchase and/or earning power.

INCOME

Definitions of assets and capital naturally influence those of income. Business income may signify either the residuum remaining after offsetting credits and debits representing revenue and costs or expenses according to accounting rules, or it may identify the amount "which is available for distribution outside the firm without contraction of the level of its operating capacity,"[8] or it may express the increase of service potentials, i.e., of the capitalized value of future expectations.[9]

PRACTICAL CONCEPTS OF DEPRECIATION

The variations in underlying terminology make a detailed evaluation of existing definitions of depreciation an expansive undertaking. Those definitions are classified by Coughlan and Strand as indicating (1) a decrease in value with the lapse of time, (2) impaired serviceability, (3) the value difference from an appraisal standard, and (4) amortized cost.[10]

That roughly corresponds with Goldberg's listing of (1) fall in market price, (2) physical deterioration, (3) fall in value, and (4) allocation of cost.[11]

Singer finds that depreciation has been referred to as meaning (1) the systematic amortization of cost without regard to value during life; (2) the exhaustion of service-units embodied in fixed assets; (3) the loss in value due to wear and tear, deterioration and obsolescence; (4) physical dete-

---

[6]AICPA, Accounting Terminology Bulletin No. 1, "Review and Resume" (*AICPA*, 1953), p. 13.

[7]American Accounting Association (AAA), "Accounting and Reporting Standards for Corporate Financial Statements and Preceding Statements and Supplements, 1957 Revision," (Madison, Wis.: AAA, School of Commerce, University of Wisconsin, 1957), p. 3.

[8]AAA, Committee on Concepts and Standards—Long-Lived Assets, "Accounting for Land, Buildings, and Equipment," Supplementary Statement No. 1, *Accounting Review*, Vol. 39 (July 1964), p. 696.

[9]Study Group on Business Income, *Changing Concepts of Business Income* (New York: Macmillan Co., 1952), pp. 8–10.

[10]Coughlan and Strand, op. cit., p. 12.

[11]Louis Goldberg, *Concepts of Depreciation* (Sydney: The Law Book Company of Australasia, Pty., Ltd., 1969), p. 4.

rioration and consequent loss in value; and (5) a means to keep real capital intact.[12]

THE SIGNIFICANCE OF THE DEFINITIONS

The definitions indicate five thoughts on what the depreciation provision represents. These concepts are influenced by whether they lean in an operational or financial direction.

Apart from the five concepts is a sixth one that adopts for reporting purposes the income-tax-motivated amount, however unrealistic. This aspect is here ignored.

The prevailing concepts are:

Operational-oriented:
    recognition of wear and tear, inadequacy and obsolescence
Financial-oriented:
    provision for replacement
    a means of income determination
    a measure of asset valuation
    a measure of the maintenance of capital

The following discussion, accordingly, deals with the concept of depreciation by reference to the operational causes of the depreciation charge and its four financial purposes and functions.

CAUSAL CONCEPT—IMPACT OF REPAIRS AND MAINTENANCE

The reference of depreciation to its causes is a favorite of textbooks. These list physical causes consisting of wear, tear and the action of elements, and functional causes consisting of gradual obsolescence, inadequacy and all other causes. Obsolescence, as considered here, is that which is the

gradual type and which is expected where improvement is constant. Sudden obsolescence requires accounting treatment only when it occurs.

The aspect of deterioration has been historically important in gaining depreciation the recognition as a legitimate business expense[13] and is still part of its definition in the 1936 uniform system of accounts for electric and gas utilities. However, physical and economic serviceableness may influence the choice of a fixed asset's rate of depreciation, but they do not identify the concept. An asset is depreciation on books even if, for a certain length of time, it becomes more effective with use. Besides, the causes of deterioration usually are difficult to separate and to measure, as they may comprise use, and abuse.

As a result, repairs and maintenance do not enter the depreciation concept. A firm's standard of maintenance affects an asset's efficiency and life; but depreciation in accounting may differ from engineering figures; using an asset does not necessarily mean using it up. Although many companies coordinate depreciation and maintenance accounting by aligning depreciation methods with estimated future maintenance and repairs, it seems better—where possible—to budget repairs and maintenance, accrue them annually, and to let depreciation follow its own rules.[14]

---

[13]Woodward, op. cit.
[14]Rufus Wixon, ed., *Accountants' Handbook* (4th ed.: New York: Ronald Press, 1956), p. 17, 21; George L. Battista and Gerald R. Crowningshield, "Accounting for Depreciation and Repair Costs," National Association of Accountants (NAA) Bulletin, Vol. 45, December 1963), p. 30—But Wendel P. Trumbull, "Differences between Financial and Tax Depreciation," *Accounting Review,* Vol. 43 (July 1968), p. 467, reports that setting up maintenance reserves is ceding to careful depreciation accounting in practice.

---

[12]Frank A. Singer, " 'Depreciation'—Better Left Unsaid," *Accounting Review,* Vol. 32 (July 1957), p. 406.

REPLACEMENT CONCEPT

External reporting of depreciation has been ascribed mainly two purposes: the economic purpose of providing for the replacement of capital goods consumed in operations, and the accounting purpose of income determination.

"Replacement" may mean physical replacement, replacement of output capacity, and replacement of value, although the concern sometimes is to restore to current assets, through the depreciation provision, the amounts diverted earlier to noncurrent assets. The first two meanings usually are implied in depreciation's replacement concept. That term must not be confused with depreciation using current replacement costs as periodic charges. Such charges may be chosen for reasons unconnected with asset replacement, such as the desire to match current dollar revenue with current dollar costs. Thus restricted, replacement depreciation may mean either (1) that depreciation is taken in order to reserve funds for asset replacement, or (2) that depreciation itself reserves funds by designating them for replacement purchases, or (3) that depreciation provides funds.

A study published by the National Association of Accountants in 1958 reveals that generally management is concerned with the effect of depreciation policy on the flow of cash to fixed assets and back, but that for various reasons it has not adopted a policy of using special depreciation procedures in order to reserve replacement funds.[15] Exceptions to the general rule are found with utilities. In some states utilities must set up sinking funds for asset replacement and use the sinking fund method of depreciation.

By itself, depreciation does not earmark funds for replacement purposes, though it is an amortization of the investment in fixed assets. Depreciation is taken on irreplaceable assets too. The funds equalling a period's depreciation are not segregated but put to many uses. Once replacement is made, it is impossible to trace the funds used for it to recovered capital, profits, or investors' contributions.

Finally, the idea that depreciation actually provides funds was found to be a fallacy long ago.[16] It is revenue that provides funds. Tax savings by depreciation do not provide funds in the industry where depreciation counts really, namely the utilities. Those tax savings generally have to be passed on to customers.[17] Where tax savings stay with the firm, depreciation does not generate funds but—like any other cost—saves them from pay-out to the government. Anyhow, funds saved by depreciation are not, in many instances, too important for asset replacement. Even total accelerated depreciation often has not come near to the amounts needed to keep modern plants well equipped.[18]

INPUT CONCEPT

The objective of depreciation, to determine net income by the assignment of plant cost as input to operations, is generally accepted today. The classical definition of this concept is that of the AICPA: "Depreciation accounting is a system of accounting which aims to distribute the cost . . . over the estimated life of the unit . . . in a systematic and rational manner. It is a process of allocation, not of valuation. . . ."[19]

---

[15]NAA, "Current Practice in Accounting for Depreciation," Research Report No. 33 (April 1958), pp. 10–13.

[16]Rufus Wixon, Ed., op. cit., pp. 17, 49f.
[17]William A. Paton, *Corporate Profits* (Homewood, Ill.: Richard D. Irwin, 1965), p. 33.
[18]Graham, Dodd and Cottle, op. cit., p. 157.
[19]AICPA, op. cit., p. 25.

This definition conceives depreciation as the expiration of prepayments in the course of business operations and as the corresponding write-off on books. Changes of the price of service potentials (assets) already paid-for are considered irrelevant. The asset cost is a historical fact; the capital, of which it forms a part, is an aggregate of various historical dollars. The cost write-offs are not meant as economic measurements of wear and tear: the remaining asset values are mere residuals on a balance sheet which is just a tabular statement of balances, functioning as footnote to the income statement.[20] The method of calculating the write-offs is "of minor importance"[21] [sic] so long as it is rational and systematic.

That leaves the choice of amortization methods wide open. Obviously, not every rational method is acceptable; it has to be reasonable in the light of surrounding circumstances. As reasonableness is judgmental, guidelines become necessary.

Hendriksen discusses four: (1) the decline in the service value of the asset, (2) the cost of services used, (3) the net service contribution, and (4) the output value of the services.[22] Item one, the decline in service value, leads right back to the valuation question, which the AICPA definition abhors.

PROBLEMS OF INPUT CONCEPT

The input concept does not only fail to provide guidance for the selection of amortization methods but also may lead to the matching of revenue measured in current dollars with expense expressed in historical dollars. Two remedies have been proposed, namely the application of price-level indexes and the use of current cost, i.e., mainly replacement costs.

A recent statement of the AICPA recommends price-level translations only for supplementary statements and declares as undesirable the restriction of translations to single items like depreciation.[23] The AAA Committee on Concepts and Standards—Long-Lived Assets recommends the recognition of holding gains and losses due to price changes.[24] Defining assets and income differently from the AICPA, the committee believes that where the economic value of service potential—i.e., the discounted value of the corresponding future cash flows—cannot be measured in ways "that meet the test of verifiable evidence," reference should be made to the current cost of securing the same or equivalent value. The committee still is primarily concerned with income determination.

However, the committee recognizes asset valuation and depreciation expense determination as interdependent; the determination of one reflects that of the other. Moonitz and Sprouse take a similar position as the AAA committee but in addition recommend periodic fixed asset revaluations.[25] To go still one step further, Ed-

[20]Herman W. Bevis, *Corporate Financial Reporting in a Competitive Economy* (New York: Macmillan Co., 1965), pp. 129–130.
[21]W. A. Paton and A. C. Littleton, *An Introduction to Corporate Accounting Standards* (Urbana, Ill.: AAA. College of Commerce and Business Administration, University of Illinois, 1954) p. 17.
[22]Eldon S. Hendiksen, *Accounting Theory* (Homewood, Ill.: Richard D. Irwin, 1965), p. 311.

[23]AICPA, Statement of the Accounting Principles Board No. 3 (1969), p. 19.
[24]AAA. Committee on Concepts and Standards—Long-Lived Assets, loc. cit., p. 695.
[25]Robert T. Sprouse and Maurice Moonitz, "A

wards and Bell stress current costs as such and not only as clues, and develop a system that integrates both historical and current costs. These writers see the difference between historical and current cost as a *holding gain* of which a part is realized by depreciation.[26]

Somewhat differently, the AAA Committee to Prepare a Statement of Basic Accounting Theory recommends the showing of historical and current costs parallel in multicolumn statements, and the reporting of both realized and unrealized holding gains.[27]

The diversity of proposals indicates the need for a concept that narrows down the choice of procedures. Even if depreciation serves primarily as an income determinant, its actual effects on asset valuation and capital maintenance determination have to be considered; those functions might furnish the needed fruitful concept.

VALUATION CONCEPT

Viewed as asset valuation, depreciation conceivably may work with: (1) present values of future cash flows attributable to the asset, or (2) with market prices, appraisals, price-level index applications, or replacement costs as indicators of those present values, or (3) with the last four as such in their own right.

Appraisal depreciation as an independent system is not used for going concerns

any more and would not present systematic, but erratic, patterns. Price-level index applications do not produce independent values but only translate given ones. The use of market prices in their own right is most prominently presented by Professor Chambers as part of an accounting system that is based on the theory of cash equivalents and which has to be accepted or refuted in total.[28] Replacement costs or current costs have been mentioned above as input measurements, not primarily concerned with asset valuation. That leaves present values for discussion.

SINKING FUND METHOD

Mathematically, present values are applications of compound interest. One extension of compound interest, the sinking fund method, was mentioned previously. This method, the application of which does not have to coincide with the establishment of an actual fund, results in increasing periodic charges due to the interest on the increasing hypothetical fund balance. Only few assets justify such charges; however, the method still is sometimes recommended for more general use.[29]

PRESENT VALUE METHODS

A related procedure is the annuity method, which arrives at equal annual charges by adding to the sinking fund depreciation the periodic interest on the unamortized asset balance. The annuity method requires the recording of imputed interest, and its total depreciation charges exceed the asset cost.

Tentative Set of Broad Accounting Principles for Business Enterprises,'' Accounting Research Study No. 3 (AICPA, 1962), p. 34.
[26]Edgar D. Edwards and Philip W. Bell, *The Theory and Measurement of Business Income* (Berkeley and Los Angeles: University of California Press, 1961), pp. 162ff.
[27]AAA, Committee to Prepare a Statement of Basic Accounting Theory (Evanston, Ill.: AAA, 1966), pp. 29.35.

[28]Raymond J. Chambers, *Accounting, Evaluation and Economic Behavior* (Englewood Cliffs, N.J.: Prentice-Hall, 1966), pp. 208–209.218.
[29]David Solomons, *Divisional Performance: Measurement and Control* (New York: Financial Executives Research Foundation, 1965), p. 135.

Exhibit 1

Year	Equivalent Annual Cash Flow	Present Factor Value at 6%	(A) Annual Cash Flow Discounted at 6%	(B) Diminution of Total Present Value
1	$4,489	0.943396	$4,235	$3,769
2	4,489	0.889996	3,996	3,996
3	4,489	0.839619	3,769	4,235
			$12,000	$12,000

It also presumes constancy of future revenue and charges other than depreciation, and assumes constant reinvestment of the cash inflow equalling the amortizations. The method is rarely used. Recording imputed interest does not appeal to most financial accountants, nor is the equality of periodic charges always realistic. Many fixed assets decline in service value much faster in the first years of use than in the later years.

It is possible, however, to modify the annuity method so as to avoid the recording of imputed interest and to obtain accelerated depreciation. This is achieved by discounting each of the annuities as of the date of asset acquisition and by using the discounted amounts as depreciation charges. The farther a charge is removed, the less will be its present value (present-value-of-annual-cash-flows method).

PRESENT VALUE—EXPIRED SERVICE POTENTIAL METHOD

Another procedure in the same direction compares the present values of the services embodied in the asset as of the beginning and as of the end of a report period and uses the difference, the expired service potential, as depreciation (balance-of-present-value method). That is the method most often

discussed nowadays.[30] It logically represents the valuation concept of depreciation. Useful results therefore would validate the concept.

Exhibit 1 illustrates both (A) the present-value-of-annual-cash-flows method and (B) the balance-of-present-value method. Given is a depreciable asset producing a net cash flow with a present value of $12,000 equally spread over three years.

In this case an interest rate of 6% is assumed. The capital recovery factor at 6% for 3 years of 0.31411 and is easily found in tables labeled correspondingly. This factor applied to $12,000 gives $4,489. The present value factors are equally easily found in tables labeled "present value of $1." Their application to $4,489 gives the

[30]W. A. Paton and W. A. Paton, Jr., *Asset Accounting: An Intermediate Course* (New York: Macmillan Co., 1952), p. 272. Harold Bierman, Jr., "Depreciable Assets—Timing of Expense Recognition," *Accounting Review*, Vol. 36 (October 1961), pp. 613–618; T. N. Young and C. G. Peirson, "Depreciation-Future Services Basis," *Accounting Review*, Vol. 42 (April 1967), pp. 338–341; Hugo Nurnberg, "Present Value Depreciation and Income Tax Allocation," *Accounting Review*, Vol. 43 (October 1968), p. 719; AAA, "Report of Committee on Managerial Decision Models," *Accounting Review*, Supplement to Vol. 44 (1969), p. 76.

Exhibit 2

	First Year	Second Year	Third Year
Service potential at beginning	$12,000	$8,231	$4,235
Present value of 2nd year's annuity	$ 4,235*		
Present value of 3rd year's annuity	3,996†	4,235‡	
Service potential left	$ 8,231	$4,235	0
Service potential expired	$ 3,769	$3,996	$4,235

* 4489 × .943396
†4489 × .889996
‡4489 × .943396

amounts in column (A). The expiration of service potentials, shown in column (B), can be computed as shown in Exhibit 2 (cents omitted).

An alternative computation is somewhat faster (cents omitted):

Year	1/1 Investment	Cash Flow	6% Interest	Depre- ciation
1	$12,000	$4,489	$720	$3,769
2	8,231	4,489	493	3,996
3	4,235	4,489	254	4,235

The interest amounts are not recorded on books but appear as profits on the income statement. Each year's opening asset balance equals the total of the remaining service potentials.

In this case, the balance-of-present-value method results in increasing charges, whereas the present-value-of-annual-cash-flows method naturally has the opposite result. However, the former method also can lead to equal and to decreasing depreciation charges—depending on the size of the individual amount representing the asset's periodic net service contributions. In such cases, both the interest rate and the annual net cash inflows have to be found. The cost of capital usually serves as interest rate. That cost can be computed by dividing the market value of a firm's common share into the firm's annual income expected by investors. The estimated service contributions may represent the prospective asset or the production of "real revenue . . . less all operating costs other than depreciation . . ." attributable to it.[31]

The previous example's result of the balance-of-present-value method, a decelerated depreciation, is usually unrealistic. As the example's assumption of equal annual service contributions is not uncommon, the method must be judged as failing to provide the valuation concept of depreciation with the necessary support of overall usefulness. That does not mean, however, that present value procedures cannot be meaningfully related to the fourth depreciation concept, that of capital maintenance. Whereas asset valuation and input measurement are functionally integrated, capital maintenance rules are independent of net asset valuation rules.[32]

[31]Isaac N. Reynolds, "Selecting the Proper Depreciation Method," *Accounting Review*, Vol. 36 (April 1961), p. 240.
[32]Keith Shwayder, "The Capital Maintenance

MAINTENANCE OF CAPITAL CONCEPT

Depreciation has been defined "as a means of measuring whether capital is retained intact for further use."[33] This definition calls for three comments. First, depreciation cost is not different from other costs as *cause* of the retention of capital, both will respect to dividend policy and otherwise.[34] Retaining capital intact is the role of revenue, i.e., recovering costs and expenses. The *measurement* of the retention is the function of the income statement, including depreciation. Second, capital and costs must be stated in the same dollars as revenue in order to make the measurement of capital maintenance meaningful, and capital must signify not merely an aggregate of historical money amounts but the purchase and/or earnings power of the business. Third, assuming absence of price-level changes, a period's plant cost consumption is fully recovered by revenue if the period shows a profit, and is partly recouped in case of a loss. In the latter situation, depreciation may measure how far (and not whether) capital has been maintained; special computations will be needed.

Accordingly, under present accounting conditions, the function of depreciation as a measure of capital maintenance presents a concept rather weak by itself. However, it is exactly this concept that provides accounting guidance. It recommends that the present value of the net cash flow of a future year attributable to a specific asset shall be the asset's depreciation in that year. Barring price changes, such depreciation will indicate, in the case of profits what part of the revenue must be reinvested to maintain the firm's earning power in the pattern of the original budget. The difference between the present value and the budgeted amount of each annual net cash flow would represent a return on capital, earned during the period from the acquisition of the service potential to the year of its consumption and realized in that year.

An example illustrates some mathematical details. Given is an asset cost of $10,000, a 6% cost of capital, and a net service (utility) contribution of $12,000 distributed over three years in the sum-of-the-years'-digits method (cents omitted).

The present value factors are the same as in the first example. The equivalent differential is computed with the equation:

$$899 = \frac{X}{2(1.06)} + \frac{X}{3(1.06)^2} + \frac{X}{6(1.06)^3} =$$

$$X\left[\frac{0.9434}{2} + \frac{0.89}{3} + \frac{0.8396}{6}\right]; X = 990.$$

The excess of the total of present values over the asset cost—$899 in this case—is either recorded and then amortized[35] or it is initially deducted from the present values. The last procedure is followed above.

ARGUMENTS AGAINST CAPITAL MAINTENANCE METHOD

Against such use of present values and the following arguments have been advanced:

1. Estimates of the asset's net service contributions are necessary.
2. The cost of capital, too, may involve judgment.

Rule and the Net Asset Valuation Rule," *Accounting Review*, Vol. 44 (April 1969), pp. 304–316.

[33]Coughlan and Strand, op. cit., pp. 1.9f.

[34]Paton and Paton, op. cit., p. 262; but William A. Paton, "Depreciation-Concept and Measurement," *Journal of Accounting* (October 1959), p. 39 stresses the understatement of depreciation as cause of impairment of capital resources.

[35]Wendell P. Trumbull, *op. cit.*, p. 465.

Year	Cash Flow	Present Value at 6%	Equivalent Differential	Present Value at 6%	Total Present Value
1	$6,000	$5,660	$495	$467	$5,193
2	4,000	3,560	330	294	3,266
3	2,000	1,679	165	138	1,541
	$12,000	$10,899	$990	$899	$10,000

3. Complications may arise due to subsequent changes in expectations.
4. The asset purchase is influenced by demand and supply. The buyer has no guarantee for the fulfillment of his expectations.[36]
5. The variety of fixed assets makes computations of present values difficult.[37]
6. The method is not applicable to non-revenue-producing items, such as personnel recreation facilities.[38]
7. The earnings power of assets is collective. The cash flow is attributable to the aggregate of assets.[39]
8. Cash savings, net service contributions, and time-adjusted accrued revenues and expenses are often discounted from the end of the year of their occurrence, whereas they occur throughout the year.[40]

The first two objections do not carry weight. Accountants are used to making judgments. Moreover, the judgment involved here is that of the decision-making and presumably well-informed management. The third objection should not be overrated. Expectations are usually capitalized only once, namely when the decision to acquire an asset is made; that decision entails the proper depreciation charges.[41] The fourth objection scarcely needs a rebuttal. Future does not hold any guarantees whatsoever. Regardless of supply and demand, no businessman buys without expecting a return of and on capital. The fifth and sixth objection have limited merit only. (Depreciation in non-profit organization is not included in this paper's discussion.) As to the seventh objection, that the earnings power of assets is collective, the rebuttal has been offered that businessmen make individual asset projections daily.[42] The last objection, finally, is taken care of by present value tables constructed on the assumption of the uniformity of cash flows during the year.

FAVORABLE ASPECTS OF CAPITAL MAINTENANCE METHOD

Favorable to the use of present values is that:

1. Interest is a factor in the cost of any fixed asset.
2. The time value of money is finding in-

[36]Paton and Paton, *op. cit.*, p. 272.
[37]Rufus Wixon, ed., *op. cit.*, pp. 17. 24f.
[38]Bierman, *op. cit.*
[39]Eugene L. Grant and Paul T. Norton, Jr., *Depreciation* (Rev. ptg.: New York: Ronald Press, 1955), p. 38.
[40]Harold Bierman, Jr., "Further Study of Depreciation," *Accounting Review*, Vol. 41 (April 1966), pp. 271–274, proposes that sales and purchases on account be time-adjusted by discounting them back to the date they are made, and then be considered part of the cash stream of that date.

[41]Bierman, "Depreciable Assets. . . ." op. cit., p. 613.
[42]Trumbull, op. cit., p. 462, n. 4.

creasing accounting recognition, e.g., in AICPA Accounting Principles Board Opinions No. 5 and No. 8.

3. People place a higher value on services to be rendered soon than on those of later delivery.

4. With present value methods, depreciation can be applied on the basis of activities instead of time intervals.

5. Present value computations are used by management in asset acquisition decisions. Usually, management will buy a plant asset if the present value of the expected net cash inflows exceeds the cost (net present value method), or if the internal rate (yield) is satisfactory. The internal rate is the rate that equates the cost of the assets with the present value of the annuity of net cash inflows attributable to the asset. The internal rate method commonly is less favored than the net present value method.

The above argument is decisive for upholding the conclusion drawn from the capital maintenance concept. According to the AAA "the use by investors of published financial statements . . . should be considered of primary importance."[43] The opportunity to appraise management's ability to realize expectations is crucial for an investor's decision to hold, buy or sell. However, perusal of a corporation's president's report with its forecasts and declarations of intentions—if those are furnished as they should be—is useless to the investor if he is not given financial statements that incorporate the thought processes underlying managerial decisions and thereby offer the opportunity to compare past expectations with present realizations. Generally speaking, financial reports contain the results of managerial decisions, should reflect the format of the decision-making process, and be consistent with its models. Compliance therewith is said to be in the interest of the company itself, because otherwise managers may be tempted to make dysfunctional decisions.[44]

EXCEPTIONS TO CAPITAL MAINTENANCE METHOD

The capital maintenance concept with its present-value-of-the-annual-cash-flows method has been found here as superior with respect to the other concepts. However, it is not a panacea either but subject to exceptions. These concern mainly three situations: the existence of industry-wide depreciation practices; a firm's lack of sophisticated accounting staff; and the multitude and variety of fixed assets in a company.

While the capital maintenance method draws support from offering investors an opportunity to judge corporate managerial efficiency, it contributes little to financial analysis through intercompany comparisons. Although such comparisons usually are difficult where depreciation is a material item, industry-wide depreciation practices may help, if the respective plants' ages and historical costs are similar. In that case sound uniform practices may prevail over the capital maintenance method.

That may be especially true for smaller companies having limited fixed asset investments. Besides, those companies will look to trade practices in depreciation for other reasons. They often will lack an accounting staff sophisticated enough to han-

---

[43]AAA, 1957 Revision. . . . op. cit., p. 7.

[44]Michael Schiff, "Effect of Variations in Accounting Methods on Capital Budgeting," *NAA Bulletin,* Vol. 46 (July 1965), p. 58; AAA, "Report of the Committee on Managerial Decision Models," loc. cit., p. 58.

dle the maintenance of capital method. In the absence of trade practices, they will use then the conventional method best suited for them.

Even in large, well-staffed companies the capital maintenance method—though otherwise applicable—may not always be practical. If the fixed assets are numerous, they often are depreciated jointly by group depreciation for similar items and composite depreciation for dissimilar ones; both commonly use a constant annual rate. Whether such depreciations are theoretically justifiable (e.g., with the previously mentioned reasoning that the earnings power of assets is collective), does not merit a discussion here. More than one firm using group or composite depreciation has experienced an unrealistic balance in its accumulated depreciation account. Any underlying theory, therefore, will not be persuasive, and the case for joint depreciations rests on expediency.

SUMMARY

In this paper five concepts of depreciation were set forth:

1. Recognition of the physical or functional deterioration of a fixed asset (causal concept).
2. Provisions for replacement of depreciable assets (replacement concept).
3. A means of income determination, at present usually through measuring operational plant input by amortization of the prepayment representing plant cost (input concept).
4. A measure of asset valuation, essentially by specifying the expiration of service potentials (valuation concept).
5. A measure of the maintenance of

capital, mainly in case of profitable operations and price-level stability (maintenance of capital concept).

In spite of some interdependence, the concepts do not have equal import. The causal concept does not typify accounting practice. The replacement concept has long been considered irrelevant for external reports. The input concept is presently dominant; however, it gives little guidance to the practice of depreciation accounting. The valuation concept provides more guidance. Nevertheless the concept fails because its logical extension, the balance-of-present value method, often yields unreasonable results. The capital maintenance concept is not quite realistic, considering the present state of accountancy. However, it provides better guidance than the valuation and input concepts; as a rule, the present value of an asset's service in a future year will be that year's depreciation expense. Acceptance of price-level adjustments will strengthen this concept.

The five concepts were discussed mainly as to their plausibility and fruitfulness. The different meanings of their components such as asset, income and capital were mentioned but not evaluated themselves. It behooves us therefore to trace the relevant depreciation concepts directly to basic accounting theory as anchorage.

The valuation concept represents the proprietary theory. That theory focuses accounting on the changes in the business wealth of the owners of a firm, is balance sheet oriented, and prevailed during the last century. The input concept represents the entity theory. This theory dominates today, stresses the business entity instead of its owners as accounting matter, and is income statement oriented. The average corporation has investors whose main interest is the earnings-per-share figure, and it is run by managers whose efficiency usually is judged by the periodic income produced. The yearly amortization of a low historical cost of fixed assets serves those managers well. The maintenance of capital concept can be aligned with the relatively recent enterprise theory. This theory sees in the large corporation an institution that is financially self-supporting, has diversified activities, and allows its stockholders in effect only the right to conventional dividends.[45] Concern about those enterprises exceeds that about their stockholders[46] and relates strongly to the maintenance of real capital. Such maintenance does not only mean security for investors, employees and customers but also contributes stability to society as a whole.

[45]Waino W. Suojanen, "Enterprise Theory and Corporate Balance Sheets," *Accounting Review*, Vol. 33 (January 1958), pp. 56–65.
[46]Bevis, Op. cit., p. 9.

QUESTIONS

1. When a closely held corporation issues preferred stock for land, the land should be recorded at the
   a. Total par value of the stock issued
   b. Total book value of the stock issued
   c. Appraised value of the land — *if known otherwise FMV of stock*
   d. Total liquidating value of the stock issued

2. A principal objection to the straight-line method of depreciation is that it
   a. Provides for the declining productivity of an aging asset
   b. Ignores variations in the rate of asset use
   c. Tends to result in a constant rate of return on a diminishing investment base
   d. Gives smaller periodic write-offs than decreasing charge methods

3. Property, plant, and equipment are conventionally presented in the balance sheet at
   a. Replacement cost less accumulated depreciation
   b. Historical cost less salvage value
   c. Original cost adjusted for general price level changes
   d. Acquisition cost less depreciated portion thereof

4. In an arm's-length transaction, Company A and Company B exchanged nonmonetary assets with no monetary consideration involved. The exchange did culminate an earning process for both Company A and Company B, and the fair values of the nonmonetary assets were both clearly evident. The accounting for the exchange should be based on the
   a. Fair value of the asset surrendered
   b. Fair value of the asset received

314

   c. Recorded amount of the asset surrendered

   d. Recorded amount of the asset received

5. As generally used in accounting, depreciation

   a. Is a process of asset valuation for balance sheet purposes

   b. Applies only to long-lived intangible assets

   c. Is used to indicate a decline in market value of a long-lived asset

   d. Is an accounting process that allocates long-lived asset cost to accounting periods

6. Use of the annuity method of calculating depreciation results in

   a. Constant charges to depreciation expense

   b. Decreasing charges to depreciation expense

   c. Increasing credits to interest income

   d. Constant credits to interest income

7. Lyle, Inc., purchased certain plant assets under a deferred payment contract on December 31, 1982. The agreement was to pay $20,000 at the time of purchase and $20,000 at the end of each of the next five years. The plant assets should be valued at

   a. The present value of a $20,000 ordinary annuity for five years

   b. $120,000

   c. $120,000 less imputed interest

   d. $120,000 plus imputed interest *time value of money*

8. For income statement purposes, depreciation is a variable expense if the depreciation method used for book purposes is

   a. Units of production

   b. Straight line

   c. Sum-of-the-year's-digits

   d. Declining balance

9. A method that excludes salvage value from the base for the depreciation calculation is

   a. Straight line

   b. Sum-of-the-year's-digits

   c. Double-declining balance

   d. Productive output

10. When a company purchases land with a building on it and immediately tears down the building so that the land can be used for the construction of a plant, the cost incurred to tear down the building should be

   a. Expensed as incurred

   b. Added to the cost of the plant

   c. Added to the cost of the land

   d. Amortized over the estimated time period between the tearing down of the building and the completion of the plant

11. A machine with a four-year estimated useful life and an estimated 15 percent

salvage value was acquired on January 1, 1982. On December 31, 1984, the accumulated depreciation using the sum-of-the-year's-digits method would be

    a. (Original cost less salvage value) multiplied by 9/10
    b. Original cost multiplied by 9/10
    c. Original cost multiplied by 9/10 less total salvage value
    d. (Original cost less salvage value) multiplied by 1/10.

12. A company using the group depreciation method for its delivery trucks retired one of its delivery trucks due to damage before the average service life of the group was reached. An insurance recovery was received. The net book value of these group asset accounts would be decreased by the

    a. Original cost of the truck
    b. Original cost of the truck less the insurance recovery received
    c. Original cost of the truck less depreciation on the truck to the date of retirement
    d. Insurance recovery received

13. When equipment is retired, accumulated depreciation is debited for the original cost less any residual recovery under which of the following depreciation methods?

	Composite depreciation	Group depreciation
a.	No	No
b.	No	Yes
c.	Yes	No
d.	Yes	Yes

14. Recognizing depletion expense is an example of the accounting process of

	Allocation	Amortization
a.	No	No
b.	No	Yes
c.	Yes	Yes
d.	Yes	No

15. A donated plant asset for which the fair value has been determined, and for which incidental costs were incurred in acceptance of the asset, should be recorded at an amount equal to its

    a. Incidental costs incurred
    b. Fair value and incidental costs incurred
    c. Book value on books of donor and incidental costs incurred
    d. Book value on books of donor

16. Depreciation continues to be one of the most controversial, difficult, and important problem areas in accounting.

Required:

  i. Explain the conventional accounting concept of depreciation accounting.
  ii. Discuss its conceptual merit with respect to (a) the value of the asset, (b) the charge(s) to expense, and (c) the discretion of management in selecting the method.
  iii. Explain the factors that should be considered when applying the conventional concept of depreciation to the determination of how the value of a newly acquired computer system should be assigned to expense for financial reporting purposes. (Income tax considerations should be ignored.)
  iv. What depreciation methods might be used for the computer system?

17. Jay Manufacturing, Inc., began operations five years ago producing probos, a new type of instrument it hoped to sell to doctors, dentists, and hospitals. The demand for probos far exceeded initial expectations, and the company was unable to produce enough probos to meet demand.

The company was manufacturing its product on equipment it built at the start of its operations, but to meet demand more efficient equipment was needed. The company decided to design and build the equipment, since that currently available on the market was unsuitable for producing probos.

In 1988 a section of the plant was devoted to development of the new equipment and a special staff of personnel was hired. Within six months a machine was developed at a cost of $170,000 which successfully increased production and reduced labor costs substantially. Sparked by the success of the new machine, the company built three more machines of the same type at a cost of $80,000 each.

Required:

  a. In addition to satisfying a need that outsiders cannot meet within the desired time, what other reasons might cause a firm to construct fixed assets for its own use?
  b. In general, what costs should be capitalized for a self-constructed fixed asset?
  c. Discuss the propriety of including in the capitalized cost of self-constructed assets:
   i. The increase in overhead caused by the self-construction of fixed assets
   ii. A proportionate share of overhead on the same basis as that applied to goods manufactured for sale
  d. Discuss the proper accounting treatment of the $90,000 ($170,000 −

$80,000) by which the cost of the first machine exceeded the cost of the subsequent machines.

18. Your client found three suitable sites, each having certain unique advantages, for a new plant facility. In order to investigate thoroughly the advantages and disadvantages of each site, one-year options were purchased for an amount equal to 5 percent of the contract price of each site. The costs of the options cannot be applied against the contracts. Before the options expired, one of the sites was purchased at the contract price of $60,000. The option on this site had cost $3,000. The two options not exercised had cost $3,500 each.

Required:
   Present arguments in support of recording the cost of the land at each of the following amounts:
   a. $60,000 · contract - for #any others are period costs
   b. $63,000
   c. $70,000 — No options — If all incurred yes.

19. *a.* Property, plant, and equipment (plant assets) generally represent a material portion of the total assets of most companies. Accounting for the acquisition and usage of such assets is, therefore, an important part of the financial reporting process.

Required:
   i. Distinguish between revenue and capital expenditures and explain why this distinction is important.
   ii. Briefly define depreciation as used in accounting.
   iii. Identify the factors that are relevant in determining the annual depreciation and explain whether these factors are determined objectively or whether they are based on judgment.
   iv. Explain why depreciation is usually shown in the sources of funds section of the statement of changes in financial position.

b. A company may acquire plant assets (among other ways) for cash, on a deferred payment plan, by exchanging other assets, or by a combination of these ways.

Required:
   i. Identify six costs that should be capitalized as the cost of the land. For your answer, assume that land with an existing building is acquired for cash and that the existing building is to be removed in the immediate future so that a new building can be constructed on that site.
   ii. At what amount should a company record a plant asset acquired on a deferred payment plan?

iii. In general, at what amount should plant assets received in exchange for other nonmonetary assets be recorded? Specifically, at what amount should a company record a new machine acquired by exchanging an older, similar machine and paying cash?

20. George Company purchased land for use as its corporate headquarters. A small factory that was on the land when it was purchased was torn down before construction of the office building began. Furthermore, a substantial amount of rock blasting and removal had to be done to the site before construction of the building foundation began. Because the office building was set back on the land far from the public road, George Company had the contractor construct a paved road which led from the public road to the parking lot of the office building.

Three years after the office building was occupied, George Company added four stories to the office building. The four stories had an estimated useful life of five years more than the remaining estimated useful life of the original office building.

Ten years later the land and building were sold at an amount more than their net book value and George Company had a new office building constructed in another state for use as its new corporate headquarters.

Required:

a. Which of the preceding expenditures should be capitalized? How should each be depreciated or amortized? Discuss the rationale for your answers.

b. How would the sale of the land and building be accounted for? Include in your answer how to determine the net book value at the date of sale. Discuss the rationale for your answer.

21. Among the principal topics related to the accounting for the property, plant, and equipment of a company are acquisitions and retirement.

Required:

a. What expenditures should be capitalized when equipment is acquired for cash?

b. Assume the market value of equipment acquired is not determinable by reference to a similar purchase for cash. Describe how the acquiring company should determine the capitalized cost of equipment purchased by exchanging it for each of the following:
   i. Bonds having an established market price
   ii. Common stock not having an established market price
   iii. Similar equipment not having a determinable market price

c. Describe the factors that determine whether expenditures relating to property plant and equipment already in use should be capitalized.

d. Describe how to account for the gain or loss on the sale of property, plant, and equipment for cash.

22. A certified public accountant is frequently called upon by management for advice regarding methods of computing depreciation. Although the question arises less frequently, of comparable importance is whether the depreciation method should be based on the consideration of assets as units, a group, or as having a composite life.

Required:

a. Briefly describe the depreciation methods based on treating assets as
 i. Units
 ii. A group or as having a composite life
b. Present arguments for and against the use of each of the two methods.
c. Describe how retirements are recorded under each of the two methods.

BIBLIOGRAPHY

Anthony, Rober N. *Accounting for the Cost of Interest.* Lexington, Mass.: Lexington Books, 1975.

Arcady, Alex T., and Charles E. Baker. "Capitalization of Interest Cost—Implementing FASB Statement No. 34." *The Ohio CPA* (Autumn 1980), pp. 137–141.

Arnett, Harold E. "APB Opinion No. 29: Accounting for Nonmonetary Transactions—Some New Perspectives." *Management Accounting* (October 1978), pp. 41–48.

Barefield, Russell M., and Eugene E. Comiskey. "Depreciation Policy and the Behavior of Corporate Profits." *Journal of Accounting Research* (Autumn 1971), pp. 351–358.

Barnea, Amir. "Note on the Cash-flow Approach to Valuation and Depreciation of Productive Assets." *Journal of Financial and Quantitative Analysis* (June 1972), pp. 1841–1846.

Baxter, W. T. "Depreciating Assets: The Forward Looking Approach to Value." *Abacus* (December 1970), pp. 120–131.

Beidelman, Carl R. "Valuation of Used Capital Assets." *Studies in Accounting Research No. 7,* American Accounting Association, 1973.

Bennett, Anthony H. M. "Depreciation and Business Decision Making." *Accounting and Business Research* (Winter 1972), pp. 3–28.

Bierman, Harold, Jr., and Thomas R. Dyckman, "Accounting for Interest During Construction." *Accounting and Business Research* (Autumn 1979), pp. 267–272.

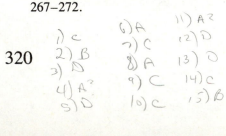

320

Burt, Oscar R. "Unified Theory of Depreciation." *Journal of Accounting Research* (Spring 1970), pp. 28–57.

Cappettini, Robert, and Thomas E. King. "Exchanges of Nonmonetary Assets: Some Changes." *The Accounting Review* (January 1976), pp. 142–147.

Castellano, Joseph F., Clarence E. Campbell, and Harper A. Roehm. "An Application of APB Opinion 29." *The Ohio CPA* (Winter 1976), pp. 17–19.

Chambers, Raymond J. "Asset Measurement and Valuation." *Cost and Management* (March–April 1971), pp. 30–35.

Cotteleer, Thomas F. "Depreciation, An Accounting Enigma." *Management Accounting* (February 1971), pp. 23–24, 27.

Coughlan, Joseph D., and William K. Strand. *Depreciation: Accounting, Taxes, and Business Decisions.* New York: Ronald Press, 1969.

Dixon, Robert L. "Decreasing Charge Depreciation—A Search for Logic." *The Accounting Review* (October 1960), pp. 590–597.

Goldberg, L. "Concepts of Depreciation." In *Studies in Accounting Theory*, edited by W. T. Baxter and Sidney Davidson. Homewood, Ill.: Richard D. Irwin, Inc., 1962, pp. 236–258.

Gray, O. Ronald. "Implementation of FASB Statement No. 34: Capitalization of Interest Cost." *The National Public Accountant* (April 1980), pp. 23–25.

Greipel, Rudolph C. "Accounting for Nonmonetary Transactions—A Review of APB Opinion No. 29." *The CPA Journal* (January 1974), pp. 34–39.

Grossman, Steven D., Alan G. Mayper, and Robert B. Welker. "Oil and Gas Disclosures—The FASB Reacts." *The CPA Journal* (May 1983), pp. 24–29.

Imhoff, Eugene A., and Paul A. Janell. "Opinion No. 29: A New Valuation Method." *Management Accounting* (March 1979), pp. 50–53.

Johnson, Orace. "Two General Concepts of Depreciation." *Journal of Accounting Research* (Spring 1968), pp. 29–37.

Lambert, S. J., and Joyce C. Lambert. "Concepts and Applications in APB Opinion No. 29." *Journal of Accountancy* (March 1977), pp. 60–68.

Lamden, Charles W., Dale L. Gerboth, and Thomas W. McRae. *Accounting for Depreciable Assets.* New York: American Institute of Certified Public Accountants, 1975.

Lev, Baruch, and Henri Theil. "A Maximum Entropy Approach to the Choice of Asset Depreciation." *Journal of Accounting Research* (Autumn 1978), pp. 286–293.

McIntyre, Edward V. "Present Value Depreciation and the Disaggregation Problem." *The Accounting Review* (January 1977), pp. 261–171.

Most, Kenneth S. "Depreciation in Economic and Accounting Theories." *Accountant* (February 25, 1971), pp. 237–240.

Mullen, Louis E. "Spotlight on Estimated Economic Life of Depreciable Assets." *The CPA Journal* (August 1973), pp. 662–666.

NAA Management Accounting Practices Committee. "Fixed Asset Accounting: The Allocation of Costs." *Management Accounting* (January 1974), pp. 43–49.

NAA Management Accounting Practices Committee. "Fixed Asset Accounting: The Capitalization of Costs." *The CPA Journal* (March 1973), pp. 193–207.

Nikolai, Loren A. "Simplifying Nonmonetary Exchanges." *The CPA Journal* (January 1977), pp. 69–71.

Paton, William A. "Depreciation—Concept and Measurement." *Journal of Accountancy* (October 1959), pp. 38–43.

Peasnell, K. V. "The CCA Depreciation Problem—An Analysis and Proposal." *Abacus* (December 1977), pp. 123–140.

Pidock, Wayne L. "Accounting for Net Salvage." *Management Accounting* (December 1970), pp. 49–52.

Snavely, Howard J. "Current Cost for Long-Lived Assets: A Critical View," *The Accounting Review* (April 1969), pp. 344–353.

Thomas, Arthur L. Studies in Accounting Research No. 9, "The Allocation Problem: Part Two." Sarasota, Fla.: American Accounting Association, 1974.

Warrell, C. J. "The Enterprise Value Concept of Asset Valuation." *Accounting and Business Research* (Summer 1974), pp. 220–226.

Wright, F. K. "Towards a General Theory of Depreciation." *Journal of Accounting Research* (Spring 1964), pp. 80–90.

Young, T. N., and C. G. Peirson. "Depreciation—Future Services Basis." *The Accounting Review* (April 1967), pp. 338–341.

7

LONG-TERM ASSETS II — INVESTMENTS AND INTANGIBLES

Investments in the securities of other corporations are made for a variety of reasons such as obtaining additional income, creating desirable relationships with suppliers, obtaining partial or full control over related companies, or adding new products. The decision to disclose these securities under the long-term investment classification rather than as current assets is based upon the concept of *managerial intent*. When management intends to use the securities for long-term purposes, they are separately classified on the balance sheet as long-term investments rather than as marketable securities, since management does not intend to convert them into cash during the next year or operating cycle.

INVESTMENTS IN COMMON STOCK

Shares of common stock may be acquired on an organized stock exchange, over the counter, or by direct sale. The recorded cost in all cases properly includes the purchase price of the securities plus any brokerage fees, transfer costs, or taxes on the transfer. When common stock is obtained in a nonmonetary transaction, its recorded cost should be based upon the fair market value of the consideration given or, if this amount is unavailable, the fair market value of the common stock received.

Subsequent to acquisition, three methods of accounting for investments in common stock are available: (1) the lower of cost or market method, (2) the equity method, and (3) the market value method.

LOWER OF COST OR MARKET METHOD

Under the lower of cost or market method, an investment in common stock is intially recorded at cost and income is recorded and reported as dividends are received. Additionally, Statement of Financial Accounting Standards No. 12 requires the securities to be carried on the balance sheet at the lower of their aggregate cost or market.[1] This process is to be accomplished by use of a valuation allowance similar to the accounting required for equity securities classified as current assets, but the amount of the charge to the valuation allowance is to be shown separately in the equity section of the balance sheet rather than against income. The provisions of FASB Statement No. 12 allow for recoveries of declines in market value not to exceed original cost. These unrealized gains and losses are to be disclosed on the balance sheet as long as the decline in the market value is deemed temporary.

EQUITY METHOD

Under the equity method, investments are initially recorded at their historical cost; however, adjustments are made to cost to account for profits and losses of the investee, based upon the investor's percentage of ownership. For example, if the investee reports a profit, the investor must report as profit its ownership percentage of the investee profit and increase the investment account by the same amount. On the other hand, dividends received result in a decrease in the carrying value of the investment account for the amount of the dividend received.

MARKET VALUE METHOD

Under the market value method, investments are also initially recorded at their cost and income is recorded for both dividends received and changes in the market price of the acquired shares. This method accounts for all upward and downward changes without regard to original cost. Market changes also result in an adjustment to the carrying value of the investment account.

Table 7.1 summaries the effect of various events on the investment account and reported income of the investor under each of the preceding alternatives.

APB NO. 18

In 1971, the Accounting Principles Board reported its initial conclusions on a study of the accounting for long-term investments in stocks and issued Opinion No. 18, "The Equity Method of Accounting for Investments in Common Stock."[2] Prior to that, the APB had concluded that the equity method was the

---

[1]Statement of Financial Accounting Standards No. 12, "Accounting for Certain Marketable Securities" (Stamford, Conn.: Financial Accounting Standards Board, 1975).
[2]Accounting Principles Board Opinion No. 18, "The Equity Method of Accounting for Investments in Common Stock" (New York: American Institute of Certified Public Accountants, 1971).

CHAPTER 7: LONG TERM ASSETS II

Table 7.1   Effects of the Lower of Cost or Market, Equity, and Market Value Methods on Investment and Income

Event	Lower of Cost or Market	Equity	Market Value
Acquire 25% of common stock of S Company for $100,000	Investment increased $100,000	Investment increased $100,000	Investment increased $100,000
Investee reports net income of $10,000	No effect on investment or income	Investment increased $2,500; income increased $2,500	No effect on investment or income
Investee pays dividends of $5,000 (25% to investor)	No effect on investment; income increased $1,250	Investment decreased $1,250; no effect on income	No effect on investment; income increased $1,250
Investor's shares increase in value by 5% of original cost	No effect on investment or income	No effect on investment or income	Investment increased $5,000; income increased $5,000
Investor's shares temporarily decline in value by 10% of original cost	Investment decreased $10,000; no effect on income; equity decreased $10,000	No effect on investment or income	Investment decreased $10,000; income decreased $10,000
Investor's shares recover in value by 7% of original cost	Investment increased $7,000; no effect on income; equity increased $7,000	No effect on investment or income	Investment increased $7,000; income increased $7,000

[handwritten annotation above Market Value column: Not generally acceptable]

most appropriate reporting technique when the investor owned a majority interest in a subsidiary but did not issue consolidated financial statements.[3] This conclusion was reaffirmed in Opinion No. 18; however, it was also noted that the equity method was not a valid substitute for consolidation.

The board went on to state that the equity method is most appropriate when an investor has the ability significantly to influence financing and operating decisions even though it holds less than 50 percent of the voting stock. Ability to exercise influence was to be determined in a number of ways, including

1. Representation on the board of directors.
2. Participation in policymaking processes.
3. Material intercompany transactions.
4. Interchange of managerial personnel.
5. Technological dependency.[4]

Nevertheless, the board noted that determining the ability to influence was not always clear and ''in order to achieve a reasonable degree of uniformity in application'' an investment of 20 percent or more of the voting stock was deemed to constitute evidence of a presumption of the ability to exercise significant influence.[5] The board therefore concluded that the equity method should be used when an investor holds 20 percent or more of the voting stock of an investee unless the surrounding circumstances indicate a lack of ability to influence.

There are circumstances in which an investor holds 20 percent or more of the outstanding common stock of an investee and does not have the ability to exercise significant influence. FASB Interpretation No. 35 suggests that the following facts and circumstances might preclude an investor from using the equity method even if an investment of 20 percent or more was held.

1. Opposition by the investee, such as litigation or complaints to governmental regulatory authorities, challenges the investor's ability to exercise significant influence.
2. The investor and investee sign an agreement under which the investor surrenders significant rights as a shareholder.
3. Majority ownership of the investee is concentrated among a small group of shareholders who operate the investee without regard to the views of the investor.
4. The investor needs or wants more financial information to apply the equity

---

[3]Accounting Principles Board Opinion No. 10, ''Omnibus Opinion—1966'' (New York: American Institute of Certified Public Accountants, 1966).
[4]Opinion No. 18, op. cit.
[5]Ibid.

method than is available to the investee's other shareholders (e.g., the investor wants quarterly financial information from an investee that publicly reports only annually), tries to obtain that information, and fails.

5. The investor tries and fails to obtain representation on the investee's board of directors.[6]

When an investor owns less than 20 percent interest or the foregoing criteria indicate that the ability to influence the investee is not present, the lower of cost or market method should be used.[7] However, the market value method is not generally accepted for most companies and may only be used in certain industries (such as mutual funds) where it is common practice.

Despite some speculation at the time that the market value might be embraced by the APB, the board did little to add to its acceptability. The use of the market value method is, of course, a departure from the historical-cost principle and the APB evidently was not prepared to take such a radical step even though the information needed to account for investments under the market value method is available in most cases. *understood without being put into writing.*

The FASB's tacit acceptance of the lower of cost or market method is not a departure from the historical-cost principle. It is simply further evidence of the overriding concern for conservatism discussed earlier, in Chapter 2.

The APB's decision to embrace the equity method was apparently based upon the objectives of accrual accounting, that is, the reporting of transactions when they occur rather than as cash is collected. The board apparently believed that cash flow needs of the investor could be satisfied by the significant influence test and that reporting needs were of primary importance.

PERMANENT DECLINE IN MARKET VALUE

When a decline in the market value of a long-term investment accounted for under the lower of cost or market method is determined to be permanent, the investment is written down, a loss is recorded, and a new cost basis is established. The recorded loss is the amount of difference between original cost and the new basis, and any previously established valuation account or unrealized loss is eliminated. Subsequent recoveries in the market value of the security are not recorded.

---

[6]"Criteria for Applying The Equity Method of Accounting for Investments in Common Stocks," FASB Interpretation No. 35. (Stamford, Conn.: Financial Accounting Standards Board, 1981), par. 4.

[7]At the time of the issuance of this Opinion, the lower of cost or market method was not established. APB No. 18 required the use of the "cost" method, which did not require companies to account for temporary declines in market value.

CHANGES IN CLASSIFICATION

When the classification of an equity security is changed from current to noncurrent status, the security is transferred at the lower of its cost or market value as of the date of transfer. This amount becomes its new cost basis, and if market is lower than cost at the date of the transfer, the difference is accounted for as a realized loss.

Note

INVESTMENTS IN PREFERRED STOCK AND BONDS

The acquisition of preferred stock as a long-term investment poses some of the same measurement problems encountered by the acquisition of common stock. While these securities generally do not carry voting rights, and their share of investee earnings is fixed, they were defined as marketable equity securities by FASB No. 12. Preferred shares are therefore carried as a part of the total equity portfolio. Cumulative or participating clauses may result in variations in yearly income but do not alter the basic reporting criteria, since preferred dividends are not a liability to the investee until declared.

Note

Investments in bonds are initially recorded at cost and it is not unusual for the purchase price of a bond to differ from its face value. These differences reflect fluctuations in market interest rates from the time the bond was initially offered for sale to the present. Any difference between the price paid for the securities and their face value should be amortized over the bonds' remaining life as an adjustment to interest income and the investment account.

difference between price paid for securities and the face value is amortized, over the remaining life

Two methods of amortization are available: straight line and compound interest. Under the *straight-line method*, the bond premium or discount is divided by the periods remaining until the bond is to be repaid. In each subsequent period an equal amount of amortization is written off against income. The rationale underlying the use of the straight-line method is its ease of computation and the belief that premium or discount amortizations are relatively minor charges. Therefore, the use of other methods would result in only minor differences.

Note compound interest method

When the compound interest method is used, a rate of return must be computed at the time the investment is acquired. This interest rate is then applied to the carrying value of the investment in each interest period resulting in a uniform rate of return. The use of this method is based upon the belief that the investment was acquired at a certain yield and that the financial statements issued in subsequent periods should reflect the effects of that decision (for a further discussion of compound interest amortization techniques, see Chapter 8).

INTANGIBLES

It is difficult to define the term *intangibles* adequately. Kohler defined it as capital assets having no physical existence and whose value depends on the rights and benefits that possession confers upon the owner.[8] However, Paton had previously noted that the lack of physical existence test was not particularly helpful and suggested that intangibles are assets more closely related to the enterprise as a whole than to any components.[9] It should be noted that many intangibles convey a sort of monopolistic right to their owners. Examples of intangibles are patents, copyrights, franchises, leaseholds, and goodwill.

Intangible assets derive their value from the special rights and privileges that they convey, and accounting for these assets involves the same problems as accounting for other long-term assets. Specifically, an initial carrying amount must be determined; this initial carrying value must be systematically and rationally allocated to the periods that receive benefit; and if the asset's value declines substantially and permanently, the unamortized carrying value must be written down. These problems are magnified in the case of intangibles because their very nature makes evidence illusive. Both the value and the useful lives of intangibles are difficult to determine.

In reviewing the topic of intangibles, the Accounting Principles Board noted that such assets might be classified on several different bases.

Identifiability—separately identifiable or lacking specific identification.
Manner of acquisition—acquired singly, in groups, or in business combinations, or developed internally.
Expected period of benefit—limited by law or contract, related to human or economic factors, or having indefinite or indeterminate duration.
Separability from an entire enterprise—rights transferable without title, salable, or inseparable from the enterprise or a substantial part of it.[10]

The foregoing definitions suggest that intangibles may be classified according to whether they are *externally acquired* (purchased from outsiders) or *internally developed*. Additionally, they may be classified as *identifiable* or *unidentifiable*. These last two classifications relate to the Type (a) and Type (b) classifications contained in ARB No. 43 and discussed later in the chapter.

ACCOUNTING FOR COST

The valuation process for intangible assets generally follows the same standards employed for other long-lived assets. Cost includes all expenditures necessary to

---

[8]Eric L. Kohler, *A Dictionary for Accountants,* 3rd ed. (Englewood Cliffs, N.J.: Prentice-Hall, 1963), p. 269.
[9]William A. Paton and William A. Paton, Jr., *Asset Accounting* (New York: Macmillan Co., 1952), pp. 485–490.
[10]Accounting Principles Board Opinion No. 17, ''Intangible Assets'' (New York: American Institute of Certified Public Accountants, 1970).

acquire an individual asset and make it ready for use. When intangibles are purchased from outsiders, assigning cost is fairly easy, and the methods used in allocating cost to groups of assets and by exchanges of other assets are similar to those discussed for tangible fixed assets.

On the other hand, companies frequently develop intangible assets internally. The Accounting Principles Board addressed the problems inherent in accounting for internally developed intangibles in Opinion No. 17. The board's conclusions are based on the identifiability characteristic defined earlier.

> *A company should record as assets the costs of intangible assets acquired from other enterprises or individuals. Costs of developing, maintaining, or restoring intangible assets which are not specifically identifiable, have indeterminate lives, or are inherent in a continuing business and related to the enterprise as a whole—such as goodwill—should be deducted from income when incurred.*[11]

The identifiability criterion alleviated much of the problem in accounting for the cost of intangible assets and is yet another example of the APB's attempts to narrow alternatives. Where a specific cost can be assigned to a specific asset, intangibles are carried forward at recorded values. Where either a specific asset or specific amount is indeterminable, no attempt should be made to carry values forward.

AMORTIZATION

The matching principle dictates that the cost of intangible assets be apportioned to the expected periods of benefit. In Accounting Research Bulletin No. 43 it was noted that this process involved two separate types of intangibles.

a. *those having a term of existence limited by law, regulation, or agreement, or by their nature (such as patents, copyrights, leases, licenses, franchises for a fixed term and goodwill as to which there is evidence of limited duration).*

b. *those having no such term of existence and as to which there is, at the time of acquisition, no indication of limited life (such as goodwill generally, going value, trade names, secret processes, subscription lists, perpetual franchises, and organization costs).*[12]

This release resulted in the adoption of a classification scheme that identified intangibles as either Type (a) or Type (b), and these terms became widely used in discussing the problems associated with recording and amortizing intangible

[11]Ibid., par. 24.
[12]Accounting Research Bulletin No. 43, "Restatement and Revision of Accounting Research Bulletins" (New York: American Institute of Certified Public Accountants, 1953), p. 6019.

330

assets. In Opinion No. 17, the terms *Type (a)* and *Type (b)* were not specifically used and the terms *identifiable* and *unidentifiable* were substituted. Additionally, in this release, the APB noted that current practices allowed for the following variations in treatment of unidentifiable intangibles: (1) retention of cost until a reduction of value was apparent, (2) amortization over an arbitrary period, (3) amortization over estimated useful life with specified minimum and maximum periods, and (4) deduction from equity as acquired.[13]

[handwritten margin note: unident-ifiable intangibles]

This review of the then current practice caused the APB to conclude that intangible assets should be amortized by systematic charges to income over the estimated period to be benefited. The board also suggested that the following factors should be considered in estimating the useful lives of intangibles.

1. Legal, regulatory, or contractual provisions may limit the maximum useful life.
2. Provisions for renewal or extension may alter a specific limit on useful life.
3. Effects of obsolescence, demand, competition, and other economic factors may reduce a useful life.
4. A useful life may parallel the service life expectancies of individuals or groups of employees.
5. Expected actions of competitors and others may restrict present competitive advantages.
6. An apparently unlimited useful life may in fact be indefinite and benefits cannot be reasonably projected.
7. An intangible asset may be a composite of many individual factors with varying effective lives.[14]

Finally, in APB Opinion No. 17, the board noted that the period of amortization should be determined from a review of the foregoing factors, but should not in any instance exceed 40 years. The straight-line method of amortization was required to be used unless another method could be demonstrated to be more appropriate.

As noted earlier, the release of this opinion narrowed alternative accounting for similar transactions; however, whether or not it created the desired result is subject to question. APB Opinion No. 17 is criticized by some because it places values on the balance sheet that relate to future expectations (for example, purchased goodwill), and others disagree with the board's conclusions because it assigns costs to arbitrary periods where there is no evidence that costs have expired (for example, perpetual franchises). Further evidence of the lack of acceptability of this pronouncement lies in the fact that originally it was part of APB No. 16, "Business Combinations"; however, since enough members of the

[13]APB Opinion No. 17, op. cit.
[14]Ibid., par. 27.

APB objected to various provisions of both Opinions, it was necessary to separate them to obtain the required majority for passage.

GOODWILL

The topic of goodwill has been of interest for many years. As initially conceived, it was viewed as good relations with customers. Such factors as a convenient location and habits of customers were viewed as adding to the value of the business. Yang described it as everything that might contribute to the advantage an established business possessed over a business to be started anew.[15] Since that time, the concept of goodwill has evolved into an earning power concept in which the value of goodwill is determined by subtracting the book value of a firm's net assets from the total value of the enterprise.

Catlett has summarized the characteristics of goodwill that distinguish it from other elements of value as follows.

1. The value of goodwill has no reliable or predictable relationship to costs which may have been incurred in its creation.
2. Individual intangible factors which may contribute to goodwill cannot be valued.
3. Goodwill attaches only to a business as a whole.
4. The value of goodwill may, and does, fluctuate suddenly and widely because of the innumerable factors which influence that value.
5. Goodwill is not utilized or consumed in the production of earnings.
6. Goodwill appears to be an element of value which runs directly to the investor or owner in a business enterprise.[16]

In assigning a value to goodwill, current practice attempts to discount the present value of expected superior earnings (expected future earnings less normal earnings for the industry). This process involves forecasting future earnings and choosing an appropriate discount rate.

The forecasting of future earnings is a risky proposition. Since the best indication of the future is the past, current revenue and expense figures should be used. However, the following points are relevant to this process.

1. The use of too few or too many years may distort projections.
2. Trends in earnings should be considered.
3. Industry trends are important.
4. Overall economic conditions can be significant.

---

[15]J. M. Yang, *Goodwill and Other Intangibles* (Ronald Press, 1927), p. 29.
[16]George R. Catlett and Norman O. Olson, *Accounting for Goodwill* (New York: American Institute of Certified Public Accountants, 1968), pp. 20–21.

In choosing the discount rate to be used in making goodwill calculations, the objective is to approximate the existing cost of capital for the company. The approximation must take into consideration existing and expected risk conditions as well as earnings potential.

The previous discussion focused upon the recording of goodwill and the method to use in estimating the amount a purchaser might be willing to pay for the intangible value of a business enterprise. Under generally accepted accounting principles as presently understood, such valuations cannot be recorded unless they are the result of an external transaction, and if goodwill is recorded, it must be amortized over a period not to exceed 40 years.

RESEARCH AND DEVELOPMENT COSTS

Large corporations are continually attempting to improve their product lines, develop new products, improve manufacturing methods, and develop improved manufacturing facilities. Accounting for the cost of the activities of the research department is a complicated process because some costs may never result in future benefits. In the past few years, many corporations have recognized the importance of developing accounting procedures that allow such costs to be capitalized and amortized on a reasonable basis. For example, one study suggested that such costs might be classified as follows.

1. *Basic research*—experimentation with no specific commercial objective.
2. *New product development*—experimental effort toward previously untried products.
3. *Product improvement*—effort toward improving quality or functional performance of current product lines.
4. *Cost and/or capacity improvement*—development of new and improved processes, manufacturing equipment, etc., to reduce operations costs or expand capacity.
5. *Safety, health, and convenience*—improvement of working conditions generally for purposes of employee welfare, community relations, etc.[17]

This classification scheme would make it easier to identify the costs that should be deferred and those that should be expensed. The authors of this study suggested that categories 1, 2, and 3 should generally be deferred and amortized, whereas 4 and 5 should be charged to expense because of the difficulty in determining the future periods expected to receive benefit.[18]

[17]Donald L. Madden, Lewis D. McCullers, and Relmond P. Van Daniker, "Classification of Research and Development Expenditures: A Guide to Better Accounting." *The CPA Journal* (February 1972), pp. 139–142.
[18]Ibid.

As noted earlier, APB Opinion No. 17 required the immediate expensing of intangible assets that are not specifically identifiable because such costs do not specifically generate revenue and have dubious future service potential. This provision was adopted to discourage the manipulation of research and development expenses. (Many companies were capitalizing them in low-profit years and writing them off in a lump sum in high-profit years.)

Later the FASB restudied the problem and issued its Statement No. 2. This release required all research and development costs to be charged to expense as incurred. To distinguish research and development costs from other costs, the FASB provided the following definitions.

Research *is planned search or critical investigation aimed at discovery of new knowledge with the hope that such knowledge will be useful in developing a new product or service or new process or technique or in bringing about a significant improvement to an existing product or process.*

Development *is the translation of research findings or other knowledge into a plan or design for a new product or process or for a significant improvement to an existing product or process whether intended for sale or use. It includes the conceptual formulation, design and testing of product alternatives, construction of prototypes, and operation of pilot plants. It does not include routine or periodic alterations to existing products, production lines, manufacturing processes and other on-going operations even though these alterations may represent improvements and it does not include market research or market testing activities.*[19]

Since many costs may have characteristics similar to research and development costs, the FASB also listed activities that would and would not be included in the category of research and development costs as follows:

Research and Development Activities	Activities Not Considered Research and Development
Laboratory research aimed at discovery of a new knowledge	Engineering follow-through in an early phase of commercial production
Searching for applications of new research findings	Quality control during commercial production including routine testing

[19]Statement of Financial Accounting Standards No. 2, "Accounting for Research and Development Costs" (Stamford, Conn.: Financial Accounting Standards Board, October 1974), par. 8.

Conceptual formulation and design of possible product or process alternatives

Testing in search for or evaluation of product or process alternatives

Modification of the design of a product or process

Design, construction, and testing of preproduction prototypes and models

Design of tools, jigs, molds, and dies involving new technology

Design, construction, and operation of a pilot plant not useful for commercial production

Engineering activity required to advance the design of a product to the manufacturing stage

Troubleshooting breakdowns during production.

Routine, ongoing efforts to refine, enrich, or improve the qualities of an existing product

Adaptation of an existing capability to a particular requirement or customer's need

Periodic design changes to existing products

Routine design of tools, jibs, molds, and dies

Activity, including design and construction engineering, related to the construction, relocation, rearrangement, or start-up of facilities or equipment

Legal work on patent applications, sale, licensing, or litigation[20]

This release virtually eliminates the problem of accounting for research and development. However, it is simply further evidence of solving accounting questions in a vacuum. The problems of asset recognition, cost expiration, matching, and the possible economic consequences of requiring all research and development to be expensed were all apparently deemed insignificant in comparison to the expediency of the moment. There is little doubt that a great deal of attention should be paid to the prevention of reporting abuses similar to those that caused the issuance of the ''separately identifiable'' clause in Opinion No. 17; however, solving such problems by fiat without regard to the overall conceptual framework of accounting does little to advance the overall theory of accounting.

[20]Ibid., pars. 9 and 10.

SUMMARY

A number of measurement problems arise in accounting for long-term investments and intangibles. Investments in common stock may be accounted for by the lower of cost or market method, the equity method, or the market value method. The requirements of accrual accounting are more closely satisfied when the equity method is used. This method is most appropriate when the investor has the ability to control or significantly influence the investee. Otherwise, the lower of cost or market method is most appropriate.

Investments in preferred stocks and bonds are recorded at cost. Income from preferred stock is recognized as dividends are received, and the investment securities are carried as a part of the total equity portfolio. Income from bonds is recognized as interest is paid. Additionally, in the case of bonds, if the cost price differs from the face value, that difference should be amortized over the life of the bonds and adjustments made in the interest and investment accounts. The straight-line or compound interest methods can be used to amortize bond premiums or discounts.

Accounting for intangibles such as patents, goodwill, and leaseholds presents a different kind of problem because the value and useful lives of these assets are often difficult to measure. Intangibles may be classified as (1) having a fixed term of existence or (2) having an indefinite term of existence. In general, accounting for intangibles is similar to accounting for other long-lived assets in that cost must be spread over their useful lives. The APB has suggested a number of criteria to consider in estimating the useful lives of intangibles, but the useful life may never exceed 40 years.

Proper accounting for research and development costs presents a number of theoretical problems. The FASB decided that all research and development costs should be expensed as incurred.

In the readings that follow, Paul Pacter examines the provisions of APB Opinion No. 18 in detail. Because this article was written before the FASB-issued Statement No. 12, it discusses the cost rather than the lower of cost or market method. The issues covered, however, are still relevant. In the second article, Harold Bierman and Roland Dukes discuss proper accounting for research and development costs under FASB No. 2.

APPLYING APB OPINION NO. 18—EQUITY METHOD

PAUL A. PACTER

APB Opinion No. 18, "The Equity Method of Accounting for Investments in Common Stock" (*J of A,* June 1971, p. 63), requires that the equity method be applied, both in consolidated financial statements and in parent-company statements prepared for issuance to stockholders as the financial statements of the primary reporting entity, to account for investments in voting stock of:

Unconsolidated subsidiaries.

Incorporated joint ventures (as defined in paragraph 3-d).

Other issuers, 50 per cent or less owned, over whose operating and financial policies the investor is able to exercise "significant influence." The Opinion presumes that, in the absence of evidence to the contrary, the ability to exercise significant influence is present for investments of 20 per cent or more of an issuer's outstanding voting stock and is absent for investments of less than 20 per cent.

The equity method should be applied to investments in common stock of a foreign issuer except when the foreign issuer is operating under conditions of exchange restrictions, controls or other uncertainties of a type which would create a reasonable doubt as to whether the earnings of the issuer will be realized in dollars by the investor (paragraphs 14–18).

Under the equity method, the investment is initially recorded at cost. The carrying amount is adjusted to recognize the investor's share of the earnings or losses of the investee subsequent to the date of investment, with the amount of the adjustment included in the determination of the investor's net income. Dividends received reduce the carrying amount of the investment. Opinion No. 18 requires that, in applying the equity method, any difference between the cost of an investment and the investor's equity in the net assets of the investee at the date of investment be accounted for as if the investee were a consolidated subsidiary (paragraph 19-b). Accordingly, the cost of the investment would first be allocated to the investor's share of the investee's net identifiable share of the investee's net identifiable assets and liabilities on the basis of their fair values. Any excess of the cost of the investment over the sum of the amounts so allocated should be considered to be goodwill (Opinion No. 16, paragraph 87). Such goodwill would be amortized, over a period not to exceed 40 years, as a reduction of the amount recognized each period by the investor as its equity in the earnings or losses of the investee (Opinion No. 17, paragraphs 28 and 29). For investments made prior to November 1, 1970, effective date of Opinion No. 17, amortization of goodwill is not required in the absence of evidence that it has a limited term of existence, although prospective amortization is encouraged (Opinion No. 17, paragraphs 33–35). An excess of the investor's equity in the investee's net assets at acquisition date over the cost of the investment should be accounted for in accordance with paragraphs 91 and 92 of Opinion No. 16. As to the question of whether to provide for deferred taxes on undistributed earnings of investee companies accounted for by the equity method, paragraph 19-j of Opinion No. 18 reaffirms the conclusions expressed in paragraph 16 of Accounting Research Bulletin No. 51, to wit, that where it is reasonable to assume that undistributed earnings of an investee will be transferred to the investor in a taxable distribution, provision for related estimated deferred income taxes, if material, should be made. If neither consolidation nor the equity method is appropriate, the cost method should be used. Under the cost method, an investment is carried at cost (in the absence of any nontemporary decline in its value, which should be recognized). Dividends received are recognized as income, except that dividends received in excess of earnings subsequent to the date of investment are considered a return of original investment. Concerning the question of accounting for a difference between the cost of an investment which will be accounted for by the cost method and the investor's equity in the underlying net assets of the investee, paragraph 20 of the ARB No. 51 provides that "appropriate recognition should be given to the possibility that, had the subsidiaries been consolidated, part of such difference would have been reflected in adjusted depreciation or amortization." Paragraph 20 had applied to both the cost and equity methods, and Opinion No. 18 supersedes it and several other paragraphs of ARB No. 51 only "to the extent that they relate to the equity method of accounting." Therefore, paragraph 20 continues to be authoritative so far as the cost method is concerned.

This article will present several examples of the application of Opinion No. 18.

Table 1

	Investment in Co. E December 31		Income Recognized	
	1970	1971	1970	1971
A. *Cost method* (investment carried at cost; dividends recognized as income)	$400	$400	$20	$20
B. *Equity method—amortization of goodwill over 40 years* (investment carried at cost plus equity in earnings minus dividends received and minus goodwill amortization; 40 per cent of Co. E's earnings, less $5 goodwill amortization, recognized as income)	419	454	39	55
C. *Equity method—no amortization of goodwill* (investment carried at cost plus equity in earnings minus dividends received; 40 per cent of Co. E's earnings recognized as income)	424	464	44	60

338

Reference will be made to particular paragraphs of this and other APB Opinions, where applicable.

EQUITY AND COST METHODS CONTRASTED

The distinction between the equity method and the cost method can be illustrated by the example which follows.

Assume that on January 1, 1970, Co. R purchased 40 of the 100 outstanding shares of Co. E stock for $400. On that date, net assets of Co. E at fair value were $500.

During 1970, Co. E earned $110 and paid cash dividends of $.50 per share. During 1971, Co. E earned $150 and paid cash dividends of $.50 per share.

Table 1 indicates Co. R's investment in Co. E and reported income thereon under (A) the cost method, (B) the equity method with amortization of goodwill over 40 years and (C) the equity method with no amortization, which is permissible under Opinion No. 18 because the investment antedated Opinion No. 17.

PARAGRAPH 19-b

As was indicated earlier, paragraph 19-b requires that any difference between the cost of an investment and the amount of the investor's equity in the net assets of the investee be accounted for as if the investee were consolidated.

Where the entire amount of this excess is deemed to be goodwill, application of the equity method is a relatively simple matter, as shown above.

Where some portion of this excess has been allocated to the investor's share of the investee's net identifiable assets and liabilities on the basis of their fair values, however, some complications may arise.

As an example, assume that a $200 excess of the cost of an investment over the

investor's equity in a 100 percent owned investee's net assets (at book value) is entirely allocated to a depreciable asset which has a remaining useful life of ten years. In this case a $20 adjustment would be made to the investor's equity in earnings of the investee in each of the ten years to reflect additional depreciation (assuming straight-line method and ignoring tax effect).

If, in the above example, the investee had sold the depreciable asset at the end of the second year of the ten-year period at a gain of $300 on its books, the investor in computing its equity in this gain would have to make the following adjustment:

Gain as reported by investee		$300
Excess of cost of investment over equity in net assets at date of investment, entirely allocated to depreciable asset	$200	
Amount of this excess which has been amortized in the first two years	40	160
Investor's reported equity in gain on sale of depreciable asset by investee		$140

It would be incorrect for the investor to recognize the entire $300 gain reported by the investee because the investor had, in effect, paid for a portion of this gain when it purchased its investment.

The reverse of the situation just discussed would be the case in which an investor allocated an amount less than the investee's book value to one of the investee's assets. This difference would be amortized as a reduction of the investee's depreciation. If the investee were to sell its assets for exactly book value, it would report no gain or loss. The investor, however, would report a gain as part of its equity in the investee's earnings.

PARAGRAPH 19-a

In applying the equity method, profits and losses arising from transactions between the investor and the investee should be eliminated until realized by the investor or investee, in the same manner as if the investee were a consolidated subsidiary (paragraph 19-a).

If the investee is wholly-owned by the investor, elimination presents no particular problem—100 percent of any unrealized profit or loss, whether on the investor's or investee's books, would be eliminated.

If, on the other hand, an investor owns less than 100 percent of an investee's outstanding voting common stock, the question arises whether 100 percent of the intercompany profit or loss should be eliminated or whether the amount of intercompany profit or loss to be eliminated should be based on the percentage of ownership of the investee by the investor. Practice in consolidation today goes both ways, paragraph 14 of ARB No. 51, which recommends elimination of 100 percent of any intercompany profit or loss, notwithstanding.

At its meeting on June 23–25, 1971, the APB discussed the question and agreed that an Unofficial Accounting Interpretation of paragraph 19-a should be prepared. It is understood that the Interpretation will conclude that the amount of intercompany profit or loss to be eliminated on the less-than-100-percent case should be based on the investor's percentage of ownership of the investee's voting common stock, regardless of whether the intercompany profit or loss is on the investee's books or the investor's.

An exception to the foregoing guidelines would arise if the transactions between the investor and the investee are clearly not at arm's-length, in which case *none* of the intercompany profit or loss should be recognized until it has been realized through a transaction with a third party.

A final note on intercompany profit elimination: If the profit is on the investee's books, the profit elimination should be reflected as a reduction of the investor's equity in the investee's income. Where the profit is on the investor's books, the profit elimination should be reflected as a reduction of the investor's gross profit.

PARAGRAPH 19-d

Paragraph 19-d of the Opinion requires that the investor's share of the investee's extraordinary items and prior period adjustments be classified as such in the investor's financial statements unless they are immaterial in the income statement of the investor.

To illustrate, assume that Co. R owns 80 percent of the outstanding shares of Co. E throughout 1971. Co. R follows the equity method of accounting for its investment in Co. E.

Exclusive of its equity in Co. E's earnings, Co. R's 1971 income before taxes is $1,000; the provision for income tax thereon amounts to $500.

Co. E's income statement for 1971 reports:

Income from operations (net of tax)	$100
Extraordinary gain on sale of land (net of tax)	200
Net income	$300

Income before taxes, before equity in earnings of Co. E, and before extraordinary item	$1,000
Income taxes	500
Income before equity in earnings of Co. E and extraordinary item	500
Equity in operating earnings of Co. E	80
Income before extraordinary item	580
Equity in extraordinary gain on sale of land by Co. E	160
Net Income	$ 740

Year	Net Income
1971	($50)
1972	(100)
1973	20
1974	50
1975	100

PARAGRAPH 19-i

If recognition by an investor of its share of losses of an investee results in reduction of the carrying amount of the investment to zero, the question arises as to whether the investor should provide for additional losses. Ordinarily, additional losses would not be provided for. However, if the investor's potential loss is not limited to the amount of its original investment (by guarantee of the investee's obligations or other commitment to provide further financial support) or if imminent return to profitable operations by the investee appears to be assured, it is appropriate for the investor to continue to apply the equity method (paragraph 19-i).

For example, on January 1, 1971, Co. R purchased all of the oustanding capital stock of Co. E for $100 cash, which is $40 in excess of the fair value of Co. E's net assets on that date.

Results of Co. E's operations from 1971 to 1975 were:

Assuming that Co. R is committed to provide continued financial support to Co. E, it would compute its investment and income thereon as shown in Table 2.

If, on the other hand, Co. R is under no obligation and does not intend to provide further financing to Co. E, it would compute its investment and income as shown in Table 3.

Note that the $39 of goodwill remaining at December 31, 1972, was written off at that date because in discontinuing application of the equity method when its investment in Co. E is reduced to zero, Co. R has implied that it has no assurance that Co. E will return to profitable operations. Note also that Co. R did not recognize its equity of $20 in Co. E's 1973 income, nor its equity of $50 in Co. E's 1974 income, nor $20 of its $100 equity in Co. E's 1975 income—a total of $90—because it had not recognized $90 of Co. E's $100 loss in 1972.

Had it been deemed appropriate to recognize the loss in value of goodwill at the end of 1971, the total loss recognized in that year would have been $90 and the investment would have been reported at $10 at December 31, 1971, which would have been written off in 1972.

PARAGRAPH 19-l

At such time as an investor's level of ownership falls below that necessary for

Table 2

Date	Equity in Net Income	Amortization of Goodwill	Income (Loss) Recognized	Equity in Net Assets	Goodwill	Investment in Co. E
Jan. 1, 1971	—	—	—	$60	$40	$100
Dec. 31, 1971	$(50)	$(1)	$(51)	10	39	49
Dec. 31, 1972	(100)	(1)	(101)	(90)	38	(52)
Dec. 31, 1973	20	(1)	19	(70)	37	(33)
Dec. 31, 1974	50	(1)	49	(20)	36	16
Dec. 31, 1975	100	(1)	99	80	35	115

Table 3

Date	Equity in Net Income	Amortization of Goodwill	Income (Loss) Recognized	Equity in Net Assets	Goodwill	Investment in Co. E
Jan. 1, 1971	—	—	—	$60	40	$100
Dec. 31, 1971	$(50)	$(1)	$(51)	10	39	49
Dec. 31, 1972	(10)	(39)	(49)	0	0	0
Dec. 31, 1973	0	0	0	0	0	0
Dec. 31, 1974	0	0	0	0	0	0
Dec. 31, 1975	80	0	80	80	0	80

CHAPTER 7: LONG TERM ASSETS II

Table 4

Year	Net Income (Loss)	Co. E. Dividends Received by Co. R		
		June 30	Dec. 31	Total
1971	$100	$1.50	$1.50	$3.00
1972	200	1.50	1.50	3.00
1973	50	3.00	3.00	6.00
1974	20	3.00	3.00	6.00
1975	(30)	1.50	1.50	3.00

continued use of the equity method, a change to the cost method is appropriate. Dividends subsequently received by the investor should be treated as a return of investment, rather than as income, to the extent that they exceed its share of the cumulative earnings of the investee subsequent to the change to the cost method. Earnings or losses of the investee previously recognized by the equity method should not be retroactively restated to the cost method (paragraph 19-l).

Assume that on January 1, 1971, Co. R purchased, for $500, 30 of the 100 outstanding shares of Co. E common stock. On this date the net assets of Co. E at fair value were $1,000.

On July 1, 1972, Co. E sold 200 additional shares of its common stock to the public, thereby reducing Co. R's ownership from 30 per cent to 10 per cent.

Net income (or loss) and dividends of Co. E for the years 1971 through 1975 were as shown in Table 4.

The $200 net income of Co. E for 1972 is assumed to have been earned evenly throughout the year.

Goodwill of $200 ($500 less 30 per cent of $1,000) will be amortized over 40 years, or $5 annually.

Under the equity method, Co. R's reported investment in Co. E and reported income therefrom would be as shown in Table 5.

If Co. E had incurred a net loss of $50 in 1975, rather than the loss of $30, no dividend income would have been recognized by Co. R in that year. The entire $3 dividend received by Co. R would be treated as a reduction of the investment (to $545 at December 31, 1975). The investment account, however, would *not* be further reduced even though the cumulative amount of dividends received since July 1, 1972 ($16.50), exceeds Co. R's 10 percent equity in Co. E's net income since July 1, 1972 ($12), and therefore $1.50 of the $6 dividend received in 1974 is, in retrospect, a return of investment (the other $3 return of investment property having been recognized in 1975).

PARAGRAPH 19-m

On January 1, 1971, Co. R purchased for $500 cash 10 percent of the outstanding shares of Co. E stock. On that date, net assets of Co. E at fair value were $3,000.

On January 1, 1973, Co. R purchased an additional 20 percent of Co. E's stock for $1,200 cash. On that date, Co. E's net assets were $4,000.

Net income of Co. E, and Co. E divi-

Table 5

Year	Income Recognized	Investment at December 31
1971	$30 equity − $5 amortization = $25	$500 + $25 income − $3 dividend = $522
1972	January 1 to June 30: $30 equity − $2.50 amortization = $27.50 July 1 to December 31: $1.50 dividend income	$522 + $27.50 − $1.50 = $548
1973	$6 dividend income	$548
1974	$6 dividend income	$548
1975	$.50 dividend income ($2.50 dividend in excess of Co. R's equity in earnings of Co. E since July 1, 1972, deemed return of investment)	$548 − $2.50 return of investment = $545.50

dends received by Co. R during the period 1971 through 1975 were:

Year	Net Income of Co. E	Co. E Dividends Received by Co. R
1971	$ 500	$ 20
1972	1,000	30
1973	1,200	120
1974	1,500	150
1975	2,000	200

The journal entries which would be made from January 1, 1971, through December 31, 1975, to reflect the above in accordance with APB Opinion No. 18 are as shown in Table 6.

INVESTMENT NO LONGER HELD

The Opinion does not discuss specifically the following transitional problem:

If an investment which had been accounted for under the cost method is no longer held by the investor at the effective date of the Opinion (or at such earlier date as its provisions are adopted by the investor for the investor's other investments), and if it would have been appropriate to account for this investment by the equity method had Opinion No. 18 been in effect when the investment was held, should the financial statements for the period during which the investment was held be retroactively restated from the cost method to the equity method even though the investment is no longer held?

This question is one which must be answered by many investors required to file with the Securities and Exchange Commission because both the general registration Form S-1 and the annual report Form 10-K (among others) require five-year earnings summaries. Also, companies which present historical summaries in their annual reports to shareholders may be confronted with this problem.

Consistent with the requirement in paragraph 21 that the Opinion "should be applied retroactively to all investments in common stock held during any portion of the period for which results of operations are presented regardless of the date the investments were acquired," it seems proper that the equity method be retroactively applied even to investments no longer held. Of course, any gain or loss previously recognized on the ultimate sale of the investment would have to be appropriately adjusted.

To illustrate, assume that on January 1, 1968, Co. R acquired a 25 percent interest in Co. E for $100, which was $40 in excess of the fair value of Co. R's share of Co. E's net assets on that date. For both book and tax purposes, Co. R accounted for its investment by the cost method.

On December 31, 1970, Co. R sold the investment for $160.

In each year 1968 through 1970, Co. E's net income was $40 and Co. R received a $5 annual cash dividend from Co. E. Accordingly, Co. R recognized $5 dividend income in each year. Upon sale of the investment at December 31, 1970, Co. R recognized a net gain, after taxes, of $45 ($160 − $100 = $60 gain on which the tax at 25 percent capital gain rate would be $15).

Co. R has adopted the provisions of Opinion No. 18 for its other investments, effective for the year ended December 31, 1971.

Table 6

January 1, 1971

Investment in Co. E Stock	500	
Cash		500

To record the purchase of a 10 percent interest in Co. E

December 31, 1971

Cash	20	
Dividend income		20

To record the receipt of a cash dividend

December 31, 1972

Cash	30	
Dividend income		30

To record the receipt of a cash dividend

January 1, 1973

Investment in Co. E Stock	1,290	
Cash		1,200
Retained earnings		90

To record the purchase of an additional 20 percent interest in Co. E and to reflect retroactively a change from the cost method to the equity method of accounting for the investment. The $90 adjustment is computed as follows:

	1971	*1972*	*Total*
Co. R equity in earnings of Co. E	$50	$100	$150
Amortization of goodwill*	(5)	(5)	(10)
Dividend received	(20)	(30)	(50)
Prior period adjustment	$25	$65	$90

---

*[$500 − (10% × 3,000)] ÷ 40 years = $5 per year.

Table 6 cont.

December 31, 1973
Investment in Co. E Stock   345
    Income on Investment in Co. E   345
To record Co. R equity in earnings of Co. E (30 percent of $1,200) less $15 amortization of goodwill. Goodwill amortization includes $5 from 1971 purchase of 10 percent interest plus $10 [$1,200 − (20% × 4,000) + 40 years] from 1973 purchase of 20 per cent interest.
Cash   120
    Investment in Co. E Stock   120
To record the receipt of a cash dividend
December 31, 1974
Investment in Co. E Stock   435
    Income on Investment in Co. E   435
30 percent of $1,500 less $15 goodwill amortization
Cash   150
    Investment in Co. E Stock   150
To record the receipt of a cash dividend
December 31, 1975
Investment in Co. E Stock   585
    Income on Investment in Co. E   585
30 percent of $2,000 less $15 goodwill amortization
Cash   200
    Investment in Co. E Stock   200
to record the receipt of a cash dividend

Co. R's financial statements for 1968 to 1970 should be restated to change the method of accounting for its investment in Co. E from cost to equity. Instead of reporting $5 annual dividend income, Co. R would recognize in each year its $10 equity (25 per cent of $40) in the earnings of Co. E. Before the gain on sale of the investment can be recomputed, two additional questions must be answered:

1. Should any of the $40 goodwill be retroactively amortized?
2. Should deferred income taxes be provided on the additional earnings recognized under the equity method during 1968–1970, and, if so, in what amount?

Concerning the goodwill question, because the investment was acquired prior to November 1, 1970, effective date of Opinion No. 17, it would not be necessary to amortize the goodwill. Even absent this grandfather clause, however, it doesn't seem appropriate to amortize the goodwill in light of the sale of the investment at substantial gain.

As to the question concerning deferred income taxes, earlier in this article it was noted that paragraph 19-j of Opinion No. 18 provides that the guides in paragraph 16 of ARB No. 51 continue to apply. Paragraph 16 of ARB No. 51 (which refers only to subsidiaries) states:

Where it is reasonable to assume that a part or all of the undistributed earnings of a subsidiary will be transferred to the parent in a taxable distribution, provision for related income taxes should be made on an estimated basis at the time

346

the earnings are included in consolidated income, unless these taxes are immaterial in amount when effect is given, for example, to dividend-received deductions or foreign-tax credits. There is no need to provide for income tax to the parent company in cases where the income has been, or there is evidence that it will be, permanently invested by the subsidiaries, or where the only likely distribution would be in the form of a tax-free liquidation.

In retrospect, we know that the ultimate distribution was not tax free because Co. R paid a $15 tax on the sale of its investment in Co. E—the gain comprised, in part, of Co. R's equity in Co. E's undistributed earnings subsequent to the date of investment. Therefore, it seems appropriate to provide for $1.25 of income tax (at the 25 percent rate) on the additional $5 of income recognized under the equity method. In other words, retroactive change to the equity method creates a timing difference (a difference between the periods in which a transaction affects taxable income and the periods in which it enters into the determination of pretax accounting income) on which deferred taxes must be provided, assuming materiality.

Under the equity method, the investment account at December 31, 1970, would have stood at $115 ($100 cost plus $30 equity in 1968–1970 Co. E earnings less $15 dividends received). The pretax gain would be restated from $60 to $45 ($160 less $115). After considering taxes, the gain would be reported as follows:

Gain, before tax effect		$45.00
Tax thereon:		
Currently payable	$15.00	
Deferred	(3.75)	11.25
Net gain		$33.75

REPORTING ON A CHANGE FROM COST TO EQUITY METHOD

Paragraphs 15 and 16 or Chapter 8 of Statement on Auditing Procedure No. 33 state:

15. *When a change has been made in the accounting principles employed during the year or years the independent auditor is reporting upon, . . . and the change has a material effect upon financial position or results of operations, he should refer in his opinion paragraph to a note to the financial statements which adequately describes the change and its effect, or describe adequately in his report the nature of the change and its effect. Where the change affects net income, disclosure should include the amount by which net income is affected after consideration of related income taxes.*

16. *Ordinarily, the disclosure would give the amount by which the current year's net income was affected as a result of the change; however, there may be instances where the effect the change would have had on the prior year's net income would be considered an appropriate disclosure.*

An example of an auditor's report in this case might be the following:

*To the Stockholders and
Board of Directors
XYZ Corporation
    We have examined the consolidated balance sheet of XYZ Corporation and subsidiaries as of December 31, 1971, and the related consolidated statements of earnings and retained earnings and changes in financial position for the year then ended. Our examination was made in accordance with generally accepted auditing standards, and accord-*

ingly included such tests of the accounting records and such other auditing
procedures as we considered necessary
in the circumstances.

*In our opinion, the financial state-
ments identified above present fairly the
financial position of the companies at
December 31, 1971, and the results of
their operations and changes in financial position for the year ended, in conformity with generally accepted accounting principles applied on a basis
consistent with that of the preceding
year after giving retroactive effect to
the change, which we approve, in the
method of accounting for the investment
in Co. S, explained in Note 2 to the
financial statements.*

Note 2 might read as follows:

*In 1971, XYZ Corporation changed its
method of accounting for its investment
in Co. S (40 percent owned), from the
cost to the equity method. Under the
new method, the investment is carried
at cost, plus the equity in undistributed
earnings since dates of acquisition, and
less amortization over a 40-year period
of the $8,714 excess of cost over the
equity in Co. S's net assets at dates of
acquisition. As a result of the change,
net earnings of the company for 1971
and 1970 and retained earnings at January 1, 1971 and 1970 were increased
by the following amounts:*

	1971	1970
Net earnings	*$1,887*	*$1,309*
Retained earnings at		
January 1	*3,346*	*2,037*

*Financial statements for 1970 have
been restated to reflect the change.*

EFFECT OF CHANGE NOT MATERIAL

Paragraphs 21 and 22 of Chapter 8 of SAP
No. 33 provide that:

21. *If a change is made in the accounting
principles employed which has no material effect on the financial statements
in the current year, but which is reasonably certain to have substantial effect in later years, it should be appropriately disclosed in a note to the
financial statements for the year in
which the change is adapted by the
client. . . .*

22. *If such a change is appropriately disclosed in a note to the financial statements as indicated above, it need not
be mentioned in the independent auditor's report. However, if such a
change is not set forth in a note to the
financial statements, it should be disclosed by the independent auditor in
his report.*

A case in point is the 1970 annual report
of Eli Lilly and Company. In Note A to its
consolidated financial statements, it is disclosed that:

*Fifty percent interests in companies lo-
cated in Spain and Japan are included
in the consolidated financial statements
for 1969 at cost and for 1970 on the
equity method of accounting. The effect
of this change is not material.*

The report of Eli Lilly's independent auditors contains no reference to the change.

AUDITOR'S REPORT COVERS BOTH YEARS

Paragraph 26 of Chapter 8 of SAP No. 33
states that:

26. *When the independent auditor reports
on all the years which have been restated as well as on the current year,
he may be giving a new opinion with
respect to the earliers years. Even
though all years covered by his report
are on a consistent basis, and the*

changes made are adequately dis-closed in the financial statements and notes, his report should make reference to the restatement in the year of change. . . .

An example of such reference is contained in the auditor's report on the 1969 and 1968 financial statements of Texaco, Inc., in which the opinion paragraph reads as follows:

In our opinion, the accompanying financial statements present fairly the financial position of Texaco, Inc., and subsidiary companies as of December 31, 1969 and 1968, and the results of their operations and the source and disposition of funds for the years then needed, in the conformity with generally applied on a consistent basis after giving retroactive effect to the change, which we approve, to the equity method of accounting for investments in certain nonsubsidiary companies, as explained in Note 2 to the financial statements.

Note 2, in part, reads:

Effective January 1, 1969, the Company adopted the equity method of accounting for its investments in companies owned 50%, and in the Arabian American Oil Company, which is owned 30%. Under this method, equity in the earnings or losses of these non-subsidiary companies is reflected currently in the Company's earnings rather than when realized through dividends. The Company's investments in these companies have been adjusted to reflect its equity in the book value of the underlying net assets of the companies. The financial statements for 1968 have been restated to a comparable basis with a reduction of $16,032,000 in net income from that previously reported and an increase in consolidated retained earnings at January 1, 1968, of $136,018,000, such amount representing the Company's equity in the net assets of these companies over the cost of the Company's investment at that date.

ACCOUNTING FOR RESEARCH AND DEVELOPMENT COSTS

HAROLD BIERMAN, JR.
ROLAND E. DUKES

The accounting profession has four basic choices available as to the method of accounting for assets:

Use cost of acquisition.
Use value estimations.

Use price level adjusted cost.
Implicitly assume the value is zero and expense the costs associated with the acquisition of the asset.

In its statement of Financial Accounting Standards No. 2, "Accounting for Research and Development Costs" (October 1974), the Financial Accounting Standards Board concludes that "all research and development costs encompassed by this

Statement shall be charged to expense when incurred.'' This practice implicitly assumes the expected value of R & D is zero. The Board reached its conclusion as a result of a reasoning process in which several preliminary premises were accepted as true. It may be possible to conclude for pragmatic reasons that the expensing decision reached by the Board is a reasonable practice, but we object to the process the Board used in arriving at the conclusion that R & D should be expensed. Specifically, the following five factors that were offered by the Board as support for its conclusion will be considered:

Uncertainty of future benefits.
Lack of causal relationship between expenditures and benefits.
R & D does not meet the accounting concept of an asset.
Matching of revenues and expenses.
Relevance of resulting information for investment and credit decisions.

Following are descriptions of these factors and evaluations of their relevance.

UNCERTAINTY OF FUTURE BENEFITS

The primary justification offered by the FASB[1] for expensing the R&D expenditures is the level of uncertainty associated with the benefits. It is argued that R&D expenditures have considerable risk where risk is defined as a large probability of failure for an individual project. In reaching its conclusion to expense R&D costs when incurred, the Board states (p. 15) that the ''high degree of uncertainty about the future benefits of individual research and development projects'' was a significant factor in reaching this conclusion. In elaborating on this conclusion, the Board cites several studies that indicate a high failure rate for research and development projects. Although the Statement is not specific on this point, it appears that because a large proportion of research and development projects are ''failures,'' the Board concludes that all R&D should be treated as failures and expensed. There are several fallacies with this conclusion.

First, it is not clear that the risks and uncertainties of company-sponsored research and development are as formidable as corporate publicists and the references cited by the Board would have us believe. In 1963, Mansfield and Hamburger[2] studied 22 major firms in the chemical and petroleum industries and found that the bulk of the R&D projects carried out by these firms were relatively safe from a technical point of view. Most of the projects were regarded as having better than a 50-50 chance of technical success. In an analysis of 70 projects carried out in the central research and development laboratories of a leading electrical equipment manufacturing company, Mansfield and Brandenburg[3] found that in more than three-fourths of the cases, the ex ante probability of technical success had originally been estimated at .80 or higher and only two projects were completed, 44 percent were fully successful technically, and only 16 percent were unsuccessful because of unanticipated technical difficulties.

[1]Financial Accounting Standards Board, Statement of Financial Accounting Standards No. 2, ''Accounting for Research and Development Costs'' (Stamford, Conn.: FASB, 1974).

[2]E. Mansfield, ''Industrial Research and Development: Characteristics, Costs, and the Diffusion of Results,'' *American Economic Review*, May 1969, p. 65.
[3]E. Mansfield, *Industrial Research and Technological Innovation* (New York: Norton, 1969).

These findings are consistent with the hypothesis that business firms do not generally begin new product or process development projects until the principal technical uncertainties have been resolved through inexpensive research, conducted either by their own personnel or by outsiders. They are also consistent with the notion that managers are averse to risk and are reluctant to pursue high risk projects when their own reputations and the funds of the company are involved. On the other hand, research and development projects sponsored by the federal government are likely to be more risky than industrial R&D because the federal government bears the financial risk. This point is also made by Scherer.[4]

Second, one has to be careful as to the definition of risk. Because of the historically high profitability of R&D efforts, it may well be that risk defined in terms of expected loss or expected monetary value may be less than many types of plant and equipment expenditures (the different tax treatments afforded the different types of expenditures also affect risk).

Bailey,[5] who computed the rate of return from R&D expenditures in the U.S. pharmaceutical industry, found a rate of return (pretax) of 35 percent in 1954 and 25 percent in 1961. Bailey explains the decrease in rate of return as being the result of increased R&D expenditures (170 percent increase between 1954 and 1961) as firms realized the high profitability of R&D in this area. Bailey does forecast decreasing returns in this industry after 1962 as a re-sult of more stringent regulations associated with introducing new products and warns of the difficulty of isolating causal relationships. Also, the measurement of profitability of R&D is difficult because there are many factors affecting earnings. But if Bailey is close to being correct, there may be less risk with R&D expenditures (if a large amount of expenditures are made, spread over a large number of projects) than with plant and equipment.

Bailey's findings are reinforced by studies by Minasian and Mansfield. Mansfield[6] found that "among the petroleum firms, regardless of whether technical change was capital-embodied or organizational, the marginal rates of return average about 40–60 percent." He found other industries also high, but not as high as for the period 1946–62. Minasian,[7] in studying firms in the chemical industry (1948–57), found the gross return on research and development to be 54 percent as compared to 9 percent for the physical capital. While Minasian defines this as a social return and not a private return, it is again evident that R&D has been very profitable. Moreover, the expected profitability affects the risk of the expenditure.

This is inconsistent with the definition of risk apparently used by the FASB, which defines risk only in terms of probability of failure. The Board does not consider the reduction in uncertainty that can be achieved by pursuing a portfolio of research and development projects. A simple example will help to illustrate this point. Suppose a firm is pursuing 100 indepen-

[4]F. M. Scherer, *Industrial Market Structure and Economic Performance* (Chicago: Rand McNally, 1970), pp. 354–356.

[5]Martin Neil Bailey, "Research and Development Costs and Returns: The U.S. Pharmaceutical Industry," *Journal of Political Economy*, January–February 1972, pp. 70–85.

[6]E. Mansfield, "Rates of Return From Industrial Research and Development," *American Economic Review*, May 1965, pp. 310–322.

[7]Jora R. Minasian, "Research and Development, Production Functions, and Rates of Return," *American Economic Review*, May 1969, pp. 80–85.

dent R&D projects. For computational ease, we assume each project costs $10,000, that each has a probability of "success" of .10 and a probability of "failure" of .90. Success results in a $200,000 present value accruing to the firm; failure results in no benefits.

Each individual project has 1 chance in 10 of being successful; this is consistent with the point made by the Board that for any individual project the probability that it will generate future benefits for the firm seems dismally low. However, the more important question is, what is the probability of making a profit from the portfolio of projects? Since each R&D project represents an independent event with two possible outcomes, the number of successes in 100 trials is a random variable whose distribution is the binomial distribution. For this example, the probability that there will be one or more successes is equal to .99997.[8] That is, the firm is virtually assured that it will realize 1 or more successes from a portfolio of 100 R&D projects.[9] This is a substantial reduction in uncertainty when compared to the .10 probability of success attached to individual projects. Moreover, the expected future benefits from the portfolio is $2 million.[10] Thus, while the Board claims a large probability of failure associated with

individual projects, it fails to consider the change in the uncertainty (defined in terms of probability of failure) associated with undertaking a portfolio of independent R&D projects.

In the above example, the $20,000 expected future benefit of each project (equal to its probability of success, .10, times the expected future benefit of success, $200,000) is greater than the $10,000 cost of each project. The expected payoff from the portfolio is twice the total cost of $1 million for all 100 research and development projects. To break even, the firm needs 5 or more successes out of 100 projects, and there is .9763 probability of this happening. Thus, rather than .10 probability of success (defined in terms of the individual project), there is .9763 probability of success (defined in terms of the profitability of the portfolio).

Since the firm does not know before it investigates which of the projects will be successful, the appropriate cost of finding the successful projects is the total cost of pursuing the portfolio of projects. Bierman, Dukes and Dyckman[11] discuss this point further with specific reference to accounting for exploration costs in the petroleum industry.

The FASB cites the low probability of success with new products. We argue that

---

[8]The probability that there will be 1 or more successes is equal to 1 minus the probability there will be zero successes. The probability of zero success is given as

$$P(0 \text{ successes}) = \frac{100!}{0!100!} [.10]^0 [.90]^{100} = .00003.$$

[9]If the probability of success for an individual project is .05, .02 or .01, then the portfolio probabilities of one or more successes are .989, .905 and .633, respectively.

[10]The expected present value from the portfolio is the sum of the expected payoffs for the individual projects:

Expected present value from portfolio

$$= \sum_{i=1}^{100} \text{Expected present value of project } i$$

$$= \sum_{i=1}^{100} [(.10)(\$200,000) + (.90)(0)]$$

$$= 100 (\$20,000) = \$2,000,000.$$

[11]Harold Bierman, Jr., Roland E. Dukes and Thomas R. Dyckman, "Financial Reporting in the Petroleum Industry," *J of A*, Oct. 74, pp. 58–64.

this low probability has not been proved. Moreover, it is not a valid measure of risk. The Board needs to define uncertainty and risk more exactly before risk of R&D can be offered as the reason for an accounting treatment. Even if it were agreed that R&D had more risk (a position we do not accept), it is still not clear that this leads to the policy conclusion of expensing the costs of R&D.

There is some uncertainty of future benefits associated with every asset currently recorded on balance sheets. Even the future real benefits that can be realized from holding cash are uncertain, especially during these times of "double-digit" inflation. More analogous to research and development, there is a high degree of uncertainty associated with investments in long-lived plant and equipment, especially in fields where the assets are extremely specialized in nature and where there is rapid technological advance. It is not clear that investments in these kinds of projects are any less uncertain in terms of the probability of making a profit than an investment in a portfolio of R&D projects. If both are uncertain, why should one be recorded differently from the other? It does not appear that using the "degree of uncertainty of future benefits" is an appropriate factor or criterion to employ in helping to resolve this issue. So long as the project has a net positive expected future benefit, uncertainty should not lead automatically to a conclusion that cost factors should be expensed.

We argue that at the portfolio level there is the possibility of a substantial reduction in uncertainty vis-à-vis the individual project level. Moreover, expected future benefits will in general be equal to or greater than the total cost of pursuing the research and development portfolio. Thus, the existence of a probability of failure cannot be

used to justify the expensing of R&D expenditures.[12]

LACK OF CAUSAL RELATION BETWEEN EXPENDITURES AND BENEFITS

In its Statement the FASB cites (p. 16) three empirical research studies that "generally failed to find a significant correlation between research and development expenditures and increased future benefits as measured by subsequent sales, earnings or share of industry sales." The Board does not specify what conclusion is to be drawn regarding the accounting treatment of research and development costs from the above statement, although it appears to consider this lack of evidence of a direct relationship between research and development costs and specific future revenue as an important factor in its conclusions.

Several points can be made regarding this factor. First, even though the studies cited by the Board were unable to detect a significant relationship between costs of research and subsequent benefits, this does not imply that such a relationship does not exist. That is, when logical deductive reasoning leads to a hypothesized relationship that cannot subsequently be empirically ob-

[12]An irrelevant argument is offered in paragraph 52 of the FASB Statement. It is stated that companies have the philosophy that "research and development expenditures are intended to be recovered by current revenues rather than by revenues from new product." This philosophy (if it does exist) should in no way affect the accounting for R&D. In addition, in evaluating new projects any sensible method of evaluation will consider the revenue (benefits) associated with the new projects. The current product revenues are irrelevant to the decision to go ahead except to the extent that they supply the cash that is used for the financing of the R&D.

served, the scientist will generally "suspend judgment" regarding the hypothesis rather than embrace the alternative hypothesis that no relationship exists. It is more appropriate to draw conclusions upon the observation of the phenomena under study rather than upon the inability to observe the phenomena.

Second, considerable research in economics does provide support for the hypothesis that research and development efforts do produce benefits for the firm. Scherer[13] reviews much of this literature when he discusses the relationship between market structures and technological innovation. Subsequent to the Scherer review, several additional studies have contributed to the evidence on the relationship between research and development and various measures of benefit to the firm. Bailey[14] found pretax rates of return from investments in research and development in the vicinity of 25 to 35 percent for the pharmaceutical firms included in this study. He also found that "earnings of the companies over time are clearly related to the number of patents held by the company." The number of patents held by a firm is an often-used surrogate for research output. In a related study, Angilley[15] found pharmaceutical sales to be significantly related to "innovative output," where innovative output was defined in terms of several measures of new pharmaceutical compounds produced by the company. Equally important, he found that his measures of innovative output were all significantly related to the amount of research and development expenditures incurred by the firm. In a

more recent study, Grabowski and Mueller[16] investigated the rates of return on investments in physical capital, in research and development and in advertising. They conclude that their result "indicates that R&D does increase the profitability of the firm over competitive levels." For the 86 firms included in their sample, "additional R&D did increase the rate of return on total capital."

Given this brief review of some of the contrary evidence, the FASB's statement (p. 16) that "a direct relationship between research and development costs and specific revenue generally has not been demonstrated . . ." is confusing and somewhat misleading. Clearly, management expects to generate positive returns from R&D. Moreover, the expected profit from large, expensive research and development portfolios is larger than the expected benefits from smaller, less costly portfolios of research and development. An inexpensive plant may turn out to be more profitable than a much more expensive plant, but this outcome does not "prove" that the plants' costs should have been expensed in both cases.

It is probably true that there is a higher variance of benefits arising from the research and development expenditures. But higher variance does not necessarily imply a higher risk is associated with such expenditures (the capital asset pricing model of Sharpe[17] is of relevance here). Applying the capital asset pricing model, the important measure of risk is the covariability of

---

[13]Scherer, especially chapters 15 and 16.
[14]Bailey, op. cit.
[15]Alan Angilley, "Returns to Scale in Research in the Ethical Pharmaceutical Industry: Some Further Empirical Evidence," *Journal of Industrial Economics*, December 1973, pp. 81–93.

[16]Henry Grabowski and Dennis Mueller, "Rates of Return on Corporate Investment, Research and Development and Advertising," unpublished working paper, Cornell University, 1974.
[17]W. F. Sharpe, "Capital Asset Prices: A Theory of Market Equilibrium Under Conditions of Risk," *Journal of Finance*, September 1964, pp. 425–442.

expected return between the individual project and the overall portfolio of securities. Expenditures on R&D to develop new products or improved old ones are likely to be less correlated with market returns than expenditures for expansion into new markets or expanding market capacity. Thus, it seems likely that many R&D expenditures will have relatively desirable risk characteristics compared to expenditures in physical capital.

In sum, it is incorrect to conclude that, because it has been difficult to observe a significant correlation between expenditures and subsequent benefits, future benefits are not generated by research and development expenditures. Moreover, considerable research does exist in which the findings support the hypothesis that research and development does generate substantive future benefits for the firm. While the Board may still determine that the expensing of research and development expenditures is an appropriate accounting policy, it is not clear that the lack of benefits argument is an appropriate supporting factor in this conclusion.

THE ACCOUNTING CONCEPT OF AN ASSET

The Board appears to be close to requiring the capitalization of research and development when it describes (p. 17) economic resources as those scarce resources for which there is an "expectation of future benefits to the enterprise either through use or sale." While R&D would qualify using this definition, the Board then discusses the criteria of measurability. We argue that the cost of R&D is subject to reasonable measurement. However, the FASB states (p. 17)

The criterion of measurability would require that a resource not be recognized

as an asset for accounting purposes unless at the time it is acquired or developed its future economic benefits can be identified and objectively measured.

Can the economic benefits of an automobile plant be objectively measured at the time it is acquired? This criterion opens the door to the reclassification to expense of many "asset" types of expenditures.

Also, the values of many assets are relatively independent of their costs. A nonregulated pipeline immediately after it has been constructed has value that is independent of its cost. As soon as any cost is incurred, it is a sunk cost and is not price or value determining.

It is probably true that R&D ranks high in variance of relationship between cost and value on specific expenditures. The lack of a one-to-one relationship between benefits and costs tends to argue in favor of a value type of accounting. But if value is excluded from consideration, at least for now, and the choice is between zero (expensing) and cost, lacking other information cost will on the average be a better estimator of value than the zero asset value resulting from the expensing of R&D.[18]

EXPENSE RECOGNITION AND MATCHING

Surprisingly the matching of revenues and expenses of earning those revenues is used as an argument by the Board in favor of expensing R&D (p. 19) because of "the general lack of discernible future benefits at the time such costs are incurred. . . ." The only reason R&D expenditures are made is to benefit future time periods by

[18]For an expansion on this point, see the article by Bierman, Dukes and Dyckman in the October *Journal of Accountancy*.

generating new revenues in those time periods. It is unlikely that R&D will increase the operating revenues of the immediate time period given the time necessary to implement R&D. To argue in favor of immediate expensing is to ignore completely one of the basic principles on which accounting stands—namely, the necessity of matching revenues and expenses. If the Board had chosen to argue that matching was not an important criterion (it wisely did not do so), then its conclusion might be understandable. But to argue that expensing of R&D is consistent with matching is a conclusion that is difficult to comprehend.

RELEVANCE OF RESULTING INFORMATION FOR INVESTMENT AND CREDIT DECISIONS

In paragraph 50 of the Statement, the Board refers to APB Statement No. 4, which indicates that certain costs are immediately "recognized as expenses because allocating them to several accounting periods is considered to serve no useful purpose." Citing evidence of the high degree of uncertainty associated with research and development and the views of security analysts and other professional investors, the Board states that "capitalization of any research and development costs is not useful in assessment of the earnings potential of the enterprise." The Board concludes that "therefore, it is unlikely that the investor's ability to predict the return on his investment and the variability of that return would be enhanced by capitalization."

There are two points to be made regarding the above reasoning and conclusions. First, the usefulness of accounting data regarding the amount of research and development costs to investors is an empirically testable question. In a study related to this issue, Dukes[19] found that the amount of research and development cost incurred and expensed during the period was significantly related to the security price of the firm. All of the firms in the Dukes study followed the accounting policy of expensing research and development costs, yet results were consistent with investors making capitalization adjustments to research and development costs in estimating the future earnings potential of the firm. That is, the "research intensity" of the firm (more precisely, the research intensity of the industry in which a firm found itself) was a significant explanatory variable in explaining the market value of the firm.

The Dukes study suggests that capitalization may serve a useful purpose in aiding the investor to predict the future return of a security. At a minimum, the study provides support to the Board's conclusion that disclosure of the amount of research and development costs is information relevant to the investment decision.

A second significant issue deals with who would be served by the requirement that research and development costs be expensed. If the results of the Dukes study are accepted, then security price behavior is more closely related to earnings computed with research and development capitalized rather than expensed. It is probably reasonable to expect security analysts and other professional investors to be able to make adjusting calculations to the reported earnings numbers, where sufficient information is supplied to adjust the basic accounting data. One is less confident, however, about the ability of nonexpert

[19]Roland E. Dukes, *Market Evaluation of Accounting Information: A Cross Sectional Test of Investor Response to Expensing Research and Development Expenditures,* unpublished Ph.D. dissertation, Stanford University, 1974.

investors to make the adjustments. For example, consider an investor who takes the accounting measures seriously and does not adjust the information, analyzing two firms both of which have reported earnings of $2 per share. However, one firm has expended (and expensed) $3 per share on R&D and the other firm has spent zero. The R&D firm would have had $5 per share of earnings if it had not purchased any R&D. The expensing of the R&D expenditures results in the two firms having the same earnings per share, thus implying equal value based on this one measure. These earnings are not comparable and the investor who views them as equivalent will be misled. There is another, related problem. Managers are very concerned with earnings per share, and they assume these numbers are used in the investment decision process. The first firm can stabilize its earnings at $2 per share by varying the amount of R&D it purchases. Thus earnings become a function of decisions to buy or not to buy R&D. It is difficult to see why the decision to buy or not to buy R&D should affect the earnings of the current year. A loss firm can reduce its loss by $1 for $1 of R&D it stops buying. This is a relatively easy way to reduce losses. The result of expensing of R&D may distort corporate decision making and lead to faulty measure of income and changes in income through time.

CONCLUSIONS

The primary purpose of this critique is to question the rationale employed by the FASB in arriving at its conclusion. It may well be that requiring all firms to disclose the amount of their research and development costs and to expense these costs is the best feasible solution. Capitalizing of such costs may not be feasible because of attendant lawsuits when the R&D is found to have less value than the recorded cost. But the resulting practice should not then be justified on the grounds that it is good accounting theory.

Virtually every time an accountant records expenditures he or she runs the risk that a later development might, with the aid of hindsight, show that the recording was "wrong." The asset may turn out to be worth much less than cost. The obvious solution for avoiding this sort of situation and resulting criticisms is to expense all costs associated with the acquisition of assets where there is some significant probability that the asset will turn out to be worth less than the cost of the asset. This "conservative" approach to asset measurement is consistent with the Board's recommendation to expense R&D expenditures. The policy decision to expense R&D costs does not appear to be based on sound accounting theory but, rather, appears to be motivated by a desire to avoid the criticism and problems resulting from situations where, after the fact, an asset is found to be worth less than the amount reported by the accountant. It ignores completely the types of errors that arise from a systematic expense overstatement, income misstatement, asset understatement and stock equity understatement. Unfortunately, criticism and lawsuits may force the adoption of such conservative practices. The way to avoid criticism that past earnings and assets have been overstated is to expense all factors associated with assets whose value is uncertain. Such a solution, however, is really a way of avoiding responsibility and is a too easy solution to an extremely difficult problem. The accountant does exercise judgment; he is an estimator and should be willing to face up to the existence of uncertainty, rather than expensing items because their ultimate value is difficult to forecast at the time the cost is incurred.

Theoretically, the accountant should provide the information most useful to society, considering the costs and benefits of the alternative accounting policies. However, the measurement of these costs and benefits is extremely difficult. Currently, all we can do is offer qualitative evaluations of alternatives rather than explicit measures.

However, Dukes[20] has offered empirical evidence of the importance of the disclosure of R&D expenditures. This evidence supports the Board's recommendation that more information relative to the magnitude of R&D expenditures be disclosed. Whatever accounting procedure is finally adopted, the disclosure of the amounts of expenditures by year will enable the analyst using the information to make the adjustments that he sees fit. If one accepts the hypothesis that capital markets are efficient in the processing of information, disclosure of the amount of the research and development expenditure is an extremely important first step. Given the basic data regarding the amount of the expenditure, an assumption of efficient capital markets implies market prices will reflect appropriate adjustments to the reported accounting numbers. The Dukes study reports findings consistent with this

conclusion. However, we are not suggesting that the ability of the market to digest data should be used as a justification for neglecting accounting practices. In the first place, the adjustment process has a cost. Second, there are many other uses of accounting data besides financial analysis for the evaluation of common stock.

When a firm suffers economic difficulty, it is likely that the accounting (book) value of its assets will exceed their economic value. Technological and social change can cause assets to lose value suddenly. It is virtually impossible for the accountant to anticipate and report these value changes and at the same time use cost-based accounting principles of asset and income measurement in a theoretically correct manner. It would be possible to expense all cost factors whose benefit stream has an element of risk, but this would result in reports that were essentially cash flow statements. The income statement prepared in accordance with theoretically correct accrual concepts is an extremely important report. While it is true that later events may indicate that estimated writeoffs of assets were too rapid or not rapid enough, the accountant has an obligation to attempt to estimate the expenses of earning the revenues of a period rather than reporting as expenses the expenditures made during the period. From the point of view of accounting theory, the expenditures for R&D, which are made in the expectation of benefiting future periods, should not be written off against the revenues of the present period. Justification for such practice must be found elsewhere, if it is to be found.

[20]Ibid.

QUESTIONS

1. Under the equity method of accounting for investments, an investor recognizes its share of the earnings in the period in which the
   a. Investor sells the investment
   b. Investee declares a dividend
   c. Investee pays a dividend
   d. Earnings are reported by the investee in its financial statements

2. Pence Corporation, which accounts for its investment in the common stock of Walsh Company by the equity method, should ordinarily record a dividend received from Walsh as
   a. An addition to the carrying value of the investment
   b. Dividend revenue
   c. A reduction of the carrying value of the investment
   d. Revenue from affiliate

3. On January 15, 1973, a corporation was granted a patent on a product. On January 2, 1982, to protect its patent, the corporation purchased a patent on a competing product that originally was issued on January 10, 1978. Because of its unique plant, the corporation does not feel the competing patent can be used in producing a product. The cost of the competing patent should be
   a. Amortized over a maximum period of 17 years
   b. Amortized over a maximum period of 13 years
   c. Amortized over a maximum period of 8 years
   d. Expensed in 1982

4. Pacer Company purchased 800 of the 1,000 outstanding shares of Queen Company's common stock for $80,000 on January 2, 1988. During 1981, Queen Company declared dividends of $8,000 and reported earnings for the year of $20,000.
   If Pacer Company uses the equity method of accounting for its investment in Queen Company, its Investment in Queen Company account at December 31, 1988 should be
   a. $96,000
   b. $89,600
   c. $86,000
   d. $80,000

5. Refer to the facts in problem (4). If Pacer Company uses the lower of cost or market method of accounting for its investment in Queen Company, its Investment in Queen Company account on December 31, 1988, should be
   a. $96,000
   b. $86,400

c. $80,000
d. $73,600

6. A large publicly held company has developed and registered a trademark during 1987. The cost of developing and registering the trademark should be accounted for by
   a. Charging it to an asset account that should not be amortized
   b. Expensing it as incurred
   c. Amortizing it over 25 years if in accordance with management's evaluation
   d. Amortizing it over its useful life or 17 years, whichever is shorter

7. Goodwill should be written off
   a. As soon as possible against retained earnings
   b. As soon as possible as an extraordinary item
   c. By systematic charges against retained earnings over the period benefited, but not more than 40 years
   d. By systematic charges to expense over the period benefited, but not more than 40 years

8. A net unrealized loss on a company's long-term portfolio of marketable equity securities should be reflected in the current financial statements as
   a. An extraordinary item shown as a direct reduction from retained earnings
   b. A current loss resulting from holding marketable equity securities
   c. A footnote or parenthetical disclosure only
   d. A valuation allowance and included in the equity section of the statement of financial position

9. Accumulated changes in the valuation allowance for a long-term marketable equity securities portfolio should be a component of
   a. Current assets
   b. Noncurrent assets (contra account)
   c. Noncurrent liabilities
   d. Net income

10. Cash dividends declared out of current earnings are distributed to an investor. How will the investor's investment account be affected by those dividends under each of the following accounting methods?

	Cost Method	Equity method
a.	Decrease	No effect
b.	Decrease	Decrease
c.	No effect	Decrease
d.	No effect	No effect

11. When an investor uses the equity method to account for investments in

360

common stock, the equity in the earnings of the investee reported in the investor's income statement will be affected by which of the following?

	Cash dividends from investee	Goodwill amortization related to purchase
a.	No	Yes
b.	No	No
c.	Yes	No
d.	Yes	Yes

12. An activity that would be expensed currently as research and development costs is the
    a. Testing in search for or evaluation of product or process alternatives
    b. Adaptation of an existing capability to a particular requirement or customer's need as a part of continuing commercial activity
    c. Legal work in connection with patent applications or litigation, and the sale or licensing of patents
    d. Engineering follow-through in an early phase of commercial production

13. Should the following fees associated with the registration of an internally developed patent be capitalized?

	Legal fees	Registration fees
a.	Yes	Yes
b.	Yes	No
c.	No	Yes
d.	No	No

14. Which of the following assets acquired in 1983 are amortizable?

	Goodwill	Trademarks
a.	No	No
b.	No	Yes
c.	Yes	Yes
d.	Yes	No

15. A purchased patent has a remaining legal life of 15 years. It should be
    a. Expensed in the year of acquisition
    b. Amortized over 15 years regardless of its useful life
    c. Amortized over its useful life if less than 15 years
    d. Amortized over 40 years

16. Which of the following amounts incurred in connection with a trademark should be capitalized?

	Cost of a successful defense	*Registration fees*
a.	Yes	No
b.	Yes	Yes
c.	No	Yes
d.	No	No

17. Victoria Company has both a current and noncurrent marketable equity securities portfolio. At the beginning of the year, the aggregate market value of each portfolio exceeded its cost. During the year, Victoria sold some securities from each portfolio. At the end of the year, the aggregate cost of each portfolio exceeded its market value.

Victoria also has long-term investments in various bonds, all of which were purchased for face value. During the year, some of these bonds held by Victoria were called prior to their maturity by the bond issuer. Three months before the end of the year, additional similar bonds were purchased for face value plus two months' accrued interest.

Required:

a. How should Victoria account for the sale of securities from each portfolio? Why?

b. How should Victoria account for the marketable equity securities portfolios at year end? Why?

c. How should Victoria account for the disposition prior to their maturity of the long-term bonds called by their issuer? Why?

d. How should Victoria report the purchase of the additional similar bonds at the date of acquisition? Why?

18. On July 1, 1987, Dynamic Company purchased for cash 40 percent of the outstanding capital stock of Cart Company. Both Dynamic Company and Cart Company have a December 31 year end. Cart Company, whose common stock is actively traded in the over-the-counter market, reported its total net income for the year to Dynamic Company, and also paid cash dividends on November 15, 1987, to Dynamic Company and its other stockholders.

Required:

How should Dynamic Company report the foregoing facts in its December 31, 1987, balance sheet and its income statement for the year then ended? Discuss the rationale for your answer.

19. On June 30, 1988, your client, the Vandiver Corporation, was granted patents covering plastic cartons that it has been producing and marketing profitably for the past three years. One patent covers the manufacturing process and the other covers the related products.

Vandiver executives tell you that these patents represent the most significant breakthrough in the industry in the past 30 years. The products have been marketed under the registered trademarks Safetainer, Duratainer, and Sealrite. Licenses under the patents have already been granted by your client to other manufacturers in the United States and abroad and are producing substantial royalties.

On July 1, Vandiver commenced patent infringement actions against several companies whose names you recognize as those of substantial and prominent competitors. Vandiver's management is optimistic that these suits will result in a permanent injunction against the manufacture and sale of the infringing products and collection of damages for loss of profits caused by the alleged infringement.

The financial vice-president has suggested that the patents be recorded at the discounted value of expected net royalty receipts.

Required:
a. What is an intangible asset? Explain.
b. i. What is the meaning of "discounted value of expected net receipts"? Explain.
   ii. How would such a value be calculated for net royalty receipts?
c. What basis of valuation for Vandiver's patents would be generally accepted in accounting? Give supporting reasons for this basis.
d. i. Assuming no practical problems of implementation and ignoring generally accepted accounting principles, what is the preferable basis of evaluation for patents? Explain.
   ii. What would be the preferable theoretical basis of amortization? Explain.
e. What recognition, if any, should be made of the infringement litigation in the financial statements for the year ending September 30, 1988? Discuss.

20. The Thomas Company is in the process of developing a revolutionary new product. A new division of the company was formed to develop, manufacture, and market this new product. As of year end (December 31, 1987), the new product has not been manufactured for resale; however, a prototype unit was built and is in operation.

Throughout 1987 the new division incurred certain costs. These costs include design and engineering studies, prototype manufacturing costs, administrative expenses (including salaries of administrative personnel), and market research costs. In addition, approximately $500,000 in equipment (estimated useful life, 10 years) was purchased for use in developing and manufacturing the preproduction prototype and will be used to manufacture the new product. Approximately $200,000 of this equipment was built specifically for the design development of the new product; the remaining $300,000 of equipment was used to manufacture the new product once it is in commercial production.

Required:

a. What is the definition of *research* and of *development* as defined in Statement of Financial Accounting Standards No. 2?

b. Briefly indicate the practical and conceptual reasons for the conclusion reached by the Financial Accounting Standards Board on accounting and reporting practices for research and development costs.

c. In accordance with Statement of Financial Accounting Standards No. 2, how should the various costs of Thomas just described be recorded on the financial statements for the year ended December 31, 1987?

21. Part *a*. The Financial Accounting Standards Board issued its Statement Number 12 to clarify accounting methods and procedures with respect to certain marketable securities. An important part of the statement concerns the distinction between noncurrent and current classification of marketable securities.

Required:

i. Why does a company maintain an investment portfolio of current and noncurrent securities?

ii. What factors should be considered in determining whether investments in marketable equity securities should be classified as current or noncurrent, and how do these factors affect the accounting treatment for unrealized losses?

Part *b*. Presented below are four unrelated situations involving marketable equity securities.

Situation I

A noncurrent portfolio with an aggregate market value in excess of cost includes one particular security whose market value has declined to less than one-half of the original cost. The decline in value is considered to be other than temporary.

Situation II

The statement of financial position of a company does not classify assets and liabilities as current and noncurrent. The portfolio of marketable equity securities includes securities normally considered current that have a net cost in excess of market value of $2,000. The remainder of the portfolio has a net market value in excess of cost of $5,000.

Situation III

A marketable equity security, whose market value is currently less than cost, is classified as noncurrent but is to be reclassified as current.

364

Situation IV

A company's noncurrent portfolio of marketable equity securities consists of the common stock of one company. At the end of the prior year the market value of the security was 50 percent of original cost, and the effect was properly reflected in a valuation allowance account. However, at the end of the current year the market value of the security had appreciated to twice the original cost. The security is still considered noncurrent at year end.

Required:

What is the effect on classification, carrying value, and earnings for each of the preceding situations? Complete your response to each situation before proceeding to the next situation.

BIBLIOGRAPHY

Abdel-khalik, A. Rashad. "Advertising Effectiveness an Accounting Policy." *The Accounting Review* (October 1975), pp. 657–670.

Barrett, M. Edgar. "Accounting for Intercorporate Investments: A Behavioral Field Experiment." *Journal of Accounting Research*. Empirical Research in Accounting (1971), pp. 50–65.

Barrett, M. Edgar. "APB Opinion No. 18: A Move Toward Preferences of Users." *Financial Analysts Journal* (July–August 1972), pp. 47–50, 52–55.

Catlett, George R., and Norman O. Olson. *Accounting for Goodwill*. Accounting Research Study No. 10. New York: AICPA, 1968.

Copeland, Ronald M., Robert Strawser, and John G. Binns. "Accounting for Investments in Common Stock." *Financial Executive* (February 1972), pp. 36–38ff.

Dukes, Roland E. "An Investigation of the Effects of Expensing Research and Development Costs on Security Prices." In *Proceedings in the Conference on Topical Research in Accounting*. Michael Schiff and George Sorter, eds. New York: New York University, 1976, pp. 147–193.

Elliot, John, Gordon Richardson, Thomas Dyckman, and Roland Dukes. "The Impact of SFAS No. 2 on Firm Expenditures on Research and Development: Replications and Extensions." *Journal of Accounting Research* (Spring 1984), pp. 85–102.

Falk, Haim, and Joseph C. Miller. "Amortization of Advertising Expenditures." *Journal of Accounting Research* (Spring 1977), pp. 12–22.

Gellein, Oscar S., and Maurice S. Newman. *Accounting for Research and Development Expenditures*. Accounting Research Study No. 14. New York: AICPA, 1973.

Gridley, F. W. "Accounting for R&D Costs." *Financial Executive* (April 1974), pp. 18–22.

Gynther, Reg S. "Some Conceptualizing on Goodwill." *The Accounting Review* (April 1969), pp. 247–255.

Johnson, Orace. "A Consequential Approach to Accounting for R&D." *Journal of Accounting Research* (Autumn 1967), pp. 164–172.

Lall, R. M. "Conceptual Veracity of Goodwill." *Accountancy* (October 1968), pp. 728–732.

Lee, T. A. "Goodwill: An Example of Will-o'-the-Wisp Accounting." *Accounting and Business Research* (Autumn 1971), pp. 318–328.

Lynch, Thomas Edward. "Accounting for Investments in Equity Securities by the Equity and Market Value Methods." *Financial Analysts Journal* (January–February 1975), pp. 62–69.

MacIntosh, J. C. C. "Problem of Accounting for Goodwill." *Accountancy* (November 1974), pp. 30–32.

Miller, Malcolm C. "Goodwill—An Aggregation Issue." *The Accounting Review* (April 1973), pp. 280–291.

Munter, Paul, and Thomas A. Ratcliff. "Accounting for Research and Development Activities." *The CPA Journal* (April 1983), pp. 54–65.

Newman, Maurice S. "Accounting for Research and Development Expenditures." *The CPA Journal* (April 1974), pp. 55–58.

O'Connor, Melvin C., and James C. Hamre. "Alternative Methods of Accounting for Long-Term Nonsubsidiary Intercorporate Investments in Common Stock." *The Accounting Review* (April 1972), pp. 308–319.

Picconi, Mario J. "A Reconsideration of the Recognition of Advertising Assets on Financial Statements." *Journal of Accounting Research* (Autumn 1977), pp. 317–326.

Sands, John E. *Wealth, Income and Intangibles*. Toronto: Toronto University Press, 1963.

Tearney, Michael G. "Accounting for Goodwill: A Realistic Approach." *Journal of Accountancy* (July 1973), pp. 41–45.

Tearney, Michael G. "Compliance with the AICPA Pronouncements on Accounting for Goodwill." *The CPA Journal* (February 1973), pp. 121–125.

Weinwurm, Ernest H. "Modernizing the Goodwill Concept." *Management Accounting* (December 1971), pp. 31–34.

8

LONG-TERM
LIABILITIES

Short-term liabilities were discussed as an element of working capital in Chapter 5. In this chapter we shall examine the nature of long-term liabilities. The emphasis will be upon the recognition and timing of events as liabilities, with specific attention to some of the more troublesome items and transactions.

The separation of liabilities into their current and noncurrent elements is important because of effects upon working capital, the current ratio, and expected future cash flows. In Chapter 5 it was noted that working capital was important as an indication of the margin or buffer available with which to meet current obligations. Changes in the amounts recorded as current obligations have a direct effect upon the determination of this buffer. Many creditor decisions are made on the basis of the relationship of debt to equity or to assets; therefore, the proper separation and recording of liabilities is important for decisionmaking.

THE RECOGNITION AND TIMING OF LIABILITIES

In earlier chapters it was noted that the recognition of items as assets is closely associated with the principles of realization and matching, and balance sheet amounts recorded as assets are, in many cases, the residual effect of income determination. The recognition of current liabilities frequently takes a similar form due to the necessities of accrual accounting; however, long-term liabilities are generally recorded as the result of specific transactions with external creditors.

The double-entry accounting system requires two or more separate and distinct recordings of each economic event. Thereafter events that are deemed to have future significance are reported on the balance sheet and separated into (1) those items that have future economic benefit-assets and (2) those items that provided funds for the acquisition of assets-liabilities and equities.

It is also important to establish criteria to enable accountants to separate the second classification of items into their liability and equity portions. This division is most easily accomplished by establishing guidelines that identify items as liabilities; all others are then recorded as equity.

Two theories of equity, the proprietary theory and the entity theory, view the right-hand side of the balance sheet somewhat differently. The proprietary theory states the fundamental accounting equation as

$$\text{assets} = \text{liabilities} + \text{equity}$$

The entity theory states this equation as

$$\text{assets} = \text{equity}$$

The basic distinction between these two theories is in the treatment of items on the right-hand side of the equation. The proprietary theory holds that some right-hand-side items are separately recorded as debt, whereas the entity theory treats all right-hand-side items as equity-holder claims with different rights. (For a more complete discussion of equity theories, see Chapter 11.)

Although the AICPA, APB, and FASB have never directly addressed the definition of liabilities on this basis, they have favored the approach implied in the proprietary theory. Recently, FASB Statement of Concepts No. 6 defined liabilities and equity as follows.

Liabilities—probable future sacrifices of economic benefits arising from present obligations of a particular entity to transfer assets or provide services to other entities in the future as a result of past transactions or events.

Equity—the residual interest in the assets of an entity that remains after deducting its liabilities. In a business enterprise the equity is the ownership interest.[1]

Previously the APB had defined liabilities and owners' equity in a somewhat similar manner and went on to state that the approach implicit in this definition is

$$\text{assets} - \text{liabilities} = \text{owners' equity}[2]$$

[1]Statement of Financial Accounting Concepts No. 6, "Elements of Financial Statements" (Stamford, Conn.: FASB, 1985), pars. 35 and 49.
[2]Accounting Principles Board Statement No. 4, "Basic Concepts and Accounting Principles Underlying Financial Statements of Business Enterprises" (New York: American Institute of Certified Public Accountants, 1970), par. 132.

CHAPTER 8. LONG TERM LIABILITIES

The definitions in FASB Statement of Concepts No. 6 and APB Statement No. 4 leave many unresolved questions. In the following section we will examine some of these questions and attempt to develop more specific criteria for the proper classification of items as liabilities.

DEBT VERSUS EQUITY

The preceding definitions require the classification of all right-hand-side balance sheet items into their liability and equity components. This requirement presupposes that all financial interest in the enterprise is either creditor or ownership, and further assumes that these distinctions are readily apparent to whomever is preparing financial statements. There are at least two fallacies in these assumptions: (1) the wide variety of securities issued by the modern complex corporation does not lend itself to simple classification schemes, and (2) there are no authoritative guidelines to use in applying the classification schemes. What one individual may view as debt another may view as equity. Therefore, it is necessary for accountants to develop additional criteria to aid in classifying the items on the right-hand side of the balance sheet. A discussion of some of the decision factors that may be used is contained in the following section.

CONSOLIDATED SET OF DECISION FACTORS

The following set of 13 factors is presented as a guide in determining the debt/equity classification in accordance with the proprietary theory. The sequence in which the factors are presented is not intended to reflect any judgment about their relative importance.

Maturity Date

Debt instruments typically have a fixed maturity date, while equity instruments do not mature. Because they do mature, debt instruments set forth the redemption requirements, and one of the requirements may be the establishment of a sinking fund in order to ensure that funds will be available for the redemption.

[handwritten margin note: Sinking fund is one of the requirements of debt instruments]

Claim on Assets

In the event of liquidation, creditors' claims take precedence over those of the owners. There are two extreme interpretations of this factor. The first is that all claims other than the first priority are equity claims. The other is that all claims other than the last are creditor claims. The problem area is everything between these two extremes: those claims that are subordinated to the first claim but take precedence over the last claim.

Claim on Income

A fixed dividend or interest rate has a preference over other dividend or interest payments and that is cumulative in the event it is not paid for a particular period is considered to indicate a debt security. On the other hand, a security that does not provide for a fixed rate, one that gives the holder the right to participate with common stockholders in any income distribution, or one whose claim is subordinate to other claims may indicate an ownership interest.

Voice in Management

The usual determinant of a voice in the management of a corporation is voting right, and this right is normally limited to common stockholders, but it may be extended to other investors if the company defaults on some predetermined conditions. For example, if interest is not paid when due or profits fall below a certain level, voting rights may be obtained, thus suggesting that the security has certain ownership characteristics.

Maturity Value

A liability has a fixed maturity value and, in addition, the value does not change throughout the life of the liability unless the company encounters serious financial problems. The owners' interest does not mature, except in the event of liquidation; consequently, there is no maturity value. The owners have a continuing financial interest in the corporation, however, and the value of that interest fluctuates with present and expected future earnings.

Intent of Parties

The courts have determined that the intent of the parties is one factor to be evaluated in ruling on the debt or equity nature of a security. Investor attitude and investment character are two subfactors that help in making the determination. Investors may be divided into those who want safety and those who want capital growth, and the investments may be divided into those that provide either safety or an opportunity for capital gains or losses. If the investor was motivated to make a particular investment on the basis of safety and if the corporation included in the issue those features normally equated with safety, then there is an indication that the security is debt rather than equity.

Preemptive Right

A security that is included in the preemptive right of common stockholders may be considered to have an equity characteristic.

Name of Security

The name given to the security—for example, bond or stock—is another of the legal factors to be considered. Because of the minimal discussion of charac-

370

teristics, this factor also appears to have substantial accounting support in determining the classification of certain securities.

Conversion Features

A security that may be converted into common stock has at least the potential to become equity if it is not currently equity. A historical study of eventual conversion or liquidation may be useful in evaluating this particular factor.

Potential Dilution of Earnings per Share

This factor might be considered as a subfactor of *conversion* because the conversion feature of a security is the most likely cause of dilution of earnings per share, other than a new issue of common stock. In any event, a security that has the potential to dilute earnings per share is assumed to have equity characteristics.

Right to Enforce Payments

From a legal point of view, creditors have the right to receive periodic interest at the agreed-upon date and to have the maturity value paid at the maturity date. The enforcement of this right may result in the corporation being placed in receivership. Owners have no such legal right; therefore, the existence of the right to enforce payment is an indication of a debt instrument. On the other hand, it may be necessary to determine the nature of the security in order to know whether the right exists.

The creditors right to enforce payment is an idication of a debt instrument

Good Business Reasons for Issuing

Determining what constitutes good business reasons for issuing a particular security rather than one with different features presents a difficult problem. Two relevant subfactors are the alternatives available and the level of capitalization. Securities issued by a company in financial difficulty or with a low level of capitalization may be ruled as equity on the grounds that only those with an ownership interest would be willing to accept the risk.

Identity of Interest Between Creditors and Owners

When the individuals who invest, through the preemptive right or otherwise, in so-called debt securities are the same individuals, or family members, who hold the common stock, an ownership interest is indicated.

An example of a security presenting this type of dilemma is redeemable preferred stock. Many companies have used these securities to raise capital; these securities typically are disclosed on the financial statements as equity even though they must be repaid like long-term debts.

The SEC recently ruled that redeemable preferred stock must be separately disclosed in the equity section of the balance sheet in order to highlight the future cash obligations necessitated by this type of security. The SEC left to the FASB the overall questions of (1) deciding if redeemable preferred stock is a liability, (2) whether the related payments are interest or dividends, and (3) whether early extinguishment could result in a reportable gain or loss. This example indicates that literature discussing the debt/equity question does not make clear the extent to which certain factors must be present, or absent, in determining whether a security should be treated as debt or as equity. However, the set of factors does provide a useful frame of reference for evaluating the classification of a particular security.

LONG-TERM DEBT CLASSIFICATION

Once a particular security has been classified as a liability, it may be recorded as either a current liability or a long-term liability. The classification of an item as a long-term liability is based upon the one-year or current-operating-cycle rule. If an existing obligation is not to be paid within one year or the current operating cycle (whichever is longer) or replaced by another current liability, it is properly classified as a long-term liability. The most frequently encountered long-term liabilities are bonds payable, long-term notes payable, lease obligations, pension obligations, deferred taxes, other long-term deferrals, and, occasionally, contingent liabilities. Leases, pensions, and taxes are discussed separately in the following chapters. In this section we examine the recording and reporting requirements for bonds, notes, deferrals, and contingencies.

BONDS PAYABLE

When additional funds are needed to expand the business or for current operations, a corporation has the choice of issuing debt or equity securities. There are four basic reasons why a corporation may wish to issue debt rather than equity securities.

1. *Bonds may be the only available source of funds.* Many small and medium-size companies may appear too risky for investors to make permanent investment.
2. *Debt financing has a lower cost.* Since bonds have a lower investment risk than stock, they traditionally have paid relatively low rates of interest. Investors acquiring equity securities generally expect a greater return. In recent years, however, market conditions have changed, and the cost of debt financing has risen. Whether or not market conditions will return to their former debt/equity cost relationship is unknown at this time.
3. *Debt financing offers a tax advantage.* Payments to debt holders in the form

372   CHAPTER 8. LONG TERM LIABILITIES

of interest are deductible for income tax purposes, whereas dividends on equity securities are not.

4. *The voting privilege is not shared.* If a stockholder wishes to maintain his or her present percentage ownership in a corporation, he or she must purchase the current ownership portion of each new common stock issue. Debt issues do not carry ownership or voting rights and therefore do not dilute voting power. Where the portion of ownership is small and holdings widespread, this consideration is probably not very important.

The use of borrowed funds is known as *trading on the equity*. The customary reason for using borrowed funds is the expectation of investing them in a capital project that will provide a return in excess of the cost of the acquired funds. The stockholders' investment serves as protection for the bondholders' principal and income, and the strength of current earnings and the debt-equity relationship both influence the rate of interest required by the debt holder. In using debt financing it should be recognized that trading on the equity increases the rate of return to common stockholders as long as the return on the project is greater than the cost of the borrowed funds. Earnings (less their related tax effect) in excess of interest payments will increase earnings per share. However, if the return falls below the stipulated bond interest rate, earnings per share will decline.

BOND CLASSIFICATIONS

Bonds frequently are classified by the nature of the protection offered by the company. Bonds that are secured by a lien against specific assets of the corporation are known as *mortgage bonds*. In the event the corporation becomes bankrupt and is liquidated, the holders of mortgage bonds have first claim against the proceeds from the sale of the assets that secured their debt. If the proceeds from the sale of secured assets are not sufficient to repay the debt, mortgage bondholders become general creditors for the remainder of the unpaid debt.

Debenture bonds are not secured by any property or assets, and their marketability is based upon the general credit of the corporation. A long period of earnings and continued favorable predictions are necessary for a company to sell debenture bonds. Debenture bondholders become general creditors of the corporation in the event of liquidation.

BOND SELLING PRICES

The decision to issue bonds and their subsequent sale may take place over a relatively long period of time. Bonds are generally sold in $1,000 denominations and carry a stated amount of interest per year, but it is not unusual for the stated and actual rates of interest to differ. Once the decision to issue bonds has been made, they are printed with a stated rate of interest that approximately equals the rate for securities of a like quality. This interest rate depends upon such factors as the relative risk of the security, the strength of the economy, and the existing bond market conditions.

Subsequently, market conditions may change, and at the time the bonds are actually sold the market interest rate necessary to sell the bonds may also have changed. Since the interest amount is already stated on the bonds, it cannot be changed; however, it is possible to sell the bonds for more than face value (thereby lowering the effective interest rate) or for less than face value (thereby raising the effective interest rate).

The rate of interest necessary to sell a bond issue is known as the *yield rate* on the bonds. If investors are willing to accept the interest rate stated on the bonds, they will be sold at their face value. However, if investors require an interest rate that is different from the stated rate, the market price of the bonds is adjusted to reflect the desired rate. The bond selling price is then determined by finding the sum of the discounted present value of the principal and interest payments at the yield rate. Bonds sold below their face value are sold at a *discount;* bonds sold above their face value are sold at a *premium.*

To illustrate, assume that the XYZ Corporation issued $100,000 of 10 percent, 10-year bonds on January 1, 1988. Interest on these bonds is to be paid annually each December 31. If these bonds are actually sold to yield 9 percent, the bond selling price would be calculated as follows.

Present value of principal	
$100,000 × 0.422411*a*	$42,241.10
Present value of interest payments	
$10,000 × 6.417658*b*	64,176.58
	$106,417.68

*a*Present value of $1:$i = 0.09$, $n = 10$.
*b*Present value of an ordinary annuity of $1:$i = 0.09$, $n = 10$.

Since investors are requiring an interest rate lower than the rate stated on the bonds, the bond selling price will be above the face value of the bonds. This increased selling price has the effect of lowering the yield rate because the actual amount of interest stipulated on the bonds will be paid to investors each interest payment date, while the amount of the principal invested has increased.

On the other hand, assume that the rate of interest required by investors is 12 percent. The bond selling price must be reduced to achieve a higher yield rate as follows.

Present value of principal	
$100,000 \times 0.321973^a$	$32,197.30
Present value of interest payments	
$10,000 \times 5.650223^b$	56,502.23
	$88,699.53

[a]Present value of $1:$i = 12$, $n = 10$.
[b]Present value of an ordinary annuity of $1:$i + 12$, $n = 10$.

In this case the yield rate is higher than the stated rate because the cash payment to investors remains the same while the amount of the principal has decreased.

Two methods may be used to allocate any premium or discounts over the life of the bonds: the straight-line method and the effective interest method. In using the *straight-line method,* the life of the bond issue is divided into the premium or discount to arrive at an amount to be amortized per period. This method gives an equal allocation per period and is advocated because of its ease in calculation.

However, the assumption of a stable interest cost per year is not realistic when a premium or discount is involved. The original selling price of the bonds was calculated by determining the yield rate necessary to sell the bonds. The issue price reflects the discounted value of future principal and interest payments. Therefore, a more valid assumption is that the yield rate should be reflected over the entire life of the bond issue. The *effective interest method* provides for such a presentation by applying the yield rate to the carrying value of the bonds in each successive period. In using this method, the premium or discount amortization is determined by taking the difference between the face amount of interest stated on the bonds and the amount of interest actually recorded under the compound interest method.

The effective interest method is theoretically preferable because it results in a stable interest rate per period and discloses a liability balance on the balance sheet equivalent to the present value of the future cash flows at the original market rate of interest. Additionally, APB No. 21 requires the use of the effective interest method unless the results obtained from the use of the straight-line method are not materially different. However, some companies use the straight-line method because it is easy to calculate, and there is a relatively minor difference between income statement and balance sheet values reported under the two methods from period to period.

ZERO COUPON BONDS

A *zero coupon bond* is a bond sold at considerably less than its face value, providing for no periodic interest payments or stated rate of interest. The interest cost to the issuer is determined by the effective interest method and allocates the total discount over the life of the bond issue. For example, if $100,000 of zero coupon bonds with a life of 10 years were issued to yield 12 percent, the issue price would be $32,197 and the unamortized discount would be $67,803.

Many accountants have questioned the logic of purchasing zero coupon bonds because of the Internal Revenue Code regulation that requires investors to include the yearly discount amortization as income prior to the time the cash interest is actually received. However, zero coupon bonds became popular with pension funds because (1) they usually do not contain a call provision and therefore the stated return is guaranteed until maturity and (2) they offer *reinvestment return,* which means that all of the interest is reinvested at the same rate of return over the life of the issue.

Zero coupon bonds were originally attractive to issuers because of the Internal Revenue Code regulation that allowed the bond discount to be amortized for tax purposes on the straight-line method. This allowed for a reduction in the effective rate of interest for the issuer in the earlier years of the bond's term. However, this treatment is no longer allowed and the attractiveness of zero coupon bonds to issuers has diminished.

CALL PROVISIONS

Long-term debt is issued under the prevailing market conditions at the time it is issued. In unfavorable market conditions it may be necessary to pay unusually high interest rates or to include promises in the *bond indenture* (the agreement between the issuing corporation and the bondholders) that inhibit the financial operation of the company. For example, the indenture may include restrictions on dividends, a promise to maintain a certain working capital position, or the maintenance of a certain debt-equity relationship.

Most companies protect themselves from the inability to take advantage of future favorable changes in market conditions by including a call provision on long-term debt. This provision allows the company to recall debt at a prestated percentage of the issue price. Since the call price is generally above the issue price (if not, it is unlikely that the company would be able to sell the debt issue), a loss or, in unusual circumstances, a gain occurs at the time the debt is recalled. (A gain will usually occur when the company is able to buy its securities on the open market at a price below face value.)

The recall, or *early extinguishment,* of debt may take two forms: (1) the borrowed funds may no longer be needed and the debt is therefore canceled, which is termed *debt retirement;* or (2) the existing debt may be replaced with another debt issue, termed *debt refunding*.

The cancellation of existing debt poses no particular accounting problem. Any gain or loss resulting from the difference between the carrying value and the call

376

price is treated as a gain or loss in the year the cancellation takes place. The theory behind this treatment is that the recall of the debt was a current decision and should therefore be reflected in the current year's income.

The argument is not quite so convincing in the case of refunding transactions. In ARB No. 43, three methods of accounting for the gain or loss from a refunding transaction were discussed.

1. Make a direct write-off of the gain or loss in the year of the transaction.
2. Amortize the gain or loss over the remaining life of the original issue.
3. Amortize the gain or loss over the life of the new issue.[3]

Recognizing the gain or loss over the remaining life of the old issue is favored by some accountants because they view this as the period of benefit—that is, a higher interest cost would have been incurred during this period if the old issue had not been refunded. Those who favor recognizing the gain or loss over the life of the new issue base their argument on the matching concept that is, the lower interest rates obtained by the refunding should be adjusted to reflect any refunding gain or loss. Finally, those accountants favoring immediate write-off argue that this method is the most logical because the value of the debt has changed over time, and paying the call price is the most favorable method of eliminating the debt.

ARB No. 43 stated a preference for the first method and allowed the second. Later, APB Opinion No. 6 allowed the use of the third method under certain circumstances.[4] In effect, these two releases frequently permitted a company to use any one of the three available methods.

After a subsequent reexamination of the topic, the APB issued its Opinion No. 26, "Early Extinguishment of Debt."[5] In this release the board took the position that all early extinguishments were fundamentally alike (whether retirements or refundings) and that they should be accounted for in the same manner. Since the accounting treatment of retirements was to reflect any gain or loss in the period of recall, it was decided that any gains or losses from refunding should also be reflected currently in income. Thus, options two and three are no longer considered acceptable under generally accepted accounting principles.

A short time later, the FASB undertook a study of the reporting requirements for gains and losses arising from early extinguishment of debt. This review was undertaken with pressure from the SEC because prevailing market conditions in

---

[3]Accounting Research Bulletin No. 43, "Restatement and Revision of Accounting Research Bulletins" (New York: American Institute of Certified Public Accountants, 1953).

[4]Accounting Principles Board Opinion No. 6, "Status of Accounting Research Bulletins" (New York: American Institute of Certified Public Accountants, 1965).

[5]Accounting Principles Board Opinion No. 26, "Early Extinguishment of Debt" (New York: American Institute of Certified Public Accountants, 1972).

1973 and 1974 allowed several companies to reacquire long-term debt at prices well below face value. For example, in 1973 United Brands was able to realize a $37.5 million gain by exchanging $12.5 million in cash and $75 million in 9⅛ percent debentures for $125 million of 5½ percent convertible subordinated debentures. This entire gain was reported as ordinary income.

Upon completion of the study, FASB Statement No. 4, "Reporting Gains and Losses from Extinguishment of Debt,"[6] was issued. This release requires all extinguishments, whether early or at scheduled maturity, to be classified as extraordinary items without regard to the criteria of "unusual nature" or "infrequency of occurrence." Additionally, the following disclosures are required.

1. A description of the extinguishment transactions, including the sources of any funds used to extinguish debt if it is practicable to identify the sources.
2. The income tax effect in the period of extinguishment.
3. The per share amount of the aggregate gain or loss net of related tax effect.[7]

Subsequently, APB No. 26 was amended by Statement of Financial Accounting Concepts No. 76, "Extinguishment of Debt." This release made the provisions of APB No. 26 applicable to all debt extinguishments, whether early or not, except those specifically exempted by other pronouncements (e.g., debt restructurings). Debt was considered to be extinguished in the following circumstances.

1. The debtor has paid the creditor and is relieved of all obligations regardless of whether the securities are canceled or held as treasury bonds by the debtor.
2. The debtor is legally released from being the primary obligor by the creditor, and it is probable that no future payment will be required (*defeasance*).
3. The debtor places cash or other essentially risk-free securities (such as government securities) in a trust used solely for satisfying both the scheduled interest payments and principal of a specific obligation, with the possibility of future payments being remote (*in substance defeasance*).

Under the third situation, known as in substance defeasance, the debt is considered extinguished even though the debtor is not legally released from being the primary obligator of the debt. The principles of in substance defeasance are as follows.

1. Government securities are purchased that have face values, maturity dates, and interest rates nearly identical to those of the debt being retired.
2. The purchased government securities and the debt being retired are placed in

---

[6]Statement of Financial Accounting Standards No. 4, "Reporting Gains or Losses from Extinguishment of Debt" (Stamford, Conn.: Financial Accounting Standards Board, 1975).
[7]Ibid., par. 9.

an irrevocable trust. The purpose of this trust is to satisfy the principal and interest obligations of the debt issue.

This treatment created a controversy among some accountants, who claimed it could allow management to manipulate income—that is, a gain on extinguishment could be recorded when the debtor has not been legally released from the obligation.

This criticism resulted in a review of the provisions of SFAC No. 76 as they related to instantaneous in substance defeasance transactions (where the interest rate on the purchased securities is higher than that on the debt). This review resulted in release of FASB Technical Bulletin 84-4. It requires a company involved in an in substance defeasance transaction to report separately the assets and debt and the interest revenue and expense. Immediate recognition of a gain on extinguishment for instantaneous in substance defeasance transactions is no longer acceptable.

CONVERTIBLE DEBT

Senior securities that are convertible into common stock have frequently played a role in corporate financing, and this role seems to be growing. The use of convertible instruments gives rise to several questions. Why do firms issue such securities? Why not issue straight bonds, preferred stock, or common stock? Are these securities really bonds and preferred stock, or are they a form of common stock? Why do buyers purchase these securities?

There is rather widespread agreement that a firm sells convertible securities for one of two primary reasons. Either the firm wants to increase equity capital and decides that convertible securities are the most advantageous way of bringing about that result, or the firm wants to increase its debt or preferred stock and discovers that the conversion feature is necessary to make the security sufficiently marketable at a reasonable interest or dividend rate. Additionally, there are several other factors that, at one time or another, may motivate corporate management to decide to issue convertible debt; among these are to

1. Avoid the downward price pressures on the firm's stock that placing a large new issue of common on the market would cause.
2. Avoid dilution of earnings and increased dividend requirements while an expansion program is getting under way.
3. Avoid the direct sale of common stock when the corporation believes that its stock is currently undervalued in the market.
4. Penetrate that segment of the capital market that is unwilling or unable to participate in a direct common stock issue.
5. Minimize the flotation cost (costs associated with selling securities).

If convertible debt is issued, the company must then decide how to disclose these securities on the balance sheet. Two methods have been advocated for recording and reporting on convertible debt: (1) allocate a part of the cost of the security to the conversion privilege through paid-in-capital and (2) treat the issue solely as debt. Those favoring the first position base their argument on the fact that a lower interest rate than might otherwise have been available usually accompanies a conversion feature. Therefore, an amount equal to the difference between the price at which the bonds might have been sold and the price at which they were sold should be allocated to paid-in capital. This position was initially embraced by the Accounting Principles Board in its Opinion No. 10,[8] but shortly thereafter was suspended in Opinion No. 12.[9]

The alternate position is that convertible debt should be treated solely as debt. This approach is based upon the inseparability of the debt and its conversion option and the lack of marketplace valuation. There was widespread opposition by corporate management to the reporting of convertible debt required in Opinion No. 10. This opposition apparently influenced the APB's decision to rescind its earlier position. Later in Opinion No. 14,[10] the APB advocated treating all convertible debt solely as debt.

It is the authors' opinion that presenting the effective interest charge on debt should take precedence over other considerations and, therefore, that a part of the convertible debt proceeds should be allocated to paid-in capital. The APB's inseparability arguments are, at best, weak and do not allow for informed decisionmaking by financial statement users. This issue is discussed in more depth in the article by Matthew Stevens, entitled "Inseparability and the Valuation of Convertible Bonds," at the end of the chapter.

LONG-TERM NOTES PAYABLE

Long-term notes payable are similar to debenture bonds in that they represent a future obligation to repay debt. Moreover, the holder of a note usually does not hold any collateral. Similarly, the promise to pay is generally accompanied by a provision for interest on the borrowed funds, and the amount of interest charged will depend on such factors as the credit standing of the borrower, the amount of current debt, and usual business customs.

[8]Accounting Principles Board Opinion No. 10, "Omnibus Opinion—1966" (New York: American Institute of Certified Public Accountants, 1966).
[9]Accounting Principles Board Opinion No. 12, "Omnibus Opinion—1967" (New York: American Institute of Certified Public Accountants, 1967).
[10]Accounting Principles Board Opinion No. 14, "Accounting for Convertible Debt and Debt Issued with Stock Purchase Warrants" (New York: American Institute of Certified Public Accountants, 1969).

During the early 1970s, the Accounting Principles Board studied the notes receivable and payable phenomenon. This study disclosed a rather unusual occurrence in that some note transactions were being conducted without an accompanying interest charge. These transactions were apparently being carried out for such purposes as maintaining favorable customer relations, maintaining current suppliers, or ensuring future services. After this study, the APB issued Opinion No. 21, "Interest on Receivables and Payables,"[11] which provided guidelines for cases in which no rate of interest was stipulated on notes or the rate stipulated was clearly inappropriate.

The provisions of Opinion No. 21, in summary form, are as follows.

1. Notes exchanged solely for cash are assumed to have a present value equal to the cash exchanged.
2. Notes exchanged for property, goods, and services should be presumed to have a proper rate of interest.
3. If no interest is stated or the amount of interest is clearly inappropriate on notes exchanged for property, goods, and services, the present value of the note should be determined by (whichever is more clearly determinable)

   a. Determining the fair market value of the property, goods, and services exchanged
   b. Determining the market value of the note at the time of the transaction

4. If neither (3a) nor (3b) is determinable, the present value of the note should be determined by discounting all future payments to the present at an imputed rate of interest. This imputed rate should approximate the rate of similar independent borrowers and lenders in arms-length transactions.[12]

When the face value of the note differs from its present value, the difference is shown as premium or discount on the face value of the note and is amortized over the life of the note by the *effective interest method* in such a manner as to reflect a constant rate of interest. This amortization will be deducted from the premium or discount each year, as in the case of bonds, in such a manner that at the time of repayment the face value and carrying value are equal.

Although Opinion No. 21 was designed to require the recording of interest on most notes receivable and payable, it specifically *exempted* the following types of transactions.

1. Normal trade transactions not exceeding a year.
2. Amounts that will be applied to the purchase of property, goods, and services.

---

[11]Accounting Principles Board Opinion No. 21, "Interest on Receivables and Payables" (New York: American Institute of Certified Public Accountants, 1971).
[12]Ibid., pars. 11–13.

3. Security deposits.
4. Customary activities of financial institutions.
5. Transactions where the rate is affected by the regulations of government agencies.
6. Transactions between parent and subsidiaries and between subsidiaries of a common parent.

The following example illustrates the application of Accounting Principles Board Opinion No. 21.

The Elliott Company sold the Kelliher Company an asset on January 1, 1988, with a book value of $5,000, accepting a noninterest bearing $10,000 five-year note in exchange. (Assume a prevailing interest rate of 8 percent and that the present value of $1 in five years at 8 percent is $0.681.)

	Elliott			Kelliher		
Jan. 1, 1988	Note receivable	$10,000		Asset	$6,810	
	Asset		$5,000	Discount on notes payable	3,190	
	Discount on notes receivable		3,190	Note payable		$10,000
	Gain		1,810			
Dec. 31 1988	Discount on notes receivable	545		Interest expense	545	
	Interest income (8% of $6,810)		545	Discount on notes payable (8% of $6,810)		545
Dec. 31, 1989	Discount on notes receivable	588		Interest expense	588	
	Interest income (8% of $7,355)		588	Discount on notes payable (8% of $7,355)		588

SHORT-TERM DEBT EXPECTED TO BE REFINANCED

In the past, some corporations attempted to improve their liquidity position by excluding that portion of short-term debt from current liabilities that was expected to be refinanced on a long-term basis. This treatment resulted in disclosure variations between companies and led to the issuance of FASB Statement No. 6, "Classification of Short Term Obligations Expected to Be Refinanced." In this release, the FASB took the position that short-term obligations cannot be disclosed as long-term liabilities unless the following conditions exist: (1) there is an intention to refinance current liabilities on a long-term basis and (2) the corporation demonstrates the ability to refinance such liabilities. The intent of the company to refinance current obligations means that working capital will not be reduced by the satisfaction of the obligation. The ability to refinance means that the company has an agreement to refinance the obligations on a long-term basis.

A company may refinance short-term debt on a long-term basis by replacing a current liability with long-term debt or ownership securities. Additionally, refinancing may be demonstrated if the current liability is extended, renewed, or replaced by other short-term debt.

A short-term obligation that is excluded from the current liability section of the balance sheet requires disclosure in the financial-statement footnotes. This disclosure must include a general description of the financing agreement and the terms of any new obligation incurred or expected to be incurred or equity securities issued or expected to be issued as a result of the refinancing.

DEFERRED CREDITS

Deferred credits are not liabilities in the usual sense of the word, in that they will not normally be satisfied by the payment of funds but rather by the performance of services. They result from the double-entry accounting system, which requires a credit for every debit. The most frequently encountered deferred credits are

1. Income received in advance.
2. Deferred taxes.
3. Unrealized gross profit on installment sales (usually no longer appropriate).

As can be seen, these items are either anticipated future revenues (prepaid income) or foreseen future expense payments (deferred taxes). But there is no assurance that all deferrals will ultimately be included in income determination. The deferral section of the balance sheet is grounded in the principle of conservatism. As discussed in Chapter 2, this principle requires that revenue recognition be postponed until there is assurance that it is earned, but expenses are to be recorded as incurred.

CONTINGENCIES

A contingency is a possible future event that will have some impact upon the firm. Although Accounting Principles Board Statement No. 4 required the disclosure of contingencies,[13] it made no effort to define or give examples of them. Among the most frequently encountered contingencies are

[13]APB Statement No. 4, op. cit.

1. Pending lawsuits.
2. Income tax disputes.
3. Notes receivable discounted.
4. Accommodation endorsements.

The decision to record contingencies should be based upon the principle of disclosure. That is, when the disclosure of an event adds to the information content of financial statements, it should be reported. Some authors have argued for basing this decision on expected value criteria. That is, if a potential claim obligation has a high probability of occurrence it should be recorded as a liability, whereas potential claim obligations with low probabilities might be better reported as footnotes.

On the other hand, the reporting of some types of contingencies may result in a self-fulfilling prophecy. For example, a frequently encountered contingency problem is the question of including the possible loss from a lawsuit in the liability section of the balance sheet. The dollar value of the loss can generally be determined by applying expected value criteria, but placing the item on the balance sheet may give the plaintiff additional evidence of the company's guilt. The corporation here is faced with the dilemma of conflicting responsibilities to its financial-statement users to disclose all pertinent information while at the same time minimizing losses.

The FASB reviewed the nature of contingencies in its Statement No. 5, "Accounting for Contingencies."[14] This release defines two types of contingencies—gain contingencies (expected future gains) and loss contingencies (expected future losses).

With respect to gain contingencies, the board took the position that these events should not usually be reflected currently in the financial statement because to do so might result in revenue recognition before realization. However, adequate disclosure should be made of all gain contingencies while exercising due care to avoid misleading implications as to the likelihood of realization.[15]

The criteria established for recording loss contingencies requires that the likelihood of loss is to be determined as follows.

Probable—the future event is likely to occur.
Reasonably possible—the chance of occurrence is more than remote but less than likely.
Remote—the chance of occurrence is slight.

---

[14]Statement of Financial Accounting Standards No. 5, "Accounting for Contingencies" (Stamford, Conn.: Financial Accounting Standards Board, 1975).
[15]Ibid.

CHAPTER 8. LONG TERM LIABILITIES

Once the likelihood of a loss is determined, contingencies are charged against income and a liability recorded if both of the following conditions are met.

1. Information available prior to the issuance of the financial statements indicates that it is probable that an asset had been impaired or a liability had been incurred at the date of the financial statements.
2. The amount of the loss can be reasonably estimated.[16]

Additionally, if no accrual of loss is made because one or both of these conditions has not been met, disclosure of the contingency should be made when there is at least a reasonable possibility that a loss may have been incurred.

Statement No. 5 indicated an FASB preference for the conservatism convention. It also resulted in the application of separate standards for the reporting of revenues and expenses. The provisions of this statement would cause one company to record a liability without a corresponding asset being recorded by the claimant company. These procedures are not conducive to the development of a general theory of accounting and are further evidence of the need to establish a broad framework within which to establish consistent accounting principles.

TROUBLED DEBT RESTRUCTURINGS

Occasionally corporations experience difficulty repaying their long-term debt obligations. These difficulties frequently result in arrangements between the debtor and the creditor that allow the debtor to avoid bankruptcy. For example, in 1976, Continental Investment Corporation satisfied $34 million of the $61 million debt owed to the First National Bank of Boston by transferring all of its stock in Investors Mortgage Group, Inc. (a subsidiary), to the bank. Accountants and financial-statement users became concerned over the lack of GAAP by which to account for these agreements. Consequently, the Financial Accounting Standards Board began a study of agreements of this type, termed *troubled debt restructurings*. This study focused on three questions. (1) Do certain kinds of troubled debt restructurings require reductions in the carrying amounts of debt? (2) If they do, should the effect of the reduction be reported as current income, deferred to a future period, or reported as contributed capital? (3) Should contingently payable interest on the restructured debt be recognized before it becomes payable?

The underlying issues in each of these questions relate to the recognition of liabilities and holding gains. A liability should be recorded at the amount of probable future sacrifice of economic benefit arising from present obligations. A

[16]Ibid., par. 8.

holding gain occurs when the value of the liability decreases. The result of the review of these questions was the release of FASB Statement No. 15, "Accounting by Debtors and Creditors for Troubled Debt Restructurings."[17]

According to FASB Statement No. 15, a troubled debt restructuring occurs when "the creditor for economic or legal reasons related to the debtor's financial difficulties grants a concession to the debtor that it would not otherwise consider."[18] A troubled debt restructuring may include, but is not limited to, one or any combination of the following.

1. Modification of terms of a debt such as one or a combination of:
    a. Reduction . . . of the stated interest rate for the remaining original life of the debt.
    b. Extension of the maturity date or dates at a stated interest rate lower than the current market rate for new debt with similar risk.
    c. Reduction . . . of the face amount or maturity amount of the debt as stated in the instrument or other agreement.
    d. Reduction . . . of accrued interest.
2. Issuance or other granting of an equity interest to the creditor by the debtor to satisfy fully or partially a debt unless the equity interest is granted pursuant to existing terms for converting the debt into an equity interest.
3. A transfer from the debtor to the creditor of receivables from third parties, real estate, or other assets to satisfy fully or partially a debt.[19]

MODIFICATION OF TERMS

A restructuring agreement involving only a modification of terms is accounted for on a prospective basis and results in one of the two following situations.

1. The amount of principal and interest to be repaid is greater than the current carrying value of the liability; therefore, no gain is recognized by the debtor.
2. The amount of principal and interest to be repaid is less than the current carrying value of the liability; therefore, a gain is recognized by the debtor.

In the event it is determined that the total amount to be repaid exceeds the carrying value of the debt on the date of the restructuring agreement, no adjustment is made to the original carrying value of the liability. However, it is necessary to determine the effective interest rate that equates the total future payments with the current carrying value. This rate is then applied to the carrying

---

[17]FASB Statement No. 15, "Accounting by Debtors and Creditors for Troubled Debt Restructurings" (Stamford, Conn.: FASB, 1977), par. 2.
[18]Ibid.
[19]Ibid., par. 5.

value of the obligation each year to determine the amount of interest expense. The difference between the recorded amount of interest expense and any cash payment reduces the carrying value of the liability.

If the total future cash payments are determined to be less than the carrying value of the obligation, the amount of the liability is reduced to the total amount of the cash to be repaid. The debtor then recognizes an extraordinary gain for the amount of this adjustment and all future payments are recorded as reductions in the amount of the liability. That is, the debt is treated as though there is no interest rate.

SATISFACTION OF THE DEBT THROUGH AN ASSET OR EQUITY SWAP

When a debtor exchanges an asset or an equity interest in satisfaction of a liability, the transfer is recorded on the basis of the fair market value of the asset or equity interest transferred. Market value is determined at the time of the exchange by the fair market value of the asset or equity exchanged, unless the fair market value of the debt satisfied is more clearly evident. An extraordinary gain is recognized for the excess of the recorded liability over the fair market value of the asset transferred. In the case of asset exchanges it is also necessary to record a gain or loss on disposition of the assets to the extent of the difference between the asset's fair market value and its carrying value.

DISCLOSURE OF RESTRUCTURING AGREEMENTS

FASB Statement No. 15 requires the following disclosures by debtors entering into restructuring agreements.

1. A description of the principal changes in terms and/or the major features of settlement for each restructuring agreement.
2. The aggregate gain on debt restructures and the related income tax effect.
3. The per share amount of the aggregate gain on restructuring net of the related income tax effect.
4. The aggregate gain or loss recognized during the period on transfers of assets.

SUMMARY

A review of the recording and reporting criteria for the components of long-term debt indicates that balance sheet items are classified as either debt or equity according to the basic concept of accounting being employed. Debt can be viewed as a separate component of the balance sheet or as part of the overall equity invested in the enterprise. The separate classification of items as debt is the generally accepted method, and a number of criteria may be used as a frame of reference in classifying specific items as debt or equity.

There are various components of long-term debt: bonds, convertible debt, long-term notes payable, deferred credits, contingencies, and so forth. The review of the accounting treatment for each of these items focused on troublesome areas and the accepted accounting treatment where definitive answers are available.

In the following readings, Matthew Stephens presents some guidelines for dealing with convertible debt, and Paul Pacter discusses some further implications of APB No. 21.

INSEPARABILITY AND THE VALUATION OF CONVERTIBLE BONDS

MATTHEW J. STEPHENS

In Opinion No. 14 the Accounting Principles Board (APB) of the American Institute of Certified Public Accountants said that no part of the proceeds received from issuing convertible bonds should be allocated to stockholders' equity. This Opinion rescinded a previous contrary statement which had been included in Opinion No. 10 and which had been temporarily suspended by Opinion No. 12.

The APB's conclusion in Opinion No. 14 was based on the inseparability of debt and the conversion option, and on practical problems of valuation, but the APB said that it gave greater weight to the inseparability argument. This statement was unfortunate because it seems to imply that the problem of inseparability of debt and the conversion option is distinct from the practical problem of valuation. Three recent articles have suggested that valuation of convertible bonds be reconsidered. All suggest that the distinction between convertible bonds and bonds with detachable stock warrants is one of form rather than substance.[1] This article will attempt to show that the inseparability of debt and equity elements is an integral part of the valuation problem and that valuation methods which ignore the inseparability of the debt and the conversion option are more formal than substantial. Furthermore, it will be shown that if the price of common stock increases rapidly, the rate of cost of convertible debt

[1]See Allen Ford, "Should Cost Be Assigned to Conversion Value," *The Accounting Review* (October 1969), pp. 818–822; Theodore M. Asner, "Convertible Debentures—Tax and Financial Accounting Treatment Today." *The Tax Adviser* (January 1970), pp. 9–15; Leroy F. Imdecke and Jerry Weygandt, "Accounting for That Imputed Discount Factor." J of A (June 1970), pp. 54–58.

is high and approaches the rate of cost of common equity very rapidly. Both current practice and the method recommended in Opinion No. 10 severely understate the cost of convertible debt in this circumstance. Finally, alternative methods of accounting for convertible bonds will be presented in order to illustrate the variability of cost measurements inherent in these methods.

CONVERTIBLES AND OPINION NO. 10

Convertible bonds may be characterized as debt instruments with an option to convert to common stock. Legally, the holder of such a bond is a creditor of the corporation until the bond is converted by the holder or redeemed by the corporation, so it is understandable why the debt feature is valued directly and the stock option is treated as a residual. Moreover, given the principal amount of the bond, the coupon rate of interest, the interest payment dates, the yield to maturity and the remaining life of the bond, the value of the debt can be easily estimated by compound interest methods. The current value of a possible future common stock position is much more difficult to estimate.

Usual thinking is that the investor in convertible bonds pays for the conversion option by accepting a lower coupon rate of interest than he would in the absence of the option. In Opinion No. 10 the APB said that the amount paid for the privilege of possible conversion could be estimated by subtracting from the price received for the convertible bonds the estimated price that would have been received had the corporation issued bonds identical in all respects but without a conversion privilege. For example, assume that a corporation issues at par $1 million principal amount of 6 per

cent, 20-year convertible bonds which pay interest semiannually. Further assume that it is estimated that if the corporation had issued similar bonds without a conversion privilege, an 8 per cent coupon rate of interest would have been necessary for the bonds to be issued at par. It can be estimated that the 6 per cent issue would have yielded $802,072 proceeds in the absence of the conversion option.[2] The entry to record the issue following Opinion No. 10 would be:

Cash	$1,000,000	
Discount on bonds payable	197,928	
Bonds payable		$1,000,000
Paid-in capital— conversion option		197,928

Bond discount would be amortized to interest expense over the life of the bonds, and, if the bonds were retired or converted prior to maturity, any remaining balance would be eliminated in the redemption entry. Upon conversion or redemption of the bonds, the conversion option account would be closed intact to other paid-in capital accounts.

---

[2]The general formula is:
Proceeds =

$$\sum_{t=1}^{M} \$I \left(\frac{1}{(1+i/2)^t} \right) + \$P \left(\frac{1}{(1+i/2)^M} \right)$$

where: M equals the number of six-month periods to maturity; i equals semiannual interest; i equals the estimated yield to maturity in the absence of a conversion option; and P equals the face amount of the bond.
Specifically, $802,072 =

$$\sum_{t=1}^{40} \$30,000 \left(\frac{1}{(1.04)^t} \right)$$

$$+ \$1,000,000 \left(\frac{1}{(1.04)^{40}} \right)$$

Bond issue costs are ignored for purposes of this article.

BONDS WITH DETACHABLE WARRANTS AND OPINIONS NOS. 10 AND 14

Before further analysis of the preceding method of recording an issue of convertible bonds, the similarity of these bonds to bonds with detachable warrants will be illustrated. Assume that in the previous example each $1,000 principal amount of bonds is convertible into 20 shares of stock, the stock currently sells for $42 per share, and the stock price has had a geometric mean rate of growth of 20 per cent per year for the last five years. As an alternative to the convertible issue, the company might have considered issuing a 6 per cent coupon bond with each $1,000 principal amount carrying 20 detachable warrants enabling the holder of a warrant to purchase one share of stock at any time over the next 20 years for $55. Assume that if this issue had been decided upon, the bonds would be issued at par and the warrants would begin trading at $10 and the bonds at $805. These figures are fair assumptions. Note that the conversion price in the convertible example was only $50 ($1,000 ÷ 20 shares) whereas the warrant exercise price is $55 per share. Such a differential can be justified because of the possibility of separable trading of the warrants as will be explained later. The $10 trading price of the warrant is a fair estimate based upon trading prices of actual warrants.

The total market values of the warrants and bonds would be $200,000 (20,000 at $10) and $805,000 respectively. The entry to record the issue would be:

Cash	$1,000,000	
Discount on bonds payable	199,000	
Bonds payable		$1,000,000
Common stock warrants outstanding		199,000

The bond discount and common stock warrants accounts would be treated the same as the discount and conversion option accounts discussed previously.

COMPARABLE EFFECTS ON CORPORATE AND INVESTOR ACCOUNTS

If the stock price does not rise above $55 over the next 20 years, the warrants would lapse and the bonds would be retired. The net effect on corporate accounts over the 20-year span would be the same as for the convertible issue except for minor differences in discount amortization. If the stock price does appreciate and remains above $55 after 20 years, it can be assumed that convertible bonds would be converted, and, if the warrant bearing issue had been utilized, the warrants would be exercised. Except for minor differences in amortization and a net inflow of $100,000 cash (20,000 warrants times the $5 difference between the warrant exercise price and the conversion price), the effect on corporate accounts over the 20 years would be the same under either alternative.

Assuming that original investors hold all securities for 20 years and ignoring taxes if the stock price does not rise above $55, the holder of the convertible bond and the holder of the bonds and warrants would be in substantially the same position over the 20-year span. If the stock price does rise above $55 at the end of 20 years, the original investors would be in substantially same position except that the investor in bonds with warrants would pay $5 more per share for his ultimate stock position.

The foregoing example serves to illustrate the similarity of convertible bonds and bonds with detachable warrants. Further, the example suggests that Opinion No. 14, which prescribes accounting for bonds with warrants in the manner illustrated above

390

but which ignores the separate value of the conversion option, does indeed exalt form over substance. However, three factors exist which create substantive differences between convertible bonds and bonds with warrants and which, in the opinion of this writer, call for different accounting treatment. These factors are:

1. Differences in taxation.
2. Differences in financing and investing consequences.
3. Differences in valuation methodology caused by the inseparability of the debt and equity components of a convertible bond.

DIFFERENCES IN TAXATION

For purposes of federal income tax, issuers of and investors in bonds with detachable warrants must allocate the issue price between the debt and warrants on the basis of their relative fair market values. Any debt discount created by the allocation is fully amortizable by the issuer, and, if original issue discount (as defined by the Internal Revenue Code) exists, such discount must be amortized by the investor. Convertible bonds, on the other hand, receive only partially similar treatment. Any debt premium which, following procedures illustrated earlier, can be attributed to the conversion feature is not amortizable, but any debt discount which might be created is not recognized for tax purposes.

It has been suggested that the IRS is moving toward full parity in the taxation of bonds with detachable warrants and convertible bonds. But regardless of the direction in which the IRS is moving, the present tax treatment of issuers of and investors in convertible bonds or bonds with detachable warrants is different. While it is generally inadvisable to have accounting principles determined by the tax law, it also seems inadvisable for the accounting profession to establish an accounting principle that equates two securities which differ with respect to a major decision variable. Since tax consequences are an important element in valuation of security investments and the decision as to the type of security to be issued, the accounting profession should proceed very cautiously before it prescribes a treatment for convertible bonds which essentially equates the accounting valuation of these securities to bonds with detachable warrants. It should also be noted that if the profession were to prescribe such treatment, the amortization per books of ''created'' debt discount would not be subject to deferred tax procedures since the difference between book and taxable income would be one of definition, not timing. The full effect of the amortization would be included in the determination of accounting income, whereas similar amortization of discount on bonds with detachable warrants would be net of the tax effects.

FINANCING CONSEQUENCES

A corporation that plans to issue either convertible bonds or bonds with detachable warrants can substantially conform the terms of each alternative. Despite such conformity, the corporation will not be indifferent as to its choice of security offering. Tax differentials which influence the choice have been discussed, but, even assuming equivalent taxation, there are two other important differences.

First, the proceeds that the corporation would receive from an issue of bonds with detachable warrants would be greater than the proceeds from an issue of convertibles because investors have more flexibility with the former type issue. This would be true even if the corporation planned to incorporate exactly the same debt features (interest rate, time to maturity, call features, etc.) and planned to conform exactly the conversion option and the warrant exercise price throughout the life of the bond (e.g., any decrease in the conversion ratio would be matched by an increase in the warrant exercise price). Because warrants can be purchased for much less than either an equivalent option in a convertible or an equivalent number of shares of stock, speculators often bid up the price of warrants much above their exercise value. Original investors in the bonds with warrants, therefore, may have a chance to take advantage of large profits from their warrants while still holding the debt security. In addition, warrants are not usually callable, so calling the bond will not terminate the stock option as is the case when convertible bonds are called. The potentially longer life of the warrant is valuable to the investor.

Second, warrants and convertible bonds affect the calculation of earnings per share in different ways. Warrants are common stock equivalents, but, because of assumptions made as to the disposition of proceeds received when warrants are exercised, it is very possible that warrants will not affect the calculation of either primary or fully diluted earnings per share for many of the periods during which the warrants are outstanding.

Whether or not convertible bonds are common stock equivalents is determined once and for always at the time of issuance. If the cash yield at issuance is less than two-thirds of the bank prime rate, the bonds are common stock equivalents; otherwise, they are not. Convertible bonds which are common stock equivalents affect the calculation of primary and fully diluted earnings per share, and convertibles which are not common stock equivalents affect only the fully diluted calculation. Thus, convertible bonds will always affect either or both of the per share calculations, as-

suming that they have a materially dilutive effect.

To what extent corporations and investors allow prospective earnings per share figures to affect financing and investment decisions is uncertain. But unless earnings per share calculations are meaningless, to the extent that planning can completely take account of the potential effects on these calculations, the choice between convertibles or bonds with detachable warrants is influenced.

VALUATION METHODOLOGY

Soon after a corporation issues bonds with detachable warrants, the bonds and warrants trade separately. The total proceeds received by the corporation can be allocated easily and rationally on the basis of the relative total market value of each security. Such an allocation is common in various accounting problems. The bonds will have to be redeemed for cash, regardless of whether or not the warrants are exercised, and interest expense is properly based upon the proceeds deemed to have been received for the bonds alone. There is no justification for not recording both the debt and equity elements.

As has been illustrated, convertible bonds are similar to bonds with warrants, but convertibles combine debt and equity features in a single security. Legally, convertible bonds represent debts of the corporation as long as the bonds are outstanding. Corporations that issue convertible bonds only plan to recognize periodic interest expense measured by the coupon rate of interest times the face value of the bonds, plus or minus the amortization of any discount or premium that arises because total proceeds received differ from the face amount of the issue. They do not plan to recognize hypothetical interest expense

CHAPTER 8. LONG TERM LIABILITIES

calculated on a premise that they might have issued straight bonds, with or without warrants, which would call for ultimate cash redemption. In fact, they usually plan that the bonds will be retired by conversion rather than cash payment.

A convertible bond is a true joint security and any method of valuation which attempts to value the joint debt and equity features separately is bound to be arbitrary. For example, compound interest methods permit easy estimation of the value of a comparable issue of bonds without the conversion feature. It is understandable, therefore, that methods which are recommended for use in allocating total proceeds between the debt and conversion option give primacy to the debt feature and treat the valuation of the option as a residual. However, if legal form is momentarily ignored and the financial nature of accounting is emphasized, substantial justification exists for emphasizing the valuation of the stock equity. Examination of investment ratings of convertible bond issues shows that relatively few receive high investment ratings as bonds. Out of 443 issues listed in *Moody's Convertible Bonds* (July 20, 1970), 387 were related. None were rated Aaa, 14 or 3.6 per cent, were rated Aa or A, and 41, or 10.6 per cent, were rated Baa. One hundred thirty-nine of those rated were rated less than Ba. This indicates that investors in most convertible bonds are expecting appreciation in stock prices and the opportunity to convert profitably. In addition, a study by Professor Brigham published in *The Journal of Finance* (March 1966) shows that almost 75 per cent of the companies he studied issued convertibles because they were primarily interested in obtaining equity, but for one reason or another, a straight issue of common stock could not be made advantageously. A large number of corporations that issue convertibles are obviously looking ahead to future conversion rather than cash retirement of the debt.

Several allocation schemes alternative to the one proposed in Opinion No. 10 certainly could be justified. For example, since many investors in and issuers of convertible bonds expect ultimate conversion, why not record the total proceeds received from an issue of convertibles as a deferred common stock equity? Granted that such a procedure would be outside the current legal framework of accounting, it would conform very well to financial expectations. Moreover, if desired, the proceeds could be divided between stock equity and debt by recording equity for an amount equal to the current stock price times the number of shares into which the bond is convertible and a liability for the balance of the proceeds. This latter element could be viewed as an advance by investors for the privilege of receiving a definite "dividend" and the right to cash redemption in the event conversion does not become profitable. Conflicting opinions as to the proper amortization of the liability and financial statement classification of the periodic interest payment would be sure to arise, but the opinions should be reconcilable.

There is no need to develop these ideas further because once it is recognized that there are several justifiable methods of allocating the proceeds received for an issue of convertible bonds, it should be recognized that the interest cost derived from any method of allocation will not be true. It is undeniable that the current procedure for recording an issue of convertible bonds often leads to an understatement of interest cost of these bonds. What is understated, however, is not an objectively measurable interest cost, but rather a subjectively estimative interest cost on an option to obtain stock equity; and interest (expected yield to the investor) on stock equity, whether this equity be in the form of a conversion option, a warrant or capital stock itself, is not recognized in the accounts.

Issues of convertible bonds or bonds with warrants involve a type of opportunity cost to the issuer because if the stock prices and convertibility or exercise of the warrants becomes assured, the corporation forgoes issuing the equivalent number of shares at the then current price. If convertibility or exercise of the warrants is not profitable ultimately, then the realized cost of the bond issue is the yield to maturity as if straight debt had been issued. But in the planning stage such cost would not be estimated as the full cost because, if it were, who could be expected to pay for the conversion option or warrant? Thus, in the financial planning stage, the expected cost of convertibles or bonds with warrants must include the expected cost of foregone future financing alternatives. However, once the decision is made to issue a certain kind of security, it does not follow that all relevant but subjectively estimated decision costs need be recognized in the accounts. Much can be said for the usefulness of the concepts of objectivity and realization in the preparation of external financial statements. Moreover, radical changes would have to be made in accounting concepts before the interest cost of all capital could be included in the accounts. Certainly, the understatement of cost of a convertible bond cannot be overcome by an ''as if'' valuation which assumes that the issuer issued two separate securities. This assumption is not true and valuations and cost estimates based upon it are more formal than substantial.

In order to estimate the full expected cost of convertible bonds, management must decide upon a particular set of contractual features such as the interest rate, call privileges, and conversion terms to be included in the bond contract. The choice of a particular combination of these features out of all possible combinations is influenced by management's view about the desired issue price, the length of life of the bonds, the future movement in stock price and whether conversion will be forced by call or encouraged by increasing the common dividend. To repeat, in an actual situation some of these factors can be estimated only subjectively, but the subsequent illustration assumes that expectations are fulfilled exactly. This would rarely, if ever, be true, but the assumption is sufficient for illustrative purposes.

Table I illustrates four methods of accounting for convertible bonds: (1) current practice, (2) APB Opinion No. 10 recommendation, (3) a 1957 American Accounting Association committee recommendation, and (4) a full cost method. Table II shows the calculation and accumulation of cost for the full cost method. The illustration is based upon the example of convertible bonds given earlier in the article and pertinent assumptions are as follows:

1. A corporation issues at par $1 million of bonds which pay 6 per cent per year compounded semiannually and which are due in 20 years. The bonds are convertible at any time into 20 shares of stock for each $1,000 face amount and are callable at any time at 105. It is assumed that the corporation would have had to pay 8 per cent compounded semiannually to issue the bonds at par if the convertible feature were not included.

2. The common stock sells for $42 per share and will pay a dividend of $.84 per share this year. The estimated growth rate of the dividend and share price is 20 per cent per year.[3]

[3]A 20 per cent per year growth rate for the future is a big assumption, but see Burroughs Corporation, which issued convertible debentures in

CHAPTER 8. LONG TERM LIABILITIES

Table 1   Alternative Methods of Accounting for Convertible Bonds

Year	Transaction	Accounts	Current Practice	APB Opinion No. 10	American Accounting Association	Full Cost
1	Issuance	Cash	$1,000,000	$1,000,000	$1,000,000	$1,000,000
		Bond discount	- 0 -	197,928*	- 0 -	- 0 -
		Bonds payable	$1,000,000	$1,000,000	$1,000,000	$1,000,000
		Paid-in capital—conversion option	- 0 -	197,928	- 0 -	- 0 -
1	Yearly interest	Interest expense	60,000	64,249	60,000	157,237
		Cash		60,000	60,000	60,000
		Bond discount	- 0 -	4,249**	- 0 -	- 0 -
		Paid-in capital—conversion option	- 0 -	- 0 -	- 0 -	97,237
2	Yearly interest	Interest expense	60,000	64,596	60,000	172,750
		Cash		60,000	60,000	60,000
		Bond discount	- 0 -	4,596**	- 0 -	- 0 -
		Paid-in capital—conversion option	- 0 -	- 0 -	- 0 -	112,750
2	Conversion	Bonds payable	1,000,000	1,000,000	1,000,000	1,000,000
		Paid-in capital—conversion option	- 0 -	197,928	- 0 -	210,000
		Loss on conversion	- 0 -	- 0 -	210,000	- 0 -
		Bond discount	- 0 -	189,083**	- 0 -	- 0 -
		common stock	1,000,000	1,008.845	1,210,000	1,210,000

*Refer to example in the early part of the article and footnote 2 for calculations.
**Assumes semiannual compounding for interest expense. Straight-line amortization would give $9.896 per year and a credit of $178,136 to dispose of the balance upon conversion.

Table II   Full Cost Accumulation Schedule

Six-Month Period	Interest Expense 7.682% Each Six Months*	Cash Payment	Capital Accumulation	Capital Balance
				$1,000,000
1	$76,820	$30,000	$46,820	1,046,820
2	80,417	30,000	50,417	1,097,237
3	84,290	30,000	54,290	1,151,527
4	88,460	30,000	58,460	1,210,000
				(rounded)

*The interest rate is obtained by solving for i in the formula:

$$\text{Proceeds} = \sum_{t=1}^{n} \$1 \, \frac{1}{(1+i)^t} + SC.Vn \, \frac{1}{(1+i)^n}$$

where

    1 equals the periodic interest payment
  SC.V equals the value of the stock upon conversion, and
    n equals the compounding periods to conversion.

In particular:

$$\$1,000,000 = \sum_{t=1}^{4} \$30,000 \, \frac{1}{(1=i)^t} + \$1,210,000 \, \frac{1}{(1=i)^4}$$

$i = 7.682\%$ or 15.364% per year compounded semiannually.

Assuming annual compounding for simplicity, i would equal 20.5% after 5 years, 21.2% after 10 years, 21.1% after 15 years, and 20.9% after 20 years. Notice how rapidly the cost of the convertible bond approaches the estimated cost of common equity if the expectation about equity (20% annual increase in share price) is fulfilled.

The after-tax rate of cost (r) to the corporation is obtained by solving for r in the formula:

$$\text{Proceeds} = \sum_{t=1}^{n} \$1(1-T_t) \, \frac{1}{(1+r)^t} \sum_{t=1}^{n} (Tt)(At) \, \frac{1}{(1+r)^t} + C.V \, \frac{1}{(1+i)^n}$$

Where prior notation is the same. T equals the corporate tax rate and A equals the periodic amortization of the difference between the proceeds and the face value of the bond. The periodic amounts of amortization would be computed under either the straight-line or compound interest method assuming that the bonds would remain outstanding the full term. The mathematical sign of the second summation is negative if bond discount is amortized and positive if premium is amortized. Only that part of bond premium which must be amortized for tax purposes should be considered.

Assuming a 50% tax rate, the after-tax cost (r) for the two-period case illustrated in Table II would be 12.560% per year compounded semiannually. Assuming annual compounding for the 5-, 10-, 15- and 20-year periods, the after-tax rates would be 18.2%, 19.6%, 19.8% and 19.9%, respectively. The after-tax rate approaches the before-tax rate very rapidly because of the assumed high rate of growth in share price. The terminal conversion value produces no tax benefit and it soon dwarfs the tax deductible interest payments.

3. It is planned to call the bonds after two years and, in fact, the bonds are called and converted at the end of the second year. The stock is selling at that time for $60.50 per share ($42 × (1.2)).

Certain observations about the entries and figures in Table 1 and the supporting Table II are warranted. First, the cost of convertible bonds under either current practice or the method recommended by Opinion No. 10 is severely misstated. Current practice is preferable, however, since it records the reality of single security issuance. Periodic interest expense is based upon the most objective information available, not upon assumptions of yield to maturity for a life span and terminal value that will probably be irrelevant.

Second, accounting for the periodic interest expense under the full cost method seems to be straightforward but only because it assumes that original expectations with respect to the life of the bonds and change in share prices are fulfilled exactly. Because situations in real life rarely happen in this way, many questions must be answered before the profession can be expected to adopt such a method. Expected costs are relevant for planning, but should such costs be accrued and reported when, in fact, they may never be realized? Should new expectations be incorporated as a basis for subsequent entries? How often should new expectations be recognized? Should prior entries be corrected when expectations change? Should information about variances around the expected values be footnoted in financial statements? The answers to these questions are beyond the scope of this article, but these problems must be resolved and their relationship to other accounting measures must be recognized before one can attempt to measure and record the true periodic cost of convertible bonds.

Third, given the present framework of accounting, the method recommended by the American Accounting Association probably does the best job of recording the full cost of convertible bonds. The timing of cost recognition leaves much to be desired from the standpoint of current evaluation of past actions, but the objectivity of the measure is unquestioned.

Finally, since the company is obviously issuing the convertible as a delayed issue of common stock, it is useful to estimate the cost of common stock equity in order to compare that cost with the cost of the convertible bond. The cost of equity—the yield investors want when they purchase the stock—cannot be measured exactly. The best that can be done is to estimate the cost from a model of the assumed behavior of the marginal investor. No ideal model exists, but there is apparent substantial agreement that the rate of cost of common equity can be approximated by adding the current dividend yield to a forecasted rate of growth.[4] In the example cited, this would yield an estimated cost of 22 per cent ($.84/$42) + 20 per cent. Comparison of this figure to the before- or after-tax rates of cost given in the notes to Table II shows that, if share prices rise as expected, the cost of convertible bonds ap-

---

1968 and called them for conversion in 1969, and Memorex, which issued convertibles in 1970. Burroughs stock price had a geometric mean rate of growth of better than 22 per cent from 1959 to 1969 and Memorex had a geometric mean rate of growth of better than 50 per cent based on average for the year prices from 1965 through 1969.

[4]Derived from a model which projects dividends into perpetuity. See M. J. Gordon and E. Shapiro, "Capital Equipment Analysis: The Required Rate of Profit," *Management Science* (October 1956), pp. 104–106.

proaches the cost of equity in the first few years that the convertible is outstanding. It should be noted that, although the model used is based upon some restrictive assumptions, particularly an assumption of perpetual growth at a constant rate, it at least allows for future growth and thus it is superior to simple earnings yield models. Models assuming different and changing patterns of growth could be used, and, while the numbers change, the difficult problem of estimation still exists.[5] Furthermore, the model shows that as managers work to enhance the value of the firm to its owners, the common stockholders, they also work in the interest of convertible bond-holders who have options on common shares.

CONCLUSIONS

A corporation planning to issue either convertible bonds or bonds with detachable warrants is looking at similar financing alternatives but alternatives which differ in important respects. They differ with respect to federal income taxation, corporate reporting standards and investor adaptability. Taxing authorities and the accounting profession might move to eliminate some of these differences, but investor adaptations cannot be conformed exactly.

Bonds with warrants are issued as a package, but the bonds and warrants trade separately. The bonds have a definite maturity date and value that must be met by the issuer regardless of what happens to the warrants, and the warrants provide a low-cost call on stock

[5]See James C. T. Mao, *Quantitative Analysis of Financial Decisions* (Toronto: Collier-Macmillan Canada Ltd., 1969), pp. 399–406.

for investors who do not want the bonds. Convertible bonds, on the other hand, are unitary in nature, and their life and terminal value more often depend upon share prices than upon the full term and principal value of the bonds. The joint nature of convertibles, in that the debt does not have a separable existence from the option, causes the essential problem in their valuation. Estimates of value of the joint components, based on assumptions about the price a corporation could obtain by issuing bonds without a conversion feature, can be made. Indeed, for certain tax purposes they must be made. But such estimates are artificial because they view convertibles as essentially debt and assume a life and terminal value that are likely to be irrelevant. It is because of legal relationships, not financial realities, that the debt features of convertibles are given priority in the process of valuation. When financial planning is given first rank, the equity features of convertibles become primarily important and typical joint valuation problem emerges. As with all joint cost problems, it is only possible to measure the inseparable components in an artificial sense; the best measure of the full cost of convertibles is obtained by viewing them as a whole, not an aggregation of separable parts. This measure of cost involves expectations and includes an opportunity cost element because the firm forgoes issuing the shares reserved for the conversion option at the price obtainable for the shares when the conversion option is exercised. The expected full cost is relevant to the decision to issue convertible bonds, but, in the interest of objectivity, current accounting principles do not permit recording the full cost of stockholder equity funds whether these funds are obtained by issuing stock or options to buy stock.

While it is debatable whether costs relevant for decision making (not only decisions whether or not to issue particular types of securities) should be included in external financial statements, it seems clear that accounting principles should not require reporting a seemingly objective measure of cost derived from an attempt to equate unequals. Until accounting principles require or permit more expectational data to be included in published financial statements, current practice or the method recommended by the American Accounting Association are the best alternatives for recording the life cycle of convertible bonds.

A SYNOPSIS OF APB OPINION NO. 21
AN EXPLANATION OF THE PROVISIONS OF THE APB OPINION ON INTEREST ON RECEIVABLES AND PAYABLES.

PAUL A. PACTER

Accounting Principles Board Opinion No. 21, "Interest on Receivables and Payables," has suffered from what the public relations people would call a bad press.

It is not—despite what one hears said every once in a while—pro forma accounting. The Opinion merely clarifies and refines existing principles of historical cost accounting. It properly puts substance over form in accounting for a type of transaction where, too often in the past, form had prevailed.

At several places in the Opinion, the APB reiterates a presumption that the rate of interest explicitly stipulated by the parties to an arm's-length trasaction represents the appropriate measure of compensation to a lender for the use of his funds. Only

where this presumption is overcome by contradictory facts in a particular situation would some other rate of interest be used in recording the transaction.

And even then, *imputation* of interest is clearly a last resort under the Opinion. If there is no interest stated by the parties to a note receivable or payable, or if the stated rate is clearly unreasonable in the circumstances, it is often possible to ascertain the unstated rate of interest *implicit* in the transaction, in which case *no* additional interest would be imputed. Only when this is impossible would interest be imputed.

Another point seems to be misunderstood: Opinion No. 21 does *not* require imputation of interest on cash loans. In fact, it prohibits imputation on notes received or issued solely for cash.

This article is an attempt to explain the provisions of the Opinion. It discusses the types of receivables and payables to which the Opinion does and does not apply, and it explains the procedures for recording receivables and payables, and any related discount or premium, in accordance with the Opinion.

A reader of this article is presumed to have a basic understanding of the concept of present value such as can be obtained by perusal, for an hour or so, of a modern intermediate or advanced level accounting principles textbook or a book on business mathematics.

The examples which are presented require the availability of present value tables. Tables I and II show, respectively, "Present Value of $1" and "Present Value of an Annuity of $1 in Arrears"[1] for 1 to 50 periods and for ½ per cent to 15 per cent interest rates. Of course, more detailed present value tables than those in Tables I and II are available which give discount factors for interest rates to the nearest eighth or sixteenth of 1 per cent. Use of such tables would eliminate the need for, and inaccuracies of, interpolation.

APPLICABILITY

The principles discussed in Opinion No. 21 should be applied to *all* receivables or payables which represent contractual *rights to receive money* or *obligations to pay money* on *fixed or determinable dates,* whether or not there is any stated provision for interest.

Certain exceptions will be mentioned below.

Notice that the Opinion does *not* apply to receivables or payables which will be settled in property, goods or services, rather than in money. *Nor* does it apply to receivables or payables which are collectible or payable on demand, or at some indeterminate future date.

Examples of the types of receivables and payables to which the Opinion applies include:

1. Notes, both secured and unsecured.
2. Debentures.
3. Bonds.
4. Mortgage notes.
5. Equipment obligations.
6. Certain accounts receivable and payable.

The following types of receivables and payables are specifically *excepted* from the provisions of Opinion No. 21:

1. Receivables or payables arising from transactions with customers or suppliers in the normal course of business which are due on customary trade terms not exceeding approximately one year.
2. Amounts which do not require repayment in cash, but rather will be applied to the purchase price of property, goods or services—for example, deposits or progress payments on construction contracts, advance payments for raw materials, advances to encourage exploration in the extractive industries.
3. Amounts intended to provide security for one party to an agreement—such as security deposits and retainages on contracts.
4. The customary cash lending activities and demand or savings deposit activities of financial institutions whose primary business is lending money.
5. Transactions where interest rates are affected by tax attributes or legal restrictions prescribed by a governmental agency—for example, industrial revenue bonds, tax-exempt obligations, government-guaranteed obligations, income tax settlements.
6. Transactions between parent and sub-

---

[1]An annuity is a series of equal payments made at equally spaced intervals of time. If the equal payments are made at the *end* of each period, it is called an "annuity in arrears." If the equal payments are made at the beginning of each period, it is known as an "annuity in advance."

sidiary companies and between subsidiaries of a common parent.

7. Contractual or other obligations assumed in connection with sales of property, goods or services—for example, a warranty for product performance.

8. Convertible debt securities (accounting for which is discussed in APB Opinion No. 14, "Accounting for Convertible Debt and Debt Issued With Stock Purchase Warrants")

TYPES OF RECEIVABLES AND PAYABLES

The Opinion classifies receivables and payables—all of which are referred to as "notes"—into three categories and prescribes the appropriate accounting to be used by both the recipient and the issuer for each category.

The classification is according to the nature of the consideration for which they were issued. The three categories are:

1. Notes received or issued solely for cash.
2. Notes received or issued for cash, but with some right or privilege also being exchanged. For example, a corporation may lend a supplier cash which is receivable five years hence with no stated interest, in exchange for which the supplier agrees to make his products available to the lender at lower than prevailing market prices.
3. Notes received or issued in a noncash exchange for property, goods or service.

The appropriate accounting for each type will be examined.

NOTE EXCHANGED SOLELY FOR CASH

When a note is received or issued solely for cash, and no other right or privilege is ex-

changed, the note should be recorded at its face amount, and any difference between the face amount and the cash proceeds exchanged should be recorded as premium or discount on the note. The interest factor for that note is presumed to be the stated interest plus or minus amortization of the recorded premium or discount. No additional interest should be imputed. The premium or discount should be amortized as interest income or expense over the life of the note in such a way as to result in a constant rate of interest when applied to the net amount outstanding at the beginning of any given period (face amount of the note plus or minus premium or discount). This is the "interest method."

To illustrate, assume that X borrows $1,000 cash from Y and agrees to repay the $1,000 with no interest five years in the future. X would record a liability of $1,000. No discount on the loan would be recorded. No interest expense would be recognized by X during the five-year period because none was provided for by the parties to the transaction. Similarly, Y would have a $1,000 receivable with no related discount and no interest earned over the five-year period.

If, however, X borrows $600 from Y and agrees to repay $1,000 five years later, the parties would record the note at its present value of $600, the amount of cash exchanged, and recognize discount on the note in the amount of $400. Over the five years the $400 discount would be amortized—as interest expense to X and as interest income to Y—using the interest method, as illustrated below. No additional interest expense or income would be imputed.

In order to amortize the $400 discount by the interest method, a determination must be made of that rate of interest which will exactly equate $1,000 to be paid five years hence with $600 today. The *discount factor* by which the $1,000 is multiplied to

Table I Present Value of $1/P= (1 = i)^{-n}$

Periods	½%	1%	2%	3%	4%	5%	6%	7%
1	0.9950 2488	0.9900 9901	0.9803 9216	0.9708 7379	0.9615 3846	0.9523 8095	0.9433 9623	0.9345 7944
2	0.9900 7450	0.9802 9605	0.9611 6878	0.9425 9591	0.9245 5621	0.9070 2948	0.8899 9644	0.8734 3873
3	0.9851 4876	0.9705 9015	0.9423 2233	0.9151 4166	0.8889 9636	0.8638 3760	0.8396 1928	0.8162 9788
4	0.9802 4752	0.9609 8034	0.9238 4543	0.8884 8705	0.8548 0419	0.8227 0247	0.7920 9366	0.7628 9521
5	0.9753 7067	0.95 4 6569	0.9057 3081	0.8626 0878	0.8219 2711	0.7835 2617	0.7472 5817	0.7129 8618
6	0.9705 1808	0.9420 4524	0.8879 7138	0.8374 8426	0.7903 1453	0.7462 1540	0.7049 6054	0.6663 4222
7	0.9656 8963	0.9327 1805	0.8705 6018	0.8130 9151	0.7599 1781	0.7106 8133	0.6650 5711	0.6227 4974
8	0.9608 8520	0.9234 8322	0.8534 9037	0.7894 0923	0.7306 9021	0.6768 3936	0.6274 1237	0.5820 0910
9	0.9561 0468	0.9143 3982	0.8367 5527	0.7664 1673	0.7025 8674	0.6446 0892	0.5918 9846	0.5439 3374
10	0.9513 4794	0.9052 8695	0.8203 4830	0.7440 9391	0.6755 6417	0.6139 1325	0.5583 9478	0.5083 4929
11	0.9466 1489	0.8963 2372	0.8042 6304	0.7224 2128	0.6495 8093	0.5846 7929	0.5267 8753	0.4750 9280
12	0.9419 0534	0.8874 4923	0.7884 9318	0.7013 7988	0.6245 9705	0.5568 4742	0.4969 6936	0.4440 1196
13	0.9372 1924	0.8786 6260	0.7730 3253	0.6809 5134	0.6005 7409	0.5303 2135	0.4688 3902	0.4149 6445
14	0.9325 5646	0.8699 6297	0.7578 7502	0.6611 1781	0.5774 7508	0.5050 6795	0.4423 0096	0.3878 1724
15	0.9279 1688	0.8613 4947	0.7430 1473	0.6418 6195	0.5552 6450	0.4810 1710	0.4172 6606	0.3624 4602
16	0.9233 0037	0.8528 2126	0.7284 4581	0.6231 6694	0.5339 0818	0.4581 1152	0.3936 4628	0.3387 3460
17	0.9187 0684	0.8443 7749	0.7141 6256	0.6050 1645	0.5133 7325	0.4362 9669	0.3713 6442	0.3165 7439
18	0.9141 3616	0.8360 1731	0.7001 5937	0.5873 9461	0.4936 2812	0.4155 2065	0.3503 4379	0.2958 6392
19	0.9095 8822	0.8277 3992	0.6864 3076	0.5702 8603	0.4746 4242	0.3957 3396	0.3305 1301	0.2765 0832
20	0.9050 6290	0.8195 4447	0.6729 7133	0.5536 7575	0.4563 8695	0.3768 8948	0.3118 0473	0.2584 1900
21	0.9005 6010	0.8114 3017	0.6597 7582	0.5375 4928	0.4388 3360	0.3589 4236	0.2941 5540	0.2415 1309
22	0.8960 7971	0.8033 9621	0.6468 3904	0.5218 9250	0.4219 5539	0.3418 4987	0.2775 0510	0.2257 1317
23	0.8916 2160	0.7954 4179	0.6341 5592	0.5066 9175	0.4057 2633	0.3255 7131	0.2617 9726	0.2109 4688
24	0.8871 8567	0.7875 6613	0.6217 2149	0.4919 3374	0.3901 2147	0.3100 6791	0.2469 7855	0.1971 4662
25	0.8827 7181	0.7797 6844	0.6095 3087	0.4776 0557	0.3751 1680	0.2953 0277	0.2329 9863	0.1842 4918
26	0.8783 7991	0.7720 4796	0.5975 7928	0.4636 9473	0.3606 8923	0.2812 4073	0.2198 1003	0.7121 9549
27	0.8740 0986	0.7644 0392	0.5858 6204	0.4501 8906	0.3468 1657	0.2678 4832	0.2073 6795	0.1609 3037
28	0.8696 6155	0.7568 3557	0.5743 7455	0.4370 7675	0.3334 7747	0.2550 9364	0.1956 3014	0.1504 0221
29	0.8653 3488	0.7493 4215	0.5631 1231	0.4243 4636	0.3206 5141	0.2429 4632	0.1845 5674	0.1405 6282
30	0.8610 2973	0.7419 2292	0.5520 7089	0.4119 8676	0.3083 1867	0.2313 7745	0.1741 1013	0.1313 6712
31	0.8567 4600	0.7345 7715	0.5412 4597	0.3999 8715	0.2964 6026	0.2203 5947	0.1642 5484	0.1227 7301
32	0.8524 8358	0.7273 0411	0.5306 3330	0.3883 3703	0.2850 5794	0.2098 6617	0.1549 5740	0.1147 4113
33	0.8482 4237	0.7201 0307	0.5202 2873	0.3770 2625	0.2740 9417	0.1998 7254	0.1461 8622	0.1072 3470
34	0.8440 2226	0.7129 7334	0.5100 2817	0.3660 4490	0.2635 5209	0.1903 5480	0.1379 1153	0.1002 1934
35	0.8398 2314	0.7050 1420	0.5000 2761	0.3553 8340	0.2534 1547	0.1812 9029	0.1301 6522	0.0936 6294
36	0.8356 4492	0.6989 2495	0.4902 2315	0.3450 3243	0.2436 6872	0.1726 5741	0.1227 4077	0.0875 3546
37	0.8314 8748	0.6920 0490	0.4806 1093	0.3349 8294	0.2342 9685	0.1644 3563	0.1157 9318	0.0818 0884
38	0.8273 5073	0.6851 5337	0.4711 8719	0.3252 2615	0.2252 8543	0.1566 0536	0.1092 3885	0.0764 5686
39	0.8232 3455	0.6783 6967	0.4619 4822	0.3157 5355	0.2166 2061	0.1491 4797	0.1030 5552	0.0714 5501
40	0.8191 3886	0.6716 5314	0.4528 9042	0.3065 5684	0.2082 8904	0.1420 4568	0.0972 2219	0.0667 8038
41	0.8150 6354	0.6650 0311	0.4440 1021	0.2976 2800	0.2002 7793	0.1352 8160	0.0917 1905	0.0624 1157
42	0.8110 0850	0.6584 1892	0.4353 0413	0.2889 5922	0.1925 7493	0.1288 3962	0.0865 2740	0.0583 2857
43	0.8069 7363	0.6518 9992	0.4267 6875	0.2805 4294	0.1851 6820	0.1227 0440	0.0816 2962	0.0545 1268
44	0.8029 5884	0.6454 4546	0.4184 0074	0.2723 7178	0.1780 4635	0.1168 6133	0.0770 0908	0.0509 4643
45	0.7989 6402	0.6390 5492	0.4101 9680	0.2644 3862	0.1711 9841	0.1112 9651	0.0726 5007	0.0476 1349
46	0.7949 8907	0.6327 2764	0.4021 5373	0.2567 3653	0.1646 1386	0.1059 9668	0.0685 3781	0.0444 9859
47	0.7910 3390	0.6264 6301	0.3942 6836	0.2492 5876	0.1582 8256	0.1009 4921	0.0646 5831	0.0415 8747
48	0.7870 9841	0.6202 6041	0.3865 3761	0.2419 9880	0.1521 9476	0.0961 4211	0.0609 9840	0.0388 6679
49	0.7831 8250	0.6141 1921	0.3789 5844	0.2349 5029	0.1463 4112	0.0915 6391	0.0575 4566	0.0363 2410
50	0.7792 8607	0.6080 3882	0.3715 2788	0.2281 0708	0.1407 1262	0.0872 0373	0.0542 8836	0.0339 4776

CHAPTER 8. LONG TERM LIABILITIES

Table I Present Value of $1/P = (1 = i)^{-n}$ (cont.)

8%	9%	10%	11%	12%	13%	14%	15%	Periods
0.925926	0.917431	0.909091	0.900901	0.892857	0.884956	0.877193	0.869565	1
0.857339	0.841680	0.826446	0.811622	0.797194	0.783147	0.769468	0.756144	2
0.793832	0.772183	0.751315	0.731191	0.711780	0.693050	0.674972	0.657516	3
0.735030	0.708425	0.683013	0.658731	0.635518	0.613319	0.592080	0.571753	4
0.680583	0.649931	0.620921	0.593451	0.567427	0.542760	0.519369	0.497177	5
0.630170	0.596267	0.564474	0.534641	0.506631	0.480319	0.455587	0.432328	6
0.583490	0.547034	0.513158	0.481658	0.452349	0.425061	0.399637	0.375937	7
0.540269	0.501866	0.466507	0.433926	0.403883	0.376160	0.350559	0.326902	8
0.500249	0.460428	0.424098	0.390925	0.360610	0.332885	0.307508	0.284262	9
0.463193	0.422411	0.385543	0.352184	0.321973	0.294588	0.269744	0.247185	10
0.428883	0.387533	0.350494	0.317283	0.287476	0.260698	0.236617	0.214943	11
0.397114	0.35535	0.318631	0.285841	0.256675	0.230706	0.207559	0.186907	12
0.637698	0.326179	0.289664	0.257514	0.229174	0.204165	0.182069	0.162528	13
0.340461	0.299246	0.263331	0.231995	0.204620	0.180677	0.159710	0.141329	14
0.315242	0.274538	0.239392	0.209004	0.182696	0.159891	0.140096	0.122894	15
0.291890	0.251870	0.217629	0.188292	0.163122	0.141496	0.122892	0.106865	16
0.270269	0.231073	0.197845	0.169633	0.145644	0.125218	0.107800	0.092926	17
0.250249	0.211994	0.179859	0.152822	0.130040	0.110812	0.094561	0.080805	18
0.231712	0.194490	0.163508	0.137678	0.116107	0.098064	0.082948	0.070265	19
0.214548	0.178431	0.148644	0.124034	0.103667	0.086782	0.072762	0.061100	20
0.198656	0.163698	0.135131	0.111742	0.092560	0.076798	0.063826	0.053131	21
0.183941	0.150182	0.122846	0.100669	0.082643	0.067963	0.055988	0.046201	22
0.170315	0.137781	0.111678	0.090693	0.073788	0.060144	0.049112	0.040174	23
0.157699	0.126405	0.101526	0.081705	0.065882	0.053225	0.043081	0.034934	24
0.146018	0.115968	0.092296	0.073608	0.058823	0.047102	0.037790	0.030378	25
0.135202	0.106393	0.083905	0.066314	0.052521	0.041683	0.033149	0.026415	26
0.125187	0.097608	0.076278	0.059742	0.046894	0.036888	0.029078	0.022970	27
0.115914	0.089548	0.069343	0.053822	0.041869	0.032644	0.025507	0.019974	28
0.107328	0.082155	0.063039	0.048488	0.037383	0.028889	0.022375	0.017369	29
0.099377	0.075371	0.057309	0.043683	0.033378	0.025565	0.019627	0.015103	30
0.092016	0.069148	0.052099	0.039354	0.029802	0.022624	0.017217	0.013133	31
0.085200	0.063438	0.047362	0.035454	0.026609	0.020021	0.015102	0.011420	32
0.078889	0.058200	0.043057	0.031940	0.023758	0.017718	0.013248	0.009931	33
0.073045	0.053395	0.039143	0.028775	0.021212	0.015680	0.011621	0.008635	34
0.067635	0.048986	0.035584	0.025924	0.018940	0.013876	0.010194	0.007509	35
0.062625	0.044941	0.032349	0.023355	0.016910	0.012279	0.008942	0.006529	36
0.057986	0.041231	0.029408	0.021040	0.015098	0.010867	0.007844	0.005678	37
0.053690	0.037826	0.026735	0.018955	0.013481	0.009617	0.006880	0.004937	38
0.049713	0.034703	0.024304	0.017077	0.012036	0.008510	0.006035	0.004293	39
0.046031	0.031838	0.022095	0.015384	0.010747	0.007531	0.005294	0.003733	40
0.042621	0.029209	0.020086	0.013860	0.009595	0.006665	0.004644	0.003246	41
0.039464	0.026797	0.018260	0.012486	0.008567	0.005898	0.004074	0.002823	42
0.036541	0.024584	0.016600	0.011249	0.007649	0.005219	0.003573	0.002455	43
0.033834	0.022555	0.015091	0.010134	0.006830	0.004619	0.003135	0.002134	44
0.031328	0.020692	0.013719	0.009130	0.006098	0.004088	0.002750	0.001856	45
0.029007	0.018984	0.012472	0.008225	0.005445	0.003617	0.002412	0.001614	46
0.026859	0.017416	0.011338	0.007410	0.004861	0.003201	0.002116	0.001403	47
0.024869	0.015978	0.010307	0.006676	0.004340	0.002833	0.001856	0.001220	48
0.023027	0.014659	0.009370	0.006014	0.003875	0.002507	0.001628	0.001061	49
0.021321	0.013449	0.008519	0.005418	0.003460	0.002219	0.001428	0.000923	50

Table II Present Value of an Annuity of $1 in Arrears

$$P = \frac{1 - (1 + i)^{-n}}{i}$$

Periods	½%	1%	2%	3%	4%	5%	6%	7%
1	0.9950 2488	0.9900 9901	0.9803 9216	0.9708 7379	0.9615 3846	0.9523 8095	0.9433 9623	0.9345 7944
2	1.9850 9938	1.9703 9506	1.0415 6094	1.9134 6970	1.8860 9467	1.8594 1043	1.8333 9267	1.8080 1817
3	2.9702 4814	2.9469 8521	2.8838 8327	2.8286 1135	2.7750 9103	2.7232 4803	2.6730 1195	2.6243 1604
4	3.9504 9566	3.9019 6565	3.8077 2870	3.7170 9840	3.6298 9522	3.5459 5050	3.4651 0561	3.3872 1126
5	4.9258 6633	4.8534 3124	4.7134 5951	4.5797 0719	4.4518 2233	4.3294 7667	4.2123 6379	4.1001 9744
6	5.8963 8441	5.7954 7647	5.6014 3089	5.4171 9144	5.2421 3686	5.0756 9206	4.9173 2433	4.7665 3966
7	6.8620 7404	6.7281 9453	6.4719 9107	6.2302 8296	6.0020 5467	5.7863 7340	5.5823 8144	5.3892 8940
8	7.8229 5924	7.6516 7775	7.3254 8144	7.0196 9229	6.7327 4487	6.4632 1276	6.2097 9381	5.9712 9851
9	8.7790 6392	8.5650 1758	8.1622 3671	7.7861 0892	7.4353 3161	7.1078 2168	6.8016 9227	6.5152 3225
10	9.7304 1186	9.4713 0453	8.9825 8501	8.5302 0284	8.1108 9578	7.7217 3493	7.3600 8705	7.0235 8154
11	10.6770 2673	10.36762825	9.7868 4805	9.2526 2411	8.7604 7671	8.3064 1422	7.8868 7458	7.4986 7434
12	11.6189 3207	11.2550 7747	10.5753 4122	9.9540 0399	9.3850 7376	8.8632 5164	8.3838 4394	7.9426 8630
13	12.5561 5131	12.1337 4007	11.3483 7375	10.6349 5533	9.9856 4785	9.3935 7299	8.8526 8296	8.3576 5074
14	13.4887 0777	13.0037 0304	12.1062 4867	11.2960 7314	10.5631 2293	9.8986 4094	9.2949 8393	8.7454 6799
15	14.4166 2465	13.8650 5252	12.8492 6350	11.9379 3509	11.1183 8743	10.3796 5804	9.7122 4899	9.1079 1401
16	15.3399 2502	14.7178 7378	13.5777 0931	12.5611 0203	11.6522 9561	10.8377 6956	10.1058 9527	9.4466 4860
17	16.2586 3185	15.5622 5127	14.2918 7188	13.1661 1847	12.1656 6885	11.2740 6625	10.4772 5969	9.7632 2299
18	17.1727 6802	16.3982 6858	14.9920 3125	13.7535 1308	12.6592 9697	11.6895 8690	10.8276 0348	10.0590 8691
19	18.0823 5624	17.2260 0850	15.6784 6201	14.3237 9911	13.1339 3940	12.0853 2086	11.1581 1649	10.3355 9524
20	18.9874 1915	18.0455 5297	16.3514 3334	14.8774 7486	13.5903 2634	12.4622 1034	11.4699 2122	10.5940 1425
21	19.8879 7925	18.8569 8313	17.0112 0916	15.4150 2414	14.0291 5995	12.8211 5271	11.7640 7662	10.8355 2733
22	20.7840 5896	19.6603 7934	17.6580 4820	15.9369 1664	14.4511 1533	13.1630 0258	12.0416 8172	11.0612 4050
23	21.6756 8055	20.4558 2113	18.2922 0412	16.4436 0839	14.8568 4167	13.4885 7388	12.3033 7898	11.2721 8738
24	22.5628 6622	21.2433 8726	18.9139 2560	16.9355 4212	15.2469 3614	13.7986 4179	12.5603 5753	11.4693 3400
25	23.4456 3803	22.0231 5570	19.5234 5647	17. 131 4769	15.6220 7994	14.0939 4457	12.7833 5616	11.6535 8318
26	24.3240 1794	22.7952 0366	20.1210 3576	17.8768 4242	15.9827 6918	14.3751 8530	13.0031 6619	11.8257 7867
27	25.1980 2780	23.5596 0759	20.7068 9780	18.3270 3147	16.3295 8575	14.6430 3362	13.2105 3414	11.9867 0904
28	26.0676 8936	24.3164 4316	21.2812 7236	18.7641 0823	16.6630 6322	14.8981 2726	13.4061 6428	12.1371 1125
29	26.9880 2423	25.0657 8530	21.8443 8466	19.1884 5459	16.9837 1463	15.1410 7358	13.5907 2102	12.2776 7407
30	27.7940 5397	25.8077 0822	22.3964 5555	19.6004 4135	17.2920 3330	15.3724 5103	13.7648 3115	12.4090 4118
31	28.6507 9997	26.5422 8537	22.9377 0152	20.0004 2849	17.5884 9356	15.5928 1050	13.9290 8599	12.5318 1419
32	29.5032 8355	27.2695 8947	23.4683 3482	20.3887 6553	17.8735 5150	15.8026 7667	14.0810 4339	12.6465 5532
33	30.3515 2592	27.9896 9255	23.9835 6355	20.7657 9178	18.1476 4567	16.0025 4921	14.2302 2961	12.7537 9002
34	31.1955 4818	28.7026 6589	24.4985 9172	21.1318 3668	18.4111 9776	16.1929 0401	14.3631 4114	12.8540 0936
35	32.0353 7132	29.4085 8009	24.9986 1933	21.4872 2007	18.6646 1323	16.3741 9429	14.4982 4636	12.9476 7230
36	32.8710 1624	30.1075 0504	25.4888 4248	21.8322 5250	18.9082 8195	16.5468 5171	14.6209 8713	13.0352 0770
37	33.7025 0372	30.7905 0994	25.9604 5341	22.1672 3544	19.1425 7880	16.7112 8734	14.7367 8031	13.1170 1660
38	34.5298 5445	31.4846 6330	26.4406 4060	22.4924 6159	19.3678 6421	16.3678 9271	14.8460 1916	13.1934 7345
39	35.3530 8900	32.1630 3298	26.9025 8883	22.8082 1513	19.5844 8484	17.0170 4067	14.9490 7468	13.2649 2846
40	36.1722 2786	32.8346 8611	27.3554 7924	23.1147 7197	19.7927 7388	17.1590 8635	15.0462 9687	13.3317 0884
41	36.9872 9141	33.4995 8922	27.7994 8945	23.4123 9997	19.9930 5181	17.2943 6796	15.1380 1592	13.3941 2041
42	37.7982 9691	34.1581 0814	28.2347 9358	23.7013 5920	20.1856 2674	17.4232 0758	15.2245 4332	13.4524 4898
43	38.6052 7354	34.8100 0806	28.6615 6233	23.9819 0213	20.3707 9494	17.5459 1198	15.3061 7294	13.5069 6157
44	39.4082 3238	35.4554 5352	29.0799 6307	24.2542 7392	20.5488 4129	17.6627 7331	15.3331 8202	13.5579 0810
45	40.2071 9640	36.0945 0844	29.4901 5987	24.5187 1254	20.7200 3970	17.7740 6082	15.4558 3209	13.6055 2159
46	41.0021 8547	36.7272 3608	29.8923 1360	24.7754 4907	20.8846 5356	17.8800 6650	15.5243 6990	13.6500 2018
47	41.7932 1937	37.3536 9909	30.2865 8196	25.0247 0783	21.0429 3612	17.9810 1571	15.5890 2821	13.6916 0764
48	42.5803 1778	37.9739 5949	30.6731 1957	25.2667 0664	21.1951 3088	18.0771 5782	15.6500 2661	13.7304 7443
49	43.3635 6028	38.5880 7871	31.0520 7801	25.5016 5693	21.3414 7200	18.1687 2173	15.7075 7227	13.7667 9853
50	44.1427 8635	39.1961 1753	31.4236 0589	25.7297 6401	21.4821 8462	18.2559 2546	15.7618 6064	13.8007 4629

Note: To convert to values of an annuity in advance, take one less period and add 1.000000.

Table II Present Value of an Annuity of $1 in Arrears (cont.)

$$P = \frac{1 = (1 + i)^{-n}}{i}$$

8%	9%	10%	11%	12%	13%	14%	15%	Periods
0.925926	0.917431	0.909091	0.900901	0.892857	0.884956	0.877193	0.869565	1
1.783265	1.759111	1.735537	1.712523	1.690051	1.668102	1.646661	1.625709	2
2.577097	2.531295	2.486852	2.443715	2.401831	2.361153	2.321632	2.283225	3
3.312127	3.239720	3.169865	3.102446	3.037349	2.974471	2.913712	2.854978	4
3.992710	3.889651	3.790787	3.695897	3.604776	3.517231	3.433081	3.352155	5
4.622830	4.485919	4.355261	4.230533	4.111407	3.997550	3.888668	3.784483	6
5.206370	5.032953	4.868419	4.712196	4.563757	4.422510	4.238305	4.160420	7
5.746639	5.534819	5.334926	5.146123	4.967640	4.798770	4.628364	4.487322	8
6.246888	5.995247	5.759024	5.537048	5.328250	5.131655	4.946372	4.771584	9
6.710081	6.417658	6.144567	5.889232	5.650223	5.426243	5.216116	5.018769	10
7.138964	6.805191	6.495061	6.206515	5.937699	5.686941	5.452733	5.233712	11
7.536078	7.160725	6.813692	6.492356	6.194374	5.917647	5.660292	5.420619	12
7.903776	7.486904	7.103356	6.749870	6.423548	6.121812	5.842362	5.583147	13
8.244237	7.786150	7.366687	6.981865	6.628168	6.302488	6.002072	5.724476	14
8.559479	8.060688	7.606080	7.190870	6.810864	6.426379	6.142168	5.847370	15
8.851369	8.312558	7.823709	7.379162	6.973986	6.603875	6.265060	5.954235	16
9.121638	8.543631	8.021553	7.548794	7.119630	6.729093	6.372859	6.047161	17
9.371887	8.755625	8.201412	7.701617	7.249670	6.839905	6.467420	6.127966	18
9.603599	8.950115	8.364920	7.839294	7.365777	6.937969	6.550362	6.198231	19
9.818147	9.128546	8.513564	7.963328	7.469444	7.024752	6.623131	6.259331	20
10.016803	9.292244	8.648694	8.075070	7.562003	7.101550	6.686957	6.312462	21
10.200744	9.442425	8.771540	8.175739	7.644646	7.169513	6.742944	6.358663	22
10.371059	9.580207	8.883218	8.266432	7.718434	7.229658	6.792056	6.389837	23
10.528758	9.706612	8.984744	8.348137	7.784316	7.282883	6.835137	6.433771	24
10.674776	9.822580	9.077040	8.421745	7.843139	7.329985	6.872927	6.464149	25
10.809978	9.928972	9.160945	8.488058	7.895660	7.371668	6.906077	6.490564	26
10.935165	10.026580	9.237223	8.547800	7.942554	7.408556	6.935155	6.513534	27
11.051078	10.116123	9.306567	8.601622	7.984423	7.441200	6.960662	6.533508	28
11.158406	10.198283	9.369606	8.650110	8.021806	7.470088	6.983037	6.550877	29
11.257783	10.273654	9.426914	8.693793	8.055184	7.495653	7.002664	6.565980	30
11.349799	10.342802	9.479101	8.733146	8.084986	7.518277	7.019881	6.579113	31
11.434999	10.406240	9.526376	8.768800	8.111594	7.538299	7.034983	6.590533	32
11.513888	10.464441	10.569432	8.800541	8.135352	7.556016	7.048231	6.600453	33
11.586934	10.517835	9.608575	8.829316	8.156564	7.571696	7.059852	6.609099	34
11.654568	10.566821	9.644159	8.855240	8.175504	7.585572	7.070045	6.616607	35
11.717193	10.611763	9.676508	8.878594	8.192414	7.597851	7.078987	6.623137	36
11.775179	10.652993	9.705917	8.899635	8.207513	7.608718	7.086831	6.628815	37
11.828869	10.690820	9.732651	8.918590	8.220993	7.618334	7.093711	6.633752	38
11.878582	10.725523	9.756956	8.935666	8.233030	7.626844	7.088747	6.638045	39
11.924613	10.757360	9.779051	8.951051	8.243777	7.634376	7.105041	6.641778	40
11.967235	10.786569	9.799137	8.964911	8.253372	7.641040	7.109685	6.645025	41
12.006699	10.813366	9.817397	8.977397	8.261939	7.646938	7.113759	6.647848	42
12.043240	10.837950	9.833998	8.988646	8.269589	7.652158	7.117332	6.650302	43
12.077074	10.860505	9.849089	8.998780	8.276418	7.656777	7.120467	6.652437	44
12.108402	10.881197	9.862808	9.007910	8.282516	7.660864	7.123217	6.654293	45
12.137409	10.900181	9.875280	9.016135	8.287961	7.664482	7.125629	6.655907	46
12.164267	10.917597	9.886618	9.023545	8.292822	7.667683	7.127744	6.657310	47
12.189136	10.933575	9.896926	9.030221	8.297163	7.670516	7.129600	6.658531	48
12.212163	10.948234	9.906296	9.036235	8.301038	7.673023	7.131228	6.659592	49
12.233485	10.961683	9.914814	9.041653	8.304498	7.675242	7.132656	6.660515	50

Assumptions:
  $600 cash loan, $1,000 to be repaid five years later.
  Effective interest rate is 10¾ per cent.

	(a) Face Amount of Loan	(b) Unamortized Discount	(c) = (a) − (b) Net Balance	(d) = 10¾% × (c) Interest*
At date of loan	$1,000	$400	$ 600	—
At end of first year	1,000	335	665	$ 65
At end of second year	1,000	264	736	71
At end of third year	1,000	185	815	79
At end of fourth year	1,000	97	903	88
At end of fifth year	1,000	- 0 -	1,000	97
				$400

*Interest expense to X (borrower). Interest income to Y (lender).

get its present value of $600 must be 0.6000 (i.e., $600/$1,000 = 0.6000). Reading across the five-period row in Table I, it can be found that at 10 per cent for five years, $1,000 would have a present value of $621. At 11 per cent for five years, $1,000 would have a present value of $593. Thus the interest rate we are looking for must be between 10 per cent and 11 per cent, and somewhat closer to 11 per cent. By interpolation, the rate can be approximated at 10¾ per cent.

In other words, at 10¾ per cent, $600 today will grow to exactly $1,000 five years from now.

Back to our example: The amount of interest which the parties would recognize in each of the five years, using the interest method, is equal to 10¾ per cent times the net amount of the loan outstanding at the beginning of the year. A schedule showing amortization of the $400 discount and the interest recognized by the interest method is presented in Exhibit A.

By the end of the five-year period, the entire $400 discount will have been amor-

tized, and $400 of interest will have been recognized. Immediately prior to repayment of the loan, the unamortized discount will have been reduced to zero, and therefore the net loan balance will stand at $1,000, as Exhibit A reveals.

It is most important to point out that we have not *imputed* interest in this example. Rather, we have merely accounted for the element of interest which was explicitly recognized in the bargained loan transaction between X and Y. It is clear that the interest element was explicitly recognized by the parties because X borrowed $600 and agreed to repay $1,000 five years in the future, the $400 difference representing interest to be paid by X and earned by Y.

To review, then: When a note is received or issued solely for cash, the note should be recorded at its face amount, and any difference between the face amount and the cash proceeds should be recorded as premium or discount on the note. Interest other than that stated in the note, plus or minus amortization of the recorded premium or discount, should not be imputed.

Assumptions:
 $100,000 five-year interest-free loan.
 Appropriate discount rate is 10 per cent.

	(a) Face Amount of Loan	(b) Unamortized Discount	(c) = (a) × (b) Net Balance	(d) = 10% × (c) Interest*
At date of loan	$100,000	$37,908	$ 62,092	—
At end of first year	100,000	31,699	68,301	$ 6,209
At end of second year	100,000	24,869	75,131	6,830
At end of third year	100,000	17,356	82,644	7,513
At end of fourth year	100,000	9,091	90,909	8,265
At end of fifth year	100,000	- 0 -	100,000	9,091
				$37,908

*Interest income to the lender/purchaser. Interest expense to the borrower/supplier.

NOTE EXCHANGED FOR CASH PLUS SOME RIGHT OR PRIVILEGE

The second category of note receivable or payable discussed in Opinion No. 21 is the note received or issued for cash but with some right or privilege also being exchanged. The right or privilege may be explicitly indicated in the note or in a related agreement between the parties involved, or it may be unstated.

The example suggested in the Opinion is that of a company which lends a supplier cash to be repaid five years later with no stated interest. In exchange, the supplier agrees to make his products available to the lender at lower than prevailing market prices.

In this case, the difference between the present value of the receivable—which would be determined by discounting all future payments on the note at an appropriate rate of interest—and the amount of the cash loaned to the supplier should be regarded as discount on the note. The discount would be accounted for by the lender as interest income over the five-year period. At the same time, the lender would record a deferred charge in an amount equal to the amount of the discount recognized. This deferred charge represents, in effect, a partial prepayment for purchases to be made in the future. The deferred charge would be amortized during the five-year contract term and added to the cost of products purchased.

In a similar manner, the supplier, at the time of the loan, would recognize discount on his note payable and also unearned income in the amount of the discount. Over the five-year period, he would amortize the discount as interest expense, and the unearned income would be recognized as having been earned.

This case is illustrated in Exhibit B, which assumes that the face or maturity amount of the five-year interest-free loan is $100,000. It assumes, further, that the appropriate rate at which to impute interests is 10 per cent. (Later in this article we will get to the question of determining an appropriate interest rate.)

The lender would record the note at its

present value of $62,092. This amount is determined by looking in the five-year row, 10 per cent column, of Table I, which shows that the present value of $1 at 10 per cent for five years is 62.0921 cents. Multiplying this by 100,000, it is found that the present value of $100,000 at 10 per cent for five years is $62,092.

To record the loan, the lender would recognize discount of $37,908, the difference between the $100,000 face amount of the loan and its present value of $62,092. The lender would also record a deferred charge of $37,908. His journal entry would be:

Deferred charge	$ 37,908	
Note receivable	100,000	
Cash		$100,000
Discount on note receivable		37,908

The journal entry to record the receipt of the $100,000 loan by the supplier would mirror the lender's entry.

Cash	$100,000	
Discount on note payable	37,908	
Note payable		$100,000
Unearned income		37,908

Both parties would amortize the discount using the interest method. The amounts of interest recognised are shown in column (d) of Exhibit B.

The lender would amortize the deferred charge as an addition to the cost of the inventory purchased during the five-year period, probably based on the estimated total number of units of inventory to be purchased. Likewise, the supplier would amortize the unearned income as additional earnings over the five years, based on his estimated sales.

In summary, if a note is received or issued for cash, but with some unstated or stated right or privilege also being exchanged, such right or privilege must be given accounting recognition by establishing a note discount or premium account.

NOTE EXCHANGED FOR PROPERTY, GOODS OR SERVICE

The third category of note receivable or payable discussed in Opinion No. 21 is the note received or issued in a noncash exchange for property, goods or service.

The Opinion states that when a receivable or payable arises in an exchange for property, goods or service in a bargained transaction entered into at arm's length, there should be a general presumption that the rate of interest stipulated by the parties to the transaction represents fair and adequate compensation to the lender for the use of the related funds. Therefore, unless this presumption is overcome by the facts of a particular situation, a rate of interest different from the rate stated by the parties should not be imputed.

The presumption that the rate of interest stipulated by the parties is fair and adequate would be overcome by the economic substance of a transaction if any of the following three conditions exist:

1. No interest is stated.
2. The stated rate of interest is unreasonable—that is, the interest rate is clearly inappropriate to the credit standing of the debtor or to the nature and terms of the transactions.
3. The stated face amount of the note is materially different from the current cash sales price for the same or similar property or services or the stated face amount is materially different from the market value of the note at the date of the transaction. If the stated face amount is materially different from the

cash price of the property or the market value of the note, it indicates that the recorded sales price and profit of the seller, and the purchase price and cost of the buyer, are misstated in the year of the transaction, and that the related interest income and interest expense in subsequent periods will also be misstated.

In any of these cases—that is, where interest is not stated, or where the stated rate of interest is unreasonable, or where the face amount of the note is materially different from the cash sales price of the property or from the market value of the note—it is necessary to *recognize interest at a rate other than that stipulated by the parties to the transaction.*

That is, either the interest factor *implicit* in the transaction must be recognized or an interest factor must be *imputed.*

In either situation—finding the implicit interest in imputing interest—it *will* be necessary to recognize interest at other than the stipulated rate. Only where it is impossible to determine the *implicit* interest rate will it become necessary to *impute* interest.

The interest rate implicit in the exchange of a note for property, goods or service may be determined if either the fair value of the property, goods or service at the date of the exchange is known or the market value of the note at the date of the exchange is known. The fair value of the property, goods or service at the date of the exchange would be the current cash sales price for the same or similar items. The market value of the note would be the proceeds which would be received if the note were discounted with an independent lender.

Therefore, even though interest on a note is not stated, or the stated interest is not reasonable, or the face amount of the note is materially different from the cash sales price of the property or from the market value of the note, interest would *not be imputed* if the fair value of the property, goods or service or the market value of the note is known.

Instead, the note would be recorded either at the fair value of the property, goods or service or at the market value of the note, whichever is more clearly determinable. The difference between the face amount of the note and the fair value of the property, goods or service or the market value of the note would be recorded as discount.

This discount will be amortized by the interest method over the term of the note in the following manner:

First, it is necessary to determine that rate of interest which equates all future payments under the note to the net recorded amount of the note, that is, face amount minus any discount. This would be done by use of present value tables. The interest rate so determined is the rate of interest implicit in the transaction.

Second, it is necessary to amortize the discount as interest by applying this implicit rate to the net balance of the note (face amount minus unamortized discount) at the beginning of each period.

To illustrate, assume that on January 1, 1971, X sells property, for which it had paid $500 to Y, receiving in return Y's noninterest-bearing note for $1,000 payable in five years. Assume, further, that X frequently sells similar items of property for a cash sales price of $600.

Ignoring for the moment any income tax implications of this transaction, how would X and Y record the sale?

X, the seller, would record a note receivable at a net amount of $600, which is equivalent to the current cash sales price for similar property, by recording the note at its face amount of $1,000 and the discount of $400. X would therefore recog-

Exhibit C

Assumptions:
  Property with a current cash sales price of $600 is sold for a noninterest-bearing $1,000 note payable in five years.
  Effective interest rate is 10¾ per cent.

	(a) Face Amount of Note	(b) Unamortized Discount	(c) = (a) − (b) Net Balance	(d) = 10¾% × (c) Interest*
January 1, 1971	$1,000	$400	$ 600	—
December 31, 1971	1,000	335	665	$ 65
December 31, 1972	1,000	264	736	71
December 31, 1973	1,000	185	815	79
December 31, 1974	1,000	97	903	88
December 31, 1975	1,000	- 0 -	1,000	97
				$400

*Interest income to X (seller). Interest expense to Y (purchaser).

nize sales revenue of $600, against which it would charge the $500 cost of the property sold, for a $100 gross margin on the sale.

Y, the purchaser, would record a $1,000 note payable and $400 related discount. It would carry the property on its books at its cost of $600.

The journal entry on the books of X, the seller, to record the sale would be:

Note receivable from Y	$1,000	
Discount on note		
receivable		$400
Sales revenue		600

On the books of Y, the purchaser, the following entry would be made:

Property	$600	
Discount on note payable	400	
Note payable to X		$1,000

The $400 discount must be amortized by the interest method. You will probably re-

call from the earlier example of the cash loan that an interest rate of 10¾ per cent equates $1,000 to be paid five years from now with $600 today. Once this rate has been determined, a schedule for amortization of the note discount, such as the one in Exhibit C would be prepared.

X would recognize interest income, and Y would recognize interest expense, by amortizing the discount over the five years in annual amounts shown in column (d) of Exhibit C. These amounts are determined by applying the 10¾ per cent implicit interest rate to the net balance of the note—face minus unamortized discount—at the beginning of each year.

To review: If the fair value of the property, goods or service exchanged for a note is known, or if the market value of the note is known, interest does not have to be imputed. Rather, the note is recorded at either the fair value of the property, goods or service or at the market value of the note, whichever is more clearly determinable, and discount is recognized. This discount is amortized over the life of the note as interest, using the interest method.

If neither the fair value of the property, goods or service nor the market value of the note is determinable, then it will be necessary to calculate the present value of the note by discounting all future payments on the note using an *imputed rate* of interest. This imputed rate should be determined at the time that the note is issued or assumed, and should be based on an interest rate appropriate on that date. Subsequent changes in prevailing interest rates are ignored.

Paragraphs 13 and 14 of the Opinion offer some guidelines for determining an appropriate imputed rate of interest which is then used to determine the present value of a note. This rate will normally be at least equal to the rate at which the issuer of the note could have obtained financing of a similar nature from an independent lender.

Thus, factors which affect the imputed rate include the credit standing of the issuer, the terms for repayment, collateral, restrictive covenants and tax considerations.

The rate of interest at which the issuer of the note could have borrowed should be used to impute interest both on the debtor's books and on the lender's.

The present value of a note is determined by discounting all future payments on the note using an imputed rate of interest. The note would be recorded at its face amount, and any excess of the face amount over the note's present value would be recorded as discount. The discount would be amortized using the interest method.

To illustrate: Assume that on January 1, 1971, X sells property costing $500,000 to Y, for which Y gives X ten $100,000 non-interest bearing notes, one of which is due each December 31 beginning December 31, 1971. If Y had arranged for the financing of its purchase of the property through an independent lender, a 10 per cent rate of interest would have been charged.

(The income tax aspects of this transaction will be illustrated in the next section of this article.)

Using Table II, it can be found that a ten-year 10 per cent annuity of $100,000 per year in arrears has a present value of approximately $614,000. That is, the present value of the ten $100,000 notes issued by Y is $614,000. Accordingly, discount on the notes in the amount of $386,000 would be recognized. This discount would be amortized as interest income to X and as interest expense to Y in amounts as shown in columns (d) of Exhibit D.

The sale would be recorded on X's books as follows:

Notes receivable from Y	$1,000,000
Discount on notes receivable	$386,000
Sales revenue	614,000

X's profit on the sale of the property would be $114,000, the $614,000 present value of the notes minus the $500,000 basis of the property sold.

The purchase would be recorded by Y as follows:

Property	$614,000
Discount on notes payable	386,000
Notes payable to X	$1,000,000

TAX ALLOCATION

The Internal Revenue Code has actually been somewhat ahead of the APB in its requirements for imputation of interest. Code Section 483, and related Regulations

Assumptions:
  Property is sold on January 1, 1971, for ten $100,000 noninterest-bearing notes payable annually at December 31.
  Interest is to be imputed at 10 per cent (in arrears).

	(a) Face Amount of Notes	(b) Unamortized Discount	(c) = (a) − (b) Net Balance	(d) = 10% × (c) Interest*
January 1, 1971	$1,000,000	$386,000	$614,000	—
December 31, 1971	900,000	324,000	576,000	$ 62,000
December 31, 1972	800,000	266,000	534,000	58,000
December 31, 1973	700,000	213,000	487,000	53,000
December 31, 1974	600,000	164,000	436,000	49,000
December 31, 1975	500,000	121,000	379,000	43,000
December 31, 1976	400,000	83,000	317,000	38,000
December 31, 1977	300,000	51,000	249,000	32,000
December 31, 1978	200,000	26,000	174,000	25,000
December 31, 1979	100,000	9,000	91,000	17,000
December 31, 1980	- 0 -	- 0 -	- 0 -	9,000
				$386,000

*Interest income to X (seller). Interest expense to Y (purchaser).

Section 1.483-1, provide that if, in an installment payment contract, interest is not stated at at least 4 per cent per year simple interest, then interest will be imputed at 5 per cent per year compounded semiannually.

Nonetheless, it is quite possible that there may be differences between the recognition for financial reporting purposes and for income tax purposes of discount or premium resulting from the determination of the present value of a note in accordance with Opinion No. 21. Such differences should be treated as timing differences for which APB Opinion No. 11 requires application of comprehensive interperiod income as tax allocation procedures.

The following example illustrates the application of tax allocation to a timing difference related to discount on a note. (This is the same example as the one in the preceding section.)

Assume that on January 1, 1971, X sells property costing $500,000 to Y for ten noninterest-bearing $100,000 notes. One note is due each December 31 beginning December 31, 1971.

Had Y arranged for similar financing of its purchase of the property through a bank, a 10 per cent rate of interest would have been charged.

Therefore, interest will be recognized at 10 per cent for financial reporting purposes.

Let us assume that, for income tax purposes, interest will be imputed at 5 per cent. (The semiannual compounding required by the IRC is being ignored for the sake of simplicity.) This example is summarized in Exhibit E.

Exhibit E

Assumptions

Property is sold on January 1, 1971, for ten $100,000 noninterest-bearing notes payable annually at December 31.

Interest is to be imputed for financial reporting purposes at 10 per cent and for income tax purposes at 5 per cent.

X's profit on the sale of the property:

	Financial Reporting Purposes	Tax Purposes	Timing Difference
Face amount of notes	$1,000,000	$1,000,000	
Discount:			
Financial reporting—10%	386,000		
Tax purposes—5%		228,000	
Present value of notes	614,000	772,000	
Cost of property sold	500,000	500,000	
Profit on sale of property	$ 114,000	$ 272,000	$158,000

X's 1971 income statement would therefore report the profit on the sale of the property, and its tax effect, as follows:

Profit		$ 114,000
Tax thereon at 50%		
Currently payable	$ 136,000	
Deferred	$ (79,000)	57,000
After-tax profit		$ 57,000

Interest income recognized by X:

	(a) Face Amount of Notes	(b) Unamortized Discount	(c) = (a) − (b) Net Balance	(d) = 10% × (c) Interest Income at 10%	(c) Tax Purposes Interest Income at 5%	(f) = (d) − (e) Reversal of Timing Difference
Jan. 1, 1971	$1,000,000	$ 36,000	$614,000	—	—	—
Dec. 31, 1971	900,000	324,000	576,000	$ 62,000	$ 39,000	$ 23,000
Dec. 31, 1972	800,000	266,000	534,000	58,000	35,000	23,000
Dec. 31, 1973	700,000	213,000	487,000	53,000	32,000	21,000
Dec. 31, 1974	600,000	164,000	436,000	49,000	29,000	20,000
Dec. 31, 1975	500,000	121,000	379,000	43,000	25,000	18,000
Dec. 31, 1976	400,000	83,000	317,000	38,000	22,000	16,000
Dec. 31, 1977	300,000	51,000	249,000	32,000	18,000	14,000
Dec. 31, 1978	200,000	26,000	174,000	25,000	14,000	11,000
Dec. 31, 1979	100,000	9,000	91,000	17,000	9,000	8,000
Dec. 31, 1980	- 0 -	- 0 -	- 0 -	9,000	5,000	4,000
				$386,000	$228,000	$158,000

At 10 per cent, the notes have a present value of $614,000. This is obtained by the use of Table II which gives the present values of annuities. Since the notes have a face value of $1 million and a present value of $614,000, discount in the amount of $386,000 would be recognized for financial reporting purposes. X's profit on the sale of the property is $114,000—the excess of the $614,000 present value of the notes over the $500,000 cost of the property.

At 5 per cent, the notes have a present value of $772,000 for tax purposes. Discount recognized for tax purposes is $228,000. The profit on the sale of the property for tax purposes is $272,000. Assuming a 50 per cent tax rate, the tax currently payable is $136,000.

The profit on the sale of the property is $158,000 greater for tax purposes than for financial reporting purposes. However, over the ten years 1971 through 1980, X will recognize for financial reporting purposes $158,000 more interest income than for tax purposes. This is evident because the $386,000 discount recognized for financial reporting purposes is exactly $158,000 more than the $228,000 discount recognized for tax purposes. The $158,000 is, therefore, a timing difference which gives rise to a deferred income tax charge in accordance with APB Opinion No. 11. This deferred income tax is recognized at the time the property is sold and will be reversed because interest income for financial reporting purposes will exceed, by $158,000, interest income reported for tax purposes.

Column (d) in the table at the bottom of Exhibit E shows the interest income which X, the seller of the property, will recognize for financial reporting purposes over the ten years at 10 per cent. Column (c) shows the amount of interest income X will report for income tax purposes. By the end of 1980, the entire $158,000 timing difference will have reversed, as column (f) indicates.

FINANCIAL STATEMENT PRESENTATION AND DISCLOSURE

The Opinion establishes certain requirements for financial requirements for financial statement presentation and disclosure of receivables and payables, as follows:

Discount or premium should be reported in the balance sheet as a direct deduction from or addition to the receivable or payable to which it relates. It should not be classified as a separate deferred charge or deferred credit.

The face amount of the note and the related discount or premium should both be disclosed. Reporting only one net amount is not acceptable.

The effective rate of interest should be disclosed.

Amortization of discount or premium should be reported as interest in the statement of income.

Issue costs related to notes should be reported in the balance sheet as deferred charges.

EFFECTIVE DATE

Opinion No. 21 is effective for transactions entered into on or after October 1, 1971.

It may be applied, in addition, to notes that had previously been recorded in the fiscal year in which October 1, 1971, occurs.

The Board's conclusions as to balance sheet presentation and disclosure—including the reporting of discount or premium as

Straight— higher

an addition to or deduction from the face amount of the related note on the balance sheet—should be applied to all notes reported in financial statements issued after October 1, 1971, regardless of when the notes were originally issued.

QUESTIONS

1. A loss from early extinguishment of debt, if material, should be reported as a component of income *This is extraordinary item*

    a. After cumulative effect of accounting changes and after discontinued operations of a segment of a business

    b. After cumulative effect of accounting changes and before discontinued operations of a segment of a business

    c. Before cumulative effect of accounting changes and after discontinued operations of a segment of a business

    d. Before cumulative effect of accounting changes and before discontinued operations of a segment of a business

2. Unamortized debt discount should be reported on the balance sheet of the issuer as

    a. A direct deduction from the face amount of the debt

    b. A direct deduction from the present value of the debt

    c. A deferred charge ← *Official answer*

    d. Part of the issue costs

3. An example of an item that is not a liability is

    a. Dividends payable in stock

    b. Advances from customers on contracts

    c. Accrued estimated warranty costs

    d. The portion of long-term debt due within one year

4. If bonds are issued initially at a discount and the straight-line method of amortization is used for the discount, interest expense in the earlier years will be

    a. Greater than if the compound interest method were used

    b. The same as if the compound interest method were used

    c. Less than if the compound interest method were used

    d. Less than the amount of the interest payments

5. Cole Manufacturing Corporation issued bonds with a maturity amount of $200,000 and a maturity 10 years from date of issue. If the bonds were issued at a premium, this indicates that

    a. The yield (effective or market) rate of interest exceeded the nominal (coupon) rate

    b. The nominal rate of interest exceeded the yield rate

every time the interest rate goes down, then the market price goes up.

QUESTIONS   415

c. The yield and nominal rates coincided

d. No necessary relationship exists between the two rates

6. "Trading on the equity" (financial leverage) is likely to be a good financial strategy for stockholders of companies having
   a. Cyclical high and low amounts of reported earnings
   b. Steady amounts of reported earnings
   c. Volatile fluctuation in reported earnings over short periods of time
   d. Steadily declining amounts of reporting earnings

7. Theoretically, a bond payable should be reported at the present value of the interest discounted at
   a. Stated interest rate for both principal and interest
   b. Effective interest rate for both principal and interest
   c. Stated interest rate for principal and effective interest rate for interest
   d. Effective interest rate for principal and stated interest rate for interest

8. A threat of expropriation of assets that is reasonably possible, and for which the amount of loss can be reasonably estimated, is an example of a (an)
   a. Loss contingency that should be disclosed, but *not* accrued
   b. Loss contingency that should be accrued and disclosed
   c. Appropriation of retained earnings against which losses should be charged
   d. General business risk which should *not* be accrued and need *not* be disclosed.

9. When it is necessary to impute an interest rate in connection with a note payable, the rate should be
   a. Two-thirds of the prime rate effective at the time the obligation is incurred
   b. The same as that used in the GNP Implicit Price Deflator
   c. At least equal to the rate at which the debtor can obtain financing of a similar nature from other sources at the date of the transaction
   d. As near zero as can be justified

10. Taft Company sells Lee Company a machine, the usual cash price of which is $10,000, in exchange for an $11,800 non-interest-bearing note due three years from date. If Taft records the note at $10,000, the overall effect will be
    a. A correct sales price and correct interest revenue
    b. A correct sales price and understated interest revenue
    c. An understated sales price and understated interest revenue
    d. An overstated interest price and understated interest revenue

11. In the situation described in problem 10, if Lee records the asset and note at $11,800, the overall effect will be
    a. A correct acquisition cost and correct interest expense
    b. A correct acquisition cost and understated interest expense

416

c. An understated acquisition cost and understated interest expense
d. An overstated acquisition cost and understated interest expense

12. How would the amortization of premium on bonds payable affect each of the following?

	Carrying value of bond	Net income
a.	Increase	Decrease
b.	Increase	Increase
c.	Decrease	Decrease
d.	Decrease	Increase

13. For a troubled debt restructuring involving only modification of terms, it is appropriate for a debtor to recognize a gain when the carrying amount of the debt
a. Exceeds the total future cash payments specified by the new terms
b. Is less than the total future cash payments specified by the new terms
c. Exceeds the present value specified by the new terms
d. Is less than the present value specified by the new terms

14. How should the value of warrants attached to a debt security be accounted for?
a. No value assigned
b. A separate portion of paid-in capital
c. An appropriation of retained earnings
d. A liability

15. For the issuer of a 10-year term bond, the amount of amortization using the interest method would increase each year if the bond was sold at a

	Discount	Premium
a.	No	No
b.	Yes	Yes
c.	No	Yes
d.	Yes	No

16. Gain contingencies are usually recognized in the income statement when
a. Realized
b. Occurrence is reasonably possible and the amount can be reasonably estimated
c. Occurrence is probable and the amount can be reasonably estimated
d. The amount can be reasonably estimated

17. An estimated loss from a loss contingency should be accrued when
a. It is probable at the date of the financial statements that a loss has been incurred and the amount of the loss can be reasonably estimated

b. The loss has been incurred by the date of the financial statements and the amount of the loss may be material

c. It is probable at the date of the financial statements that a loss has been incurred and the amount of the loss may be material

d. It is probable that a loss will be incurred in a future period and the amount of the loss can be reasonably estimated

18. When the issuer of bonds exercises the call provision to retire the bonds, the excess of the cash paid over the carrying amount of the bonds should be recognized separately as a (an)

a. Extraordinary loss

b. Extraordinary gain

c. Loss from continuing operations

d. Loss from discontinued operations

19. An investor purchased a bond as a long-term investment on January 1. Annual interest was received on December 31. The investor's interest income for the year would be lowest if the bond was purchased at

a. A discount

b. A premium

c. Par

d. Face value

20. A two-year note was issued in an arm's-length transaction at face value solely for cash at the beginning of this year. There were no other rights or privileges exchanged. The interest rate is specified at 10 percent per year. Principal and interest are payable at maturity. The prevailing rate of interest for a loan of this type is 15 percent per year. What annual interest rate should be used to record interest expense for this year and next year?

	This year	Next year
a.	10 percent	15 percent
b.	10 percent	10 percent
c.	15 percent	10 percent
d.	15 percent	15 percent

21. Carpenter Company is being sued for $2,000,000 for an injury caused to a child as a result of alleged negligence while the child was visiting the Carpenter Company plant in March 1988. The suit was filed in July 1988. Carpenter's lawyer states that it is probable that Carpenter will lose the suit and be found liable for a judgment costing anywhere from $200,000 to $900,000. However, the lawyer states that the most probable judgment is $400,000.

Required:
How should Carpenter report the suit in its 1988 financial statements?

418

Discuss the rationale for your answer. Include in your answer disclosures, if any, that should be made in Carpenter's financial statements or notes.

22. Part *a*. The two basic requirements for the accrual of a loss contingency are supported by several basic concepts of accounting. Three of these concepts are periodicity (time periods), measurement, and objectivity.

Required:

Discuss how the two basic requirements for the accrual of a loss contingency relate to the three concepts listed above.

Part *b*. The following three independent sets of facts relate to (1) the possible accrual or (2) the possible disclosure by other means of a loss contingency.

Situation I

A company offers a one-year warranty for the product that it manufactures. A history of warranty claims has been compiled and the probable amount of claims related to sales for a given period can be determined.

Situation II

Subsequent to the date of a set of financial statements, but prior to the issuance of the financial statements, a company enters into a contract that will probably result in a significant loss to the company. The amount of the loss can be reasonably estimated.

Situation III

A company has adopted a policy of recording self-insurance for any possible losses resulting from injury to others by the company's vehicles. The premium for an insurance policy for the same risk from an independent insurance company would have an annual cost of $2,000. During the period covered by the financial statements, there were no accidents involving the company's vehicles that resulted in injury to others.

Required:

Discuss the accrual of a loss contingency and/or type of disclosure necessary (if any) and the reason(s) why such a disclosure is appropriate for each of the three independent sets of fact above. Complete your response to each situation before proceeding to the next situation.

23. On October 1, 1984, Janine Company sold some of its five-year, $1,000 face value, 12 percent term bonds dated March 1, 1984, at an effective annual interest rate (yield) of 10 percent. Interest is payable semiannually and the first interest payment date is September 1, 1984. Janine uses the interest method of amortization. Bond issue costs were incurred in preparing and selling the bond issue.

On November 1, 1984, Janine sold directly to underwriters, at lump-sum price, $1,000 face value, 9 percent serial bonds dated November 1, 1984, at an effective annual interest rate (yield) of 11 percent. A total of 25 percent of these serial bonds are due on November 1, 1986, a total of 30 percent on November 1, 1988. Interest is payable semiannually and the first interest payment date is May 1, 1985. Janine used the interest method of amortization. Bond issue costs were incurred in preparing and selling the bond issue.

Required:

a. How would the market price of the term bonds and the serial bonds be determined?

b. i. How would all items related to the term bonds, except for bond issue costs, be presented in a balance sheet prepared immediately after the term bond issue was sold?

   ii. How would all items related to the serial bonds, except for bond issue costs, be presented in a balance sheet prepared immediately after the serial bond issue was sold?

c. What alternative methods could be used to account for the bond issue costs for the term bonds in 1984?

d. How would the amount of interest expense for the term bonds and the serial bonds be determined for 1984?

24. Angela Company is a manufacturer of toys. During the year, the following situations arose.

• A safety hazard related to one of its toy products was discovered. It is considered probable that liabilities have been incurred. Based on past experience, a reasonable estimate of the amount of loss can be made.

• One of its small warehouses is located on the bank of a river and could no longer be insured against flood losses. No flood losses have occurred after the date that the insurance became unavailable.

• This year, Angela began promoting a new toy by including a coupon, redeemable for a movie ticket, in each toy's carton. The movie ticket, which cost Angela $2, is purchased in advance and then mailed to the customer when the coupon is received by Angela. Angela estimated, based on past experience, that 60 percent of the coupons would be redeemed. Forty percent of the coupons would be actually redeemed this year, and the remaining 20 percent of the coupons are expected to be redeemed next year.

Required:

a. How should Angela report the safety hazard? Why? Do not discuss deferred income tax implications.

b. How should Angela report the noninsurable flood risk? Why?

c. How should Angela account for the toy promotion campaign in this year?

25. Business transactions often involve the exchange of property, goods, or services for notes or similar instruments that may stipulate no interest rate or an interest rate that varies from prevailing rates.

   a. When a note is exchanged for property, goods, or services, what value should be placed upon the note

     i. If it bears interest at a reasonable rate and is issued in a bargained transaction entered into at arm's length? Explain.

     ii. If it bears no interest and/or is not issued in a bargained transaction entered into at arm's length? Explain.

   b. If the recorded value of a note differs from the face value,

     i. How should the difference be accounted for? Explain.

     ii. How should this difference be presented in the financial statements? Explain.

26. Part *a*. The appropriate method of amortizing a premium or discount on issuance of bonds is the effective interest method.

Required:

     i. What is the effective interest method of amortization and how is it different from and similar to the straight-line method of amortization?

     ii. How is amortization computed using the effective interest method, and why and how do amounts obtained using the effective interest method differ from amounts computed under the straight-line method?

Part *b*. Gains or losses from the early extinguishment of debt that is refunded can theoretically be accounted for in three ways.

     i. Amortized over the life of old debt.

     ii. Amortized over the life of the new debt issue.

     iii. Recognized in the period of extinguishment.

Required:

     i. Discuss the supporting arguments for each of the three theoretic methods of accounting for gains and losses from the early extinguishment of debt.

     ii. Which of the preceding methods is generally accepted and how should the appropriate amount of gain or loss be shown in a company's financial reports.

27. On January 1, 1988, Plywood Homes, Inc., issued 20-year, 4 per cent bonds having a face value of $1,000,000. The interest on the bonds is payable semiannually on June 30 and December 31. The proceeds to the company were $975,000 (i.e., on the day they were issued the bonds had a market value of $975,000). On June 30, 1988, the company's fiscal closing date, when the bonds were being traded at 98½, each of the following

amounts was suggested as a possible valuation basis for reporting the bond liability on the balance sheet.

a. $975,625 (proceeds, plus six months' straight-line amortization)

b. $1,000,000 (face value).

c. $1,780,000 (face value plus interest payments).

    i. Distinguish between nominal and effective interest rates.

    ii. Explain the nature of the $25,000 difference between the face value and the market value of the bonds on January 1, 1988.

    iii. Between January 1 and June 30, the market value of the company's bonds increased from $975,000 to $985,000. Explain. Discuss the significance of the increase to the company.

    iv. Give the arguments for and/or against each of the suggested alternatives for reporting the bond liability on the balance sheet.

BIBLIOGRAPHY

Anton, Hector R. "Accounting for Bond Liabilities." *Journal of Accountancy* (September 1956), pp. 53–56.

Bevis, Herman. "Contingencies and Probabilities in Financial Statements." *Journal of Accountancy* (October 1968), pp. 37–41.

Carpenter, Charles G., and Joseph F. Wojdak. "Capitalizing Executory Contracts: A Perspective." *New York CPA* (January 1971), pp. 40–47.

Castellano, Joseph F., and Gerald E. Keyes. "An Application of APB Opinion No. 21." *The Ohio CPA* (Summer 1972), pp. 86–91.

Clancy, Donald K. "What is a Convertible Debenture? A Review of the Literature in the U.S.A." *Abacus* (December 1978), pp. 171–179.

Collier, Boyd, and Curtis Carnes. "Convertible Bonds and Financial Reality." *Management Accounting* (February 1979), pp. 47, 48, 52.

Cramer, Joe J., Jr. "The Nature and Importance of Discounted Present Value in Financial Accounting and Reporting." *The Arthur Andersen Chronicle* (September 1977), pp. 27–39.

Falk, Haim, and Stephen L. Buzby. "What's Missing in Accounting for Convertible Bonds?" *CA Magazine* (July 1978), pp. 40–45.

Ford, Allen. "Should Cost Be Assigned to Conversion Value?" *The Accounting Review* (October 1969), pp. 818–822.

Henderson, M. S. "Nature of Liabilities." *Australian Accountant* (July 1974), pp. 328–330, 333–334.

Hughes, John S. "Toward a Contract Basis of Valuation in Accounting." *The Accounting Review* (October 1978), pp. 882–894.

Imdieke, Leroy F., and Jerry J. Weygandt. "Accounting for that Imputed Discount Factor." *Journal of Accountancy* (June 1970), pp. 54–58.

Jacobsen, Lyle E. "Liabilities and Quasi Liabilities." In Morton Backer, ed. *Modern Accounting Theory.* Englewood Cliffs, N.J.: Prentice-Hall, Inc., 1966. pp. 232–249.

King, Raymond D. "The Effect of Convertible Bond Equity Values on Dilution and Leverage." *The Accounting Review* (July 1984), pp. 419–431.

Kulkarni, Deepak. "The Valuation of Liabilities." *Accounting and Business Research* (Summer 1980), pp. 291–297.

Ma, Ronald, and Malcolm C. Miller. "Conceptualizing the Liability." *Accounting and Business Research* (Autumn 1978), pp. 258–265.

McCullers, Levis D. "An Alternative to APB Opinion No. 14." *Journal of Accounting Research* (Spring 1971), pp. 160–164.

Melcher, Beatrice. *Stockholders' Equity.* New York: American Institute of Certified Public Accountants, 1973.

Meyers, Stephen L. "Accounting for Long Term Notes." *Management Accounting* (July 1973), pp. 49–51.

Miller, Jerry D. "Accounting for Warrants and Convertible Bonds." *Management Accounting* (January 1973), pp. 26–28.

Moonitz, Maurice. "The Changing Concept of Liabilities." *Journal of Accountancy* (May 1960), pp. 41–46.

Savage, Charles L. "Review of APB Opinion No. 28—Early Extinguishment of Debt." *The CPA Journal* (April 1973), pp. 283–285.

Shoenthal, Edward R. "Contingent Legal Liabilities." *The CPA Journal* (March 1976), pp. 30–34.

Sprouse, Robert T. "Accounting for What-You-May-Call-Its." *Journal of Accountancy* (October 1966), pp. 45–53.

Waxman, Robert N. "Review of APB Opinion No. 21—Interest on Receivables and Payables." *The CPA Journal* (August 1972), pp. 627–633.

9

INCOME
TAX
ALLOCATION

Financial reports are prepared with certain objectives in mind, and these objectives influence the ultimate form and content of the reports. For example, the objectives of reports prepared for managerial use may differ considerably from those of reports prepared for the Securities and Exchange Commission or other regulatory agencies. Similarly, the objectives of reports prepared for the Internal Revenue Service differ from the objectives of financial statements prepared for investors and other third-party users.

The differing objectives of the Internal Revenue Code and generally accepted accounting principles are the primary causes of differences in the manner income is determined for income tax purposes and financial accounting purposes. That is, the objective of the Internal Revenue Code is to provide revenue for the operation of the government, and on occasion the Code may be used to regulate the economy. This objective differs considerably from the objective of financial statements prepared under generally accepted accounting principles for use by external users such as stockholders and potential investors. These reports are designed to provide financial information intended to be useful in making economic decisions.

The different objectives of the Internal Revenue Code and GAAP may result in income measurement differences. Therefore, the income tax allocation issue revolves around the questions of whether and how to account for the tax effects of differences between taxable income and pretax financial accounting income. Some accountants believe it is inappropriate to give any accounting recognition to the tax effects of these differences. Others believe that recognition is appropriate but disagree on the method to use. There is also disagreement over the appropriate tax rate to use and whether the amounts should be discounted to their

424

present values. Finally, there is a lack of consensus over whether allocation should be applied comprehensively to all differences or only those expected to reverse in the future. We will examine these issues in detail in the following sections.

PERMANENT AND TIMING DIFFERENCES

An objective of financial accounting is the appropriate matching of revenues and related expenses. Therefore, the income tax expense disclosed on the income statement should be based upon the income reported for financial accounting purposes. However, differences between this financial accounting income and taxable income may arise because of (1) permanent differences and (2) timing differences. The generally accepted accounting treatment for permanent and timing differences was established by Accounting Principles Board Opinion No. 11, "Accounting for Income Taxes." This opinion has been slightly modified by several subsequent pronouncements but continues to provide the guidelines for accounting for income taxes in published financial reports.

Permanent differences arise because of federal economic policy or because Congress may wish to alleviate a provision of the tax code that falls too heavily upon one segment of the economy. There are three types of permanent differences.

1. Revenue recognized for financial accounting reporting purposes that is never taxable—for example, interest on municipal bonds and life insurance proceeds payable to a corporation upon the death of an insured employee.
2. Expenses recognized for financial accounting reporting purposes that are never deductible for income tax purposes—for example, life insurance premiums on officers and amortization of goodwill.
3. Income tax deductions that do not qualify as expenses under generally accepted accounting principles—for example, percentage depletion in excess of cost depletion and the special dividend deduction.

Permanent differences may affect either financial accounting income or taxable income, but not both. A corporation that has nontaxable revenue or additional deductions for income tax reporting purposes will report a relatively lower taxable income as compared to pretax financial accounting income than it would have if these items were not present, whereas a corporation with expenses that are not tax deductible will report a relatively higher taxable income.

When the only difference between financial accounting and taxable income is determined to be a permanent difference, the amount of income tax expense is equivalent to the amount of taxes actually paid. Therefore, where permanent differences exist, financial reporting follows the tax treatment.

TIMING DIFFERENCES

Timing differences between taxable and financial accounting income occur either because revenue is recognized in one period for income tax purposes and in a different period for accounting purposes or because expenses are recognized in either an earlier or later period for accounting purposes than for tax purposes.

Timing differences may also be caused by factors other than the differing objectives of income taxation and financial reporting. For example, business managers usually want to recognize all corporate expenses at the earliest possible moment for tax purposes and thereby reduce or postpone the payment of taxes. Therefore, management decisions that are designed to affect the timing of tax payments are a major source of timing differences. When a timing difference occurs, this difference will reverse in some later period. Consequently, in the absence of a subsequent tax rate change, it is presumed that the total amount of taxes will be the same over an extended period of time even though the amount of income tax reported on the financial statement and the income tax return may differ from year to year. Thus, an allocation of income tax expense between periods is necessary for the appropriate matching of revenue and expense. This is termed *interperiod tax allocation.*

According to Accounting Principles Board Opinion No. 11, the amount of income tax expense shown on the financial accounting income statement should be related to the amount of income shown on that statement, whereas the amount of income tax shown on the income tax return is the amount actually payable.[1] The difference between income tax expense and income tax payable results in a deferred debit or a deferred credit. Accounting for this difference has caused considerable controversy among accountants because the deferral must be recorded as either an asset or a liability. The basic question involved is, Does a timing difference create an asset or liability that is consistent with the definition of these elements from Statement of Concepts No. 6?

The FASB maintains that deferred taxes are assets and liabilities. Therefore, it is necessary to determine the amount of financial accounting income that will be taxable either in the current period or in future periods before recording timing differences. Timing differences relate to individual items of revenue and expense and may be classified into four groups. The first two items result in financial accounting income exceeding taxable income in the year the timing difference originates. The third and fourth result in taxable income exceeding financial accounting income in the year the timing difference originates.

1. *Revenues recognized for financial accounting purposes prior to the time they are included in the determination of taxable income.* For example, revenue on

---

[1]Accounting Principles Board Opinion No. 11, ''Accounting for Income Taxes'' (New York: American Institute of Certified Public Accountants, 1967).

installment sales should normally be recognized at the time of sale for financial accounting purposes but is recognized as cash is collected for tax purposes; or when revenue from an investment is recognized under the equity method for financial accounting purposes but in a subsequent period as dividends are received for tax purposes.

2. *Expenses deducted to determine taxable income prior to the time they are reported for financial accounting purposes.* For example, a fixed asset may be depreciated by an accelerated method for tax purposes and by the straight-line method for financial accounting purposes; or interest and taxes on a self-construction project may be deducted as incurred to arrive at taxable income but capitalized as a part of the cost of the fixed asset for financial accounting.

3. *Revenues included in the determination of taxable income prior to their recognition for financial accounting purposes.* For example, rent received in advance is taxable when received but is not reported for financial accounting purposes until the service actually has been provided; or gains on "sale and leasebacks" are taxed at the date of sale, but are reported over the life of the lease contract for financial accounting purposes.

4. *Expenses charged against financial accounting income prior to the time they are allowed as deductions to arrive at taxable income.* For example, product warranty costs should be estimated and recorded as expenses in the year of sale for financial accounting purposes but may be deducted only when actually incurred in the determination of taxable income; or a contingent liability from a pending lawsuit should be expensed for financial accounting purposes if a loss is deemed probable but is not deductible in arriving at taxable income until it is actually paid.

Each of these timing differences requires the use of interperiod income tax allocation procedures in order to properly match income tax expense against accounting income, to properly match taxes payable against taxable income, and to properly recognize deferred income taxes.

As indicated earlier, the purpose of the tax law is to raise revenue for the government and not necessarily to accomplish the best matching of revenues and expenses or any of the other specific external accounting objectives. Therefore, (1) if the Internal Revenue Code and GAAP differ on the time to record revenues and expenses or (2) if the firm chooses to use an accounting practice that results in financial accounting income that is different from the income reported for tax purposes because it wishes to postpone the payment of taxes, generally accepted accounting principles require that the determination of income tax expense be based upon accounting income. The amount recorded as tax expense is based upon financial accounting income, while the amount of income tax payable, as reported in the tax return, is recorded as a liability.

The difference between the amount of income tax expense and the amount of income tax payable is recorded as deferred income tax. Whether this amount is to be recorded as an asset or as a liability depends upon the direction of timing difference. Since this difference is assumed to reverse in later periods, over the long run the income tax expense and income tax payable will normally be the same.

METHODS OF ALLOCATION

The preceding discussion assumed that an income tax timing difference originating in one year will exactly reverse in a subsequent period. However, this may not be a realistic assumption for two reasons.

1. An entity may experience different levels of income between the originating year and reversing year of a timing difference. Therefore, the reversal may be taxed at a different rate than the originating difference because of the graduated tax provisions of the Internal Revenue Code.
2. Congress may change either the tax code or the methods of determining taxable income between the originating and reversing years.

The Accounting Principles Board reviewed these factors and noted that the amount of the timing difference could be determined by one of three procedures: the deferred, liability, or net of tax methods. The first is an income statement oriented method, while the latter two are balance sheet oriented.

The *deferred method* of interperiod income tax allocation is income statement oriented because of its strong emphasis upon the matching concept. Advocates also point out that it avoids any assumption about future tax rates and eliminates the need to make future adjustments to balance sheet accounts for changes in tax rates or levels. Under this method, the amount of tax applicable to current income tax timing differences is calculated on the basis of the tax rates in effect when the differences originate and the amount is not adjusted for any future changes in tax rates. Thus, if accounting income is $1,000 more or less than the tax income, and the tax rate is 46 percent, the amount of deferred tax will be $460 until the timing reversal, irrespective of tax rate changes. The taxes thus determined are deferred currently and allocated to income tax expense of those periods in which the timing differences reverse. Until such time as the reversal occurs, the tax effects of transactions that reduce taxes currently payable are reported as deferred credits and the tax effects of transactions that increase taxes currently payable are reported as deferred debits.

Opponents of the deferred method consider it theoretically unacceptable because the deferred amounts do not qualify as assets or liabilities under the definitions contained in SFAC No. 6. They also argue that the deferred tax accounts are merely suspense accounts employed for the convenience of shifting tax effects between periods.

428   CHAPTER 9: INCOME TAX ALLOCATION

The *liability method* of interperiod income tax allocation is a balance sheet valuation oriented process. Under this method, the amount of tax applicable to current income tax timing differences is calculated on the basis of the tax rates expected to be in effect in the periods in which the timing differences reverse. Furthermore, the initial computation is considered tentative and therefore subject to adjustment if the tax rates or conditions change in the future. This treatment clearly indicates the valuation concept underlying the liability method.

Under the liability method, when the amount reported as income tax expense exceeds the amount of income tax payable, there is a presumption that the firm has an obligation to pay a higher tax in the future. With this presumption, the firm reports a liability for the amount expected to be paid. When the amount reported as income tax expense is less than the amount of income tax payable, there is a presumption that the firm has generated a prepaid tax. Therefore, the firm reports an asset equal to the tax benefit available in future periods.

Critics of the liability method maintain that using expected future tax rates could produce complicated computations and adjustments. They also maintain that there is no current legal obligation to deferred taxes. Rather, the obligation arises from earning taxable income in the future.

The *net of tax* approach considers taxability and tax deductibility as factors in the valuation of individual assets and liabilities. Thus, part of the value of the asset is reduced, apart from any decrease in value attributable to use. This means that accelerated depreciation hastens the value decline, and therefore the tax effects of timing differences should be recognized in the valuation of the particular assets and liabilities. Proponents of the net of tax approach believe that it best reflects the tax attributes of the economic value of the related assets and liabilities. Opponents criticize it as being overly complex. Moreover, they argue that it hides tax effects in the related asset and liability accounts.

Accounting Principles Board Opinion No. 11 stated a preference for the deferred method over the other two methods. Thus, the amount of deferred tax is established on the basis of the rate in effect when the difference occurs and not when the difference is expected to reverse, or in the valuation of the individual assets and liabilities.[2]

Another issue is whether the amount of deferred taxes should be discounted to reflect the time value of money (from a practical standpoint, discounting could virtually eliminate many noncurrent deferred tax balances with long reversal periods). Those who advocate discounting state that it recognizes the real economic benefits of postponing payment and the opportunity cost of not doing so. Advocates also point out that discounting is required in several circumstances such as leases and pensions. Opponents of discounting point out that deferred tax

---

[2]The FASB recently reexamined this issue and indicated a preference for the liability method. However, this issue was not fully resolved at the time of publication of this text.

payments are in effect interest-free loans to the government and, accordingly, the appropriate discount rate is 0 percent. Therefore, discounting is irrelevant since the discounted and undiscounted amounts would be the same.

Applying the Allocation Method to Timing Differences

Application of the allocation method is relatively simple when only one item caused the timing difference and there is only a single originating or reversing difference in any one year. However, large corporations generally encounter many separate timing originating and reversing differences each year. In these cases two procedures may be used to compute the amount of income tax to defer. They are the gross change method and the net change method.

Both of these methods combine individual timing differences arising from similar types of transactions. For example, all warranty cost timing differences would be grouped. Subsequently, if the *gross change method* is used, the tax effects of originating differences are separated from the tax effects of reversing differences to determine the impact on deferred taxes. Thereafter, the tax effects of originating differences are based upon the current tax rate and the tax effects of reversing differences are based upon the rate in effect in the year the reversing difference originated.

In contrast, under the *net change method* the current tax rate is applied to the difference between group originating and reversing differences. Under this method, reversing timing differences are not based upon the rate in existence in the year of origination.

The gross change method is theoretically preferable under current generally accepted accounting principles because it is similar to the method used to account for individual timing differences. Additionally, the use of the net change method can distort the valuation of the deferred income tax account balance if timing differences occur over a number of years when the company experienced different tax rates.

Once the amount of deferred tax has been established, one remaining accounting issue is the application of the appropriate allocation technique. Allocation may be accomplished by either the partial allocation or comprehensive allocation methods, and the use of either method can affect the extent to which interperiod tax allocation is accomplished.

PARTIAL VS. COMPREHENSIVE ALLOCATION

In the preceding section we discussed the methods of interperiod tax allocation and the measurement of tax effects. In this section we shall review whether accounting for timing differences should be limited only to certain differences (partial allocation) or should apply to all timing differences (comprehensive allocation).

430

Most corporations will encounter many originating and reversing timing differences in any one year. Under *partial allocation* income tax expense is only deferred on the net difference expected to reverse in the future. Therefore, there is a general presumption that the amount of income tax expense for a period should be the amount of income tax actually payable during that period. This concept is essentially an argument for nonallocation based upon the view that the timing differences result in an indefinite postponement of the tax payable; therefore, there is no reason to reflect a greater charge to income tax expense in the current period than is actually paid. For example, in their dissent from Opinion No. 11, Biegler, Davidson, and Queenan argued for partial allocation and asserted,

> *To the extent that comprehensive allocation deviates from accrual of income tax reasonably expected to be paid or recovered, it would result 1) in accounts carried as assets which have no demonstrable value and which are never expected to be realized, 2) in amounts carried as liabilities which are mere contingencies and 3) in corresponding charges or credits to income for contingent amounts.*[3]

Those who argue for partial allocation recognize some exceptions, but these exceptions pertain only to instances where there is some specific and nonrecurring difference in taxable income and accounting income. If these nonrecurring items are considered to have sufficient impact upon the income determination for a period, a deferral of income taxes and an allocation to future periods are considered to be warranted. These circumstances obviously would be unusual and infrequent; therefore, the partial allocation view is essentially, as stated previously, a nonallocation point of view.

Comprehensive allocation views the difference between accounting income and taxable income as a revolving account much like accounts payable. Thus, when a company is growing or maintaining a stable replacement pattern, the total of the deferred income tax account will normally increase or remain constant. The partial allocationists say this practice is really a permanent postponement or an indefinite postponement that is not being reversed. The argument for comprehensive allocation, on the other hand, suggests that while the account may have an increasing balance, the components of that account are constantly changing just as with any other operating account. Thus, as one timing difference reverses, some new timing difference is being generated that causes the account total or balance to increase.

Proponents of comprehensive allocation emphasize the matching of revenue and expense also in determining periodic income. This emphasis suggests that balance sheet amounts result primarily from the income measurement process. For example, Hicks asserted,

[3]Ibid., following par. 67.

Balance sheet items may properly represent amounts which have been tem-
porarily diverted from the stream of a company's transactions and are being
held for use in determining net income in a subsequent year. This is true of
amounts carried forward for inventories, for fixed assets, for deferred re-
search and development expenditures, for items of unearned income. It is also
true for the balance sheet amounts, be they charges or credits, resulting from
income tax allocation.[4]

Tax allocation is therefore considered necessary for a proper matching of revenues and expenses.

Another aspect of this argument is that while the deferred income tax account
will normally have a credit balance, and thus will be reflected as a liability, it is a
special type of liability that has no claimant. The Internal Revenue Service does
not have a claim for that amount and neither does any other creditor. Furthermore, as has been pointed out by Price Waterhouse & Co.,

Not a single source document can be unearthed to support the . . . excess
charges against income (resulting from inter-period tax allocation). The
source documents behind income tax costs are tax returns and canceled
checks. But the . . . deferred tax is over and above what these show. This is
not true of the unchanging or increasing amount of accounts payable in the
balance sheet. These can be backed up by an itemized list of vendor's invoices
showing to whom, and when, each individual amount is payable; and, in
short order, there will be canceled checks to complete the evidence.[5]

The Price Waterhouse position suggests that the deferred amount is not really a
liability at all but rather some unique segregation of owners' equity, since the
total amount will come due only under some unusual circumstances. Such circumstances would require that the company have a less than stable asset replacement policy, be in a declining growth pattern, and at the same time be earning a
profit such that these deferred taxes would begin coming due. That seems to be
an unlikely combination of circumstances.

In 1984, the FASB reviewed the partial vs. comprehensive allocation question. This review was prompted by changes in the tax laws such as accelerated
cost recovery system depreciation and investment tax credit basis reductions.
Such changes have accentuated the problems of accounting for income taxes for
smaller companies. These changes in the tax law have also served to increase
complaints about *standards overload* (discussed in Chapter 1) for many small
businesses. The FASB review revealed that substantially changing the method of
accounting for deferred taxes might cause large fluctuations in reported net
income at a time when tax rates are also changing. Business executives voiced

---

[4]Earnest L. Hicks, "Income Tax Allocation," *Financial Executive* (October 1963), pp. 47–49.
[5]Is Generally Accepted Accounting for Income Taxes Possibly Misleading Investors?" *Price Waterhouse & Co. Review* (New York: 1967), p. 27.

concern that profit fluctuations might have an adverse effect on stock prices, that shareholders might demand higher dividends, and that employees might seek higher wages. The FASB therefore concluded that comprehensive allocation should be used to account for deferred income taxes.

SPECIAL AREAS OF ACCOUNTING FOR INCOME TAXES

At the time APB Opinion No. 11 was issued, the board exempted several types of transactions from its provisions. These areas required additional study because (1) it was unclear whether they should be treated as permanent or timing differences and (2), if they were to be treated as timing differences, what tax rate was applicable. Later, in APB Opinions No. 23 and No. 24, the board discussed four of these special areas of accounting for income taxation that were considered to have unique characteristics: (1) undistributed earnings of subsidiaries, (2) bad debt reserves of savings and loan associations, (3) amounts designated as policyholders' surplus by stock life insurance companies, and (4) investments in subsidiaries carried under the equity method.

The first three of these areas were discussed in Opinion No. 23. In connection with the undistributed earnings of subsidiaries, the board concluded,

Including undistributed earnings of a subsidiary in the pretax accounting income of a parent company, either through consolidation or accounting for the investment by the equity method, may result in a timing difference, in a difference that may not reverse until indefinite future periods, or a combination of both types of differences, depending on the intent and action of the parent company.[6]

As such, undistributed earnings should be accounted for as timing differences unless the presumption that these earnings would be transferred to the parent could be overcome by existing evidence. Such evidence might include specific plans for reinvestment of earnings of the subsidiary.

The board concluded that in accounting for differences between taxable income and pretax accounting income attributable to bad debt reserves of savings and loan associations, consideration should be given to the fact that the difference might not reverse until some indefinite future period and might never reverse. Consequently, the board decided that savings and loan associations "should not provide income taxes on this difference."[7]

This same line of reasoning held for tax deferral or nondeferral for policyholder surplus of stock life insurance companies. The conclusion here again was that the difference might not reverse until indefinite future periods or might

[6]Accounting Principles Board Opinion No. 23, "Accounting for Income Taxes—Special Areas" (New York: American Institute of Certified Public Accountants, 1972), par. 9.
[7]Ibid., par. 23.

not ever reverse. Thus, the recommendation was that "stock life insurance companies should not accrue income taxes on the difference between taxable income and pretax accounting income attributable to amounts designated as policyholders' surplus."[8] In both the case of bad debt reserves of savings and loan associations and policyholder surplus of stock life insurance companies, the decision was to account for these items as permanent differences. Thus, while APB Opinion No. 23 maintained the general principle of comprehensive tax allocation, it did establish the indefinite reversal concept. Subsequently, FASB Interpretation No. 22, "Applicability of Indefinite Reversal Criteria to Timing Differences," explicitly limited the indefinite reversal concepts to the items identified in APB No. 23.

In APB Opinion No. 24, the board addressed the question of accounting for income taxes on investments in common stock accounted for by the equity method. As previously discussed in Chapter 7, when the equity method of accounting for an investment is considered appropriate, the investor company must record as income its relative share of the earnings of the investee. Thus, a timing difference occurs between taxable income and pretax accounting income attributable to earnings of the investee that have been recorded by the investor. The tax effects are related to "probable future distributions of dividends or to anticipated realization on disposal of the investment, and therefore have the essential characteristics of timing differences."[9] In reviewing this question, the board concluded,

> If evidence indicates that an investor's equity in undistributed earnings of an investee will be realized in the form of dividends, an investor should recognize income taxes attributable to the timing differences as if the equity in the earnings of the investee that the investor included in income were remitted as a dividend during the period, recognizing available dividend-received deductions and foreign tax credits. Income taxes of the investor company should also include taxes that would have been withheld if the undistributed earnings had been remitted as dividends. If evidence indicates that an investor's equity in undistributed earnings of an investee will be realized by ultimate disposition of the investment, an investor should accrue income taxes attributable to the timing difference at capital gains or other appropriate rates, recognizing all available deductions and credits.[10]

In summary, it is necessary to defer income taxes on investments in common stock carried under the equity method; the only question remaining is the proper tax rate to apply.

[8]Ibid., par. 28.
[9]Accounting Principles Board Opinion No. 24, "Accounting for Income Taxes" (New York: American Institute of Certified Public Accountants, 1972), par. 7.
[10]Ibid., par. 8.

ACCOUNTING FOR THE INVESTMENT TAX CREDIT

The Internal Revenue Code of 1954 made provision for an investment tax credit; however, it was not until the early 1960s that it was made available to businesses.

The investment tax credit is an example of the federal government using the Internal Revenue Code to regulate the economy. Its purpose is to stimulate investment in assets by corporations by allowing a tax deduction directly from taxes payable for a percentage of any qualified investment in new or used assets. The investment tax credit, perhaps more than any other single item, gave rise to the conflict in accounting as to the proper method to use in recording differences between income taxes actually payable and the amount of tax based on pretax accounting income. In 1962, APB Opinion No. 2[11] focused on the effect of the investment tax credit on the reporting of net income. The discussion in that Opinion indicated that three concepts might be considered in accounting for the substance of the investment credit.

According to the first concept, the investment tax credit is a subsidy to the company from the federal government in the form of a contribution to capital. The second concept is that the investment tax credit is intended to be a tax reduction and, therefore, should be related to the taxable income in the year in which the tax credit arises. The third concept holds that the investment tax credit constitutes a cost reduction of the asset acquired. Thus, the amount to be charged to future periods as an amortization of the cost of the asset should be reduced by the amount of the investment tax credit.

In Opinion No. 2, the APB expressed a preference for the cost reduction concept. It stated that the subsidy is the least rational of the three concepts because it runs counter to the conclusion that the investment tax credit increases the net income of some future accounting period. However, in terms of actual impact, some consider the subsidy concept to be the most appropriate because the purpose of the investment tax credit is to stimulate the economy by giving some particular benefit to a company that makes an investment in assets. This mechanism is similar to a city employing an industrial development commission to give special tax considerations, land, or other resources to a business that locates in the community.

Although the board concluded that the cost reduction method was the most appropriate, some companies and their accounting firms believed that tax reduction was the proper concept to be applied to the investment tax credit. These firms insisted that the credit was given to reduce the tax in a particular period and that this reduction of tax should be included in the accounting records of the period in which the credit was given. For that reason, some companies refused to

---

[11]Accounting Principles Board Opinion No. 2, "Accounting for the Investment Credit" (New York: American Institute of Certified Public Accountants, 1962).

account for the investment tax credit as specified in Opinion No. 2. To complicate the matter further, the Securities and Exchange Commission issued Accounting Series Release No. 96 in 1963, which stated that, because of the differences of opinion among various groups and firms, the commission would accept statements prepared in accordance with either the recommendations of Opinion No. 2 or the reduction of tax method.

Due to the opposition by companies and CPA firms, and the fact that the SEC was willing to accept either the tax reduction or cost reduction method, the APB relented and issued Opinion No. 4.[12] This Opinion concluded that due to the lack of general acceptance of Opinion No. 2, either of the two methods would be acceptable. The APB also stated that it still believed the most appropriate method was to treat the amount of the investment tax credit as a reduction in the cost of the acquired asset.

These two Opinions, with No. 4 being, in effect, a retraction from the position established in No. 2, contributed to a rather shaky beginning for the APB. This controversy indicated a clear recognition that the Accounting Principles Board had no authority except the general acceptance of its Opinions, and that companies, accounting firms, or the SEC might take positions in opposition to its Opinions.

INTRAPERIOD INCOME TAX ALLOCATION

In order to portray properly the relationship between the various revenue and expense items in a period, it may be necessary to allocate the tax expense for that period to the various components of the financial statements Tax allocation within a period to the various components of the financial statements is termed *intraperiod tax allocation*. Income tax expenses may be shown for such items as net income from continuing operations, gains or losses resulting from the disposal of a segment of a business, the gain or loss attributable to that discontinued segment of business, and the cumulative effect of changes in the accounting principles. There is also the possibility of extraordinary gains or losses and, in rare circumstances, adjustments to prior periods' income. Each of these items requires a determination of the income tax expense attributable to its respective portion of net income. The matching concept provides the rationale for intraperiod tax allocation. That is, income tax expense is matched against the various compo-

---

[12]Accounting Principles Board Opinion No. 4 (amending No. 2), ''Accounting for the Investment Credit'' (New York: American Institute of Certified Public Accountants, 1964).

nents of net income in order to "fairly present" the after-tax impact of these items on income.

OPERATING LOSSES

An operating loss occurs when the amount of expense is greater than the revenue for the period. The Internal Revenue Code allows corporations reporting operating losses to carry these losses back and forward to offset other reported taxable income (currently back three years and forward fifteen). The basic accounting question is when to recognize carrybacks and carryforwards in published financial statements. With respect to carrybacks, the APB stated,

> *The tax effect of any realizable loss carrybacks should be recognized in the determination of net income (loss) of the loss periods. The tax loss gives rise to a refund (or claim for refund) of past taxes, which is both measurable and currently realizable; therefore the tax effect of the loss is properly recognizable in the determination of the net income (loss) for the loss period. Appropriate adjustments of existing net deferred tax credits may also be necessary in the loss period.*[13]

Tax carrybacks do not present a very difficult accounting problem, since previously profitable operations allow the tax effect to be reflected in the current period income as a reduction of the current period loss. On the other hand, loss carryforwards raise the following question: Does the carryforward meet the asset definition and related measurement criteria at some time prior to realization? It should be noted that future profitable operations generally are not assured in the period of loss. Unless there is net income in future periods, no benefits will be received from the loss carryforwards, and thus, according to the APB, the "tax benefits of loss carryforwards would not be recognized until they are actually realized, except in unusual circumstances when realization is assured beyond any reasonable doubt at the time when any loss carryforwards arise."[14]

The board further described the circumstances under which realization of a tax benefit from a loss carryforward would appear to be assured beyond any reasonable doubt by establishing that both of the following conditions must exist.

> *(a) the loss results from an identifiable, isolated and nonrecurring cause and the company either has been continuously profitable over a long period or has suffered occasional losses which were more than offset by taxable income in subsequent years, and (b) future taxable income is virtually certain to be*

[13]Op. cit., APB Opinion No. 11, par. 44.
[14]Ibid., par. 45.

large enough to offset the loss carryforward and during the carryforward period.[15]

These conditions have placed both the company and its public accounting firm in the position of guaranteeing future profitable operations when operating losses are recorded as assets. Therefore, few, if any, operating loss carryforwards are recorded as assets by publicly held corporations.

Critics of the assured-beyond-reasonable-doubt criteria believe a relaxed recognition standard would result in better matching and comparability. They also assert that a more relaxed standard would be more consistent with the going-concern assumption and point out that the current standard is among the most stringent under GAAP.

FINANCIAL REPORTING OF INCOME TAXES

The principle of disclosure requires that the amount of deferred income tax be reflected on the balance sheet. The proper placement of this amount depends on whether it has resulted from net taxes to be paid in the future or net taxes prepaid on future income. The FASB also concluded, in its Statement No. 37, that clarification of the classification of deferred income taxes was necessary. This release states,

> *A deferred charge or credit is related to an asset or liability if reduction of the asset or liability causes the timing difference to reverse. A deferred charge or credit that is related to an asset or liability shall be classified as current or noncurrent based on the classification of the related asset or liability. A deferred charge or credit that is not related to an asset or liability because (a) there is no associated asset or liability or (b) reduction of an associated asset or liability will not cause the timing difference to reverse shall be classified based on the expected reversal date of the specific timing difference. Such classification disregards any additional timing difference that may arise and is based on the criteria used for classifying other assets and liabilities.*[16]

The amount of the deferred account should be separated into two categories: the net current amount and the net noncurrent amount. That is, the amount of deferred income tax that is related to current assets or current liabilities should be shown as current, and the remainder should be shown as a long-term item. Additionally, with respect to operating losses, the APB stated,

---

[15]Ibid., par. 47.

[16]Statement of Financial Accounting Standards No. 37, "Balance Sheet Classification of Deferred Income Taxes" (Stamford, Conn.: FASB 1980), par. 4.

Refunds of past taxes or offsets to future taxes arising from recognition of the tax effects of operating loss carrybacks or carryforwards should be classified either as current or noncurrent. The current portion should be determined by the extent to which realization is expected to occur during the current operating cycle.[17]

As discussed previously, the total amount of income tax expense for the period should be categorized on the basis of the items that caused the tax to be changed—normal operations, extraordinary items, disposal of a segment of a business, etc. In addition, there should be a disclosure of the taxes estimated to be currently payable, the tax effect of timing differences, and the tax effect of operating losses. The APB also set forth the following additional disclosures that should be made about income taxation.

1. *amounts of any operating loss carryforwards not recognized in the loss period, together with expiration dates (indicating separately amounts which, upon recognition, would be credited to deferred tax accounts)*
2. *significant amounts of any other unused deductions or credits, together with expiration dates*
3. *reasons for significant variations in the customary relationships between income tax expense and pretax accounting income, if they are not otherwise apparent from the financial statements or from the nature of the entity's business.*[18]

The board further emphasized that the net of tax method discussed previously should not be used for financial statement purposes. All timing differences should be accounted for in the income statement and balance sheet but not included in the valuation of assets or liabilities.

The Securities and Exchange Commission has also adopted new disclosure requirements for corporations issuing publicly traded securities. The disclosures required include (1) a reconciliation of the difference between income and tax expense and the amount of tax expense that would have been reported by applying the normal tax rate to reported income (in other words, what special benefits of the tax code applied to the company?) and (2) the amount of any timing difference that was due to the deferral of investment tax credits. These disclosure requirements are intended to provide information on the effective tax rate of the corporation.

---

[17]Op. cit., APB Opinion No. 11, par. 58.
[18]Ibid., par. 63.

SUMMARY

Interperiod income tax allocation is considered necessary in order to achieve a proper matching of revenues and expenses when there is a timing difference in the recognition of revenues or expenses for accounting and tax purposes. The amount of tax expense reflected on the accounting income statements is to be based upon the amount of accounting income, while the tax payable is related to the amount of taxable income.

The Accounting Principles Board recommended that the amount of deferred tax be calculated by the *deferred method,* which is based upon the tax rate in effect when the timing difference occurs. In addition, the concept of comprehensive allocation, which views the deferred tax account as revolving, was originally recommended by the APB. This portion has recently been reaffirmed by the FASB.

Several areas of accounting for income tax present special problems. In general, the position of the Accounting Principles Board was that if timing differences might not reverse until some indefinite future period, or might never reverse, tax allocation was not appropriate.

Operating loss carrybacks can be recognized in the period of loss, since realization is assured. Loss carryforwards, however, should not be recognized in the period of loss, since realization is not assured except under certain specific circumstances.

In the readings for this chapter, Barry Robbins and Steven Swyers discuss the significance of predicting timing difference reversals and Arthur Wyatt, Richard Dieter, and John Stewart reconsider the accounting implications of tax allocation.

ACCOUNTING FOR INCOME TAXES: PREDICTING TIMING DIFFERENCE REVERSALS

BARRY P. ROBBINS
STEVEN O. SWYERS

Accounting for income taxes—long a subject of controversy—has been a major project of the Financial Accounting Standards Board since 1982. Since the board issued a discussion memorandum on the subject the following summer, more than 400 letters of comment have been received in Stamford.[1]

[1]Financial Accounting Standards Board discussion memorandum, *An Analysis of Issues Relat-*

Public hearings were held in April 1984,[2] and an exposure draft of a proposed statement of financial accounting standards is expected in the fourth quarter of this year. (Although recently the FASB tentatively agreed that some form of comprehensive allocation should be continued, the board may change its position before issuing the draft.)

The most important issues in accounting for income taxes concern accounting for timing differences. Timing differences occur when revenues and expenses are reported in financial statements in a period earlier or later than they are included in taxable income. Timing differences originate in one period and reverse in subsequent periods, at which time their cumulative effect on taxable income and financial reporting pretax income is the same.

The following methods of accounting for the tax effects of timing differences are among the alternatives discussed in the FASB discussion memorandum:

- Taxes payable.
- Partial allocation.
- Comprehensive allocation under the deferred method.
- Comprehensive allocation under the liability method.

The conceptual and pragmatic merits and deficiencies of each method are described in the discussion memorandum, along with the related issue of whether the tax effects of timing differences should be discounted.

SIGNIFICANCE OF PREDICTING REVERSALS

One aspect of timing differences that has received little attention may well be important. Except for the taxes payable approach, all of the alternatives cited, including discounting, are affected by the ability to predict the period in which timing differences will reverse, although the significance of the year of reversal on the measurement of income tax expense and net income varies with each method and the circumstances to which it is applied. Predicting the reversal period of timing differences also will be necessary if the FASB adopts certain recommendations on expanded disclosure of the future effect of timing differences on companies.

The importance of a reliable prediction of the periods in which timing differences will reverse is not a new phenomenon, nor is it occasioned solely by the board's reconsideration of accounting for income taxes. Comprehensive allocation under the deferred method, as currently required by Accounting Principles Board Opinion no. 11[3] and related pronouncements, requires such a prediction when net operating loss and investment tax credit carryforwards are recognized by releasing or drawing down existing deferred tax credits related to timing differences scheduled to reverse during the carryforward period. Prediction of timing difference reversal is also required in estimating the fair value of assets acquired and liabilities assumed in a business combination accounted for as a purchase when those assets and liabilities have different book and tax bases.

Clearly, predictions of timing difference

ed to *Accounting for Income Taxes* (Stamford: FASB, August 1983).

[2]For a report on the hearings, see Bill Liebtag, "FASB Income Tax Hearings Show Diverse Opinions Still Exist on 1960s APB Opinions," J of A, June 1984, pp. 46–54.

[3]Accounting Principles Board Opinion no. 11, *Accounting for Income Taxes* (New York: AICPA, 1967).

reversals are already important, but they will become more so if the FASB adopts partial allocation, comprehensive allocation under the liability method or discounting.

Advocates of partial allocation believe that deferred tax credits should not be established for timing differences of a recurring nature the reversal of which would be offset by new originating timing differences from similar transactions and, accordingly, would not result in actual tax payments. In applying partial allocation, it is necessary to predict the years in which existing timing differences will reverse and whether future originating timing differences will be sufficient to offset all or only part of the tax effects anticipated on such reversals. Income tax expense could be affected if actual reversals in a given year differ from amounts previously estimated.

The liability method, used in conjunction with either comprehensive or partial allocation, attempts to measure the expected future tax effects of the reversal of timing differences. In applying this method, it is necessary to schedule cumulative timing differences by year of expected reversal if (1) different tax rates or statutory limitations on investment tax credit utilization have been enacted for future periods or (2) tax carryforwards exist (to determine whether the carryforwards will expire before all cumulative timing differences reverse). Given a situation in which a future tax rate change has been enacted, it is easy to see how an inaccurate estimate of the period in which a timing difference will reverse could result in a misstatement of income tax expense and the deferred tax liability.

The ability to predict the periods in which timing differences will reverse is likely to have its most significant effect on the measurement of income tax expense and net income if deferred taxes are discounted. Discounting deferred tax liabilities and assets would require that timing differences be scheduled by expected year of reversal or, with respect to tax carryforwards, by expected year of realization. The tax effects of such timing differences would be calculated and then discounted to present value using a separate calculation for each year of expected reversal. Since the discount period is a key factor in measuring present value, an accurate prediction of the period of reversal is of considerable importance.

IMPLEMENTATION CONSIDERATIONS

Because of the potential significance of predicting and scheduling timing difference reversals, more focus is needed on possible implementation problems. The lack of attention paid to these problems in no way reflects the complexities that are involved, nor should preparers, auditors and standard setters be lulled into an ill-founded sense of complacency. Problems will arise. Such problems can be resolved, but their resolution will require guidelines as well as the exercise of judgment.

It may be helpful to think of timing differences as falling into three possible categories, classified according to the difficulty of predicting reversals. For the sake of convenience, we will refer to these categories as 1, 2 and 3.

Category 1. At the low end of the difficulty scale are category 1 timing differences, in which reversal does not depend on future events. The reversal period for these timing differences can be predicted reliably when the timing differences originate. The prediction generally involves only a straightforward mechanical calculation and should present no problems.

Examples of category 1 timing differences include certain installment sales and sale–leaseback transactions. The total profit on installment sales generally is recognized at the time of sale for financial reporting purposes (timing difference origination) and as cash is received for tax purposes (timing difference reversal). If the installment sale contract specifies the dates on which cash payments are due, the reversal period of the timing difference is likewise specified, provided that the possibility of late payments is not a significant concern.

In a sale–leaseback transaction the seller–lessee usually reports any gain on the sale as taxable income at the time of sale. Financial reporting for such transactions is prescribed by FASB Statement no. 28, which requires that the gain or part of it be recognized in income over the term of the leaseback.[4] The reversal of the timing difference follows the specified term of the leaseback, which is known when the timing difference originates.

Category 2. Category 2 timing differences, like those in category 1, are not dependent on future events for their reversal. They are more complex, however, because they originate over several periods and reverse over several periods. Although the reversals follow a predetermined schedule, the association of specific originations with specific reversals requires the selection of an arbitrary ordering (for example, Fifo, Lifo or average). Once an ordering assumption has been made, category 2 timing differences are equivalent to category 1 timing differences; the reversal periods can be predicted reliably by using a straightforward mechanical calculation.

The principal example of a category 2

timing difference is depreciation. Often, depreciation for financial reporting purposes follows the straight-line method, whereas tax depreciation uses the accelerated methods and shortened recovery periods available under the accelerated cost recovery system (ACRS). In these circumstances tax depreciation will exceed book depreciation in the early years of the life of the asset, with book depreciation exceeding tax depreciation in later years.

A similar situation exists, but in reverse, when a lease is classified as a capital lease for financial reporting purposes and as an operating lease for tax purposes. Charges to expense in the financial statements, comprising depreciation and interest, will exceed the tax deduction for rent expense in the early years of the lease; the timing difference will reverse over several years toward the end of the lease term.

Category 3. Surprisingly prevalent, as well as most complex, are category 3 timing differences, the reversal of which does depend on future events. Predicting the periods of reversal may be difficult, and estimates may be subject to change over time. A list of 10 category 3 timing differences is found in exhibit 1. The balance of this article focuses on the timing differences in this category—that is, on the problems involved in predicting reversals; suggestions for resolving these problems are also advanced.

Over the past few years, several public companies have adopted the modified-units-of-production (MUP) method of depreciation, principally for steelmaking machinery and equipment and drilling rigs used in the oil service industry; the method is also widely used by forest products companies. The use of MUP is for financial statement purposes, whereas ACRS or its tax predecessor remains in use for tax purposes. MUP is a hybrid of straight-line and pure units-of-production depreciation.

[4] FASB Statement no. 28, *Accounting for Sales with Leasebacks* (Stamford: FASB, 1979).

The method assigns to a productive asset a range of estimated useful lives in years; the depreciation charge in any given period reflects a single useful life within this range, determined by the production level or usage in the period. The difficulty in predicting timing difference reversals is that future book depreciation depends on future levels of operation; it is even possible that years of timing difference reversal will be followed by years of timing difference origination for the same asset.

Although future operating levels depend in part on external factors, management should use the best forecasts available to project these levels and, hence, future book depreciation. Forecasts may be available from several sources: sales or operating budgets, capital budgets, long-range plans or a variety of external economic projections. The minimum and maximum useful lives inherent in MUP depreciation set limits on the possible incidence of timing difference reversal. As with other depreciation timing differences, an ordering assumption is necessary once future book depreciation has been projected.

Similar timing differences, with similar problems, are found in the extractive industries, in which costs may be capitalized for financial reporting purposes and charged to expense as incurred for tax purposes. An example is intangible drilling costs in the oil and gas industry. Amortization of these costs depends on future operating levels (that is, extraction of oil and gas reserves) as well as on estimates of remaining reserves.

Revenue recognition on long-term construction contracts may produce timing differences the reversal of which similarly depends on future activity levels. The timing difference is created by recognizing revenue and profit on the percentage-of-completion method for books and the completed-contract method for tax; it reverses when the contract is completed. The reliability of projecting contract completion depends on such factors as the size of the project, progress to date, technological difficulty and time limits imposed by the contract. Potential problems with labor and environmental conditions also contribute to the uncertainty. All these factors should be considered when predicting timing difference reversals.

Timing differences 3 through 6 in the exhibit involve changes in the value of assets that are recognized in the financial statements before being recognized in the tax return. The timing differences reverse when the particular asset is disposed of (through sale or otherwise). Inventory obsolescence reserves are recognized for book purposes when the impairment of value becomes probable; they are deductible for tax purposes, however, only when the related inventory is disposed of or offered for sale at the impaired price.

In certain industries (for example, insurance, broker–dealers, investment companies) investments in securities are carried at market value; that is, unrealized appreciation or depreciation is recognized in the financial statements. For tax purposes, however, appreciation or depreciation becomes taxable or deductible only when realized, which occurs when the securities are sold.

APB Opinion no. 18 provides that the equity method be used to account for certain investments in common stock,[5] whereas the tax rules generally require that such investments be accounted for using the cost method. Under the equity method the investor recognizes its proportionate share of investee earnings as they accrue; under the cost method the investor recognizes income only to the extent of dividends. In the common situation in which investee earnings exceed dividend payments, the timing difference will reverse on the sale of the investment.

An arranged exchange transaction involves the sale of an asset and the purchase of another asset, with the transaction structured as a nonmonetary exchange to defer the payment of income taxes. Gain on the sale of the asset generally is recognized in the financial statements at the time of sale.

The basis of the asset sold becomes, for tax purposes, the basis of the asset purchased. If the asset involved is land, the gain is taxable only if and when the purchased land is sold.

The event that triggers a timing difference reversal in these situations—the sale or other disposal of an asset—is primarily a management decision, one that is influenced by external conditions. The estimated period of reversal should be based on management's current intention with respect to the asset. Predicting the period of reversal for obsolete inventory should not be difficult because, presumably, the inventory will be disposed of within a relatively short period of time.

For other assets, however, management's current intention may be to retain the asset for the foreseeable future. This intention is likely in the case of investments accounted for by the equity method and land obtained in an arranged exchange transaction for the construction of a major corporate facility. These situations are similar to the "indefinite reversal" timing differences described in APB Opinion no. 23,[6] and it may be difficult to predict the period of reversal with any reasonable accuracy. The ramifications of this difficulty depend on the reason timing difference reversals must be projected. For examlpe, discounting the tax effects of such timing differences may result in not providing deferred taxes because the discount period could be indefinite.

Another timing difference the reversal of which may not be anticipated in the foreseeable future is the use of the Fifo inventory method for financial reporting and the Lifo method for tax purposes (or

[5]APB Opinion no. 18, *The Equity Method of Accounting for Investments in Common Stock* (New York: AICPA, 1971).

[6]APB Opinion no. 23, *Accounting for Income Taxes—Special Areas* (New York: AICPA), par. 12.

vice versa) when permissible. The timing difference reverses either when liquidations of Lifo inventory layers occur as a result of declines in inventory levels or when current prices decline. Predicting such events, and their extent, may be difficult. Many businesses require a minimum, or base stock, inventory level; it is likely that liquidations below this level would not be expected.

Timing differences 8 through 10 in the exhibit involve liabilities. Warranty expense is recognized in the financial statements coincident with sales recognition for the products expected to give rise to future warranty claims. A tax deduction for warranty costs is available only when the claims are honored. The company's historical experience with the timing of warranty claims and the contractual warranty period should provide a reasonable basis for predicting the timing difference reversal.

Timing differences related to certain stock compensation arrangements are unusual in that the period of reversal may be largely outside management's control, constrained only by the terms of the compensation plan. For example, compensation cost for stock appreciation rights and nonqualified stock options in which the exercise price is less than market value of the stock at the date of grant typically is recognized in the financial statements over the vesting period of the award. The company receives a tax deduction, however, in the year the employee reports ordinary income in his or her tax return—usually the year the right or option is exercised.

Within the limits set by the plan, the exercise date is the result of a unilateral decision made by the employee based on stock market conditions and his personal financial situation. There may be little or no basis for selecting any particular year within the exercise period as being the most likely period of timing difference reversal. In such situations it may be prudent for management to project a reversal year that is the most conservative given the reason timing difference reversals must be projected.

Companies often continue to pay health and life insurance premiums for former employees after their retirement. The accounting for these postemployment benefits is currently on the FASB's agenda. The board's current views, if ultimately adopted in a final standard, would require that such costs be accrued and charged to expense during the service lives of employees who are expected to receive such benefits.[7]

These arrangements generally are not funded, and the tax deduction is taken on a cash basis when the premiums are paid. Since the reversal of this timing difference occurs when premium payments are made, predicting the amounts and timing of these payments is necessary. The calculation is needed to determine the financial statement accrual for the cost of postemployment benefits and, thus, could serve a dual role. An ordering assumption is necessary in predicting timing difference reversal because the book accrual will occur over several years, as will the actual premium payments.

The category 3 timing differences discussed are illustrative only, not all-inclusive. Additional examples include timing differences related to bad-debt reserves, marketable securities carried at the lower of cost or market and loss provisions made in connection with protracted litigation. Differences in measuring pen-

[7]See FASB Preliminary Views, *Employers' Accounting for Pensions and Other Postemployment Benefits* (Stamford: FASB, November 1982).

sion expense for financial reporting versus tax purposes also may become more prevalent when the FASB completes its reconsideration of employers' accounting for pensions.

STILL AN OPEN QUESTION

This discussion of the significance of predicting the periods of timing difference reversal and the implementation problems that may be encountered is not intended to discourage consideration of any of the alternative methods of accounting for income taxes. An informed consideration of these alternatives, however, must acknowledge the practical implications highlighted in this analysis. Predicting timing difference reversals may be more judgmental than conventional wisdom suggests; the dialogue on accounting for income taxes should proceed with this in mind.

TAX ALLOCATION REVISITED

ARTHUR R. WYATT
RICHARD DIETER
JOHN E. STEWART

Income tax allocation remains a subject of debate and controversy. Stated in simple terms, it involves accounting for the tax effects of items of income or expense that enter into the determination of taxable income in different periods from those that are included in financial reporting income (i.e., "timing differences").

BACKGROUND

In January 1982, the FASB announced a major project to reconsider APB Opinion No. 11 (1967), which sets forth the present accounting rules for deferred income taxes. To date, the FASB has issued a Discussion Memorandum (DM) and published certain research undertaken on its behalf. FASB's tentative timetable called for written com-

ments on the DM in January 1984 and a public hearing in April 1984. The issuance of an Exposure Draft of a Standard is scheduled to occur in late 1984 and a final statement sometime in 1985.

Possible solutions identified in the DM vary from doing away with deferred income taxes entirely (i.e., no tax allocation), to providing deferred income taxes for some, but not all timing differences ("partial" allocation), to retaining comprehensive tax allocation (providing deferred income taxes for substantially all timing differences) as required presently by APB Opinion No. 11. In implementing any concept of interperiod tax allocation, the alternatives identified include (a) the deferral method required by APB Opinion No. 11, (b) the liability method, and (c) the net-of-tax method. The DM also considers accounting for investment tax credits, foreign tax and other credits, as well as net operating loss carry-forwards, but these matters will not be dealt with in this article.

WHY RECONSIDER AT THIS TIME?

A decision by the FASB to reconsider the accounting for income taxes has arisen for several reasons. Whether one classifies a particular reason as primary or secondary is largely dependent on one's viewpoint, and can vary based on which constituency one belongs to (user, preparer, academic, or auditor). To the FASB, perhaps the primary reason is the progress the Board has made to date in the development of a conceptual framework for accounting. In Statement of Financial Accounting Concepts (SFAC) No. 3, the Board has called into question the nature and balance-sheet deferred tax credits and charges that result from the application of the tax allocation method prescribed by APB Opinion No. 11.

External events have also brought into question the appropriateness of the accounting presently called for, including the passage of ERTA 1981, and specifically the accelerated cost recovery system. The result of this tax legislation has increased the amount of deferred income taxes on the liability side of corporate balance sheets, and it is presumed that this increase will accelerate. This has added to the confusion among some users and preparers of financial statements about what these growing balances represent economically.

For example, some believe these growing balances will never be "paid" on a net basis, since the *aggregate* balance will not decrease, particularly in an inflationary environment, as long as the company continues to acquire new property to replace older property. Thus, some propose to do away with such deferred income taxes (a partial tax allocation approach). Others would retain these deferred tax balances, but would view them as accounting liabilities that should be adjusted for tax rate changes (a liability method). Some holding this view would also propose that these liabilities for future taxes be discounted for the time value of money (not now permitted). Still others view deferred income tax balances as adjustments of the carrying amount of assets, since the use of an asset's tax deductibility effectively takes up a portion of the asset's cost and, correspondingly, a portion of the company's cost of the asset is recovered through tax reductions (a net-of-tax approach).

A third reason that the Board is reconsidering APB Opinion No. 11 relates to the 1981 Tax Act's impact on smaller companies. Under the Tax Act, asset depreciable lives for financial reporting purposes will frequently differ from lives used for tax purposes. Thus, smaller companies that have in the past used the same book and tax lives are no longer able to follow that approach. As a result, they have to deal with deferred tax accounting for the first time. This is viewed by some as onerous and not meeting the needs of small, privately held companies.

Another reason is that deferred income tax accounting under present authoritative literature has become extremely complex. Growing criticism exists, that the various accounting requirements are inconsistent and that the results of applying the concepts of APB Opinion No. 11 can only be described in terms of a mechanical process. Some believe that the time devoted to coping with the complexities and inconsistencies is not cost-beneficial when compared with the usefulness of the resultant information.

Lastly, the Board is aware that accounting standards setters in countries other than the U.S. have reached conclusions that differ, in some respects significantly, from those presently followed in the United States. The Board has as a consideration in the establishment of accounting principles a need to recognize the international business community. For example, the United Kingdom has in the past few years adopted a form of partial tax allocation in response to changing tax regulations.

At the outset, let us acknowledge that deferred tax balances have, in some cases, become quite significant for individual companies and, with the recent tax law changes, may grow at an accelerated pace. Further, it seems clear that some preparers and users of financial statements are confused over what these growing balances represent. We believe that present financial reporting for the tax effects of timing differences does not contribute to reducing this confusion, because it does not in all cases reflect what deferred tax balances represent economically. Our views expressed in this article recognize the economic effects of business judgments made in tax planning decisions that, if adopted, should serve to reduce confusion among preparers and users and aid in their understanding of the economic consequences of income tax timing differences.

WHETHER TO ALLOCATE

In debating the issue of tax allocation, perhaps the single most important issue is whether tax allocation should be comprehensively based (account for the tax effect of substantially all timing differences) or whether a partial or no tax allocation approach better portrays the economic consequences of the tax effect of timing differences. It is indisputable, in our view, that the factors giving rise to tax timing differences are economic events that produce economic consequences. Therefore the central focus should not be on whether those economic events and related consequences need to be reflected in the finan-

cial reporting process, but rather how best to reflect those consequences.

Comprehensive tax allocation associates the tax consequences of a revenue, expense, gain, or loss with the period in which accounting recognition is given to those items and is consistent with accrual accounting. Accrual accounting associates revenues, expenses, gains, and losses with periods and with each other so as to reflect an enterprise's performance during a period. There is a direct economic relationship between identifiable transactions reflected in the financial statements and the related income tax effects. Each of those transactions has a tax effect as evidenced by the emphasis placed on structuring individual transactions in light of their income tax consequence. The FASB has concluded in SFAC No. 1 that the primary focus of financial reporting is information about earnings and its components; and that information about earnings based on accrual accounting generally provides a better indication of an enterprise's present and continuing ability to generate favorable cash flows than information limited to the financial effects of cash receipts and payments.

We believe the "no allocation" and partial tax allocation approaches are not based on sound premises, often produce results that are not meaningful, and result in mismatching of benefits and costs. For example, as an enterprise claims accelerated tax depreciation, it sacrifices a future benefit and in exchange enjoys a current tax reduction. The "no allocation" and partial allocation approaches may report only one side of the exchange—the reduction in taxes currently payable—but ignore the other side—the cost associated with the giving up of an asset's tax deductibility.

As another example, a significant amount of revenue that is recognized in financial reporting income may be included in taxable income the next period—for instance, a large volume of installment sales. Under a "no allocation" approach, and possibly under a partial allocation notion, the financial statements for the first period would report all the income but none of the tax. For the second period, the financial statements would report all the tax and none of the income. In our view, these results are not useful for making investment and credit decisions.

It is arithmetically inescapable that timing differences reverse—they are not permanent. It also is clear that the reversal of individual timing differences has a cash flow impact—in the form of larger tax payments than those that would be required if the reversals were not occurring. As a result, the cost associated with the tax impact of the originating difference should be reported in the current period. When the timing difference reverses, either the tax impact will be settled in cash, or new transactions arising in the reversal period will tend to offset the reversal by creating a new timing difference that will reverse in a later period. The use of the tax deductibility of a future asset acquisition to offset a reversing difference is the use of a different economic resource that should not be ignored when that timing difference originates. It is just as real a sacrifice as the payment of taxes.

Assets and liabilities result from past or current transactions. We believe it is not appropriate to omit accounting for an event because a "yet to be committed" and "yet to be recorded" future transaction (for example, a future originating timing difference—accelerated depreciation—on a "to be acquired" fixed asset) may nullify it. Anticipating future transactions is more applicable to cash flow and financial planning and analysis than to accounting. Accrual accounting under the historical-cost model addresses the economics of transac-

tions that *have occurred* and the economic consequences of *those transactions*. It is based on a going-concern concept and not on a projection of future transactions (e.g., future growth). A present effect of a timing difference exists based on past events. Future events have their own tax effects that will be reflected and accounted for when they occur. For example, if a future event negates a past liability, that effect should be recognized in the subsequent period and not be anticipated.

The partial allocation approach, in effect, says that when a timing difference arises, it is appropriate to offset it with the tax-reducing capability of the asset that will be acquired in the future when the currently arising timing difference reverses. However, the company does not yet own or control the asset it will acquire in the future. We believe no part of it (including its tax-reducing capability) should be reported as an asset (or liability reduction) before it is acquired.

Tax planning techniques often permit the taxpayer temporarily to shift taxable income among periods. Comprehensive allocation objectively reflects the accounting recognition of economic events and restricts the management of net income. Partial or "no allocation" methods of tax allocation can create a significant temptation to manage income, and, under certain circumstances, can lead to classic abuses. In our view, reported earnings are suspect if one can improve net income by purchasing plant and equipment close to year end (or enter into other tax deferral transactions) in order to reduce the tax bill. Earnings are derived from using assets, not from purchasing them, and accrual basis earnings do not flow from tax planning techniques that temporarily shift tax payments. Under comprehensive allocation, income recognition is based on generally accepted accounting principles, not tax regulations.

WHETHER COMPREHENSIVE INCOME TAX ALLOCATION GIVES RISE TO AN ASSET, LIABILITY, OR A VALUATION ACCOUNT, OR A COMBINATION

In implementing a comprehensive method of tax allocation, various alternative schemes have been proposed. The central issue is the nature of the balance that arises in providing for the tax effect of a timing difference.

Under the liability method, the tax effects of a timing difference are represented as tax liabilities to be paid in the future or prepaid taxes. Under the net-of-tax notion, the tax effects of timing differences represent reductions (''valuation'' accounts as defined in SFAC No. 3 such as accumulated depreciation) to the particular assets or liabilities giving rise to the timing differences. Historically, in the debates on the issue of tax allocation, positions generally were taken on an ''either-or'' basis. In our view, such an approach is not necessarily appropriate because different timing differences do, in fact, have different economic substance. Stated otherwise, different timing differences have different fundamental characteristics such that different methods of reflecting their tax effects are necessary.

Economically, some timing differences give rise to estimated tax assets and liabilities, while the tax effects of other timing differences affect the carrying amount of the asset or liability giving rise to the timing difference (i.e., a net-of-tax display). The economic nature of the timing difference and, therefore, the nature of the item for accounting purposes depends on whether the timing difference impacts taxable income currently or whether its impact on taxable income will occur in a future period. Expressed in a different manner, the key distinguishing feature is whether the expense or revenue item that is the sub-ject of a timing difference is first recognized by inclusion in the tax return in determining taxable income or first recognized in financial reporting income.

This distinction is of key significance because it determines when the tax reduction (cash benefit), tax payment, (cash outflow) or other economic benefit or detriment from the timing difference occurs. If the tax economic benefit or detriment is to occur in future periods based on a current or past transaction (i.e., the item has entered the income statement, but it has not yet been reflected in a tax return—such as gross profit from installment sales), the timing difference gives rise to an estimated tax asset or liability that will be settled in the future. Until settled, the tax effect of this timing difference should be displayed as a separate asset or liability because it involves an estimated future receipt of an economic benefit or a future sacrifice of economic resources resulting from a current or past transaction. The settlement of the tax asset or liability will occur when the item enters the tax return.

Conversely, if the tax economic benefit or detriment from the timing difference has already occurred (i.e., the timing difference has been recognized in a tax return, but is yet to be reflected in the income statement, such as accelerated tax depreciation), the tax effect of the timing difference cannot give rise to an estimated tax asset or liability that will be settled in the future because it has already been received or given up. The tax effect that arises in this situation is not an amount payable (liability) to the government because the transaction giving rise to the tax effect has already appeared in an income tax return. The amount will never appear in a future tax return and, therefore, is never again an element used in determining taxable income. Rather, the tax effect of the timing difference is a measurable present cash inflow or outflow or other current economic benefit or detriment that affects the carrying amount of the asset or liability giving rise to the timing difference.

Two simple examples illustrate this point. If the cost of a $30,000 fixed asset acquired on the last day of *year* one were deducted for tax purposes immediately at a 50 percent tax rate, should the emphasis in tax allocation be on the $15,000 current cash savings (tax benefit) realized today (a recovery of asset cost and the using up of tax deductibility), or on the $15,000 that will be "paid" in the future when the timing difference reverses (assuming depreciation over several future years for financial reporting purposes)? Introducing the variable of a tax rate change helps focus on the matter. If it is known in *year* one that the tax rate will increase to 60 percent in the *second* and subsequent years, should the tax effect of the timing difference still be measured at $15,000, since that is the historic *year* one tax reduction from deducting the cost of the asset, or should the tax effect be measured at $18,000, since that is the amount of tax that will be "payable" when the timing difference reverses?

We believe the appropriate economic effect (and economic consequence) to be accounted for is the $15,000 of current cash savings realized today. Assuming the case of a tax rate increase to 60 percent in the second and subsequent years, the $18,000 is not a liability, but more of an opportunity cost (i.e., the tax benefit that might have been obtained had the asset been deducted for tax purposes in subsequent years). In the case at hand, the tax deductible attribute of the asset itself will produce tax benefits of $15,000—no more and no less—despite the tax rate increase, and that tax effect all occurs in the first year contributing to recovering the cost of the asset.

In effect, the income tax effect is equivalent to a "valuation" or accumulated amortization account similar to accumulated depreciation (a cost allocation process), and represents the using up of a portion of the cost of the tax deductibility of the asset, i.e., the tax-reducing capacity of the asset is consumed (or used up) more rapidly in the tax return than in the financial statements. Thus the appropriate accounting is to reflect the reduction in the future benefits to be derived from the asset by reducing the carrying amount of the asset. Since the cash flows related to the tax benefit are part of the total cash flows derived from the asset, they are integral to the recovery of the cost of the asset. The cost of an asset should be allocated to the periods in which the cost is recovered. The provision for deferred taxes in this case represents an allocation of cost, not a provision for a future liability.

On the other hand, if an installment sale produces financial reporting profits of $30,000 in *year* one that will be included in the tax returns of *years* two and three, this $30,000 has not yet been subjected to tax at the end of *year* one, but will be in subsequent years. In this case (assuming knowledge of the future tax rate change from 50 percent to 60 percent), a liability for future taxes of $18,000 exists at the end of *year* one to be paid in *years* two and three when the gross profit is reported as part of taxable income. A liability is incurred in *year* one generated by the past economic event of consummating a sale for accounting purposes in that year. That liability (future sacrifice of economic resources as a result of a current transaction) should be measured in that year by the best estimate of the amount that will be payable in the year(s) the gross profit is expected to be included in a tax return.

The timing difference classification method outlined earlier is consistent with the FASB's conceptual framework—specifically, its definitions of elements of financial statements in SFAC No. 3.

Take, for example, timing differences that enter the tax return before the income statement. SFAC No. 3 defines expenses as "outflows or other using up of assets. . . ." The using up of tax deductibility by claiming accelerated tax depreciation is the using up of an asset. SFAC No. 3 states that the common characteristic possessed by any asset is its "service potential" or "future economic benefit." Certainly the ability to reduce income taxes in the future is a future economic benefit, and when that benefit has been sacrificed, there has been a using up of a portion of the cost of the asset. SFAC No. 3 indicates that an asset continues as an asset until some circumstance destroys the future benefit or removes the enterprise's ability to attain it. When that occurs, the appropriate accounting as indicated above is to reflect the reduction in the future benefits to be derived from the asset by reducing the carrying amount of the asset.

For timing differences that enter into the determination of financial reporting income before taxable income, the estimated tax asset/liability presentation is consistent with SFAC No. 3. For example, deferred taxes payable for this type of timing difference meet the definition of a liability. Their extinction will involve a future sacrifice of economic benefits as a result of past transactions or events. The past transactions or events are those that generated current period pre-tax accounting income. The future sacrifice of economic benefits will occur in the form either of cash or the use of the tax deductibility of future asset additions (new timing differences) to offset reversing timing differences. Under SFAC No. 3, the existence of a legally enforceable claim is not a prerequisite for an obligation to qualify as a liability, if the future payment of cash or other transfer of assets to settle the obligation is otherwise probable.

Another example in which a timing difference first entering into the determination of financial reporting income before entering into the determination of taxable income is an accrued expense; for example, a product warranty accrual. Its future deductibility represents an asset to the entity—the tax benefit resulting from deducting the item for tax purposes in the future. This asset is of an estimated nature because the item has not yet entered into the determination of taxable income.

MEASURING TAX ALLOCATION EFFECTS

Two issues are involved with measuring the effect of tax allocation: (a) the impact of changing tax rates, and (b) consideration of the time value of money.

TAX RATE CHANGES

We believe the accounting for tax rates and tax rate changes depends on the classification of the timing difference in accordance with the classification method outlined in the previous section. The primary focus should be on the tax rate in effect when the timing difference is, or will be, reflected in determining taxable income.

- The tax effect of timing differences that are accounted for as estimated tax assets or liabilities initially should be estimated based on the tax rate expected to be in effect when the tax asset or liability is settled, i.e., when the timing difference reverses. These estimated tax assets and liabilities should be adjusted in subsequent periods for changes in tax rates not anticipated in initially recording the tax effect to reflect properly the ultimate settlement amount of the estimated tax asset or liability.

The tax effect of timing differences that are accounted for on a net-of-tax basis should be based on the tax rate currently in effect in the period in which the timing differences arise (i.e., the tax rate that the items are subject to in the current period tax return). Obviously, since the tax effect in these circumstances is known (i.e., has already become currently ''collectible'' or payable) and by definition cannot change, no adjustments for subsequent tax rate changes would be appropriate.

DISCOUNTING

In our view, the time value of money has important economic effects that should be reported in financial statements prepared under an historical-cost model. Accordingly, to the extent that the tax effect of a timing difference is a monetary liability or receivable (e.g., an estimated tax asset or liability that represents a future cash flow), the time period between recognition and payment or receipt should be accounted for. Consequently:

- For timing differences in which the item is included in the tax return before the income statement, discounting for the time value of money is not necessary for two reasons:
  1. The tax impact has already become currently ''collectible'' or payable and, therefore, involves no delayed future cash flow of consequence, and
  2. The tax effect is not an estimated liability or an estimated asset.
- For timing differences that result from reflecting the item in the income statement before the tax return, an estimated

tax liability or tax asset is established. Discounting for these types of timing differences is appropriate. This position is consistent with the economics and the nature of the item (an estimated future cash flow).

The combination of our views concerning (a) accounting for the tax effects of certain timing differences as estimated tax assets and liabilities and (b) discounting leads to results that in some cases need further elaboration. In most instances, the reversal of a timing difference is scheduled, predictable, or otherwise reasonably able to be estimated. In more limited circumstances, however, the reversal is not estimated to occur in the foreseeable future. Perhaps the best example is earnings of foreign subsidiaries. In most circumstances, earnings of foreign subsidiaries do not enter the U.S. tax return until remitted, and the company may have decided to reinvest these earnings indefinitely in the subsidiaries' operations. In these instances, a current measurement of the tax effect of the timing difference at a discounted amount approaches zero. As a practical matter, if the discounted amount is not significant, no deferred taxes should be provided.

CONCLUSION

We believe current reconsideration of the existing accounting requirements for tax allocation is appropriate. The method proposed in this article starts with a belief that comprehensive tax allocation is the *only* method that is consistent with accrual accounting and that is objectively determinable. A divergence of views exists on how best to implement and measure comprehensive tax allocation. In the authors' view, different timing differences have different economic consequences and, therefore, different measurement and display approaches are called for. This distinction recognizes fundamental economic differences that lead to a result that is understandable, objectively determined, conceptually sound, and consistent with the FASB's conceptual framework developed to date.

QUESTIONS

1. With respect to the difference between taxable income and pretax accounting income, the tax effect of the undistributed earnings of a subsidiary included in consolidated income should normally be
   a. Accounted for as a timing difference
   b. Accounted for as a permanent difference
   c. Ignored because it must be based on estimates and assumptions
   d. Ignored because it cannot be presumed that all undistributed earnings of a subsidiary will be transferred to the parent company
2. Income tax allocation procedures are not appropriate when
   a. An extraordinary loss will cause the amount of income tax expense to be less than the tax on ordinary net income
   b. An extraordinary gain will cause the amount of income tax expense to be greater than the tax on ordinary net income
   c. Differences between net income for tax purposes and financial reporting occur because tax laws and financial accounting principles do not concur on the items to be recognized as revenue and expense
   d. Differences between net income for tax purposes and financial reporting occur
3. Which of the following would cause a deferred tax expense?
   a. Amortization of goodwill
   b. Use of equity method where undistributed earnings of a 30 percent owned investee are related to probable future dividends
   c. Premiums paid on insurance carried by company (beneficiary) on its officers or employees
   d. Income taxed at capital gains rates
4. Differences between taxable income and pretax accounting income arising from transactions that, under applicable tax laws and regulations, will not be offset by corresponding differences or "turn around" in future periods is a definition of
   a. Permanent differences
   b. Timing differences
   c. Intraperiod tax allocation
   d. Interperiod tax allocation

5. The tax effect of a difference between taxable income and pretax accounting income attributable to losses of a subsidiary is normally recognized for
   a. Neither carrybacks nor carryforwards
   b. Both carrybacks and carryforwards
   c. Carrybacks but not carryforwards
   d. Carryforwards but not carrybacks

6. Which of the following is not affected by tax allocation within a period?
   a. Income before extraordinary items
   b. Extraordinary items
   c. Adjustments of prior periods
   d. Operating revenues

7. Under the comprehensive deferred interperiod method of tax allocation, deferred taxes are determined on the basis of
   a. Tax rates in effect when the timing differences originate without adjustment for subsequent changes in tax rates
   b. Tax rates expected to be in effect when the items giving rise to the timing differences reverse themselves
   c. Net valuations of assets or liabilities
   d. Averages determined on an industry-by-industry basis

8. The accounting recognition of the benefit from a tax loss carryforward in most situations should be reported as
   a. A reduction of the loss in the year of the loss
   b. A prior period adjustment in whichever year the benefit is realized
   c. An extraordinary item in the year in which the benefit is realized
   d. An item on the retained earnings statement, not the income statement

9. Intraperiod income tax allocation arises because
   a. Items included in the determination of taxable income may be presented in different sections of the financial statements
   b. Income taxes must be allocated between current and future periods
   c. Certain revenues and expenses appear in the financial statements either before or after they are included in taxable income
   d. Certain revenues and expenses appear in the financial statements but are excluded from taxable income

10. Assuming no prior period adjustments, would the following affect net income?

	Interperiod income tax allocation	Intraperiod income tax allocation
a.	Yes	Yes
b.	Yes	No
c.	No	Yes
d.	No	No

11. A machine with a 10-year useful life is being depreciated on a straight-line basis for financial statement purposes, and over 5 years for income tax purposes under the accelerated cost recovery system. Assuming that the company is profitable and that there are and have been no other timing differences, the related deferred income taxes would be reported in the balance sheet at the end of the first year of the estimated useful life as a
    a. Current liability
    b. Current asset
    c. Noncurrent liability
    d. Noncurrent asset

12. Smith Corporation owns only 25 percent of the voting stock of Jones Corporation but exercises significant influence over its operating and financial policies. The tax effect of differences between taxable income and pretax accounting income attributable to undistributed earnings of Jones Corporation should be
    a. Accounted for as a timing difference
    b. Accounted for as a permanent difference
    c. Ignored because it must be based on estimates and assumptions
    d. Ignored because Smith holds less than 51 percent of the voting stock of Jones

13. A company has four "deferred income tax" accounts arising from timing differences involving (1) current assets, (2) noncurrent assets, (3) current liabilities, and (4) noncurrent liabilities. The presentation of these four "deferred income tax" accounts in the statement of financial position should be shown as
    a. A single net amount
    b. A net current and a net noncurrent amount
    c. Four accounts with no netting permitted
    d. Valuation adjustments of the related assets and liabilities that gave rise to the deferred tax

14. In preparing financial statements a corporation is expected to follow the practice of comprehensive income tax allocation. At various times three methods of allocation have been used: the deferred method, the liability method, and the net-of-tax method. Discuss the theoretical justification for interperiod income tax allocation. (Do not discuss the theoretical aspects of intraperiod tax allocation.)

15. The following differences enter into the reconciliation of financial net income and taxable income of the A. P. Baxter Corporation for the current year.
    a. Tax depreciation exceeds book depreciation by $30,000.
    b. Estimated warranty costs of $6,000 applicable to the current year's sales have not been paid.

c. Percentage depletion deducted on the tax return exceeds cost depletion by $45,000. *Permanent differences*

d. Unearned rent revenue of $25,000 was deferred on the books but appropriately included in taxable income. *Temporary differences*

e. A book expense of $2,000 for life insurance premiums on officers' lives is not allowed as a deduction on the tax return. *Permanent diff.*

f. Baxter took a $7,000 deduction from expensing research and development cost for tax purposes, but those costs were capitalized for financial reporting. *Temp. differences*

g. Gross profit of $80,000 was excluded from taxable income because Baxter had appropriately elected the installment sale method for tax reporting, but all gross profit from installment sales was recognized at the time of the sale for financial reporting. *Temporary difference*

Consider each reconciling item independently of all others and explain whether each item would enter into the calculation of income taxes to be allocated. For any that are included in the income tax allocation calculation, explain the effect of the item on the current year's income tax expense and the way the amount would be reported on the balance sheet. (Tax allocation calculations are not required.)

16. Eneri Company's president has heard that deferred income taxes can be variously classified in the balance sheet.

Required:
   Identify the conditions under which deferred income taxes would be classified as a noncurrent item in the balance sheet. What justification exists for such classification?

17. Deferred income taxes are required under generally accepted accounting principles. Accounting Principles Board Opinion No. 11 requires the use of the deferred method of comprehensive interperiod tax allocation. Two ways to account for timing differences under the deferred method are (1) the gross change method and (2) the net change method.

Required:
   a. Describe the gross change method.
   b. Describe the net change method.

18. Accounting for income taxes involves various issues, and a thorough understanding of overall terms is necessary.

Required:
Compare and contrast the following terms as they relate to accounting for income taxes.
   a. Permanent and timing differences.
   b. Interperiod and intraperiod tax allocation.

c. Comprehensive and partial income tax allocation.

d. Liability and deferred methods of tax allocation.

e. Tax loss carrybacks and carryforwards.

19. The Primrose Company appropriately uses the deferred method for interperiod income tax allocation.

Primrose reports depreciation expense for certain machinery purchased this year using the accelerated cost recovery system (ACRS) for income tax purposes and the straight-line basis for accounting purposes. The tax deduction is the larger amount this year.

Primrose received rent revenues in advance this year. These revenues are included in this year's taxable income. However, for accounting purposes, these revenues are reported as unearned revenues, a current liability.

Required:

a. What is the theoretical basis for deferred income taxes?

b. How would Primrose determine and account for the income tax effect for the depreciation and rent? Why?

c. How should Primrose classify the income tax effect of the depreciation and rent on its balance sheet and income statement? Why?

20. The financial statements of the Shinn Corporation recognize profits on installment sales when the merchandise is shipped. The profits on such sales, however, are reported in the corporate income tax returns on the installment basis.

Under this tax-reporting method, the corporation will defer for tax purposes $10,000 of profits on $50,000 of accounts receivable at year end. All related expenses will be reported in the financial statements and in the federal income tax return. The corporation plans to carry $4,800 as a liability for federal income taxes to be paid in future years.

Required:

a. Interperiod tax allocation is necessary because there are differences in the timing of revenues and expenses between financial statements and federal income tax returns. List the categories of circumstances that result in such timing differences and give examples of them.

b. Explain the following interperiod tax allocation concepts.

   i. Liability concept

   ii. Deferred concept

   iii. Net-of-tax concept

c. The propriety of applying the liability concept to deferred taxes on installment sales is questioned sometimes because no legal debtor--creditor relationship underlies the "liability for federal income taxes to be paid in future years." Write a rebuttal to this argument.

21. Part *a*. Income tax allocation is an integral part of generally accepted accounting principles. The applications of intraperiod tax allocation (within a period) and interperiod tax allocation (among periods) are both required.

Required:
  i. Explain the need for intraperiod tax allocation.
 ii. Accountants who favor interperiod tax allocation argue that income taxes are an expense rather than a distribution of earnings. Explain the significance of this argument. Do not explain the definitions of expense or distribution of earnings.
iii. Indicate and explain whether each of the following independent situations should be treated as a timing difference or a permanent difference.
   (a) Estimated warranty costs (covering a three-year warranty) are expensed for accounting purposes at the time of sale but deducted for income tax purposes when incurred.
   (b) Depreciation for accounting and income tax purposes differs because of different bases of carrying the related property. The different bases are a result of a business combination treated as a purchase for accounting purposes and as a tax-free exchange for income tax purposes.
   (c) A company properly uses the equity method to account for its 30 percent investment in another company. The investee pays dividends that are about 10 percent of its annual earnings.
 iv. Discuss the nature of the deferred income tax accounts and possible classifications in a company's statement of financial position.

Part *b*. The investment tax credit can be accounted for by one of two ''generally accepted'' methods for accounting purposes.

Required:
Identify and explain these two accounting methods for the investment tax credit. Do not discuss income tax computations of the investment credit.

BIBLIOGRAPHY

Arthur Andersen & Co. *Accounting for Income Taxes*. Chicago: Arthur Andersen & Co., 1961.

Barton, A. U. ''Company Income Tax and Interperiod Allocation.'' *Abacus* (September 1970), pp. 3–24.

Baylis, A. W. ''Income Tax Allocation—A Defense.'' *Abacus* (December

1971), pp. 161–172. See also A. D. Barton, "Reply to Mr. Baylis." *Abacus* (December 1971), pp. 173–175.

Beaver, William, and Roland E. Dukes. "Interperiod Tax Allocation and Delta-Depreciation Methods: Some Empirical Results." *The Accounting Review* (July 1973), pp. 549–595.

Bevis, Donald J., and Raymond E. Perry. *Accounting for Income Taxes.* New York: AICPA, 1969.

Bierman, Harold, and Thomas R. Dyckman. "New Look at Deferred Taxes." *Financial Executive* (January 1974), pp. 40ff.

Black, Homer A. "Interperiod Allocation of Corporate Income Taxes." *Accounting Research Study No. 9.* New York: AICPA, 1966.

Chambers, R. J. "Tax Allocation and Financial Reporting." *Abacus* (December 1968), pp. 99–123.

Cramer, Joe J., Jr., and William J. Schrader. "Investment Tax Credit." *Business Horizons* (February 1970), pp. 85–89.

Godlick, Neil B., and Richard P. Miller. "Applying APB Opinions Nos. 23 and 24." *Journal of Accountancy* (November 1973), pp. 55–63.

Hill, Thomas. "Some Arguments Against the Interperiod Allocation of Income Taxes." *The Accounting Review* (July 1957), pp. 528–537.

Laibstain, Samuel. "New Look at Accounting for Operating Loss Carry--Forwards." *The Accounting Review* (April 1971), pp. 342–351.

Moonitz, Maurice. "Some Reflections on the Investment Credit Experience." *Journal of Accounting Research* (Spring 1966), pp. 47–61.

Moore, Carl L. "Deferred Income Tax—Is It a Liability?" *New York CPA* (February 1970), pp. 130–138.

Norgaard, Corine T. "Financial Implications of Comprehensive Income Tax Allocation." *Financial Analysts Journal* (January–February 1969), pp. 81–85.

Nurnberg, Hugo. "Critique of the Deferred Method of Interperiod Tax Allocation." *New York CPA* (December 1969), pp. 958–961.

Pointer, Larry Gene. "Disclosing Corporate Tax Policy," *Journal of Accountancy* (July 1973), pp. 56–61.

Price Waterhouse & Co. *Is Generally Accepted Accounting for Income Taxes Possibly Misleading Investors?* New York: Price Waterhouse & Co., 1967.

Raiburn, Michael H., Michael R. Lane, and D. D. Raiburn. "Purchased Loss Carryforwards: An Unresolved Issue." *Journal of Accountancy* (November 1983), pp. 98–108.

Revsine, Lawrence. "Some Controversy Concerning Controversial Accounting Changes." *The Accounting Review* (April 1969), pp. 354–358.

Rosenfield, Paul, and William C. Dent. "No More Deferred Taxes." *Journal of Accountancy* (February 1983), pp. 44–55.

Smith, Willis A. "Tax Allocation Revisited—Another Viewpoint." *The CPA Journal* (September 1984), pp. 52–56.

Stamp, Edward. "Some Further Reflections on the Investment Credit." *Journal of Accounting Research* (Spring 1967), pp. 124–128.

Throckmorton, Jerry J. "Theoretical Concepts for Interpreting the Investment Credit." *Journal of Accountancy* (April 1970), pp. 45–52.

Voss, William M. "Accelerated Depreciation and Deferred Tax Allocation." *Journal of Accounting Research* (Autumn 1968), pp. 262–269.

Watson, Peter L. "Accounting for Deferred Tax on Depreciable Assets." *Accounting and Business Research* (Autumn 1979), pp. 338–347.

Weber, Richard P. "Misleading Tax Figures: A Problem for Accountants." *The Accounting Review* (January 1977), pp. 172–185.

Wheeler, James E., and Willard H. Galliart. *An Appraisal of Interperiod Income Tax Allocation.* New York: Financial Executives Research Foundation, 1974.

Williams, Edward E., and M. Chapman Findly. "Discounting Deferred Tax Liabilities: Some Clarifying Comments." *Journal of Business Finance and Accounting* (Spring 1975), pp. 121–133.

Wolk, Harry I., and Michael G. Tearney. "Income Tax Allocation and Loss Carry-Forwards: Exploring Unchartered Ground." *The Accounting Review* (April 1973), pp. 292–299.

10

LEASES
AND
PENSIONS

This chapter deals with two significant accounting topics that did not fit neatly into previous chapters dealing with assets and liabilities: (1) leases and (2) pensions. Leases have posed unique accounting problems for many years. These problems are evidenced by the examination of the subject in four APB Opinions and the comprehensive FASB Statement No. 13. The topic of pensions has also been controversial, and federal government reporting requirements have fostered additional interest in the subject.

ACCOUNTING FOR LEASES

A lease is an agreement between two parties whereby assets are rented for a period of time. These agreements usually require the lessee to maintain the leased property and pay any expenses related to the assets such as property taxes and insurance. Therefore, the out-of-pocket costs of leasing assets by the lessee typically include the rental payments plus the maintenance costs. Insofar as the lessor is concerned, rental revenues are included in the operating revenues of the company and depreciation expense on the leased property should be recorded as an operating expense.

Unfortunately, some lease agreements are in substance long-term installment purchases of assets that are structured to gain tax or other benefits to the parties. Since leases may take different forms, it is necessary to examine the underlying nature of the original transaction to determine the appropriate method of accounting for these agreements. That is, they should be reported in a manner that describes the intent of the lessor and lessee rather than the form of the agreement.

Over the years, two predominant methods for allocating lease revenues and expenses to the periods covered by the lease agreement have emerged in accounting practice. One method, termed a *capital lease,* is based upon the view that the lease constitutes a device through which the lessor finances the acquisition of assets by the lessee and, as such, is in substance a purchase agreement. The other method is termed an *operating lease* and is based upon the view that the lease constitutes a rental agreement between the lessor and lessee.

In November 1976, the Financial Accounting Standards Board issued Statement No. 13, "Accounting for Leases." This Statement superseded APB Opinion No. 5, "Reporting of Leases in Financial Statements of Lessee"; APB Opinion No. 7, "Accounting for Leases in Financial Statements of Lessors"; APB Opinion No. 27, "Accounting for Lease Transactions by Manufacturer or Dealer Lessors"; and APB Opinion No. 31, "Disclosure of Lease Commitments by Lessees." A major purpose of Statement No. 13 was to achieve a greater degree of symmetry of accounting between lessees and lessors. In an effort to accomplish this goal, the Statement established standards of financial accounting and reporting for both lessees and lessors. One of the problems associated with the four Opinions issued by the APB was that they allowed differences in recording and reporting the same lease by lessors and lessees. Adherence to FASB Statement No. 13 substantially reduces (though does not completely eliminate) this possibility.

The conceptual foundation underlying Statement No. 13 is based on the view that "a lease that transfers substantially all of the benefits and risks incident to the ownership of property should be accounted for as the acquisition of an asset and the incurrence of an obligation by the lessee and as a sale or financing by the lessor."[1] This viewpoint leads immediately to three basic conclusions: (1) The characteristics that indicate that substantially all of the benefits and risks of ownership have been transferred to the lessee must be identified. These leases should be recorded as if they involved the purchase and sale of assets (*capital leases*). (2) The same characteristics should apply to both the lessee and lessor; therefore, the inconsistency in accounting treatment that previously existed would be eliminated. (3) Those leases that do not meet the characteristics identified in (1) should be accounted for simply as rental agreements (*operating leases*).

CRITERIA FOR CLASSIFYING LEASES

In Statement No. 13, the FASB outlined specific criteria to assist in classifying leases as either capital or operating leases. In the case of the lessee, if at its

---

[1]Statement of Financial Accounting Standards No. 13, "Accounting for Leases" (Stamford, Conn.: Financial Accounting Standards Board, 1976), par. 60. This Statement was later amended in 1980 to incorporate several FASB pronouncements that expanded upon the principles outlined in the original pronouncement.

inception the lease meets any one of the following four criteria, the lease is classified as a capital lease; otherwise, it is classified as an operating lease.

1. The lease transfers ownership of the property to the lessee by the end of the lease term. This includes the fixed noncancelable term of the lease plus various specified renewal options and periods.
2. The lease contains a bargain purchase option. This means that the stated purchase price is sufficiently lower than the expected fair market value of the property at the date the option becomes exercisable and that exercise of the option appears, at the inception of the lease, to be reasonably assured.
3. The lease term is equal to 75 percent or more of the estimated remaining economic life of the leased property unless the beginning of the lease term falls within the last 25 percent of the total estimated economic life of the leased property.
4. The present value at the beginning of the lease term of the minimum lease payments, which is specifically defined and excludes that portion of the payments representing executory costs such as insurance, maintenance, and taxes to be paid by the lessor, equals or exceeds 90 percent of the fair value of the leased property less any related investment tax credit retained by the lessor. (This criterion is also ignored when the lease term falls within the last 25 percent of the total estimated economic life of the leased property).[2]

In the case of the lessor (except for leveraged leases, discussed later), if a lease meets any one of the preceding four criteria plus *both* of the following additional criteria, it is classified as a capital lease.

1. Collectibility of the minimum lease payments is reasonably predictable.
2. No important uncertainties surround the amount of unreimbursable costs yet to be incurred by the lessor under the lease.[3]

ACCOUNTING AND REPORTING BY LESSEES

Historically, the primary concern in accounting for lease transactions by lessees has been the appropriate recognition of assets and liabilities on the lessee's balance sheet. This concern has overridden the corollary question of revenue recognition on the part of lessors. Therefore, the usual position of accountants has been that if the lease agreement was in substance an installment purchase, the "leased" property should be accounted for as an asset by the lessee, together with its corresponding liability. Failure to do so results in an understatement of assets and liabilities on the balance sheet. Lease arrangements that are not considered installment purchases constitute *off-balance sheets financing* arrange-

[2]Ibid., par. 7.
[3]Ibid., par. 8.

ments (discussed in Chapter 4) and should be properly disclosed in the notes to financial statements.

As early as 1962, the accounting research division of the AICPA recognized that there was little consistency in the disclosure of leases by lessees and that most companies were not capitalizing leases. It therefore authorized a research study on reporting of leases by lessees. Among the recommendations of this study were the following:

> *To the extent, then, that leases give rise to property rights, those rights and related liabilities should be measured and incorporated in the balance sheet.*
>
> *To the extent, then, that the rental payments represent a means of financing the acquisition of property rights which the lessee has in his possession and under his control, the transaction constitutes the acquisition of an asset with a related obligation to pay for it.*
>
> *To the extent, however, that the rental payments are for services such as maintenance, insurance, property taxes, heat, light, and elevator service, no asset has been acquired, and none should be recorded. . . .*
>
> *The measurement of the asset value and the related liability involves two steps: (1) the determination of the part of the rentals which constitutes payment for property rights, and (2) the discounting of these rentals at an appropriate rate of interest.*[4]

The crucial difference in the conclusion of this study and the existing practice was the emphasis on *property rights* (the right to use property), as opposed to the *rights in property*—ownership of equity interest in the property.

The APB considered the recommendations of this study and agreed that certain lease agreements should result in the lessee recording an asset and liability. However, the board concluded that the important criterion to be applied was whether the lease was in substance a purchase, that is, rights in property, rather than the existence of property rights. This, in effect, means that the APB agreed that assets and liabilities should be recorded when the lease transaction was in substance an installment purchase in the same manner as other purchase arrangements. The APB, however, did not agree that the right to use property in exchange for future rental payments gives rise to the recording of assets and liabilities, since no equity in property is created.

In response to the views expressed in the preceding paragraphs, the APB asserted in Opinion No. 5 that a noncancelable lease, or a lease cancelable only upon the occurrence of some remote contingency, was probably in substance a purchase if either of the two following conditions exists.

---

[4]John H. Myers, Accounting Research Study No. 4. ''Reporting of Leases in Financial Statements'' (New York: American Institute of Certified Public Accountants, 1962), pp. 4–5.

CHAPTER 10: LEASES AND PENSIONS

1. The initial term is materially less than the useful life of the property, and the lessee has the option to renew the lease for the remaining useful life of the property at substantially less than the fair rental value.
2. The lessee has the right, during or at the expiration of the lease, to acquire the property at a price which at the inception of the lease appears to be substantially less than the probable fair value of the property at the time or times of permitted acquisition by the lessee.[5]

The presence of either of these two conditions was seen as convincing evidence that the lessee was building an equity in the property.

The APB went on to say that one or more of the following circumstances tend to indicate that a lease arrangement is in substance a purchase.

1. The property was acquired by the lessor to meet the special needs of the lessee and will probably be usable only for that purpose and only by the lessee.
2. The term of the lease corresponds substantially to the estimated useful life of the property, and the lessee is obligated to pay costs such as taxes, insurance, and maintenance, which are usually considered incidental to ownership.
3. The lessee has guaranteed the obligations of the lessor with respect to the leased property.
4. The lessee has treated the lease as a purchase for tax purposes.[6]

In addition, the lease might be considered a purchase if the lessor and lessee were related even in the absence of the preceding conditions and circumstances. In that case,

A lease should be recorded as a purchase if a primary purpose of ownership of the property by the lessor is to lease it to the lessee and (1) the lease payments are pledged to secure the debts of the lessor or (2) the lessee is able, directly or indirectly, to control or influence significantly the actions of the lessor with respect to the lease.[7]

These conclusions have caused controversy in the financial community because some individuals believe that they result in disincentives to leasing. Those holding this view maintain that noncapitalized leases provide the following benefits.

1. Improved accounting rate of return and debt ratios, thereby improving the financial picture of the company.

---

[5]Accounting Principles Board Opinion No. 5, "Reporting of Leases in Financial Statements of Lessees" (New York: American Institute of Certified Public Accountants, 1964), par. 10.
[6]Ibid., par. 11.
[7]Ibid., par. 12.

2. Better debt ratings.

3. Increased availability of capital.

On the other hand, the advocates of lease capitalization hold that these arguments are in essence attempts to deceive financial-statement users. That is, a company should fully disclose the impact of all of its financing and investing activities and not attempt to hide the economic substance of external transactions.

CAPITAL LEASES

The views expressed in APB Opinion No. 5 concerning the capitalization of those leases that are "in substance installment purchases" are significant from a historical point of view for two reasons. First, in FASB No. 13, the FASB based its conclusion on the concept that a lease that "Transfers substantially all of the benefits and risks of the ownership of property should be accounted for as the acquisition of an asset and the incurrence of an obligation by the lessee, and as a sale or financing by the lessor." Therefore, the concept of "in substance installment purchases" was rejected by the board. Second, to a great extent, the accounting provisions of FASB Statement No. 13 applicable to lessees generally follow APB Opinion No. 5.

When a lessee enters into a capital lease agreement, both an asset and a liability are recorded at the lower of the following.

1. Sum of the present value of the *minimum lease payments* at the inception of the lease (see following discussion).

2. The fair value of the leased property at the inception of the lease.

The rules for determining minimum lease payments were specifically set forth by the board. In summary, those payments that the lessee is obligated to make or can be required to make with the exception of executory costs should be included. Consequently, the following items are subject to inclusion in the determination of the minimum lease payments.

1. Minimum rental payments over the life of the lease.

2. Payment called for by a bargain purchase option.

3. Any guarantee by the lessee of the residual value at the expiration of the lease term.

4. Any penalties that the lessee can be required to pay for failure to renew the lease.[8]

These two are usually not together

[8]FASB Statement No. 13, op. cit., par. 5.

Once the minimum lease payments or fair market value are determined, the next step is to compute the present value of the lease payments. The interest rate to be used in this computation is generally the lessee's incremental borrowing rate. This is the rate the lessee would have been charged had he or she borrowed funds to buy the asset with repayments over the same term. If the lessee can readily determine the implicit interest rate used by the lessor and if that rate is lower than his or her incremental borrowing rate, then the lessee is to use the lessor's implicit rate for calculating the present value of the minimum lease payments.

Capital lease assets and liabilities are to be separately identified in the lessee's balance sheet or in the accompanying footnotes. The liability should be classified as current and noncurrent on the same basis as all other liabilities, that is, according to when the obligation must be paid.

Unless the lease involves land, the asset recorded under a capital lease is to be amortized by one of two methods. Leases that meet either criterion 1 or 2 on page 465 are to be amortized in a manner consistent with the lessee's normal depreciation policy for owned assets; that is, the assets economic life to the lessee is used as the amortization period. Leases that do not meet criterion 1 or 2 but meet either criterion 3 or 4 are to be amortized in a manner consistent with the lessee's normal depreciation, using the lease term as the period of amortization. In conformity with APB Opinion No. 21, "Interest on Receivables and Payables," Statement No. 13 requires that each minimum payment under a capital lease be allocated between a reduction of the liability and interest expense. The allocation is to be made in such a manner that the interest expense reflects a constant rate on the outstanding balance of the obligation (i.e., the effective interest method). Thus, as with any loan payment schedule, each successive payment has more allocated to principal and less to interest; however, the rate of interest on the outstanding balance remains the same over the life of the loan. This procedure results in the loan being reflected on the balance sheet at the present value of the future cash flows discounted at the effective interest rate.

DISCLOSURE REQUIREMENTS FOR CAPITAL LEASES

Statement No. 13 also provides for the disclosure of additional information for capital leases. The following information should be disclosed in the lessee's financial statements or in the accompanying footnotes.

1. The gross amount of assets recorded under capital leases as of the date of each balance sheet presented by major classes according to nature or function.
2. Future minimum lease payments as of the date of the latest balance sheet presented, in the aggregate and for each of the five succeeding fiscal years.

3. The total minimum sublease rentals to be received in the future under noncancelable subleases as of the date of the latest balance sheet presented.
4. Total contingent rentals (rentals on which the amounts are dependent on some factor other than the passage of time) actually incurred for each period for which an income statement is presented.[9]

A later section of this chapter provides an illustration of these disclosure requirements together with requirements for lessors.

OPERATING LEASES

All leases that do not meet any of the four criteria for capitalization are to be classified as operating leases by the lessee. Failure to meet any of the criteria means that the lease is simply a rental arrangement and, in essence, should be accounted for in the same manner as any other rental agreement, with certain exceptions. The rent payments made on an operating lease are normally charged to expense as they become payable over the life of the lease. An exception is made if the rental schedule does not result in a straight-line basis of payment. In such cases, the rent expense is to be recognized on a straight-line basis unless the lessee can demonstrate that some other method gives a more systematic and rational periodic charge.

In the 1973 APB Opinion No. 31, "Disclosure of Lease Commitments by Lessees," the board observed that many different users of financial statements were dissatisfied with the information being provided about leases. The board did not address the question of capitalization, since that topic had already been placed on the agenda of the FASB. Instead, the APB directed its attention to the information that should be disclosed about noncapitalized leases. Many of the requirements of this Opinion are also continued in the section of FASB Statement No. 13 dealing with operating leases.

1. *For operating leases having initial or remaining noncancelable lease terms in excess of one year:*
   a. *Future minimum rental payments required as of the date of the latest balance sheet presented in the aggregate and for each of the five succeeding fiscal years.*
   b. *The total of minimum rentals to be received in the future under noncancelable subleases as of the date of the latest balance sheet presented.*
2. *For all operating leases, rental expense for each period for which an income statement is presented, with separate amounts for minimum rentals, contingent rentals and sublease rentals.*

---

[9]Ibid., par. 16.

3. *A general description of the lessee's leasing arrangements including, but not limited to the following:*
   a. *The basis on which contingent rental payments are determined.*
   b. *The existence and terms of renewals or purchase options and escalation clauses.*
   c. *Restrictions imposed by lease agreements, such as those concerning dividends, additional debt, and further leasing.*[10]

The board concluded that the preceding accounting and disclosure requirements for capital and operating leases would give users information useful in assessing a company's financial position and results of operations. The requirements also provide many specific and detailed rules, which should lead to greater consistency in the presentation of lease information by lessees.

ACCOUNTING AND REPORTING BY LESSORS

The major concern in accounting for leases in the financial statements of lessors is the appropriate allocation of revenues and expenses to the periods covered by the lease. This concern contrasts with the lessee's focus on the balance sheet presentation of leases. As a general rule, lease agreements include a specific schedule of the date and amounts of payments to be made by the lessee to the lessor. The fact that the lessor knows the date and amount of payment does not, however, mean that revenue should be recorded in the period of receipt. Accrual accounting frequently gives rise to situations in which revenue is recognized in a period other than when payment is received in order to measure more fairly the results of operations.

The nature of the lease and the rent schedule may make it necessary for the lessor to recognize revenue which is more or less than the payments received in a given period. Furthermore, once revenue is recognized, the lessor must allocate the acquisition and operating costs of the leased property, together with any costs of negotiating and closing the lease, to the accounting periods receiving benefits in a systematic and rational manner consistent with the timing of revenue recognition. The latter point is consistent with the usual application of the matching principle in accounting, that is, determining the amount of revenue to be recognized in a period and then ascertaining which costs should be matched with that revenue.

The criterion for choosing between accounting for lease revenue by either the capital or operating methods historically was based upon the accounting objective of fairly stating the lessor's periodic net income. Whichever method would best accomplish this objective should be followed. FASB Statement No. 13 has

---

[10]Ibid., par. 16.

now set forth specific criteria for determining the type of lease as well as the reporting and disclosure requirements for each type.

According to FASB Statement No. 13, if at its inception a lease agreement meets the lessor criteria for classification as a capital lease, the lessor is to classify it either as a *sales-type lease* or a *direct financing lease*, whichever is appropriate. All other leases, except leveraged leases (discussed in a separate section), are to be classified as operating leases.

SALES-TYPE LEASES

A capital lease should be recorded as a *sales-type lease* by the lessor when there is a manufacturer's or dealer's profit (or loss). This implies that the leased asset is an item of inventory and the seller is computing a gross profit on the sale. Hence sales type leases arise when manufacturers or dealers use leasing as a means of marketing their products.

Figure 10.1 depicts the major steps involved in accounting for sales-type leases by the lessor. The amount to be recorded as gross investment (a) is the total amount of the minimum lease payments over the life of the lease, plus any unguaranteed residual value accruing to the benefit of the lessor. Once the gross investment has been determined, it is to be discounted to its present value (b) using an interest rate that causes the aggregate present value at the beginning of the lease term to be equal to the fair value of the leased property less any investment tax credit retained by the lessor. The rate thus determined is referred to as the interest rate implicit in the lease.

Figure 10.1   Accounting steps for sales-type leases

Gross investment (a)	XX
minus	
Present value of gross investment (b)	XX
equals	
Unearned income (c)	XX
Gross investment (a)	XX
minus	
Unearned income (c)	XX
equals	
Net investment (d)	XX
Sales (e)	XX
minus	
Cost of goods sold (f)	XX
equals	
Profit or loss (g)	XX

The difference between gross investment (a) and the present value of the gross investment (b) is to be recorded as unearned interest income (c). The unearned interest income is to be amortized to income over the life of the lease using the interest method described in APB Opinion No. 21. Applying the interest methods results in a constant rate of return on the net investment in the lease. The difference between gross investment (a) and the unearned interest income (c) is the amount of net investment (d), which is the same as the present value of the gross investment (b) and is to be classified as a current or noncurrent asset on the same basis as applied to other assets in a classified balance sheet. Revenue on sales-type leases is thus reflected by two different figures: (1) the gross profit (or loss) on the sale in the year of the lease agreement and (2) interest on the remaining net investment over the life of the lease agreement.

For sales-type leases, the initial direct costs associated with obtaining the lease agreement are written off when the sale is recorded at the inception of the lease. These costs are disclosed as selling expenses on the income statement.

DIRECT FINANCING LEASES

When no manufacturer's or dealer's profit (or loss) is recorded, a capital lease should be accounted for as a direct financing lease by the lessor. Under the direct financing method, the lessor is essentially viewed as a lending institution for revenue recognition purposes. If a lessor records a capital lease under the direct financing method, each payment must be allocated between interest revenue and investment recovery. In the early periods of the agreement, a significant portion of the payment will be recorded as interest, but each succeeding payment will result in a decreasing amount of interest revenue and an increasing amount of investment recovery due to the fact that the amount of the net investment is decreasing.

In reporting direct financing leases, the FASB adopted the approach of recording the total minimum lease payments as a receivable on the date of the transaction with the difference between that amount and the asset cost being treated as unearned income. When each rental payment is received, the receivable is reduced by the full amount of the payment. At the same time, a portion of the unearned income is transferred to earned income and with each payment this amount becomes smaller.

Figure 10.2 illustrates the accounting steps for direct financing leases. Gross investment (a) is determined the same as in sales-type leases, but unearned income (c) is computed as the difference between gross investment and the cost (b) of the leased property. The difference between gross investment (a) and unearned income (c) is net investment (d), which is the same as (b) in the sales type lease.

Initial direct costs (e) in financing leases are to be charged against income as incurred, but an amount equal to those costs is deducted from the unearned

Figure 10.2   Accounting steps for financing leases

Gross investment (a)	XX
minus	
Cost (b)	XX
equals	
Unearned income (c)	XX
Gross investment (a)	XX
minus	
Unearned income (c)	XX
equals	
Net investments (d)	XX
Unearned income (c)	XX
minus	
Initial direct costs (e)	XX
equals	
Unearned income to be amortized (f)	XX

income (c) in the same period. The amount of unearned income to be amortized (f) in accordance with the "interest method" is reduced by any initial direct costs. As a result, the net investment is increased by an amount equal to the initial direct costs. Consequently, a new effective interest rate must be determined in order to apply the interest method to the declining net investment balance. Under direct financing leases the only revenue recorded by the lessor is disclosed as interest revenue over the lease term. Initial direct costs increase the amount disclosed as the net investment. Therefore, the interest income reported represents both interest and a write-off of the initial direct cost in proportion to the interest income on the original amount of the net investment.

DISCLOSING REQUIREMENTS FOR SALES-TYPE AND DIRECT FINANCING LEASES

In addition to the preceding specific procedures to be followed in accounting for sales-type and direct financing leases, the FASB established certain disclosure requirements. The following information is to be disclosed when leasing constitutes a significant part of the lessor's business activities in terms of revenue, net income, or assets.

1. The components of the net investment in leases as of the date of each balance sheet presented:
   a. Future minimum lease payments to be received with deduction for any executory costs included in payments and allowance for uncollectibles.

b. The unguaranteed residual value.

c. Unearned income.

2. *Future minimum lease payments to be received for each of the five succeeding fiscal years as of the date of the latest balance sheet presented.*

3. *The amount of unearned income included in income to offset initial direct costs charged against income for each period for which an income statement is presented. (For direct financing leases only.)*

4. *Total contingent rentals included in income for each period for which an income statement is presented.*

5. *A general description of the lessor's leasing arrangements.*[11]

The board indicated its belief that these disclosures by the lessor, as with the disclosures by lessees, would aid the users of financial statements in their assessment of the financial condition and results of operations of lessors. Note also that these requirements make the information disclosed by lessors and lessees more consistent.

OPERATING LEASES

Those leases that do not meet the criteria for sales-type or direct financing classification are accounted for as operating leases by the lessor. Essentially this means that the leased property is treated like other property. That is, the leased property is included with or near other property, plant, and equipment in the lessor's balance sheet and is depreciated following the lessor's normal depreciation policy.

Rental payments are to be recognized as revenue when they become receivables unless the payments are not made on a straight-line basis. In that case, as with the lessee, the recognition of revenue is to be on a straight-line basis. Initial direct costs associated with the lease are to be deferred and allocated over the lease term, also on a straight-line basis. However, if these costs are not material, they may be charged to expense as incurred.

If leasing is a significant part of the lessor's business activities, the following information is to be disclosed for operating leases.

1. *The cost and carrying amount, if different, of property on lease or held for leasing by major classes of property according to nature or function, and the amount of accumulated depreciation in total as of the date of the latest balance sheet presented.*

2. *Minimum future rentals on noncancelable leases as of the date of the latest balance sheet presented, in the aggregate and for each of the five succeeding fiscal years.*

---

[11]Ibid., par. 23.

3. *Total contingent rentals included in income for each period for which an income statement is presented.*

4. *A general description of the lessor's leasing arrangements.*[12]

As with the disclosure requirements for sales-type and direct financing leases, the test of significance should be in terms of revenue, net income, or assets as separate indicators.

LESSEE AND LESSOR DISCLOSURE ILLUSTRATION

The following illustration of accounting and disclosure by lessees and lessors is based upon Appendixes C and D of FASB Statement No. 13.[13] In the example, the leased property is an automobile.

LEASE TERMS AND ASSUMPTIONS

The terms and assumptions of the lease are as follows.

Lessor's cost of the leased property (automobile)	$5,000
Fair value of the leased property at inception of the lease (1/1/87)	$5,000
Estimated economic life of the leased property	5 years

The lease has a fixed noncancelable term of 30 months, with a rental of $135 payable at the beginning of each month. The lessee guarantees a residual value of $2,000 at the end of the lease and will receive any excess of sales price over that amount. The lessee pays executory costs. The lease is renewable periodically on a decreasing rate, the rentals specified are fair, the estimated residual is reasonable, and no investment tax credit is available. The lessee depreciates the owned automobiles on a straight-line basis. The incremental borrowing rate is 10.5 percent per year. There are no initial direct costs of negotiating and closing the transaction. At the end of the lease term the asset is sold for $2,100.

COMPUTATION OF MINIMUM LEASE PAYMENTS (LESSEE AND LESSOR)

The minimum lease payments are computed as follows.

Minimum rental payments over the lease term ($135 × 30 months)	$4,050
Lessee guarantee of the residual value at the end of the lease term	2,000
Total minimum lease payments	$6,050

[12]Ibid., par. 23.
[13]Ibid., pars. 121–122.

The lessor's implicit interest rate in this lease is 12.036 percent, which is the rate implicit in the recovery of the fair value of the property at the inception of the lease ($5,000) through the minimum lease payments (30 monthly payments of $135 and the lessee's guarantee of the $2,000 residual value).

CLASSIFICATION OF THE LEASE

The lease can be classified by examining it in relation to the criteria discussed earlier.

Criterion 1 is not met because the lease does not transfer ownership of the property to the lessee by the end of the lease term.

Criterion 2 is not met because the lease does not contain a bargain purchase option.

Criterion 3 is not met because the lease term is not equal to 75 percent or more of the estimated economic life of the property.

Criterion 4 is met in the lessee's case because the present value ($5,120) of the minimum lease payments using his incremental borrowing rate (10.5 percent) exceeds 90 percent of the fair value of the property at the inception of the lease. In the lessor's case, the present value ($5,000) of the minimum lease payments using the implicit rate also exceeds 90 percent of the fair value of the property. As a result of meeting the present-value test, the lessee will classify the lease as a capital lease and, assuming that the two additional criteria are met, the lessor will classify the lease as a direct financing lease because there is no manufacturers' or dealers' profit.

The preceding present values were determined as follows.

	Lessee's Computation Using the Incremental Borrowing Rate of 10.5% Because it is Lower Than the Implicit Rate	Lessor's Computation Using the Implicit Rate of 12.036%
Minimum lease payments:		
Rental payments	$3,580	$3,517
Residual guarantee by lessee	1,540	1,483
	$5,120	$5,000
Fair value of the property at inception of the lease	$5,000	$5,000

BALANCE SHEET PRESENTATION

The lessee and lessor would report the lease in their balance sheets as follows.

Lessee Company
Balance Sheet

Assets		*Liabilities*	
Leased property under		*Current:*	
capital leases, less		Obligations under	
accumulated amortization	XXX	capital leases	XXX
		Noncurrent:	
		Obligations under	
		capital leases	XXX

The lessee should also explain the various terms and conditions of the lease in a footnote.

Lessor Company
Balance Sheet

Assets	
Current assets:	
Net investment in direct financing leases	XXX
Noncurrent assets:	
Net investment in direct financing leases	XXX

The lessee and lessor would also describe the lease in a footnote.

SALES AND LEASEBACKS

In a sale and leaseback transaction, the owner of property sells the property and then immediately leases it back from the buyer. Such transactions frequently occur when companies have limited cash resources or when they result in tax advantages. Tax advantages occur because the sales price of the asset is usually its current market value and this amount generally exceeds the carrying value of the asset on the seller's books. Therefore, the tax-deductible periodic rental payments are higher than the previously recorded amount of depreciation expense.

Most sales and leaseback transactions are treated as a single economic event according to the lease classification criteria previously discussed on page 465. That is, the lessee-seller records the lease as capital or operating and the gain or loss on the sale is amortized over the lease term. However, in certain circumstances where the lessee retains significantly smaller rights to use the property, any gain or loss may be immediately recognized. In these cases it is argued that two distinctly different transactions have occurred because the rights to use have changed.

LEVERAGED LEASES

A leveraged lease is defined as a special leasing arrangement involving three different parties: (1) the equity holder—the lessor; (2) the asset user—the lessee; and (3) the debt holder—a long-term financer.[14] A leveraged lease may be illustrated as follows:

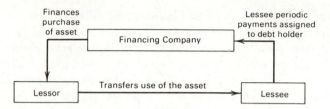

The major issue in accounting for leveraged leases is whether the transaction should be recorded as a single economic event or as separate transactions. All leveraged leases must meet the criteria for direct financing leases; however, a leveraged lease might be accounted for as a lease with an additional debt transaction, or as a single transaction. The FASB determined that a leveraged lease should be accounted for as a single transaction, and provided the following guidelines.

The lessee records the lease as a capital lease. The lessor records the lease as a direct financing lease and the investment in capital leases is the net result of several factors.

1. *Rentals receivable, net of that portion of the rental applicable to principal and interest on the nonrecourse debt.*
2. *A receivable for the amount of the investment tax credit to be realized on the transaction.*
3. *The estimated residual value of the leased asset.*
4. *Unearned and deferred income consisting of the estimated pretax lease income (or loss), after deducting initial direct costs remaining to be allocated to income over the lease term and the investment tax credit remaining to be allocated to income over the lease term.[15]*

Once the original investment has been determined, the next step is to project cash receipts and disbursements over the term of the lease, then compute a rate of return on the net investment in those years in which it is positive. Annual cash flow is the sum of gross lease rental and residual value (in the final year), less loan interest payments plus or minus income tax credits or charges, less loan

---

[14]A fourth party may also be involved when the owner-lessor initially purchases the property from a manufacturer.
[15]FASB Statement No 13, op. cit., Par. 43.

principal payments, plus investment tax credit realized. The rate to be used in the computation is that "which when applied to the net investment in the years in which the net investment is positive will distribute the net income to those years."[16]

In a footnote to an illustration of the allocation of annual cash flow to investment and income, Statement No. 13 includes the following comment.

> *[The rate used for the allocation] is calculated by a trial and error process. The allocation is calculated based upon an initial estimate of the rate as a starting point. If the total thus allocated to income differs under the estimated rate from the net cash flow the estimated rate is increased or decreased, as appropriate, to devise a revised allocation. This process is repeated until a rate is selected which develops a total amount allocated to income that is precisely equal to the net cash flow. As a practical matter, a computer program is used to calculate [the allocation] under successive iterations until the correct rate is determined.*[17]

This method of accounting for leveraged leases was considered to associate the income with the unrecovered balance of the earning asset in a manner consistent with the investor's view of the transaction. Income is recognized at a level rate on net investment in years in which the net investment is positive and is thus identified as "primary" earnings from the lease.

ACCOUNTING FOR THE COST OF PENSION PLANS

For many years, employers have been concerned with providing for the retirement needs of their work force. This concern has resulted in the adoption of pension plans on a massive scale since World War II. Generally, companies provide for pension benefits by making periodic payments to an outside third party, termed a funding agency. This agency then assumes the responsibility for investing the pension funds and making the periodic payments to the recipients of benefits.

The two most frequently encountered types of pension plans are defined contribution plans and defined benefit plans. In a *defined contribution plan,* the employer promises to contribute a certain sum into the plan each period. For example, the employer may promise to contribute 8 percent of the employee's salary each year. However, no promise is made concerning the utlimate benefits to be paid. Benefits are ultimately determined by the return on the invested pension funds.

[16]Ibid., par. 44.
[17]Ibid., par. 123.

In a *defined benefit plan,* the amount of pension benefits to be received in the future are defined by the terms of the plan. For example, the retirement plan of one company promises that an employee retiring at age 65 will receive 2 percent of the average of the highest 5 years' salary for every year of service. Therefore, an employee working for this company for 30 years would receive a pension for life equal to 60 percent of the average of his or her highest 5 salary years. In defined benefit plans, it is necessary for the employer to determine the annual contribution necessary to meet the benefit requirements in the future.

Accounting for defined contribution plans is relatively straightforward. Since the risk for future benefits is borne by the employee, the employer's only expense is the annual promised contribution to the pension plan. This amount of contribution is the periodic pension expense. Additionally, the employer's financial statements should disclose the existence of the plan, the employee groups covered, the basis for determining contributions, and any significant matters affecting comparability from period to period (such as amendments increasing the annual contribution percentage).

On the other hand, accounting for defined benefit plans is much more complex. In these plans, the pension benefits to be received in the future are affected by uncertain variables such as turnover, mortality, length of employee service, compensation levels, and the earnings of the pension fund assets. In defined benefit plans, the risks are borne by employers because they must make large-enough contributions to meet the pension benefits promised. As a result, the amount of periodic pension expense may not be equal to the cash contributed to the plan.

Since the future pension benefits are affected by uncertain variables, employers hire actuaries to assist in determining the amount of periodic contributions necessary to satisfy future requirements. The actuary takes into consideration the future benefits promised and the characteristics of the employee group (such as age and sex). He or she then makes assumptions about such factors as employee turnover, future salary levels, and the earnings rate on the funds invested, and arrives at the present value of the expected benefits to be received in the future. The employer then determines the funding pattern necessary to satisfy the future obligation.

The employer's actuarial funding method may be either a cost approach or a benefit approach. A *cost approach* estimates the total retirement benefits to be paid in the future and then determines the equal annual payment that will be necessary to fund those benefits. The annual payment necessary is adjusted for the amount of interest assumed to be earned by funds contributed to the plan.

A *benefit approach* determines the amount of pension benefits earned by employee service to date and then estimates the present value of those benefits. Two benefit approaches may be used: (1) the accumulated benefit approach and (2) the benefits/years of service approach. The major difference between these two methods is that under the *accumulated benefits approach,* the annual pension expense and liability are based on existing salary levels; whereas under the *benefits/years of service approach* (also called the *projected unit credit method*) the annual pension expense and liability are based upon the estimated final pay at retirement. The liability for pension benefits under the accumulated benefits approach is termed the *accumulated benefits obligation,* whereas the liability computed under the benefits/years of service approach is termed the *projected benefit obligation.*

Even though the approaches have been defined, accounting for the cost of pension plans has caused a great deal of controversy over the years and several authoritative pronouncements have been issued. In the following sections we will trace the evolution of pension accounting standards.

HISTORICAL PERSPECTIVE

The rapidly increasing number of pension plans coming into existence following World War II caused accountants to question the then current treatment of accounting for pension costs. A major factor behind this concern was the fact that many new pension plans gave employees credit for their years of service before adoption of the plan. The point at issue was the most appropriate treatment of costs associated with past service. In Accounting Research Bulletin No. 47, "Accounting for Costs of Pension Plans," the Committee on Accounting Procedure of the AICPA stated its preference that costs based on current and future service should be systematically accrued during the expected period of active service of the covered employees and that costs based on past services should be charged off over some reasonable period, provided the allocation is made on a systematic and rational basis and does not cause distortion of the operating results in any one year.

As the number of pension plans grew, however, the APB observed that despite ARB No. 47, accounting for the cost of pension plans was inconsistent from year to year, both among companies and within a single company. Sometimes the cost charged to operations was equal to the amount paid into the fund during a given year; at other times no actual funding occurred, and the amortization of past service cost ranged up to 40 years.

Accounting inconsistencies and the growing importance of pension plan costs prompted the APB to authorize Accounting Research Study No. 8, "Accounting for the Cost of Pension Plans." This study was published in 1965 and, after careful examination of its recommendations, the APB issued Opinion No. 8, "Accounting for the Cost of Pension Plans" in 1966. Since the conclusions of the APB were generally similar to those of the research study, we shall review only the Opinion here.

APB Opinion No. 8 identified the basic problems associated with accounting

482   CHAPTER 10: LEASES AND PENSIONS

for the cost of pension plans as (1) measuring the total amount of costs associated with a pension plan, (2) allocating the total pension costs to the proper accounting periods, (3) providing the cash to fund the pension plan, and (4) disclosing the significant aspects of the pension plan on the financial statements.

The conclusions expressed by the APB concerning these questions were based to a large extent on two basic beliefs or assumptions. First, the board believed that most companies will continue the benefits called for in a pension plan even if the plan is not fully funded on a year-to-year basis. Therefore, the cost should be recognized annually whether or not funded. Second, the board adopted the view that the cost of all past service should be charged against income after the adoption or amendment of a plan and that no portion of such cost should be charged directly to retained earnings.

Normal Cost

In APB Opinion No. 8, several issues were addressed and various terms were introduced. In the following paragraphs we will examine these issues and terms as originally defined by the APB; however, it should be noted that subsequent pronouncements have modified these definitions. The current expense provision of pension cost was termed normal cost in APB Opinion No. 8. This was the amount that should be expensed each year based upon the current number of employees and the actuarial cost method being used. As noted earlier, the actuarial cost method must take into consideration such factors as employee turnover, mortality, and the treatment of actuarial gains and losses.

Past Service Cost

When a pension plan is adopted, the employees are given credit for previous years of service. These benefits are referred to as *past service cost* and should be charged as expense in current and future periods. Past service cost is calculated by determining the present value of the amount of future benefits accruing to the current employee group. Prior to the issuance of APB No. 8, many companies charged past service costs against retained earnings as prior period adjustments. This policy was based upon the theory that the benefits of employee service had been obtained in prior periods; therefore, the cost associated with those benefits should be charged to previous periods. APB No. 8 eliminated this treatment of past service costs, and later pronouncements concurred.

Prior Service Cost

Prior service costs are pension costs assigned to years prior to the date of a particular actuarial valuation. Prior service cost arises as a result of an amendment to the original pension agreement or changes in the actuarial assumptions of the pension plan. When the pension agreement is amended or the underlying assumptions change, it becomes necessary to recalculate the expected future benefits accruing to the current employee group. This calculation is similar to the determination of past service cost.

Actuarial Gains and Losses

As noted earlier, pension cost for any period is based upon several assumptions. These assumptions frequently do not coincide with actual results. It is therefore necessary to make periodic adjustments so that actual experience is recognized in the recorded amount of annual pension expense. APB Opinion No. 8 termed the deviations between the actuarial assumptions and actual experience *actuarial gains and losses*.

The amount of any actuarial gain or loss was to be recognized over current and future periods by one of two acceptable methods.

1. *Spreading*. The net annual actuarial gains and losses are applied to current and future costs through an adjustment to either normal cost or past service cost each year.
2. *Averaging*. An average of the sum of previously expensed annual actuarial gains and losses and expected future actuarial gains and losses is applied to normal cost.

Basic Accounting Method

Prior to the time APB Opinion No. 8 was issued, the board could not completely agree on the most appropriate measure of cost to be included in each period. Consequently, it was decided that annual cost should be measured by an acceptable actuarial cost method, consistently applied, that produces an amount between a specified minimum and maximum. (In this context, an acceptable actuarial cost method should be rational and systematic and should be consistently applied so that the cost is reasonably stable from year to year.)

The minimum annual provision (see Fig. 10.3) for pension cost could not be less than the total of

1. Normal cost (cost associated with the years after the date of adoption or amendment of the plan).
2. An amount equivalent to interest on any unfunded past or prior service cost.
3. If indicated, a provision for vested benefits (benefits that are not contingent on the employee continuing in the service of the company).

The maximum annual provision (see Fig. 10.3) for pension cost could not be more than the total of

1. Normal cost.
2. Ten percent of the past service cost (until fully amortized).

484   CHAPTER 10: LEASES AND PENSIONS

Figure 10.3   Minimum and maximum provision for annual pension cost.

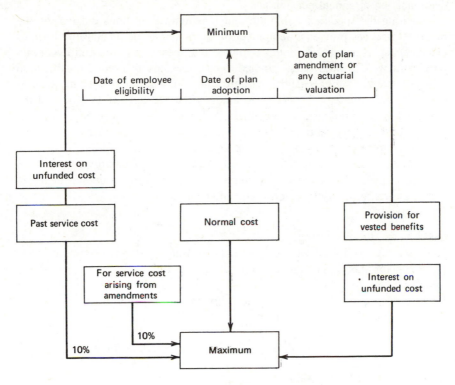

3. Ten percent of the amounts of any increase or decrease in prior service cost arising from amendments of the plan (until fully amortized).

4. Interest equivalents on the difference between provisions, that is, pension costs and amounts funded.

The board's disagreement revolved around two differing viewpoints regarding the nature of pension cost. One view held that pensions are a means of promoting efficiency by (1) providing for the systematic retirement of older people and (2) fulfilling a social obligation expected of a business enterprise. Accordingly, pension costs are associated with the plan itself rather than specific employees, and the amount of pension expense is the amount that must be contributed annually in order to keep the plan in existence indefinitely. The alternate view was that pensions are a form of supplement benefit to the current employee group, so that the amount of pension expense in any period is related to specific employees. Therefore, the amount of pension expense is established by determining the benefits expected to become payable to specific employees in the future. Under either view annual pension expense would include normal costs. However, only the second view would include past and prior service costs in the determination of annual pension cost.

Requiring the specified minimum and maximum provisions did narrow the range of practices previously employed in determining the annual provision of pension cost. However, it should be noted that these minimum and maximum provisions were arbitrarily determined. Thus, the only theoretical justification for their use was a higher degree of uniformity. In addition, the board decided that only the difference between the amount charged against income and the amount funded should be shown in the balance sheet as accrued or prepaid pension cost. The unamortized and unfunded past and prior service cost was not considered to be a liability by the board and was not required to be disclosed on the balance sheet. This decision caused a great deal of controversy and has resulted in many debates among accountants over the proper amount of future pension costs to be disclosed on financial statements.

Disclosure Requirements

A review by the FASB of the information disclosed by companies offering pension plans indicated that more informative disclosures were necessary. FASB Statement No. 36, "Disclosure of Pension Information," was the result of this review. According to this release, the following information must be disclosed for a company's pension agreement.

1. *A statement that such plans exist, identifying or describing the employee groups covered.*
2. *A statement of the company's accounting and funding policies.*
3. *The provision for pension cost for the period.*
4. *The actuarial present values of accumulated vested plan benefits and plan net assets available for benefits.*
5. *The nature and effect of significant matters affecting comparability for all periods presented, such as changes in accounting methods (actuarial cost method, amortization of past and prior service cost, treatment of actuarial gains and losses, etc.), changes in circumstances (actuarial assumptions, etc.) or adoption or amendment of a plan.*
6. *Description of significant actuarial assumptions and the methods used to determine fair value of assets and actuarial value of accumulated benefits.*
7. *Other postretirement benefits, accounting policy followed, and recorded cost.*[18]

---

[18]FASB Statement No. 36, "Disclosure of Pension Information" (Stamford, Conn.: Financial Accounting Standards Board, 1980), par. 8.

Additionally, the following information must also be disclosed and prepared in accordance with the provisions of FASB Statement No. 35 (discussed in a following section): (1) the actuarial present value of vested and nonvested accumulated plan benefits, (2) the plan's net assets available for benefits, (3) the assumed rates of return used in determining the present values of vested and nonvested plan benefits, and (4) the date as of which the benefit information was determined.

THE PENSION LIABILITY ISSUE

In 1981, the FASB proposed a significant change in the method to account for pension cost. The board enumerated several reasons for these proposed changes. First, the number of pension plans had grown enormously since the issuance of APB Opinion No. 8 in 1966. A research study performed by Coopers and Lybrand indicated there were approximately 500,000 private pension plans in the United States in 1979, with total plan assets in excess of $320 billion. There have also been significant changes in laws, regulations, and economic factors affecting pension plans, not the least of which was double-digit inflation.

A second reason cited by the FASB for studying pension accounting was that pension information is inadequate, despite the increased disclosures mandated by SFAS No. 36. Finally, the flexibility of permitted actuarial methods resulted in a lack of comparability among reporting companies, according to some financial-statement users.

The basic issues involved in the FASB's proposal entitled "Preliminary Views" were:

1. What is the period over which the cost of pensions should be recognized? In 1981, pensions costs could be recognized over 30–40 years, which is generally longer than the current work force is expected to continue working.
2. How should pension costs be spread or allocated to the individual periods? The basic question here is whether the practice of choosing among a variety of acceptable costs and funding methods meets the needs of financial statement users.
3. Should information about the status of pensions be included in the statement of changes in financial position? This was undoubtedly the most controversial of the issues considered.

The position taken in the FASB's "Preliminary Views" would have required an employer that sponsors a defined benefit pension plan to recognize a net pension liability (or asset) on its balance sheet. This disclosure would be comprised of the following three components: *the pension benefit obligation* less *the plan's net assets available for benefits* plus or minus *a measurement valuation allowance*. This calculation of pension cost coincides with the view that pension expense should be recognized in the period in which the employees render their services.

One of the organizations that opposed the position of the "Preliminary View" was the AICPA task force on pension plans and pension costs. This group's opposition was expressed in several general areas.

1. The amounts involved do not meet the definition of assets or liabilities under FASB Concepts Statement No. 3 (now SFAC No. 6).
2. A pension arrangement is essentially an executory contract which under existing generally accepted accounting principles is accounted for only as the covered services are performed.
3. Too much subjectivity is involved in determining the amount of the net pension liability—that is, the number is too "soft" to be reported in basic financial statements.
4. Finally, the FASB has not demonstrated the need to amend APB Opinion No. 8 extensively.

Despite this opposition, the FASB remained determined to change previous pension accounting methods. Under the method originally advocated in "Preliminary Views," the pension benefit obligation would be comprised of an accrual for benefits earned by the employees but not yet paid, including prior service credits granted when a plan is initiated or amended. The obligation would include both vested and nonvested benefits and would be measured based on estimates of future compensation levels.

The measure of the pension benefit obligation proposed was called the *actuarial present value of accumulated benefits with salary progression*. It is consistent with the measurement method required under FASB Statement No. 36, with one key difference. The liability under SFAS No. 36 pertains to accumulated benefits and does *not* take into account any future salary increases, where the proposed method would have required a forecast of salary growth for pension plans that define benefits in terms of an employee's future salary. Since most sponsors utilize financial pay plans, the salary growth assumption would result in pension benefit obligations larger than those previously being reported.

On the other hand, if plan assets exceeded the benefit obligation, a company would report a net pension asset on its balance sheet. The plan's investment assets available for benefits would be measured at fair value, consistent with FASB Statement No. 35, "Accounting and Reporting for Defined Benefit Pension Plans" (discussed later in this chapter).

The third component of the net pension liability is the measurement valuation allowance. This component was intended to reduce the volatility of the net pension liability inherent in the prediction of future events, such as changes in the pension benefit obligation and the plan assets, due to experience gains and losses or changes in actuarial assumptions.

Under "Preliminary Views," the amount of annual pension expense that an employer would recognize was the sum of the following amounts.

1. The increase in the pension benefit obligation attributable to employee service during the period (conceptually similar to "normal cost").
2. The increase in the pension benefit obligation attributable to the accrual of interest on the obligation (resulting from the fact that the obligation is the discounted present value of estimated future payments).
3. The increase in plan assets resulting from earnings on the assets at the assumed rate (reducing the periodic pension expense).
4. The amortization of the measurement valuation allowance, which may either increase or decrease the pension expense. Actuarial gains or losses would be included in the measurement of valuation allowance.

STATEMENT OF FINANCIAL ACCOUNTING STANDARDS NO. 87

After deliberating the issues addressed in "Preliminary Views" for several years, the FASB reached a consensus in 1985 and issued SFAS No. 87 "Employers' Accounting for Pensions." This release took the position that pension information should be prepared on the accrual basis and retained three fundamental aspects of past pension accounting: (1) delaying recognition of certain events, (2) reporting net cost, and (3) offsetting assets and liabilities.

The delayed-recognition feature results in systematic recognition of changes in the pension obligation (such as plan amendments). It also results in changes in the value of assets set aside to meet those obligations.

The net cost feature results in reporting as a single amount the recognized consequences of the events that affected the pension plan. Three items are aggregated to arrive at this amount: (1) the annual cost of the benefits promised, (2) the interest cost resulting from the deferred payment of those benefits, and (3) the result of investing the pension assets.

Offsetting means that the value of the assets contributed to a pension plan and the liabilities recognized as pension cost in previous periods are disclosed as a single net amount in the employer's financial statements.

The members of the FASB expressed the view that understandability, comparability, and the usefulness of pension information will be improved by narrowing the range of methods available for allocating the cost of an employee's pension to individual periods of service. The board also expressed the view that the pension plan's benefit formula provides the most relevant and reliable indicator to how pension costs and pension benefits are incurred. Therefore, three changes in previous pension accounting were required by SFAS No. 87.

1. A standardized method of measuring net pension cost. The board indicated that this method was intended to improve comparability and understandability

by recognizing the cost of an employee's pension over that employee's approximate service period.

2. Immediate recognition of a pension liability when the accumulated benefit obligation exceeds the fair value of the pension assets (recall from our earlier discussion that the accumulated benefit obligation is the liability for pension benefits computed under the accumulated benefits approach and does not take future salary increases into consideration).

3. Expanded disclosures intended to provide more complete and current information than can be practically incorporated into the financial statements at this time.

Pension Cost

Under the provisions of SFAS No. 87, net pension cost is comprised of several components reflecting different aspects of the benefits earned by employees and the method of financing those benefits by the employer. The following components are required to be included in the net pension cost recognized by an employer sponsoring a defined benefit pension plan.

1. Service cost.
2. Interest cost.
3. Actual return on plan assets.
4. Amortization of unrecognized prior service cost.
5. Amortization of gains and losses.
6. Amortization of the unrecognized net obligation or unrecognized net asset at the date of the initial application of SFAS No. 87 (the transition amount).

The *service cost* component is determined as the actuarial present value of the benefits attributed by the pension formula to employee service for that period. This requirement means that one of the benefit approaches discussed earlier must be used as the basis for assigning pension cost to an accounting period. It also means that the benefits/years of service approach should be used to calculate pension cost for all plans that use this benefit approach in calculating earned pension benefits. The FASB's position is that the terms of the agreement should form the basis for recording the expense and obligation, and the plan's benefit formula is the best measure of the amount of cost incurred each period. The discount rate to be used in the calculation of service cost is the rate at which the pension benefits could be settled, such as by purchasing annuity contracts from an insurance company. This rate is termed the *settlement-basis discount rate*.

The *interest cost* component is determined as the increase in the projected benefit obligation due to the passage of time. Recall that the pension liability is recorded on a discounted basis and accrues interest each year. The interest cost component is determined by accruing interest on the previous year's pension liability at the settlement-basis discount rate.

490

The actual *return on plan assets* component is the difference between the fair value of these assets from the beginning to the end of the period, adjusted for contributions, benefits, and payments. That is, the interest and dividends earned on the funds actually contributed to the pension fund will reduce the amount of net pension cost for the period.

Prior service cost is the total cost of retroactive benefits at the date the pension plan is initiated or amended. Prior service cost is assigned to the expected remaining service period of each employee expected to receive benefits. (As a practical matter, the FASB allows for a simplified method of assigning this cost to future periods; the company may assign this cost on a straight-line basis over the average remaining service life of its active employees.)

Gains and losses are changes in either the projected benefit obligation or plan assets. They result from experience different from what was assumed or from changes in assumptions. The gain or loss component of pension cost consists of two elements. (A) The yearly difference between the actual return on plan assets and the expected return. This amount is recognized currently as a *return adjustment*. (B) The amortization of any unrecognized gain or loss from previous periods. The FASB adopted what was termed the *corridor approach* in the recognition of gains and losses for the part (B) element. This approach reduces the amount of gain or loss recognized as adjustments to pension cost. Recognition of gains and losses is not required unless any unrecognized gain or loss at the beginning of the year is in excess of 10 percent of the greater of the projected benefit obligation or the market value of the plan assets. If amortization is required, the amount to be recognized is the excess amount (the gain or loss in excess of the corridor) divided by the average remaining service period of the employees expected to receive benefits. The rationale for the use of the corridor approach is that some of these gains and losses will offset each other over time and therefore volatility is reduced.

SFAS No. 87 requires significant changes in pension accounting from what was previously required in APB Opinion No. 8. As a result, the board decided to allow for a relatively long transition period. Most companies will not be required to follow the provisions of SFAS No. 87 until the 1987 calendar year. Additionally, the minimum liability provision (discussed in the next section) need not be reported until calendar year 1989. Since these changes are so significant, an *unrecognized net obligation* or *unrecognized net asset* will frequently result when changing to the new reporting requirements. Therefore, the provisions of SFAS No. 87 require companies to determine, on the date the provisions of this statement are first applied, the amount of (1) the projected benefit obligation and (2) the amount of the fair value of the plan assets. This will result in either an unrecognized net obligation or unrecognized net asset. This amount, termed the *transition amount,* should be amortized on a straight-line basis over the average remaining service period of employees expecting to receive benefits.

Minimum Liability Recognition

When a plan is initiated or amended, the increase in prior service cost to be amortized in future periods is not recorded. Recall that the FASB's original position on this issue, expressed in "Preliminary Views," was that a liability existed when the projected benefit obligation exceeded the plan assets or that an asset existed if the reverse was true. Since agreement on this issue could not be reached, the board developed a compromise position which requires recognition of a liability, termed the *minimum liability,* when the accumulated benefit obligation exceeds the fair value of the plan assets. It is important to note that the minimum liability is based upon the accumulated benefit obligation and not the projected benefit obligation. As a result, future salary levels are not taken into consideration in computing the minimum liability.

The debit to offset any recognized minimum liability is not recorded as a component of annual pension cost. This amount is generally recognized as an intangible asset because unfunded accumulated benefits usually result from plan amendments that are expected to benefit future periods. However, in the event the amount of minimum liability exceeds the amount of the existing prior service cost, this excess is not considered to have future economic benefit and must be classified as a reduction of equity instead of an intangible asset. The intangible asset or reduction in equity is not amortized. The required amount of minimum liability is reassessed annually, and any necessary adjustment is made directly to either the intangible asset or stockholders' equity. The following example illustrates the applications of the provisions of SFAS No. 87.

The Stevens Company has a defined benefit pension plan covering all of its 100 full-time employees. Prior to January 1, 1987, the cumulative pension expense recognized equaled its contributions. On January 1, 1987, Stevens adopted SFAS No. 87. On the date of transition the projected benefit obligation and plan assets are

Projected benefit obligation	$3,000,000
Fair value of plan assets	1,700,000
Unrecognized net obligation	$1,300,000

Additional Information

1.	The benefits per years of service approach indicates that the actuarial present value of the benefits earned during the period were	$ 180,000
2.	The settlement basis discount rate is	9%
3.	The expected rate of return is	9%
4.	The actual return on plan assets during 1987 was	$ 120,000
5.	The employees' average remaining service period is	10 years
6.	Accumulated benefit obligation 12/31/87	$2,200,000

Components of Pension Cost

Service Cost (given)	$ 180,000

Interest Cost (9% × $3,000,000)	$ 270,000
Actual return on plan assets	($ 120,000)
Prior service cost	0
Return adjustment [($1,700,000 × .09) − 120,000]	($ 33,000)
Prior Service Cost	0
Gain or loss (no element (B) gain or loss is recognized since the unrealized gain or loss at the beginning of the period is 0.)	0
Transition amount (Net underfunding at transition—that is, the projected benefit obligation is less than the fair value of plan assets, or $3,000,000 − 1,700,000 = $1,300,000. This amount is amortized over the average employee service life of 10 years)	130,000
Pension Expense	$ 427,000

Calculation of the Minimum Liability

The unfunded accumulated benefits at the end of 1987 were $500,000 ($2,200,000 − 1,700,000). This amount will be recorded as a pension liability and as an intangible asset (note that it is an intangible asset because there is no unrecognized prior service cost).

Disclosures

SFAS No. 87 requires employers to disclose information beyond that previously required. Perhaps the most significant of these new disclosures are the components of net pension cost and the funding status of the plan. Specifically, employers sponsoring defined benefit plans must disclose the following information.

1. A description of the plan including employee groups covered, type of benefit formula, funding policy, types of assets held, significant nonbenefit liabilities if any, and the nature and effect of significant matters affecting comparability of information for all periods presented.
2. The amount of net periodic pension cost for the period showing separately the service cost component, the interest cost component, the actual return on assets for the period, and the net total of other components.
3. A schedule reconciling the funded status of the plan with amounts reported in the employer's statement of financial position, showing separately
   a. The fair value of plan assets.
   b. The projected benefit obligation identifying the accumulated benefit obligation and the vested benefit obligation.
   c. The amount of unrecognized prior service cost.
   d. The amount of unrecognized prior net gain or loss.
   e. The amount of any remaining unrecognized net obligation or net asset existing at the date of initial application of SFAS No. 87.

f. The amount of any additional liability recognized.

g. The amount of net pension asset or liability recognized in the statement of financial positions (this is the net result of combining the preceding six items).

h. The weighted average assumed discount rate and the weighted average expected long-term rate of return on plan assets.

The annual pension cost reported by corporations under SFAS No. 87 will undoubtedly be different than disclosed under the provisions of APB Opinion No. 8. The magnitude of these differences will depend on such factors as the pension plan's benefit formula, employees' remaining service periods, investment returns, and prior accounting and funding policies. Companies that have underfunded pension plans with a relatively short future employee service period may be required to report significantly higher pension expense.

In releasing SFAS No. 87, the board stated that this pronouncement was a continuation of its evolutionary search for more meaningful and more useful pension accounting information. The board also stated that while it believes that the conclusions it reached are a worthwhile and significant step in that direction, these conclusions are not likely to be the final step in the evolution. Table 10.1 compares the evolution of these standards from APB Opinion No. 8 through "Preliminary Views" to SFAS No. 87.

ACCOUNTING FOR THE PENSION FUND

Until 1980, accounting practice often relied on the actuary's funding and cash flow considerations for measuring pension costs and accumulated pension benefits. At that time, Accounting Principles Board Opinion No. 8, "Accounting for the Costs of Pension Plans," stated that accounting for pension expense and related liabilities was separate and distinct from actuarial costing for funding purposes. However, according to FASB Statement No. 35, "Accounting and Reporting by Defined Benefit Pension Plans," the status of plans for financial reporting purposes is to be determined by actuarial methodology designed not for funding purposes but, rather, for financial reporting purposes.

Neither the FASB nor its predecessors had issued authoritative accounting standards specifically applicable to pension plans. Therefore, the financial reporting by those plans varied widely. Statement No. 35 establishes accounting and reporting standards designed to correct this shortcoming.

The primary objective of FASB No. 35 is to provide financial information that is useful in assessing a pension plan's current and future ability to pay benefits when due. In attempting to accomplish this objective, Statement No. 35 requires that pension plan financial statements include four basic categories of information:

Table 10.1   Comparison of Previous Accounting Practice With FASB's "Preliminary Views" and Statement of Financial Accounting Standards No. 87

Issue	Previous Accounting	Preliminary Views	SFAS No. 87
Recognition of a liability.	A liability recognized equal to accumulated expense based on an acceptable actuarial method less amounts funded.	Recognizes a net pension liability (or asset) based on services rendered by the employees, using an actuarial method the FASB concludes is most appropriate for accounting purposes.	Recognition of a liability if periodic cost exceeds contributions to the plan. Additional "minimum liability" recognized when the accumulated benefit obligation exceeds the fair value of the plan assets.
Recognition of plan assets as employer's assets.	Not recognized as employer's assets.	Recognizes plan assets as an offset against the pension obligation. Could result in a net asset.	Not recognized as employer's assets
Measurement of pension liability and expense.	Based on a number of actuarial cost methods that achieve systematic and rational allocation of pension cost.	Proposes one method as most appropriate for accounting purposes: the projected-unit-credit method for final pay and career-average pay plans, and the accumulated benefits method for flat benefit plans.	Based upon the terms of the pension agreement. Uses the accumulated benefits approach for plans based upon existing salary levels and the benefits per years of service approach for plans based upon future salary levels.

(continued)

Table 10.1 (Continued)

Accounting for changes in the plan, including a new one that gives credit for past service.	No immediate recognition of an accounting liability. Pension expense and the related actuarial liabilities are recognized over a number of future periods.	Recognizes the increased pension benefit obligation (liability) and records an intangible asset representing expected future economic benefits. Pension expense would include amortization of prior service cost over the average remaining service period of active plan participants.	No immediate recognition of the liability. Recognizes increased pension expense over the expected remaining service period of employees expected to receive benefit.
Accounting for actuarial gains or losses (measurement changes).	Included in pension expense in a systematic and rational manner (i.e., spread or averaged over a period of 10 to 20 years).	Establishes a measurement valuation allowance, consisting of realized and unrealized experience gains and losses and effects of changes in actuarial assumptions, which would be a component of the net pension liability. Recognizes measurement changes prospectively through amortization of the measurement valuation allowance based on the average remaining service period of active plan participants.	No immediate recognition of the liability. Corridor approach adopted. Ten percent of the excess of any annual gain or loss in excess of the greater of the projected benefit obligation or the market value of the plan assets is recognized over the average service period of employees expected to receive benefits.

Source: Adapted from Coopers & Lybrand, Executive Alert Newsletter, Dec.–Jan. 1985, p. 14.

1. Net assets available for benefits.
2. Changes in net assets during the reporting period.
3. The actuarial present value of accumulated plan benefits.
4. The significant effects of factors such as plan amendments and changes in actuarial assumptions on the year-to-year change in the actuarial present value of accumulated plan benefits.

Information about net assets must be available for plan benefits at the end of the plan year and must be prepared on the accrual basis of accounting.

The statement also sets standards for information regarding participants' accumulated plan benefits. Accumulated plan benefits are defined as those future benefit payments attributable under the plan's provisions to employees' service rendered to date. Information about these accumulated benefits may be presented either at the beginning or at the end of the plan year. Accumulated plan benefits are to be measured at their actuarial present value, based primarily on history of pay and service and other appropriate factors.

THE EMPLOYEE RETIREMENT INCOME SECURITY ACT

In 1974 Congress passed the Employee Retirement Income Security Act (ERISA), also known as the Pension Reform Act of 1974. The basic goals of this legislation were to create standards for the operation of pension funds and to correct abuses in the handling of pension funds.

ERISA establishes guidelines for employee participation in pension plans, vesting provisions, minimum funding requirements, financial statement disclosure of pension plans, and the administration of the pension plan. Shortly thereafter, the FASB undertook a study of the impact of ERISA on APB Opinion No. 8. The conclusions of this study are contained in FASB Interpretation No. 3:

1. *The Pension Reform Act of 1974 is concerned with pension cost funding requirements. The fundamental concept of APB Opinion No. 8, that the amount of pension cost expense is not necessarily determined by funding policies, is not affected by ERISA.*
2. *No change in the computation of the required minimum, and maximum provisions is required by ERISA.*
3. *Compliance with ERISA's participation vesting or funding requirements may change the amount of expense that might otherwise have been incurred.*
4. *Any additional expenses incurred because of compliance with the provisions of ERISA shall be charged to current and future periods subsequent to the date the pension plan became subject to ERISA's provisions.*[19]

[19]FASB Interpretation No. 3 "Accounting for the Cost of Pension Plans Subject to the Employee Retirement Income Security Act of 1974" (Stamford, Conn.: FASB, 1974).

In essence, FASB Interpretation No. 3 states that the provisions of APB Opinion No. 8 were not affected by ERISA. However, compliance with the act's requirements can increase the amount of pension cost charged to expense in current and future periods over what it would have been prior to the enactment of ERISA. The provisions of SFAS No. 87 are also not affected by ERISA. The pronouncements of the APB and the FASB are concerned with periodic expense and liability recognition. The provisions of ERISA are mainly concerned with the funding policies of pension plans.

SUMMARY

Statement of Financial Accounting Standards No. 13 sets forth clear criteria for identifying leases that are to be capitalized by lessees and treated as sales-type or direct financing leases by lessors. The criteria were designed to achieve symmetry in accounting between lessees and lessors. The achievement of symmetry, however, will depend upon such things as whether comparable interest rates are used by the lessee and lessor in calculating the present value of the minimum lease rentals, whether the two certainty criteria applied by the lessor are met, and whether current leasing techniques are continued or new off–balance sheet techniques are found. Thus, the statement may achieve its stated objective, or it may simply cause the demise of current leasing activities and the creation of some different approaches for securing and providing the use of the assets.

Accounting for the cost of pension plans continues to be a controversial issue. Although both the Accounting Principles Board and the Financial Accounting Standards Board have addressed this issue, a complete consensus has not been achieved. There still are a variety of views on what constitutes a company's liability and periodic expense for a pension plan. Similarly, there are differing views on how to measure and disclose pension assets and liabilities on financial statements. In the articles that follow, Timothy Lucas and Betsy Ann Hollowell discuss the possible recognition of future pension obligations and John W. Coughlan discusses several problems associated with applying FASB Statement No. 13.

PENSION ACCOUNTING: THE LIABILITY QUESTION

TIMOTHY S. LUCAS
BETSY ANN HOLLOWELL

Financial reports are not telling the whole story about pensions. But how should that story be told? Should some part of the pension obligation not currently recognized as a liability be included on the balance sheet of the employer? Is there an unrecorded liability for pensions under existing generally accepted accounting principles?

We want to discuss this aspect of pension accounting for three reasons. First, the many questions in the pension accounting area are so complex that they all cannot be effectively discussed at once, and the answer to the liability question does not appear to depend on answers to other questions. Second, and more important, the question is one of the most significant in terms of the changes from current accounting that could result from the Financial Accounting Standards Board's pension accounting project. That significance can help us to achieve our primary objective—to stimulate thinking about and discussion of the issues involved in the board's project. Third, a majority of the speakers at the FASB's July 13–15 public hearings in New York on its discussion memorandum (DM), *Employers' Accounting for Pensions and Other Postemployment Benefits,*[1] took positions 'against including pension obligations on employers' balance sheets and provided a variety of supporting arguments. We believe an interesting case can be made *for* recognizing pension liabilities, and that case should be considered and debated by those who are interested in pension accounting questions.[2]

To understand better how the weight of pension liabilities can affect major decisions of management, consider the following report in the press: "Esmark announced recently that it was putting its meat-packing subsidiary, Swift Fresh Meats Division, on the market—and fund-

[1] Financial Accounting Standards Board Discussion Memorandum, *Employers' Accounting for Pensions and Other Postemployment Benefits* (Stamford, Conn.: FASB, 1981).

[2] The liability question is one of eight issues addressed in the DM. This article does not attempt to cover other closely related questions, including how to measure the liability if it is to be recorded and the nature of the offsetting debit that arises if a liability is recorded. Measuring or determining the amount of the liability is complex and involves two problems. First, any measure of the pension obligation involves estimating future events, such as how long retirees will live and how many employees will leave before vesting or die before retiring. Second, even after all the estimates are made, there are different attributes of the obligation that may be measured, including vested benefits, accumulated benefits and prior service cost determined under one or more actuarial cost methods. Determining the amount that might be recorded as a liability is beyond the scope of this article, but it involves understanding events related to the growth of the pension obligation as an employee's career progresses from hiring to retirement. The possible choices with regard to the nature of the offsetting debit that arises if a liability is recorded discussed in the DM include recording the debit as an intangible asset or as some kind of charge on the income statement.

ing the subsidiary's 'sizable' unfunded pension liabilities.

"'They had to do that to make it saleable,' one Esmark analyst commented."

The same article also included a description of another situation: "One instance where pension liabilities were not adequately covered in the original deal—and later came back to haunt a firm—involved the spin-off in 1976 of Facet Enterprises from The Bendix Corp. The divestiture was ordered by the Federal Trade Commission, and Bendix formed Facet as a subsidiary, transferred certain business units to Facet and in 1976 distributed all of the stock of Facet to the common stockholders of Bendix. Included in the transfer to Facet were large unfunded pension liabilities.

"Facet eventually filed suit against Bendix, charging the company was aware of 'highly detrimental financial consequences' the transfer of the obligation would have on Facet."[3]

Facet Enterprises subsequently notified the Pension Benefit Guaranty Corp. that it was terminating the pension plan, which covered some twenty-two hundred employees and retirees. Facet said that terminating the pension plan was necessary to rescue its financially troubled automotive parts divisions and that the plan's unfunded liabilities of about $31 million exceeded the net worth of the three units it covered.

At about the same time, *Fortune* reported

> When Kaiser Steel was considering liquidation last September . . . some people saw an opportunity for a quick profit in the stock. They believed the sell-off of Kaiser's various properties would fetch considerably more than the

$44 per share its stock was going for. This reasoning, however, overlooked the company's unfunded vested pension liability of about $9 per share and the even larger amount Kaiser says it would have had to fork over to provide health insurance and other benefits to retirees. When Kaiser's directors eventually voted not to liquidate, they gave as one reason the size of these burdens. The board concluded the liquidation value could actually be below the $44 market price."[4]

In these situations, which unfortunately are not unique, a pension obligation had an unexpected and newsworthy effect on the economic potential and well-being of the company. The pension obligation was not suddenly created in any of these situations. It existed all along, but it was not reported as a liability. Although each company had prepared financial statements in accordance with GAAP, the pension situation was not fully understood, even by knowledgeable readers of those statements.

CURRENT PENSION GAAP

Employer accounting for pensions is based, at present, on Accounting Principles Board Opinion no. 8, *Accounting for the Cost of Pension Plans*,[5] as amended by FASB Statement no. 36, *Disclosure of Pension Information*.[6] Opinion no. 8 allows pension cost to be determined under any of a number of acceptable actuarial

[4]Mary Greenebaum, "The Market Has Spotted Those Pension Problems," *Fortune*, December 1, 1980, p. 146.
[5]Accounting Principles Board Opinion no. 8, *Accounting for the Cost of Pension Plans* (New York: AICPA, 1966).
[6]FASB Statement no. 36. *Disclosure of Pension Information* (Stamford, Conn.: FASB, 1980).

[3]Maria Crawford Scott, "Pension Liabilities May Hurt Merger," *Pensions and Investments*, October 13, 1980, p. 4.

CHAPTER 10: LEASES AND PENSIONS

cost methods. Typically, the method used to determine funding of a pension plan (the annual contribution to the pension fund or trust) is also used for accounting.

Under current GAAP, most balance sheets do not include a line item labeled "pension liability." Nevertheless, under Opinion no. 8 part of the pension obligation is recorded as a liability. The amount of liability recorded (debit expense, credit liability) typically is equal to the amount of liability discharged by the contribution (debit liability, credit cash). This is because contributions to the pension plan are recorded as discharges of the pension liability and because most companies fund pension cost accrued. The resulting net liability—the amount appearing on the balance sheet—is zero. But the amount expensed and contributed to the plan cannot be called an unrecorded liability in the usual sense. It does not appear on the balance sheet only because the transfer of assets to the pension fund is regarded as payment of the liability. If, instead, we view the transfer as a segregation or setting aside of assets, it would be logical to add the accumulated amounts expensed (the liability) and the assets held by the plan to the balance sheet.

But for most employers and most plans another part of the pension obligation has not yet been expensed, recorded as a liability or "discharged" by contributions to the plan. The pension obligation that is not recorded as a liability under current GAAP results, primarily, from plan amendments. Parts of that obligation also may result from establishment of new plans and from cumulative experience gains and losses, but for simplicity we will focus on plan amendments. When a pension plan is amended to increase benefits, the increased benefits usually are granted based on service, including service rendered before the date of the change. In some cases benefits also are increased for former employees who are already retired. After such an amendment, the employer's pension obligation is larger than it was before. It is this incremental obligation that some believe should be recorded as a liability. This view is based on the idea that the employer has an obligation for benefits already earned by employees. The amount of benefits earned (however measured) will not necessarily coincide with the accumulation of prior years' normal costs and amortization of prior service costs recorded under Opinion no. 8.

For convenience, let's assume that we are dealing with a typical company that sponsors a single-employer, defined-benefit pension plan. The plan provides a retirement income benefit of, say, $50 per month for each year of an employee's service. In the current year, the company amends the plan to increase the benefits to $60 per month per year of service for all active employees and for retirees who are receiving pensions. The amendment provides for increased benefits based on all of an employee's years of service, past as well as future. Actuaries will review the change and compute the new, increased amount of contribution the company will pay over a period of years to find the increased benefits. The accounting question is, When the plan is amended, does a recordable liability arise for that part of the increased benefits attributed to past years of service?

Opinion no. 8 accounting reflects such an amendment prospectively, usually based on the way the cost of the amendment will be funded. No increase in liability is recorded immediately as a result of the event that occurred when the plan was amended. Instead, it is provided for and recorded as expense and a liability a little bit at a time.

Whether a recordable liability arises

when the plan is amended depends on what kinds of things belong on balance sheets. Accountants and users of financial statements generally understand the nature of items on balance sheets, including liabilities. That knowledge makes the balance sheet useful. Liabilities such as accounts payable, notes payable and bonds payable all have something in common. And, most important, all accounts, notes and bonds payable are included. If each company had the flexibility to omit some of these items in preparing its balance sheet, disclosing the omitted items in the footnotes, the usefulness of the balance sheet would be reduced. Analysts would doubtless add the "footnote liabilities" to those on the statement and construct their own adjusted balance sheets (as some do today with pension disclosures), but the convenience of having a complete balance sheet would be lost and some users might be misled because they expect all liabilities to be included.

The FASB has begun the process of describing the kinds of things that belong on the right-hand side of a balance sheet by providing a definition of liabilities. Financial Accounting Concepts Statement no. 3, *Elements of Financial Statements of Business Enterprises,* defines liabilities as "probable future sacrifices of economic benefits arising from present obligations of a particular entity to transfer assets or provide services to other entities in the future as a result of past transactions or events."[7]

The concepts statement also identifies three essential characteristics of a liability inherent in the definition: ". . . (a) it embodies a present duty or responsibility to one or more other entities that entails settlement by probable future transfer or use of assets at a specified or determinable date, on occurrence of a specified event, or on demand, (b) the duty or responsibility obligates a particular enterprise, leaving it little or no discretion to avoid the future sacrifice, and (c) the transaction or other event obligating the enterprise has already happened."[8]

In addition, it discusses other features often found in liabilities:

Liabilities commonly have other features that help identify them—for example, most liabilities require the obligated enterprise to pay cash to one or more identified other entities and are legally enforceable. However, those features are not essential characteristics of liabilities. Their absence, by itself, is not sufficient to preclude an item's qualifying as a liability. That is, liabilities may not require an enterprise to pay cash but to convey other assets, to provide or stand ready to provide services, or to use assets. And as long as payment or other transfer of assets to settle an existing obligation is probable, the identity of the recipient need not be known to the obligated enterprise before the time of settlement. Similarly, although most liabilities rest generally on a foundation of legal rights and duties, existence of a legally enforceable claim is not a prerequisite for an obligation to qualify as a liability if the future payment of cash or other transfer of assets to settle the obligation is otherwise probable.[9]

A careful reading of the above excerpts reveals that the definition of liabilities is primarily a description of current practice; it is not a radical change but a formal de-

---

[7]Financial Accounting Concepts Statement no. 3, *Elements of Financial Statements of Business Enterprises* (Stamford, Conn.: FASB, 1980), par. 28.

[8]Ibid., par. 29.
[9]Ibid., par. 29.

CHAPTER 10: LEASES AND PENSIONS

scription of the kinds of things that we already think of as liabilities. Accountants are likely to agree, for example, that accrued salaries payable is a liability because the company has a responsibility or obligation to employees who have performed services for which they have not yet been paid. The obligation probably will be satisfied by paying the accrued amounts (transferring assets) at a future date, and the event that obligated the company (the performance of the services) has already occurred.

On the other hand, a budgeted expenditure to replace a machine is not a liability, even though the transfer of assets may be virtually certain and the need to replace the machine acute. The budgeted expenditure does not entail the essential obligation—the duty or responsibility to another entity. That obligation will be created by a future event.

The same understanding of a liability (as formalized by Concepts Statement no. 3) can be used in considering the pension liability question. In the example described earlier, when the plan is amended is there an obligation to make a probable future payment? Has the event that obligated the company already happened? It seems clear to us that a case can be made for an affirmative answer to those questions. If so, the pension obligation is similar to other obligations that are recorded as liabilities, and the balance sheet would be incomplete—its usefulness diminished—if the pension liability was excluded, just as it would be incomplete without bank loans or accounts payable.

The news excerpts quoted earlier suggest that economic decisions sometimes are affected by the failure of decision makers to fully understand or consider pension obligations. As noted, the pension obligations that are not recorded and may therefore be overlooked result primarily from plan amendments. The incremental pension obligations that result from a plan amendment are now recorded as liabilities only over future periods. If those obligations were included on the balance sheet as liabilities when incurred, it seems to us, they would be less likely to be overlooked, and the balance sheet would provide a more complete picture of the financial position of the company. We also noted that some analysts adjust present balance sheets to consider some measure of pension obligations. If, as we have suggested, the unrecorded pension obligation looks like other obligations afforded balance sheet status, why do some people still want to exclude pension obligations from balance sheets?

ARGUMENTS FOR AND AGAINST DEFERRED RECOGNITION OF PENSION LIABILITIES

The remainder of this article explores some of the reasons advanced for continuing the present practice of deferred recognition of pension liabilities resulting from plan amendments. Our opinions as to why those reasons have not been convincing also are discussed. The arguments for and against recognition generally apply equally to the obligation resulting from plan amendments and to that resulting from other factors such as experience gains and losses.

The company's obligation is only to make contributions. Some people suggest that the company does not have an obligation directly to the employees but only an obligation to make scheduled contributions to the plan. They conclude that there is no liability if contributions called for (by the actuary) have been made.

We believe this confuses the existence of a liability with its maturity date. If there is an obligation to the plan—an obligation to make future contributions—resulting from past events such as plan amendments and past service, that obligation may qualify as a liability. The fact that the contributions are scheduled for payment in future years does not mean that the obligation should remain unrecorded; most liabilities have scheduled future payment dates. The obligation to the plan and the obligation to the employees are two different ways to describe the same thing. The crucial question is whether there is a present obligation as a result of past transactions or events, not the identification of the obligee.

In addition, the idea that the existence of the pension plan or trust as a separate legal entity somehow avoids what would otherwise be the company's liability leads to other questions. Suppose a company set up a similar trust to be funded over a period of years to pay off a major lawsuit settlement. Should the full amount of the agreed on settlement be recorded as a liability or is it only an obligation of the trust?

It is not a legal liability. Some argue that the pension liability should be excluded from the balance sheet because it is not a "legal" liability. As the excerpt we quoted from Concepts Statement no. 3 notes, legal status is not required for an obligation to be recorded as a liability. In addition, the meaning of the term *legal liability* in this context is unclear. Pension obligations have been held to be legally enforceable in various circumstances.

It will never have to be paid. If a pension plan is assumed to continue in effect, the liability will never be fully paid since there will always be active employees whose pensions are not yet payable. Some people suggest that the pension obligation need not be recorded on this basis.

The same thing may be said, however, of many other liabilities. For example, if a company continues in business, it is unlikely ever to reduce the balance of accounts payable to zero, but it is still considered useful to record and report the total amount of the obligation at the end of each period. This argument seems to be more relevant to funding decisions than to accounting questions.

The amount of the obligation can't be measured. Some argue that the pension obligation should be excluded from the balance sheet because it is too uncertain or too hard to measure. They note that several future events must be estimated to calculate the amount of the obligation and that it is expected that these estimates will have to be adjusted as experience unfolds. The need to estimate and project future events is not unique to pensions. Accounting unavoidably involves many estimates and must be able to deal with changes in those estimates. The best current estimate of the amount of the pension obligation, based on the experience and knowledge of the professional actuary, is useful information. Pension accounting is already based on the same estimates; the only difference is that the amounts are spread over a number of future periods.

Spreading the effect of a plan amendment over a number of future periods tends to obscure, rather than report, the effect of the change. The obligation for future pension payments or contributions clearly is greater after a plan amendment than it was before the amendment. Financial Accounting Concepts Statement no. 1, *Objectives of Financial Reporting by Business Enterprises,* states

"Financial reporting should provide information about the economic resources of an enterprise, the claims to those resources (obligations of the enterprise to transfer resources to other entities and owners' equity), and the effects of transactions, events, and circumstances that change its resources and claims to those resources."[10]

[10]Financial Accounting Concepts Statement no. 1, *Objectives of Financial Reporting by Business*

Since the plan amendment is an event that changes the employer's obligation—an event that increases employees' claims to the company's resources—financial statements should reflect that event.

The increased benefits are granted in exchange for future service. Some suggest that increases in pension benefits are granted in anticipation of future employee services, even though the amount of increase may be computed based on the number of years of prior service. In this view, the employer would be unlikely to increase benefits unless he expected to receive something of value in return. Since the value of past services cannot be enhanced retroactively, the employer must expect to receive benefits in the form of future services. The suggested conclusion is that the liability arises only as the future service is rendered.

The use of this line of reasoning for benefit increases granted to those already retired is based on the idea that current employees will provide services in exchange for benefits paid to other individuals already retired because they expect to receive similar increases after they retire.

The problem with that argument is it does not address whether the employer has a liability—a present obligation to transfer assets as a result of past transactions or events. After a plan amendment becomes effective, that obligation exists. What the employer receives in return for incurring the liability is another issue. An asset can exist as a result of the amendment, for example, if employees are motivated to work harder. Concepts Statement no. 3 has defined assets as "probable future economic benefits obtained or controlled by a particular entity as a result of past transactions or events."[11] Whether an intangible asset ex-

ists after a plan amendment is beyond the scope of this article.

Liability recognition would have economic consequences. Some suggest that recognizing the unrecorded pension liability would cause some employers to go bankrupt, to be denied access to credit markets or to be unwilling to improve pension plans. These and other predicted economic consequences are perceived as undesirable. They are said to be costs that exceed any possible benefit that might result from changes in pension accounting.

The FASB addressed the relationship between economic consequences and accounting standards in Financial Accounting Concepts Statement no. 2, *Qualitative Characteristics of Accounting Information:*

> *While rejecting the view that financial accounting standards should be slanted for political reasons or to favor one economic interest or another, the Board recognizes that a standard-setting authority must be alert to the economic impact of the standards that it promulgates. The consequences of those standards will usually not be easy to isolate from the effects of other economic happenings, and they will be even harder to predict with confidence when a new standard is under consideration but before it has gone into effect. Nevertheless, the Board will consider the probable economic impact of its standards as best it can and will monitor that impact as best it can after a standard goes into effect. For one thing, a markedly unexpected effect on business behavior may point to an unforeseen deficiency in a standard in the sense that it does not result in the faithful representation of economic phenomena that was intended. It would then be necessary for the standard to be revised.*
>
> *Neutrality in accounting is an impor-*

Enterprises (Stamford, Conn.: FASB, 1978), par. 40.
[11]Concepts Statement no. 3, par. 19.

tant criterion by which to judge accounting policies, for information that is not neutral loses credibility. If information can be verified and can be relied on faithfully to represent what it purports to represent—and if there is no bias in the selection of what is reported—it cannot be slanted to favor one set of interests over another. It may in fact favor certain interests, but only because the information points that way, much as a good examination grade favors a good student who has honestly earned it.

The italicized words deserve comment. It was noted earlier in this Statement that reliability implies completeness of information, at least within the bounds of what is material and feasible, considering the cost. An omission can rob information of its claim to neutrality if the omission is material and is intended to induce or inhibit some particular mode of behavior.[12]

The board also has recognized its responsibility to limit changes in existing practice to situations in which the perceived benefits exceed the perceived costs of the change.

Economic consequences, however, can work both ways. There also may be economic consequences of failing to change accounting rules that do not reflect economic reality or that are not neutral and unbiased. The costs of not improving accounting are probably as hard to measure as the costs of changes, but they may be significant.

The economic consequences argument against recognizing the pension liability presumes that markets and decision makers will not become aware of the liability if it is not recorded. It also assumes that situation to be desirable. That assumpion conflicts with the basic objective of reporting neutral and unbiased information that is relevant to decision makers.

Consider, for example, the suggestion that recording the pension liability will deny some companies access to credit. Decisions to grant or deny credit to a particular company are not made by the FASB; they are made by people, such as bankers, who are concerned with the ability of the company to repay. Credit decisions are based, in part, on accounting information, and those who must decide to grant or deny credit rely on having unbiased information, including information about a company's liabilities. It is inappropriate for the FASB to refuse to recognize a liability that exists just because knowledge of that liability might cause the banker to deny credit to a particular company. Indeed, that may be a persuasive reason to require recognition of the liability.

CONCLUSION

Based on our work to date, we are not convinced by the arguments against recording a liability when a pension plan is established or amended. We believe that an accounting liability does exist and that including it with other liabilities in the balance sheet will significantly improve the usefulness of financial statements.

CPAs may or may not agree with our conclusion. However, even if they, and the members of the FASB, ultimately do agree, a number of important related questions must be resolved before any change in pension accounting can be implemented, including

- What is the appropriate measure of the liability? Is it vested benefits, accumulat-

[12]Financial Accounting Concepts Statement no. 2, *Qualitative Characteristics of Accounting Information* (Stamford, Conn.: FASB, 1980), pars. 106, 107, 108.

ed benefits, prior service cost or something else?

- If a liability is recorded, what is the nature of the offsetting debit? Is it expense, an extraordinary charge, an intangible asset or something else?
- How should the assets held by the plan be reflected on the employer's balance sheet? Depending on the measure of the liability, plan assets might exceed the liability for many companies.

These and other related issues are now being considered as part of the FASB's project on employers' accounting for pensions and other postemployment benefits. The answers to the issues may have a significant effect on how financial statements reflect pension activities. We encourage accountants to help in finding answers that improve financial reporting by participating in the board's process.

REGULATION, RENTS AND RESIDUALS

JOHN W. COUGHLAN

Everybody except the landlord seems to want to regulate rents. Even the Financial Accounting Standards Board has gotten into the act by regulating the manner of accounting for rents. In FASB Statement no. 13, *Accounting for Leases,*[1] the FASB proposes the following "basic concept" in distinguishing between "capital leases" and "operating leases":

Copyright © 1980 by the American Institute of Certified Public Accountants, Inc. *Journal of Accountancy.* February 1980. Reprinted by permission.
Author's note: The author would like to thank Paul Rosenfield, CPA, director of the AICPA accounting standards division, for helpful suggestions received during the preparation of this article.

[1] Financial Accounting Standards Board Statement no. 13, *Accounting for Leases* (Stamford, Conn.: Financial Accounting Standards Board, November 1976), employs the term "capital lease" from the lessee's perspective only. For the lessor, it divides capital leases into "sales-type leases" and "direct financing leases." Since there is no comment here about the distinction between sales and financing leases, and since both correspond to what from the lessee's perspective is referred to as a capital lease, the term capital lease will be used for both lessee and lessor. The purpose of this article is to probe the basic flaws in the capital vs. operating distinction; therefore, the extension of these flaws to sales, financing and leveraged leases will not be discussed. Likewise, the concern will be the quilt (Statement no. 13) rather than the patches (FASB Statement nos. 17, *Accounting for Leases—Initial Direct Costs;* 22, *Changes in the Provisions of Lease Agreements Resulting From Refundings of Tax-Exempt Debt;* 23, *Inception of the Lease;* 26, *Profit Recognition on Sales-Type Leases of Real Estate;* 27, *Classification of Renewals of Extensions of Existing Sales-Type or Direct Financing Leases;* 28, *Accounting for Sales With Lease-backs;* and 29, *Determining Contingent Rentals;* and FASB interpretations nos. 19, *Lessee Guarantee of the Residual Value of Leased Property;* 21, *Accounting for Leases in a Business Combination;* 23, *Leases of Certain Property Owned by a Governmental Unit or Authority;* 24, *Leases Involving Only Part of a Building;* 26, *Accounting for Purchase of a Leased Asset by the Lessee During the Term of the Lease;* and 27, *Accounting for a Loss on a Sublease*). It must be obvious that any quilt which requires 13 patches in three years must be rent beyond repair. In mid-January the FASB announced plans to issue this year a single pronouncement that would integrate Statement no.

*. . . a lease that transfers substantially
all of the benefits and risks . . . should
be accounted for as the acquisition of an
asset and the incurrence of an obligation
by the lessee and as a sale or financing
by the lessor. All other leases should be
accounted for as operating leases. In a
lease that transfers substantially all of
the benefits and risks of ownership, the
economic effect on the parties is similar,
in many respects, to that of an installment purchase . . . (paragraph 60).*

The distinction is one of common sense:
since corporate controllers and accounting
practitioners are traditionally blessed with
this commodity, there would have been no
problem in applying this "rewards and
risks" distinction.

Statement no. 13 did no stop here, however. It imposed additional criteria purport-
edly to assist in applying the basic concept.
In doing so, it created a complex[2] document with fundamental flaws that go to the
very essence of the distinction:

- It introduces two criteria—(a) and (b)—
  that are clearly implicit in another criterion—(d)—and are therefore redundant.
- It introduces a rate for discounting purposes—the "incremental borrowing
  rate"—in circumstances in which it is
  unlikely the rate can ever be used but
  expresses faith that it is this rate which
  will "generally" be used for the lessee's
  accounting for capital leases.
- Its excessive regulatory zeal leads to arbitrary distinctions capable, for example,
  of putting two almost identical lessors
  (say, two "rent a car" companies) in
  different industrial classifications, one
  renting machinery (operating leases) and
  the other making loans (capital leases).

---

13 and all the amendments and interpretations of
that statement.
[2]For a good analysis of some of the complexities

THE LESSOR'S CRITERIA

The lessor shall treat as a capital lease—
that is, shall interpret as a lease involving a
sale or financing event—any lease that
meets both of the following two requirements (pars. 7 and 8):

- It must meet any one of four criteria,
  which are designated (a), (b), (c) and (d).
- There must be no important uncertainties
  about certain future cash flows.

The first requirement is an "or" proposition: it is enough if a lease meets any of
the four criteria. However, it can easily be
demonstrated that, if criterion (d) belongs
on the list, there is no need for (a) or (b).

CRITERION (D)

It is no exaggeration to say that everything
in the first test turns on criterion (d):

> *The present value at the beginning of the
> lease term of the minimum lease pay-
> ments . . . equals or exceeds 90 percent
> of . . . the fair value of the leased prop-
> erty . . . to the lessor at the inception of
> the lease. . . . A lessor shall compute
> the present value of the minimum lease
> payments using the interest rate implicit
> in the lease . . . (par. 7).*

EXAMPLE 1

A lessor leases an automobile with a fair
value of $5,000 at $135 per month for 30
months, with the initial payment to occur at
inception. At the end of 30 months, the

---

of Statement no. 13, see Raymond J. Clay, Jr.,
and William W. Holder, "A Practitioner's
Guide to Accounting for Leases," JofA. Aug.
77, pp. 62–68. See also J. Kenneth Alderman
and C. Wayne Alderman, "Accounting for
Leases," JofA. June 79, pp. 74–79.

CHAPTER 10: LEASES AND PENSIONS

Exhibit 1   Illustration of Criterion (d)

	Minimum Lease Payments	×	Discount Factors	=	Present Values
Month 1	$ 135	×	$1/(1.01)^0$	=	$ 135
Month 2	135	×	$1/(1.01)^1$	=	134
Month 30	135	×	$1/(1.01)^{29}$	=	101
					3,517*
Month 31	2,000	×	$1/(1.01)^{30}$	=	1,483
Totals	$6,050				$5,000

lessee is to return the car, the lessor is to sell it and the lessee guarantees it will be worth $2,000 at that time. If it sells for less than $2,000, the lessee will make up the difference. The $2,000 is referred to as a "guaranteed residual value." Criterion (d) requires that the minimum lease payments—which include the guaranteed residual—be discounted by use of the "interest rate implicit in the lease," which is 1 percent per month compounded monthly, as shown in exhibit 1. The example is drawn from Appendix C of Statement no. 13, which points out that the present value of the minimum lease payments is $5,000 and that it is 100 percent of fair value. Is it a coincidence the present value works out to exactly 100 percent rather than 98 percent or 103 percent?

It is no happenstance: it is no coincidence. It is a consequence of the definition of the interest rate implicit in the lease. This rate discounts the minimum lease payments to the fair value of the property at the inception of the lease. In the example, the interest rate implicit in the lease is i in equation 1, as follows:

EQUATION 1

$$5,000 = 135/(1 + i)_0 + 135/(1 + i)^1 + \, + 135/(1 + i)^{29} + 2000/(1 + i)^{30}$$

In solving this equation for i, it will be found that the implicit rate is approximately .01 in decimal form or 1 percent per month.

The present value computed by means of this implicit rate is exactly 100 percent of fair value because we are locked in a circle. The implicit rate is that rate which equates the present value of the minimum lease payments to the fair value at the inception of the lease. If the minimum lease payments are then discounted by this implicit rate, it should be no surprise that their present value is exactly equal to the fair value. What is involved is two applications of the above equation 1: in the first application, the $5,000 is treated as known and the accountant solves for the unknown i, finding it to be 1 percent; in the second, the 1 percent is known and employed to discount the minimum lease payments to the unknown present value, which—surely to nobody's surprise—turns out to be the same $5,000 with which the accountant began!

Were there nothing else than what has been described, all leases without exception would meet criterion (d). O. J. Simpson sprinting through the airport would have to tarry with the complexities of capital leases and Statement no. 13 would be nonsense. However, there is "something else"—the "unguaranteed residual value" (URV), defined as the estimated residual value of the leased property at the end of the lease exclusive of any portion guaranteed by the lessee. Statement no. 13 defines the interest rate implicit in the lease as follows:

> *The discount rate that, when applied to (i) the minimum lease payments . . . and (ii) the unguaranteed residual value . . . accruing to the benefit of the lessor, causes the aggregate present value at the beginning of the lease term to be equal to the fair value of the leased property . . . to the lessor at the inception of the lease . . . (par. 5(k)).*

EXAMPLE 2

Assume the same lease except that now, while it is reasonable to suppose that the auto will be worth $2,000 after 30 months, the lessee makes no guarantee concerning residual value, which accordingly becomes a URV. From the quotation above, it is apparent that the URV is included in the determination of the implicit interest rate so that it is the same 1 percent per month that solves equation 1, with the discounted values appearing as follows: 5,000 = 3,517 + 1,483.

The term with the asterisk is the present value of the minimum lease payments, and the final term is the present value of the URV. While the URV plays a role in the determination of the implicit rate, it is not included in the present value used in criterion (d). Indeed, it is the presence of the URV in the implicit rate definition and its absence from (d) that saves Statement no. 13 from a vicious circle. Since the present value of the minimum lease payments to be used in (d)—the asterisked 3,517—is less than 90 percent of the 5,000 fair value, (d) is not met and the lease is an operating lease. The important thing to notice is that the present value is other than 100 percent of fair value. This can only happen within the Statement no. 13 framework if there is a URV. Furthermore, it is only if this URV is substantial in relation to the minimum lease payments that criterion (d) can be failed.

THE REDUNDANCY OF CRITERIA (A) AND (B)

The redundancy of criteria (a) and (b) can now be seen. Criterion (a) states: "The lease transfers ownership of the property to the lessee by the end of the lease. . . ." While the leased property may have some residual value at termination, it can have none accruing to the lessor. Any lease meeting (a)—that is, transferring ownership by the end of the lease term—will have no URV to the lessor, and the implicit rate, no matter what the fair value and the minimum lease payments, will always discount minimum lease payments to exactly 100 percent of fair value. A lease that meets (a) must meet (d).

Criterion (b) states: "The lease contains a bargain purchase option." Since the bargain purchase option is included in minimum lease payments and title is assumed to pass, there can be no URV accruing to the lessor, and the lease must have a present value of 100 percent of fair value and thereby meets (d).

If either (a) or (b) is met, by definition alone, there can be no URV to the lessor and (d) must be met. Since requirement 1 is met if one of the four lettered criteria is met, there is no need to check (a) or (b) if (d) is met. A list that includes (d) has no need for (a) or (b).

CRITERION (C)

It would be convenient if it could be demonstrated that leases meeting criterion

CHAPTER 10: LEASES AND PENSIONS

(c)—". . . lease term . . . is equal to 75 percent or more the estimated economic life of the leased property . . ."—automatically meet (d). Unfortunately, it is possible (but difficult) to construct examples to the contrary.

Nevertheless, for the sake of simplicity, (c) should be eliminated for the very good reason that the great majority of leases that meet (c) also meet (d). Bear in mind that that URV for a lease covering 75 percent or more of economic life will, because of the partial obsolescence of the asset and its need for greater maintenance, be small and the present value of that URV will be but a small part of the value at inception. (Indeed, paragraph 75 of Statement no. 13 so states.) Accordingly, it is apparent that, because of the circle previously cited, almost all leases meeting (c) meet (d) and, therefore, (c) may on practical grounds also be considered redundant.

A SIMPLIFIED CRITERION

The first requirement for a capital lease from the lessor's viewpoint—namely, that it meet one or more of the lettered criteria—has now been condensed into the single criterion (d). In so condensing, it is recognized that there are a few leases that meet (c) (just barely) and nevertheless fail (d) (just barely). It is further recognized that there are no leases that meet (a) or (b) that do not meet (d).

Can the retention of (a) to (b) be justified because a lack of knowledge might make it impossible to apply (d)? Suppose, for example, the lessor could not determine fair value and could not, therefore, apply (d). But any assistance that (a), (b) or (c) would provide in such a case would be nugatory. Statement no. 13's prescribed lessor accounting for capital leases requires a knowledge of the implicit rate, which in turn requires a knowledge of the same fair value and cash flow information that is required to apply (d). If the criterion (d) information is not available, there is no point using (a) to (c) to determine the operating or capital character of a lease since the information needed to account for a capital lease is also not available.

The Statement no. 13 requirements for a capital lease may accordingly be simplified by dropping (a), (b) and (c) and by using only (d) or its shadow, the URV, so that the lessor's two requirements may be stated as follows:

- The URV must be small or nominal.[3]
- There must be no important uncertainties about certain future cash flows.

In a quest for an even more concise statement of the capital lease requirement, return to the URV and ask why it should make a difference. Consider any lease, such the one in example 2, with a sufficiently large URV to fail criterion (d) and be classified as an operating lease. Now let the lessee guarantee the residual value as in example 1; recalling the circle, the present value will be 100 percent of fair value and the lease will meet (d) and will be classified as a capital lease. While the total to be received is identical—at least on an expected value basis—more of it is guaranteed. A guarantee of residual value is sufficient to convert all operating leases to capital leases.

Apparently the Statement no. 13 view is that there is no problem accounting for the lease payments as a long-term receivable

---

[3]This approach is similar to that in a statement of position issued by the accounting standards division of The American Institute of CPAs, which did not specify an exact percentage but, instead, suggested capitalization when the residual value was expected to be "nominal" (JofA, Oct. 75, p. 14 and Dec. 75, p. 26.).

with appropriate recognition of interest income if there is little uncertainty about cash flows and some assurance that the lessor will recover his investment and earn a positive interest rate, whereas important elements of uncertainty pertaining to the future cash flows—particularly if there is some doubt about the ability to fully recover the fair value of the leased asset—should lead to the operating classification. Seen from the perspective, it is risk and uncertainty—the natural human tendency to fear the dark—that is the enemy of the capital lease. The simplified two-point criterion suggested above might be further condensed since both points deal with uncertainties about future cash flows. One could replace the two-point test with a one-point test relating to the subjective probability of recovering the fair value of the leased property and (possibly) some positive amount of interest:

- Capital leases are those for which there is at least an X probability of recovering the fair value of the leased asset.

One hopes that the practitioner would be permitted to rely on his judgment to pick the probability (it might be stated in terms of a reasonable expectation), but the FASB could (and undoubtedly would) prescribe a probability. Such a simplified test (if passed) would in all likelihood lead to the same leases being classified as capital leases as those using the Statement no. 13 criteria and (if failed) would lead to the same leases being classified as operating leases as those using the statement's criteria. Where the classifications of particular leases differed, the difference would generally result from arbitrary consequences of the overly complex criteria in Statement no. 13 rather than from differences in the underlying purposes.

THE INCREMENTAL BORROWING RATE

Turning to the lessee, a curious aspect of Statement no. 13 is the introduction of a new interest rate "the incremental borrowing rate"—which may play some role in the classification scheme but cannot play any role (despite the statement's suggestions to the contrary) in the accounting.

The lessee's incremental borrowing rate is defined as the "rate that, at the inception of the lease, the lessee would have incurred to borrow over a similar term the funds necessary to purchase the leased asset" (par. 5 (1)). Following is another version of criterion (d) that includes certain wording omitted in the excerpt printed on page 508.

The present value at the beginning of the lease term of the minimum lease payments . . . equals or exceeds 90 percent of . . . the fair value of the leased property . . . to the lessor. . . . A lessee shall compute the present value of the minimum lease payments using his incremental borrowing rate . . . unless (i) it is practicable for him to learn the implicit rate computed by the lessor and (ii) the implicit rate computed by the lessor is less than the lessee's incremental borrowing rate. If both of those conditions are met, the lessee shall use the implicit rate (par. 7 (d)).

Assuming the lessee knows the implicit rate,[4] it can be demonstrated that the im-

[4]Surely a reasonable assumption despite Statement no. 13's suggestion to the contrary in the above excerpt of (d). All that is needed to infer the implicit rate are three items of information: the minimum lease payments, the URV and the fair value of the leased property to the lessor at

plicit rate will always be employed in the accounting whether it is higher or lower than the incremental borrowing rate. Suppose first the implicit rate is less than the

---

the inception of the lease. Since the minimum lease payments are the principle subject matter of the lease agreement, presumably the lessee knows as much about them as the lessor. Possibly the lessor knows more about URV than the lessee. Recall from the previous analysis, however, that the URV cannot be too great if the lease is classified as a capital lease. Given that the lessee is correct in classifying a lease as a capital lease, it follows that the URV will not be too substantial and it is therefore unlikely that the lessee's estimate can be sufficiently erroneous to make a material difference to his computation of the implicit rate.

This leaves the fair value of the leased property to the lessor at the inception of the lease. Much of the personality (office equipment, computers, fleets of trucks, etc.) to which Statement no. 13 is currently being applied has a well-established purchase price that is readily available to the lessee: to the extent it is not, antitrust efforts at the federal level are increasingly making it available. Accordingly, it may be concluded that, for most of the leased property to which Statement no. 13 is currently applied, the lessee may make almost as good an estimate of the implicit rate as the lessor. The FASB also appears to believe that the lessee can infer within limits that implicit rate; since the first draft of this article was written, the FASB has issued an exposure draft of a proposed statement requiring the lessee in certain circumstances to make a "reasonable estimate" of the implicit rate.

Even in those rare cases in which no reasonable estimate of the implicit rate can be made, the conclusion in this article—that the incremental borrowing rate will never be used—still stands. Admittedly, with regard to certain personality and some reality, usually with perpetual life, the lessor may have better information with regard to fair value. But it still cannot be inferred that the incremental borrowing rate will play a role because the lessee's ignorance of fair value will prevent application of the all-important criterion (d), the 90-percent-of-fair-value test! Such leases rarely meet criterion (a) or (b) and usually cannot meet (c). The ignornace of fair value pre-

incremental borrowing rate[5] so that, following the above quotation, the implicit rate is used for classification purposes in criterion (d). The implicit rate will also be used for the accounting. *The incremental borrowing rate plays no role.*

Now suppose the incremental borrowing rate is lower. From the above quotation, it is apparent this incremental rate will be employed to test criterion (d): if the test is met, one might assume, other things being equal, that the incremental borrowing rate would play a role in the accounting. But here is a key passage:

> *The lessee shall record a capital lease as an asset and an obligation at an amount equal to the present value at the beginning of the lease term of minimum lease payments.* . . . However, if the amount so determined exceeds the fair value of the leased property at the inception of the lease, the amount recorded as the asset and obligation shall be the fair value. . . . *The discount rate to be used in determining present value of the minimum lease payments shall be that prescribed for the lessee in paragraph 7(d)(par. 10, emphasis supplied).*

If there is no URV, the present value as discounted by the implicit rate is exactly

---

vents the lessee not only from knowing the implicit rate but also from classifying the lease as a capital lease and having an opportunity to use the incremental borrowing rate.

[5]There are good reasons to think the implicit rate will be less. Statement no. 13 treats capital transactions as being, in part at least, credit transactions, and the mere fact that the lessee in effect "borrows" from the lessor rather than from his next best source of credit (the incremental borrowing rate) would suggest the lessor's interest rate—the implicit rate—is lower.

100 percent of fair value. Since it is now hypothesized that the incremental borrowing rate is less than the implicit rate, it is apparent that the similar present value using the lower incremental borrowing rate will exceed 100 percent of fair value. Observing the italicized limitation to fair value in the above quotation, it seems obvious that the lessee will capitalize the fair value, which is based on the implicit rate, not the incremental rate: the other prescriptions in Statement no. 13 (particularly paragraph 12) make it apparent that it is the implicit rate which will be used in all subsequent accounting. *The incremental borrowing rate still plays no role in the accounting.*

The best illustration is example 1, but this time regarded from the lessee's viewpoint. This example is straight from Statement no. 13, which specifies that while the implicit rate is 1 percent per month the incremental borrowing rate is only .875 percent per month. The present value using this lower incremental borrowing rate is $5,120 which, as observed in Statement no. 13, exceeds the fair value of $5,000. The illustration of lessee accounting in the statement accordingly involves a capitalization of the fair value of $5,000 (which implies use of the implicit rate, not the incremental borrowing rate), and the subsequent entries are based throughout on the implicit rate. When there is no URV or only a small one, the present value using the lower incremental borrowing rate will exceed fair value and *the incremental borrowing rate cannot play a role.*

Even if there is a substantial URV (see the appendix, page 516, for a detailed analysis), the conclusion still stands, *the incremental borrowing rate can play no role in the accounting.*

Unfortunately, this analysis cannot be reconciled with the explicit assumption in Statement no. 13 that the lessee will "generally" use the incremental borrowing rate:

"With respect to the rate of interest to be used in determining the present value of the minimum lease payments for recording the asset and obligation under a capital lease, the Board concluded the rate should generally be that which the lessee would have incurred to borrow for a similar term the funds necessary to purchase the leased asset (the lessee's incremental borrowing rate)" (par. 93).

May one conclude that the architects of the labyrinth also get lost in its corridors?

THIRD-PARTY GUARANTORS

It has been demonstrated that there is only one interest rate in Statement no. 13, the implicit rate, and it was previously demonstrated that, using this implicit rate, only (d) of the lettered criteria need be tested. Recalling that criterion (d) is always met and that all leases are capital leases unless there is a URV, it is to be hoped that no excess of regulatory zeal, and no desire to specify everything, has led the FASB to make any mistakes in the concept or definition of this central concept of URV.

EXAMPLE 3A

Hurts Rent-A-Car leases automobiles on a daily basis. The rental fee for a day, net of certain executory costs (such as maintenance), is $51. Hurts does not insure these cars since it serves as its own insurance company. An auto has a fair value of $5,000 when rented, and Hurts anticipates it will be worth $5,000 when returned 24 hours later. The lessee pays the $51 when he returns the auto. By solving the following equation for i

$$5,000 = 5,051/(1 + i)$$

it will be found that the implicit rate is approximately 1 percent per day compounded daily. The minimum lease payment is $51; if this amount is discounted one day at 1 percent, it will have a present value of $50, which is far below 90 percent of the fair value, or $4,500. Accordingly, (d) is not met, the lease will be classified as an operating one, the auto will remain on Hurts's books (where it will be depreciated) and the $51 will be recognized as rental revenues.

EXAMPLE 3B

Mavis Rent-A-Car owns title to autos, hands keys to its customers and employs maintenance mechanics, but these peripherals are simply a clever "cover" for its real business, which is making one-day loans at usurious interest rates. Mavis keeps only $50 of each daily rental fee and requires the lessee to use the other $1 to buy a contract with an independent insurance company, which guarantees the auto will be worth $5,000 when returned. Since the cash flow expectations are approximately the same as for Hurts. Mavis will compute the implicit rate in the same fashion and will discover the implicit rate to be 1 percent per day. But, since the definition of URV states that it is the estimated residual value of the leased property "exclusive of any portion guaranteed by the lessee *or by a third party unrelated to the lessor*" (par. 5 (i), emphasis supplied), the Mavis $5,000 is a guaranteed residual; as such it is an integral part of the minimum lease payments since such payments include "any guarantee of the residual value . . . by a third party unrelated to either the lessee or the lessor, provided the third party is financially capable of discharging the obligations that may arise from the guarantee" (par. 5 (j) ii). Now test criterion (d) by discounting the minimum lease payments—the full $5,050—at the implicit rate of 1 percent:

$$5,050/1.01 = 5,000$$

Since there is no URV, it is not surprising that the present value is exactly 100 percent of fair value but, since (d) is met, it may come as a considerable shock to Mavis to find it is in the short-term loan business rather than in auto leasing. Lapses in logic and obfuscating complexities aside, can there be merit to a pronouncement that puts Hurts in car renting and Mavis in loan sharking?

ACCOUNTING AND AUTHORITY

The tale of two leases, the operating lease and the capital lease, is neither the best nor the worst of FASB statements. Surely its emphasis on future cash flows and on present values, while foreshadowed to some extent in prior pronouncements (notably Accounting Principles Board Opinion nos. 21, *Interest on Receivables and Payables;* 5, *Reporting of Leases in Financial Statements of Lessee;* 7, *Accounting for Leases in Financial Statements of Lessors;* 27, *Accounting for Lease Transactions by Manufacturer or Dealer Lessor;* and 31, *Disclosure of Lease Commitments by Lessees*), must be counted among its more positive and forward-looking developments.[6] Just as surely, its implicit belief that accounting requires authority, and authority of a complex and stifling character, must constitute its most negative and backward-looking features.

In matters of social interaction, where differences of opinion must be resolved in some manner, authority in the form of laws, legislatures, judges and juries may be

[6]Also see a research study that has had much to do with the development of thought regarding leases: John H. Myers, Accounting Research Study no. 4, *Reporting of Leases in Financial Statements* (New York: AICPA, 1962).

necessary. If accounting falls in this arena—and there is a growing opinion that it does as witness the existence of the FASB and the Cost Accounting Standard Board—the path ahead is clear. There will be an increasing amount of regulation, and it will be imposed with the muscle of the federal government. The official pronouncements will have the full force of law but will follow the model so carefully set since 1935 by the committee on accounting procedure of the American Institute of Accountants (a predecessor of the AICPA), the APB and the FASB. These official pronouncements will differ in no important respect from their predecessors except that they may be more voluminous and more costly. One hopes that there is a better road.

Usefulness—not authority—is the final arbiter of accounting. If its "economic consequence" is a better allocation of scarce resources, then it needs no authority. If it does not perform a useful function in that sense, then no authority will help.[7]

APPENDIX

If there is no URV, or only a small one, then the incremental borrowing rate is completely irrelevant to the accounting. It will be demonstrated in this appendix that, even with a substantial URV, there is little possibility that the incremental borrowing rate can play any role in the accounting.

Observe first that a substantial URV usually leads to the lease's being classified as an operating lease and therefore pro-

[7]See also John W. Coughlan, *Guide to Contemporary Theory of Accounts* (Englewood Cliffs, N. J.: Prentice-Hall, 1965), p. 1, and Accounting Principles Board Statement no. 4, *Basic Concepts and Accounting Principles Underlying Financial Statements of Business Enterprises* (New York: AICPA, 1970), par. 21.

vides no opportunity to employ the incremental borrowing rate (see example 2, page 510).

What is required is a URV that is small enough to permit the lease to meet criterion (d) but, at the same time, large enough so that, using the lower incremental borrowing rate, the present value will be less than fair value. (Otherwise fair value and the implicit interest rate will be employed.) Whether such a small-enough, large-enough URV is even possible depends on the meaning of "fair value."

EXAMPLE 4

The lessee acquires the use of an asset with a five-year life by making rental payments of $1,000 per year at the beginning of each of the first three years. At the beginning of the fourth, with two years of life to go, the asset reverts to the lessor, at which date it is expected to be worth $471, its URV. The lessee's incremental borrowing rate is 10 percent and, assuming the asset has a fair value to the lessor at the inception of the lease of $2,800, the implicit rate is 20 percent; as shown in exhibit 2.

Statement no. 13 is unambiguous re-

Exhibit 2 Two Interpretations of "Fair Value"

	Present Values	
	at 10%	at 20%
$1,000	$1,000	$1,000
1,000	909	833
1,000	827	694
Minimum lease payments	$2,736	2.527 FV B
Unguaranteed residual value ($471)	273	
Total		$2,800 FV A

garding the application of (d) in this situation. The lessee would use his incremental borrowing rate and the appropriate present value is accordingly $2,736 from the above tabulation. Criterion (d) requires that this present value equal or exceed 90 percent of the "fair value . . . *to the lessor* . . . "(emphasis supplied). That fair value to the lessor would include the present value of the URV and would accordingly be the $2,800 in the tabulation. Clearly the $2,736 using the incremental borrowing rate exceeds 90 percent of fair value, and Statement no. 13 would require capitalization. So far there's no problem, and the incremental borrowing rate has played a role in the classification scheme.

But now turn to the accounting and consider Statement no. 13's limitation in paragraph 10 (see page 513) of the amount capitalized to the fair value. Two interpretations of fair value are possible, and both lead to problems for Statement no. 13:

- If the fair value limitation refers to fair value to the lessor (the $2,800 labeled "FV A" in the tabulation), the same fair value that is used in criterion (d) for classification purposes would be employed in the accounting, and the amount capitalized would be the $2,736 from the tabulation: this is less than FV A of $2,800, and the subsequent accounting would indeed be based on 10 percent, the incremental borrowing rate. But now observe that because the URV must be not great (for fear of failing (d)), the difference in the amount capitalized as between using the two interest rates is trivial. Further, while the interest rates (10 percent vs. 20 percent) differ considerably, an exploration of the net effect on the income statement in the ensuing years should convince the reader that, if both interest expense and depreciation are considered, the net impact on the in-

come statement is negligible. The incremental borrowing rate, if appropriate at all, gives results that cannot differ much from the implicit rate; therefore, the accountant who wants to simplify Statement no. 13 may employ the implicit rate in all cases and, if ever called to account, may simply quote the boldface sentence that appears in all FASB statements, including no. 13: "The provisions of this Statement need not be applied to immaterial items." Even allowing for this interpretation, it may be concluded that *the incremental borrowing rate can play no material role in the accounting.*

But this interpretation is difficult to allow. To arrive at such a result, one must include in fair value the present value of the URV. While URV may be relevant to the lessee's classification of a lease as operating or capital, and criterion (d) so implies, it is hardly conceivable that URV can have any relevance to the subsequent accounting for leases classified as capital leases. In deciding whether a lease is operating or capital, it may make sense for the lessee to inquire whether he acquires the full service potential of the leased asset or whether there is a substantial URV that reverts to the lessor. But in limiting the capitalized present value to fair value, it makes little sense to include in the limitation the present value of the unguaranteed residual, a residual that goes to the lessor and that is surely irrelevant to the lessee except possibly for classification purposes.

- It is far more meaningful to interpret paragraph 10 in terms of the fair value relating to the service potential acquired by the lessee. While Statement no. 13, in defining the implicit rate (paragraph 5 (k)), specifies fair value to the lessor and again, in stating criterion (d), refers to the lessor, its paragraph 10 limitation is in the discussion of lessee accounting and omits the crucial words "to the lessor" even though the term "fair value" is used twice: ". . . if the amount so determined exceeds the fair value of the leased property at the inception of the lease, the amount recorded as the asset and obligation shall be the fair value." To make sense out of this fair value limitation, it must surely be fair value to the lessee.

But this fair value to the lessee is simply the present value of the minimum lease payments discounted by the implicit rate. It is the $2,527 labeled "FV B" in the tabulation. Since it is hypothesized throughout this appendix that the incremental borrowing rate is lower than the implicit rate, the present value using the lower incremental borrowing rate will always be higher than that using the implicit rate; therefore, the fair value limitation must always be binding and that fair value will be capitalized and amortized by use of the implicit rate, not the incremental borrowing rate. *Given that the implicit rate is known, the incremental borrowing rate can never play any role in the accounting.*

QUESTIONS

1. Under the capital method of accounting for leases the excess of aggregate rentals over the cost of leased property should be recognized as revenue of the lessor
   a. In increasing amounts during the term of the lease
   b. In constant amounts during the term of the lease
   c. In decreasing amounts during the term of the lease
   d. After the cost of leased property has been fully recovered through rentals
2. When measuring the present value of future rentals to be capitalized as part of the purchase price in a lease that is to be accounted for as a purchase, identifiable payments to cover taxes, insurance, and maintenance should be
   a. Included with the future rentals to be capitalized
   b. Excluded from future rentals to be capitalized
   c. Capitalized but at a different discount rate and recorded in a different account than future rental payments
   d. Capitalized but at a different discount rate and for a relevant period that tends to be different than that for future rental payments
3. Equal monthly rental payments for a particular lease should be charged to rental expense by the lessee for which of the following?

	Capital lease	Operating lease
a.	Yes	No
b.	Yes	Yes
c.	No	No
d.	No	Yes

518   CHAPTER 10: LEASES AND PENSIONS

4. In a lease that is recorded as a sales-type lease by the lessor, the difference between the gross investment in the lease and the sum of the present values of the components of the gross investment should be recognized as income
   a. In full at the lease's expiration
   b. In full at the lease's inception
   c. Over the period of the lease using the interest method of amortization
   d. Over the period of the lease using the straight-line method of amortization

5. For a six-year capital lease, the portion of the minimum lease payment in the third year applicable to the reduction of the obligation should be
   a. Less than in the second year
   b. More than in the second year
   c. The same as in the fourth year
   d. More than in the fourth year

6. Based solely upon the following sets of circumstances, indicated below which set gives rise to a sales type or a direct financing lease of a lessor:

	Transfers ownership by end of lease?	Contains bargain purchase provision?
a.	No	Yes
b.	Yes	No
c.	Yes	Yes
d.	No	No

7. Generally accepted accounting principles require that certain lease agreements be accounted for as purchases. The theoretical basis for this treatment is that a lease of this type
   a. Effectively conveys all of the benefits and risks incident to the ownership of property
   b. Is an example of form over substance
   c. Provides the use of the leased asset to the lessee for a limited period of time
   d. Must be recorded in accordance with the concept of cause and effect

8. The appropriate valuation of an operating lease on the statement of financial position of a lessee is
   a. Zero
   b. The absolute sum of the lease payments
   c. The present value of the sum of the lease payments discounted at an appropriate rate
   d. The market value of the asset at the date of the inception of the lease.

9. A six-year capital lease entered into on December 31, 1981, specified equal minimum annual lease payments due on December 31, 1983. Minimum payment applicable to which of the following increased over the corresponding December 31, 1982, minimum payment?

	Interest expense	Reduction of liability
a.	Yes	Yes
b.	Yes	No
c.	No	Yes
d.	No	No

10. Office equipment recorded under a capital lease containing a bargain purchase option should be amortized
   a. Over the period of the lease using the interest method of amortization
   b. Over the period of the lease using the straight-line method of amortization
   c. In a manner consistent with the lessee's normal depreciation policy for owned assets
   d. In a manner consistent with the lessee's normal depreciation policy for owned assets except that the period of amortization should be the lease term

11. APB Opinion No. 8 set minimum and maximum limits on the annual provision for pension cost. An amount that was always included in the calculation of both the mimimum and maximum limit is
   a. Normal cost
   b. Amortization of past service cost
   c. Interest on unfunded past and prior service costs
   d. Retirement benefits paid

12. In accounting for a pension plan, any difference between the pension cost charged to expense and the payments into the fund should be reported as
   a. An offset to the liability for prior service cost
   b. Accrued or prepaid pension cost
   c. An operating expense in this period
   d. An accrued actuarial liability

13. Benefits under a pension plan that are not contingent upon an employee's continuing service are
   a. Granted under a plan of defined contribution
   b. Based upon terminal funding
   c. Actuarially unsound
   d. Vested

14. According to SFAS No. 87, "Employer's Accounting for Pensions," gains and losses should be *a.* Fully allocated to current and future periods

b. Offset against pension expense in the year of occurrence

c. Allocated if any unrecognized gain or loss at the beginning of the year is in excess of 10 percent of the greater of the projected benefit obligation or the market value of the plan assets

d. Disclosed in a note to the financial statements only

15. According to SFAS No. 87, prior service costs should be

a. Charged to retained earnings as a cost relating to the past

b. Amortized over the service period of each employee expected to receive benefits

c. Taken into consideration only by expensing interest on the unfunded amount

d. Recorded in full as a liability at their discounted present value

16. According to SFAS No. 87, which of the following is never recorded as a component of annual pension cost?

a. Amortization of the intangible asset recorded as the offset to the minimum pension liability

b. Amortization of prior service cost

c. Amortization of gains and losses

d. Amortization of the transition amount

17. On January 1, 1984, Lani Company entered into a noncancelable lease for a machine to be used in its manufacturing operations. The lease transfers ownership of the machine to Lani by the end of the lease term. The term of the lease is eight years. The minimum lease payment made by Lani on January 1, 1984, was one of eight equal annual payments. At the inception of the lease, the criteria established for classification as a capital lease by the lessee were met.

Required: *Transfer*

a. What is the theoretical basis for the accounting standard which requires certain long-term leases to be capitalized by the lessee? Do not discuss the specific criteria for classifying a specific lease as a capital lease.

b. How should Lani account for this lease at its inception and determine the amount to be recorded? *Pg 465 As asset*

c. What expenses related to this lease will Lani incur during the first year of the lease, and how will they be determined? *Interest exp & Dep. exp.*

d. How should Lani report the lease transaction on its December 31, 1984, balance sheet? *The asset as non-current*

18. Doherty Company leased equipment from Lambert Company. The classification of the lease makes a difference in the amounts reflected on the balance sheet and income statement of both Doherty Company and Lambert Company. *Bal. sheet*

QUESTIONS *Liab* 521

Current 6830
Accrued liab 3170
L.T. liab (31699-6830)

Asset
P & Pm
Leased assets - - - 41,698
Less acc amt. (4170)
37528

Required:

Pq 465 a. What criteria must be met by the lease in order that Doherty Company classify it as a capital lease? ~Title transfered, Bargain Purchase,~ ~75% of economic life~

465 b. What criteria must be met by the lease in order that Lambert Company classify it as a sales-type or direct financing lease?

c. Contrast a sales-type lease with a direct financing lease.

19. On January 1, Borman Company, a lessee, entered into three noncancelable leases for brand-new equipment, Lease J, Lease K, and Lease L. None of the three leases transfers ownership of the equipment to Borman at the end of the lease term. For each of the three leases, the present value at the beginning of the lease term of the minimum lease payments, excluding that portion of the payments representing executory costs such as insurance, maintenance, and taxes to be paid by the lessor, including any profit there-on, is 75 percent of the excess of the fair value of the equipment to the lessor at the inception of the lease over any related investment tax credit retained by the lessor and expected to be realized by the lessor.

The following information is peculiar to each lease:

- Lease J does not contain a bargain purchase option; the lease term is equal to 80 percent of the estimated economic life of the equipment.
- Lease K contains a bargain purchase option; the lease term is equal to 50 percent of the estimated economic life of the equipment.
- Lease L does not contain a bargain purchase option; the lease term is equal to 50 percent of the estimated economic life of the equipment.

Required:

a. How should Borman Company classify each of the three leases and why? Discuss the rationale for your answer.

b. What amount, if any, should Borman record as a liability at the inception of the lease for each of the three leases?

c. Assuming that the minimum lease payments are made on a straight-line basis, how should Borman record each minimum lease payment for each of the three leases?

20. Part *a.* Capital leases and operating leases are the two classifications of leases described in FASB pronouncements from the standpoint of the lessee.

Required:

a. Describe how a capital lease would be accounted for by the lessee both at the inception of the lease and during the first year of the lease, assuming the lease transfers ownership of the property to the lessee by the end of the lease.

b. Describe how an operating lease would be accounted for by the lessee both at the inception of the lease and during the first year of the lease,

522   CHAPTER 10: LEASES AND PENSIONS

assuming equal monthly payments are made by the lessee at the beginning of each month of the lease. Describe the change in accounting, if any, when rental payments are not made on a straight-line basis. Do not discuss the criteria for distinguishing between capital leases and operating leases.

Part *b*. Sales-type leases and direct financing leases are two of the classifications of leases described in FASB pronouncements, from the standpoint of the lessor.

Required:
Compare and contrast a sales-type lease with a direct financing lease as follows:
a. Gross investment in the lease.
b. Amortization of unearned interest income.
c. Manufacturer's or dealer's profit.
Do not discuss the criteria for distinguishing between the leases described above and operating leases.

21. Milton Corporation entered into a lease arrangement with James Leasing Corporation for a certain machine. James's primary business is leasing and it is not a manufacturer or dealer. Milton will lease the machine for a period of three years, which is 50 percent of the machine's economic life. James will take possession of the machine at the end of the initial three-year lease and lease it to another, smaller company that does not need the most current version of the machine. Milton does not guarantee any residual value for the machine and will not purchase the machine at the end of the lease term. Milton's incremental borrowing rate is 10 percent and the implicit rate in the lease is 8½ percent. Milton has no way of knowing the implicit rate used by James. Using either rate, the present value of the minimum lease is between 90 percent and 100 percent of the fair value of the machine at the date of the lease agreement.

James is reasonably certain that Milton will pay all lease payments, and, because Milton has agreed to pay all executory costs, there are no important uncertainties regarding costs to be incurred by James.

Required:
a. With respect to Milton (the lessee) answer the following.
   i. What type of lease has been entered into? Explain the reason for your answer.
   ii. How should Milton compute the appropriate amount to be recorded for the lease or asset acquired?
   iii. What accounts will be created or affected by this transaction and

how will the lease or asset and other costs related to the transaction be matched with earnings? *Fixed asset acquired through lease*

iv. What disclosures must Milton make regarding this lease or asset?

b. With respect to James (the lessor) answer the following.

   i. What type of leasing arrangement has been entered into? Explain the reason for your answer. *Direct finance*

   ii. How should this lease be recorded by James and how are the appropriate amounts determined? *Debt for the total receivable a credit unearned income*

   iii. How should James determine the appropriate amount of earnings to be recognized from each lease payment? *Debt Lease pmt receivable*

   iv. What disclosures must James make regarding this lease? *Credit equipt, & unearned Revenue — Capital lease*

22. To meet the need for its expanding operations. Johnson Corporation obtained a charter for a separate corporation whose purpose was to buy a land site, build and equip a new building, and lease the entire facility to Johnson Corporation for a period of 20 years. Rental to be paid by Johnson was set at an amount sufficient to cover expenses of operation and debt service on the corporation's 20-year serial mortgage bonds. During the term of the lease, the lessee has the option of purchasing the facilities at a price that will retire the bonds and cover the costs of liquidation of the corporation. Alternatively, at the termination of the lease, the properties will be transferred to Johnson for a small consideration. At the exercise of the option or at the termination of the lease, the lessor corporation will be dissolved.

Required:

a. Under certain conditions, generally accepted accounting principles provide that leased property be included in the balance sheet of a lessee even though legal title remains with the lessor.

   i. Discuss the conditions that would require financial-statement recognition of the asset and the related liability by a lessee.

   ii. Describe the accounting treatment that should be employed by a lessee under the conditions you described in your answer to part i.

b. Unless the conditions referred to in (a) are present, generally accepted accounting principles do not embrace asset recognition of leases in the financial statements of lessees. However, some accountants do advocate recognition by lessees that have acquired *property rights*. Explain what is meant by property rights and discuss the conditions under which these rights might be considered to have been acquired by a lessee.

c. Under the circumstances described in the case, how should the Johnson Corporation account for the lease transactions in its financial statements? Explain your answer.

23. Pension accounting has become more closely associated with the method of determining pension benefits.

Required:

a. Discuss the following methods of determining pension benefits.

Pg 480 i. Defined contribution plan — *The employer promises to contribute a certain sum into the plan each period.*

481 ii. Defined benefit plan — *The amt of pension benefits to be received in the*

b. Discuss the following actuarial funding methods. *future are defined by the terms of the plan.*

Pg 481 i. Cost approach

481 ii. Benefit approach

✓ **24.** Statement of Financial Accounting Standards No. 87, "Employers Accounting for Pensions," requires a new method of accounting for pension cost.

Required:

a. Discuss the following components of annual pension cost.

483 i. Service cost

ii. Interest cost

iii. Actual return on plan assets

19 483 iv. Amortization of unrecognized prior service cost

vi. Amortization of the transition amount

b. Discuss the composition and treatment of the minimum liability provision.

BIBLIOGRAPHY

Abdel-Khalik, A. Rashad, Robert B. Thompson, and Robert E. Taylor. "The Impact of Reporting Leases Off the Balance Sheet on Bond Risk Premiums: Two Exploratory Studies." *Economic Consequences of Financial Accounting Standards.* FASB, 1978, pp. 103–155.

Abrams, Reuben W. "Accounting for the Cost of Pension Plans and Deferred Compensation Contracts." *New York CPA* (April 1970), pp. 300–307.

Anton, Hector R. "Leveraged Leases—A Marriage of Economics, Taxation and Accounting." In DR Scott Memorial Lectures in Accountancy, vol. 6. Edited by Alfred R. Roberts. Columbia, Mo.: University of Missouri, 1974, pp. 81–113.

Bowman, Robert G. "The Debt Equivalence of Leases: An Empirical Investigation." *The Accounting Review* (April 1980), pp. 237–253.

Brownler, E. Richard, and S. David Young. "Pension Accounting: A New Proposal." *The CPA Journal* (July 1985), pp. 28–34.

Bullock, Clayton L. "Accounting Conventions and Economic Reality." *The CPA Journal* (July 1974), pp. 19–74.

Cassell, Jules M., and Diana W. Kahn. "FASB Statement No. 35: Not Enough About the Future?" *Financial Executive* (December 1980), pp. 44–51.

Clay, Raymond J., and William W. Holder. "A Practitioner's Guide to Accounting for Leases." *Journal of Accountancy* (August 1977), pp. 61–68.

Collins, William A. "Accounting for Leases-Flowcharts." *Journal of Accountancy* (September 1978), pp. 60–63.

Deaton, William C., and Jerry J. Weygandt. "Disclosures Related to Pension Plans." *Journal of Accountancy* (January 1975), pp. 44–51.

DeFliese, Philip L. "Accounting for Leases: A Broader Perspective." *Financial Executive* (July 1974), pp. 14–23.

Deitrick, James W., and C. Wayne Alderman. "Pension Plans: What Companies Do- and Do Not-Disclose." *Management Accounting* (April 1980), pp. 24–29.

Deming, John R. "An Analysis of FASB No. 13." *Financial Executive* (March 1978), pp. 46–51.

Dewhirst, John F. "A Conceptual Approach to Pension Accounting." *The Accounting Review* (April 1971), pp. 365–373

Dieter, Richard. "Is Lessee Accounting Working?" *The CPA Journal* (August 1979), pp. 13–19.

Doley, Lane Alan. "The Valuations of Reported Pension Measures for Firms Sponsoring Defined Benefit Plans." *The Accounting Review* (April 1984), pp. 177–198.

Elam, Rick. "Effect of Leases Data on the Predictive Ability of Financial Ratios." *The Accounting Review* (January 1975), pp. 25–43.

FASB Discussion Memorandum. *Accounting for Leases*. Stamford, Conn.: Financial Accounting Standards Board, 1974.

Finnerty, Joseph F., Rich N. Fitzsimmons, and Thomas W. Oliver. "Lease Capitalization and Systematic Risk." *The Accounting Review* (October 1980), pp. 731–739.

Goldberg, Seymour. "Pension Planning and the CPA." *Journal of Accountancy* (May 1984), pp. 68–72.

Goldstein, Leo. "Unfunded Pension Liabilities May Be Dangerous to Corporate Health." *Management Accounting* (April 1980), pp. 20–22.

Grant, Edward B., and Thomas R. Weirich. "Current Developments in Pension Accounting." *The National Public Accountant* (July 1980), pp. 11–15.

Grinnel, D. Jacque, and Richard F. Kochanek. "The New Accounting Standards for Leases." *The CPA Journal* (October 1977), pp. 15–21.

Hawkins, David F., and Mary M. Wehle. *Accounting for Leases*. New York: Financial Executives Research Foundation, 1973.

Hawkins, David. "Objectives, Not Rules for Lease Accounting." *Financial Executive* (November 1970), p. 34.

Hicks, Ernest L. "Accounting for the Cost of Pension Plans." Accounting Research Study No. 8. New York: AICPA, 1965.

Ingberman, Monroe, Joshua Ronen, and George H. Sorter. "How Lease Capitalization Under FASB Statement No. 13 Will Affect Financial Ratios." *Financial Analysts Journal* (January–February 1979), pp. 28–31.

Kirk, Donald J. "Pension Accounting: Where the FASB Now Stands." *Journal of Accountancy,* (June 1980), pp. 82–88.

Langenderfer, Harold Q. "Accrued Past-Service Pension Costs Should Be Capitalized." *New York CPA* (February 1971), pp. 137–143.

Lorensen, Leonard, and Paul Rosenfield. "Vested Benefits—A Company's Only Pension Liability." *Journal of Accountancy* (October 1983), pp. 64–76.

Ma, Ronald. "Accounting for Long-Term Leases." *Abacus* (June 1972), pp. 12–34.

Myers, John H. *Reporting of Leases in Financial Statements.* New York: American Institute of Certified Public Accounts, 1962.

Philips, G. Edward. "Pension Liabilities and Assets. *The Accounting Review* (January 1968), pp. 10–17.

Schuchart, J. A., and W. L. Sanders, Jr. "Pension Fund Considerations." *Management Accounting* (March 1972), pp. 49–52.

Shachner, Leopold. "The New Accounting for Leases." *Financial Executive* (February 1978), pp. 40–47.

Smith, Jack L. "Actuarial Cost Methods—Basics for CPA." *Journal of Accountancy* (February 1977), pp. 62–66.

Smith, Jack L. "Needed: Improved Pension Accounting and Reporting." *Management Accounting* (May 1978), pp. 43–46.

Stone, Mary C. "The Changing Picture for Pension Accounting." *The CPA Journal* (April 1983), pp. 32–42.

Swieringa, Robert J. "When Current is Noncurrent and Vice Versa." *The Accounting Review* (January 1984), pp. 123–130.

Walken, David M. "Accounting for Reversions from Pension Plans." *Journal of Accountancy* (February 1985), pp. 64–70.

Whittred, G. P. "Accounting for the Extractive Industries: Use or Abuse of the Matching Principle?" *Abacus* (December 1978), pp. 154–159.

Wyatt, Arthur R. "Leases Should Be Capitalized." *The CPA Journal* (September 1974), pp. 35–58.

Zises, Alvin. "The Pseudo-Lease—Trap and Time Bomb." *Financial Executive* (August 1973), pp. 20–25.

11

EQUITY

In Chapter 8, two equity theories, the proprietary theory and the entity theory, were introduced. These and several other theories may provide a frame of reference for the presentation of financial statements. When viewing the applicability of the various theories of equity, it is important to keep in mind that the purpose of a theory is to provide a rationale or explanation for some action. The proprietary theory gained prominence because the interests of the owner(s) were seen as the guiding force in the preparation of financial statements. However, as the interests of other users became more significant, accountants made changes in financial report formats without adopting a particular equity theory.

In the following discussion, the student should keep in mind that the adoption of a particular theory could influence a number of accounting and reporting procedures. Also note that the theories represent a point of view toward the firm for accounting purposes that is not necessarily the same as the legal view of the firm.

THEORIES OF EQUITY

PROPRIETARY THEORY

According to the proprietary theory, the firm is owned by some specified person or group. The ownership interest may be represented by a sole proprietor, a partnership, or by a number of stockholders. The assets of the firm belong to these owners and any liabilities of the firm are also their liabilities. Revenues received by the firm immediately increase the owner's net interest in the firm and, likewise, all expenses incurred by the firm immediately decrease the net proprietary interest in the firm. This equity theory holds that all profits or losses

528

immediately become the property of the owners, and not the firm, whether or not they are distributed. Therefore, the firm exists simply to provide the means to carry on transactions for the owners and the net worth or equity section of the balance sheet should be viewed as

$$\text{assets} - \text{liabilities} = \text{proprietorship}$$

Additionally, financial reporting is based upon the premise that the owner is the primary focus of these reports. The proprietary theory is particularly applicable to sole proprietorships where the owner is the decisionmaker. When the form of the enterprise becomes more complex, and the ownership and management become separated, this theory becomes less acceptable. An attempt has been made to retain the concepts of the proprietary theory in the corporate situation; however, many accountants have asserted that it cannot meet the requirements of the corporate form of organization.[1] Nevertheless, we still find significant accounting policies that can be justified only through the acceptance of the proprietary theory. For example, the calculation and presentation of earnings-per-share figures is relevant only if we assume that those earnings belong to the shareholders prior to the declaration of dividends.

ENTITY THEORY

The rise of the corporate form of organization, which was accompanied by the separation of ownership and management, limited the liability of owners, and the legal definition of a corporation as a person encouraged the evolution of new theories of ownership. Among the first of these theories was the entity theory, which may be expressed as

$$\text{assets} = \text{equities}$$

The entity theory, like the proprietary theory, is a point of view toward the firm and the people concerned with its operation. This viewpoint places the firm, and not the owners, at the center of interest for accounting and financial reporting purposes. The essence of the theory is that creditors as well as stockholders contribute resources to the firm, and the firm exists as a separate and distinct entity apart from these groups. The assets and liabilities belong to the firm and not the owners. As revenue is received, it becomes the property of the entity and expenses incurred are obligations of the entity. Any profits are the property of the entity and accrue to the stockholders only when a dividend is declared. Under

---

[1]See, for example, William J. Vatter, "Corporate Stock Equities," Part 1, in *Modern Accounting Theory,* Morton Backer, ed. (Englewood Cliffs, N.J.: Prentice-Hall, 1966), p. 251.

this theory all of the items on the right-hand side of the balance sheet, except retained earnings that belong to the firm, are viewed as claims against the assets of the firm, and individual items are distinguished by the nature of the claim. Certain of these items are identified as creditor claims and others as owner claims; but, nevertheless, they are claims against the firm as a separate entity.

Goldberg has illustrated the difference between the proprietary and entity theories by way of an example involving a small child in possession of his or her first unit of monetary exchange.

> *Suppose that a small child is given, say £1, with which he can do whatever he likes. If (as is most unlikely) he is not familiar with the idea of ownership, he will think (i) "Here is £1"; and (ii) "This £1 is mine." These thoughts comprise the essence of the proprietary viewpoint and of double entry, for if the child were a born accountant, he would express the same thoughts as (i) "There exists an asset," and (ii) "I have a proprietary interest in that asset." That is to say, the £1 is regarded from two aspects: (1) as something that exists—an asset; and (ii) as belonging to somebody—my asset. Suppose further that, until the child can decide what he will do with the £1 he puts it in a money box. The entity theory can be introduced here by personalizing the money box—it involves adopting the point of view that the money box now has the £1 and owes £1 to the child.[2]*

Imbedded in this illustration is the fundamental distinction between the proprietary and entity theories—perceptions of the right-hand side of the balance sheet. Individuals who view net income as accruing only to owners will favor the proprietary approach, whereas those taking a broader view of the nature of the beneficiaries of income will favor the entity approach.

OTHER THEORETICAL APPROACHES

Several authors have noted inadequacies in the entity and proprietary approaches and have developed additional viewpoints or perspectives from which to rationalize the recording function. The most notable of these new viewpoints are the fund theory, the commander theory, the enterprise theory, and the residual equity theory. Each of these theories will now be considered separately.

Fund Theory
Vatter attacks the proprietary theory as too simplistic for modern corporate reporting.[3] On the other hand, he sees no logical basis for viewing the corpora-

---

[2]Louis Goldberg. *An Inquiry into the Nature of Accounting* (American Accounting Association. Monograph No. 7, 1963), p. 126.

[3]William J. Vatter, *The Fund Theory of Accounting and Its Implications for Financial Reports* (Chicago, Ill.: University of Chicago Press, 1947).

530

tion as a person in the legal sense. From this perspective, Vatter argues that the corporation is the people it represents.

The fund theory attempts to abandon the personal relationship advocated by the proprietary theory and the personalization of the firm advocated by the entity theory. Under the fund approach, the measurement of net income plays a role secondary to satisfying the special interests of management, social control agencies (e.g., government agencies), and the overall process of credit extension and investment. The fund theory is expressed by the following equation.

$$assets = restrictions \ on \ assets$$

This theory explains the financial recording of an organization in terms of three features, defined as follows.

1. *Fund*—an area of attention defined by the activities and operations surrounding any one set of accounting records, and for which a self-balancing set of accounts is created.
2. *Assets*—economic services and potentials.
3. *Restrictions*—limitations on the use of assets.

Each of these features is applied to each homogeneous set of activities and functions within the organization, thus providing a separate accounting for each area of economic concern.

The fund theory has not gained general acceptance in financial accounting. Its somewhat radical change from current practices and the added volume of bookkeeping it would require have inhibited its adoption. The use of the fund approach in government accounting is principally attributed to the legal restrictions typically imposed upon each fund, thus requiring a separate accounting for each.

Commander Theory
The entity theory adopts the point of view of the business entity, while the proprietary viewpoint takes on the viewpoint of the proprietor. But, asks Goldberg, "What of the point of view of the managers, that is, of the activity force in a . . . company?"[4] Goldberg argues that this question is of major importance because of the divergent self-interested viewpoints of owners and managers in large-scale corporations. In fact, so relevant is this divergence, "that in recent years a whole new field of study, going under the name of 'management accounting' and an ancillary literature have grown up, in which the emphasis is laid upon accountants for information to enable them (the managers) to carry out their function of control of property with a view to its increase."[5]

The commander approach is offered as a replacement for the proprietary and

[4]Goldberg, op. cit., p. 152.
[5]Ibid. p. 152

entity theories because it is argued that the goals of the manager (commander) are at least equally important to those of the proprietor or entity. The proprietary, entity, and fund approaches emphasize persons, personalization, and funds, respectively, but the commander theory emphasizes control. Everyone who has resources to deploy is viewed as a commander.

The commander theory, unlike the proprietary, entity, and fund approaches, has applicability to all organizational forms (i.e., sole proprietorship, partnership, and corporation). The form of organization does not negate the applicability of the commander view because the commander can take on more than one identity in any organization. In a sole proprietorship or partnership, the proprietor or partners are both owners and commanders. Under the corporate form, both the managers and stockholders are commanders in that they each maintain some control over resources (i.e., managers control the enterprise resources and stockholders control returns on investment emerging from the enterprise).

The commander theory argues that the notion of control is broad enough to encompass all relevant parties to the exclusion of none. The function of accounting, then, takes on an element of stewardship, to whom resource increments flow is not relevant. Rather, the relevant factor is how the commander allocates resources to the benefit of all parties. Although it is not on the surface a radical move from current accounting practices, the commander theory has generated little reaction in accounting circles.

Enterprise Theory

Under the enterprise theory, the business unit, most notably those listed on national or regional stock exchanges, is viewed as a social institution composed of capital contributors having "a common purpose or purposes and, to a certain extent, roles of common action."[6] Management within this framework essentially maintains an arm's-length relationship with owners and has as its primary responsibilities: (1) the distribution of adequate dividends and (2) the maintenance of friendly terms with employees, consumers, and government units. Because this theory applies only to large nationally or regionally traded issues, it is generally considered to have only minor impact on accounting theory.

Residual Equity Theory

Residual equity is defined by Staubus as "the equitable interest in organization assets which will absorb the effect upon those assets of any economic event that no interested party has specifically agreed to."[7] Here, the common shareholders

---

[6]Waino Soujanen, "Enterprise Theory and Corporate Balance Sheets." *The Accounting Review* (Janaury 1958), p. 56.

[7]George J. Staubus, "The Residual Equity Point of View in Accounting." *The Accounting Review* (January 1959), p. 3.

hold the residual equity in the enterprise by virtue of having the final claim upon income, yet they are the first to be charged for losses. The residual equity holders are vital to the firm's existence in that they are clearly the highest-risk takers and provide a substantial volume of capital during the firm's developmental stage. Again, as with the fund, commander, and enterprise theories, the residual equity approach has gained little attention in financial accounting circles.

RECORDING EQUITY

The American economy is generally characterized by three forms of business organization: sole proprietorships, partnerships, and corporations. Because of the efficiency of its production and distribution systems the corporation has emerged as the major form of business organization in most industries. Several advantages accrue to the corporate form and help to explain its emergence. Among these are

1. *Limited liability*—Stockholders are only liable for the amount of their original investment (unless that investment is less than the par value of the shares). Creditors may not look to owners for debt repayments as is possible in the case of sole proprietorships and partnerships.
2. *Continuity*—The corporation's life is not affected by the death or resignation of owners.
3. *Investment liquidity*—Corporate shares may be freely exchanged on the open market. Many shares are listed on national security exchanges, which improves their marketability.
4. *Variety of ownership interest*—Shares of corporate stock usually contain four basic rights: the right to vote for members of the board of directors of the corporation and thereby participate in management, the right to receive dividends, the right to receive assets upon the liquidation of the corporation, and the preemptive right to purchase additional shares in the same proportion to current ownership interest if new issues of stock are marketed. Any or all of these rights may be sacrificed by shareholders in return for special privileges. This results in an additional class of stock termed *preferred stock,* which may have either or both of the following features.
   a. Preference as to dividends.
   b. Preference as to assets in liquidation.

The corporate form of business organization allows management specialists to be employed. The owners thereby gain an expertise not normally available in sole proprietorships or partnerships. Evidence of the extent of this advantage can be found in the growth of business schools in the major universities. Almost every student in these programs is in training to obtain employment in a large corporation.

As noted in the previous discussion, two major types of stock may be found in any corporation, preferred stock and common stock. Preferred stockholders give up one or more of the rights usually accruing to stockholders for preference as to dividends or to assets in liquidation. Common stockholders retain such rights and have a residual claim on both the earnings and assets in liquidation. In addition to disclosing the legal claims these ownership groups have against the assets of the corporation, separation of the ownership groups gives information on the sources of capital, dividend requirements, and priorities in liquidation.

A corporation's capital section usually is subdivided into several components. These components are classified by source in the following manner.

I. Paid-in capital (contributed capital)
   A. Legal capital-par, stated value, or entire proceeds if no par or stated value accompanies the stock issue
   B. Additional paid-in capital—amounts received in excess of par or stated value
II. Unrealized capital
III. Earned capital
   A. Appropriated
   B. Unappropriated

Each of these components is discussed in further detail in the following sections.

PAID-IN CAPITAL

The limited liability advantage of the corporate form of business organization provides that creditors may look only to the assets of the corporation to satisfy their claims. This factor has caused various states to enact laws that attempt to protect creditors and inform them of the true nature of the assets and liabilities of individual corporations. Additionally, state laws generally protect creditors by establishing the concept of *legal capital*—the amount of net assets that cannot be distributed to stockholders. These laws vary from state to state, but the par or stated value of the outstanding shares generally constitutes a corporation's legal capital. State laws generally require legal capital to be reported separately from the total amount invested. As a result, ownership interests are classified as capital stock or additional paid-in capital in excess of par value. The classification *additional paid-in capital* includes all amounts originally received for shares of stock in excess of par or stated value. In unusual cases, stock may be sold for less than par value. In the event the corporation is liquidated, the holders of these securities could be required to pay the corporation the amount of the difference between the original investment and par value to protect creditors.

Stock Subscriptions

Large corporations frequently sell entire issues of stock to a group of investment advisors, or *underwriters,* who then attempt to resell the shares to the public. The

534

corporation is thereby relieved of the responsibility of selling and recording the individual share transactions over long periods of time. The underwriters record the new shareholders and incur the selling costs. However, when the corporation is unable or unwilling to sell stock through underwriters, records must be kept of each transaction with the new shareholders.

It is a common occurrence for individuals to contract to purchase shares on an installment basis. These potential shareholders, termed *subscribers,* usually receive the rights of ownership upon subscription but do not receive any shares until payment for all subscribed shares has been received. That is, each installment received is viewed as a percentage payment on each contracted share, and no shares are issued until all are paid in full. In some states, capital stock subscribed is viewed as a part of legal capital even though the shares are not outstanding. In other states, the subscribed shares are included in legal capital only after they have been fully paid and issued.

SPECIAL FEATURES

Securities other than common stock may contain provisions that allow (1) the holders of these securities to become common stockholders, (2) the corporation to reacquire these securities, or (3) the rate of return on the securities to fluctuate. Among these features are convertible provisions, call provisions, cumulative provisions, participating provisions, and redemption provisions. These provisions may be found most frequently on preferred stock, but some may also be found on long-term debt, as was discussed in Chapter 8.

Conversion

A convertible feature is included on preferred stock to make it more attractive to potential investors. Usually, a conversion feature is attached to allow the corporation to sell its preferred shares at a relatively lower dividend rate than is found on other securities with the same degree of risk. The conversion rate is normally set above the current relationship of the market value of the common share to the market value of the preferred convertible shares. For example, if the corporation's common stock is selling at $10 per share and the preferred stock has a selling price of $100 per share, the conversion rate might be set at eight shares of common for one preferred. All other things being equal, it would appear to be profitable for the preferred shareholders to convert to common when the value of the common shares rose above $12.50 per share. However, it is normal for the market price of the preferred shares to fluctuate in proportion to the market price of the common; therefore, an individual would not be able to make a profit by simply converting one type of security to another. Convertible stock is attractive to investors because the exchange ratio tends to tie the market price of the preferred stock to the market price of the common stock.

When preferred stock is converted to common stock, the proper accounting treatment is to transfer the par value of the preferred, plus a proportionate share of any additional paid-in capital on the preferred stocks, to common stock. If this amount differs from the par or stated value of common stock, it should be apportioned between par or stated value and additional paid-in capital on common stock.

Call Provisions

Call provisions allow the corporation to reacquire preferred stock at some predetermined amount. Call provisions are included on securities by corporations because of uncertain future conditions. Current conditions dictate the return on investment that will be attractive to potential investors, but conditions may change so that a lower return may be offered in the future. Additionally, market conditions may make it necessary to promise a certain debt-equity relationship at the time of issue. Call provisions allow the corporation to take advantage of future favorable conditions and indicate how the securities may be retired. The existence of a call price tends to set an upward limit on the market price of nonconvertible securities, since investors will not normally be inclined to purchase shares that could be recalled momentarily at a lower price.

Cumulative Provisions

Preferred shareholders normally have a preference as to dividends. That is, no common dividends may be paid in any one year until all preferred dividends for that year are paid. Corporations usually also include added protection for preferred shareholders in the form of a cumulative provision. These agreements state that if all or any part of the stated preferred dividend is not paid in any one year, the unpaid portion accumulates and must be paid in subsequent years before any dividend can be paid on common stock. Any unpaid dividend on cumulative preferred stock constitutes a dividend in arrears and should be disclosed on the financial statements even though it is not a liability until actually declared by the board of directors of the corporation. However, dividends in arrears are important in predicting future cash flows and as an indicator of financial flexibility and liquidity.

Participating Provisions

Participating provisions allow preferred stockholders to share with common shareholders dividends in excess of a normal return on a per share basis, in some predetermined ratio. For example, a participating provision might indicate that preferred shares are to participate in dividends on a 1:1 basis with common on all dividends in excess of $5 per share. This provision would require that any payments of more than $5 per share to the common stockholder also be made on a dollar-for-dollar basis to each share of preferred.

536

Redemption Provision

A redemption provision indicates that the preferred stock may be exchanged by the shareholder for cash in the future. The redemption provision may include a mandatory maturity date or specify a redemption price. Redeemable preferred stock has several of the debt characteristics discussed earlier in chapter 8. In fact, the Securities and Exchange Commission requires separate disclosure of such shares in its reports because of their special nature. At present the FASB does not require similar treatment, although footnote disclosure is required.

STOCK OPTIONS AND WARRANTS

Many corporations have agreements with employees and security holders that may result in the issuance of additional shares of common stock. These agreements can significantly affect the amount of common stock outstanding, and the method of accounting for them should be carefully evaluated.

Stock Options

Executive stock option plans have become an important element of the compensation package for corporate officers over the years. These plans allow corporate officials to purchase a stated number of shares of stock at an established price for some predetermined period. In the past, stock option plans were especially advantageous because of income tax regulations that taxed proceeds at the capital gains rate when the securities purchased under stock option plans were sold. Current tax laws have substantially reduced the tax advantage of stock options; nevertheless, they are still used by many corporations as a part of the total compensation package.

Stock option plans are most valuable when the option price is lower than the market price. For this reason, stock option plans are viewed as an incentive that influences the holders of options to try to increase corporate profits, and thereby increase the value of the company's common shares on the stock market. These plans have a potentially dilutive effect upon other shareholders, since exercising options causes additional stockholder claims against the same amount of income. The relative effects of this potential dilution versus the effect of management's incentive to increase profits should be examined by current and potential shareholders. Such measurements are, of course, quite difficult.

In 1972 the Accounting Principles Board reviewed the problems associated with accounting for stock options and issued Opinion No. 25, "Accounting for Stock Issued to Employees,"[8] Two types of plans were defined, noncompensatory and compensatory.

[8]Accounting Principles Board Opinion No. 25, "Accounting for Stock Issued to Employees" (New York: American Institute of Certified Public Accountants, 1972).

A *noncompensatory stock option plan* was defined as one not primarily designed as a method of compensation, but rather as a source of additional capital or of more widespread ownership among employees. Four essential characteristics of noncompensatory plans were defined: (1) the participation of all full-time employees, (2) the offering of stock on an equal basis or as a uniform percentage of salary to all employees, (3) a limited time for exercise of the option, and (4) a discount from market price that would not differ from a reasonable offer to stockholders. When these conditions are met, the corporation is not required to record any compensation expense.

Compensatory stock option plans, on the other hand, involve the recording of an expense, and the timing of the measurement of this expense can greatly affect its impact. The six possible measurement dates originally discussed in ARB No. 43 were reviewed in Appendix B to Opinion No. 25. These dates are:

1. The date of the adoption of an option plan.
2. The date on which an option is granted to a specific individual.
3. The date on which the grantee has performed any conditions precedent to exercise of the option.
4. The date on which the grantee may first exercise the option.
5. The date on which the option is exercised by the grantee.
6. The date on which the grantee disposes of the stock acquired.[9]

The APB concluded that compensation should be measured on the first date on which both the number of shares to be received by a particular individual and the option price are known. In most cases this will be the date on which the option is granted to a specific individual. The compensation is the difference between the market price of the stock on the measurement date and the price the employee is required to pay.

The determination of the measurement date is of primary importance for compensatory stock option plans. In some plans the date of the grant is the measurement date and, therefore, the amount of compensation is known. In other plans the measurement date is later than the date of the grant and the annual compensation expense must be estimated.

If the date of the grant and the measurement date are the same, deferred compensation and common stock options are established for the total amount of compensation cost. The deferred compensation cost is offset against the common stock options in the stockholders' equity section and amortized to expense over the period of benefit. In the event the measurement date is later than the date of the grant, total compensation cost cannot be measured on the date of the grant.

[9]Ibid., par. 6.

Therefore, annual compensation expense is estimated and common stock options are recorded during each period until the measurement date is reached.

Occasionally, available stock options may not be exercised. In the event an option is not exercised prior to the expiration date, previously recognized compensation cost is not affected; however, on the expiration date, the value of any previously recorded common stock options is transferred to additional paid-in capital.

Many accountants believe that the established procedures for recognizing common stock options result in understated income statement and balance sheet valuations. It should be noted that employees accepting stock options are accepting an investment in the firm in lieu of additional cash compensation. The ultimate value of this investment lies somewhere between zero—when the market price never exceeds the option price—and a very large return—when the market price rises substantially above the option price. Some accountants have advocated recording the value of the option at the expected value that lies between these two extremes; however, this procedure would result in a more subjective valuation. The recording and measurement of common stock option plans will undoubtedly continue to be a controversial issue in the near future.

Stock Warrants

Stock warrants are certificates that allow holders to acquire shares of stock at certain prices within stated periods. These certificates are generally issued under one of two conditions.

1. As evidence of the preemptive right of current shareholders to purchase additional shares of common stock from new stock issues in proportion to their current ownership percentage.
2. As an inducement originally attached to debt or preferred shares to increase the marketability of these securities.

Accounting for the preemptive right of existing shareholders creates no particular problem. These warrants need not be recorded except as memoranda in the formal accounting records. In the event warrants of this type are exercised, the shares of stock issued are measured at the amount of cash exchanged.

Warrants attached to other securities require a separate valuation because they may be traded on the open market. The amount to be attributed these types of warrants depends on their value in the securities market. Their value is measured by determining the relationship of the price of the warrant to the total market price of the security and warrant, and applying this percentage to the proceeds of the security issue. This procedure should be followed whether the warrants are associated with bonds or preferred stock.

In Opinion No. 14, the Accounting Principles Board supported this approach when it stated,

> The Board is of the opinion that the portion of the proceeds of debt securities issued with detachable stock purchase warrants which is applicable to the warrants should be accounted for as paid-in capital. The allocation should be based on the relative fair value of the two securities at the time of issuance.[10]

If the warrants are exercised, their value will be added to the cash received to arrive at the carrying value of the common stock. In the event the warrants are not exercised within the designated period, the portion of the cost of the security allocated to the warrants will remain on the books as paid-in capital.

UNREALIZED CAPITAL

Unrealized capital arises from events not connected with the issuance of stock or the normal profit-directed operations of the company. Unrealized capital results from the need to recognize assets or changes in value of other balance sheet items that have been excluded from the components of income by an authoritative body. The recognition issues for these items are discussed elsewhere in the text. The major examples of unrealized capital are (1) donated capital arising from the recognition of donated assets (discussed in Chapter 6), (2) unrealized losses on long-term investments in equity securities (discussed in Chapter 7), and (3) unrealized gains and losses on some foreign currency transactions (discussed in Chapter 12).

RETAINED EARNINGS

Legal restrictions in most states only allow corporations to pay dividends when there are accumulated earnings. These restrictions have resulted in the division of owners' equity into paid-in capital and earned capital. Although some states allow dividends from paid-in capital in the event of deficits, corporate managements generally do not wish to deplete capital, and distributions of this type are rare.

Retained earnings represent the accumulated net profits of a corporation that have not been distributed as dividends. It also should be noted, however, that accumulated retained earnings do not necessarily mean that a corporation has the cash available with which to pay dividends. Accumulated earnings allow corpo-

---

[10]Accounting Principles Board Opinion No. 14, "Accounting for Convertible Debt and Debt Issued with Stock Purchase Warrants" (New York: American Institute of Certified Public Accountants, 1969), par. 16.

rations to distribute dividends; the actual funds to pay these dividends must be available or acquired from other sources.

In many cases the retained earnings balance disclosed on the financial statements is divided into appropriated and unappropriated sections. The appropriated section indicates that the corporation does not plan to distribute as dividends that portion of the retained earnings balance. Appropriations may arise from legal restrictions, contractual restrictions, or internal decisions. Again it should be noted that an appropriation does not provide the funds with which to accomplish stated objectives, and it can be argued that these disclosures might be just as effective as footnotes.

Stock Dividends

As noted previously, corporations may have accumulated earnings but not have the funds available to distribute these earnings as cash dividends to stockholders. In such cases the company may elect to distribute some of its own shares of stock as dividends to current stockholders. Distributions of this type are termed *stock dividends,* and when they are minor relative to the total number of shares outstanding, retained earnings are reduced by the market value of the shares distributed. Capital stock and additional paid-in capital are increased by the par value of the shares and any excess, respectively. In theory, a relatively small stock dividend will not adversely affect the previously established market value of the stock. The rationale behind stock dividend distributions is that the stockholders will receive additional shares with the same value per share as those previously held. Nevertheless, stock dividends are not income to the recipients. They represent no distribution of corporate assets to the owners and are simply a reclassification of ownership interest.

Stock Splits

A procedure somewhat similar to stock dividends but with a different purpose is a *stock split.* The most economical method of purchasing and selling stock in the stock market is in blocks of 100 shares, and this fact affects the marketability of the stock. The higher the price of the individual shares of stock, the fewer the number of people able to purchase them in blocks of 100. For this reason many corporations wish to maintain the price of their shares of stock within certain ranges. When the price climbs above that range, the firm may decide to issue additional shares to all existing stockholders (or split the stock). In a stock split every stockholder receives a stated multiple of the number of shares currently held (usually 2 or 3 for 1), which lowers the market price per share. In theory, this lower price should be calculated by dividing the current price by the multiple of shares in the split, but intervening variables in the marketplace frequently affect prices simultaneously. A stock split does not cause any change in the stockholder's equity section except to increase the number of actual shares outstanding and reduce the par or stated value per share. No additional values are assigned to the shares of stock issued in a stock split because no distribution of assets or reclassification of ownership interests occurs.

A question sometimes arises as to whether a stock dividend is in actuality a stock split and should be treated accordingly. In a stock dividend, no material change in the market price of the shares is anticipated, whereas stock splits are undertaken specifically to change the market price. A large stock dividend can cause market prices to decline regardless of the terminology attached to the distribution. A rule of thumb is that if a stock dividend is at least 20 to 25 percent of the outstanding shares, the distribution should be recorded in a manner similar to a stock split. Stock distributions of this magnitude are termed *large stock dividends*. When large stock dividends are recorded, standard practice is to capitalize an amount of retained earnings equal to the par value of the shares issued.

TREASURY STOCK

Capital may be reduced by formally repurchasing and canceling outstanding shares of stock; however, the corporation may informally reduce capital by acquiring shares on the open market but not canceling them. These shares are termed *treasury stock*. Reacquisition of a company's own stock reduces both assets and stockholder equity and results in a legal restriction on retained earnings.

Two methods of accounting for treasury stock are found in current practice, the cost method and the par-value method. Under the *cost method*, the presumption is that the shares acquired will be resold and two events are assumed: (1) the purchase of the shares by the corporation and (2) the reissuance to a new stockholder. The reacquired shares are recorded at cost and this amount is disclosed as negative stockholders' equity by deducting it from total capital until the shares are resold. Any difference between the acquisition price and the sales price is generally treated as an adjustment to paid-in capital (unless sufficient additional paid-in capital is not available to offset any "loss"; in such cases retained earnings is charged).

Under the *par-value method*, it is assumed that the corporation's relationship with the original stockholder is ended. Therefore, legal capital and additional paid-in capital are reduced for the original issue price of the reacquired shares. Any difference between the original issue price and the reacquisition price is treated as an adjustment to additional paid-in capital (unless a sufficient balance is not available to offset a "loss" and retained earnings is charged). The reacquired shares are disclosed as a deduction from capital stock until they are reissued.

542

The disclosure of treasury stock on the financial statements is not clearly defined by generally accepted accounting principles. For example, APB Opinion No. 6 stated,

> *When a corporation's stock is acquired for purposes other than retirement (formal or constructive), or when ultimate disposition has not yet been decided, the cost of acquired stock may be shown separately, as a deduction from the total capital stock, capital surplus, and retained earnings, or may be accorded the accounting treatment appropriate for retired stock, or in some circumstances may be shown as an asset.[11]*

This Statement, in effect, allows for virtually any presentation of treasury stock desired by a corporation and disregards the realities of the acquisition of such shares. Treasury stock is clearly not an asset because a company cannot own itself, and treasury shares are not paid dividends. Similarly "gains" and "losses" on treasury stock transactions should not be reported on the income statement because of the possibility of income manipulation. The presentation of treasury shares on the financial statements should be reviewed in conjunction with the FASB's conceptual framework project, and a presentation that more closely resembles the purpose of the acquisition of treasury shares should be required.

QUASI-REORGANIZATIONS

A corporation which suffers losses over an extended period of time may find it difficult to attract new capital. That is, debt holders and stockholders wish to receive a return on their investments, but a period of unprofitable operations may restrict the corporation's ability to offer interest and dividend payments. This is particularly true for stockholders who cannot receive dividends unless there is a positive retained earnings balance.

In such cases a corporate reorganization allowed under the provisions of state law may be attempted as an alternative to bankruptcy. These situations are termed *quasi-reorganizations,* and the company is given a fresh start by eliminating the deficit balance in retained earnings and writing down any overvalued assets. If a quasi-reorganization is undertaken, the corporation must clearly disclose its plan to the stockholders and receive their formal approval. The steps involved in a quasi-reorganization are

1. Assets are written down to their fair market value against retained earnings or additional paid-in capital.

---

[11]Accounting Principles Board Opinion No. 6, "Status of Accounting Research Bulletins" (New York: American Institute of Certified Public Accountants, 1965), par. 12.

2. The retained earnings deficit is eliminated against additional paid-in capital or legal capital.
3. The zero retained earnings balance is dated and this date is retained until it loses its significance (typically 5 to 10 years).

SUMMARY

There are a number of theoretical approaches to the recording and reporting of ownership equity. The proprietary and entity theories are the two major approaches, but recently theorists have developed new viewpoints. These include the fund, commander, enterprise, and residual equity theories.

In addition to an understanding of the theoretical bases of equity reporting, it is important to know the generally accepted accounting principles for the proper recording of equity. Preferred stock, common stock, additional paid-in capital, subscriptions, options, and warrants all require somewhat different accounting procedures.

Also related to equity accounting is the concept of retained earnings—the undistributed net profits. Although these earnings exist in an accounting sense and allow the distribution of cash dividends, the actual funds for such distribution may not be available. In addition, stock dividends, stock splits, treasury stock, and quasi-reorganization all affect the reporting of equity securities, and each of these has its own reporting requirements.

In the following readings, Arthur Lorig reviews the theories of equity and examines the conflicts between the proprietary and entity theories through a series of questions. Brian Haley and Thomas Ratcliffe discuss the implications of stock options on the earnings of a business enterprise.

SOME BASIC CONCEPTS OF ACCOUNTING AND THEIR IMPLICATIONS

ARTHUR N. LORIG

PART I

There are certain basic over-all concepts regarding the fundamental nature of busi-

ness and other organizations from which one reasons to arrive at some accounting decisions, including aspects of classification, measurement and reporting. These concepts are variously termed theories, schools of thought, viewpoints, conventions, approaches, methods of viewing, and even doctrines. They are so different from one another that they lead to different conclusions or accounting decisions. This often results in controversy and sometimes confusion and misunderstanding.

Two of the concepts are widely held— the proprietary and the entity concepts. Other concepts or theories have been proposed as being improvements upon or more realistic than the two mentioned. These include the fund theory, the enterprise theory and the residual equity theory. However, thus far they have found so little recognition or support in accounting literature and practice that they will receive only slight consideration here.

Although the proprietary and entity theories are used widely, they often are not recognized as basic concepts. Many practicing accountants seem never to have even heard of them. In arriving at conclusions in some areas of accounting, these accountants have not sought to establish a premise from which to reason, but instead have merely assumed one or the other of the two concepts without being aware of the assumptions. Furthermore, not being conscious of their assumptions, they sometimes unknowingly shift from one to the other in treating different problems of even the same business organization. Some of their conclusions and decisions as a result may be inconsistent and even incongruous, and at odds with decisions made by other accountants on the same problems.

There is a possibility that, if practicing accountants understood the concepts and could agree on one as being the more acceptable and therefore the one which should be adopted, the differences resulting from the use of divergent concepts might be eliminated. Perhaps pointing out the areas of conflicting thought which have resulted will generate enough interest on the part of the accountants to induce them to take some action to select one concept

and adhere to it. It is that hope which initially prompted the study.

This paper is divided into two parts. Definitions and a somewhat general discussion of the concepts were found to be necessary and are taken up in Part I. The areas of conflict arising out of the existence of he differing concepts are disclosed in Part II. Readers who tend to be impatient with theoretical discussions may wish to turn to Part II first to see if the disclosures are of interest to them.

SHOULD ONE CONCEPT SUFFICE?

There is, of course, the question of whether it is possible to have one basic concept apply to all accounting entities, or whether the different types of such entities naturally require different concepts. For example, is the corporate structure so unlike that of a sole proprietorship that a different basic theory should be used? Do governments and other non-profit organizations have unique characteristics which call for a basic concept different from one suited to a profit-making enterprise? Should a corporate family, a parent and subsidiary companies, adopt a special viewpoint for its accounting different from that of a single corporation?

First, let it be pointed out that a legal entity, such as a corporation, is not identical with an accounting entity. The latter is not in any way limited by legal provisions. An accounting entity is one for which a self-balancing group of accounts is provided (assuming double-entry accounting, which is generally considered essential to complete accounting). It may go well beyond corporate limits to include many related corporations. At the other extreme, it may involve only a small fund of a municipality with very few accounts, such as a special revenue or agency fund. To reason basically about an accounting entity from a legal limitation standpoint would be a mistake.

Disregarding, then, any legal differences, are there other factors which might necessitate different accounting approaches for various types of accounting entities? Writers on this subject think not. Even two writers with views directly adverse in their preferences of a basis theory agree that one should suffice.[1] That also seems to be the belief of the chief advocate of the fund theory.[2] It was an assumption made at the start of this study, and no reasons were found later to abandon it.

EQUITIES

It will be apparent as the discussion proceeds that the theories are concerned directly only with items which appear on the credit side of the balance sheet. These items are referred to collectively as equities. They are claims against, or equitable rights in, the assets (or the values reflected in the assets) reported on the debit side. Of necessity, consideration will be given to the two major types of equities—outside and inside, or creditors and proprietors— with their several subclassifications; and to the possibility of a third type, the equity of the accounting entity itself. While this last may not seem sensible at this point, the need for considering such a possibility will be shown later.

The equities are sometimes thought of as

[1]See George Husband, "The Corporate-Entity Fiction and Accounting Theory," *The Accounting Review*, September 1938, p. 242; and Walter G. Kell. *The Equities Concept and Its Application to Accounting Theory* (unpublished doctoral thesis) Graduate College of the University of Illinois, Urbana, Ill., 1952, p. 2.
[2]William J. Vatter, *The Fund Theory of Accounting and Its Implication for Financial Reports* (Chicago: The University of Chicago Press, 1947).

sources of capital, which in effect they are, with a few possible exceptions such as taxes payable and claims for damages. The sources are divided into short-term (current liabilities) and long-term (bonds, stocks and retained earnings), the long-term group being of particular importance in the entity theory.

Before taking up the main subject of this study—a disclosure of the conflicting thoughts arising out of adhering to differing basic concepts—it seems desirable to define the concepts themselves. This is not an easy task because of the considerable confusion existing in accounting literature regarding the two main theories, the entity and proprietary theories. But that very confusion points to the need for defining the terms.

THE PROPRIETARY CONCEPT

According to the proprietary theory, the business or other organization being accounted for belongs to one or more persons thought of as proprietors or owners, and their viewpoint is reflected in the accounting. The assets are regarded as their assets and the liabilities as their liabilities. The business is merely a segregated portion of their financial interests, accounted for separately because it is convenient or necessary for various reasons to do so. The balance sheet equation expressing this viewpoint is "Assets − Liabilities = Proprietorship."

For accounting purposes, a corporation is looked upon as not different fundamentally from a sole proprietorship, the stockholders simply being an association of individuals joined together in owning the one business. The corporation as a legal entity is nothing more than "a device of a representative nature by means of which the associations' business affairs may be conveniently adminstered with certain legal privileges and within certain legal limitations.''[3]

The emphasis in accounting is upon the proprietors' equity, and a major purpose of the accounting is to determine the proprietors' net income or the changes in the proprietorship. The undistributed or retained earnings are assumed to belong to the proprietors.

Just who constitute the proprietors in a business corporation is not entirely clear. Certainly the common stockholders are included. The preferred stockholders also are generally considered in that category, though normally they have no voice in operating the business. In practice, the financial return to them is always considered a distribution and is chargeable only to net profits current or accumulated, and payable only when declared in the form of a dividend. Both classes of stockholders, therefore, are distinctly different from the creditor group, and this distinction is basic in the proprietary concept. Hence, for purposes of this study, the proprietors in a business corporation will be assumed to include all stockholders.

SOME CRITICISMS OF THE PROPRIETARY CONCEPT

Y. C. Chow raises the question whether perhaps all long-term investors—stockholders and bond or mortgage holders—may not be assumed to be proprietors.[4] This appears to be the view of some entity theorists in claiming there is too little difference between the two groups to justify basing a general accounting theory on the distinction. Nevertheless, an overwhelming majority of accountants consider only shareholders as owners.

The proper answer to the question who are the proprietors is most readily seen in a case of a small business enterprise. Assume a situation where a very few individual entrepreneurs seek to conduct business for profit. They have available the several forms of business organization from which to choose—individual proprietorships for each, a partnership, or corporation. Presumably they will select the form which best meets their balanced desires of high profit (including minimizing taxes), little risk, continued existence, ease of sale of interests, etc. Whichever form they select could permit them to obtain additional funds through long-term borrowing without giving up any of their effective control over the business operations. The basic accounting theory could be the same regardless of the form of organization selected, and the distinction between creditors and owners need not vary because of the form of organization.

Another objection raised against the proprietary viewpoint is that is is impossible to determine the profits of individual common stockholders of a corporation, some and possibly most of whom acquire their shares by purchase on the market at various prices. The simple notion of corporate profit being a personal gain of the proprietors, as called for in the proprietary concept, is said not to be applicable.[5] The reasoning in this objection is not clear. Even if the profit to an individual shareholder takes into account factors external to the business which are not shown on the

---

[3]Robert T. Sprouse, "The Significance of the Concept of the Corporation in Accounting Analyses," *The Accounting Review,* July 1957, p. 370.

[4]Y. C. Chow, "The Doctrine of Proprietorship," *The Accounting Review,* April 1942, pp. 162–163.

[5]Vatter, op. cit., p. 4.

books of the accounting entity, this should not argue against the proprietary concept. The stockholder's share of the increase in the proprietorship (the residual equity) of the business is easily calculated. What further calculation must be made to determine his net gain or loss is his personal affair. It is not a concern of the other members of the associated individuals, the stockholders, represented in the proprietorship.[6]

Husband answers the objection differently. He calls attention to

> the usual accounting assumption that new stockholders always step into the shoes of original stockholders. From this point of view the book values are their values. More realistically, however, only the placing of accounting on an economic basis can actually solve this problem. The accountant's problem here is one of convention, not of reality.[7]

Other characteristics said to raise questions as to the applicability of the proprietary concept are that the stockholders' control through voting is passive and of doubtful significance: that the invested capital cannot be withdrawn at will; that the managers are responsive to the wishes of other equity interests, too: and that these other equities also assume risks and have a claim on income. There is truth in each of these.

But why they negate the proprietary viewpoint is not at all clear. Basically the stockholders are the owners with control and bear the greatest risk and their rights constitute the residual equity. The managers may be removed by the stockholders and hence tend to serve stockholder's interests above other interests.

Furthermore, recent developments have resulted in some merging of executives' economic interests with those of stockholders. A very high percentage of large businesses have stock option plans for their executives. Executive incentive bonus plans also are now being used by the majority of large industrial companies. Both have resulted in increased managements' interest in enhancing profits and have done much to identify their interests with those of the proprietors.[8]

THE ENTITY CONCEPT

According to the entity concept, the business or other unit being accounted for must be considered as entirely apart from the shareholders or other owners. Not only is there a complete self-balancing set of accounts for the entity: the entity is conceived of as having a separate existence—an arms-length relationship with its owners. The relation to the owners is regarded as not particularly different from that to the long-term creditors. The balance sheet equation does not distinguish between creditors and proprietors but is simply "Assets = Equities." The accounting and reporting are for the entity itself as entirely separate from the owners.

Beyond this simple statement of what the entity concept is lies uncertainty and

---

[6] The problem is not greatly different from that of determining the current profit on the sale of an item unrealistically carried in inventory at a value far below its current market cost because of using the Lifo method of valuation. We accept the book profit on the sale, knowing it is unrealistic when judged by the current purchase cost of the item. If we wish to know the margin of current profit, we make a separate determination.

[7] George Husband, "The Equity Concept in Accounting," *The Accounting Review,* October 1954, p. 558.

[8] William H. White, *The Changing Criteria in Investment Planning* (Washington, D.C.: The Brookings Institution, 1962), pp. 21–23.

even confusion. The nature of the equities side of the equation is not clear. Decided differences of opinion on this point are expressed in accounting literature. Some writers seem to want to maintain the distinction between creditors and owners yet treat them similarly in the accounting.[9] Others regard proprietors as creditors,[10] and the widespread use of "Liabilities" as a heading for the whole credit side of the balance sheet indicates this is commonly held opinion.[11]

Among the recent writers on the entity concept, there seems to be universal agreement that the income of a corporation is not income of the stockholders—that it becomes their income only when and to the extent that dividends are declared.[12] This means that the retained earnings belong to the corporation itself and measure its equity in itself,[13] as meaningless as that concept might be. One writer suggests that

even the "business capital supplied by stockholders to the corporation does not represent the equity of the former, but rather that of the latter."[14]

Much emphasis is given by entity theorists to the following views and facts regarding an incorporated business:

The stockholders have practically the same relation to the corporation as the bondholders.

They do not own the profit made by the company.

They are mere investors in the corporation with practically no say in its operation.

The properties are owned by the corporation itself, not the stockholders.

The accounting and financial reporting are for all interested parties, including the entity's administration. They are not intended specifically for the stockholders.

These indicate the stockholders are closer to a creditor status than the creditors are to an owners' status. And since under the entity concept the stockholders and long-term creditors are to be treated similarly, it is logical that both classes should be regarded as creditors. As stated earlier, this is acknowledged by some of the entity theorists and it will be the assumption in this study.[15]

---

[9]Walter Kell claims that, although stockholders are considered to be "outsiders" under this theory, this does not indicate a stockholder is a creditor. Op. cit., p. 84.

[10]See Stephen Gilman, *Accounting Concepts of Profit* (New York: The Ronald Press Company, 1939), pp. 25, 26, 51. Also see Husband (1938), op. cit., p. 244.

[11]Of the 600 corporate balance sheets studied by the staff of the American Institute of Certified Public Accountants for the year 1962, about 49% used the single word "Liabilities" to head the credit side. The trend seems to be away from using it, however. Kell reports that in 1950 the ratio was 286/477 or 60%, and that a study by Field in 1936 showed the ratio as 86%. See Kell, op. cit., pp. 94–95.

[12]A. C. Littleton states that in early concepts of the entity theory, "profit was but an additional 'indebtedness' to the sources of the property in use." See his *Accounting Evaluation to 1900* (New York: American Institute Publishing Company, Inc., 1933), p. 194.

[13]Some writers favoring the entity theory seem reluctant to accept this inevitable conclusion, claiming that the retained earnings are rightfully

part of the stockholders' equity even though the income is not theirs. See Gilman, op. cit., p. 61, and Kell, op. cit., pp. 85 and 162.

[14]David H. Li, "The Nature of Corporate Residual Equity under the Entity Concept," *The Accounting Review*, April 1960, p. 261.

[15]The entity theorists who do not regard stockholders as creditors prefer to consider long-term creditors as somewhat equivalent to stockholders. To them, interest on borrowings is a distribution of income, not an expense. But their position is less tenable, and certainly less consistent with the idea of a separate entity, than the one maintained here.

Hence, it will be accepted herein that, under the entity theory, the credit side of the balance sheet consists of liabilities except for undistributed earnings which belong to the entity itself. Furthermore, inasmuch as the theory extends to all accounting entities, partners and sole proprietors also hold such a creditor relationship to their respective business enterprises under that theory.

CRITICISMS OF THE EQUITY CONCEPT

Perhaps the chief criticisms of the entity concept will arise from the unusual accounting decisions or principles which logically must follow from adopting it in dealing with accounting problems. These decisions will be discussed later. Here it is intended to point out other objections.

A major criticism is that the creditor relationship between the accounting entity and the owners is unrealistic and hence an improper basis upon which to build a theoretical accounting structure. The common stockholders of a corporation cannot be creditors because if they were it should be possible to determine the amounts owed and to ultimately pay them off. And even if it were possible to pay them off, it could only be by liquidating the corporation and paying them not only their recorded investment but the accumulated earnings—an acknowledgment that those earnings did belong to them all along. This is not in conformity with the entity theory.

A main reason why Sprague considered the entity theory unsatisfactory is that the rights of the proprietor are so very different from the rights of creditors. Proprietors' rights involve dominion over the assets and the power to use them as they choose or even sell them—the creditors' not being able to interfere except under extraordinary circumstances. The rights of the creditors are limited to definite sums which do not shrink when assets shrink, while the proprietors' rights are elastic, they suffering losses, expenses, and shrinkage and benefiting from profits, revenues and increases of value.[16] Canning objected to the use of the term "liabilities" to head the righthand side of the balance sheet because it is "seriously confusing and misleading."[17]

Another basis for criticism is disclosed in a simple comparison. A corporation is not a person but merely a device, created to benefit the originators. It is, in a sense, a machine. As viewed under the entity concept, it may be likened to a machine that has become personified and has declared a form of independence from its creator and owner, denying any closer relation or greater responsibility to him than to one who loaned money used in building it. In the case of the machine, it clearly is an unacceptable viewpoint: in the case of the corporation, it should be also.

In a similar manner it is possible to compare a business entity, as viewed under the entity theory, with a government created by men to serve their interests. The individuals given the responsibilities of seeing that the governments' functions are carried out often assume it has a separate existence. They tend to forget it is merely a useful device or servant of its creators and begin to regard it as having a will of its own with a right to determine its own functions and even to expect service of its citizens. "Ask not what your country can do for you but what you can do for your country" is the admonition of one well-known public administrator. In like manner a cor-

[16]Charles E. Sprague, *The Philosophy of Accounts* (New York: The Ronald Press Company, 1912), p. 47.
[17]John B. Canning, *The Economics of Accountancy* (New York: The Ronald Press Company, 1929), p. 55.

poration may mistakenly be regarded as entitled, through its management, to act independently of the stockholders' wishes and to expect them to allow the use of their money with little to say as to how it should be used. The concept of an independent entity with its own motivations and interests seems unjustified in both cases and even dangerous to the long-run welfare of the originators.

When the entity theory is applied to noncorporate situations, its flaws become more apparent. Partners and sole proprietors have difficulty conceiving of themselves as of the same general nature as their long-term creditors and recognizing that the profits are not theirs until withdrawn. When approached with the concept, they are perplexed and, if inclined to be courteous, change the subject hurriedly because of danger of getting angry.

Carried to an extreme situation, the entity concept would dictate that an individual's personal possessions be accounted for as a separate entity, distinct from himself. Then those possessions owe him for their worth, and the income from his investments does not really become his until he consumes it. The concept appears somewhat ludicrous when applied to such a situation.

OTHER THEORIES

An "enterprise theory" has been proposed as being more realistic than the entity theory for those corporations with common stock listed on stock exchanges and hence subject to considerable control by governments.[18] A corporation is viewed as concerned with its place in society and having as its main objectives survival and growth.

Its management feels no great responsibility to the owners and attempts to satisfy them only to the extent of "conventionally adequate dividends." This responsibility is considered somewhat on a par with that of paying high wages to employees or maintaining friendly relations with governments, the public and consumers.

This theory could have only very limited application[19] and is therefore not useful as a general over-all theory. Furthermore, it does not seem to accord with observable attempts of management to withstand labor unions' demands and to seek lower interest costs in order to improve profits. Nor can it be said that survival and growth are incompatible with stockholders' desires; many of them prefer the resultant capital gains in preference to high cash dividends.

Eugene V. Rostow wrote of the seeming ineffective stockholders' control of management and of the latter's responsibility to other groups. And yet he concluded ihat the objectives of the corporation should be, and are, to provide profits and operate according to economic laws.[20] He believes the rule of long-term profit maximization is more in accord with public expectancy than any other alternatives.[21]

Another proposal is one made by William Vatter, which he calls the fund theory.[22] In this theory he avoids personalizing the entity. Rather, he divides the entity into various areas of interest devoid of direct relationship to any group of per-

[18]Waino W. Suojanen, "Enterprise Theory and Corporate Balance Sheets." *The Accounting Review,* January 1958, pp. 56–65.

[19]This theory could apply to only a few thousand out of close to a million corporations existent in the United States.
[20]Eugene V. Rostow, "To Whom and For What Ends is Corporate Management Responsible," Chapter 3 in Edward S. Mason (ed.), *The Corporation in Modern Society* (Cambridge: Harvard University Press, 1959), p. 67.
[21]Ibid., p. 70.
[22]Vatter, op. cit.

sons, each area to have its own self-balancing set of accounts. Those individuals concerned with the equity would be expected to use the accounting reports for the areas in which their interests lie.

This proposal appears to have been scientifically conceived but it has demerits, too. One writer critically points out that Vatter's "statement of operations" is not an income statement but contains additional data, such as appear in a source and application of funds statement, and items usually relegated to footnotes, such as unrealized gains. The reader of the financial reports is expected to calculate net income according to his own concept of what that calculation should include.[23] This writer knows of no adoption of the fund theory during the fifteen years which have passed since the proposal was published. Hence it will not be considered further here.

One other proposal will be mentioned—that the basic theory in accounting be from the point of view of the residual equity.[24] The residual equity in a corporation is that of common stockholders who have the final claim on income and who are the first to be charged with a loss. Under this concept, all prior claims to income would be regarded as costs, including dividends to preferred stockholders and even Class A common dividends.[25] Again this writer knows of no case where this view is adhered to and will not consider it further in this treatise.

PART II

CONFLICTS IN PRINCIPLES AND PRACTICE ARISING OUT OF THE PROPRIETARY AND ENTITY CONCEPTS

Thus far, explanations have been given of the important proprietary and entity concepts now generally used by accountants (often unknowingly) as the bases for accounting principles and decisions. It is now intended to take up the main objective of this study—to disclose and briefly discuss the conflicts in accounting thought and action that have arisen out of the use of the two concepts. Hopefully, this might make accountants aware of the suspect nature of some of their decisions. It also should point out the seriousness of using two very different concepts somewhat indiscriminately.

The conflicts to be examined will be introduced in the form of questions, with "yes" and "no" answers given for the proprietary and entity concepts. Brief discussions or explanations will follow when considered desirable.

[23]Loyd C. Heath, "A Critical Review of the Fund Theory of Accounting and its Implications for Financial Reports," an unpublished paper.
[24]This is described in George J. Staubus, "The Residual Equity Point of View in Accounting." *The Accounting Review*, January 1959, pp. 3–31. Kell also discusses it, op. cit., pp. 116–118.

[25]Y. C. Chow, op, cit., p. 162.

	Proprietary Concept	Entity Concept
1. *Are the net earnings of a business to be considered income of the stockholders (or other owners)?* Under the entity concept, the income is that of the business enterprise itself until dividends are declared or distribution otherwise made.	Yes	No

2. *Should earnings per share be reported?*   Yes   No

The earnings per share has real significance to stockholders under the proprietary theory. Under the entity concept the earnings do not belong to the stockholders and the amount per share would carry misleading inferences.

3. *Are corporate retained earnings, or earned surplus, part of the stockholders' equity?*   Yes   No

According to the entity theory, the retained earnings must be regarded as belonging to the entity itself. Some entity theorists hesitate to admit this, but there can be no alternative if the stockholders are not to receive income until distribution is made. Certain types of capital surplus, such as donated surplus, appreciation surplus, and surplus arising through reorganizations, also belong to the entity. However, capital surplus arising out of sale of capital stock at a premium is regarded as part of the stockholders' equity under both concepts.

4. *Do the two taxes, corporate income tax and personal income tax on corporate cash dividends, result in double taxation?*   Yes   No

Under the proprietary concept, the income of the corporation is the income of the stockholders and hence tax is levied twice on the same income. However, there is a probability that some companies are able to pass along part of the burden of the corporate income tax to their customers through their sale prices. In such cases the tax burden on the stockholders would not truly be double.

5. *May the income of corporations be taxed justifiably to the stockholders at the time it is earned by the corporation, prior to its distribution as dividends?*   Yes   No

In this respect stockholders, under the proprietary theory, are comparable to members of a partnership and are properly subject to tax on undistributed corporate income. It appears, then, that theoretically a choice develops between the alternatives of accepting as justified either double taxation or a personal tax on proportional shares or undistributed profits.[26] In the latter case, the government might tax the corporate profits tentatively and, when dividends are received by shareholders and

---

[26]Actually, such a choice already is available to certain small business corporations through Subchapter S of the Internal Revenue Code. Under carefully defined conditions, corporate income is permitted as if they were members of a partnership.

included in their taxable income, allow their share of the
corporate tax as a credit on their personal tax.

6. *Should cash dividends be regarded as an expense to the
   corporation?*   No   Yes
   Herein lies an injustice in the federal income tax. The
   entity theory is adhered to by the government in levying a
   corporate income tax, but the proprietary theory must be
   the basis used in denying the corporation a deduction of
   the dividends as an expense.

7. *May a parent and subsidiary companies be accounted for
   as one economic unit through use of consolidated statements?*   Yes   No
   When, as under the entity theory, the relationship is debt-
   or and creditor, a consolidated picture is not proper.
   Under the proprietary theory, the subsidiaries' income
   belongs to the stockholders, including a parent company,
   at the time it is earned and hence may be included with
   the parents' own earnings through consolidation. To prepare consolidated statements is to espouse the proprietary
   concept.

8. *Should a parent company take up on its books its proportionate share of it subsidiaries' profits and losses?*   Yes   No

9. *Are consolidated corporate income tax returns justified?*   Yes   No

10. *Is a dividend declared out of retained earnings and paya-
    ble in capital stock (a stock dividend) to be regarded as
    income to the recipients?*   No   Yes
    Under the entity concept, inasmuch as the stock dividend
    would entail a transfer from retained earnings (represent-
    ing the corporation's equity in itself) to capital stock
    (representing a liability to the stockholders), it must be
    regarded as an income to the stockholders. However, a
    premium on capital stock is a part of the stockholder's
    equity and a dividend, cash or stock, charged against
    such a premium account would not be income to the
    stockholders.

11. *Should a cash dividend declared immediately after stock
    is purchased be considered as income to the new stock-
    holder?*   No   Yes
    According to the entity theory, no corporate earnings are
    income to the stockholder until received as a dividend.
    Hence, unless the amount is regarded as stockholder in-

	Proprietary Concept	*Entity Concept*

come at this time, it never would be. Under the proprietary theory, the former stockholder received income when the corporation earned it. Being undistributed, it is assumed logically to be included in the price of the stock and its receipt now would be merely a return of capital to the new owner.

12. *Should preferred stock dividends in arrears be recorded as a corporate expense, and a liability for it set up?*   **No**   **Possibly**

The answer under the entity concept is difficult to determine. The stockholder does not own corporation income until a dividend is declared. And yet a preferred stockholder has a preferred claim which is practically certain to be met if corporation income is ample. And since a dividend is expense under this concept, it would seem highly irregular not to recognize such an accrual of probable expense.

13. *May a corporate deficit be shown on the debit side of the balance sheet?*   **No**   **Yes**

As long as the business is a going concern, it could be expected that the deficit might be offset by future earnings which are now owned by the stockholders. Hence it seems improper under the entity concept to show a reduced liability to the stockholders to the amount of the deficit. In case liquidation is anticipated, the deficit is expected to be used later to reduce the liability to stockholders. In this respect it is similar to a sinking fund which normally is shown on the debit side of the balance sheet. However, liquidation is a very limited experience for a firm and the location of the deficit under those conditions is of little importance so long as it is carefully identified.

14. *May discount on capital stock with reason be charged to retained earnings?*   **Yes**   **No**

The retained earnings do not belong to the stockholders under the entity concept, and the discount is an offset to the liability shown in the capital stock account. To wipe out the discount against retained earnings would result in an increase in the liability to the stockholders. Under the proprietary theory, the retained earnings do belong to the stockholders, and the charge-off of discount would not affect the position of that group.

SOME BASIC CONCEPTS OF ACCOUNTING AND THEIR IMPLICATIONS

	Proprietary Concept	Entity Concept

15. *May gain on the acquisition of treasury stock be credited to retained earnings?* No Yes

The gain on the treasury stock transaction is a net gain to the entity under the entity concept, for the liability to stockholders is reduced in an amount greater than that paid out. Furthermore, the transaction with the former stockholder is completed and the gain is realized, just as a gain in paying off a liability is realized. Under the proprietary theory opinion is divided on this question but the majority opinion favors recording the treasury stock at cost and reporting it as a deduction from the total of capital stock and related surplus items.

16. *Is cost the best basis of asset value to use in financial reports?* Probably not Yes

Since under the entity concept the stockholders are regarded as creditors, it would be inaccurate to show as liabilities more or less than the amounts invested. And to reflect any gain or loss in asset values, resulting from price changes, in the entity's equity in itself would be rather meaningless.[27] On the other hand, under the proprietary concept where accounting is for the owners, there is real doubt whether adhering to cost is as satisfactory as reporting the more realistic current values, especially for inventories and investments.

17. *Should the calculated book value per share of common stock include a proportionate part of retained earnings?* Yes No

The retained earnings do not belong to the stockholders under the entity concept. Hence the book value cannot properly include any part of those earnings. This can lead to absurd results as in the case of a certain closely held corporation with capital stock of $2,000 and retained earnings in excess of $500,000.

18. *Is the common account form of balance sheet (debits on the one side, credits on the other) the clearest form for presenting the financial position?* No Yes

The equation for the entity concept is "Assets = Equities (or Liabilities)" and this corresponds to the account form. The equation for the proprietary concept is "Assets −

---

[27]Gilman states, "The entity, as such, is not concerned with economic measures of valuation but rather symbolizes in terms of money various transactions reflecting a charge and discharge relationship between entity and proprietor. . . . From the entity viewpoint valuation at cost is natural," op. cit., p. 55.

556

Liabilities = proprietorship'' and the report form of statement of financial position expresses that relationship most clearly.

19. *Do stock market values provide a logical basis for valuing common capital stock held as investments?*   Yes   No
Stock market values do assume that both past and future earnings of a corporation belong to the stockholders and therefore reflect the proprietary point of view.

CONCLUSION

The above questions are those which occurred to the writer or were found in the course of this study. While undoubtedly not presenting a complete list of the problems arising out of the selection of one or the other of the two basic concepts, they are thought to be inclusive enough to reveal how important to accounting practice and theory the selection of proper concept is.

An examination of the answers indicates that the proprietary concept is adhered to by accountants in a large majority of their decisions regarding the questions. In this writer's opinion, in only three questions (numbers 5, 16, and 18) is the entity viewpoint the one generally favored. In all of the other sixteen questions, the proprietary viewpoint seems to be the one generally held.

Is there a way to determine if one concept can be found to be entirely correct and the other wrong? This writer knows of none. The law does not provide a way, and lawyers appear to be just as inconsistent or as uncertain in their views on the corporate entity as the accountants.[28]

Can we possibly conduct accounting without personal points of view—i.e., thoroughly objectively? Vatter suggested his fund theory as a means of doing this, but it has not taken hold. Raby stated that the entity concept can be maintained objectively,[29] but to this writer he was not convincing. His argument that management's responsibilities are to the entity, not to the stockholders or creditors or employees or society,[30] means that the responsibilities are to an inanimate creation, and that seems inconceivable. One does not feel responsible to a machine.

Accounting is a tool, and requires a classification in the form of accounts and groupings or accounts for summarizing transactions. In setting up such a classification, we must have points of view. It may be the long-term investors, or all the equities, or the common stockholders, or perhaps the government's (as to when a separate set of accounts is prepared for a utility to satisfy governmental demand for information). And one of those interests must be a dominant one, and it naturally would be the one which created the business entity.

[28]See Robert T. Sprouse, ''Legal Concepts of the Corporation.'' *The Accounting Review.* January 1958, pp. 37–49.

[29]William L. Raby, ''The Two Faces of Accounting.'' *The Accounting Review,* July 1959, p. 461.
[30]Ibid., p. 455.

The thought occurs that possibly we could allow individual selection of a basic concept out of the several possibilities, as we do between cash and accrual accounting. For some the entity theory might seem the best selection, as for a very large corporation. For smaller corporations and partnerships and sole proprietorships the proprietary theory would seem more appropriate. Were this permitted, it should be expected that whatever the selection in a given instance, it be adhered to consistently.

However, there would be less confusion to the users of financial statements if one of the two main concepts were selected for all accounting entities, and used consistently by each entity. From his study, the writer concluded that the proprietary concept is the more realistic and theoretically accurate and practical, and more in conformity with actual practice. Its adoption as the basic concept to be used for all accounting entities would be a boon to improved clarity in accounting.

ACCOUNTING FOR INCENTIVE STOCK OPTIONS

BRIAN W. HALEY
THOMAS A. RATCLIFFE

Accounting principles covering compensation in the form of stock options were originally promulgated in 1948 as Accounting Research Bulletin (ARB) No. 37. In 1953, ARB No. 37, revised to reflect the enactment of Sec. 130A of the Internal Revenue Code (IRC), was restated as ARB No. 43, Chapter 13B. The principles enunciated under ARB No. 43 remain in effect for the traditional stock option plan. However, in 1972, AFB Opinion No. 25 redefined the measure of compensation to account for the more complex plans based on variable factors. In 1978, FASB Interpretation No. 28 clarified the accounting for variable plans consistent with the principles of APB Opinion No. 25.

Reprinted with permission of *The CPA Journal,* Copryright´ 1982, New York State Society of Certified Public Accountants.

ACCOUNTING FOR STOCK OPTIONS

The accounting for compensatory stock options[1] revolves around two critical elements:

- Identification of the compensation elements to be measured; and
- The measurement date.

COMPENSATION ELEMENTS

The compensation amount can be viewed from the perspective of the employer. The

[1]APB Opinion No. 25 (Para. 7) specifies four criteria which must be met to classify an option as noncompensatory. These criteria should be applied to any plan. However, such application to plans under Sec. 422, 422A and 424 will show them to be compensatory. In addition, Para. 7 promulgates plans under Sec. 423 to be noncompensatory but omits plans under other sections.

Committee on Accounting Procedure (CAP), when it issued the ARBs on this subject recognized that, from the standpoint of the employee, there is an inherent value in a restricted future right to purchase shares, even if the purchase price is initially set at or above fair market value. However, the complex interaction of positive and negative variables make it impractical to measure any such value.[2] Furthermore, from the viewpoint of the employer corporation, the value of the option to the employee cannot represent a measurable cost if, at the date of grant, the corporation could realize an amount equal to or in excess of the fair market value of the optioned shares. From this, it follows that the corporation will incur a cost if the employee has a right to purchase the optioned shares at an amount below fair value. Therefore, it was concluded (later referred to as a "practical solution" by the APB) that the value to the employee and the cost to the employer is to be the excess of the fair value of the shares over the option price, such fair value being established by the quoted market price. If quoted market prices are not available or are not representative of the actual value, a "best estimate" of the market value should be used.

MEASUREMENT DATE

Having specified the relevant compensation elements, the date to measure those elements is of critical importance since the fair value, option price and the number of shares subject to the option may vary over the option term. ARB 43 suggested six potential dates for measuring compensation. These dates were: (1) the plan adoption date, (2) the option grant date, (3) the date when condition precedents are satisfied,

---

[2]Such factors include a known purchase price, restriction on right to receive, absence of commissions, tax consequences and transfer restrictions.

(4) the date the option is first exercisable, (5) the actual exercise date, and (6) the stock disposition date. The date of grant was selected as the appropriate point to evaluate the cost to the employer, since this is the time the parties agreed to the valuation of the option to be given in exchange for the services to be rendered. In addition, this is the date on which the corporation forgoes the principal alternative use of the shares it places in option. The fact that the corporation could have obtained more or less on its shares in the future is not relevant to the compensation which was agreed to at the date of grant. Choosing the date of grant as the time to measure the compensation is consistent with the accounting treatment normally accorded compensation paid in other forms of noncash consideration, i.e., at the time the parties agree to the amount of compensation. However, this position proved to be unworkable when applied to option arrangements based on variable factors. In such situations, the number of shares under the option or the option price may change depending on future events such as earnings or stock market values. As a consequence, Opinion No. 25 (Para. 10b) redefined the measurement date to be the first date on which both the following are known:

- The number of shares that an individual employee is entitled to receive; and
- The option or purchase price, if any.

Thus, for traditional plans, the measurement date remains the date of grant with compensation being measured on the date of grant values for the quoted market price of the stock and the option exercise price. This compensation amount is then recognized over the one or more periods in which the employee performs the agreed on services. However, when the measurement date is later than the grant date (as in variable plans), compensation expense should be accrued each period subsequent to the date of grant based on the quoted market price of the stock at the end of each period. If the market price should change between periods, the estimated compensation expense should be prospectively accounted for in the period of change as a change in accounting estimate. This treatment is also applicable to phantom or shadow stock plans (e.g., stock appreciation rights), as will be discussed later in this article.

These are the general rules for computing and recognizing compensation expense for stock options issued to employees. However, before proceeding to their application to incentive stock options, three other points must be considered.

DEFERRED TAXES

As discussed on the authors' article on the tax aspect of this topic in *The CPA Journal's* September 1982 issue, the employer corporation is entitled to a tax deduction for compensation expense when the stock option plan is nonstatutory. The tax deduction is measured, normally, at the date of exercise (as opposed to the date of grant) as the excess of the fair market value (at exercise date) over the option price. Thus, not only will the income tax deduction be recognized at a time different from the financial statements (timing differences) but the wage amount for tax purposes will normally also differ from accounting amounts (permanent differences). To the extent the accounting expense is deductible for tax purposes, it gives rise to a timing difference which should be reflected in the deferred tax provision (i.e., a reduction of tax expense). To the extent the amount of the tax deduction varies from accounting expense, such permanent difference will not be taken into income but will represent an adjustment of paid-in capital. Therefore, if the tax deduction exceeds the accounting expense, the tax benefit will increase paid-in capital in the period of the tax reduction (i.e., when the option is exercised). Conversely, if the tax deduction is less than the accounting expense, paid-in capital will be reduced in the period in which the additional liability results.

Of course, if the option plans are statutory, no tax deduction is allowed for the compensation, resulting in a permanent difference. Therefore, the compensation related to the statutory option plan will not affect the deferred tax provision.

MODIFICATION OF EXISTING PLANS

APB Opinion No. 25 (Par. 11e) provides as follows:

Renewing a stock option or purchase right or extending its term establishes a new measurement date as if the right were newly granted.

The option being modified should be treated as not being exercised and the previous amounts of wages recognized as well as deferred tax charges associated with the recognized expense should be reversed and reflected in current year earnings. The modified option is then treated as a new option giving rise to a new measurement date, compensation amount and accrual period. The elimination of the "old option" could have a favorable impact on earnings (restoration of prior periods expense in the current period—if any recognized) while the "new option" could have a negative impact.

Note that paid-in capital will not be affected for permanent tax differences as such differences only arise when the option is exercised.

EXAMPLE 1

FASB IN No. 28, Appendix B

Date of Grant	January 1, 1982
Expiration Date	December 31, 1991
Vesting	100% at the end of 1985
Number of Shares Under Option	1000
Option Price	$10 per share

Market Price Assumption
Quoted market price per share at
December 31 of subsequent years:

1982	$11
1983	12
1984	15
1985	14
1986	15
1987	18

CASH SETTLEMENTS

Cash paid to an employee to settle an earlier grant of option should measure compensation expense. Thus, if the cash payment differs from the originally recognized compensation amount, compensation expense should be adjusted as a change in accounting estimate.

ACCOUNTING TREATMENT FOR INCENTIVE STOCK OPTIONS

This portion of the article is divided into two segments. The first considers the accounting for newly granted incentive stock options. The second addresses itself to the conversion of pre-1981 stock option plans to qualify for incentive option treatment.

OPTION PLANS GRANTED INITIALLY AS INCENTIVE STOCK OPTIONS

On the surface, the incentive stock option appears to be similar to the old statutory plans and, therefore, should have a similar accounting treatment. Since Sec. 422A(b)(4) prohib-

its the granting of the option at an exercise price below fair market value, the accounting treatment should be easy—there will not be any. The value of the stock, at the date of grant, is equal to the option price and, as a result, the employer company has incurred no cost. There will not be any problems with the deferred tax provision, since the difference between compensation expense for accounting and tax (no deduction allowable) is permanent. The employee corporation merely has to record the consideration received (ostensibly the option price amount) and the stock issued when the option is exercised.

Now the problem area. As discussed in our earlier article on the tax consequences of stock options, no consideration will ever be received. The employee will only go through the formality of tendering his own stock (as little as one share) and getting in return sufficient shares to equal the full appreciation in the option shares. In substance, all that results is a stock appreciation right which is defined by FASBIN No. 28 as:

Awards entitling employees to receive . . . stock . . . in an amount equiv-

EXHIBIT 1

Computation of Annual Compensation—Incentive Stock Option

		Cumulative Compensation				Accrual of Expense By Year					
Date	Market Price	(1) No. Shares Issuable	(2) Aggregate Compensation	Percent Accrued	Accrual To Date	1982	1983	1984	1985	1986	1987
12/31/82	$11	91	$1001	× 25%	$ 250	$250					
12/31/83	12	167	2004	× 50%	752 / 1002		$752				
12/31/84	15	333	4995	× 75%	2744 / 3746			$2744			
12/31/85	14	286	4004	× 100%	258 / 4004				$258		
12/31/86	15	333	4995	× 100%	991 / 4995					$991	
12/31/87	18	444	7992	× 100%	2997 / 7992						$2997

(1) Number of Shares Issuable
1982: $1000 \times (1-10/11) = 90.9$ (Round to 91)
1983: $1000 \times (1-10/12) = 166.6$ (Round to 167)
1984: $1000 \times (1-10/15) = 333.3$ (Round to 333)
1985: $1000 \times (1-10/14) = 285.7$ (Round to 286)
1986: $1000 \times (1-10/15) = 333.3$ (Round to 333)
1987: $1000 \times (1-10/18) = 444.4$ (Round to 444)

(2) Aggregate compensation for shares issuable upon exercise of option to be allocated to periods in which service performed.

alent to any excess of the market value of a stated number of shares of the employer company's stock over a stated price.

To illustrate the accounting, assume the same facts as found in Example 1.

The computation of the annual compensation is shown in Exhibit 1. The results are the same (except for rounding) as that shown in FASBIN No. 28 (Example 1). The only difference is that FASBIN No. 28 computed the aggregate compensation based on the shares under the option times the per share aggregate appreciation. Under the pyramid acquisition of shares, the total shares under the option will not be issued. The shares that will be issued are only those which, in the aggregate, will equal the appreciation in the option shares. Therefore, to compute the compensation amount, the issuable shares are multipled by the current fair market value. The result is the same as in the FASBIN No. 28.

ACCOUNTING TREATMENT FOR THE CONVERSION OF PRE-1981 OPTIONS

The conversion of profitable pre-1981 stock options can bring a windfall to the employee. However, such conversion can have an equally significant adverse impact on company financial statements.

In considering this impact, a conclusion must be made on whether the modification of a pre-1981 option represents the creation of a new option or would merely represent the continuation of the old one. APB Opinion No. 25 (Para. 11e) does not provide much assistance. It merely stipulates that the renewal or extension of an option will be considered the granting of a new option for measurement date purposes. However, the normal modifications in a conversion can include not only the extension of a term (which certainly will cause a new measure-

ment date), but also the abbreviation of a term (to 10 or five years, as appropriate) and the increase or decrease of the option price (to market value at date of grant). The theoretical basis for considering a term extension as a new option is the fact that, in substance, it is a new option. The parties just did not go through the formalities of letting the old option expire, followed by a new grant. This same line of thought does not apply to the reduction of a term. Here, it could be argued that no new measurement date need be set as the employer's original cost and the employee's original gain are not modified (i.e., excess of market value over option price). The alteration of the option price does change the employer's originally negotiated obligation and, therefore, could represent a "theoretical" basis for setting a new measurement date. However, FASB Technical Bulletin 82-2 states that an increase in the option price to 100 percent of fair value at the date of grant to qualify under ERTA 81 does not result in a new measurement date.[3]

An incentive stock option by virtue of the employee's right to tender existing shares for lower priced option shares, is not a stock option but, in substance, is a stock appreciation right. The authors submit that the conversion of a stock option plan into a stock appreciation right cannot be considered a technical modification of a continuing plan for measurement date purposes. In substance, the old option has been cancelled and a new compensation package arranged, resulting in a new and significantly larger, obligation to the employer.

[3]FASB Technical Bulletin 82-2, "Accounting for the Conversion of Stock Options into Incentive Stock Options as a Result of the Economic Recovery Tax Act of 1981," Para 9.

Returning to ARB No. 43, let's reconsider why the grant day was deemed to be the proper measurement date. This date was selected because it was the date on which the two parties agreed to the value of the consideration for the employee's future services and the date on which the corporation gave up the principal alternative use of the shares placed under the option. In short, it is the date on which the corporation incurred a cost. However, when the options are converted into stock rights, the compensation package no longer resembles the originally negotiated one. Where the corporation was once obligated to issue stock on the receipt of a specific amount of consideration, it is now obligated to issue a different number of shares in return for no consideration. If the real cost to the employer was actually determined at the date of grant (presuming no variable plan was negotiated at that time), it can readily be seen that the new obligation bears no resemblance to the cost which was originally incurred. Following the precept that the incurrence of an obligation must give rise to either an asset or an expense, it can be said that the additional obligation incurred on the date of conversion must impact on the financial statements. Finally, it should be noted that a new cost has been incurred because the elements of compensation have changed. The number of shares under the option have not only changed but are no longer known since they are now contingent on future market values while the option price has dropped to zero. The criteria under APB Opinion No. 25 for a measurement date are no longer met, thus requiring the accounting treatment promulgated for variable plans.

In conclusion, a conversion of a stock option arrangement into a stock appreciation right represents the termination of the option and the issuance of a new right. The recognized compensation expense in the prior period must be restored to income in the year of conversion, deferred tax credits must be adjusted and current compensation expense, if any, must be recorded for the new plan.

As an example of how significant a conversion of previously granted plans to "incentive" treatment can be, consider the following facts:

In 1976 XYZ Corporation initiated a

EXAMPLE 2

1. Options are 100 percent vested;
2. Fair market value at the end of 1981 is $60;
3. Data on options originally granted (for each stockholder):

Option Year	Option Shares	Value at Grant Date	Option Price	Total Expense	Aggregate Accrual as of 12/13/81
1976	1000	25	$20	$5,000	2,333
1977	1000	30	25	5,000	2,000
1978	1000	35	30	5,000	1,666
1979	1000	50	45	5,000	1,333
				$20,000	7,332

4. The aggregate accrual is based on the 15 year option term period.
5. Due to the appreciation in stock, the full wage expense will be deductible for tax purposes. Therefore, the wage expense has been reflected in each year's deferred tax provision. The effective tax rate is 50 percent each year.

564

EXAMPLE 3

A. The average exercise price (restated to market value at date of grant) is $35. (25 + 30 + 35 + 50) + 4;
B. The number of issuable shares, per employee, if pyramiding is elected is 1,667 shares. SI = 4000 × (1 − 35/60) = 1,667;
C. Total impact on earnings:
   1. Cost incurred on new plan:

Shares issuable	$1,667	
Current value	× 60	
	100,000	
Number of employees	20	$2,000,000

   2. Restoration of prior year accruals:

Accrual per employee	$7,332	
Number of employees	× 20	(146,640)

   3. Reversal of deferred tax charges:

Compensation accrual	$146,640	
Tax rate	× 50%	73,320
		$1,926,680

nonstatutory stock option program for 20 of its key employees. The plans were granted at the beginning of each year with an option price exactly $5 less than the quoted market price. Each option covered 1000 shares resulting in an annual $5000 compensation amount per employee, considered to be reasonable. Each option was granted for a period of 15 years.

After the enactment of ERTA 1981, the 20 employees are interested in converting their options to incentive stock options. To make the conversions, the option terms must be shortened to 10 years and the original exercise prices must be increased to the quoted market prices as of the date of grant. The 20 employees are willing to accept these concessions because of the tax benefits associated with incentive plans and the fact they will not have to generate the cash needed to exercise their options. They will use pyramiding. (See authors' article in September 182 issue for discussion and illustration of pyramiding).

The board of directors is favorably inclined to elect such treatment since, after all, it is "getting out of" the originally agreed on compensation amount representing the $5 discount per share or $400,000 (1000 shares × 4 options × $5 × 20 employees) while the number of shares under each option remains the same. However, before proceeding, the board has asked its accountant what the effect will be on earnings based on the facts shown in Example 2.

If the conversion of the plans to incentive plans results in their treatment as a newly granted plan, the charge to earnings will be $1,926,680, computed as in Example 3.

What appeared to be a relief of $400,000 in incurred compensation cost was, in reality, the benefit from eliminating the earlier options in lieu of granting the new stock appreciation rights which carry a cost of $2,000,000.

If the employer had agreed to reimburse the employees for the original discounts given up, then the options should be treated as being settled and not cancelled. The original compensation amount computed on the appropriate measurement dates remains the same. Therefore, no additional expense would be charged to earnings. The corporation would have to establish an unearned compensation account for $253,360 ($400,000 − $146,640).

CONCLUSION

The accounting treatment for newly granted incentive options presents no new problems. The accounting for variable plans, as promulgated under APB Opinion No. 25 and FASBIN interpretation No. 28 should be followed. However, it may be necessary for the FASB to clarify the accounting for converting plans. Until the FASB does so, interested parties should beware. If such conversions do, in fact, cause the creation of new plans, as concluded here, the negative impact on earnings could be significant.

QUESTIONS

1. Compensatory stock options were granted to executives on January 1, 1987, with a measurement date of June 30, 1988, for services to be rendered during 1987, 1988, and 1989. The excess of the market value of the stock over the option price at the measurement date was reasonably estimimable at the date of grant. The stock option was exercised on October 31, 1989. Compensation expense should be recognized in the income statement in which of the following years?

	1987	1988	1989
a.	No	No	Yes
b.	No	Yes	Yes
c.	Yes	No	No
d.	Yes	Yes	Yes

2. For a compensatory stock option plan for which the date of grant and the measurement date are the same, compensation cost should be recognized in the income statement
   a. At the date of retirement
   b. Of each period in which services are rendered
   c. At the exercise date
   d. At the adoption date of the plan
3. For a compensatory stock option plan for which the date of grant and the measurement date are different, compensation cost should be recognized in the income statement
   a. At the later of grant or measurement date
   b. At the exercise date
   c. Of each period in which the services are rendered
   d. At the adoption date of the plan

566

4. Payment of a dividend in stock
   a. Increases the current ratio
   b. Decreases the amount of working capital
   c. Increases total stockholders' equity
   d. Decreases book value per share of stock outstanding

D

5. The directors of Corel Corporation, whose $40 par value common stock is currently selling at $50 per share, have decided to issue a stock dividend. The corporation has an authorization for 200,000 shares of common, has issued 110,000 shares of which 10,000 shares are now held as treasury stock, and desires to capitalize $400,000 of the retained earnings balance. To accomplish this, the percentage of stock dividend that the directors should declare is
   a. 10
   b. 8
   c. 5
   d. 2

B

(handwritten working:)
Shares issued   110,000
held treasury stock   10,000
share outstanding   100,000
Retained earnings to be ~ 400,000 capitalized
Market value of shares = 50
$\frac{8000}{110,000} = 7.3\%$
$\frac{8000}{100,000} = 8\%$
$\frac{400,000}{50} = 8000$ New stock to be issued

6. On December 31, 1988, when the Conn Company's stock was selling at $36 per share, its capital accounts were as follows

Capital stock (par value $20, 100,000 shares issued)	$2,000,000
Premium on capital stock	800,000
Retained earnings	4,550,000

If a 100 percent stock dividend were declared and the par value per share remained at $20
   a. No entry would need to be made to record the dividend
   b. Capital stock would increase to $5,600,000   100,000 x 20 =
   c. Capital stock would increase to $4,000,000
   d. Total capital would decrease

C

7. A company has not paid dividends on its cumulative nonvoting preferred stock for 20 years. Healthy earnings have been reported each year, but they have been retained to support the growth of the company. The board of directors appropriately authorized management to offer the preferred shareholders an exchange of bonds and common stock for all the preferred stock. The exchange is about to be consummated. Which of the following best describes the effect of the exchange on the company?
   a. The statute of limitations applies; hence, cumulative dividends of only seven years need to be paid on the preferred stock exchanged.
   b. The company should record an extraordinary gain for income determination purposes to the extent that dividends in arrears do not have to be paid in the exchange transaction.
   c. Gain or loss should be recognized on the exchange by the company, and the exchange would have to be approved by the Securities and Exchange Commission.

D

QUESTIONS

567

     d. Regardless of the market value of the bonds and common stock, no gain or loss should be recognized by the company on the exchange, and no dividends need to be paid on the preferred stock exchanged.

8. A restriction of retained earnings is most likely to be required by the
     a. Exhaustion of potential benefits of the investment credit
     b. Purchase of treasury stock
     c. Payment of last maturing series of a serial bond issue
     d. Amortization of past service costs related to a pension plan

9. A feature common to both stock splits and stock dividends is
     a. A reduction in total capital of a corporation
     b. A transfer from earned capital to paid-in capital
     c. A reduction in book value per share
     d. Inclusion in conventional statement of source and application of funds

10. Assuming the issuing company has only one class of stock, a transfer from retained earnings to capital stock equal to the market value of the shares issued is ordinarily a characteristic of
     a. Either a stock dividend or a stock split
     b. Neither a stock dividend nor a stock split
     c. A stock split but not a stock dividend
     d. A stock dividend but not a stock split

11. When a stock option plan for employees is compensatory, the measurement date for determining compensation cost is the
     a. Date the option plan is adopted, provided it precedes the date on which the options may first be exercised by less than one operating cycle
     b. Date on which the options may first be exercised (if the first actual exercise is within the same operating period) or the date on which a recipient first exercises any of his options
     c. First date on which are known both the number of shares that an individual employee is entitled to receive and the option or purchase price, if any
     d. Date each option is granted

12. As a minimum, how large in relation to total outstanding shares may a stock distribution be before it should be accounted for as a stock split instead of a stock dividend?
     a. No less than 2 to 5 percent
     b. No less than 10 to 15 percent
     c. No less than 20 to 25 percent
     d. No less than 45 to 50 percent

13. The dollar amount of total stockholders' equity remains the same when there is a (an)
     a. Issuance of preferred stock in exchange for convertible debentures
     b. Issuance of nonconvertible bonds with detachable stock purchase warrants

deficit is a debit balance, or negative in the retained earnings. (handwritten)

c. Declaration of a stock dividend

d. Declaration of a cash dividend

14. A company with a substantial deficit undertakes a quasi-reorganization. Certain assets will be written down to their present fair market value. Liabilities will remain the same. How would the entries to record the quasi-reorganization affect each of the following?

C (handwritten)

	Contributed capital	Retained earnings
a.	Increase	Decrease
b.	Decrease	No effect
c.	Decrease	Increase
d.	No effect	Increase

15. What is the most likely effect of a stock split on the par value per share and the number of shares outstanding?

A (handwritten)

	Par value per share	Number of shares outstanding
a.	Decrease	Increase
b.	Decrease	No effect
c.	Increase	Increase
d.	No effect	No effect

16. Gilbert Corporation issued a 40 percent stock split-up of its common stock that had a par value of $10 before and after the split-up. At what amount should retained earnings be capitalized for the additional shares issued?

a. There should be no capitalization of retained earnings

b. Par value

B (handwritten)

c. Market value on the declaration date

d. Market value on the payment date

17. How would the declaration and subsequent issuance of a 10 percent stock dividend by the issuer affect each of the following when the market value of the shares exceeds the par value of the stock?

D (handwritten)

	Common stock	Additional paid-in capital
a.	No effect	No effect
b.	No effect	Increase
c.	Increase	No effect
d.	Increase	Increase

18. A company with a $2,000,000 deficit undertakes a quasi-reorganization on November 1, 1988. Certain assets will be written down by $400,000 to their

present fair market value. Liabilities will remain the same. Capital stock was $3,000,000 and additional paid-in capital was $1,000,000 before the quasi-reorganization. How would the entries to accomplish these changes on November 1, 1988, affect each of the following?

	Capital stock	Total stockholders' equity
	No effect	No effect
	No effect	Decrease
c.	Decrease	Decrease
d.	Decrease	No effect

19. How would a stock split affect each of the following?

	Assets	Total stockholders' equity	Additional paid-in capital
a.	Increase	Increase	No effect
b.	No effect	No effect	No effect
c.	No effect	No effect	Increase
d.	Decrease	Decrease	Decrease

20. The purchase of treasury stock
    a. Decreases common stock authorized
    b. Decreases common stock issued
    c. Decreases common stock outstanding
    d. Has no effect on common stock outstanding

21. For a compensatory stock option plan for which the date of grant and the measurement date are different, compensation cost should be recognized in the income statement
    a. At the later of grant or measurement date
    b. At the exercise date
    c. At the adoption date of the plan
    d. Of each period in which the services are rendered

22. For numerous reasons a corporation may reacquire shares of its own capital stock. When a company purchases treasury stock, it has two options as to how to account for the shares: the cost method and the par-value method.

    Required:
       Compare and contrast the cost method and the par value method for each of the following.
    a. Purchase of shares at a price less than par value

570

b. Purchase of shares at a price greater than par value

c. Subsequent resale of treasury shares at a price less than purchase price, but more than par value

d. Subsequent resale of treasury shares at a price greater than both purchase price and par value

e. Effect on net income

23. Carrol, Inc., accomplished a quasi-reorganization effective December 31, 1987. Immediately prior to the quasi-reorganization, the stockholders' equity was as follows:

Common stock, par value $10 per share
  authorized issued and outstanding
  400,000 shares $4,000,000
Additional paid-in capital   600,000
Retained earnings (deficit)   (900,000)

Under the terms of the quasi-reorganization the par value of the common stock was reduced from $10 per share to $5 per share and equipment was written down by $1,200,000.

Required:
Discuss the accounting treatment necessary to accomplish this quasi-reorganization.

24. Raun Company had the following account titles on its December 31, 1988, trial balance:

Six percent cumulative convertible preferred stock, $100 par value
Premium on preferred stock
Common stock, $1 stated value
Premium on common stock
Retained earnings

The following additional information about the Raun Company was available for the year ended December 31, 1988.

1. There were 2,000,000 shares of preferred stock authorized, of which 1,000,000 were outstanding. All 1,000,000 shares outstanding were issued on January 2, 1985, for $120 a share. The Aa Corporate bond interest rate was 8.5 percent on January 2, 1985, and 10 percent on December 31, 1988. The preferred stock is convertible into common stock on a one-for-one basis until December 31, 1985; thereafter, the preferred stock ceases to be convertible and is callable at par value by the company. No preferred stock has been converted into common stock, and there were no dividends in arrears at December 31, 1988.

2. The common stock has been issued at amounts above stated value per share since incorporation in 1955. Of the 5,000,000 shares authorized, there were 3,500,000 shares outstanding at January 1, 1988. The market

price of the outstanding common stock has increased slowly, but consistently, for the last five years.

3. The company has an employee stock option plan where certain key employees and officers may purchase shares of common stock at 100 percent of the market price at the date of the option grant. All options are exercisable in installments of one-third each year, commencing one year after the date of the grant, and expire if not exercised within four years of the grant date. On January 1, 1988, options for 70,000 shares were outstanding at prices ranging from $47 to $83 a share. Options for 20,000 shares were exercised at $47 to $79 a share during 1988. No options expired during 1988, and additional options for 15,000 shares were granted at $86 a share. Of these, 30,000 were exercisable at that date at prices ranging from $54 to $79 a share.

4. The company also has an employee stock purchase plan through which the company pays one-half and the employee pays one-half of the market price of the stock at the date of the subscription. During 1988, employees subscribed to 60,000 shares at an average price of $87 a share. All 60,000 shares were paid for and issued late in September 1988.

5. On December 31, 1988, there was a total of 355,000 shares of common stock set aside for the granting of future stock options and for future purchases under the employee stock purchase plan. The only changes in the stockholders' equity for 1988 were those described previously, 1988 net income, and cash dividends paid.

Required:

a. Prepare a stockholders' equity section of the balance sheet of Raun Company at December 31, 1988: substitute, where appropriate. X's for unknown dollar amounts. Use good form and provide full disclosure. Write appropriate footnotes as they should appear in the published financial statements.

b. Explain how the amount of the denominator should be determined to compute primary earnings per share for presentation in the financial statements. Be specific as to the handling of each item. If additional information is needed to determine whether an item should be included or excluded or the extent to which an item should be included, identify the information needed and the way the item would be handled if the information were known. Assume Raun Company had substantial net income for the year ended December 31, 1988.

25. Stock options are widely used as a form of compensation for corporate executives.

a. Identify five methods that have been proposed for determining the value of executive stock options.

b. Discuss the conceptual merits of each of these proposed methods.

572

26. On January 1, 1987, as an incentive to improved performance of duties. Recycling Corporation adopted a qualified stock option plan to grant corporate executives nontransferable stock options to 500,000 shares of its unissued $1 par value common stock. The options were granted on May 1, 1987, at $25 per share, the market price on that date. All of the options were exercisable one year later and for four years thereafter providing that the grantee was employed by the corporation at the date of exercise.

The market price of this stock was $40 per share on May 1, 1988. All options were exercised before December 31, 1988, at times when the market price varied between $40 and $50 per share.

Required:
a. What information on this option plan should be presented in the financial statements of Recycling Corporation at (1) December 31, 1987, and (2) December 31, 1988? Explain.
b. It has been said that the exercise of such a stock option would dilute the equity of existing stockholders in the corporation.
   i. How could this happen? Discuss.
   ii. What conditions could prevent a dilution of existing equities from taking place in this transaction? Discuss.

27. The proprietary theory, the entity theory, and the funds theory are three approaches to accounting for equities.
a. Describe briefly each of these theories.
b. State your reasons for emphasizing the application of one of these theories to each of the following.
   i. Single proprietorship
   ii. Partnership
   iii. Financial institutions (banks)
   iv. Consolidated statements
   v. Estate accounting

28. The total owners' equity (excess of assets over liabilities) is usually shown under a number of subcaptions on the balance sheet of a corporation.

Required:
a. List the major subdivisions of the stockholders' equity section of a corporate balance sheet and describe briefly the nature of the amounts that will appear in each section.
b. Explain fully the reasons for subdividing the amount of stockholders' equity, including legal, accounting, and other considerations.
c. Describe four different kinds of transactions that will result in paid-in or permanent capital in excess of legal or stated capital.
d. Various accounting authorities have recommended that the terms *paid-in surplus* and *earned surplus* not be used in published financial state-

ments. Explain briefly the reason for this suggestion and indicate acceptable substitutes for the terms.

29. The directors of Lenox Corporation are considering issuing a stock dividend. They have asked you to discuss the proposed action by answering the following questions.

    a. What is a stock dividend? How is a stock dividend distinguished from a stock split from a legal standpoint? From an accounting standpoint?

    b. For what reasons does a corporation usually declare a stock dividend? A stock split?

    c. Discuss the amount, if any, of retained earnings to be capitalized in connection with a stock dividend.

30. *Part a.* A corporation's capital (stockholders' equity) is a very important part of its statement of financial position.

    Required:
    Identify and discuss the general categories of capital (stockholders' equity) for a corporation. Be sure to enumerate specific sources included in each general category.

    Part b. Stock splits and stock dividends may be used by a corporation to change the number of shares of its stock outstanding.

    Required:
    i. What is meant by a stock split effected in the form of a dividend?
    ii. From an accounting viewpoint, explain how the stock split effected in the form of a dividend differs from an ordinary stock dividend.
    iii. How should a stock dividend which has been declared but not yet issued be classified in a statement of financial position? Why?

    Part *c.* Jones Company has adopted a traditional stock option plan for its officers and other employees. This plan is properly considered a compensatory plan.

    Required:
    Discuss how accounting for this plan will affect net earnings and earnings per share. (Ignore income tax considerations and accounting for income tax benefits.)

BIBLIOGRAPHY

Alvin, Gerald. "Accounting for Investment and Stock Rights: The Market Value Method." *The CPA Journal* (February 1973), pp. 126–131.

Bird, Francis A., Lewis F. Davidson, and Charles H. Smith. "Perceptions of External Accounting Transfers under Entity and Proprietary Theory." *The Accounting Review* (April 1975), pp. 233–244.

574

Birnberg, Jacob G. "An Information Oriented Approach to the Presentation of Common Stockholders' Equity." *The Accounting Review* (October 1964), pp. 963–971.

Boudreaux, Kenneth J., and Stephen A. Zeff. "A Note on the Measure of Compensation Implicit in Employee Stock Options." *Journal of Accounting Research* (Spring 1976), pp. 158–162.

Chang, Emily C. "Accounting for Stock Splits." *Financial Executive* (March 1969), pp. 79–80, 82–84.

Committee on Tax and Financial Entity Theory. "Report of the Committee on Tax and Financial Entity Theory." *The Accounting Review,* supplement to Vol. 48 (1973), pp. 187–192.

Foster, Taylor W., III, and Don Vickrey. "The Information Content of Stock Dividend Announcements." *The Accounting Review* (April 1976), pp. 360–370.

Goldberg, Louis. *An Inquiry into the Nature of Accounting.* American Accounting Association, Monograph No. 7, 1963.

Gynther, Reginald S. "Accounting Concepts and Behavioral Hypotheses." *The Accounting Review* (April 1967), pp. 274–290.

Hawkins, David F., and Walter J. Campbell. *Equity Valuation: Models, Analysis and Implications.* New York: Financial Executives Research Foundation. 1978.

Husband, George. "The Corporate-Entity Fiction and Accounting Theory." *The Accounting Review* (September 1938), pp. 241–253.

Li, David, H. "The Nature of Corporate Residual Equity under the Entity Concept." *The Accounting Review* (April 1960), pp. 197–201.

Lowe, Howard D. "The Classification of Corporate Stock Equities." *The Accounting Review* (July 1961), pp. 425–433.

Melcher, Beatrice. "Stockholders' Equity." Accounting Research Study No. 15. New York: AICPA, 1973.

Millar, James A. "Split or Dividend: Do the Words Really Matter?" *The Accounting Review* (January 1977), pp. 52–55.

1964 Concepts and Standards Research Committee—The Business Entity. "The Entity Concept." *The Accounting Review* (April 1965), pp. 358–367.

Pusker, Henri C. Accounting for Capital Stock Distributions (Stock Split-Ups and Dividends). "*New York CPA* (May 1971), pp. 347–352.

Rogers, Donald R., and R. W. Schattke. "Buy-Outs of Stock Options: Compensation or Capital?" *Journal of Accountancy* (August 1972), pp. 55–59.

Scott, Richard A. "Owners' Equity, the Anachronistic Element." *The Accounting Review* (October 1979), pp. 750–763.

Simons, Donald R., and Jerry J. Weygandt. "Stock Options Revisited: Accounting for Option Buy-Outs." *The CPA Journal* (September 1973), pp. 779–783.

Smith, Clifford W., Jr., and Jerold L. Zimmerman. "Valuing Employer Stock Option Plans Using Option Pricing Models. *Journal of Accounting Research* (Autumn 1976), pp. 357–364.

Smith, Ralph E., and Leroy F. Imdieke. "Accounting for Stock Issued to Employees." *Journal of Accountancy* (November 1974), pp. 68–75.

Soujanen, Waino. "Enterprise Theory and Corporate Balance Sheets." *The Accounting Review* (January 1958), pp. 56–65.

Sprouse, Robert T. "The Significance of the Concept of the Corporation in Accounting Analyses." *The Accounting Review* (July 1957), pp. 369–378.

Staubus, George J. "The Residual Equity Point of View in Accounting." *The Accounting Review* (January 1959), pp. 3–13.

Thomas, Paula Bevels, and Larry E. Farmer. "Accounting for Stock Options and SARs: The Equality Question." *Journal of Accountancy* (June 1984), pp. 92–98.

Vatter, William J. "Corporate Stock Equities." *Modern Accounting Theory*. Morton Backer, ed. Englewood Cliffs, N.J.: Prentice-Hall, 1966.

Vatter, William J. *The Fund Theory of Accounting and Its Implications for Financial Reports*. Chicago, Ill.: University of Chicago Press, 1947.

Weygandt, Jerry J. "Valuation of Stock Option Contracts." *The Accounting Review* (January 1977), pp. 40–51.

12

ACCOUNTING FOR MULTIPLE ENTITIES

Business enterprises have found it beneficial to operate in conjunction with each other since the inception of the corporate form of organization. This cooperation may vary from corporate joint ventures in which two or more corporations join together as a partnership for a particular project, such as drilling an offshore oil well, to the sale of one company to another. The accounting for acquisitions of one company by another is complicated by the various terms that may be used to describe the acquisition. Such terms as *consolidation, combination, merger, pooling of interest,* and *purchase* have all been used interchangeably despite the fact that they are not all the same and some are subclassifications of others. In this chapter we shall focus upon the three main aspects of accounting for multiple entities: (1) the acquisition of one company by another—*combinations*, (2) the reporting of parent and subsidiary relationships—*consolidations* and *segment reporting*, and (3) the reporting of results of nondomestic subsidiaries—*foreign currency translation*.

BUSINESS COMBINATIONS

The uniting of two or more separate business organizations into a single entity has been an observable phenomenon since the late 1800s. Wyatt has divided these events into three categories.

The classical era—the period from 1890 to 1904, following the passage of the Sherman Act. These combinations were generally accomplished through a holding company whose purpose was vertical integration of all operations from acquisition of raw materials to sale of the product.

Second wave—the period from the end of World War I to the end of the 1920s. These combinations were generally piecemeal acquisitions whose purpose was to expand the operations of the acquiring company.

Third wave—the period from the end of World War II until the present. These again were piecemeal acquisitions designed to strengthen competitive position, diversify into new areas, or keep up with technological changes.[1]

In addition to the foregoing reasons, several other factors may cause a business organization to consider combining with another organization.

Tax consequences—the purchasing corporation may accrue the benefits of operating loss carryforwards from acquired corporations. Additionally, the previous owners of the acquired corporation may be entitled to capital gains treatment on the proceeds from the sale of their stock.

Growth and diversification—the purchasing corporation may wish to acquire a new product or enter a new market.

Financial considerations—a larger asset base may make it easier for the corporation to acquire additional funds from capital markets.

Competitive pressure—economies of scale may alleviate a highly competitive market situation.

Profit and retirement—the seller may be motivated by a high profit or the desire to retire.[2]

After the Securities and Exchange Commission was established during the 1930s, two methods of accounting for business combinations evolved: *purchase* and *pooling of interests*. These methods are described in more detail in the following comments.

In accounting for business combinations it is essential to recall that fair reporting of the results of economic events for a particular enterprise is the essence of the accounting process. These reports should not be biased in favor of any group and must be based upon the underlying substance of the economic events. There are two methods of achieving majority ownership in another corporation: (1) the acquiring corporation purchases the voting stock of the acquired corporation for cash or (2) the acquiring corporation exchanges its voting stock for the voting stock of the acquired corporation. The essential question then becomes: is the economic substance of these events different enough to warrant different methods of accounting?

As we noted earlier, two methods of accounting for business combinations are available: (1) purchase and (2) pooling of interests. Under the *purchase* method,

---

[1]Arthur R. Wyatt, *A Critical Study of Accounting for Business Combinations* (New York: American Institute of Certified Public Accountants, 1963), pp. 1–5.

[2]Ibid., pp. 6–8.

the assets of the acquired company are recorded at their market value in the same manner as was discussed in Chapter 6 for group purchases of assets. That is, the individual *fair market value* of each asset is recorded. Any liabilities assumed by the acquiring company are then deducted from this amount and any excess or deficiency between the net assets received and the cash paid is recorded as *goodwill*. Additionally, reported income for the new combined company will include the acquiring company's income for the entire year and the acquired company's income since the date of acquisition.

The *pooling of interests* method accounts for the combination as the uniting of ownership interests. That is, it is not accounted for as an acquisition but rather as a fusion of two or more previously separate entities. The recorded amounts of assets and liabilities of the merging companies are added together on the balance sheet of the combined corporation and goodwill is *not* recorded. Similarly, the remaining equity accounts of both companies are combined and any difference between the net fair market value of the new companies and the fair market value of the stock exchanged to achieve the combination is deducted from other contributed capital and then from retained earnings. Additionally, income for the new reporting unit includes the income since the last reporting date for each of the previously separate companies. For example, if P Corporation acquired S Corporation on December 15, 1987, the combined corporation may report S's net income for the entire year.

In the question posed earlier on the propriety of using different recording and reporting techniques, it should be noted that two distinctly different economic events may occur in a business combination. When cash is exchanged, only one ownership group remains and only one entity survives. When voting stock is exchanged, all the previous owners are still present, and the companies have simply united to carry on their previously separate operations. It would therefore seem appropriate to use the purchase method for cash transactions and the pooling of interest method for stock exchanges.

The Accounting Principles Board reviewed this entire question and in 1970 issued its Opinion No. 16, ''Business Combinations.''[3] The board found merit in the use of both methods and did not propose that one method be used to the exclusion of the other. The APB noted that the two methods were not alternatives for accounting for the same transaction and established specific criteria for determining whether or not a combination should be accounted for as a purchase or a pooling of interests. All transactions that involve the exchange of cash are to be recorded as purchases, whereas exchanges of voting stock are to be reported as pooling of interests subject to some specific criteria. If any of the criteria are violated, the combination must be recorded as a purchase. These criteria are

[3]Accounting Principles Board Opinion No. 16. ''Business Combinations'' (New York: Accounting Principles Board, 1970).

classified as (1) attributes of the combining companies, (2) manner of combining interests, and (3) absence of planned transactions. In essence, they were established to ensure that a combination could not be recorded as a pooling of interests where one group of stockholders achieved an advantage over another, or where the combined corporation did not plan to carry on the activities of the previously separate companies. These requirements are summarized as follows.

ATTRIBUTES OF THE COMBINING COMPANIES

1. Each of the combining companies is autonomous and has not been a subsidiary or division of another corporation within two years before the plan of combination is initiated.
2. Each of the combining companies is independent of the other combining companies. (*independent* means no more than 10 percent investment in the outstanding voting stock of any combining company at the date of acquisition).

MANNER OF COMBINING INTERESTS

1. The combination is effected in a single transaction or is completed in accordance with a specific plan within one year after the plan is initiated.
2. A corporation offers and issues only common stock with rights identical to those of the majority of its outstanding voting common stock in exchange for substantially all of the voting common stock interest of another company at the date the plan of combination is consummated (*substantially all* means 90 percent or more of the outstanding voting common stock at the date the plan is consummated).
3. None of the combining companies changes the equity interest of the voting common stock in contemplation of effecting the combination within two years before the plan is initiated or between the date the plan is initiated and the date it is consummated. (Such changes might include distribution to stockholders, exchanges, retirements, or additional issuances.)
4. Each of the combining companies reacquires shares of voting common stock only for purposes other than business combinations, and no company requires more than a normal number of shares between the date the combination is initiated and consummated (normal reacquisition determined by pattern prior to initiation of the plan).
5. The ratio of the interest of an individual common stockholder to those of other common stockholders in a combining company remains the same as a result of the exchange of stock to effect the combination. (The proportion of shares

received is equal to each individual stockholder's relative proportion of previous ownership.)

6. The voting rights to which the common stock ownership interests in the resulting combined corporation are entitled are exercisable by the stockholders; the stockholders are neither deprived of nor restricted in exercising those rights for a period.
7. The combination is resolved at the date the plan is consummated and no provisions of the plan relating to the issue of securities or other considerations are pending.

ABSENCE OF PLANNED TRANSACTIONS

1. The combined corporation does not agree directly or indirectly to retire or reacquire all or part of the common stock issued to effect the combination.
2. The combined corporation does not enter into other financial arrangements for the benefit of former stockholders of a combining company, such as a guaranty of loans secured by stock issued in the combination, which in effect negates the exchange of equity securities.
3. The combined corporation does not intend or plan to dispose of a significant part of the assets of the combining companies within two years after the combination other than disposals in the ordinary course of business of the formerly separate companies and to eliminate duplicate facilities or excess capacity.[4]

It should be emphasized that pooling of interests is only appropriate when there is an exchange of voting stock and each of the foregoing conditions has been met. Where a combination has been effected by a cash transaction or any *one* of the foregoing conditions has been violated, the purchase method must be used. Additionally, when the purchase method is appropriate for combinations involving the exchange of voting common stock, the fair market value of the securities exchanged is the measure of the acquition price.

CONSOLIDATIONS

When a business organization acquires control over one or more others through the acquisition of a majority of the outstanding voting stock, the entity concept is enhanced by preparing financial statements for the group of companies. The entire group is considered as a unified whole, and in most cases it is appropriate

[4]Ibid., pars. 46–48.

to present consolidated financial statements where one corporation has control over another.

The criteria for the preparation of consolidated financial statements were originally described in Accounting Research Bulletin No. 51 as follows.

1. A parent-subsidiary relationship must exist. (The parent must own at least 51 percent of the subsidiary.)
2. The parent exercised control over the subsidiary. (Where the courts are exercising control as in a bankruptcy, consolidation is not appropriate.)
3. The parent plans to maintain control over the subsidiary during the near future. (Subsidiaries which are to be sold in the near future should not be consolidated.)
4. The parent and subsidiary should operate as an integrated unit and non-homogeneous operations should be excluded.
5. The fiscal years of the units should approximate each other. (Generally, they should fall within 93 days of each other, or appropriate adjustments should be made to reflect similar closing dates.)[5]

The underlying philosophy of Accounting Research Bulletin No. 51 is the presentation of a single, though fictional, entity with economic but not legal substance. In the preparation of consolidated financial statements, two overriding principles prevail. The first is balance sheet oriented while the second is income statement oriented.

1. The entity cannot own or owe itself.
2. The entity cannot make a profit by selling to itself.

The result of the first principle is to eliminate all assets on one company's books that are offset by liabilities on the other. For example, an account receivable on the parent's books relating to a corresponding account payable on the subsidiary's books. In the preparation of consolidated statements, the account receivable of the parent is eliminated against the account payable of the subsidiary. In applying the second principle, all intercompany sales and profits are eliminated. For example, a sale by one company is offset against a purchase by an affiliated company. (A detailed discussion of the preparation of consolidated financial statements is beyond the scope of this text.)

MINORITY INTEREST

When a portion of the stock of a subsidiary is owned by investors outside the parent company, this ownership is referred to as *a minority interest.* The value of

---

[5]Accounting Research Bulletin No. 51, ''Consolidated Financial Statements'' (New York: American Institute of Certified Public Accountants, 1959).

CHAPTER 12: ACCOUNTING FOR MULTIPLE ENTITIES

this investment results from holding shares in an affiliated company, and the determination of equity, the payment of dividends, and the basis for a claim should a liquidation ensue are all based upon a claim against a particular subsidiary. Therefore, the minority interest must gauge its financial status from the subsidiary company, not the parent or the consolidated group. The minority interest is calculated as the percentage ownership in the subsidiary net assets at the date of acquisition, plus the percentage of earnings since acquisition.

The classification of minority interest on consolidated financial statements has posed a problem. Some accountants view minority interest as a liability, whereas others view it as a part of equity. Under the proprietary theory, all amounts due to nonstockholders are considered liabilities, and accountants holding this viewpoint would prefer to report the minority interest as a long-term liability. On the other hand, the entity theory views all items on the right-hand side of the balance sheet as equity, and those favoring the entity viewpoint do not prefer the separate classification of the minority interest.

In actual practice, minority interest has been disclosed under three different classifications on published financial statements.

1. As a liability.
2. Separately presented between liabilities and stockholders' equity.
3. As a part of equity.

Accounting Research Bulletin No. 51 did not take a position on the classification of minority interest in financial statements. Nevertheless, it is the authors' opinion that minority interest should be included as a part of stockholders' equity. Presenting these amounts as liabilities or quasi-liabilities is not in accord with the established theoretical bases for debt determination discussed in Chapter 8. Minority interests have residual claims against assets that are in the nature of equity. The inclusion of minority interest as a part of equity adds to the presentation of the various sources of capital and is more theoretically sound.

SEGMENTAL REPORTING

The growth of business combinations has created companies with diversified operations termed *conglomerates*. The result of this process has been the aggregation of financial information from various lines of business in one set of financial reports. Each new business combination results in the loss of some information to the investing public because previously reported data is now combined with existing data in consolidated financial reports.

The reporting of financial information on a less than total enterprise basis is termed *segmental reporting*. In previous years generally accepted accounting principles did not usually require less than total enterprise reporting except in limited areas. For example, ARB No. 43 recommended certain disclosures about foreign operations. APB No. 18 required disclosure of certain information about companies accounted for by the equity method of accounting, and APB No. 30 required the disclosure of information about discontinued segments. However, segmental information became an increasing part of corporate reporting during the 1970s because of two factors.

1. In 1969, the Securities and Exchange Commission required line-of-business reporting in registration statements, and in 1970 these requirements were extended to the 10-K reports.
2. In 1973, the New York Stock Exchange urged that line-of-business reporting, similar to that provided on the 10-K reports, be included in the annual reports to stockholders.

The proponents of segmental reporting base their arguments on two points.

1. Various types of operations may have differing prospects for growth, rates of profitability, and degrees of risk.
2. Since management responsibility is frequently decentralized, the assessment of management ability requires less than total enterprise information.[6]

Subsequent study of the problem resulted in the issuance of FASB Statement No. 14 in 1976.[7] This pronouncement requires a corporation issuing a complete set of financial statements to disclose

1. The enterprise's operations in different industries.
2. Its foreign operations and export sales.
3. Its major customers.[8]

In requiring these disclosures, FASB No. 14 provided the following definitions.

1. *Industry segment*—component of an enterprise engaged in providing a product or service or group of related products and services primarily to unaffiliated customers for a profit.
2. *Reportable segment*—an industry segment for which information is required to be reported by this segment.
3. *Revenue*—sales to unaffiliated customers and intersegment transactions similar to those with unaffiliated customers.
4. *Operating profit or loss*—revenue minus all operating expenses including the allocation of corporate overhead.

[6]*An Analysis of Issues Related to Financial Reporting for Segments of a Business Enterprise*, FASB Discussion Memorandum (Stamford, Conn.: Financial Accounting Standards Board, 1974), pp. 6–7.
[7]Statement of Financial Accounting Standards No. 14, "Financial Reporting for Segments of a Business Enterprise" (Stamford, Conn.: Financial Accounting Standards Board, 1976).
[8]Ibid.

5. *Identifiable assets*—tangible and intangible enterprise assets that are used by the industry segment.[9]

The major problems associated with these disclosures are (1) the determination of reportable segments, (2) the allocation of joint costs, and (3) transfer pricing. In determining its reportable segments, an enterprise is required to identify the individual products and services from which it derives its revenue, group these products by industry lines and segments, and select those segments that are significant with respect to the industry as a whole. These procedures require a considerable amount of managerial judgment, and the following guidelines are presented.

1. *Existing profit centers*. The smallest units of activity for which revenue and expense information is accumulated for internal planning and control purposes—represent a logical starting point for determining industry segments.
2. *Management organization*. The company's internal organizational structure generally corresponds to management's view of the major segments.
3. *Investor expectations*. The information provided should coincide with the type of information needed by the public.
4. *Competitive factors*. Although the disclosure of all industry segment information might injure a company's competitive position, the required disclosures are not more detailed than those typically provided by an enterprise operating within a single industry.[10]

The problems of the allocation of joint costs and transfer pricing also cause some difficulty in reporting segmental information. Joint costs should be allocated to the various segments in the most rational manner possible; however, since the allocation process is frequently quite arbitrary, this process may have a profound effect upon reported segmental income.

The transfer pricing problem arises when products are transferred from division to division, and one division's product becomes another's raw material. In many cases these interdivisional transfers are recorded at cost plus an amount of profit. Most accountants advocate eliminating the profit from interdivisional transfers before they are reported as segmental information.

Once the grouping of products and services by industry lines has been accomplished FASB No. 14 requires companies to provide answers to the following questions.

1. Which of its segments meets the definition of reportable segments?
2. What information should be disclosed for each reportable segment?

[9]Ibid., par. 10.
[10]Ibid., par. 13.

3. Where should the required information be disclosed on the financial statements?

Reportable Segments

FASB No. 14 requires that each industry segment that is significant to the enterprise as a whole be identified as a *reportable segment* and suggests the following separate tests for significance.

1. Its revenue, including unaffiliated customers and intersegment transfers, is 10 percent or more of combined revenue to all unaffiliated customers and intersegment transfers.
2. The absolute amount of profit or operating loss is 10 percent or more of the greater in absolute amount of
   a. The combined operating profit of all industry segments that did not incur an operating loss.
   b. The combined operating loss of all industry segments that incurred an operating loss.
3. Its identifiable assets are 10 percent or more of the combined identifiable assets of all industry segments.[11]

Additionally, it is required that the combined revenue from sales to all unaffiliated customers of all reportable segments constitutes at least 75 percent of the combined revenue from sales to unaffiliated customers of all industry segments. Furthermore, the disclosure of segmental information is not required where an enterprise is regarded as operating predominantly in a single industry (revenue, profits, and assets each constitute more than 90 percent of related combined totals for all industry segments).

Disclosed Information

FASB Statement No. 14 requires the following information to be presented for each of the reportable segments.

1. Revenue.
2. Profitability.
3. Identifiable assets.
4. Other disclosures.
   a. Depreciation, depletion, and amortization for each segment.
   b. Capital expenditures for each segment.
   c. Equity method investees that are vertically related and the geographic location of such investees.

[11]Ibid., par. 15.

d. Changes in accounting principles (as defined by APB No. 20) which relate to industry segments.[12]

Method of Disclosure

Three alternative methods of disclosure of segmental information are allowed by FASB No. 14.

1. Within the body of the financial statements, with appropriate explanatory disclosures.
2. Entirely in the footnotes to the financial statements.
3. In a separate schedule that is included as an integral part of the financial statements.

In analyzing segmental information, the user should keep in mind that the comparison of a segment from one enterprise with a similar segment from another enterprise has limited usefulness unless both companies use similar disaggregation procedures. The procedures for the allocation of common costs to various segments are particularly crucial to this process, and unless similar allocation procedures are followed, comparisons may be completely distorted.

FOREIGN CURRENCY TRANSLATION

There has been a substantial increase in foreign operations by U.S. corporations in recent years. As one might expect, this growth of multinational firms has given rise to several unavoidable problems in international business dealings. One of these problems is accounting for the different monetary systems in different countries. More specifically, the issue is, how does a U.S.-based corporation measure monetary unit differences and changes in those differences in its foreign branches and subsidiaries?[13]

The problem arises in the following manner. The foreign subsidiary handles its transactions in foreign currency, which may include anything from long-term borrowing agreements for assets acquired to credit sales carried on accounts receivable. When management or outside investors wish to evaluate the company's operations as a whole, it becomes necessary to express all activities, foreign and domestic, in common financial terms. Since useful comparisons and calculations can only be made if measures of the company's profitability are

---

[12]Ibid., par. 22.

[13]It has been argued that in reality it is impossible to isolate the translation process from general price level adjustments, since foreign exchange rates do to some extent reflect changes in the price level. But even though inflationary relationships between countries may be indirectly reflected in official exchange rates, translation is still considered to be an independent process.

expressed in a common unit of measurement, usually the domestic currency, foreign monetary measures must be converted to domestic units. This process is known as translation.

In translating foreign currency, the foreign exchange rate defines the relationship between two monetary scales. The foreign currency is stated as a ratio to the U.S. dollar, and this ratio becomes the multiplying factor to determine the equivalent amount of domestic currency. For example, if the British pound (£) is quoted as $1.20 and an American subsidiary acquired an asset valued at £10,000, the translation into dollars would be $12,000 (10,000 × $1.20). Foreign exchange rates change over time in response to the forces of supply and demand and to the relative degree of inflation between countries. These changes are classified into three types—fluctuation, devaluation, and revaluation. *Fluctuation* denotes a rate change within the narrow margin allowed by the International Monetary Fund (IMF) (a deviation of 2¼ percent above or below that country's official exchange rate). If an entirely new support level of the foreign currency is allowed by the IMF and the dollar rate falls, it is called *devaluation*. *Revaluation* occurs when the dollar rate of the foreign currency rises to a new support level.

It is important to note that the translation process in no way changes the inherent characteristics of the assets or liabilities measured. That is, translation is a single process that merely restates an asset or liability initially valued in foreign currency in terms of a common currency measurement by applying the rate of exchange factor; it in no way restates historical cost. Translation is a completely separate process just as adjusting for general price level changes is a separate process. The translation process is analogous to price level adjustments in that neither changes any accounting principles; they merely change the unit of measurement. (See Chapter 13 for a discussion of price level adjustments.)

If the exchange rate remained constant between a particular foreign country and the United States, translation would be a relatively simple process involving a constant exchange rate. However, recent history indicates that this is an unlikely occurrence, and a method of translation must be established that adequately discloses the effect of changes in exchange rates on financial statements. However, there has been considerable debate among accountants on how to achieve this objective. In the following sections we will review the proposals advocated by several individuals and groups.

Historically, four methods of translation were proposed by various authors prior to the release of any official pronouncements by the APB or FASB: the current-noncurrent method, the monetary-nonmonetary method, the current rate method, and the temporal method.[14]

---

[14]See Leonard Lorensen, *Reporting Foreign Operations of U.S. Companies in U.S. Dollars.* Accounting Research Study No. 12 (New York: American Institute of Certified Public Accountants, 1972).

CURRENT-NONCURRENT METHOD

The current-noncurrent method is based upon the distinction between current and noncurrent assets and liabilities. It was initially recommended by the American Institute of Certified Public Accountants (AICPA) in 1931, and updated in Accounting Research Bulletin No. 43 in 1953.[15] Simply stated, this method provides that all current items (cash, receivables, inventory, and short-term liabilities) are to be translated at the foreign exchange rate existing at the balance sheet date. The noncurrent items (plant, equipment, property, and long-term liabilities) are to be translated using the rate in effect when the items were acquired or incurred (the historical rate). The rationale for the dichotomy between current and noncurrent items is that those items that will not be converted into cash in the upcoming period (noncurrent) are not affected by changes in current rates. Thus, in using this method, the assumption is made that items translated at the historical exchange rate are not exposed to gains and losses owing to changes in the currency rate in contrast to current items, which are exposed. In 1965, ARB No. 43. Chapter 12 was modified by Accounting Principles Board Opinion No. 6 to allow long-term payables and receivables to be translated at the current rather than historical rate if this treatment resulted in a better representation of a company's position.[16] With respect to the income statement, ARB No. 43 requires revenues and expenses to be translated at the average exchange rate applicable to each month, except for depreciation, which is translated at the historical rate.

MONETARY-NONMONETARY METHOD

The monetary-nonmonetary method was first advocated by Samuel Hepworth,[17] and the National Association of Accountants' support of Hepworth's method in 1960 resulted in more widespread acceptance of its provisions.[18]

The monetary-nonmonetary method requires that a distinction be made between monetary items (accounts representing cash or claims on cash, such as receivables, notes payable, and bonds payable) and nonmonetary items (accounts physical in nature, such as land, inventory, plant, and equipment). Monetary items are translated at the exchange rate in effect at the balance sheet date, while

---

[15]Accounting Research Bulletin No. 43 (New York: American Institute of Certified Public Accountants, 1953), Chapter 12.

[16]Accounting Principles Board Opinion No. 6, "Status of Accounting Research Bulletins" (New York: American Institute of Certified Public Accountants, 1965), par. 18.

[17]Samuel Hepworth, "Reporting Foreign Operations," *Michigan Business Studies* (University of Michigan, 1956).

[18]National Association of Accountants, "Management Accounting Problems in Foreign Operations," NAA Research Report No. 36 (New York, 1960).

nonmonetary items retain the historical exchange rate. Table 12.1 summarizes the results of the application of these two methods for a corporation that has experienced a devaluation. Prior to the devaluation one unit of foreign currency was worth $0.50, whereas after devaluation it was worth $0.25.

As Table 12.1 shows, the only difference between the two methods in the reporting of assets is in the translation of inventories. If the current-noncurrent method is used, inventories are considered to be current assets (sensitive to foreign exchange gains and losses) and are translated at the current rate, while the monetary-nonmonetary method classifies inventories as nonmonetary assets that are subsequently translated at the historical or preexisting rate. A conflict also arises in translating long-term debt. The current-noncurrent approach uses the historical translation rate, whereas the monetary-nonmonetary method considers it to be monetary and uses the current rate. This difference between the two methods disappears, however, if the current-noncurrent approach is modified as required by APB No. 6, which allows the application of the current rate where it is considered to be more appropriate. In any event, both approaches result in a foreign exchange gain or loss in order to balance the assets and equities, thereby creating a reporting problem. That is, how should a gain or loss on foreign currency translation be reported on the financial statements? (We will discuss this issue later in the chapter.)

While these two translation methods dominated accounting practices for approximately 40 years, the late 1960s and the early 1970s produced a proliferation of new proposals for dealing with foreign exchange problems. After 1971, when the dollar was devalued and allowed to float on the world monetary market, the dissatisfaction with the traditional methods came to the forefront. Most authors advocating new approaches contend that new problems surfaced in 1971 because foreign currencies were appreciating rather than depreciating in relation to the dollar, and that these problems could not be resolved by the traditional approaches. Two other methods, the current rate method and the temporal method, have been advocated as alleviating this problem.

CURRENT RATE METHOD

The current rate method has been used by companies in England, Scotland, and Wales since the British pound was devalued in 1967. The current rate method simply involves translating *all* assets and liabilities at the rate in effect on the balance sheet date (current rate). It is therefore the only method that translates fixed assets at current rather than historical rates, and no division of items into current or monetary is necessary. Proponents of the current rate method claim that it most clearly represents the true economic facts, because stating all items currently presents the true earnings of a foreign operation at that time—particularly since from the investor's point of view the only real earnings are those that can actually be distributed.

Table 12.1 Currency Translation by Current-Noncurrent and Monetary-Nonmonetary Methods

	Balance Sheet in FC* 12-31-8X	Current-Noncurrent		Monetary-Nonmonetary	
		Translation Rate	Balance Sheet in DC+	Translation Rate	Balance Sheet in DC+
Assets:					
Cash	$120	0.25	$ 30	0.25	$ 30
Receivables	80	0.25	20	0.25	20
Inventories	80	0.25	20	0.50	40
Property, plant land and equipment	120	0.50	60	0.50	60
Total assets	$400		$130		$150
Liabilities and Owners' Equity					
Payables	$ 40	0.25	$ 10	0.25	$ 10
Bank note (long-term)	200	0.50	100	0.25	50
Capital	160	0.50	80	0.50	80
Foreign exchange gain (loss)	—		(60)		10
Total liabilities and owners' equity	$400		$130		$150

*FC = foreign currency.
+ DC = domestic currency.
Rate before devaluation = 0.50.
Rate after devaluation = 0.25.

While the current rate method has drawn some support, it is not without critics. Proponents argue that it presents true economic facts by stating all items at the current rate while keeping operating relations intact, since depreciation and amortization are not exposed to the current rate translation. However, critics attack the use of the current rate for fixed assets, stating that the resulting figure on the translated consolidated balance sheet does not represent the historical cost. They therefore conclude that until the entire reporting system is changed, the current rate method will not be acceptable.

TEMPORAL METHOD

In 1972, Lorensen advocated another approach, called the temporal principle of translation.[19] Monetary measurements under this method depend on the temporal characteristics of assets and liabilities, that is, the time of measurement of the specific financial statement evaluations of each individual item. Lorensen sums up the principle by stating,

> *Money and receivables and payables measured at the amounts promised should be translated at the foreign exchange rate in effect at the balance sheet date. Assets and liabilities measured at money prices should be translated at the foreign exchange rate in effect at the dates to which the money prices pertain.*[20]

This principle is simply an application of the fair value principle in the area of foreign translation. By stating foreign money and foreign money receivables and payables at the balance sheet rate, supposedly the foreign currency's command over U.S. dollars is measured. (Lorensen believes this attribute, command over U.S. dollars, to be of paramount importance.) Nevertheless, the results from the use of this method are generally identical to the monetary-nonmonetary method except when the inventory valuation is based upon the lower of cost or market rule.

Lorensen's main concern was that the generally accepted accounting principles being followed should not be changed by the translation process. Consequently, he strongly opposed any translation method that ultimately changed the attributes of a balance sheet account (e.g., historical cost being transformed into replacement cost or selling price). Unfortunately, the temporal method, which produces essentially identical results to the monetary-nonmonetary method, does not provide any solution to the problem of reporting change gains and losses that plague the traditional methods.

It must be stressed that none of these methods of translation provide a perfect

[19]Leonard Lorensen, op. cit.
[20]Ibid., p. 19.

representation of valuation and worth because of the nature of the world's monetary systems. A country's currency is basically a one-dimensional scale that measures and compares economic values within that one political entity. Thus, even the best translation method attempting to restate a foreign asset or liability in terms of domestic currency will inevitably be limited in its representation of economic reality.

THE FASB AND FOREIGN CURRENCY TRANSLATION

The Financial Accounting Standards Board took this entire question under advisement again and originally issued its Statement No. 8, "Accounting for the Translation of Foreign Currency Transactions and Foreign Currency Financial Statements."[21] The significant provisions of this pronouncement are summarized.

1. The overall objective of foreign currency translation is to measure and express, in dollars and in conformity with U.S. generally accepted accounting principles the assets, liabilities, revenue, and expenses initially measured in foreign currency.
2. The following translation principles are to apply.
   a. Record each transaction at the exchange rate in effect at the transaction date.
   b. Adjust all cash and amounts owed to or by the enterprise by the current rate at the balance sheet date.
   c. Adjust assets carried at market price into an equivalent dollar price on the balance sheet date.
3. For all other assets the particular measurement basis (e.g., historical cost, replacement cost, market, etc.) should be used to determine the translation rate.
   a. Accounts carried at prices in past exchanges should be translated at the historical rate.
   b. Accounts carried at current prices should be translated at the current rate.
4. Revenue and expenses should be translated in a manner that produces approximately the same dollar amount that would have resulted had the underlying transactions been translated into dollars on the dates they occurred. (An average rate may be used except for expenses that relate to specific assets and liabilities. In such cases, the same rate used to translate the assets and liabilities must also be used for related revenues and expenses.)

---

[21]Statement of Financial Accounting Standards No. 8, "Accounting for the Translation of Foreign Currency Transactions and Foreign Currency Financial Statements," (Stamford, Conn.: Financial Accounting Standards Board, 1975).

5. Exchange gains or losses can occur because of (a) changes in the relationship between currencies during the year, (b) conversion of foreign currency during the year, or (c) the settlement of receivables or payables at rates different from those at which the items were recorded. Such gains and losses should be included in the determination of net income for the period in which the rate changes.

6. Forward exchange contracts are agreements to exchange currencies at a predetermined rate on a specific date in the future. The purpose of such contracts may be to hedge either a foreign currency commitment, or a foreign currency exposed net asset position, or exposed net liability position, or to speculate. In general, gains and losses from forward exchange contracts should be included in the determination of net income for the period in which the rate changes. Gains or losses intended to be a hedge of an identifiable foreign currency commitment should be deferred subject to the following criteria.

   a. The life of the forward contract entered into extends at least to the anticipated transaction date.

   b. The forward contract is denominated in the same currency as the commitment and the amount is the same or less than the amount of the commitment.

   c. The commitment is firm and uncancelable.[22]

It should be noted that this statement did not specifically advocate any one of the translation methods previously discussed, and none were adopted intact. Nevertheless, the general objectives of translation advocated by the FASB were most closely satisfied by the temporal method because this method retains the measurement bases of the foreign statements just as well under exchange prices as it does under historical cost accounting.

Statement of Financial Accounting Concepts No. 52

The requirements of FASB No. 8 produced some perceived distortions in financial reporting that resulted in questions by many accountants and financial-statement users as to the relevance, reliability, and predictive value of the information presented. Among these perceived distortions were the following.

1. The results of the application of FASB Statement No. 8 were economically incompatible with reality. That is, since nonmonetary items such as inventory were translated at the historical rate, a loss could be reported during a period in which a foreign currency actually strengthened in relation to the dollar.

2. Inappropriate matching of costs and revenues. For example, sales were measured and translated at current prices, whereas inventory was measured and translated at historical rates.

[22]Ibid., par. 27.

3. The volatility of earnings. FASB Statement No. 8 required all translation gains and losses to be included in income. However, exchange rate changes are unrealized and frequently short-term in nature. This produces a so-called yo-yo effect upon earnings. Critics contended that this reporting requirement tended to obscure long-term trends.

The FASB took these criticisms under advisement and later replaced Statement No. 8 with Statement No. 52, "Foreign Currency Translation."[23] The following translation objectives were adopted in this release.

1. To provide information that is generally compatible with the expected economic efforts of a rate change on an enterprise's cash flow and equity.
2. To reflect in consolidated statements the financial results and relationships of the individual consolidated entities in conformity with U.S. generally accepted accounting principles.

FASB Statement No. 52 adopts the *functional currency* approach to translation. An entity's functional currency is defined as the currency of the *primary economic environment* in which it operates, which will normally be the environment in which it expends cash. Most frequently the functional currency will be the local currency, and four general procedures are involved in the translation process when the local currency is defined as the functional currency.

1. The financial statements of each individual foreign entity are initially recorded in that entity's functional currency. For example, a Japanese subsidiary would initially prepare its financial statements in terms of yen, as that would be the currency it generally uses to carry out cash transactions.
2. The foreign entity's statements must be adjusted (if necessary) to comply with generally accepted accounting principles in the United States.
3. The financial statements of the foreign entity are translated into the reporting currency of the parent company (usually the U.S. dollar). Assets and liabilities are translated at the current exchange rate at the balance sheet date. Revenues, expenses, gains, and losses are translated at the rate in effect at the date they were first recognized.
4. Exchange gains and losses are accumulated and reported as a separate component of stockholders' equity in the unrealized capital section.

FASB No. 52 went on to define two situations in which the local currency would not be the functional currency.

1. The foreign country's economic environment is highly inflationary (over 100

[23]Statement of Financial Accounting Standards No. 8, "Foreign Currency Translation" (Stamford, Conn.: Financial Accounting Standards Board, 1981.)

percent cumulative inflation over the past three years such as recently experienced by Argentina and Brazil).

2. The company's investment is not considered long-term.

In these cases the foreign company's functional currency is defined by the U.S. dollar and the financial statements are translated using the FASB Statement No. 8 approach, with exchange gains and losses being reported as a component of income.

Translation versus Remeasurement

Under the provisions of SFAS No. 52, translation is the process of expressing financial statements measured in one unit of currency (the reporting currency). The translation process is performed for the purpose of preparing financial statements and assumes that the foreign accounts *will not* be liquidated into U.S. dollars. Therefore, translation adjustments are disclosed as a part of stockholders' equity rather than as adjustments to income.

Remeasurement is significantly different from translation and is the process of measuring transactions originally denominated in a different unit of currency (e.g., purchases of a German subsidiary of a U.S. company payable in French francs). Remeasurement is required when

1. A foreign entity operates in a highly inflationary economy.
2. The accounts of an entity are maintained in a currency other than its functional currency.
3. A foreign entity is a party to a transaction that produces a monetary asset or liability denominated in a currency other than its functional currency.

Remeasurement is virtually the same process as described earlier under the temporal method. That is, the financial-statement elements are restated according to their original measurement bases. It assumes that an exchange of currencies will occur at the exchange rate prevailing on the date of remeasurement. This produces a foreign exchange gain or loss if the exchange rate fluctuates between the date of the original transaction and the date of the assumed exchange. Therefore, any exchange gain or loss is included in income in the period in which it occurs.

Forward Exchange Contracts

As noted earlier, *forward exchange contracts* are agreements to exchange currencies at a predetermined rate on a specific date in the future. These agreements are frequently used to protect a company from experiencing exchange gains or losses when a transaction with a foreign entity is settled at an amount different from the amount at which it was initially recorded. Two viewpoints have been advocated in accounting for transactions of this type.

1. *One transaction*—all aspects are viewed as part of a single transaction. That is, commitments to buy or sell currency necessary to settle a foreign payable or receivable are viewed as a part of the purchase or sale transaction.
2. *Two transaction*—the purchase or sale of goods is viewed as separate from any commitment to buy or sell foreign currency to settle the foreign payable or receivable.

Forward exchange contracts may be associated with four types of situations, each of which is viewed somewhat differently under the provisions of FASB Statement No. 52.

1. A hedge of a recorded but unsettled foreign currency transaction.
2. A hedge of an identifiable foreign currency commitment.
3. Speculating in foreign currency.
4. Hedging a net investment.

A recorded but unsettled foreign currency transaction arises when a company has an exposed liability position (a liability in a foreign currency) or an exposed asset position (a receivable in a foreign currency). These situations are similar, so only the liability position will be discussed. A U.S. company purchases inventory and agrees to pay a French company 100,000 francs in 30 days. The U.S. company is in an exposed liability position. To avoid the risk of an exchange rate increase, the U.S. company enters into a forward exchange contract whereby it agrees to purchase 100,000 francs at the exchange rate in effect on the date the inventory was purchased (this contract is defined as a *hedge* because it protects the company from experiencing an exchange rate loss). In the event the exchange rate between the dollar and the franc changes prior to the settlement of the liability, an exchange gain or loss is recorded as a component of net income. This treatment is an application of the two-transaction approach by the FASB. The rationale for this treatment is that cost or revenue was determined by the initial purchase or sale transaction and not by any subsequent agreement to exchange currencies.

A hedge of an identifiable foreign currency commitment occurs when a U.S. company purchases goods from a foreign entity to be delivered and paid for in the foreign company's currency in the future. The U.S. company, wishing to protect itself from the risks of exchange rate fluctuation, contracts with a currency dealer to purchase a specified amount of the foreign currency on the date of the purchase. In these situations any exchange gain or loss is deferred until the actual date the goods are acquired. This is an example of the one-transaction approach and is supported because both the purchase or sale and the forward exchange contract are future commitments.

Speculating in a foreign currency occurs when a company enters into an agreement to buy or sell a foreign currency that does not relate to the purchase or sale of goods. Any exchange gains or losses from speculating in foreign currency are recognized currently in income.

Hedging a net investment involves dealing in a foreign currency to offset the effects of changes on exchange rates on the parent company's total investment in a foreign operation. For example, several U.S. companies recently borrowed pesos to hedge agains the effect of the possible devaluation of that currency on their investments in Mexico. Accounting for any gains or losses depends upon whether the dollar or the foreign currency is the functional currency. If the dollar is the functional currency (which should be normal because devaluation normally takes place in highly inflationary economies), remeasurement is required and any gain or loss is reported on the income statement. If the foreign currency is the functional currency, any gain or loss is reported as a separate component of stockholders' equity as unrealized capital.

In analyzing foreign currency translation information, investors should keep in mind that it is a mixture of exceptional complexity. That is, foreign currency exchange reporting is inextricably intertwined with accounting for business combinations. The question of what constitutes the net income of a consolidated corporation with foreign subsidiaries may never be fully answerable.

SUMMARY

There are several aspects to consider in accounting for multiple entities: (1) recording the acquisition of one company by another—combinations, (2) recording and reporting of parent and subsidiary relations—consolidations and segment reporting, and (3) reporting the results of nondomestic subsidiaries—foreign currency translation.

In accounting for business combinations, two methods of acquisition may be used. A subsidiary may be acquired by a cash exchange or by an exchange of voting stock. Additionally, two methods of accounting—the purchase and the pooling of interests methods—may be used to record these acquisitions. These two methods are not alternatives for recording the same transaction. Exchanges of voting stock that satisfy certain criteria are to be recorded as pooling of interests; all other combinations are to be recorded as purchases.

Accounting for consolidations involves three major problems: (1) the presentation of consolidated assets, liabilities, and equity; (2) the presentation of consolidated net income; and (3) the presentation of minority interest. Guidelines have been established for handling each of these problems. In addition, FASB No. 14 has set out requirements for proper accounting of segmental reporting.

The major problem in the accounting for foreign subsidiaries is the translation of economic events reported in foreign currency into U.S. dollars. Several methods of accomplishing foreign currency translation were discussed along with the requirements of FASB No. 8 and FASB Statement No. 52.

In the readings that follow, John Dewhirst discusses some additional issues raised by APB No. 16 in accounting for business combinations, and Howard Donaldson and Alan Reinstein discuss some implications of the application of FASB Statement No. 52, "Foreign Currency Translation."

ACCOUNTING FOR BUSINESS COMBINATIONS—THE PURCHASE VS. POOLING OF INTERESTS ISSUE

JOHN F. DEWHIRST

In recent years no single accounting controversy has generated as much discussion and conflict in the United States as the struggle of the Accounting Principles Board of the American Institute of Certified Public Accountants (AICPA) to establish principles of accounting for business combinations. The struggle culminated in the issue of *Opinion 16—Business Combinations*, summarized as follows:

The Board finds merit in both the purchase and pooling of interests methods of accounting for business combinations and accepts neither method to the exclusion of the other. The arguments in favor of the purchase method of accounting are more persuasive if cash or other assets are distributed or liabilities are incurred to effect a combination, but arguments in favor of the pooling of interests method of accounting are more persuasive if voting common stock

is issued to effect a combination of common stock interests.

The Board also concludes that the two methods are not alternatives in accounting for the same business combination. A single method should be applied to an entire combination.[1]

In Canada, an empirical study of Canadian experience with business combinations accounting has been published, but no principles of accounting for business combinations have been issued to date by the Canadian Institute of Chartered Accountants (CICA).[2] In view of the present situation in Canada, this article will analyze the purchase vs. pooling controversy and make recommendations on principles of accounting for business combinations.

Reprinted with permission from CA magazine, published by the Canadian Institute of Chartered Accountants, Toronto, Canada, September 1972.

[1]The Accounting Principles Board. "Business Combinations." *Opinion No. 16* (New York: AICPA, August 1970), p. 294.

[2]S. Martin et al., *Business Combinations in the 1960's: A Canadian Profile* (Toronto: CICA, 1969).

BUSINESS COMBINATIONS, AND POOLING AND PURCHASE—SOME DEFINITIONS AND IMPLICATIONS

Opinion No. 16 (AICPA) specifies that:

A business combination occurs when a corporation and one or more incorporated or unincorporated businesses are brought together into one accounting entity. The single entity carries on the activities of the previously separate, independent entities.[3]

A business combination is classified as a purchase when:

Consideration other than (voting) equity shares is exchanged and one group of shareholders gives up its ownership interest in the assets it formerly controlled.[4]

While, a business combination is classified as a pooling of interests when:

Voting equity shares are exchanged and both groups of shareholders continue their ownership interests in the combined companies.[5]

A business combination, therefore, represents the joining together of two formerly separate accounting entities as one entity, and the applicability of purchase or pooling

accounting methods to the combination depends primarily on *the consideration exchanged,* i.e., voting common stock to qualify as pooling and nonvoting stock, liabilities, and/or assets to qualify as purchase. In addition, the choice between purchase and pooling hinges further on whether proportionate ownership interests have been maintained. Pooling assumes that the ownership interests of the combining companies are preserved in the combined companies, and purchase accounting assumes that only the purchaser company's ownership interest survives.

The business combinations accounting issue is important because the two proposed methods—purchase and pooling—can result in very different postcombination statements of financial position and results of operations. The pooling accounting method carries forward the net book values of both parties to the combination, along with their retained earnings balances. The purchase accounting method, on the other hand, carries forward the net book values of the assets of the purchaser company and states the net assets of the purchased company at fair market value. In addition, purchase accounting carries forward the retained earnings of the purchaser company only.

The main problem in resolving the business combination accounting controversy is to differentiate between substance and form, with substance providing the foundation for our choice of accounting. In this process, the overall business combinations accounting controversy can be factored into several sub-issues. Each sub-issue can be analyzed separately, and the interaction of the conclusions reached for each sub-issue, hopefully, will point the way to the appropriate accounting for business combinations.

---

[3]*Opinion No. 16,* op. cit., p. 281.
[4]R. C. Holsen, "Another Look at Business Combinations," in A. R. Wyatt, *A Critical Study of Accounting for Business Combinations,* Accounting Research Study No. 5 (New York: AICPA, 1963), p. 110.
[5]Ibid.

THE ENTITY CONCEPT, THE CORPORATION AND ITS RELATION TO SHAREHOLDERS

The entity concept in financial accounting specifies that accounting is done for specific business entities. In Hendriksen's words:

> The main reason for the significance of this concept is that it defines the area of interest and thus narrows the possible objects and activities and their attributes that may be selected for inclusion in financial reports.
>
> One approach to the definition of the accounting entity is to determine the economic unit which has control over resources, accepts responsibilities for making and carrying out commitments, and conducts economic activity. Such an accounting entity may be either an individual, a partnership, or a legal corporation, or consolidated group.
>
> An alternative approach is to define the entity in terms of the area of economic interest of particular individuals, groups or institutions.[6]

The entity concept and its interpretation underlies much of the controversy over purchase vs. pooling. For example, purchase accounting implies that one of the two parties to a business combination purchases the other party, resulting in the termination of one entity (the purchased company) and the continuation of the other entity (the purchaser). Pooling accounting, on the other hand, implies that both parties to the combination survive as entities in combined form. *The resolution of the "surviving entity" question is important*

because entity considerations affect postcombination stockholders' equity accounting, and can be used to determine the need for a new basis of accounting (revaluation of assets).

It is generally accepted in financial accounting that as long as a specific business entity survives as a going concern, no new basis of accounting arises. That is, assets are recorded at fair market value when purchased and they remain on the books at their acquisition cost in accordance with the cost concept. When an entity purchases one asset or the entire bundle of assets that constitute a going concern from another entity, it is generally accepted that the appropriate basis of valuation on the purchaser's books is fair market value (for the asset or going concern) and the basis of accounting on the books of the company being purchased is not relevant.

In the area of stockholders' equity classification, it is generally accepted to carry forward from period to period the retained earnings of an entity that still qualifies as a going concern. In the case of pooling, if both entities are held to survive in a "federal" form, then it is legitimate to carry forward the retained earnings of both companies. Under purchase accounting, however, it is not appropriate to carry forward the retained earnings of the purchased or dissolved party to the combination because they applied only to that terminated entity. As a result, the retained earnings of the purchaser are carried forward and the retained earnings of the purchased company become "invested capital" of the purchaser.

Given the differences in the potential applicability of generally accepted accounting principles to combination accounting *depending upon the nature of the business entity (entities) that survives a combina-*

---

[6]E. S. Hendriksen, *Accounting Theory*, rev. ed. (Homewood, Ill.: R. D. Irwin, 1970), p. 99.

tion, the determination of the nature of the surviving entity under different conditions is crucial for our analysis.

As in all areas of the business combinations accounting controversy the matter of separating substance from form becomes exceedingly important. Some of the important questions that have to be resolved in determining the nature of the surviving entity (entities) include:

1. Does the legal form of the survivor matter, for example, whether one or both of the combining parties remain as legal corporations, or a new legal corporation is formed and both previous legal entities disappear?
2. Does the maintenance of proportionate owners' interests in the combined companies indicate that both entities survive in a federation?
3. Does the fact that the owners of one of the parties to the combination emerge with "effective control" over the combination because of their superior size and voting strength mean that the smaller party ceases to exist as an entity, federated or otherwise?
4. Does the fact that the combined companies constitute a new "economic entity" with a very different economic nature than the two precombination companies indicate that a new entity is formed and both prior entities cease to exist?

Questions such as these must be analyzed carefully if the proper accounting is to result.

It is generally accepted that legal entity status, while in many situations an indicator of the boundaries of an accounting entity, is not the chief criterion for distinguishing accounting entities to serve as a focus for accounting. For example, legally separate entities (parents and subsidiaries) are combined in the preparation of consolidated financial statements which purport to show the financial position and results of operations of a *single* accounting entity. As a result, the legal form of the corporate combination should not be the major determinant of the nature of the surviving entity.

The maintenance of proportionate ownership interests is the major justification for the pooling of interests approach to accounting. The assumption under pooling is that "the entity" is synonymous with proportionate ownership of common voting stock, and that when a combination is effected by exchanging voting stock the perpetuation of *both entities* is accomplished. That is, the original corporate entities are not really involved and "the combination is in substance an arrangement among stockholders who exchange mutual risks and benefits."

Several challenges can be hurled against the assumption that the exchange of common voting shares so that proportionate interests are maintained is in substance *solely an arrangement among stockholders* and does not constitute the termination of one or more of the original entities. First, the idea that a "pooling" combination is in substance solely "an arrangement among stockholder groups" is a naive interpretation of contemporary business reality in the great majority of cases. It might be a reasonable interpretation of the facts when a former legally separate subsidiary is merged with its former parent,[7] or possibly when two "closely-held" corporations of

---

[7]APB *Opinion No. 16,* op. cit., par. 5, states that "the term business combination in this opinion excludes . . . a transfer of net assets or exchange of shares between companies under common control . . . such as between a parent corporation and its subsidiary. . . ." In my article the joining of a legally separate parent and subsidiary is termed a business combination but not one of substance, only form, and one in which the pooling of interests method should be applied.

similar size join together by exchanging voting stock. In the more common case of a combination involving one or more companies whose common shares are "widely-held," however, it is unrealistic to assume that the combination is effected by stockholders. Rather, the action is planned, negotiated, and executed by the "professional" managements of both firms, and the shareholders generally have only token, *ex post facto* involvement.

Second, the relative size or dominance of the two parties to the combination is believed by many observers to far outweigh the significance of the perpetuation of proprortionate ownership interest in widely-held corporations. Many of these observers would maintain that it is a gross misrepresentation of the facts to imply, as pooling accounting implies, that *both* entities survive when one party to the combination clearly dominates post-combination business decisions, policy-making, dividend declarations, and so forth, through its superior voting power and control of the board of directors and management. In other words, ownership without the powers and control that are associated with ownership is tantamount to a loss of effective proportionate ownership and the relegation to the status of an ordinary investor. And, since the great majority of business combinations involve one party who is dominant, and who achieves effective voting control over the combined companies, one entity disappears (the smaller party) and the other entity survives (the dominant party).

Third, changes in the "economic nature" of the combined companies (compared to the sum of the individual predecessor companies) can be interpreted as a signal that *one or both* of the parties to the combination cease to exist as an entity. In the social science of economics, questions of resource combination, resource use, and resource productivity and earning power predominate over questions of resource ownership. From the point of view of economics, therefore, whether or not a new entity arises would appear to hinge on whether the combination leads to expectations of: major changes in cost structure (fixed vs. variable cost, and economies of scale); changes in asset composition and structure; changes in capital structure (debt vs. equity); changes in seasonal, cyclical and trend cash flow patterns, revenue patterns, expense patterns, and earnings patterns. Changes such as these imply that a new economic entity has emerged and there is no justification for claiming that one or more of the parties to the combination survives as an economic entity (i.e., their basic economic nature is changed by the combination).

In summary, an analysis of the implications of the entity concept for business combinations accounting suggests that in the vast majority of cases *when common voting shares are exchanged* (i.e., cases in which one party achieves effective control of the combined companies), only a dominant entity survives and one of the original entities ceases to exist. In a similar fashion, when one entity purchases another entity and the *consideration exchanged is cash or any form except proportionate common voting shares,* the purchased entity ceases to exist and the purchaser entity survives. In a third less common situation, *where two entities of similar size combine* so that neither party to the combination dominates the combined companies and where the combination is accompanied by several opportunities for the introduction of economies of scale and synergy *resulting in a significant change in the economic nature of the two entities,* it can be held that neither entity survives and that a new economic entity is created by the combination.

As a consequence, when a dominant entity is combined with a smaller entity, *re-*

gardless of the form of the consideration exchanged and the dominant entity is deemed to be the only one to survive, a new basis of accountability (fair market value) is required for the dissolved entity only, and only the retained earnings of the dominant entity are brought forward. In a situation where the two parties to the combination are of similar size and power, and where there are abundant opportunities for changes in the post-combination economic nature of the parties, a new economic entity is created. Both old entities dissolve, a new basis of accountability for *both* parties is established, and the retained earnings from *neither* party is carried forward.[8]

THE GOING CONCERN CONCEPT

Though not mentioned specifically by many observers, the going concern concept is relevant to the resolution of the purchase vs. pooling controversy. Implicit in the arguments of the supporters of pooling accounting, and closely related to the discussion of the entity concept above, is the assumption that no new basis of accounting (revaluation) is called for, and that the retained earnings of both companies involved in the combination can be carried forward, because *no new going concern is created.*

[8]There is some controversy over whether or not retained earnings should be carried forward when two entities combine and are deemed to form a "new economic entity" (see G. Mulcahy, "Accounting for Business Combinations," *CCA* (July 1972), p. 46). The position in my article of not carrying forward the retained earnings of either party to the combination when a new entity results is based on accepted accounting practice. Personally, however, I do not have strong feelings one way or another on the issue, and I could accept carrying forward the retained earnings of both parties as long as they were properly labelled and disclosed.

Precedent exists, however, to suggest that when there is a major "rupture" or "discontinuity" in a going concern such as a financial reorganization, a new basis of accountability does arise. For example, when a company is on the brink of bankruptcy and its asset values are overstated on the "books" in relation to any foreseeable estimate of revenues that they might generate, it is generally acceptable to write them down to "reasonable" values in order to make future accounting-determined earnings and dividends possible. In other words, the expected earning power of the assets determines that assets are overvalued, and the need for a "fresh start" in the basis of accounting is recognized. In Byrd's words:

> *A reorganization enables a company to obtain a fresh start without the expense and disruption involved in creating a new corporate entity. Typically a reorganization results in the write-down of overvalued assets and the elimination of a deficit. There is usually an adjustment in the long-term liabilities and a reduction in the par value of share capital. The adjustments clear the way for showing profits and paving dividends in future years. . . . After a reorganization the limited company is considered to be starting fresh—in effect as a new corporate entity.[9]*

For related reasons, a significant change in the economic prospects and make-up of a combination over the prospects and make-up of the sum of the separate entities before combination, suggests that a discontinuity has occurred in the going concern

[9]H. A. Finney, H. E. Miller, and K. F. Byrd, *Principles of Accounting: Intermediate,* 6th ed., Canadian ed. (Scarborough, Ont.: Prentice-Hall, 1966), p. 810.

status of the corporations prior and after combination, and a "fresh start" or new basis of accounting is required. In this situation, however, since economic prospects are likely to be *enhanced* by the combination, an upward revaluation of assets is suggested.

THE COMBINATION AS AN EXCHANGE TRANSACTION

In *Accounting Research Study No. 5,* Wyatt concluded that a business combination ". . . is basically an exchange event in which two economic interests bargain to the consummation of an exchange of assets and/or equities."[10] Also, according to Paton and Littleton:

> The activities of the specific business enterprise, with respect to which the accountant must supply pertinent information, consist largely of exchange transactions with other enterprises. Accounting undertakes to express these exchanges quantitatively. The basic subject matter of accounting is therefore the measured consideration involved in exchange activities, especially those which are related to services acquired (cost, expense) and services rendered (revenue, income).[11]

"Measured consideration," in this case, represents the cash price or cash equivalent price of other consideration exchanged as determined by "unrestricted negotiations between independent parties" in an armslength transaction. "In cases in which the consideration employed in acquiring goods or services is in the form of capital stock. . . . The proper measure of actual cost in such circumstances is the amount of money which could have been raised through the issue of the securities."[12]

It goes without saying that the great majority of business combinations constitute significant exchange transactions between independent, arms-length parties (except possibly the combination of a formerly legally separate parent and subsidiary), and as a consequence it is a signal for the determination of the "measured consideration" exchanged and the recording in the combined companies' books of this consideration. At the same time, to justify the carrying forward of the book values of both parties to the combination as pooling supporters do, we would have to ignore reality and assume that no exchange transaction took place between independent corporate parties.

CONSISTENCY OF RESULTS OVER TIME

One of the major reported drawbacks of purchase accounting and one of the alleged advantages of pooling, stems from the potential "inconsistency" between pre- and post-combination earnings and earnings per share when purchase accounting methods are applied. Company managements, quite understandably, want post-merger results to be as consistent and comparable as possible with the sum of the combining companies' premerger results. The application of purchase accounting in a combination normally results in a change in the valuation of tangible assets and the introduction of purchased goodwill, which can have the effect of reducing post-merger

[10]A. R. Wyatt, *A Critical Study of Accounting for Business Combinations,* Accounting Research Study No. 5 (New York: AICPA, 1963), p. 104.
[11]W. A. Paton and A. C. Littleton, *An Introduction To Corporate Accounting Standards* (Madison, Wis.: American Accounting Association, 1962), p. 11.

[12]Ibid., pp. 26–28.

earnings, earnings per share and realign many of the key financial ratios calculable from the balance sheet and income statement.

In addition, assuming unrealistically that there are no *new* economic benefits from combination, post-merger results will generally tend to be poorer when purchase accounting is applied, than the sum of the pre-merger results of the combining companies. Purchase accounting produces poorer results because of the attendant upward valuation of the purchased company and the resulting higher future expense write-offs. Therefore, regardless of whether purchase, pooling or some alternative form of accounting is appropriate for business combinations from an accounting theory point of view, company managements will be encouraged to promote pooling accounting because it normally presents their future performance in a more favourable light. The finding of a major Canadian study that the great majority of Canadian business combinations were accounted for as purchases does not change the above tendency, because Canadian accounting principles allow purchase accounting to become "pseudo-purchase accounting" (the opportunity to avoid amortizing goodwill against revenues and not requiring companies to write up tangible assets and identifiable intangibles) and have the same impact on future results as if pooling accounting was actually implemented.[13]

Hendriksen maintains that it is misleading in most combinations to assume that the sum of the prior combination earnings of the two parties is in any way comparable to the after combination earnings when he states:

It has also been recommended that when prior results of operations are presented for comparative purposes, the previous data (of the separate parties) should also be restated on a pooling basis as if the combination had taken place in an earlier period. The apparent objective is to show meaningful trends of income and earnings per share data that can be used for predictive purposes. However, this is a misuse of comparative data, because a discontinuity has occurred. The combined firm is not the same as a group of separate firms and it is misleading to assume that nothing has happened. Furthermore, the combination generally results in a new capitalization and new relationships among the equity holders. It is misleading to assume that these new capitalization relationships existed in an earlier period under entirely different circumstances.[14]

Research has established that many company managements appear to base investment decisions on the potential impact of these decisions on externally reported financial accounting results, rather than on the basis of the inherent economic merits of each project.[15] As a consequence, pooling accounting, which assumes that the prior-combination results of the two companies are comparable to post-combination results, might encourage managers to use the wrong data for decision making. In addition, some observers believe that much of the impetus for the disastrous history of the conglomerate movement in the United

[14]Hendriksen, op. cit., p. 547.
[15]E. M. Lerner and A. Rappaport, "Limit DCF in Capital Budgeting," *Harvard Business Review* (September–October 1968), pp. 133–139.

[13]S. Martin, et al., op. cit.

States and the phenomenon of "merger by numbers" can be traced to the availability of the pooling of interests accounting device, and conglomerate managements' practices of basing their merger decisions on projected short-run pooling of interests—determined earnings per share and price-earnings ratios.

REVALUATION OF ONLY ONE PARTY TO THE COMBINATION

A major complaint of the supporters of pooling accounting, and a well-founded complaint in the opinion of the author *in some circumstances,* is the "inconsistent" practice, when purchase accounting is applied, of stating the purchased company's net assets at fair market value while carrying forward the book value of net assets of the company designated to be the purchaser. Besides claiming that this action results in an inconsistent treatment of both parties to the combination, some supporters of pooling maintain that this practice results in mixing together different valuation bases and making the resulting accounting data less meaningful.

Contrary to the opinions of some supporters of pooling accounting, the use of pooling accounting does not result in consistent valuation bases for both parties to the combination because the historical cost book values of both companies are composed of mixed valuation bases. That is, even though the assets are recorded at historical cost, they were purchased in different time intervals when the current cost levels and purchasing power of the dollar differed. In addition, in the most common combination situation (where one company buys the other company, or where one company is dominant and emerges with effective control after an exchange of shares)

one entity continues and the other entity dissolves. In this situation, generally accepted accounting principles dictate that there is no need to establish a new basis of accounting (revaluation) for the continuing entity (the purchaser, or dominant party), while a new basis of accounting is required for the purchased or minor party.

The objection of some pooling supporters does make sense, however, in combinations involving companies of similar size where one cannot claim in any reasonable manner that one company dominates the other company or vice versa. About all one can verify in these situations is that one of the two parties *initiated* the combination proposal; but this, in itself, is not sufficient justification for a new basis of accounting for only one of the parties at the exclusion of the other.

THE CONSIDERATION EXCHANGED—SUBSTANCE OR FORM

As mentioned above, regardless of all ancillary reasons for distinguishing between the applicability of purchase or pooling accounting in a given business combination, the single operational criterion that has emerged to distinguish the appropriateness of the two alternatives is whether the combination is effected by means of an exchange of common voting stock or some other form of consideration. If common stock is exchanged the combination is viewed as a pooling requiring no revaluation of either of the combining company's assets.

In a "naive" bookkeeping sense, the consideration transferred is important because if one company purchases the assets of stock of another company, the double-entry mechanism requires that debits equal credits after the acquisition. In other words, if cash and/or bonds transferred exceed the historical cost net book value of the assets of the acquired company, a debit "short-fall" is created by the transaction, and the double-entry system requires that the event be recorded as a purchase with the attendant recognition of purchased goodwill.

On the other hand, if common shares are exchanged for net assets or shares of the acquired company, the "recording value" of the acquired company is not determined directly by the act of exchanging consideration, and the accountant faces the additional responsibility of placing a value or dollar assignment to the consideration given up (or received). In this situation, the double-entry mechanism does not force him to record an imbalance between debits and credits. Any imbalance that does arise will be strictly a function of the value he assigns to the consideration exchanged. In a very fundamental sense, therefore, the primary practical reason for the two alternative methods stems from the accountant's opportunity to place a value on the consideration exchanged interacting with the double-entry mechanism.

Aside from the mechanics of the double-entry system and the discretion allowed the accountant in selecting a valuation, are there differences in substance between the several types of consideration that may be exchanged in a business combination? Are these differences in consideration exchanged important enough to justify two radically different methods of accounting for business combinations?

From the point of view of the common shareholders in both companies involved in the combination, all forms of consideration that might be exchanged are equally important. To the shareholders, the combination represents an exchange of resources (cash, or other assets) or potential resources (un-

issued bonds or common stock), for the resources, earning power, and possibly, the management talent inherent in the other company involved in the combination.

The form of the consideration given is not of critical importance to common shareholders of both companies, *rather it is the resource values given up regardless of form vs. the resource values received.* The cost or value of any consideration given, on either side of the combination, is ultimately the opportunity cost of the resources (or potential resources in the case of common stock) involved (i.e., the return forgone by not using those resources in their next most profitable use). The form of the consideration exchanged, therefore, does not appear to justify in itself two different methods of accounting for business combinations. And, since differences in the form of consideration exchanged appear to be the major rationalization supporting pooling of interest accounting, one can conclude that pooling accounting is of questionable validity.

Because the value of the consideration given on either side of the combination, regardless of form, is the opportunity cost of the resources exchanged, and because the minimum required rate of return on new investment projects or the cost of capital to the company is the recognized opportunity cost of finance in corporations, the pooling method gives rise to further criticisms. Implicit in the pooling method is the assumption that the cost of capital to the acquiring firm can be equated to the historical cost net book value of the acquired company. This unusual conclusion is justified because the common stock issued by the acquiring company is valued at the net book value of the assets of the acquired company regardless of the fair market value of the shares exchanged.

Related to this unrealistic assumption about the opportunity cost of capital im-

CHAPTER 12: ACCOUNTING FOR MULTIPLE ENTITIES

plicit in pooling accounting is the additional charge that the pooling of interests accounting device results in the inappropriate conversion of hidden stockholders' equity values into post-combination net income. This charge is based on the observation that issued stock and net assets received are not valued at fair market value, resulting in future post-combination net income being overstated by an unrealistically low level of expenses as the expired assets are matched with revenues. If the consideration exchanged was valued at fair market value as in the case of *internal* expansion, owners' equity, associated assets, future expenses and net income would be realistically determined.

THE COMBINATION DECISION

REASONS FOR BUSINESS COMBINATIONS

The reasons for business combinations are many[16] and in a given prospective combination *one or more* of the following objectives normally apply: (1) to obtain an established research capability, (2) to obtain established management and/or employee skills, (3) to obtain economies of scale in production and marketing, (4) to

obtain liquid assets or financing capability, (5) to obtain control over sources of raw materials and parts, (6) to diversify into a stable line to help offset seasonal or cyclical unstable markets, (7) to obtain expertise in a new technology, (8) to accomplish vertical integration, (9) to reduce competition, and (10) to improve the position of stockholder-owners with respect to income tax law and estate tax law.[17]

In addition, a business combination is often considered to be an alternative to *internal growth or expansion for several reasons:* (1) the time required to enter a new industry or achieve other objectives is often shortened substantially, (2) the desired facilities and trained personnel might be less costly, (3) the large scale financing required might be handled more easily and cheaply through a direct exchange of shares than through the public capital markets, and (4) the risks of combining with an established concern might be less than venturing into a new industry or achieving other objectives by means of internal expansion.[18]

THE COMBINATION DECISION PROCESS

As discussed above, the reasons for business combinations are many and in a particular combination situation the two parties might have different reasons. Regardless of the reasons, however, the quantitative aspects of the combination decision process are best described as a form of investment or capital budgeting decision. Both parties will undertake the following steps:

---

[16]Many "nonquantitative" considerations are also important in business combination decisions, for example, the role that management of the potential acquisition will play in the companies after combination. Nonquantitative factors are especially important in the bargaining strategy stage. See G. E. MacDougal and F. V. Malek, "Master Plan or Merger Negotiations," *Harvard Business Review* (January–February 1970), pp. 77–82; J. S. R. Shad, "The Financial Realities of Mergers," *Harvard Business Review* (November–December 1969), pp. 138–141; R. M. Hexter, "How to Sell Your Company," *Harvard Business Review* (May–June 1968), pp. 71–77; and W. F. Rockwell, Jr., "How to Acquire a Company," *Harvard Business Review* (May–June 1968), pp. 121–132.

[17]J. F. Weston and E. F. Brigham, *Managerial Finance,* 2d ed. (Toronto: Holt, Rinehart and Winston, 1962), pp. 631–638.
[18]Ibid.

1. *Place a present value on their own company as it is now.* The extent of this analysis will differ depending on the nature of the combination and can vary all the way from both parties determining an ''intrinsic value'' for their own common shares, to valuing the companies as a whole. In valuing the company as a whole the procedure followed includes: a) forecasting future net *cash* profits (cash revenues minus cash expenses) by year over the expected life of the company; b) present-valuing the forecasted net cash profits by means of an appropriate discount rate. The appropriate discount rate in the majority of situations is the opportunity cost of capital (the policy-set required minimum rate of return or cut-off rate for new capital investment proposals) to the company.

2. *Place a present value on the other company who is a party to the combination.* The methodology will be the same as described in (1) above.

3. Both companies independently estimate the *incremental* cash profits that will result from the economies, cross-fertilization, and synergy created by the combination. They will then present-value these incremental cash profits to determine the value-added by the combination.

4. Both companies estimate *their own* contribution to the incremental cash profits of the combination, discount these at their own cost of capital, and arrive at ''their share'' of the value-added.

5. Each company now adds its estimate of the value of their own company as it is now [(1) above] to their estimate of their share added [(4) above] to arrive at their floor or base positions for negotiation.

6. Room for bargaining exists if each company's floor or base position for nego-

tiation is *below* the value assigned by the other party to the combination. If the reverse holds true, the combination will not take place.

Room for bargaining can exist because both parties to the combination: (1) make independent (and probably different) estimates of future net cash profits for their company and the other party, (2) both companies probably have different expectations as to the economic results of the combination, and their own and the other party's contribution to these incremental economic results, (3) both parties probably have different cost of capital rates (or, minimum required rates of return for new capital investment proposals).

THE POINT OF VIEW OF THE USER OF ACCOUNTING INFORMATION

The American Accounting Association in A Statement of Basic Accounting Theory maintains that:

> *Accounting information is the chief means of reducing the uncertainty under which external users act as well as a primary means of reporting on stewardship. . . . Most decisions based on accounting information involve some kind of prediction. Common samples include forecasts of future earnings, of probable repayment of debt, and of likely managerial effectiveness.*
>
> *Those external users who have or contemplate having a direct relationship with an enterprise must decide, on the basis of all available information, whether to affiliate with or to modify an existing relationship with the firm.*
>
> *It is not the function of the accountant to dictate the decision models for users of accounting data. However, to the ex-*

tent that there is a consensus with regard to all or part of a specific decision model, the accountant should select, process, and report relevant data.[19]

Further, when comparing the point of view of economics, which focuses on the decision-making processes of individuals and entities, with the point of view of accounting. Edwards and Bell state:

The overwhelming test of the adequacy of accounting data as developed for any particular period must be their comparability with the expectations originally specified for that period. Where economics deals with a set of expectations and an expected profit which represents a summary of these expectations, accounting attempts to develop a list of actual events and the actual profits which result from them.[20]

Taking the American Accounting Association point of view and combining it with Edwards and Bell's statement, we find that financial accounting information is relevant or useful to external users to the extent that it:

1. Aids them to predict variables that are important in making sound decisions (i.e., provides data specified by their decision models), and
2. Serves to explain the actual results achieved by the firm over time in a manner that is comparable with the expectations originally held by the users.

From the point of view of one important user—the present and prospective common stockholder—what variables about the firm's economic behaviour are relevant? First and foremost, the common stock investor is interested in predicting the future timing and rate of growth in dividends per share and market price per share. At the same time, in formulating his expectations about the future he is also interested in reports of the actual performance of the company to compare with his original expectations. The future timing and rate of growth in dividends per share and market price per share depend very much on the attained and expected timing and rate of growth of earnings per share: therefore, the investor is interested in an earnings per share calculation that will explain what economic progress has actually been achieved, and how useful the reported earnings per share will be in predicting future economic progress.

In the business combination decision, the common stock investor realizes that company management chose to invest company resources (including those in which he has an equity) into a combination with another company rather than into some alternative use, including the possibility of achieving the same objectives through internal expansion. He also realized that those resources (including the use of potential resources such as unissued common shares) have a cost. At a minimum the cost to the company and the cost to him as a shareholder is the cost of capital to the company or the required minimum rate of return on new capital investments: while at the maximum, the cost to the company is the return forgone by not investing those resources in their next most profitable employment. If the company invests in projects (including combinations) that earn *less* than the cost of capital, the common shareholder is likely to suffer a dilution in the value of his equity in the business.

[19]AAA Committee, *A Statement of Basic Accounting Theory* (Evanston, Ill. American Accounting Association, 1966), pp. 19–22.
[20]E. O. Edwards and P. W. Bell, *The Theory and Measurement of Business Income* (Berkeley and Los Angeles: University of California Press, 1961), p. 4.

From the common shareholder's point of view, therefore, his main interest in the combination decision is to assess the values or resources given up by his company against the values or resources contributed by the other party to the combination. If the combination promises to generate a rate of return in excess of the cost of capital of the resources his company devotes to it, the shareholder will expect higher earnings and earnings per share, as well as greater dividends per share and/or a greater increase in market price per share.

From the point of view of relevant information to the common stockholder-user of financial accounting data, therefore, it would appear that the following accounting methods would result in an earnings per share figure that is more consistent with his decision model than an earnings per share figure based on pooling accounting: (1) an accounting method that will report the fair market value of the resources given up or exchanged, and (2) an after-combination earnings per share figure determined by matching combination fair market value costs with the higher revenues that are expected to result from the combination.

The pooling accounting method will not produce results that are consistent with the stockholders' decision model because pooling implies that the consideration exchanged represents a sacrifice equivalent to the net historical cost book value of the acquired company. The net historical cost book value of the acquired company, however, bears no relationship to the fair market value or the cost of capital inherent in the consideration exchanged. Pooling also results in unrealistic future earnings per share figures because the higher future revenues generated by the benefits of combination will be matched with irrelevant costs, to produce in the usual case a gross overstatement of future net earnings attributable to the combination.

When fair market value is assigned to the tangible and intangible assets of the acquired company, future expense matching will be consistent with the revenues that flow from the synergy and economies of the combination, and future predictions of earnings per share based on these earnings figures are likely to be more reliable. In addition, companies that expand by means of mergers and acquisitions will be more directly comparable with companies that choose to expand by internal growth.

Fair market value is also superior to the pooling approach in providing data to shareholders and/or management to measure the success or failure of the company management's combination decision. The discussion above on the combination decision process demonstrates that the managements of both companies *base their combination decision on whether the expected future earnings from the combination* discounted by the cost of capital *will exceed the fair market value of the consideration given in exchange*. To turn around and report the actual future earnings based on anything other than the fair market value of the consideration exchanged will result in financial accounting data which is inconsistent with the specifications of management's original combination decision, and will also tend to make "bad" merger decisions look "good," and "good" merger decisions look "phenomenal."

SUMMARY OF THE ANALYSES OF SUB-ISSUES AND RECOMMENDATIONS FOR BUSINESS COMBINATIONS

The *weight of the preceding analyses* generates considerable doubt about the validity of the concept of pooling of interests accounting, except possibly in situations where nothing of substance has happened, for example, when a parent combines with a "controlled" subsidiary. In all situations where cash or any form of consideration is exchanged other than common shares, one of the previous parties to the combination ceases to exist and purchase accounting is normally appropriate. However, in cases where the combination results in major economic changes to *both* original parties: for example, where two companies of similar size combine and there are several changes in the economic nature of the combined firms, regardless of the form of consideration exchanged, *both companies should be revalued at fair market value* to reflect the fact that a new economic entity emerges with assets of substantially different earning power than *either* predecessor.

PRACTICAL CONSIDERATIONS OF THE PROPOSED BASIS FOR BUSINESS COMBINATIONS

MARKET VALUE FOR FAIR MARKET VALUE PURPOSES

The selection of fair market value to assign to the purchased company's net assets and both companies' net assets in the case of the creation of a new economic entity can be difficult in practice for many reasons. In the first place, when shares are exchanged, several possible valuation points of view are possible. For example, in the case of a purchase situation (where a dominant firm merges with a smaller firm) the fair market value of the smaller firm's net assets can be based on (a) the dominant firm's estimate of the value of its shares exchanged, (b) the smaller firm's estimate of the value of the dominant firm's shares, and (c) the capital market's estimate of the value of the dominant firm's shares.

Likewise, in the situation where two companies (Company A and B) of similar size and enhanced economic prospects combine to form Company AB, calling for a revaluation of both parties, the fair market value of the combined companies can differ depending upon whether the accountant considers (a) Company A's estimate of the value of Company AB, (b) Company B's estimate of the value of Company AB, (c) Company A's estimate of the value of Company A, (d) Company B's estimate of the value of Company A, (e) Company A's estimate of the value-added to the combination in total and by each of Companies A and B, (f) Company B's estimate of the value-added to the combination in total and by each of Company A and B, and (g) the capital market's estimate of the combination of Company AB's share value.

The discussion demonstrates that the accountant will be faced with an overwhelming array of possible "fair market values," even if he has access to the negotiation working papers of both parties to the combination. In addition, these fair market values can differ significantly from one party to the other, because of the differences in expectations between the parties, and differences in the cost of capital to both parties. As a consequence, *the accountant should select the capital market value of the shares exchanged shortly after combination, as an impartial, market-determined, objective basis for the determination of fair market value and associated combination goodwill for accounting purposes.*

FAIR MARKET VALUE WHERE CAPITAL MARKET PRICES ARE UNAVAILABLE OR UNREALISTIC

In those few situations where the after-combination capital market price of the shares exchanged is not available or is unrealiable because, for example, the market for the stock is "thin," or the stock is not listed or traded over the counter, another approach to valuation must be used. A less desirable but reasonable alternative approach would be *to revalue only the tangible assets and identifiable intangible assets at fair market value* (e.g., replacement cost), thereby refraining from computing and recording combination goodwill. This second approach would be less desirable and not as realistic as the first approach mentioned above, and would only be used by the accountant in those situations where market conditions surrounding the stock exchanged were such that any share price chosen would not be objective or reliable enough to qualify as fair market value for accounting purposes.

DETERMINING THE TYPE OF COMBINATION AND THE APPROPRIATE ACCOUNTING METHODS

According to the analyses presented above, three possible combination situations might arise with three different methods of accounting applicable. In the first situation (and probably an infrequent combination situation), a combination takes place in which nothing of economic substance happens. For example, regardless of the form of consideration exchanged (stock, cash, bonds, etc.) the combination of a former separate legal entity subsidiary with a former separate legal entity parent company, results in no change in economic substance. Because the parent controlled the subsidiary before combination all foreseeable economic advantages have already been exploited, and the combination is one of form and not economic substance. In this situation, no new basis of accounting is called for by the combination and the book values of the former companies are brought forward.

Second, the great majority of combination situations encountered will involve a large, dominant firm with a much smaller firm. In most of these cases the major

changes of economic substance that result from the combination (e.g., earnings, revenues, etc.) are attributable to the restructuring and prospects of the smaller firm component. The larger firm component of the combination will likely remain substantially unchanged in an economic sense from its pre-combination economic make-up. In this situation, *regardless of the form of consideration exchanged,* a new basis of accounting will be applied to the net assets of the smaller party, and no new basis of accounting applied to the dominant party.

Third, a much smaller number of combination situations encountered will involve two entities of similar size, whose joining together will result in material changes in economic results and structure. In essence, a new economic entity is born out of the combination and material economic changes are expected to occur to both original parties to the combination. In these situations, a new basis of accounting (valuation at fair market value) is required for *both* parties to the combination to reflect the economic substance inherent in the event.[21]

When deciding to which of the three categories a particular combination belongs, the accountant can look to the following for guidance: (1) the precombination relationship of the two parties (e.g., subsidiary and parent), (2) the relative sizes of the two

---

[21]Two alternative methods have been reported by Gertrude Mulcahy to account for a business combination where a "new economic entity" is held to be created and an acquirer cannot be identified to qualify for purchase accounting. One method consists of arbitrarily selecting one of the combining firms as the "acquirer" and applying purchase accounting, and the other alternative would be to arbitrarily designate the combination as a pooling. Both alternatives are inferior to the "new economic entity" approach recommended in my article because they are not based on the underlying economic conditions inherent in the combination. (See G. Mulcahy. op. cit., p. 45.)

parties (e.g., as indicated by sales, net income, assets, stockholders' equity, and so forth), (3) all available information surrounding the combination event, from the internal documents (e.g., minutes) of the two parties to the information reported by external sources, to assess the degree of expected economic change.

THE RELATED ISSUE OF ACCOUNTING FOR GOODWILL

In Canada, there are several options available at present for dealing with combination goodwill: (1) goodwill can be left on the books unamortized, (2) it can be amortized systematically over a reasonable period in the future, and (3) it can be written off immediately against surplus. In the United States, on the other hand, Accounting Principles Board *Opinion No. 17* does not allow the immediate write-off of combination goodwill and requires that goodwill be amortized systematically over a period of not more than forty years from the date of combination. Also, in Canada, while it is recommended in the *CICA Handbook* that *tangible* and *identifiable intangible* assets of purchased companies be revalued at fair market value, in practice virtually no Canadian companies do so. Instead, all of the excess of consideration paid over book value of the acquired company is assigned to "purchased" goodwill[22] The effect of these practices and options in goodwill accounting in Canada is to result in virtually all cases of purchase accounting having the *same effect* on post-combination earnings and earnings per share as the outright application of pooling accounting.

The analysis of the issue of accounting for goodwill is beyond the scope of this

article, however the author believes that the issue of business combinations accounting should be decided and principles issued *before* the principles of accounting for combinations goodwill are decided.[23] Otherwise, in Canada we are likely to experience the intense problems faced by the American Institute of Certified Public Accountants when they first attempted to do away with pooling accounting and at the same time forbid the immediate write-off of purchased goodwill against surplus.

CONCLUSION

The analysis of several sub-issues in the pooling vs. purchase accounting controversy including the application of relevant accounting concepts and the information needs of stockholder users of accounting information has led to the following recommendations. Pooling accounting lacks theoretical merit and is not consistent with the information needs of stockholder investors and should be virtually abandoned. What is now known as purchase accounting should be retained and applied to the great majority of combinations involving a dominant party with a small party, re-

---

[22]S. Martin, et al., op. cit.

[23]The issue of accounting for goodwill is a controversial one and can have a major impact on the net result of business combination accounting. For a discussion of some of the positions, see G. Mulcahy, ibid., p. 46, and particularly Catlett and Olsen, *Accounting for Goodwill*, ARS No. 10 (New York: AICPA, 1968), and R. Gynther, "Some Conceptualizing on Goodwill," *Accounting Review* (April 1969), pp. 247–255. In my opinion Catlett's and Olsen's analysis and recommendation to write purchase goodwill off against surplus immediately after combination flies in the face of the economic facts of the situation, and Gynther's analysis and recommendations are closer to my own thinking on the subject.

gardless of the form of consideration exchanged. When two companies of similar size combine with prospects of material economic change arising out of combination, both parties, net assets should be restated at fair market value to give recognition to the birth of a new economic entity.

IMPLEMENTING FAS NO. 52: THE CRITICAL ISSUES

HOWARD DONALDSON
ALAN REINSTEIN

Multinational corporations must adopt new foreign currency translation principles as a result of Financial Accounting Standard No. 52, "Foreign Currency Translation." FAS No. 52, issued in December 1981, improves upon FAS No. 8 in that volatile translation adjustments are no longer included in income in local functional currency countries, financial statement results and relationships are compatible with the primary economic environment, and more liberal treatment is afforded to effective hedges. But FAS No. 52 will cause some problems of its own.

Since it becomes binding for fiscal years beginning on or after December 1982, extended and precise planning for its implementation is imperative, because a comprehensive plan must be developed which encompasses procedures to provide for the following:

- Establish or re-evaluate the short- and long-range objectives of foreign operations.
- Consult with representative management personnel including accounting, treasury, tax, marketing, division, and field staff.
- Consider all relevant financial factors including, but not necessarily limited to, cash flow, financing, market structure, and hedging techniques.
- Appraise major implementation issues.
- Prepare financial projections under varying circumstances.
- Monitor the process.

As an aid to companies beginning the process, this article will explore a series of issues raised by FAS No. 52, issues already dealt with by a multinational company (Burroughs Corporation). These issues are timing and method of adoption; determination of the functional currency; translation and remeasurement of foreign financial statements; and the minimization of exchange gains and losses in income.

TIMING AND METHOD OF ADOPTION

Upon adoption, prior years may be restated retroactively or reported on a pro forma basis. Either presentation requires disclosure of the nature of restatement and its effect on income before extraordinary items, net income, and related earnings per share for each period presented.

Retroactive restatement will reveal how operating income has been affected by recent severe currency movements, demonstrate the impact of the new standard upon future financial statements, and allow better financial comparisons. But restatement is expensive. Because adoption must occur at the beginning of the year, retroactive restatement should be elected only when the trends of translation gains and losses under FAS No. 8 are material. Even then, restatement of prior years may not be warranted because the comparisons made possible will not reveal some essential information: Restatement will not, for example, reflect management action, which could have been taken to minimize exchange exposure had FAS No. 52 been in effect. There are at least three reasons for this:

- Under FAS No. 52, short-term U.S. dollar intercompany balances on foreign financial statements produce exchange gains and losses in income when the local currency is the functional currency. Under FAS No. 8, these exchange gains and losses were offset with translation gains and losses, and thereby did not affect income.
- Under FAS No. 52, remeasurement of deferred income taxes yields exchange gains and losses in income, when the U.S. dollar is the functional currency. Under FAS No. 8, translation of deferred income taxes had no exchange effect in income.
- Under FAS No. 52, hedging transactions, such as forward exchange contracts, must be designated before deferral of exchange gains and losses is permitted. FAS No. 8 did not require this designation.

DETERMINATION OF FUNCTIONAL CURRENCY

Identifying each foreign entity's functional currency should be done carefully, because it will determine the method used to translate the foreign financial statements into U.S. dollars, possibly the most time-consuming and important decision required under FAS No. 52. Unlike its predecessor, FAS No. 52 defines the functional currency as the currency of the primary economic environment in which the entity operates (i.e., generally, the currency used to generate and expend cash), and distinguishes between self-contained foreign entities and extensions of the parent company.

Self-contained foreign entities, displaying autonomy over their daily operating affairs, independence from their parent's economic environment, and discretionary control over their use of cash, should adopt their local currency as the functional one. Foreign entities considered as extensions of their parent company's operations usually should adopt their parent company's currency, generally the U.S. dollar, as their own because they will normally incur transactions with their parent company which significantly affect their cash flows through acquisition and sale of assets and primary financing.

Determining the functional currency should follow an objective evaluation of how alternative choices will affect cash flow, sales price, sales market, expenses, financing, and intercompany transactions—all factors discussed in Appendix A of FAS No. 52.

When a single functional currency is not clearly identifiable, the following additional factors should be considered:

- National sovereignty implications, including currency control, and economic and tax policies.

- Generally accepted industry practices, especially if pricing and other transaction attributes are tied to a specific currency.
- Dividend policy, including the practice of converting available funds into U.S. dollars for remittance to the parent company.
- The expected life of the foreign investment.

Some specific situations that suggest using the U.S. dollar as the functional currency include the following:

- U.S. dollar-denominated billings.
- Significant importation of inventory with minor local marketing, service, and administrative costs.
- Manufacturing of subassemblies for inclusion in products manufactured and sold in the U.S.
- A foreign finance agent for a U.S. company.
- A foreign sales branch of a U.S. manufacturing company.
- A foreign construction or development joint venture having limited life.

The U.S. dollar or parent company currency is required as the functional currency when the cumulative 3-year inflation rate exceeds 100 percent, which represents only a 26-percent inflation rate compounded annually. Under FAS No. 8, highly inflationary environments were not considered because the U.S. dollar was always used as the measuring base. However, under FAS No. 52, when the local currency is the functional currency, significant nonmonetary accounts such as inventories and capital assets lose all relevant relationship to cost or value in any currency. **Table 1** illustrates the problem.

Use of the U.S. dollar as the functional currency will prevent nonmonetary assets from "disappearing," because the use of historical exchange rates freezes the U.S. dollar value of these assets.

Management should also consider employing the U.S. dollar as the functional currency when the cumulative 3-year inflation rate nears 100 percent with no abatement foreseen. In addition, management should consider using the most recent 3-year period ending on the last day of the latest period reported, although any 3-year period may be used for this test.

Each foreign entity must be measured in its functional currency and the result translated into the reporting company's currency for purposes of preparing their consolidated financial statements, a two-step conversion process. Under FAS No. 52, remeasurement into the functional currency is necessary when the foreign entity's

Table 1   Cost of Fixed Assets in Argentina

Original Cost		
December 1974	100,000,000 pesos	
Translated Into U.S. Dollars	Exchange Rate	
December 1974	.2	$20,000,000
December 1980	.000495	$ 49,500
December 1981	.000094	$ 9,400

618   CHAPTER 12: ACCOUNTING FOR MULTIPLE ENTITIES

Table 2   Remeasurement of Beginning Deferred Income Taxes

Beginning Period	Local Currency Amount	Exchange Rate	Deferred Income Taxes	Retained Earnings
FAS No. 8 Translation	50,000	.65(Hist.)	$32,500	$209,500
FAS No. 52 Remeasurement	50,000	.60(Curr.)	30,000	
Decrease in deferred income taxes; increase in retained earnings			$ 2,500	2,500
Retained Earnings as Restated				$212,000

books or specific accounts are not maintained in the functional currency, while translation into the reporting currency is required when the functional currency is not the reporting currency. Consequently, when the functional currency is the U.S. dollar, remeasurement will obviate the need for translation. Under FAS No. 8, conversion into the reporting company currency was a one-step process because the U.S. dollar was always used as the measuring base.

REMEASUREMENT

Remeasurement under FAS No. 52 is similar to the translation principle required by FAS No. 8. In fact, when the U.S. dollar is the functional currency, this process parallels FAS No. 8's translation process, producing congruent accounting results and placing no additional burden on preparers of financial statements. The likeness of these two approaches can be demonstrated by comparing the listing of accounts converted at historical exchange rates in Appendix B of FAS No. 52 and Appendix A of FAS No. 8. Inventories, prepaid expenses, and capital assets are included in both appendixes. Although equity accounts are not listed in Appendix B of FAS No.

52, it appears that they should also be remeasured using historical exchange rates. In addition, as in the past, detailed records of inventory and capital assets will be necessary to keep track of these assets and charge appropriate cost of sales and depreciation amounts using historical exchange rates. Furthermore, the lower of cost or market test should be applied to inventory after remeasurement into the functional currency, because FAS No. 52 requires all measurements in the functional currency.

However, FAS No. 52 requires remeasurement of deferred income taxes at current rather than historical exchange rates, as was mandated by FAS No. 8. This process produces a one-time adjustment to beginning retained earnings resulting from conversion of beginning period deferred income taxes at the current exchange rate, as illustrated in **Table 2.**

This difference between the current and historical exchange rates at the start of the period yields a $2,500 decrease in deferred income taxes and a corresponding increase in retained earnings. During subsequent periods, exchange-rate changes will affect the measurement of deferred income taxes and result in exchange gains and losses in income similar to other monetary accounts such as cash and receivables.

TRANSLATION

After the remeasurement procedure, translation is the second step of the two-step conversion process used to express foreign financial statements in the reporting currency. This conversion process produces translation adjustments because assets and liabilities are converted at current exchange rates while equity accounts are converted at historical exchange rates. These translation adjustments are excluded from income because translation is performed only for preparation of the reporting company financial statements and does not anticipate liquidation of the foreign investment or exchange into U.S. dollars. Essentially, translation under FAS No. 52 values functional currency net assets at the dollar equivalent using the current exchange rate and requires an adjusting entry to balance the dollar net worth. Previously, FAS No. 8 required companies to report translation exchange gains and losses for monetary accounts in current income.

Because FAS No. 52 must be adopted at the start of the year, beginning translation adjustments in equity will result from the difference between nonmonetary accounts suh as inventories, capital assets, and deferred income taxes translated at current exchange rates under FAS No. 52 and historical exchange rates under FAS No. 8, as illustrated in **Table 3.**

Stated differently, the beginning period translation adjustment may be computed from the difference between how FAS No. 52 and FAS No. 8 measure net assets. The $92,500 beginning translation adjustment of Table 3 is a reduction of equity, which is compatible with the reduction in current exchange rates. In addition, FAS No. 52 requires any income taxes related to translation adjustments to be recorded in equity in accordance with Accounting Principles Board Opinion Nos. 11, 23, and 24. Because a separate component of equity is used to record translation adjustments, beginning retained earnings is not affected unless prior year financial statements are restated.

Under FAS No. 52, U.S. dollar financial statements will more closely reflect the local currency financial results and relationships for self-contained entities because all assets and liabilities are converted at the same current exchange rate. Consequently, financial ratios of the U.S. dollar and local currency statements are also similar. Given the current trend of a stronger U.S. dollar resulting in declining U.S. dollar equivalent exchange rates, lower product cost and depreciation values are reflected in the FAS No. 52 U.S. dollar income statement, resulting in higher gross margin, as illustrated in **Table 4.**

Current period exchange rate fluctuations affecting net assets are reflected in the translation adjustment account, directly impacting equity. Declining U.S. dollar equivalent exchange rates produce results similar to that of **Table 5.**

The decline in the U.S. dollar equivalent exchange rate is applied to beginning net assets and current period net income, increasing the translation adjustment account from $92,500 to $140,000 and thereby reducing equity.

Upon sale or "substantially complete liquidation" of a foreign investment, the related translation adjustment recorded in equity should be realized. Because FAS No. 52 does not totally define "upon substantially complete liquidation," some professional judgment will be required to determine when realization should occur.

Information systems will be affected minimally by remeasurement, while some system changes will be required for translation, resulting in less recordkeeping for financial reporting because historical dollar vintage accounts are no longer necessary

CHAPTER 12: ACCOUNTING FOR MULTIPLE ENTITIES

Table 3 Beginning Translation Adjustment Computation

Beginning Period Accounts	Local Currency Balance	FAS No. 8		FAS No. 52		
		Historical Exchange Rate	Amount	Current Exchange Rate	Amount	Beginning Translation Adjustment
Inventory	300,000	.65	$195,000	.60	$180,000	$(15,000)
Net plant & equipment	1,000,000	.68	680,000	.60	600,000	(80,000)
Deferred income taxes	(50,000)	.65	(32,500)	.60	(30,000)	2,500
	1,250,000		$842,500		$750,000	$(92,500)

Table 4   Income Statement Accounts

| Income Statement Accounts | Local Currency Amount | FAS No. 8 | | FAS No. 52 | |
		Historical Exchange (H) Rate	Amount	Current Average Exchange Rate	Amount
Revenue	1,500,000	.55	825,000	.55	825,000
Product cost	(670,000)	.65(H)	(435,500)	.55	(368,500)
Gross margin	830,000		389,500		456,500
Depreciation	(270,000)	.68(H)	(183,600)	.55	(148,500)

for nonmonetary assets and liabilities. However, historical vintage accounts may be essential for income tax purposes, intercompany margin elimination from affiliated company equipment, and identification of the effect of FAS No. 52 in the year of adoption for management's benefit. Under FAS No. 52, additional system changes will be necessary to disclose appropriately the activity in the translation adjustment account, including beginning and ending balances, aggregate translation adjustment, allocated income taxes, and amount realized in income as a result of sale or liquidation of a foreign investment.

MINIMIZING THE IMPACT OF EXCHANGE GAINS AND LOSSES

Under FAS No. 52, when the U.S. dollar is the functional currency, exchange gains and losses recorded in income resemble FAS No. 8 results except for the impact of deferred income taxes. Like FAS No. 8, exchange gains and losses are produced from foreign-denominated transactions or balances, such as a Swiss franc receivable included in British pound financial statements and translation of monetary accounts such as cash, receivables, payables, and debt. However, exchange gains and losses resulting from U.S. dollar-denominated transactions included in foreign financial statements are exactly offset by the translation process and, therefore, do not affect income. To minimize the impact of these exchange gains and losses, the "neutrality concept" should be used to balance the foreign-denominated transactions and monetary accounts. For example, a forward ex-

Table 5
COMPUTATION OF ENDING TRANSLATION ADJUSTMENT ACCOUNT

	Amount
Beginning translation adjustment per Table 3	$(92,500)
Beginning net assets × annual decrease in exchange rates (195,000) × (.60 − .50)	(19,500)
Net income × decrease from average to year-end exchange rate (560,000 × (.55 − .50)	(28,000)
Translation Adjustment Ending Balance	$(140,000)

CHAPTER 12: ACCOUNTING FOR MULTIPLE ENTITIES

change contract could be used to sell Swiss francs at a future date, thereby creating a Swiss franc liability to exactly offset the foreign receivable in the British financial statements. In addition, if a wholly owned British company holds net monetary assets of 100,000 pounds, a corporation might choose to liquidate pound assets or purchase pound liabilities of 100,000 pounds.

When the local currency is the functional currency, foreign denominated transactions including U.S. dollar trade accounts contained in overseas financial statements will produce exchange gains and losses in income. These foreign denominated transactions, particularly U.S. dollar accounts, are most likely to occur on intercompany activity between a multinational corporation's affiliated companies. To minimize this exchange impact, forward exchange contracts typically are purchased to permit the company to buy foreign currency forward at a fixed rate. However, a premium or discount representing the difference between the current spot rate and the forward rate must be paid. **Table 6** illustrates how a forward exchange contract is used to minimize the exchange impact on a U.S. dollar-denominated payable account with the parent company. Assume a foreign entity purchases equipment billed in 37,500 U.S. dollars from the parent company, creating a U.S. dollar liability in their books. To minimize any impact of exchange fluctuations, a $37,500 forward exchange contract is purchased creating an identical U.S. dollar receivable. On July 1, a dollar was valued at .55 (i.e., spot rate (SR)), the forward rate (FR) was .52, while on December 31, the spot rate was .50. Thus, the potential 6818 local currency exchange loss was minimized

Table 6   Use of Forward Exchange Contract to Hedge U.S. $ Intercompany Payable Local Currency Subsidiary Records (July 1, 1982 to December 31, 1982)

	Due Jan. 1, 1983	Local Currency Exchange (Gain) Loss*
Loss on U.S. $ Intercompany Payable:		
July 1, 1982 $37,500 ÷ .55 SR**	(68,182)	
Dec. 31, 1982 $37,500 ÷ .50 SR	(75,000)	6,818
Gain on Forward Exchange Contract, U.S. $ Asset:		
July 1, 1982 $37,500 ÷ .55 SR	68,182	
Dec. 31, 1982 $37,500 ÷ .50 SR	75,000	(6,818)
Computation of Premium		
$37,500 ÷ .55 SR (July 1, 1982)	68,182	
$37,500 ÷ .52 FR***	72,115	3,933
Foreign Local Currency Exchange Loss		
		3,933

*Translated into U.S. dollars at weighted average exchange rate.
**SR = Spot Rate
***FR = Forward Rate

by the payment of the 3,933 local currency premium.

FAS No. 52 permits exchange gains and losses resulting from long-term intercompany borrowings between affiliated companies to be recorded in the translation adjustment component of equity, net of related deferred income taxes. Long-term in this context means that settlement is not planned or anticipated. In Table 6, if the U.S. dollar intercompany payable were determined to be long-term, the U.S. dollar equivalent of 6,818 local currency could be transferred to equity. Thus, the resulting impact of exchange rate movements on income is further minimized to the extent intercompany financing is long-term, obviating the necessity for a forward exchange contract.

HEDGING AN INVESTMENT

The effect of exchange rate movements on a net foreign investment affects equity through the translation adjustment account under FAS No. 52. Table 5 illustrated how a decrease in exchange rates applied to net assets reduced U.S. dollar reported equity in foreign financial statements. The opposite occurs when exchange rates increase.

The exchange gain or loss exposure on equity has increased significantly because of the inclusion of inventories and capital assets. Under FAS No. 8, inventories and capital assets did not produce exchange gains and losses, because they were converted at historical exchange rates. Recognizing that hedging, like any other insurance policy, expends corporate resources, firms should consider the cost-benefits of hedging a net foreign investment to minimize adverse translation effects.

In addition, other issues should be evaluated when considering a net investment hedging policy, including the following: assets to keep pace with inflation; ability to raise prices for exchange rate movements; timing differences of exchange impact in equity versus income; and overall impact of exchange on retained earnings and translation adjustment account.

FAS No. 52 permits using designated forward exchange contracts or any other foreign currency transactions to hedge net investments. Exchange gains and losses, including premiums and discounts related to such hedging devices, should be recorded in the translation adjustment component of equity, net of any related deferred income taxes provided. However, the amount transferred to equity may not exceed the current period translation adjustment resulting from translation of net assets.

Table 7 illustrates a hedge of a net investment. The parent company borrows 195,000 local currency at the beginning of the period to hedge its 195,000 local currency net investment. The decrease in ex-

Table 7
HEDGE OF A NET INVESTMENT

	Equity Gain (Loss)
Local currency debt × annual decrease in exchange rate 195,000 × (.60 − .50)	$19,500
Current period increase in translation adjustment account—see Table 5. (140,000 − 92,500)	(47,500)
Change in Translation Account During 1982	$(28,000)

Note: Gains on the foreign currency transaction loan exceeding $47,500 should be reported in the Income Statement.

CHAPTER 12: ACCOUNTING FOR MULTIPLE ENTITIES

change rates produces a 19,500 local currency gain recorded in equity, which helps offset the current period translation loss of 47,500 local currency. The parent company could have also elected to increase its local currency borrowings as its net investment increased during the period, which would have further reduced the translation loss in equity.

A company entering into significant foreign currency commitments such as the purchase of inventory or capital assets may find it advantageous to ''freeze'' the cost of its functional currency by entering into an immediate forward exchange contract. Because this event represents a commitment rather than a transaction, the accounting transaction is not recognized until goods or services are received. FAS No. 52, like FAS No. 8, permits the gain or loss and premium or discount on the contract to be deferred and included in the measurement of the related foreign currency transaction until the underlying transaction is recorded. In Table 6, if a commitment to purchase the inventory had been entered into earlier in the year, the cost of the commitment could have been ''frozen'' with the forward exchange contract. Both the gain and premium recorded during the commitment period could have been deferred and included in the cost of the related asset.

Under FAS No. 52, more liberal criteria are permitted for hedging a commitment provided the commitment is firm and resulting gains and losses are not deferred when it causes losses to be recorded in later periods. However, under FAS No. 52, hedges must be designated and effective. FAS No. 52 permits any foreign currency transaction, including those denominated in currencies moving in tandem, to hedge a commitment, whereas FAS No. 8 only permitted forward exchange contracts denomi-

nated in the same currency. In addition, FAS No. 8 required forward contracts to extend from the commitment date to the anticipated transaction date or later.

All consolidation journal entries should be reviewed to determine if they are affected by the new translation method, particularly for entities using a local functional currency and recognizing profits on affiliated company equipment shipments. Intercompany profits should be eliminated using exchange rates in effect on the dates of sales or transfers or some other reasonable approximation; this may require maintaining vintaged accounts for significant intercompany inventory and capital assets, depending upon the method used. Assume in Table 4 that gross margin is created from intercompany shipments, affording higher gross margin under FAS No. 52 because product cost is translated at a lower current exchange rate. This result requires additional elimination of gross margin from intercompany inventory and capital assets residing in the balance sheet when the local currency is the functional currency.

ACCOUNTING HAZARDS

When the requirements of FAS No. 52 are applied to individual operations, other areas of generally accepted accounting principles will be affected, including constant dollar and current cost information; equity investments; changes in accounting policies; consolidating purchase adjustments; discontinued operations; segment information; and capitalization of interest cost.

Multinational corporations with significant foreign operations are faced with the task of implementing new foreign currency translation principles. These new principles, however, raise complex issues that require careful planning.

QUESTIONS

1. Consolidated statements are proper for Neely, Inc., Randle, Inc., and Walker, Inc., if

a. Neely owns 80 percent of the outstanding common stock of Randle and 40 percent of Walker; Randle owns 30 percent of Walker.

b. Neely owns 100 percent of the outstanding common stock of Randle and 90 percent of Walker; Neely bought the stock of Walker one month before the balance sheet date and sold it seven weeks later. NO

c. Neely owns 100 percent of the outstanding common stock of Randle and Walker; Walker is in legal reorganization.

d. Neely owns 80 percent of the outstanding common stock of Randle and 40 percent of Walker; Reeves, Inc., owns 55 percent of Walker.

(handwritten: A) Neely Inc 80% 40% Randle 30% WALKER; Direct 40% indirect 24% 80% x 30%; Total 64%)

2. On October 1, Company X acquired for cash all of the outstanding common stock of Company Y. Both companies have a December 31 year end and have been in business for many years. Consolidated net income for the year ended December 31 should include net income of

a. Company X for 3 months and Company Y for 3 months

b. Company X for 12 months and Company Y for 3 months

c. Company X for 12 months and Company Y for 12 months

d. Company X for 12 months, but no income from Company Y until Company Y distributes a dividend

(handwritten: B)

3. Which of the following types of transactions or situations would preclude a company from accounting for a business combination as a pooling of interests?

a. Immediately after the combination the acquiring corporation reacquires the stock issued to effect the combination.

b. The combined company sells assets that were acquired in the combination, which represent duplicate facilities.

c. The acquiring corporation acquires only 90 percent of the voting common stock of the other corporation in exchange for its voting common stock.

d. The combination is effected within 9 months of the initiation of the plan of combination.

(handwritten: A)

4. On December 1, 1988, Company B was merged into Company A with Company B going out of existence. Both companies report on a calendar-year basis. This business combination should have been accounted for as a pooling of interests, but it was mistakenly accounted for as a purchase. As a result of this error, what was the effect upon Company A's net earnings for the year ended December 31, 1988?

a. Overstated if B had a net loss from December 1, 1988, to December 31, 1988

(handwritten: D)

b. Understated if B had a net loss from January 1, 1988, to November 30, 1988

c. Overstated if B had net earnings from December 1, 1988, to December 31, 1988

d. Understated if B had net earnings from January 1, 1988, to November 30, 1988

5. Using the information from Question 4, what was the effect of this error upon A's asset valuations at December 1, 1988?

a. Overstated under any circumstances

b. Understated under any circumstances

c. Overstated if the fair value of B's assets exceeded their book value

d. Understated if the fair value of B's assets exceeded their book value

6. Arkin, Inc., owns 90 percent of the outstanding stock of Baldwin Company. Curtis, Inc., owns 10 percent of the outstanding stock of Baldwin Company. On the consolidated financial statements of Arkin, Curtis should be considered as

a. A holding company

b. A subsidiary not to be consolidated

c. An affiliate

d. A minority interest

7. A sale of goods, denominated in a currency other than the entity's functional currency, resulted in a receivable that was fixed in terms of the amount of foreign currency that would be received. Exchange rates between the functional currency and the currency in which the transaction was denominated changed. The resulting gain should be included as a (an)

a. Separate component of stockholders' equity

b. Deferred credit

c. Component of income from continuing operations

d. Extraordinary item

8. Which of the following is not a consideration in segment reporting for diversified enterprises?

a. Allocation of joint costs

b. Transfer pricing

c. Defining the segments

d. Consolidation policy

9. Which of the following is the appropriate basis for valuing fixed assets acquired in a business combination accounted for as a purchase carried out by exchanging cash for common stock?

a. Historic cost

b. Book value

c. Cost plus any excess of purchase price over book value of asset acquired

d. Fair value

10. A subsidiary may be acquired by issuing common stock in a pooling-of-interests transaction or by paying cash in a purchase transaction. Which of the following items would be reported in the consolidated financial statements at the same amount regardless of the accounting method used?

    a. Minority interest

    b. Goodwill

    c. Retained earnings

    d. Capital stock

11. Goodwill represents the excess of the cost of an acquired company over the

    a. Sum of the fair values assigned to identifiable assets acquired less liabilities assumed

    b. Sum of the fair values assigned to tangible assets acquired less liabilities assumed

    c. Sum of the fair values assigned to intangible assets acquired less liabilities assumed

    d. Book value of an acquired company

12. The theoretically preferred method of presenting minority interest on a consolidated balance sheet is

    a. As a separate item within the deferred credits section

    b. As a reduction from (contra to) goodwill from consolidation, if any

    c. By means of notes or footnotes to the balance sheet

    d. As a separate item within the stockholders' equity section

13. Meredith Company and Kyle Company were combined in a purchase transaction. Meredith was able to acquire Kyle at a bargain price. The sum of the market or appraised values of identifiable assets acquired less the fair value of liabilities assumed exceeded the cost to Meredith. After revaluing noncurrent assets to zero there was still some "negative goodwill." Proper accounting treatment by Meredith is to report the amount as

    a. An extraordinary item

    b. Part of current income in the year of combination

    c. A deferred credit and amortize it

    d. Paid-in capital

14. Which of the following is a potential abuse that can arise when a business combination is accounted for as a pooling of interests?

    a. Assets of the investee may be overvalued when the price paid by the investor is allocated among specific assets.

    b. Liabilities may be undervalued when the price paid by the investor is allocated to the specific liabilities.

    c. An undue amount of cost may be assigned to goodwill, thus potentially allowing for an overstatement of pooled earnings.

    d. Earnings of the pooled entity may be increased because of the combination only and *not* as a result of efficient operations.

15. How should long-term debt assumed in a business combination be shown under each of the following methods?

	Purchase	Pooling of interests
a.	Recorded value	Recorded value
b.	Recorded value	Fair value
c.	Fair value	Fair value
d.	Fair value	Recorded value

16. On November 1, 1988, Company X acquired all of the outstanding common stock of Company Y in a business combination accounted for as a pooling of interests. Both companies have a December 31 year end and have been in business for many years. Consolidated net income for the year ended December 31, 1988, should include net income for 12 months of

	Company X	Company Y
a.	Yes	Yes
b.	Yes	No
c.	No	No
d.	No	Yes

17. When translating foreign currency financial statements, which of the following accounts would be translated using current exchange rates?

	Property, plant, and equipment	Inventories carried at cost
a.	Yes	Yes
b.	No	No
c.	Yes	No
d.	No	Yes

18. How would the retained earnings of a subsidiary acquired in a business combination usually by treated in a consolidated balance sheet prepared immediately after the acquisition?
a. Excluded for both a purchase and a pooling of interests
b. Excluded for a pooling of interests but included for a purchase
c. Included for both a purchase and a pooling of interests
d. Included for a pooling of interests but excluded for a purchase

19. In financial reporting for segments of a business enterprise, the operating profit or loss of a segment should include

	Reasonably allocated common operating costs	Traceable operating costs
a.	No	No
b.	No	Yes
c.	Yes	No
d.	Yes	Yes

20. In a business combination, how should plant and equipment of the acquired corporation generally be reported under each of the following methods?

	Pooling of interests	Purchase
a.	Fair value	Recorded value
b.	Fair value	Fair value
c.	Recorded value	Recorded value
d.	Recorded value	Fair value

21. The profitability information that should be reported for each reportable segment of a business enterprise consists of
   a. An operating profit-or-loss figure consisting of segment revenues less traceable costs and allocated common costs
   b. An operating profit-or-loss figure consisting of segment revenues less traceable costs but not allocated common costs
   c. An operating profit-or-loss figure consisting of segment revenues less allocated common costs but not traceable costs
   d. Segment revenues only

22. A supportive argument for the pooling-of-interests method of accounting for a business combination is that
   a. It was developed within the boundaries of the historical-cost system and is compatible with it
   b. One company is clearly the dominant and continuing entity.
   c. Goodwill is generally a part of any acquisition.
   d. A portion of the total cost is assigned to individual assets acquired on the basis of their value.

23. A foreign subsidiary's functional currency is its local currency that has not experienced significant inflation. The weighted average exchange rate for the current year would be the appropriate exchange rate for translating

	Wages expense	Sales to customers
a.	Yes	Yes
b.	Yes	No
c.	No	No
d.	No	Yes

24. A subsidiary's functional currency is the local currency that has not experienced significant inflation. The appropriate exchange rate for translating the depreciation on plant assets in the income statement of the foreign subsidiary is the

   a. Exit exchange rate
   b. Historical exchange rate
   c. Weighted average exchange rate over the economic life of each plant asset
   d. Weighted average exchange rate for the current year

25. The Whit Company and the Berry Company, a manufacturer and retailer, respectively, entered into a business combination whereby the Whit Company acquired for cash all of the outstanding voting common stock of the Berry Company.

   Required:

   a. The Whit Company is preparing consolidated financial statements immediately after the consummation of the newly formed business combination. How should the Whit Company determine in general the amounts to be reported for the assets and liabilities of Berry Company? Assuming that the business combination resulted in goodwill, indicate how the amount of goodwill is determined.
   b. Why and under what circumstances should Berry Company be included in the entity's consolidated financial statements?

26. The Bert Company and the Lyle Company entered into a business combination accounted for as a pooling of interests.

   Required:

   a. How should the expenses related to effecting the business combination be handled, and why?
   b. How should the results of operations for the year in which the business combination occurred be reported? Why is this reporting appropriate?

27. Reporting forward exchange contracts continues to be a significant issue in accounting for foreign currency translation adjustments.

   Required:

   a. Discuss the one-transaction and two-transaction approaches to reporting forward exchange contracts.
   b. Discuss the proper accounting treatment for each of the following types of forward exchange contracts.
      i. Hedge of a recorded but unsettled foreign currency transaction.
      ii. Hedge of an identifiable foreign currency commitment.
      iii. Speculating in foreign currency.
      iv. Hedging a net investment.

28. In SFAS No. 52, the Financial Accounting Standards Board adopted standards for financial reporting of foreign currency exchanges. This release adopts the functional currency approach to foreign currency translation.

Required:
a. Discuss the functional currency approach to foreign currency translation.
b. Discuss the terms *translation* and *remeasurement* as they relate to foreign currency translation.

29. Part *a.* In order properly to understand current generally accepted accounting principles with respect to accounting for and reporting upon segments of a business enterprise, as stated by the Financial Accounting Standards Board in its Statement No. 14, it is necessary to be familiar with certain unique terminology.

Required:
 With respect to segments of a business enterprise, explain the following terms:
  i. Industry segment. — *like oil a gas*
  ii. Revenue. — *sales outside plus other sales segment*
  iii. Operating profit and loss. *Revenue minus*
  iv. Identifiable assets.
Part *b.* A central issue in reporting on industry segments of a business enterprise is the determination of which segments are reportable.

Required:
  i. What are the tests to determine whether or not an industry segment is reportable?
  ii. What is the test to determine if enough industry segments have been separately reported upon and what is the guideline on the maximum number of industry segments to be shown? *the industry segment has to be reported of 75%*

30. The board of directors of Kessler Corporation, Bar Company, Cohen, Inc., and Mason Corporation are meeting jointly to discuss plans for a business combination. Each of the corporations has one class of common stock outstanding. Bar also has one class of preferred stock outstanding. Although terms have not yet been settled, Kessler will be the acquiring or issuing corporation. Because the directors want to conform to generally accepted accounting principles, they have asked you to attend the meeting as an advisor.
Consider the following questions independently of the others and answer each in accordance with generally accepted accounting principles. Explain your answers.
a. Assume that the combination will be consummated August 31, 1988. Explain the philosophy underlying the accounting and how the balance

sheet accounts of each of the four corporations will appear on Kessler's consolidated balance sheet on September 1, 1988, if the combination is accounted for as a

 i. Pooling of interests.

 ii. Purchase.

b. Assume that the combination will be consummated August 31, 1988. Explain how the income statement accounts of each of the four corporations will be accounted for in preparing Kessler's consolidated income statement for the year ended December 31, 1988, if the combination is accounted for as a

 i. Pooling of interests.

 ii. Purchase.

c. Some of the directors believe that the terms of the combination should be agreed upon immediately and that the method of accounting to be used (whether pooling of interests, purchase, or a mixture) may be chosen at some later date. Others believe that the terms of the combination and the method to be used are very closely related. Which position is correct?

d. Kessler and Mason are comparable in size; Cohen and Bar are much smaller. How do these facts affect the choice of accounting method?

e. Bar was formerly a subsidiary of Tucker Corporation, which has no other relationship to any of the four companies discussing combination. Eighteen months ago Tucker voluntarily spun off Bar. What effect, if any, do these facts have on the choice of accounting method?

f. Kessler holds 2,000 of Bar's 10,000 outstanding shares of preferred stock and 15,000 of Cohen's 100,000 outstanding shares of common stock. All of Kessler's holdings were acquired during the first three months of 1988. What effect, if any, do these facts have on the choice of accounting method?

g. It is almost certain that Mrs. Victor Mason, Sr., who holds 5 percent of Mason's common stock, will object to the combination. Assume that Kessler is able to acquire only 95 percent (rather than 100 percent) of Mason's stock, issuing Kessler common stock in exchange.

 i. Which accounting method is applicable?

 ii. If Kessler is able to acquire the remaining 5 percent at some future time—in five years, for instance—in exchange for its own common stock, which accounting method will be applicable to this second acquisition?

h. Since the directors feel that one of Mason's major divisions will not be compatible with the operations of the combined company, they anticipate that it will be sold as soon as possible after the combination is consummated. They expect to have no trouble in finding a buyer. What effect, if any, do these facts have on the choice of accounting method?

31. Because of irreconcilable differences of opinion, a dissenting group within the management and board of directors of the Algo Company resigned and formed the Bevo Corporation to purchase a manufacturing division of the Algo Company. After negotiation of the agreement, but just before closing and actual transfer of the property, a minority stockholder of Algo notified Bevo that a prior stockholder's agreement with Algo empowered him to prevent the sale. The minority stockholder's claim was acknowledged by Bevo's board of directors. Bevo's board then organized Casco, Inc., to acquire the minority stockholder's interest in Algo for $75,000, and Bevo advanced the cash to Casco. Bevo exercised control over Casco as a subsidiary corporation with common officers and directors. Casco paid the minority stockholder $75,000 (about twice the market value of the Algo stock) for his interest in Algo. Bevo then purchased the manufacturing division from Algo.

   a. What expenditures are usually includable in the cost of property, plant, and equipment acquired in a purchase?

   b.   i. What are the criteria for determining whether to consolidate the financial statements of Bevo Corporation and Casco, Inc.?

      ii. Should the financial statements of Bevo Corporation and Casco, Inc., be consolidated? Discuss.

   c. Assume that unconsolidated financial statements are prepared. Discuss the propriety of treating the $75,000 expenditure in the financial statements of the Bevo Corporation as

      i. An account receivable from Casco.

      ii. An investment in Casco.

      iii. Part of the cost of the property, plant, and equipment.

      iv. A loss.

32. The most recently published statement of consolidated earnings of National Industries, Inc., appears as follows.

Charles Norton, a representative of a firm of security analysts, visited the central headquarters of National Industries for the purpose of obtaining more information about the company's operations.

In the annual report, National's president stated that National was engaged in the pharmaceutical, food processing, toy manufacturing, and metal working industries. Mr. Norton complained that the published statement of earnings was of limited utility in his analysis of the firm's operations. He said that National should have disclosed separately the profit earned in each of its component industries. Further, he maintained that several items appearing on the statement of consolidated retained earnings should have been included on the statement of earnings, namely, a gain of $633,400 on the sale of the furniture division in early March of the current year and an assessment for additional income taxes of $164,900 resulting from an examination of the returns covering the years ended March 31, 1987 and 1988.

NATIONAL INDUSTRIES, INC.
Statement of Consolidated Earnings
for the Year Ended March 31, 1988

Net sales	$38,041,200
Other revenue	407,400
Total revenue	38,448,600
Cost of products sold	27,173,300
Selling and administrative expenses	8,687,500
Interest expense	296,900
Total cost and expense	36,157,700
Earnings before income taxes	2,290,900
Provision for income taxes	1,005,200
Net earnings	$ 1,285,700

Required:
a. Explain what is meant by the term *conglomerate company*.
   i. Discuss the accounting problems involved in measuring net profit by industry segments within a company.
b. i. With reference to National Industries' statement of consolidated earnings, identify the specific items where difficulty might be encountered in measuring profit by each of its industry segments and explain the nature of the difficulty.
c. i. What criteria should be applied in determining whether a gain or loss should be excluded from the determination of net earnings?
   ii. What criteria should be applied in determining whether a gain or loss that is properly includable in the determination of net earnings should be included in the results of ordinary operations or shown separately as an extraordinary item after all other terms of revenue and expense?
   iii. How should the gain on the sale of the furniture division and the assessment of additional taxes each be presented in National's financial statements?

33. Part *a*. The Financial Accounting Standards Board discusses certain terminology essential to both the translation of foreign currency transactions and foreign currency financial statements in its Statement No. 8. Included in the discussion is a definition of and distinction between the terms *measure* and *denominate*.

Required:
   Define the terms *measure* and *denominate* as discussed by the Financial Accounting Standards Board and give a brief example that demonstrates the

distinction between accounts measured in a particular currency and accounts denominated in a particular currency.

Part *b*. There are several methods of translating foreign currency transactions or accounts reflected in foreign currency financial statements. Among these methods are current/noncurrent, monetary/nonmonetary, current rate, and the temporal method (the method adopted by the Financial Accounting Standards Board).

Required:

Define the temporal method of translating foreign currency financial statements. Specifically include in your answer the treatment of the following four accounts.

    i. Long-term accounts receivable.
    ii. Deferred income.
    iii. Inventory valued at cost.
    iv. Long-term debt.

BIBLIOGRAPHY

Arnold, Jerry, William W. Holder, and M. Herschelmann. "International Reporting Aspects of Segment Disclosure." *International Journal of Accounting* (Fall 1980), pp. 124–135.

Backman, Jules. "Economist Looks at Accounting for Business Combinations." *Financial Analysts Journal* (July–August 1970), pp. 39–48.

Baldwin, Bruce A. "Segment Earnings Disclosure and the Ability of Security Analysts to Forecast Earnings Per Share." *The Accounting Review* (July 1984), pp. 376–384.

Bartlett, Thomas M., Jr. "Problems in Accounting for a Business Purchase." *Financial Executive* (April 1973), pp. 52–71.

Baxter, George C., and James C. Spinney. "A Closer Look at Consolidated Financial Statement Theory." *CA Magazine* (January 1975), pp. 31–36.

Benjamin, James J., and Steven D. Grossman. "Foreign Currency Translation: An Update." *The CPA Journal* (February 1981), pp. 38–42.

Beresford, Dennis R., Norman N. Strauss, and John R. Klein. "A Summary of the FASB's Inflation Accounting Rules." *Financial Executive* (January 1980), pp. 12–19.

Bergstein, Sol. "More on Pooling of Interest." *Journal of Accountancy* (March 1972), pp. 83–86.

Brenner, Vincent C. "Empirical Study of Support for APB Opinion No. 16." *Journal of Accounting Research* (Spring 1972), pp. 200–208.

Briloff, Abraham J. "Dirty Pooling." *The Accounting Review* (July 1967), pp. 489–496.

Brown, Frank A., and Philip L. Kintzele. "The Effects of FASB Statement No. 14 on Annual Reports." *The Ohio CPA* (Summer 1979), pp. 98–103.

Burton, John C. *Accounting for Business Combinations: A Practical and Empirical Comment.* New York: Financial Executives Research Foundation, 1970.

Choi, Frederick D. S., and Gerhard G. Mueller. *An Introduction to Multinational Accounting.* Englewood Cliffs, N.J.: Prentice-Hall, Inc., 1978.

Cohen, Stuart. "Segment Reporting by Diversified Corporations." *Massachusetts CPA Review* (March–April 1979), pp. 15–20.

Dewberry, J. Terry. "A New Approach to Business Combinations." *Management Accounting* (November 1979), pp. 44–49.

Eigen, Martin M. "Is Pooling Really Necessary?" *The Accounting Review* (July 1965), pp. 563–570.

Eiteman, Dean S. *Pooling and Purchase Accounting.* Ann Arbor: University of Michigan, 1967.

Evans, Thomas G. "Some Concerns About Exposure After the FASB's Statement No. 8." *Financial Executive* (November 1976), pp. 28–30.

Fantl, Irving L. "Problems with Currency Translation—A Report on FASB No. 8." *Financial Executive* (December 1979), pp. 33–37.

Foster, William C. "Does Pooling Present Fairly?" *The CPA Journal* (December 1974), pp. 36–41.

Foster, William C. "The Illogic of Pooling." *Financial Executive* (December 1974), pp. 16–21.

Fotenos, James F. "Accounting for Business Combinations: A Critique of APB Opinion Number 16." *Stanford Law Review* (January 1971), pp. 330–346.

Fritzemeyer, Joe R. "Accounting for Business Combinations: The Evolution of an APB Opinion." *Journal of Accountancy* (August 1969), pp. 35–49.

Gagnon, Jean-Marie. "Purchase-Pooling Choice: Some Empirical Evidence." *Journal of Accounting Research* (Spring 1971), pp. 52–72.

Gitres, David L. "Negative Goodwill Paradox." *The CPA Journal* (December 1978), pp. 45–48.

Gunther, Samuel P. "Lingering Pooling Problems." *The CPA Journal* (June 1973), pp. 459–463.

Harmon, David Perry, Jr. "Pooling of Interests: A Case Study." *Financial Analysts Journal* (March–April 1968), pp. 82–88.

Hayes, Donald J. "Translating Foreign Currencies." *Harvard Business Review* (January–February 1972), pp. 6–18.

Horwitz, B., and R. Kolodny. "Segment Reporting: Hindsight After Ten Years." *Journal of Accounting, Auditing and Finance* (Fall 1980), pp. 20–35.

Lauver, R. C. "The Case for Poolings." *The Accounting Review* (January 1966), pp. 65–74.

Lurie, Adolph. "Segment Reporting—Past, Present, and Future." *The CPA Journal* (August 1979), pp. 27–30.

Lurie, Adolph. "Selecting Segments of a Business." *Financial Executive* (April 1980), pp. 34–44.

Mednick, Robert. "Companies Slice and Serve Up their Financial Results under FASB 14." *Financial Executive* (March 1979), pp. 44–56.

Moonitz, Maurice. *The Entity Theory of Consolidated Statements*. Brooklyn, N.Y.: The Foundation Press, 1951.

Norr, David. "Improved Foreign Exchange Disclosure for the Investor." *Financial Analysts Journal* (March–April 1977), pp. 17–20.

Rappaport, Alfred, and Eugene M. Lerner. *A Framework for Financial Reporting by Diversified Companies*. New York: National Association of Accountants, 1969.

Rappaport, Alfred, and Eugene M. Lerner. *Segment Reporting for Managers and Investors*. New York: National Association of Accountants, 1972.

Rodriguez, Rita M. "FASB No. 8: What Has It Done for Us?" *Financial Analysts Journal* (March–April 1977), pp. 40–47.

Rule, John E. "The Practical Business Effect of Exchange-Rate Fluctuations." *The Arthur Andersen Chronicle* (September 1977), pp. 63–75.

Sapienza, Samuel R. "Business Combinations." In Morton Backer, ed., *Modern Accounting Theory*. Englewood Cliffs, N.J.: Prentice-Hall, Inc., 1966, pp. 339–365.

Sapienza, Samuel R. "Distinguishing between Purchase and Pooling." *Journal of Accountancy* (June 1961), pp. 35–40.

Sapienza, S. R. "Divided House of Consolidations." *The Accounting Review* (July 1960), pp. 503–510.

Savage, Allan H., and B. J. Linder. "Meeting the Requirements of Line of Business Reporting." *Financial Executive* (November 1980), pp. 38–44.

Savage, Linda, and Joel Siegel. "Disposal of a Segment of a Business." *The CPA Journal* (September 1978), pp. 32–37.

Schrader, William J., Robert E. Malcom, and John J. Willingham. "In Support of Pooling." *Financial Executive* (December 1969), pp. 54–63.

Seidler, Lee J. "An Income Approach to the Translation of Foreign Currency Financial Statements." *The CPA Journal* (January 1972), pp. 26–35.

Shank, John K., Jesse F. Dillard, and Richard J. Murdock. *Assessing the Economic Impact of FASB No. 8.* New York: Financial Executives Research Foundation, 1979.

Shank, John K., Jesse F. Dillard, and Richard J. Murdock. "FASB No. 8 and the Decision Makers." *Financial Executive* (February 1980), pp. 18–23.

Shank, John K. "FASB Statement No. 8 Resolved Foreign Currency Accounting—or Did It?" *Financial Analysts Journal* (July–August 1976), pp. 55–61.

Shwayder, Keith R. "Accounting for Exchange Rate Fluctuations." *The Accounting Review* (October 1972), pp. 747–760.

Slesinger, Reuben E. "Conglomeration: Growth and Techniques." *Accounting and Business Research* (Spring 1971), pp. 145–154.

Snavely, Howard J. "'Pooling' Is Good Accounting." *Financial Analysis Journal* (November–December 1968), pp. 85–89.

Snavely, Howard J. "Pooling Should Be Mandatory." *The CPA Journal* (December 1975), pp. 23–26, and (April 1976), pp. 5–6.

Solomons, David. *Divisional Performance: Measurement and Control.* Homewood, Ill.: Richard D. Irwin, Inc., 1968.

Sprouse, Robert T. "Diversified Views about Diversified Companies." *Journal of Accounting Research* (Spring 1969), pp. 137–159.

Steedle, Lamont F. "Disclosure of Segment Information—SFAS 14." *The CPA Journal* (October 1983), pp. 34–47.

Watt, George C., Richard M. Hammer, and Marianne Burge. *Accounting for the Multinational Corporation.* New York: Financial Executives Research Foundation, 1978.

Willey, Russell W. "In Defense of FASB No. 8." *Management Accounting* (December 1979), pp. 36–40.

Wyatt, Arthur R. *A Critical Study of Accounting for Business Combinations.* New York: American Institute of Certified Public Accountants, 1963.

Wyatt, Arthur R. "Inequities in Accounting for Business Combinations." *Financial Executive* (December 1972), pp. 28–35.

13

CURRENT VALUE AND GENERAL PURCHASING POWER ACCOUNTING

this chapter is always in.

The use of historical-cost information in accounting records and financial statements has been a generally accepted accounting principle for a number of years. The widespread acceptance of this convention can be attributed to its objectivity and the transactions approach to income determination. Many accountants believe that only external exchanges should be measured and reported. Consequently, events that do not involve transactions are frequently ignored. For example, unrealized increases in asset values are rarely recorded, since no external arm's-length transaction has occurred.

Under the historical-cost concept, transactions are measured on the basis of the number of original dollars involved. Such measurements are considered to be "objective," since the amount of cost, or revenue, can be easily verified by referring to invoices, checks, deposit receipts, and other documents. Thus, *verifiability*—which essentially means that two accountants with similar knowledge and experience could review and evaluate a transaction and reach approximately the same conclusion—and *objectivity* are accounting concepts that have been closely related to the historical-cost concept over the years.

The significance of objectivity as a major criterion for the recognition and measurement of accounting information has been questioned by various financial-statement user groups for over 50 years. This criticism arises because the use of historical-cost information frequently results in income not being recognized during the period in which it occurs (for example, holding gains), and because income is often overstated in periods of inflation. Two accounting problems are created by changing prices.

1. Valuation problem—the value of individual assets changes in relation to all other assets in the economy, irrespective of any changes in the general level of prices.
2. Measurement unit problem—the value of the measurement unit changes because prices change in general.

Opposition to historical cost has resulted in the development of two basically different viewpoints on the type of financial information that should be presented to account for the effect of changing prices and values on an enterprise. One viewpoint advocates statements prepared on the basis of current value. Current value is related to the economic concept of well-offness discussed in Chapter 2. This viewpoint addresses the valuation problem. A second viewpoint proposes financial statements that utilize historical cost and then adjust this information to account for the effect of the overall change in prices (price-level-adjusted financial statements). This viewpoint addresses the measurement unit problem.

There are several alternative methods of determining current value, such as entry price or replacement cost, exit or selling price, and the discounted present value of expected future cash flows. Similarly, price-level financial statements have been referred to under a variety of different names such as stabilized accounting, inflation accounting, financial reporting in units of general purchasing power, and constant dollar accounting. In the following sections we will discuss the general nature of these concepts and review the evolution of the reporting requirements to account for changes in current value and price.

CURRENT VALUE ACCOUNTING

The concept of *capital maintenance,* discussed in Chapter 2, indicates that no income is recognized until capital has been maintained and costs recovered. This concept requires all assets and liabilities to be stated at their current values, and various methods have been advocated to accomplish this objective.

The most common approaches to current-value measurement are: (1) entry price or replacement cost, (2) exit value or selling price, and (3) discounted present value of expected future cash flows. Each of these approaches will be discussed briefly in order to demonstrate their strengths, weaknesses, and characteristics in comparison to measuring in units of general purchasing power.

ENTRY PRICE OR REPLACEMENT COST

The concept of entry price or replacement cost accounting is not new, having been experimented with in the 1920s. Renewed interest in the concept was generated by the work of Edwards and Bell,[1] first published in 1961. This approach to asset valuation and income determination was also advanced by Sprouse and Moonitz[2] and a committee of the American Accounting Association,[3] among others.

When the value of a firm's assets is determined on the basis of entry price, the emphasis is on the cost of replacing the assets with similar assets. That is, what would it cost to purchase other assets similar to the ones the firm is now using? Each asset is therefore valued on the basis of what it would cost to replace it with a similar asset in a similar condition.

The replacement cost concept poses some immediate measurement problems. The firm may be able to determine precisely the replacement cost for inventories and certain other assets; however, for many assets, particularly the physical plant, there may not be a ready market from which to acquire replacement assets. Therefore, it may be impossible to determine precisely the cost of replacement. In such cases the firm may be required to appraise the assets in order to arrive at an approximation of their current replacement value. (An additional problem is that appraisals are typically exit values representing the current selling price of the assets.)

An alternative approach to approximate replacement cost is to use a specific purchasing power index. This differs from a general purchasing power index in that a specific index relates to a particular type of asset or business.

A specific index is designed to measure what has happened to a specific segment of the economy rather than the economy in total. An appropriate index is chosen and applied to the assets to obtain a measure of their replacement value.

An important note of caution about replacement cost is in order. Whether the replacement cost is determined by appraisal or by a specific index, the result is only an approximation of current value. Many critics of general purchasing power adjustments assert that the general index is irrelevant because it does not relate to the specific company. By the same token, a specific index may not relate perfectly to the assets of a given firm; thus, the specific index may be closer to value than a general index, but the result is still approximate. The actual value can only be determined when an exchange occurs.

[1]E. O. Edwards and P. W. Bell. *Theory and Measurement of Business Income* (Berkeley, Calif.: University of California Press, 1961), pp. 33–69.

[2]Robert T. Sprouse and Maurice Moonitz, "A Tentative Set of Board Accounting Principles for Business Enterprises," *Accounting Research Study No. 3* (New York: American Institute of Certified Public Accountants, 1962).

[3]American Accounting Association, *A Statement of Basic Accounting Theory.* (Evanston, Ill., American Accounting Association, 1966).

EXIT VALUE OR SELLING PRICE

A second concept for value determination is exit value or selling price. This valuation approach, which was first advocated by McNeal,[4] in the 1930s, requires an assessment of each asset from a disposal point of view. That is, all assets—inventory, plant, equipment, etc.—are valued on the basis of what the selling price would be if the firm chose to dispose of its assets.

This concept poses several measurement problems. First, there is the basic problem of determining a selling price for the assets, such as property, plant, and equipment, for which there is no ready market. Second, there is a question as to which selling price should be used. For example, should the value be based upon forced liquidation prices or prices arising from sales in the normal course of business? The latter approach may be feasible for assets such as inventory but may be impracticable, if not impossible, for the physical plant, since it would not be disposed of in the normal course of operation.

One can argue that replacement costs are more relevant measures of the current value of fixed assets, whereas exit values are better measures of the current value of inventory items. Since management intends to use rather than sell fixed assets, their value in use is what it would cost to replace them. On the other hand, inventory is purchased for resale. Hence, its value is directly related to its selling price to customers.

DISCOUNTED CASH FLOW

A third approach to the measurement of asset value is discounted cash flow. According to this concept, the present value of the future cash flows expected to be received from the assets and liabilities is the relevant value of the assets and liabilities disclosed on the balance sheet. Income is then measured as the difference between the present value of the assets and liabilities at the end of the period and their present value at the beginning of the period. This measurement process is similar to the economic concept of income and is perhaps the closest approximation of the actual value of the assets.

A strong argument can be made for the concept of discounted cash flow. All assets are presumed to be acquired for the future service potential they can provide the firm. Furthermore, there is a presumption that the initial purchase price was paid because of a belief that the asset would generate sufficient revenue in the future to make its acquisition worthwhile. Thus, either implicitly or explicitly, the original cost was related to the present value of expected cash flows. This concept, in effect, says that the same rationale that was applied to the

[4]Kenneth McNeal, *Truth In Accounting* (Philadelphia: University of Pennsylvania Press, 1939).

original purchase should be applied at the end of each period to measure current value and periodic income.

There are three major measurement problems with the concept of discounted cash flow. First, the concept depends on an estimate of future cash flows by time periods. As a result, both the amount of cash to be generated in the future and the timing of that cash flow must be determined.

The second problem arises once the amount and timing of the cash flow has been estimated. In order to determine the current value of those future flows, they must be discounted to the present, since it is obvious that with purchasing power changes a dollar received in the future is not as valuable as a dollar received today. A discount factor must, therefore, be selected and applied to the estimates of future cash flows.

A third problem is created by the fact that the assets of a firm are interrelated. Revenues are generated by the combined use of a company's resources. Therefore, even if the company's future cash flows and the appropriate discount rate could be precisely determined, it would not be practicable to determine exactly how much each asset contributed to those cash flows. As a result, the discounted present value of individual firm assets cannot be determined and summed to determine the present value of a company.

Use of present-value techniques to measure current value can only be as valid as the estimates of future cash flows, the timing of those flows, and the appropriateness of the discount factor. To the extent that these estimates are valid, the measurement of the present value of future service potential is probably the most relevant measurement to disclose on the balance sheet, that is, relevant in the sense that the balance sheet would provide information about the ability of the assets to produce income in the future. As indicated previously, if assets are measured in this manner, net income will be the difference between the end-of-year and beginning-of-year balances.

FINANCIAL REPORTING IN UNITS OF GENERAL PURCHASING POWER

As indicated in Chapter 1, a basic principle of accounting is the measurement of transactions in terms of dollars. There is also an implicit, if not explicit, assumption that the dollar is a stable measuring unit, since dollar measurements are added, subtracted, multiplied, and divided. However, the purchasing power of the dollar changes; hence, the stable-dollar assumption has never been completely valid. Nevertheless, the position of the authoritative bodies over the years has been that the amount of change in prices has been relatively insignificant. Although this position may have been accepted in the earlier days of accounting, there has been a growing consensus that the measuring unit must be adjusted to reflect the impact of inflation.

HISTORICAL PERSPECTIVE

The literature on the impact of changes in value of the measuring unit is rather lengthy. The following comments are not intended to be a comprehensive survey of this literature; instead, they are provided to illustrate the development of current thought on the subject.

The most comprehensive of the early efforts to bring about changes in the measuring unit can be attributed to Henry Sweeney. In the early 1930s he published a series of articles on the subject, and his book, *Stabilized Accounting*,[5] published in 1936, set forth the procedures for adjusting financial statements to a common-sized dollar. Sweeney was motivated by the belief that it is impossible to develop meaningful financial statements when elements are measured in different-sized dollars.

In 1947,[6] 1948,[7] and 1953,[8] the Committee on Accounting Procedure of the American Institute of Certified Public Accountants addressed itself to the accounting problems created by the rather dramatic increase in the general level of prices following World War II. The major concern of the committee was the amount of depreciation expense being charged against current income, that is, the historical-cost depreciation write-off of the assets was much lower than current costs. However, the committee concluded that depreciation expense should be based on historical cost. In each of these documents, the committee also gave its full support to the use of supplementary financial schedules, explanations, or footnotes which management might use to explain that enterprise profits sufficient to replace productive facilities at current prices must be retained to remain in business.

In 1963 the AICPA issued a research study on the effects of price level changes. *Accounting Research Study No. 6*[9] strongly suggested that unless financial statements were adjusted for changes in the general purchasing power of the dollar they were likely to be misleading. The study further proposed the methods and procedures for making the necessary adjustments. (The adjustment procedures will be discussed in a later section of this chapter.)

The Accounting Principles Board reacted to ARS No. 6 and inflation in 1969

---

[5]Henry W. Sweeney, *Stabilized Accounting* (New York: Harper & Bros., 1936).

[6]Accounting Research Bulletin No. 33, "Depreciation and High Costs" (New York: American Institute of Certified Public Accountants, 1947).

[7]Committee on Accounting Procedure, letter to American Institute of Certified Public Accountants members reaffirming the recommendations of Accounting Research Bulletin No. 33, October 1948.

[8]Accounting Research Bulletin No. 43, Chapter 9, Section A, "Depreciation and High Costs" (New York: American Institute of Certified Public Accountants, 1953).

[9]Staff of the Accounting Research Division, *Accounting Research Study No. 6*, "Reporting the Financial Effects of Price-Level Changes." (New York: American Institute of Certified Public Accountants, 1963).

when it issued APB Statement No. 3.[10] In essence, the board said that it agreed with ARS No. 6 that price-level-adjusted statements contain much useful information that would not otherwise be available to the users of historical dollar financial statements. Therefore, it was concluded that general price level information could be presented as a supplement to the basic historical dollar financial statements but not an integral part of the basic statements.

The APB went on to state that the degree of inflation or deflation in an economy might become so great that historical dollar statements would lose their significance, but such was not the case in the United States at that time. In a footnote, the board observed that it had not determined the degree of inflation or deflation which might cause general price level statements to become more meaningful than historical-cost statements.

In 1974, the Financial Accounting Standards Board decided that inflation had become a significant enough problem, to warrant some further action and issued a proposed statement entitled "Financial Reporting in Units of General Purchasing Power."[11] This statement, which was rejected in 1976, would have required the following information, at a minimum, to be presented in units of general purchasing power for each period for which an income statement was presented.

1. *Total revenue.*
2. *Depreciation of property, plant and equipment.*
3. *Net general purchasing power gain or loss from holding monetary assets and liabilities. (If a complete or condensed general purchasing power income statement is presented, this amount shall be presented as a separate item.)*
4. *Income from continuing operations (that is, income including net general purchasing power gain or loss from holding monetary assets and liabilities but before discontinued operations, extraordinary items, and the cumulative effect of accounting changes.)*
5. *Net income.*
6. *Net income per common share.*
7. *Cash dividend per common share.*[12]

There was a further requirement that, for each date for which a balance sheet is presented, the following information, at a minimum, shall be presented in units of general purchasing power.

1. *Inventories.*
2. *Working capital.*

[10]Accounting Principles Board Statement No. 3, "Financial Statements Restated for General Price-Level Changes" (New York: American Institute of Certified Public Accountants, 1969).
[11]Proposed Statement of Financial Accounting Standards, "Financial Reporting in Units of General Purchasing Power" (Stamford, Conn.: Financial Accounting Standards Board, 1974).
[12]Ibid., p. 17.

3. Total property, plant, and equipment, net of accumulated depreciation.
4. Total assets.
5. Total common stockholders' equity.[13]

Despite the FASB's failure to act, in 1976 the SEC decided that inflation had become a serious enough problem to warrant disclosure of some of its effects in financial statements. Accounting Series Release No. 190 (discussed in Chapter 6) required certain companies to disclose data on the replacement cost of their productive capacity and inventories.

In 1979, the FASB again opened the question of the effects of changing prices on financial reporting. This review resulted in the publication of FASB Statement No. 33, "Financial Reporting and Changing Prices."[14] As a result, most large companies were required to report both constant-dollar and current-cost data as supplemental information.

The general requirements of ASR No. 190 and FASB Statement No. 33 are contrasted in Table 13.1.

In addition to the historical aspects of this problem, there are several key conceptual issues involved in measuring with units of general purchasing power that need to be considered.

MEANING AND SIGNIFICANCE OF GENERAL PURCHASING POWER ADJUSTMENTS

The concept of general purchasing power deals with the inflationary or deflationary forces operating in the economy as a whole that have a general impact on the purchasing power of the dollar. (The remainder of this discussion will examine inflation; however, in the event of deflation, the same rationale would apply, only in reverse.) This concept does not refer to a dollar spent on a specific good; rather, it refers to dollars spent in general throughout the economy.

The basic rationale of general purchasing power adjustments is simply that two items should be measured with the same-size dollar so that they can be properly added together to get a valid result. This total is not intended to reflect what the items are worth, since this process is not concerned with value. Rather, the purpose is to measure all items with a common sized unit so that the impact of changes in the general purchasing power of the dollar can be determined. Consequently, if the desire is to measure some aspect of the economy using dollars, then those dollars should have the same purchasing power significance. Otherwise one might measure X in 1980 dollars and Y in 1988 dollars.

---

[13]Ibid.
[14]FASB Statement No. 33, "Financial Reporting and Changing Prices" (Stamford, Conn.: Financial Accounting Standards Board, 1979).

	Statement No. 33	**ASR No. 190**
APPLICABILITY		
Entities	Public companies	Registrants
Size tests	At least: $125 million of inventories and gross properties *or* $1 billion of total assets	Inventories and gross properties at least: $100 million *and* 10% of total assets
Reported in	Annual Reports (including Form 10-K)	Form 10-K
Reported for	Consolidated entity	Consolidated entity and each complete set of other statements
MEASUREMENT		
Approach	Current cost and constant dollar	Replacement cost
Focus	Replace assets (service potential) presently owned	Replace existing productive capacity
Assets covered	Inventories and properties (net), generally	Inventories and properties (gross and net), generally
Exceptions	Current cost—unprocessed natural resources and income-producing real estate	Land, oil and gas reserves, long-term construction contracts, productive capacity not to be replaced, and miscellaneous others
	Constant dollar—none	
Value ceiling	Use net realizable value or value in use when	None—but disclose net realizable value when

Table 13.1 (cont.)

	Statement No. 33	**ASR No. 190**
	lower than amounts under dual measurement approach	lower than replacement cost
Income measurement?	Yes, for both measurement methods	No—users cautioned against computing revised income
Depreciation	Same methods used in primary financial statements (generally)	Straight line

Source: Financial Reporting Developments, Ernst and Whinney, ''Inflation Accounting: Implementing FASB Statement No. 33,'' (December 1979), pp. 44–45.

For example, suppose the historical cost of two different items was $10, but one was purchased in 1980 and the other in 1988. Under current accounting practice the two would be added together and totaled as $20. However, there is clearly a difference in purchasing power in 1980 and 1988 because of the inflationary effect between those years. Therefore, if changes in purchasing power are to be considered the $10 from 1980 should be adjusted to the same-sized dollars as the $10 from 1988. The adjustment would be as follows, assuming 50 percent inflation from 1980 to 1988.

	Unadjusted	**Adjustment Factor (%)**	**Adjusted**
1980	$10	150	$15
1988	10	100	10
	$20		$25

The adjusted number simply means that the two amounts equal $25 of 1988 purchasing power, since the $10 in 1980 would have purchased one and one-half times more than the $10 in 1988.

The adjustment, of course, could have been in the opposite direction, in which case both amounts would be stated in 1980-size dollars. In that case, the adjustment would be as follows.

	Unadjusted	Adjustment Factor (%)	Adjusted
1980	$10	100	$10.00
1988	10	66 2/3	6.67
	$20		$16.67

This type of adjustment also expresses all amounts in the same-size dollars, but they are dollars of some previous period. The position of the FASB, and virtually all advocates of price level adjustments, is that it is more meaningful to express items in terms of current dollars. Hence, the first illustration reflects the preferred treatment.

Whichever approach is followed, the rationale is the same: all amounts are measured in the same-size monetary unit. For example, in measuring the fixed assets of a firm at the end of 1988, assets purchased in 1960 or any other year would be restated in terms of 1988 dollars; the total amount of fixed assets would be reflected in a common measuring unit.

The adjusted amount of fixed assets does not, and is not intended to, reflect the value of the assets, just as the unadjusted amount does not indicate value. To reiterate, the purpose of the adjustment is to measure all of the amounts with a common unit so that the mathematical processes of addition, subtraction, multiplication, and division can be legitimately accomplished. Therefore, these adjustments are not a departure from generally accepted accounting principles. The current concepts of revenue and expense recognition, depreciation methods, inventory valuation, and so forth are still applied.

The purpose of the adjustment for changes in general purchasing power is not only rather simple but, in the opinion of many supporters, absolutely essential. As indicated in Chapter 1, a fundamental accounting assumption is that the dollar is a stable measuring unit. Therefore, the various amounts on the financial statement can be manipulated mathematically. Clearly, accountants have been aware that the dollar is not completely stable, but there has been a general presumption that the rates of inflation and deflation either offset each other or were insignificant over time. Thus, the dollar has been treated as though it is to be essentially stable over time.

Since 1940, however, the movement of prices has been generally upward and the concept of stability no longer appears to be valid. Thus, in order to give the stable-dollar assumption validity, historical costs must be adjusted for changes in purchasing power. Purchasing power adjustments require an agreement on the proper index to use in order to measure in a common unit. However, the members of the financial community have not reached a consensus regarding which index to use. Some believe the consumer price index should be used, others believe a manufacturing type index should be used, and Accounting Research Study No. 6 and the exposure draft issued by the FASB recommended a general index based upon the gross national product—the GNP implicit price deflator index. The rationale for using the GNP deflator is that it reflects a broad segment of the economy and it takes into consideration more variables than any of the other indexes. However, FASB Statement No. 33 required the use of the consumer price index for all urban consumers (CPIUC). This index was chosen mainly because it is available on a monthly basis.

The use of the consumer price index is criticized because it is a general index and because it does not apply to the total economy and, therefore, may have little relevance to a particular business. This argument can be related to personal situations as well as to businesses. In a given year, suppose the cost of living, in general, increases by 10 percent. Depending upon their consumption patterns, some individuals would suffer more than a 10 percent decrease in purchasing power while others might suffer less or might even gain. For example, a person owning a home with fixed monthly mortgage payments would not have lost purchasing power on the dollars paid on the debt. The person renting on a month-to-month basis would probably have had a rent increase; therefore, each dollar spent on housing would have less purchasing power this year than in the previous year. This logic apparently was a factor in the FASB's decision to require the disclosure of both constant-dollar and current-cost information as discussed in the following sections.

STATEMENTS OF FINANCIAL ACCOUNTING STANDARDS NO.'S 33 AND 82

In 1980 the Financial Accounting Standards Board released its Statement of Financial Accounting Standards No. 33, "Financial Reporting and Changing Prices." This pronouncement required certain companies to experiment with the disclosure of information on the effects of changing prices on business enterprises. In general, SFAS No. 33 established a size test to determine if a company must comply with its provision (public companies with over $1 billion of assets or $125 million of inventories and property and equipment) and described the method for restating information on a constant-dollar and current-cost basis.

Later, in 1984, the FASB amended SFAS No. 33. This amendment, published as SFAS No. 82, "Financial Reporting and Changing Prices: Elimination of Certain Disclosures," was in response to an Exposure Draft issued by the board. A substantial majority of the comments received on this Exposure Draft supported the elimination of the requirement to disclose historical-cost/constant-dollar information. The reasons cited by the respondents for this position were (1) the elimination of confusion on the part of financial-statement users, (2) the elimination of complexity, (3) the reduction of the cost of compliance, and (4) the greater usefulness of current-cost information.

Specifically SFAS No. 82 eliminated the requirement for supplementary disclosure of constant dollar information for enterprise disclosing current cost/constant dollar information.

Companies meeting the size test are now required to disclose the following as supplementary information:

1. Income from continuing operations on a current cost/constant dollar basis.
2. Purchasing power gain or loss.
3. Increases or decreases in current cost amounts of inventory and property, plant and equipment.
4. Current cost amounts of inventory, and property plant and equipment at year-end.

In the following sections we will review the specific current-value and constant-dollar provisions of SFAS No. 33. This review will focus on methods of preparing the required information and the necessary disclosures. It is important to remember that although many of the constant-dollar provisions of SFAS No. 33 are no longer required for most corporations, companies that disclose this information must continue to follow the established guidelines. Additionally, an enterprise may now substitute historical-cost/constant-dollar information for the required current-cost information if there is no material difference between the amount of income from continuing operations that would be disclosed by the two methods.

CURRENT-COST ACCOUNTING UNDER FASB STATEMENT NO. 33

Current-cost accounting, as defined by the FASB, is an attempt to restate certain assets on the basis of their ''value to the business.'' Comprehensive application of current-cost accounting is not required by FASB Statement No. 33. Current-cost measurements are only required for inventories, property plant and equipment, and the related expenses. Additionally, current-cost measurements of liabilities are not required.

The following reasons were cited by the FASB for requiring only partial application of current-cost accounting.

1. Inventories and property, plant and equipment are normally the most significant assets of the companies affected by the FASB Statement No. 33. They also are most affected by specific price changes.
2. The FASB wished to restrict the costs of compliance with FASB Statement No. 33.
3. Current-cost measurements of some assets, such as goodwill and patents, may be too unreliable and subjective to serve any useful purpose.
4. The FASB did not wish to address the liability measurement issue at the time it was debating inflation accounting

Under FASB Statement No. 33, current-cost accounting is used to determine the following supplemental disclosures each year.

1. Income from continuing operations.
2. Increases or decreases in the current-cost amounts of inventory and property, plant and equipment. These amounts were to be disclosed both before and after the effects of general inflation.
3. Current cost of inventories and property, plant and equipment (net) at the latest balance sheet date.

The primary feature of the current-cost method is the separation of operating profit and holding gains (increases in the current cost of assets). For example, assume a company purchases inventory at $5,000 and subsequently sells it for $6,500 when the current cost of the inventory was $5,400. Historical cost and current cost incomes would be determined as follows.

	Historical Cost	Current Cost
Sales	$6,500	$6,500
Cost of goods sold	5,000	5,400
Income	$1,500	$1,100

The FASB believes that the current-cost presentation is more likely to provide a basis for assessing future cash flows. That is, the relationship of cost of goods sold to sales will probably remain stable over time when selling prices are determined by current costs. Whether or not these holding gains should be disclosed as income has not been decided by the FASB. The decision is based upon which capital maintenance theory is used. The two choices available are financial capital maintenance and physical capital maintenance.

Financial Capital. Capital is defined as the quantity of financial resources (dollars) invested in a business. Income is determined by the difference between revenues and the dollars (either nominal or constant dollars) invested in financial resources used to generate that revenue. In our preceding example the financial capital theory would say that total income was $1,500 even though it may be better to distinguish between operating profit ($1,100) and the results of holding activities ($400). The $400 increase in current cost would be described as a "holding gain," which connotes its status as income. It recognizes that a company could be better off as a result of wise (or fortunate) timing of its purchases, that is, before the price increases. Traditional historical-cost accounting generally reflects the financial capital theory.

Physical Capital. Capital is defined as the productive capacity (i.e., operating capability) of an enterprise. Income is not earned until an enterprise provides for maintenance (replacement) of its productive capacity, which is often represented by its inventories and properties. Essentially, the physical capital maintenance theory is concerned with providing an income figure that is a starting point in determining "distributable income." In our preceding example, the physical capital theory would say that only $1,100 of income has been earned rather than $1,500 because the $400 current-cost increase would be termed a "capital maintenance adjustment" and would not appear on the income statement, but would be shown as a direct adjustment to equity. While adoption of the physical capital maintenance theory would be a significant change over current GAAP, a similar concept is apparent in the Lifo inventory accounting method.

Until the FASB comes to a final decision on capital maintenance, it expects the disclosures required under Statement No. 33 to permit users to treat them as they see fit. That is, users may combine current-cost increases with income from continuing operations, or disregard them.

The disclosure of constant-dollar/current-cost information was also required by FASB Statement No. 33, in addition to current-cost increases measured before the effect of general inflation. For example, assume from the previous example that the increase in inflation between the time of the purchase of the inventory to the time of sale was 5 percent. The increase in current cost net of inflation would be determined as follows.

Increase in current costs	$400
Effect of general inflation ($5,000 × 0.05)	250
Increase in current cost net of general inflation	$150

This disclosure is intended to inform users how the increase in the current cost of a firm's inventories and properties compares with the rate of general inflation. In the event the rate of inflation is in excess of current cost, a negative amount would be reported as a decrease in current cost net of general inflation. Such disclosure is intended to indicate by how much the specific prices of these assets changed relative to general prices.

CONSTANT-DOLLAR ACCOUNTING UNDER FASB STATEMENT NO. 33

The adjustment of financial statement elements via constant-dollar accounting was an attempt to report all financial statement elements in dollars of the same purchasing power. FASB Statement No. 33 originally required constant-dollar accounting in three different areas.

1. As an adjustment to historical-cost figures to report in dollars of fixed purchasing power (historical cost–constant dollar).
2. As an adjustment to current cost to determine the effect of inflation upon inventories and productive capacity (current cost–constant dollar).
3. As an adjustment to five-year summary information to remove the effect of inflation from trend data (five-year summary–constant dollar).

These constant-dollar measurements were to be stated in constant dollars represented by the *average level* over the fiscal year of the consumer price index for all urban consumers. The use of the fiscal-year average is a departure from previous proposals that employed an end-of-year index. However, the use of the fiscal-year average simplifies the computation of income from continuing operations in that revenues and expenses generally will already reflect constant dollars (except for cost of goods sold and depreciation) because revenues are usually earned and expenses usually incurred fairly evenly throughout the year. (A year-end index was allowed to be used if comprehensive constant-dollar financial statements were presented.)

Historical Cost–Constant Dollar

The requirements of FASB Statement No. 33 resulted in only a partial application of constant-dollar accounting. The board intended to simplify the adjustment process by requiring only the restatement of those items most frequently affected by inflation inventories: property, plant, and equipment; monetary assets; and monetary liabilities. However, a company could have elected to disclose comprehensive constant-dollar financial statements.

Historical-cost–constant-dollar measurement under the provisions of Statement No. 33 is a five-step process.

1. Determine the year of acquisition (or the year of historical-cost measurement) for each item. This is termed the base year.
2. Determine the average consumer price index corresponding to the base year.
3. Determine the average consumer price index for the current period.
4. Restate the historical cost to the current-year average constant dollars by multiplying it by the current-year index over the base-year index.
5. Determine that the adjusted amount does not exceed recoverable amounts (net realizable value or value in use).[15]

For example, assume that an asset was acquired in 1980 for $20,000. The average consumer price index for 1980 was 116.3. The asset is being restated in

---

[15]Net realizable value is defined as the net amount of cash expected to be obtained from the sale of the asset. This amount would be used for all assets about to be sold. Value in use is the net present value of future cash flows expected to be derived from the use of an asset and is used when the asset is not expected to be sold.

1988 when the average consumer price index is 217.6 and the adjusted amount does not exceed the recoverable amount. The asset would be restated as follows.

1. $20,000.
2. 116.3.
3. 217.6.
4. $20,000 × 217.6/116.3 = $37,420.46.
5. $37,420.46, since the adjusted amount does not exceed the recoverable amount.

FASB Statement No. 33 requires two historical-cost–constant-dollar disclosures for the current year.

1. Income from continuing operations.
2. Purchasing power gain or loss on net monetary items.

Income from Continuing Operations

To meet the minimum requirements of FASB No. 33, income from continuing operations is adjusted by converting cost of goods sold, depreciation, amortization, and depletion to average-for-the-year constant dollars. Additionally, if inventories or property and plant and equipment were recorded at net realizable value or value in use (as defined previously), these write-downs were to be included in the computation of income from continuing operations and disclosed.

FASB Statement No. 33 goes on to state that these amounts

1. Need only be used for a group of assets when the amount is *materially* and *permanently* lower.
2. Need not be considered for individual assets unless they are used independently of other assets.

Purchasing Power Gains or Losses

Purchasing power gains and losses result from holding monetary assets and liabilities. Monetary items are those assets and liabilities that are fixed as to the dollar amount the firm has on hand, will receive, or will disburse. For example, if the firm has $1,000 receivable from a customer, $1,000 is the amount to be received, irrespective of the level of inflation or deflation. The same is true for monetary liabilities, such as bonds payable where the amount to be paid is the face value of the bond, which is fixed. Among the items commonly identified as *monetary* are

Cash.
Receivables (including allowances).
Accounts and notes payable.
Accrued expenses payable.
Bonds payable.
Other long-term debt.

The more common *nonmonetary* items are:

Marketable securities.
Inventories (except those produced under fixed-price contracts).
Prepaid expenses.
Property, plant, and equipment and the related accumulated depreciation.
Deferred income.
Patents, goodwill, and other intangibles.
Provision for guarantees.
Minority interest.
Preferred stock.
Common stock.
Additional paid-in capital.

The reason for identifying and distinguishing between monetary and nonmonetary items is that inflation and deflation have a different impact on each. For example, assume that a firm holds $100,000 of accounts receivable during a period of inflation. When the $100,000 is collected some time in the future, the cash will not have as much purchasing power as it has today. (The amount of loss in purchasing power depends upon both the time period and the rate of inflation.) Therefore, the firm will suffer a loss in purchasing power as a result of holding a monetary asset during an inflationary period. Just the opposite is true for holding monetary liabilities. If the firm owed $100,000, the dollars used to pay the debt in the future will not have as much purchasing power as when the dollars were borrowed. Thus, the firm will have a gain as a result of holding monetary liabilities during an inflationary period.

The effect of inflation on nonmonetary items is significantly different from the effect on monetary items because the nonmonetary items have the potential to keep pace with inflation, since their dollar amount is not fixed. For example, if the inflation rate is 10 percent during the year, property, plant, and equipment items similar to the ones owned by the firm would probably cost more dollars at the end of the year than at the beginning. Consequently, purchasing power gains and losses are *not* computed for nonmonetary items.

The gain or loss on net monetary items (monetary assets minus monetary liabilities) is disclosed separately and is not included in income from continuing operations. This requirement was intended to improve understanding by investors of the monetary components of working capital requirements and the amount of debt included in the capital structure of the company.

The purchase power gain or loss is determined by comparing the net monetary items at the beginning of the year and the end of the year and adjusting these amounts to fiscal-year averages. The result measures the average gain or loss in purchasing power experienced during the year. In a period of inflation, (1) a purchasing power gain will result from holding net monetary liabilities and (2) a purchasing power loss will result from holding net monetary assets. The following example illustrates the computation of purchasing power gains and losses.

Company A

	December 31	
	1988	**1987**
Monetary Items		
Cash	$ 20,000	$ 15,000
Accounts Receivable	80,000	75,000
Notes Receivable	115,000	100,000
Monetary Assets	$215,000	$190,000
Notes Payable	30,000	30,000
Accounts Payable	50,000	70,000
Long-term Debt	150,000	140,000
Monetary Liabilities	$230,000	$240,000
Net Monetary Liabilities	$ 15,000	$ 50,000

	Purchasing Power Gain or Loss		
	Historical Dollar	**Conversion Factor**	**Constant Dollars**
1. Balance 1/1/88	$50,000	217.6 (1988 avg. index) / 202.4 (1987 year-end index)	$53,754.94
2. Net Change	(35,000)	A	(35,000.00)
3. Balance 12/31/88	15,000	217.6 (1988 avg. index) / 230.0 (1988 year end index)	(14,191.30)
Purchasing Power Gain			$ 4,563.64B

A Assumed to be stated in average 1988 dollars.
B 1–2–3.

In computing the price level gain or loss, the ending monetary position adjusted for inflation for the year, $18,754.94 ($53,754.94 − 35,000), is compared to the actual monetary liabilities adjusted to the average dollar level, $14,191.30, resulting in a price level gain of $4,563.64.

FIVE-YEAR SUMMARY INFORMATION·

An additional requirement of FASB Statement No. 33 was the disclosure of the following summary information in constant dollars for each of its five most recent fiscal years.

Net Sales and Other Operating Revenues
Historical-Cost–Constant-Dollar Information

1. Income from continuing operations.
2. Income per common share from continuing operations.
3. Net assets at fiscal year end.

Current-Cost Information

1. Income from continuing operations.
2. Income per common share from continuing operations.
3. Net assets at fiscal year end.
4. Increases or decreases in the current-cost amounts of inventories and property, plant, and equipment, net of inflation.

Other Information

1. Purchasing power gain or loss on net monetary items.
2. Cash dividends declared per common share.
3. Market price per common share at fiscal year end.
4. Level of the consumer price index used to compute income from continuing operations. (Either the average-for-the-year index or the end-of-year index may be used if a company presents comprehensive supplementary constant-dollar financial statements. All other companies *must* use the average CPI.)

This information may be stated in one of two ways:

1. Average-for-the-year constant dollars or end-of-year constant dollars, whichever is used for the measurement of income from continuing operations for the current fiscal year.
2. Dollars having a purchasing power equal to that of dollars of the base period used by the Bureau of Labor Statistics in calculating the consumer price index (currently 1967).

Inasmuch as most business managers desire growth and expansion for their companies, the requirement to publish five-year summary information was expected to result in the following corporate policies.

1. The presentation of dividends on a real basis may cause dividend rates to rise with the rate of inflation so that equity capital sources are maintained.

2. The disclosure of net assets in real dollars may improve the internal analysis of return on investment by focusing upon the real rates of return.
3. The disclosure of revenues on a real basis may indicate that real sales are declining and cause management to raise prices more frequently.

The prospect of continued inflation and the requirements of FASB Statement No. 33 were expected to encourage managers to evaluate their businesses in real-dollar items. Among the specific changes expected were an increase in the number of companies shifting to Lifo inventory costing, increased investments in more productive equipment, the retirement of inefficient productive capacity, an attempt to improve accounts receivable turnover, and a reduction of the amount of cash on hand. Additionally, the requirement to report financial operations on a real, inflation-adjusted basis was expected to prompt managers to measure internal operating performances and new investment proposals on this basis. Such evaluations could improve reported results on an inflation-adjusted basis if both the original evaluation of projects and financial reporting are made on the same basis. However, as noted earlier, the FASB found that much of the information disclosed in SFAS No. 33 was not being used. As a result, the cost of providing this information exceeded the benefits provided and the disclosure of much of this information is no longer required.

SUMMARY

In recent years, continuing inflation has caused dissatisfaction with historical-cost financial statements in units of money. A variety of adjustments have been proposed to increase the relevance of financial statements and their ability to express the actual value of the assets they are measuring. In 1979, the FASB issued its Statement No. 33, "Financial Reporting and Changing Prices." This release requires the supplemental disclosure of the impact of general inflation and current cost on financial statements. However, in 1984 SFAS No. 33 was amended by SFAS No. 82 which eliminated certain current-cost disclosures.

Current-value accounting, another form of adjustment, may use entry or replacement costs, exit or selling price, or discounted present value. Each of these methods gives only an approximation of asset value because the actual value can be determined only by an exchange. Constant-dollar–current-cost accounting required by FASB No. 33 is a partial application of current-value accounting.

The adjustment of financial statements to units of general purchasing power (constant-dollar–historical-cost accounting) does not require any departure from present generally accepted accounting principles. Instead, its purpose is to present items on the financial statements in common-sized dollars. The adjustment process requires that a distinction be made between monetary and nonmonetary items because there are purchasing power gains and losses on the former but not on the latter.

Various individuals and organizations have proposed a number of compromises in the adjustment process, but at this time the procedures that will finally become generally accepted are not known. In the article that follows, Edward Swanson suggests some changes in accounting for financial reporting and changing prices.

ACCOUNTING FOR CHANGING PRICES: SOME MIDCOURSE CORRECTIONS

EDWARD P. SWANSON

The lengthy struggle to develop an accounting standard on a controversial topic finally reached a milestone in September 1979, when the Financial Accounting Standards Board issued Statement no. 33, *Financial Reporting and Changing Prices.*[1] The FASB, fearing the milestone would be a millstone, emphasized that the standard was only an experiment and committed itself to a comprehensive review within five years.

The board then awaited what it expected would be significant criticism. Such criticism seemed unavoidable, since there was little agreement among the FASB's diverse constituents—managers, investors, creditors, auditors and others—about the best method of accounting for changing prices. Surprisingly, however, the criticism that followed publication was mild, at least by the standards of an organization accustomed to controversy.

The business community appeared resigned to the need for an FASB standard requiring disclosure of some form of data adjusted for changing prices. Prices were increasing at an astounding rate for the U.S. The current accounting system, which explicitly assumes prices are constant (the "assumption of a constant monetary unit"), was increasingly being viewed as inadequate. The Securities and Exchange Commission, moreover, had apparently "softened up" the FASB's constituents by issuing Accounting Series Release no. 190, *Notice of Adoption of Amendments to Regulation S-X Requiring Disclosure of Certain Replacement Cost Data,*[2] which required disclosure of certain replacement cost information by large companies. Much of the FASB's constitu-

[1]Financial Accounting Standards Board Statement no. 33, *Financial Reporting and Changing Prices* (Stamford: FASB, 1979).

[2]Securities and Exchange Commission Accounting Series Release no. 190, *Notice of Adoption of Amendments to Regulation S-X Requiring Disclosure of Certain Replacement Cost Data,* March 23, 1976.

ency believed that an FASB standard almost had to provide more useful information—ASR no. 190 data weren't suitable even for calculating an adjusted-income total.

A good deal has happened since Statement no. 33 was issued: The board has issued additional statements on accounting for changing prices by companies with assets in certain specialized industries, such as forest products and income-producing real estate. An unprecedented research program has been implemented by the FASB. The board has issued Statement no. 70, *Financial Reporting and Changing Prices: Foreign Currency Translation,*[3] which rescinds the requirement that companies with significant foreign operations disclose historical cost/constant dollar (HC/C$) data. And on December 27, 1983, the FASB issued the Invitation to Comment (IC) *Supplementary Disclosures about the Effects of Changing Prices,*[4] which discusses potential midcourse corrections in Statement no. 33 and related pronouncements.

This article reviews the controversy about how best to report the impact of changing prices, provides an update on FASB actions and other activities since September 1979 and discusses key sections of the FASB's IC.

OVERVIEW OF THE CONTROVERSY

The major issue in the debate over how best to reflect the impact of changing prices concerns the extent to which general versus

[3]FASB Statement no. 70, *Financial Reporting and Changing Prices: Foreign Currency Translation* (Stamford: FASB, 1982).

[4]FASB Invitation to Comment *Supplementary Disclosures about the Effects of Changing Prices* (Stamford: FASB, December 27, 1983).

specific price changes should be incorporated into the supplementary disclosures. Proponents of the HC/C$ method argue that inflation is the problem; an adequate solution, therefore, is the adjustment of historical cost amounts using an index incorporating a broad range of price changes, either the Consumer Price Index (CPI) or the Gross National Product Implicit Price Deflator.

Proponents of current cost argue that the decision usefulness of historical cost data declines, even if there is no general inflation, when prices change in the specific goods and services purchased by a company. They argue that cost of goods sold, depreciation and possibly other expenses should be based on current, rather than on historical, costs. If both general prices (inflation) and specific prices change, then many current cost advocates would adjust accounting information for both types of price changes. Using this current cost/constant dollar (CC/C$) method, all assets, liabilities, revenues and expenses for the prior year that are to be reported in the current period's financial report first must be increased by the rate of general inflation. This adjustment for inflation is designed primarily to facilitate comparisons of results from consecutive periods. In addition, gains or losses in purchasing power from holding cash, receivables, payables and other monetary items during inflationary periods would be recognized.

The FASB's response in Statement no. 33 was to require large companies to report, on an experimental basis, both HC/C$ and CC/C$ information. The experiment consists of using both methods for a trial period, collecting information on the usefulness and costliness of the two methods and then choosing one of the methods at the end of the experimental period. Of course, many decisions about the implementation of the chosen method also will be made, based in part on information obtained during the experimental period.

Several events occurred prior to the publication of Statement no. 33 that illuminate the FASB's decision to require both HC/C$ and CC/C$ information. Although academics have studied and debated for decades the usefulness of these two methods, as well as of others, the first authoritative pronouncement in the U.S. by a standard-setting group was issued in 1969 by the former Accounting Principles Board.[5] It encouraged, but didn't require, supplementary disclosures using the HC/C$ method. Only a few companies complied by issuing such information.

The FASB was formed in 1973 and at the end of 1974 issued an exposure draft (ED), *Financial Reporting in Units of General Purchasing Power,*[6] which also would have required HC/C$ information. The proposed date for implementation was January 1, 1976, but a final standard was never issued. Instead, the SEC intervened, issuing ASR no. 190, which required supplementary disclosure in form 10-K reports of selected replacement cost information. The FASB had little practical choice but to avoid confrontation with the SEC. Further consideration of the FASB ED was deferred indefinitely.

ASR no. 190 was especially important because it "softened up" the FASB's constituents for Statement no. 33, particularly the requirement that current cost data be disclosed. ASR no. 190 required disclosure of inventory, fixed assets, costs of sales and depreciation expense on a replacement cost basis. Replacement cost was to be measured as the cost to replace productive capacity at the latest technology, a controversial provision that precluded calculating replacement cost income for companies employing older technology.

These companies deduct relatively low capital costs as depreciation in their historical cost statements but incur relatively high labor and operating costs because of the older technology in use. Purchase of equipment that incorporates the latest technology would often be more costly than purchase of equipment incorporating the technology in use, but some of this higher capital cost would be offset by savings in labor and operating costs. Therefore, if income is calculated by substituting replacement cost depreciation, which reflects the higher costs of the latest technology, for historical cost depreciation, both high capital and high labor costs would be deducted. As a result, an estimate of labor- and operating-cost savings must be added back to calculate replacement cost income. Companies weren't required to provide such estimates, however, and few did so. Critics of ASR no. 190 regarded this inability to calculate replacement cost income as a fatal flaw.

The weaknesses in ASR no. 190, as well as the SEC's general commitment to support standard setting by the private sector, provided an opportunity for the FASB to reassert its leadership in the area of accounting for changing prices. The board again began deliberations and still seemed to favor the HC/C$ method. The SEC, however, led by former chairman Harold E. Williams, was outspoken in its demand that any FASB pronouncement include current cost disclosures. At the end of 1978 the FASB issued an ED, *Financial Reporting and Changing Prices,*[7] of a standard that would have required supplementary dis-

[5]Accounting Principles Board Statement no. 3, *Financial Statements Restated for General Price-Level Changes* (New York: AICPA, 1969).
[6]FASB Exposure Draft *Financial Reporting in Units of General Purchasing Power* (Stamford: FASB, December 31, 1974).

[7]FASB ED *Financial Reporting and Changing Prices* (Stamford: FASB, December 28, 1978).

closures using either the CC/C$ or the HC/C$ method. The board nevertheless included guidelines that encouraged adoption of the CC/C$ method. Respondents during the exposure period indicated that companies would use these guidelines as a loophole to avoid developing current cost data. The guidelines subsequently were omitted from Statement no. 33 and replaced by a provision requiring disclosures using both methods. (See exhibit 1, which summarizes the major provisions of Statement no. 33.)

Statement no. 33 is, then, a product not only of technical and theoretical considerations but also of political factors. Few issues have illustrated so clearly the nature of the standard-setting process. The FASB was caught in the middle—pressured by management, which preferred the HC/C$ method, and explicitly constrained by the SEC on the nature of the final standard that it would accept. Some years ago, Charles T. Horngren described the relationship between the SEC and the APB as one of decentralized management, with the SEC as

---

Exhibit 1

Summary of Financial Accounting Standards Board Statement no. 33, *Financial Reporting and Changing Prices*

Applicability

Size test:
Publicly traded companies with beginning-of-the-year total assets of more than $1 billion or total inventory and property, plant and equipment (before deducting accumulated depreciation) of more than $125 million.

Industry:
Assets used in operations of certain specialized industries are covered by separate standards.

Required disclosures

Income statement:
Costs of goods sold, depreciation (in aggregate) and income from continuing operations must be disclosed on both a historical cost/constant dollar (HC/C$) basis and a current cost/constant dollar (CC/C$) basis. Two other new items must also be disclosed but not included in income: (1) the purchasing power gain or loss on net monetary items and (2) the increase or decrease in the current cost of inventory and property, plant and equipment (net of inflation). Any write-downs to lower recoverable amounts and foreign currency translation adjustments must be reported.

Balance sheet:
Net assets at year-end should be presented on both a CC/C$ and an HC/C$ basis. The current costs of inventory and property, plant and equipment at year-end must be disclosed in nominal dollars.

For the last five years the following items must be reported after adjustment for changes in the Consumer Price Index (CPI) to report all items in the average dollar for the current year:

- Net sales and other operating revenues.
- HC/C$ information.
  1 Income from continuing operations.
  2 Income per common share from continuing operations.
  3 Net assets at fiscal year-end.
- Current cost information.
  1 Income from continuing operations.
  2 Income per common share from continuing operations.
  3 Net assets at fiscal year-end.
  4 Increases or decreases in the current cost amounts of inventory and property, plant and equipment (net of inflation).
- Other information.
  1 Purchasing power gain or loss on net monetary items.
  2 Cash dividends declared per common share.
  3 Market price per common share at fiscal year-end.
  4 Average level of CPI.

Only sales, dividends and market price per share must be reported for years prior to adoption of the standard.

Narrative:
Explanations of the information and discussions of its significance in the circumstances of the enterprise are required.

top management and the APB as middle management.[8] The same relationship holds today, but now the FASB is middle management. As with other middle management, the FASB ordinarily is allowed extensive freedom because of greater expertise. The

[8]Charles T. Horngren, "Accounting Principles: Private or Public Sector?" JofA, May 72, pp. 37–41, and "The Marketing of Accounting Standards," JofA, Oct. 73, pp. 61–66.

SEC retains its position as top management, with the power to constrain and veto decisions by the FASB.

FASB STATEMENTS FOR SPECIALIZED ASSETS

Managers in many industries believe that estimating the cost to replace their assets presents unique measurement problems. Representatives of several industries argued that their companies should be exempt from the CC/C$ provisions of Statement no. 33. The FASB decided that determining current cost for the following specialized assets deserved separate consideration; timberlands and growing timber, mineral-ore bodies, proved oil and gas reserves and income-producing real estate property. Other industries, including financial institutions, public utilities and insurance companies, didn't receive special consideration. Although the FASB agreed to give further consideration to disclosure of CC/C$ data by companies with specialized assets, all companies were required to present HC/C$ data. Calculating HC/C$ data for specialized assets doesn't present unique measurement problems because inventory, plant and equipment and related expenses are adjusted for changes in the CPI for All Urban Users (CPI-U). The relevance of these HC/C$ data is highly suspect, however.

The measurement problems encountered in estimating the current cost of specialized assets are complex. Current cost is measured by estimating either a current market buying price or the current cost of some other method of acquisition (for example, growth, exploration and development, construction). The choice between these two general approaches of measuring current cost usually should reflect the acquisition method normally used by the enterprise. Acquisition by a method other than purchase often should be used. The relevance and reliability of the resulting CC/C$ data have been questioned both by representatives of the industries and by external users. The FASB, consequently, allowed companies with specialized assets to substitute HC/C$ measures for CC/C$ measures in the initial year of Statement no. 33. Four task forces were set up to develop reports on the unique problems encountered in measuring the current cost of specialized assets.

In April 1980 the FASB issued an ED, *Financial Reporting and Changing Prices: Specialized Assets,*[9] of a proposed statement that would have required disclosure of CC/C$ information for all specialized assets. In addition, disclosure of estimated fair values would have been required for timberlands and growing timber, proved oil and gas reserves and income-producing real estate properties. (*Fair value* may be defined as the exchange price that could reasonably be expected to be paid in a transaction between a willing buyer and a willing seller.) Fair values of mining assets would not have been required because of the inadequacy of systems for estimating such values. Certain other disclosures, tailored to the nature of each of the industries, also were proposed.

This ED was never issued as a final standard. The four votes required for passage of a standard could be obtained only if the disclosures were voted on separately by type of specialized asset. In other words, the four (or more) board members who agreed on a particular set of disclosures varied by type of specialized asset, and no four board members could agree when all the specialized assets were considered in a single standard. It was necessary, then, to issue three standards: Statements nos. 39, *Financial Reporting and Changing Prices: Specialized Assets—Mining and Oil and Gas;*[10] 40, *Financial Reporting and Changing Prices: Specialized Assets—Timberlands and Growing Timber;*[11] and

[9] FASB ED *Financial Reporting and Changing Prices: Specialized Assets* (Stamford: FASB, April 21, 1980).
[10] FASB Statement no. 39, *Financial Reporting and Changing Prices: Specialized Assets—Mining and Oil and Gas* (Stamford: FASB, 1980).
[11] FASB Statement no. 40, *Financial Reporting and Changing Prices: Specialized Assets—Timberlands and Growing Timber* (Stamford: FASB, 1980).

Exhibit 2   Measurement methods required for specialized assets

FASB statement	Type of specialized asset	Measurement methods
39[1]	Mineral-ore bodies	CC/C$
40	Timberlands and growing timber	CC/C$ but can substitute HC/C$
41	Income-producing real estate	CC/C$ but can substitute HC/C$
69	Proved oil and gas reserves	(1) CC/C$ but can substitute HC/C$ (2) Standardized measure of discounted future net cash flows for proved reserves

[1]Financial Accounting Standards Board Statement no. 69, *Disclosures about Oil and Gas Producing Activities,* superseded disclosures required for oil and gas assets in Statement no. 39, *Financial Reporting and Changing Prices: Specialized Assets—Mining and Oil and Gas.*

41, *Financial Reporting and Changing Prices: Specialized Assets—Income-Producing Real Estate.*[12] Subsequently, Statement no. 69, *Disclosures about Oil and Gas Producing Activities,*[13] which was issued for the purpose of reducing the disclosure burden for oil and gas companies, modified the measurement methods in Statement no. 39 for such companies. Exhibit 2, above, summarizes the measurement methods that must be used for the various types of specialized assets.

Two important points should be noted: First, fair value information is not required for any of the specialized assets. Recall that, under the provisions of the ED, such information would have been required for all specialized assets but mining assets. Second, in measuring specialized assets other than mining assets, HC/C$ data can be substituted for CC/C$ data. These data, then, are potentially misleading: HC/C$ data aren't a good surrogate for CC/C$ data in most cases because the CPI-U isn't a reliable surrogate for changes in prices of the specialized assets.

In addition to the standards discussed above, the FASB has issued two statements that amend Statement no. 33 to provide relief to industries with unique measurement problems. Statement no. 46, *Financial Reporting and Changing Prices: Motion Picture Films,*[14] allows companies that produce motion pictures to substitute HC/C$ data for CC/C$ data. Films are really specialized assets, and this standard allows such assets to be measured using the

[12]FASB Statement no. 41, *Financial Reporting and Changing Prices: Specialized Assets—Income-Producing Real Estate* (Stamford: FASB, 1980).
[13]FASB Statement no. 69, *Disclosures about Oil and Gas Producing Activities* (Stamford: FASB, 1982).

[14]FASB Statement no. 46, *Financial Reporting and Changing Prices: Motion Picture Films* (Stamford: FASB, 1981).

same shortcut allowed for several other specialized assets. Statement no. 54, *Financial Reporting and Changing Prices: Investment Companies,*[15] exempts investment companies from the provisions of Statement no. 33. Representatives of this industry wanted to avoid presentation of the five-year summary of operating results adjusted to a constant dollar basis using the CPI-U. They also wanted to avoid a new performance indicator that would compare their operating returns to the rate of inflation. (There is no theoretical justification for exempting the investment industry from the five-year summary. The industry had planned to sue the board over this issue, and the FASB wanted to avoid potentially costly litigation.)

FASB RESEARCH PROGRAM

The FASB has undertaken several activities as part of a research program to encourage a productive and meaningful experiment. The board has published a research report that summarizes empirical research on accounting for changing prices[16] and has issued an IC that suggests areas for additional research.[17] It has encouraged research by people in various fields—industry, practice, universities, government and others. In January 1983 the FASB sponsored a conference to examine research findings from a series of projects it either encouraged (often bringing researchers and sponsors together) or, in a few cases, sponsored itself. Conference participants were given the opportunity over a two-day period to question and react to 17 research studies, identify key issues for further study and suggest ways of making the remainder of the changing-prices experiment more meaningful. (The views expressed here on some of the changes needed in Statement no. 33 have been influenced in some cases by discussions at this conference.) An overview of the conference is now available from the FASB.[18]

Another element in the FASB's research program, and one of special importance, is the data base of changing-prices disclosures. A computer tape containing the quantitative disclosures required by Statement no. 33, as well as codes that identify certain nonquantitative information, is now available from Value Line Data Services. Data for 1979, 1980, 1981 and 1982 are currently available. The data base has been developed by the FASB with substantial assistance from the major accounting firms, faculty and students at Columbia University and corporate sponsors. The ready availability of these data in an easily usable form is likely to stimulate use by Wall Street, corporate management and academic researchers.

FUTURE OF ACCOUNTING FOR CHANGING PRICES

The December 1983 IC discusses several potential changes in accounting for changing prices. It is restricted to issues directly related to rescinding or amending Statement no. 33 and does not consider funda-

---

[15]FASB Statement no. 54, *Financial Reporting and Changing Prices: Investment Companies* (Stamford: FASB, 1982).

[16]Paul Frishkoff, *Financial Reporting and Changing Prices: A Review of Empirical Research* (Stamford: FASB, 1982).

[17]FASB IC *On the Need for Research on Financial Reporting and Changing Prices* (Stamford: FASB, June 15, 1981).

[18]Robert N. Freeman, "Research Conference Launches FASB Review of Statement 33," *Highlights of Financial Reporting Issues* (Stamford: FASB, 1983). A notebook containing papers from the conference also can be purchased from the FASB.

mentally different approaches to accounting for changing prices. It identifies four issues that the board is likely to address in 1984. The first two issues solicit views about whether changing-prices disclosures should be continued. The other two issues concern potential amendments to Statement no. 33 if some form of disclosures is continued. The IC emphasizes that, if changing-prices disclosures are continued, changes would be restricted to those that could be implemented in the near future, without significantly changing either the nature of the disclosures or the cost of preparing the data.

The four issues can be summarized as follows:

1. Are the Statement no. 33 disclosures as a whole a generally useful supplement to the financial statements for assessing the effects of changing prices on business enterprises? If so, how are the data used? If not, why not, and what other information would be useful?
2. Should the FASB continue to require either the current or revised disclosures? If yes, should the requirement remain experimental or become a permanent part of financial reporting?
3. Which specific Statement no. 33 disclosures are useful and should be continued? Which should be deleted? What additional disclosures would be useful? Should a more standardized format be required?
4. What changes, if any, should be made to improve the relevance and reliability of current cost measures for fixed assets and depreciation?

Of these issues the second—whether or not to continue some form of disclosures— is obviously the most critical to the future of accounting for changing prices. The FASB requests feedback on the use of Statement no. 33 data to help it decide whether to continue the disclosures. Surveys and interviews have already disclosed that the CC/C\$ data are used to some extent, but the HC/C\$ data are virtually never used.[19]

The relative emphasis of the discussion in the IC favors continuing some form of disclosures, either as an experiment or as a permanent part of financial reporting.[20] Of particular note, the following three counterarguments are presented in response to the argument that changing-prices disclosures are no longer needed because inflation has subsided: First, the effects of inflation are cumulative, so the effects of past inflation will take many years to work their way through the financial statements. Second, if Statement no. 33 is rescinded now and high rates of inflation return, the start-up costs to revive changing-prices disclosures might be greater than the costs of continuing these disclosures without interruption. Third, the data are not so useful in the first few years because a long-term series of observations is needed to conduct trend analyses.

If some form of accounting for changing prices is continued, the discussion in the IC favors no longer requiring a dual set of disclosures. The presentation of two differ-

---

[19]See Arthur Young, *Financial Reporting and Changing Prices: A Survey of Preparers' Views and Practices* (New York: AY, 1981), and William C. Norby, ''Applications of Inflation-Adjusted Accounting Data,'' *Financial Analysts Journal,* March–April 1983, pp. 33–39.

[20]The 10-paragraph discussion of the second issue in the IC clearly favors continuation of some disclosures (either as an experiment or as a permanent part of financial reporting). The first 5 paragraphs present the case for continuation of some disclosures. The sixth paragraph presents arguments for halting the experiment, but the next 3 paragraphs refute these arguments. The last paragraph is neutral, requesting feedback from readers.

ent types of data, both of which are adjusted for changing prices, has been widely criticized as generating confusion. This viewpoint was expressed, for example, by participants at the January 1983 FASB Conference on Financial Reporting and Changing Prices, who by a wide margin favored dropping the HC/C$ method. The IC discusses three alternatives, each of which would eliminate the requirement for both HC/C$ and CC/C$ data: (1) disclose either HC/C$ or CC/C$ data but not both, (2) disclose only HC/C$ data or (3) disclose only CC/C$ data.

The first alternative would have companies with significant amounts of inventory and property, plant and equipment continue to disclose CC/C$ data, whereas others would disclose HC/C$ data. It is suggested that this approach would not impair the comparability of the CC/C$ disclosures because companies with material amounts of inventory and fixed assets would continue to report CC/C$ data; for other companies the CC/C$ and HC/C$ disclosures required by Statement no. 33 are not significantly different. This alternative was proposed in the ED that preceded Statement no. 33 but was rejected in favor of a dual set of disclosures. The discussion in the IC favors the approach of the first alternative.[21]

The second alternative would require companies to disclose only HC/C$ data. The primary advantage cited for disclosing only HC/C$ is that the data are less costly to prepare and verify than CC/C$ data. It is also argued that, although the two methods are conceptually different, for many companies the reported amounts are similar. The FASB seems unlikely to adopt this alternative for two reasons: First, financial analysts do not regard the data as useful. Second, the FASB, in Statement no. 70, has already rescinded the requirement to disclose HC/C$ for companies with significant foreign operations. This disclosure requirement was rescinded because companies with foreign operations would have had to identify reliable price indexes for each functional currency in which they conduct operations and then make numerous calculations. It seems unlikely that the FASB would reimpose on these companies a requirement to prepare HC/C$ data.

The third alternative would require CC/C$ disclosures for companies with significant amounts of inventory and property, plant and equipment and rescind the disclosure requirements for other companies. The IC contains no discussion of this alternative, so it may not be under serious consideration. The IC does indicate, however, that requiring current cost disclosures for a more comprehensive set of assets and liabilities (and all companies would then report current cost data) could be considered at a later date but not in 1984.

In summary, the IC leans toward continuing to require some form of disclosures of the effects of changing prices. It favors requiring companies with significant amounts of inventory and property, plant and equipment to disclose CC/C$ data and others to disclose HC/C$ data. Some modifications in the disclosure requirements are also proposed.

MODIFICATIONS TO CURRENT COST MEASUREMENTS

The IC discusses the following modifications to Statement no. 33 that might increase the relevance and reliability of cur-

[21]The discussion of this alternative is seven paragraphs long, whereas the combined discussion of the other two alternatives is only three paragraphs long. In addition, although no preference is stated, this alternative is listed first in the IC.

rent cost measures for fixed assets and depreciation:

1. Reduce the flexibility in selecting price indexes; that is,
   a. Requires indexes based on used-asset prices if available.
   b. If indexes based on new-asset prices or direct pricing methods based on technologically different assets are used, require explicit adjustment for, and disclosure of, the effects of technological change.
2. Require separate determination of depreciation methods, estimates of useful lives and salvage values.
3. Revise the lower recoverable amount (LRA) provision of Statement no. 33. Either provide more guidance for estimating LRA or eliminate this provision.
4. Require more detailed management discussions of the disclosures.

Each of these potential modifications could increase the usefulness of current cost data.

The first modification is considered because companies have relied almost exclusively on indexes based on new-asset prices.[22] When original acquisition costs are multiplied by such price indexes, the result is an estimate of cost of reproduction (new). That cost may include the cost of technological improvements that are not part of the actual asset owned by the company. In this case the estimate of current cost will be overstated unless adjustments are made for differences in "service potential" between a new asset and the asset in use. The board intended that such adjustments be made when it required deduction of "an allowance for the operating disadvantages of the asset owned (higher operating costs or lower output potential). . . ."[23] Few companies, however, have made such adjustments. The magnitude of the measurement error caused by this situation is believed to be significant. Alfred King, for example, estimates that indexed amounts are 20 percent to 70 percent higher than fair market value.[24]

Unfortunately, correcting this situation may be controversial. Used-asset price indexes are available for assets in only a few industries, such as computers, airlines and automobiles. For other assets only new-asset prices are available. It would then be necessary to adjust for differences, if any, in useful life, output capacity, nature of services and operating costs between new assets and the actual assets in use. Such adjustments could significantly increase the costs of data preparation. To reduce costs the FASB should involve industry associations. They could provide leadership in developing techniques of adjusting for service potential changes and maintain data bases of changes in service potential for widely held groups of assets. Despite the additional costs, it is critical to the future of the experiment that the FASB require improved measurements of current costs.

The second modification proposed to improve the decision usefulness of State-

[22]FASB Statement no. 33 doesn't explicitly state a preference from among methods that can be used to measure current costs, although indexation is listed first. This is an important change from the ED preceding it, which expressed a preference for direct pricing (using either current invoice prices or prices from vendors), unit pricing and indexation in this order. This change encouraged companies to rely on indexes based on new-asset prices.

[23]FASB Statement no. 33, par. 180c.
[24]Alfred King, "The Development of Current Cost: Alternative Approaches in Foreign Countries and the U.S.," *Research on Financial Reporting and Changing Prices* (Stamford: FASB, 1983), p. 69.

ment no. 33 data would be to require the use of more accurate useful lives in calculating depreciation. Statement no. 33 encourages companies to use the same methods, useful lives and salvage values as are used in the primary financial statements: "There is a *presumption* that depreciation methods, estimates of useful lives, and salvage values of assets *should be the same* for purposes of current cost, historical cost/constant dollar, and historical cost/nominal dollar depreciation calculations. However, if the methods and estimates used for calculations in the primary financial statements have been chosen partly to allow for expected price changes, different methods and estimates *may* be used for purposes of current cost and historical cost/constant dollar calculations."[25]

The IC asks whether it may be more appropriate to presume that Statement no. 33 useful lives, salvage values and depreciation methods should be different, since most companies consider expected inflation when establishing depreciation schedules for the primary statements. The answer would seem to be yes, particularly for useful lives. Most companies base depreciation expense on useful lives much shorter than actual lives; in part this has been done to provide support for the use of short lives for tax purposes. Companies could calculate depreciation using realistic economic lives at little additional cost. In addition, companies should be encouraged to use different depreciation methods and salvage values if it is believed that that would improve the usefulness of the data.

The third potential modification discussed in the IC would be either to provide more guidance in estimating LRA or to eliminate the LRA provision. Recoverable amount equals selling price minus costs of disposal for assets about to be sold and the net present value of future cash flows from the use of other assets. Recoverable amount is instrumental to the Statement no. 33 definition of current cost accounting: "A method of measuring and reporting assets and expenses associated with the use or sale of assets, at their current cost or *lower recoverable amount* at the balance sheet date or at the date of use or sale."[26]

Yet, in practice, few companies other than utilities have applied the LRA provision. This lapse is understandable because Statement no. 33 declares that write-downs to LRA are necessary only when judged to be materially and permanently lower than current cost (or HC/C$ amounts). Moreover, Statement no. 33 provides no guidelines on how to calculate the present value of future cash flows from use. One way to resolve this problem would be to retain the LRA provision only for assets about to be sold. The problems encountered in calculating net present value of future cash flows from use are probably intractable. Specifically, how can future cash flows be traced to individual assets or even to groups of assets?

The fourth potential modification considered to improve the usefulness of current cost measurements would be to require more detailed management discussion of how the data have been calculated. Analysts would be more likely to use the data if their comparability among companies could be assessed. At a minimum, information should be required about measurement methods, service potential adjustments, selection of depreciation lives and LRA determinations.

[25]FASB Statement no. 33, par. 61. Emphasis added.

[26]Ibid., par. 22b. Emphasis added.

MODIFICATIONS TO DISCLOSURE FORMAT

Two potential modifications to the format used to present the data are discussed in the IC. One proposal would require a reconciliation of beginning-of-the-year and end-of-the-year stockholders' equity in average-for-the-year dollars. The IC provides an illustration of a standardized format for CC/C$ (see exhibit 3, on this page). This reconciliation would improve the quality of the data by ensuring that all income statement items, when restated in average-for-

Exhibit 3   Reconcillation of stockholders' equity (in average for the year dollars)[1]

Beginning-of-the-year stockholders' equity		$XXX
Income from continuing operations	$XX	
Purchasing power gains and losses	XX	
Increases or decreases in the specific prices of inventory and property, plant and equipment (net of inflation)	XX	
Translation adjustment	XX	
Net change in stockholders' equity, excluding transactions with stockholders		XXX
Dividends		XXX
Other transactions with stockholders		XXX
End-of-the-year stockholders' equity		$XXX

[1] This table is reproduced from paragraph 53 of the FASB Invitation to Comment *Supplementary Disclosures about the Effects of Changing Prices.*

the-year dollars, articulate with calculations of net assets at the beginning and end of the year. A second, although unstated, advantage is that it may reduce criticism of the board for not having decided on a bottom-line income number. Purchasing power gains and losses, changes in specific prices, and other items are currently displayed separately and cannot be added to income from continuing operations. Including these amounts in a reconciliation, rather than presenting them separately, may reduce the impression the board does not know what to do with these items.

The second proposed format modification is to eliminate use of the base period (1967) for the CPI-U in the five-year summary of key operating items. At present companies can report amounts in either average-for-the-year dollars or base-year dollars. All companies would use average-for-the-year dollars except those few that present comprehensive financial statements restated into year-end dollars. These latter companies would continue to have the option of using either year-end or average-for-the-year dollars. This proposal should not be controversial because few companies have reported in base-period dollars. Moreover, most readers of financial reports think in terms of the recent purchasing power of the dollar.

CONCLUSION AND RECOMMENDATION

Since rates of inflation have recently declined dramatically, those in the business community opposed to disclosing any form of accounting information adjusted for changing prices have already begun to exert pressure on the FASB to rescind, rather than to revise, Statement no. 33. At a minimum, the FASB may not receive the activist support from the SEC that is necessary for bold initiatives.

Given these factors, the FASB should strive to extend the experiment for another three to five years. This extension would postpone some difficult decisions—decisions that may be impossible to make in a period of low inflation and with possibly lukewarm support from the SEC. A lengthening of the experimental period is needed, as well, to improve the quality of the data and to give users more time fully to understand and utilize the data. Of special importance is the fact that users need trend data and only recently have had access to five-year trends. Researchers also need more time; research findings are tentative because data have been available for only a few years.

It is urged here that the experiment with accounting for changing prices should be continued. The accounting profession is ill served by persisting in its adherence to an accounting system that explicitly assumes there is no inflation—that is, assumes a stable monetary unit. It would be foolhardy to undo the hard-earned progress made to date, during what may be a temporary interlude in inflation. And progress has been made—at least if one accepts the theory of progress cited by Arthur Bloch: "Progress does not consist in replacing a theory that is wrong with one that is right. It consists in replacing a theory that is wrong with one that is more subtly wrong."[27]

[27]Arthur Bloch, *Murphy's Law Book Two: More Reasons Why Things Go Wrong* (Los Angeles: Price/Stern/Sloan Publishers, Inc., 1982), p. 51.

QUESTIONS

1. Following are four observations regarding the amounts reported in financial statements that have been adjusted for general price level changes. Which observation is valid?
   a. The amount obtained by adjusting an asset's cost for general price level changes usually approximates its current fair value.
   b. The amounts adjusted for general price level changes are not departures from historical cost.
   c. When inventory increases and prices are rising, last-in, first-out (Lifo) inventory accounting has the same effect on financial statements as amounts adjusted for general price level changes.
   d. When inventory remains constant and prices are rising, Lifo inventory accounting has the same effect on financial statements as amounts adjusted for general price level changes.

2. In accordance with FASB Statement No. 33, the consumer price index for all urban consumers was used to compute information on a
   a. Historical-cost basis
   b. Current-cost basis

   c. Constant-dollar basis

   d. Nominal-dollar basis

3. A method of accounting based on measures of historical prices in dollars, each of which has the same general purchasing power, is

   a. Current-cost–constant-dollar accounting

   b. Current-cost–nominal-dollar accounting

   c. Historical-cost–constant-dollar accounting

   d. Historical-cost–nominal-dollar accounting

4. If constant-dollar–historical-cost balance sheets are prepared, they should be presented in terms of

   a. The general purchasing power of the dollar at the latest balance sheet date

   b. The general purchasing power of the dollar in the base period

   c. The average general purchasing power of the dollar for the latest fiscal period

   d. The general purchasing power of the dollar at the time the financial statements are issued

   e. None of the above

5. The restatement of historical dollar financial statements to reflect general price level changes results in presenting assets at

   a. Lower of cost or market values

   b. Current appraisal values

   c. Costs adjusted for purchasing power changes

   d. Current replacement cost

   e. None of the above

6. During a period of deflation an entity would have the greatest gain in general purchasing power by holding

   a. Cash

   b. Plant and equipment

   c. Accounts payable

   d. Mortgages payable

   e. None of the above

7. Which of the following methods of reporting attempts to eliminate the effect of the changing value of the dollar?

   a. Discounted net present value of future cash flows

   b. Historical cost restated for changes in the general price level

   c. Replacement value

   d. Retirement value

8. In preparing price level financial statements, monetary items consist of

   a. Cash items plus all receivables with a fixed maturity date

   b. Cash, other assets expected to be converted into cash, and current liabilities

most all liabilities are monetary investment

    c. Assets and liabilities whose amounts are fixed by contract or otherwise in terms of dollars regardless of price level changes. *This is monetary investment*

    d. Assets and liabilities which are classified as current on the balance sheet

    e. None of the above

9. In preparing price level financial statements, a nonmonetary item would be

    a. Accounts payable in cash

    b. Long-term bonds payable

    c. Accounts receivable → *most receivable are fixed in amount.*

    d. Allowance for uncollectible accounts

    e. None of the above *{Accumulated Depv.} answer*

10. When computing information on a historical-cost–constant-dollar basis, which of the following is classified as nonmonetary?

    a. Allowance for doubtful accounts

    b. Accumulated depreciation of equipment

    c. Unamoritzed premium on bonds payable

    d. Advances to unconsolidated subsidiaries

11. A method of accounting based on measures of current cost or lower recoverable amount, without restatement into units having the same general purchasing power, is

    a. Historical-cost–constant-dollar accounting

    b. Historical-cost–nominal-dollar accounting

    c. Current-cost–constant-dollar accounting

    d. Current-cost–nominal-dollar accounting

12. When computing information on a historical-cost–constant-dollar basis, which of the following is classified as nonmonetary?

    a. Accumulated depreciation of equipment

    b. Advances to unconsolidated subsidiaries

    c. Allowance for doubtful accounts

    d. Unamortized premium on bonds payable

13. When computing information on a historical-cost–constant-dollar basis, which of the following is classified as monetary?

    a. Goodwill arising from a business combination concluded last year

    b. Deferred investment tax credits related to equipment

    c. Obligation under warranties expiring in one year

    d. Allowance for doubtful accounts on long-term receivables

14. During a period of inflation, an account balance remains constant. With respect to this account, a purchasing power loss will be recognized if the account is a

    a. Monetary asset

    b. Monetary liability

    c. Nonmonetary asset

    d. Nonmonetary liability

15. In current-value (fair value) financial statements
    a. General price level gains or losses are recognized on net monetary items
    b. Amounts are always stated in common purchasing power units of measurements
    c. All balance sheet items are different in amount than they would be in a historical-cost balance sheet
    d. Holding gains are recognized
16. When does a general purchasing power loss occur, and when is it recognized?
    a. It occurs when holding net monetary assets during inflation and is recognized in units-of-general-purchasing-power financial statements.
    b. It occurs when holding net monetary liabilities during inflation and is recognized in units-of-general-purchasing-power financial statements.
    c. It occurs when holding net monetary assets during inflation and is recognized in units-of-general-purchasing-power and units-of-money financial statements.
    d. It occurs when holding net monetary liabilities during inflation and is recognized in units-of-general-purchasing-power and units-of-money financial statements.
17. FASB Statement No. 33 requires that the current cost for inventories be measured as the
    a. Recoverable amount regardless of the current cost
    b. Current cost regardless of the recoverable amount
    c. Higher of current cost or recoverable amount
    d. Lower of current cost or recoverable amount
18. When computing information on a historical-cost–constant-dollar basis, which of the following is classified as nonmonetary?
    a. Cash surrender value of life insurance
    b. Long-term receivables
    c. Allowance for doubtful accounts
    d. Inventories, other than inventories used on contracts
19. If constant-dollar financial statements are prepared, purchasing power gain or loss results from which of the following?

	Monetary assets and liabilities	Nonmonetary assets and liabilities
a.	Yes	Yes
b.	Yes	No
c.	No	Yes
d.	No	No

20. When computing information on a historical-cost–constant-dollar basis, which of the following is classified as nonmonetary?

Long-term investment is included in

inventory is not included in monetary

a. Obligations under warranties
b. Accrued expenses payable
c. Unamortized premium on bonds payable
d. Refundable deposits

21. Financial reporting should provide information to help investors, creditors, and other users of financial statements. Statement of Financial Accounting Standards No. 33 required large public enterprises to disclose certain supplementary information.

Required:

a. Describe the historical-cost–constant-dollar method of accounting. Include in your discussion how historical-cost amounts are used to make historical-cost–constant-dollar measurements.

b. Describe the principal advantage of the historical-cost–constant-dollar method of accounting over the historical cost method of accounting.

c. Describe the current-cost method of accounting.

d. Why would depreciation expense for a given year differ using the current-cost method of accounting instead of the historical-cost method of accounting? Include in your discussion whether depreciation expense is likely to be higher or lower using the current-cost method of accounting instead of the historical-cost method of accounting in a period of rising prices, and why.

22. There has been a good deal of criticism of the traditional historical-cost records and the data they reflect, especially during times of inflation or deflation. In order to assist in the interpretation of accounting reports as normally prepared, many accountants have suggested that conventional financial statements first be prepared with recorded cost data, and then, as a supplementary technique, these statements be converted into dollars having a uniform purchasing power through applying price indices to the recorded dollar amounts. These accountants have had considerable difference of opinion as to whether to use a ''general'' price index, such as the wholesale commodity price index or the cost-of-living index, or a more ''specific'' price index that is more applicable to the industry involved or to the particular items being converted (for instance, using a construction index for the conversion of plant and equipment items, or a special price index constructed for a specific industry). Give arguments in favor of and against each of these two types of indices.

23. Part <i>a.</i> Advocates of current-value accounting propose several methods for determining the valuation of assets to approximate current values. Two of the methods proposed are replacement cost and present value of future cash flows.

Required:

Describe each of the two methods cited and discuss the pros and cons of the various procedures used to arrive at the valuation for each method.

Part *b*. The financial statements of a business entity could be prepared by using historical cost or current value as a basis. In addition, the basis could be stated in terms of unadjusted dollars or dollars restated for changes in purchasing power. The various permutations of these two separate and distinct areas are shown in the following matrix.

	Unadjusted Dollars	Dollars Restated for Changes in Purchasing Power
Historical cost	1	2
Current value	3	4

Block 1 of the matrix represents the traditional method of accounting for transactions in accounting today, wherein the absolute (unadjusted) amount of dollars given up or received is recorded for the asset or liability obtained (relationship between resources). Amounts recorded in the method described in block 1 reflect the original cost of the asset or liability and do not give effect to any change in value of the unit of measure (standard of comparison). This method assumes the validity of the accounting concepts of going concern and stable monetary unit. Any gain or loss (including holding and purchasing power gains or losses) resulting from the sale or satisfaction of amounts recorded under this method is deferred in its entirety until sale or satisfaction.

Required:

For each of the remaining matrix blocks (2, 3, and 4), respond to the following questions. Limit your discussion to nonmonetary assets only.

a. How will this method of recording assets affect the relationship between resources and the standard of comparison?

b. What is the theoretical justification for using each method?

c. How will each method of asset valuation affect the recognition of gain or loss during the life of the asset and ultimately from the sale or abandonment of the asset? Your response should include a discussion of the timing and magnitude of the gain or loss and conceptual reasons for any difference from the gain or loss computed using the traditional method.

Complete your discussion for each matrix block before proceeding to the discussion of the next matrix block.

✓24. A common objective of accountants is to prepare meaningful financial statements. To attain this objective, many accountants maintain that the financial statements must be adjusted for changes in price level. Other accountants believe that financial statements should continue to be prepared on the basis of unadjusted historical cost.

Required:

a. List the arguments for adjusting financial statements for changes in price level.

b. List the arguments for preparing financial statements only on the basis of unadjusted historical cost.

c. In their discussions about accounting for changes in price levels and the methods of measuring them, uninformed individuals have frequently failed to distinguish between adjustments for changes in the price levels of specific goods and services and adjustments for changes in the general purchasing power of the dollar. What is the distinction? What are "price level adjustments"? Discuss.

BIBLIOGRAPHY

Anthony, Robert N. "A Case for Historical Costs." *Harvard Business Review* (November–December 1976), pp. 69–79.

Backer, Morton, and Richard Simpson. *Current Value Accounting.* New York: Financial Executive Research Foundation, 1973.

Bartlett, Ralph, T., and Thomas H. Kelly. "Will FAS No. 33 Solve Inflation Accounting Problems?" *Management Accounting* (April 1980), pp. 11–14.

Baxter, W. T. *Accounting Values and Inflation.* Maidenhead, Berkshire, England: McGraw-Hill Book Company (U.K.) Limited, 1975.

Bedford, Norton M., and James C. McKeown. "Comparative Analysis of Net Realizable Value and Replacement Costing." *The Accounting Review* (April 1972), pp. 333–338.

Bradford, William D. "Price-Level Restated Accounting and the Measurement of Inflation Gains and Losses." *The Accounting Review* (April 1974), pp. 296–305.

Casler, Darwin J., and Thomas W. Hall. "Firm-Specific Valuation Accuracy Using a Composite Price Index." *Journal of Accounting Research* (Spring 1985), pp. 110–122.

Chambers, R. J. "NOD, COG, and PuPu: See How Inflation Teases." *Journal of Accountancy* (September 1975), pp. 56–62.

Chippindale, Walter, and Phillip L. Defliess, eds. *Current Value Accounting. A Practical Guide for Business.* New York: Amacom, 1977.

Davidson, Sidney, and Roman L. Weil. "Inflation Accounting: What Will General Price-Level Adjusted Income Statements Show?" *Financial Analysts Journal* (January–February 1975), pp. 27–31, 70–84.

Devon, Philip C. "Price-Level Reporting and its Value to Investors." *Accounting and Business Research* (Winter 1978), pp. 19–24.

Dyckman, T. R. "Investment Analysis and General Price-Level Adjustments— A Behavioral Study." *Studies in Accounting Research No. 1.* Evanston, Ill.: American Accounting Association, 1969.

Edwards, Edgar O. "The State of Current Value Accounting." *The Accounting Review* (April 1975), pp. 235–245.

Freeman, Robert N. "Alternative Measures of Profit Margin: An Empirical Study of the Potential Information Content of Current Cost Accounting." *Journal of Accounting Research* (Spring 1983), pp. 42–64.

Friedman, Lawrence A. "An Exit-Price Income Statement." *The Accounting Review* (January 1978), pp. 18–30.

Gay, William C., Jr. "Inflation, Indexation and Violation of Human Rights." *Price Waterhouse Review* (1978, Vol. 23, No. 2), pp. 20–29.

Gill, Charles W., and S. Thomas Moser. "Inflation Accounting at the Crossroads." *Journal of Accountancy* (January 1979), pp. 70–78.

Giroux, Gary A., Steven D. Grossman, and Stanley H. Kratchman. "Accounting for the Impact of Inflation: The Experience of the Oil Companies." *Oil & Gas Tax Quarterly* (December 1980), pp. 331–348.

Giroux, Gary A., Steven D. Grossman, and Stanley H. Kratchman. "What FAS No. 33 Does to Bank Financial Statements." *Management Accounting* (January 1981), pp. 42–47.

Griffin, Paul, ed. *Financial Reporting and Changing Prices: The Conference.* Stamford, Conn.: FASB, 1979.

Gynther, R. S. *Accounting for Price-Level Changes: Theory and Procedures.* Oxford, England: Pergamon Press, 1966.

Hakansson, Nils H. "On the Relevance of Price-Level Accounting." *Journal of Accounting Research* (Spring 1969), pp. 22–31.

Heath, Loyd C. "Distinguishing Between Monetary and Nonmonetary Assets and Liabilities in General Price-Level Accounting." *The Accounting Review* (July 1972), pp. 458–468.

Heintz, James A. "Price-Level Restated Financial Statements and Investment Decision Making." *The Accounting Review* (October 1973), pp. 679–689.

Ijiri, Yuji. "The Price-Level Restatement and Its Dual Interpretation." *The Accounting Review* (April 1976), pp. 227–243.

Ijiri, Yuji. "A Defense for Historical Cost Accounting." In Robert R. Sterling, ed., *Asset Valuation and Income Determination*. Houston: Scholars Book Co., 1971, pp. 1–14.

King, Alfred M. "Price-Level Restatement: Solution or Problem?" *Management Accounting* (November 1976), pp. 16–18.

Kohler, Eric L. "Why Not Retain Historical Cost?" *Journal of Accountancy* (October 1963), pp. 35–41.

Largay, James A., III and John Leslie Livingstone. *Accounting for Changing Prices*. New York: John Wiley & Sons, Inc. 1976.

Matolcsy, Z. P. "Evidence on the Joint and Marginal Information Content of Inflation—Adjusted Accounting Income Numbers." *Journal of Accounting Research* (Autumn 1984), pp. 555–569.

Mautz, Robert K. "A Few Words for Historical Cost." *Financial Executive* (January 1973), pp. 23–27, 64.

McDonald, Bill, and Michael H. Morris. "The Relevance of SFAS 33 Inflation Accounting Disclosures in the Adjustment of Stock Prices to Inflation." *The Accounting Review* (July 1984), pp. 432–446.

Moonitz, Maurice. "Restating the Price-Level Problem." *CA Magazine* (July 1974), pp. 27–31.

Morris, R. C. "Evidence of the Impact of Inflation Accounting on Share Prices." *Accounting and Business Research* (Spring 1975), pp. 82–90.

Paton, William A. "Cost and Value in Accounting." *Journal of Accountancy* (March 1946), pp. 192–199.

Paton, William A. "Measuring Profits under Inflation Conditions: A Serious Problem for Accountants." *Journal of Accountancy* (January 1950), pp. 16–27.

Perrin, John R. "Illusory Holding Gains on Long-Term Debt." *Accounting and Business Research* (Summer 1974), pp. 234–236.

Revsine, Lawrence. "On the Correspondence between Replacement Cost Income and Economic Income." *The Accounting Review* (July 1970), pp. 513–523.

Revsine, Laurence. *Replacement Cost Accounting*. Englewood Cliffs, N.J.: Prentice-Hall, Inc., 1973.

Revsine, Lawrence, and Jerry J. Weygandt. "Accounting for Inflation: The Controversy." *Journal of Accountancy* (October 1974), pp. 72–78.

Roehm, Harper A., and Joseph F. Castellano. "Inflation Accounting: A Compromise." *The CPA Journal* (September 1978), pp. 38–47.

Rosen, L. S. *Current Value Accounting and Price-Level Restatements*. Toronto: Canadian Institute of Chartered Accountants, 1972.

Rosenfield, Paul. "The Confusion Between General Price-Level Restatement and Current Value Accounting." *Journal of Accountancy* (October 1972), pp. 63–68.

Rosenfield, Paul. "Current Replacement Value Accounting—A Dead End." *Journal of Accountancy* (September 1975), pp. 63–73.

Samuelson, Richard A. "Should Replacement Cost Changes Be Included in Income?" *The Accounting Review* (April 1980), pp. 254–287.

Schaefer, T. F. "The Information Content of Current Cost Income Relative to Dividends and Historical Cost Income." *Journal of Accounting Research* (Autumn 1984), pp. 647–656.

Scott, George M. *Research Study in Current-Value Accounting Measurement and Utility*. New York: Touche Ross Foundation, 1978.

Seed, Allen H., III. *Inflation: Its Impact on Financial Reporting and Decision Making*. New York: Financial Executives Research Foundation, 1978.

Staubus, George J. "The Effects of Price-Level Restatements on Earnings." *The Accounting Review* (July 1976), pp. 574–589.

Sterling, Robert R. "Relevant Financial Reporting in an Age of Price Changes." *Journal of Accountancy* (February 1975), pp. 42–51.

Stickney, Clyde P., and David O. Green. "No Price Level Adjusted Statements, Please." *The CPA Journal* (January 1974), pp. 25–31.

Sweeney, Henry W. *Stabilized Accounting*. New York: Harper & Brothers, 1936.

Tierncy, Cecelia. "Price-Level Adjustments—Problem in Perspective." *Journal of Accountancy* (November 1963), pp. 56–60.

Touche Ross & Co. *Current Value Accounting: Economic Reality in Financial Reporting*. New York: Touche Ross & Co. 1975.

Trienens, Howard J., and Daniel U. Smith. "Legal Implications of Current Value Accounting." *Financial Executive* (September 1972), pp. 44–77.

Vickrey, Don W. "General Price-Level Adjusted Historical Cost Statements and the Ration-Scale View." *The Accounting Review* (January 1976), pp. 31–40.

Wilcox, Edward B., and Howard C. Greer. "The Case against Price-Level Adjustments in Income Determination." *Journal of Accountancy* (December 1950), pp. 492–504.

14

FINANCIAL
REPORTING
AND
DISCLOSURE
REQUIREMENTS

In the preceding chapters of this text we have attempted to give a concise yet comprehensive explanation of current generally accepted accounting principles. We have given primary attention to those principles promulgated by the Financial Accounting Standards Board in its role as the body of the accounting profession authorized to issue financial accounting standards. The discussion, therefore, has frequently been directed toward the identification of transactions to be treated as accounting information, the appropriate measurement of those transactions, criteria for the classification of the data in the financial statements, and the reporting and disclosure requirements of the various APB Opinions and FASB Standards.

As indicated in Chapter 1, these processes are all part of the conceptual framework of accounting and involve the concept of disclosure. However, various disclosure techniques are available and the selection of the best method depends upon the nature of the information and its relative importance. The most common types of disclosure can be classified as follows.

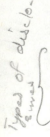

1. The financial statements.
2. Footnotes to the financial statements.
3. Supplementary statements and schedules.
4. The auditor's certificate.

The *financial statements* should contain the most relevant and significant information about the corporation expressed in quantitative terms. The form and arrangement of the financial statements should be such as to insure that the most vital information is readily apparent to the financial-statement users.

The *footnotes* should be used to present information that cannot be easily incorporated into the financial statements themselves. However, footnotes should never be used to substitute for the proper valuation of a financial-statement element nor should they be used to contradict information contained in the financial statements. The most common examples of footnotes are

Note! The proper way to use the "FooTH NOTES"

1. Schedules and exhibits such as long-term debt.
2. Explanations of financial statement items such as pensions.
3. General information about the company such as subsequent events or contingencies.

Supplementary statements and schedules are intended to improve the understandability of the financial statements. They may be used to highlight trends such as five-year summaries or be required by FASB pronouncements such as information on current costs.

The *auditor's certificate* is a form of disclosure in that it informs the users of the reliability of the financial statements. That is, an unqualified opinion should indicate more reliable financial statements than would a qualified or adverse opinion.

The presentation of this information also involves a decision on the level of sophistication of the financial-statements users. That is, should the information be understandable to the relatively uninformed investor or to individuals working with the information on a day-to-day basis such as security analysts? The FASB answered this question when it stated in Statement of Financial Accounting Concepts No. 1 that financial information should be comprehensible to those who have a reasonable understanding of business and economic activities and are willing to study the information with reasonable diligence.

The purpose of this chapter is to draw additional attention to the special importance of disclosure in financial reporting. The following prominent sources clearly indicate this importance.

1. Positions taken by private-sector authoritative bodies in various publications.
2. Pronouncements by the Securities and Exchange Commission.
3. Findings and conclusions of efficient market research.
4. Findings and conclusions of agency theory research.
5. Findings and conclusions of human information processing research.

The focus on these sources does not imply that other sources are not important. Virtually every organization that has any connection with the discipline of accounting, finance, investment, or management has been active in assessing financial reporting and disclosure needs and requirements. The views of the sources cited above often conflict, but they nevertheless indicate the concern of various individuals and organizations over how best to satisfy the needs of financial-statement users. In the following sections we will review the disclosure issues addressed by each of these sources.

PRIVATE-SECTOR AUTHORITATIVE BODIES

A casual perusal of the Accounting Research Bulletins (ARBs), Opinions of the Accounting Principles Board, and Standards of the Financial Accounting Standards Board provides unmistakable evidence of the increased attention given to disclosure by the groups authorized to issue accounting pronouncements. The Accounting Research Bulletins contain only three disclosure captions. One of these pertains to income taxes, another to long-term leases, and the third to contingencies, and in each case the discussion is rather brief. Of course, there are several references to disclosure contained in the text of the ARBs, but the primary attention is directed to recording and reporting procedures.

The increased concern with disclosure becomes apparent in APB Opinion No. 5, "Reporting of Leases in Financial Statements of Lessees," issued in September 1964, which contains three paragraphs under the disclosure caption. From that point forward approximately one-half of the APB opinions contain such captions, frequently with several paragraphs devoted to the topic, and almost every one includes a reference to disclosure. Similary virtually every FASB Statement includes a section on disclosures.

APB OPINION NO. 22

APB Opinion No. 22, "Disclosure of Accounting Policies," provides another good example of the increased concern for disclosure. In that Opinion the board reviewed the overall question of the impact of various alternative accounting policies on net income, and noted that these policies could have a significant effect on the usefulness of financial statements in making economic decisions. The APB concluded that the disclosure of this information was essential for financial-statement users.

Accordingly, the board stated that the accounting policies followed by the entity and the methods used in applying these policies should be disclosed as a "Summary of Significant Accounting Policies" preceding the footnotes or as the first footnote. In particular, it was stated that accounting methods and procedures that involved the following cases should be disclosed.

1. A selection from existing acceptable alternatives.
2. Principles and methods peculiar to the industry in which the reporting entity operates.
3. Unusual or innovative applications of generally accepted accounting principles.

The board's principle objective in issuing this Opinion was to give information that allows investors to utilize existing data in comparing firms across and between industries. Nevertheless, Opinion No. 22 has been criticized as not going far enough. That is, simply saying that one company uses a 10-year straight-line depreciation method whereas another uses an 8-year double declining balance method adds little to the information content of financial statements. A more important question is the effect upon income of using one accounting procedure instead of another. Those who criticize Opinion No. 22 on this basis would prefer industry-by-industry standards or additional information that would allow more exact comparisons to be made.

AICPA CODE OF PROFESSIONAL ETHICS

The number of lawsuits in which accountants have been named as defendants has no doubt had an impact on the increased emphasis on disclosure. However, the accounting profession, through its code of ethics and auditing standards, has long recognized the need for adequate disclosure.

Accountants that belong to the AICPA must follow that organization's Code of Professional Ethics. This document addresses the disclosure issues of adequate auditing procedures, the use of acceptable accounting principles, and independence. The code states that a member of the AICPA "shall not permit his name to be associated with financial statements in such a manner as to imply that he is acting as an independent public accountant unless he has complied with the applicable generally accepted auditing standards promulgated by the Institute."[1] In addition, a member must not express an opinion that financial statements are in conformity with generally accepted accounting principles "if such statements contain any departure from an accounting principle promulgated by the body designated by Council [FASB] to establish such principles"[2] unless the member can provide evidence that the FASB approach would have been misleading in the particular case. Thus, ethical standards require compliance with the increased disclosure requirements contained in the APB and FASB pronouncements.

An earlier version of the Code of Professional Ethics was more specific, perhaps because the official pronouncements about disclosure were inadequate at that time.

a member . . . may be held guilty of an act discreditable to the profession if

a. he fails to disclose a material fact known to him which is not disclosed in the financial statements but disclosure of which is necessary to make the financial statements not misleading; or
b. he fails to report any material misstatement known to him to appear in the financial statement; or
c. he is materially negligent . . . or

[1]American Institute of Certified Public Accountants, Code of Professional Ethics (New York: 1973), p. 22.
[2]Ibid.

d. he fails to acquire sufficient information . . . or

e. he fails to direct attention to any material departure from generally accepted accounting principles or to disclose any material omission of generally accepted auditing procedures applicable in the circumstances.[3]

Auditing activities have long been guided by ten generally accepted auditing standards. These standards are grouped according to general standards (three), standards of fieldwork (three), and standards of reporting (four). The third standard of reporting is the one most specifically concerned with the adequacy of disclosure. That standard asserts that "informative disclosures in the financial statements are to be regarded as reasonably adequate unless otherwise stated in the report." In an elaboration on that standard, the Committee on Auditing Procedures of the AICPA stated,

> *The fairness of presentation of financial statements in conformity with generally accepted accounting principles comprehends the adequacy of disclosures involving material matters. These matters relate to the form, arrangement, and content of the financial statements with their appended notes; the terminology used; the amount of detail given; the classification of items in the statements; the bases of amounts set forth, for example, with respect to such assets as inventories and plant; liens on assets; dividend arrearages; restrictions on dividends; contingent liabilities; and the existence of affiliated or controlling interests and the nature and volume of transactions with such interests. This enumeration is not intended to be all-inclusive but simply indicative of the nature and type of disclosures necessary to make financial statements sufficiently informative.*[4]

The concept of independence is also defined in the Code. In general, this concept requires the complete separation of the business and financial interests of the public accountant from the client corporation. Two main conditions might cause the CPA to be considered not independent.

1. Any direct financial interest or any material indirect financial interest in the client company.
2. Any connection with the issuance of securities of a client company as a promoter, underwriter, director, officer, or employee.

The positions taken by the AICPA in the Code of Professional Ethics indicate that the AICPA is seriously concerned with providing adequate disclosures to the

---

[3]American Institute of Certified Public Accountants. Code of Professional Ethics (New York: 1962), p. 31.

[4]Committee on Auditing Procedures, Statement on Auditing Standards No. 1, "Codification of Auditing Standards and Procedures" (New York: 1973), p. 78.

users of financial statements. Failure to abide by the provisions of the Code can cause a CPA to be barred from membership in the AICPA, a very serious action.

SECURITIES AND EXCHANGE COMMISSION

The Securities and Exchange Commission (SEC) is the agency charged with administering the Securities Act of 1933, the Securities Exchange Act of 1934, and the Foreign Corrupt Practices Act of 1977. These acts stress the need to provide prospective investors with full and fair disclosure of the activities of a company offering and selling securities to the public.

The Securities Act of 1933 regulates the initial public distribution of a corporation's securities. The disclosure issue addressed by the 1933 act is the protection of the public from fraud when a company is initially issuing securities to the general public (issuing securities to the public for the first time is termed *going public.*) The disclosure system necessary under this legislation has developed over the years and emphasizes the disclosure of "relevant information." The disclosure requirements include the filing of a registration statement and a prospectus for review by the SEC. Once a registration statement is filed, it becomes effective on the twentieth day after filing unless the SEC requires amendments. This 20-day period is termed the *waiting period,* and it is unlawful for a company to offer to sell securities during this period. It should be emphasized that the registration of securities with the SEC does not insure investors from loss, and it is unlawful for anyone to suggest that registration prevents possible losses. The registration of securities under the provisions of the 1933 act is designed to provide adequate disclosures of material facts to allow investors to assess the degree of potential risk.

The Securities Exchange Act of 1934 regulates the trading of securities of publicly held companies. The disclosure issues addressed by the 1934 act are the personal duties of corporate officers and owners (*insiders*) and the corporate reporting requirements. Periodic reporting for publicly held companies is termed *being public.* The disclosure system developed under this act deals primarily with the formal content of the information contained in the corporate annual reports and interim reports issued to shareholders. One of the major goals of this legislation is to insure that any *corporate insider* (broadly defined as any corporate officer, director, or 10-percent-or-more shareholder) does not achieve an advantage in the purchase or sale of securities because of a relationship with the corporation. Thus, the 1934 act establishes civil and criminal liabilities for insiders making false or misleading statements when trading corporate securities. The specific SEC reporting requirements for going public and being public are beyond the scope of this text. In the following paragraphs we will focus upon some of the major disclosure issues adopted by the SEC.

THE SEC'S INTEGRATED DISCLOSURE SYSTEM

The dual reporting system generated by the 1933 and 1934 acts frequently resulted in reporting much of the same information several times in slightly different forms. Additionally, the audited financial statements included in the annual report to shareholders were not explicitly covered by either piece of legislation.

In 1980, the SEC adopted a new integrated disclosure system for virtually all of the reports covered by the 1933 and 1934 acts. The new system was accomplished by revamping the two basic regulations of the SEC. These are Regulation S-X, which establishes the requirement for audited financial statements, and Regulation S-K, which covers other types of disclosure. The major change in Regulation S-X was that the audited financial statements included in the annual reports must conform and be identical to those required in the prospectus and all other reports filed with the SEC.

The major changes in Regulation S-K were (1) a requirement to include five years of selected data to highlight trends and (2) a revision of the requirements for management's discussion and analysis of financial condition and results of operations. The main items now required to be analyzed and discussed by management are

1. Unusual or infrequent events that materially affect the reported amount of income.
2. Trends or uncertainties having or expected to have a significant impact on reported income.
3. Changes in volume or price and the introduction of new products that materially affect income.
4. Factors that might have an impact on the company's liquidity or ability to generate enough cash to maintain operations.
5. Commitments for capital projects and anticipated sources of funds to finance these projects.
6. The impact of inflation on the company's operations (narrative presentation for companies not covered by FASB Statement No. 33).
7. Companies are encouraged but not required to provide financial forecasts.

The Securities Act of 1933 is primarily implemented through the requirement that a nonexempt firm that desires to offer securities for public sale must file a registration statement with the SEC and provide the investor with a prospectus. The prospectus contains most of the information provided to the SEC in the registration statement; therefore, we will only review the registration statement. Furthermore, the review will be limited to SEC Form S-1, the general form to be used by all security issuers that are not required to use any of the many other S series forms.

The disclosure requirements of Form S-1 are listed in two parts as shown in Figure 14.1. Part I information must be included in the prospectus, while Part II lists additional information that may be required.

Figure 14.1   Requirements of SEC Form S-1

Part I	Part II
1. Distribution spread	22. Marketing arrangements
2. Plan of distribution	23. Other expenses of issuance
3. Use of proceeds	24. Relationship with registrants of
4. Sales other than for cash	experts named in statements
5. Capital structure	25. Sales to special parties
6. Summary of earnings	26. Recent sales of unregistered
7. Organization of registrant	securities
8. Parents of registrant	27. Subsidiaries of registrant
9. Description of business	28. Franchises and concessions
10. Description of property	29. Indemnification of directors and
11. Organization within five years	officers
12. Pending legal proceedings	30. Treatment of proceeds from
13. Capital stocks being registered	stock being registered
14. Long-term debt being registered	31. Financial statements
15. Other securities being registered	
16. Directors and executive officers	
17. Remuneration of directors and officers	
18. Options to purchase securities	
19. Principal holders of securities	
20. Interest of management in certain transactions	
21. Certified financial statements	

Source. K. Fred Skousen, *An Introduction to the SEC* (Cincinnati: South-Western Publishing Co., 1976), p. 61.

The Securities Exchange Act of 1934 established extensive reporting requirements to provide continuous full and fair disclosure. Again, there are numerous forms, and the corporation must select those that are appropriate for presenting the desired disclosure. The most common forms are

1. Form 10, for registration of a class of security for which no other form is specified.

2. Form 10-K, the annual report to be used when no other form is specified. This form is the annual report counterpart of Form 10, which is used for registration.
3. Form 10-Q, a quarterly report of operations used by all firms.
4. Proxy statement, which is used when the firm makes a proxy solicitation for stockholder meetings.

Of these, Form 10-K is usually considered to be the most important because it is the annual report, which must be filed within 90 days after the end of the firm's fiscal year. The new disclosure rules adopted by the SEC restructured Form 10-K. This restructuring was intended to encourage companies to combine Form 10-K with the annual shareholders' report, thereby satisfying the purposes of both reports. The major disclosure items of Form 10-K are shown in Figure 14.2.

Figure 14.2   Requirements of SEC Form 10-K

Part I	Part II	Part III	Part IV
1. Business 2. Properties 3. Pending legal proceedings 4. Security ownership of certain beneficial owners and management	5. Market for the registrant's common stock and related security holder matters 6. Selected financial data 7. Management's discussion and analysis of financial condition and results of operations 8. Financial statements and supplemental data	9. Directors and executive officers of the registrant 10. Management remuneration and transactions	11. Exhibits financial statements and reports

Additionally, the chief executive officer, the chief financial officer, the chief accounting officer, and a majority of the board of directors must sign Form 10-K.

This requirement is intended to encourage the directors to devote the needed attention to reviewing the form and to obtain professional help whenever it is necessary.

The fact that much of the information provided to the SEC must be certified by an independent certified public accountant has been a significant factor in the growth and importance of the public accounting profession. Accumulating information for the various reports, as well as assisting in their preparation, also requires substantial internal accounting effort, which has contributed to the growth and prestige of that segment of accounting.

Both internal and independent accountants, however, probably consider the SEC a mixed blessing at best, because of the detailed information required and the legal liability involved. The 1933 act makes clear that anyone connected with the registration statement is liable to investors for the accuracy of the statements. The external accountants liability under this act has been summarized as follows.

1. *Any person acquiring securities described in the Registration Statement may sue the accountant, regardless of the fact that he is not the client of the accountant.*

2. *[The plaintiff's] claim may be based upon an alleged false statement or misleading omission in the financial statements, which constitutes his prima facie case. The plaintiff does not have the further burden of proving that the accountants were negligent or fraudulent in certifying to the financial statement involved.*

3. *The plaintiff does not have to prove that he relied upon the statement or that the loss which he suffered was the proximate result of the falsity or misleading character of the financial statement.*

4. *The accountant has thrust upon him the burden of establishing his freedom from negligence and fraud by proving that he had, after reasonable investigation, reasonable ground to believe and did believe that the financial statements to which he certified were true not only as of the date of the financial statements, but beyond that, as of the time when the Registration Statement became effective.*

5. *The accountant has the burden of establishing by way of defense or in reduction of alleged damages, that the loss of the plaintiff resulted in whole or part from causes other than the false statements or the misleading omissions in the financial statements. Under the common law it would have been the plaintiff's affirmative case to prove that the damages which he claims he sustained were proximately caused by the negligence or fraud of the accountant.*[5]

[5]Saul Levy, *C.P.A.* Handbook (New York: American Institute of Certified Public Accountants, 1952), p. 39.

The magnitude of this liability has almost certainly been a factor in the continual increase in both voluntary and required financial statement disclosures. In addition, the SEC is constantly expanding and asserting its role in providing the investor with full and fair disclosure.

ORGANIZATION STRUCTURE OF THE SEC

The Securities and Exchange Commission is directed by four commissioners appointed by the president with the approval of the U.S. Senate. Each commissioner is appointed for a five-year term and one member is designated by the president as the chairman of the SEC.

The SEC is administered from its Washington, D.C., headquarters but has regional and branch offices in the major financial centers of the United States. The commission is assisted by a professional staff of accountants, engineers, lawyers, and securities analysts. These individuals are assigned to the various offices throughout the United States.

The SEC is organized into the following five divisions.

1. *Market Regulation*—responsible for the regulation of national securities exchanges and security brokers and dealers.
2. *Corporate Regulation*—responsible for the regulation of public utilities and serves in an advisory function to federal courts in corporate reorganization or bankruptcy cases.
3. *Investment Management*—responsible for regulating investment companies (companies engaged in trading corporate securities).
4. *Corporation Finance*—responsible for reviewing all registration statements, prospectuses, quarterly and annual reports, proxy statements, and sales literature for corporations offering securities for sale to the public.
5. *Division of Enforcement*—responsible for determining whether the available evidence supports allegations or complaints filed against publicly held companies.

DUTIES OF PUBLIC ACCOUNTANTS

Public accountants engaged in practicing before the Securities and Exchange Commission must conform to both SEC requirements and the AICPA Code of Professional Ethics. A public accountant is considered to be practicing before the SEC if he or she prepares any portion of a registration statement, application, or report and allows his or her name to be associated with the filing. The SEC is particularly sensitive to the *independence* of public accountants, which, as noted earlier, is defined in the Code of Ethics as complete separation from the financial and business interests of the client.

Regulation S-X contains the SEC's independence requirements. That rule states two conditions that will cause the public accountant to be considered not independent.

1. Any direct financial interest or any material indirect financial interest in the issuer.
2. Any connection with the issuer of the securities as a promoter, underwriter, director, officer, or employee.

The 1933 act establishes the liability of public accountants to third parties when the accountant makes an untrue statement of a material fact (or omits a material fact) in a registration statement. The accountant's main defense in such cases is *due diligence*. That is, after reasonable investigation, he or she had reasonable grounds to believe that the facts as presented by the client were true.

Under the 1934 act, the accountant has the responsibility of acting in good faith. If an investor acted upon false and misleading financial statements filed with the SEC, the accountant must prove that he or she had no knowledge that the financial statements were false or misleading. That is, the test is *gross negligence*, which means that the accountant acted with less care than would be exercised by a reasonable person under the circumstances.

FOREIGN CORRUPT PRACTICES ACT OF 1977

The Foreign Corrupt Practices Act (FCPA) was enacted by Congress in 1977. It has been viewed as the culmination of a trend toward upgrading the ethical behavior of American firms engaged in international trade. The FCPA has two main elements. The first makes it a criminal offense to offer bribes to political or governmental officials outside the United States and imposes fines upon offending firms. It also provides for fines and imprisonment of officers, directors, or stockholders of offending firms.

The second element of FCPA is the requirement that all public companies must (1) keep reasonably detailed and accurate records which accurately and fairly reflect company financial activity and (2) devise and maintain a system of internal control that provides reasonable assurance that transactions were properly authorized, recorded, and accounted for. This element is an amendment to the Securities and Exchange Act of 1934 and therefore applies to all corporations that are subject to the 1934 act's provisions. The disclosure issues involved in this legislation are the prevention of bribery of foreign officials and the maintenance of adequate financial records.

EFFICIENT MARKET RESEARCH

Economists have argued for many years that in a free market economy with perfect competition, price is determined by (1) the availability of the product (supply) and (2) the desire to possess that product (demand). According to this theory, the price of the particular product is then determined by a consensus in the marketplace. This process is generally represented by the following diagram.

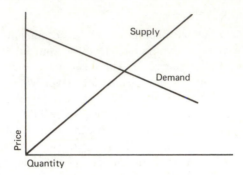

It is also argued that this model is not completely operational in the marketplace because the following assumptions about the perfectly competitive market are routinely violated by the nature of our economic system.

1. All economic units possess complete knowledge of the economy.
2. All goods and services in the economy are completely mobile and can be easily shifted within the economy.
3. Each buyer and seller must be so small in relation to the total supply and demand that neither has an influence on the price or demand in total.
4. There are no artificial restrictions placed on demand, supply, or prices of goods and services.

The best example of the supply and demand model may be in the securities market, particularly when we consider that stock exchanges provide a relatively efficient distribution system and that information concerning securities is available through many different outlets. Examples of these information sources are

1. Published financial statements from the companies.
2. Quarterly earnings reports released by the corporation through the news media.
3. Reports of management changes released through the news media.
4. Competitor financial information released through financial reports or the news media.
5. Contract awardings announced by the government or private firms.
6. Information disseminated to stockholders at annual stockholders' meetings.

THE EFFICIENT MARKET HYPOTHESIS

According to the supply and demand model, price is determined by the purchaser's knowledge of relevant information about the product. This model has been refined in the securities market to become known as the efficient market hypothesis (EMH). The disclosure issues addressed by the EMH are (1) what information about a company is of value to an investor and (2) does the form of the disclosure of various types of corporate information impact upon the understandability of that information?

According to EMH, a market for securities can be described as efficient if it reflects all available information and reacts instantaneously to new information. Discussions of EMH in academic literature have varied in the definition of all available information and have resulted in three separate forms of the efficient market hypothesis: the *weak form,* the *semistrong form,* and the *strong form.* The efficient market hypothesis holds than an investor cannot make an *excess return* (a return above what should be expected for the security, given market conditions and the risk associated with the security) by knowledge of particular pieces of information.

WEAK FORM

The weak form of the EMH is essentially an extension of the random walk theory as expressed in financial literature. According to this theory, the historical price of a stock provides an unbiased estimate of the future price of that stock, and several studies have supported this argument.[6] However, the argument that stock prices are random does not mean that fluctuation takes place without cause or reason. On the contrary, it suggests that price changes take place because of investor knowledge about perceived earnings potential or alternative investment opportunities.

According to the weak form of the EMH, an investor cannot make excess returns by simple knowledge of past prices. For example, suppose a certain group of securities with a known risk yields an average return on investment of 10 percent (this average is composed of returns above and below that figure). According to the weak form of the EMH, the stock market incorporates all information on past prices into the determination of the current price. Therefore, the charting of the trends of security prices adds no additional information to the investor. If this form of the EMH is correct, an investor could do just as well by randomly selecting a portfolio of securities as he could by charting the past prices

---

[6]See, for example, E. Fama, "The Behavior of Stock Market Prices," *Journal of Business* (January 1965), pp. 285–299.

of securities and selecting the portfolio on that basis. (It is important to note here that the EMH is based upon a portfolio of securities and average returns on investments, not on individual purchases of securities.) The implications of this form of the EMH are that some of the information provided by security analysts is useless, that is, these individuals have correctly maintained that trends in prices are good indicators of future prices. However, knowledge of this information will not aid an investor, because it has already been incorporated into the price determination process in the marketplace.

SEMISTRONG FORM

The difference between the weak, semistrong, and strong forms of the EMH lies in the amount of information assumed to be incorporated into the determination of security prices. Under the semistrong form of the EMH, all publicly available information including past stock prices is assumed to be important in determining security prices. In other words, if this form of the EMH is correct, no investor can make an excess return by use of publicly available information because this information has already been considered by the marketplace in establishing security prices. The implication of this form of the EMH for accountants is that footnote disclosure is just as relevant as information in the body of financial statements. Additionally, it suggests that the accounting procedures adopted by a particular organization will have no effect if an investor can convert to the desired method. The results of studies on this form of EMH have been generally supportive.

STRONG FORM

According to the strong form of the EMH, all information, including security price trends, publicly available information, and insider information, is impounded into security prices in such a way as to leave no opportunity for excess returns. The implications of this form of the EMH for accountants is that all information available, whether external or internal, will be considered by the marketplace. That is, as soon as a piece of information is known by anyone in a corporation, that information is immediately incorporated into the determination of a security's price in the market. This form, in effect, says that published accounting information is no more valuable than any other type of available information, whether publicly available or not.

Most of the evidence testing this form of the EMH suggests that it is not valid. However, one study of mutual funds, whose managers are more likely to have insider information, indicated that such funds did no better than an individual investor could expect to do if he had purchased a diversified portfolio with similar risk, and, in fact, many did worse than randomly selected portfolios would have done.[7] This study tends to support the strong form of the EMH.

The efficient market hypothesis presents an interesting research challenge for accountants. Research strategies must be designed to test each of the EMH forms so that more solid conclusions can be drawn. The EMH is important to accountants because it provides evidence on the manner in which information about business enterprises is incorporated into the price of corporate securities, and research of this nature will allow investor-oriented accounting principles to be developed.

AGENCY THEORY

Financial accounting theory attempts to specify which events to record, how the recorded data should be manipulated, and the manner in which the data should be presented. As discussed earlier, theory has developed pragmatically; that is, if a practice or method has been used to satisfy a particular reporting need in the past by a large number of accountants, its continued use is acceptable. Except for the works of Paton[8] and Canning,[9] no attempt to develop a comprehensive theory of accounting was made before World War II. Since that time there has been an increasing demand for such a theory; indeed, in the last two decades the efforts to satisfy this demand have permeated accounting literature. These efforts rely heavily on theories developed in mathematics, economics, and finance.

There are two basic types of theory: descriptive and normative. Descriptive theories are attempts to explain observed phenomena. The extreme diversity of accounting practices and application has made development of a comprehensive description of accounting difficult. Concurrently, to become a theory, description must have explanatory value. For example, not only must the use of historical cost be observed, that use must also be explained.

Normative theories are based on a set of goals, but there is no set of goals that is universally accepted by accountants. Normative accounting theories are usually acceptable only to those individuals who agree with the assumptions upon which they are based. Nevertheless, most accounting theories are normative because they are based upon some particular objectives of financial reporting.

Attempts to describe financial statements and the accounting theories from which they originate, and to explain their development based on the economic

[7]See, for example, J. Williamson, "Measuring Mutual Fund Performance." *Financial Analysis Journal* (November–December 1972), pp. 78–84.

[8]William A. Paton, *Accounting Theory—With Special Reference to the Corporate Enterprise* (New York: The Ronald Press, 1922).

[9]John B. Canning, *The Economics of Accountancy* (New York: The Ronald Press, 1929).

theories of prices, agency, public choice, and economic regulation, have been grouped under the title *agency theory*. Agency theory offers a consistent and relatively complete explanation for accounting theories and standards.

The basic assumption of agency theory is that individuals maximize their own expected utilities and are resourceful and innovative in doing so. Therefore, the disclosure issue raised by agency theory is a particular individual's expected benefit from a particular course of action. That is, how might a manager or stockholder benefit from a corporate decision?

An *agency* is defined as a relationship by consent between two parties, whereby one party (agent) agrees to act on behalf of the other party (principal). For example, the relationship between shareholders and managers of a corporation is an agency relationship, as is the relationship between managers and auditors and, to a greater or lesser degree, that between auditors and shareholders.

Inherent in this theory is the assumption that there is a conflict of interest between the owners of a firm (shareholders) and the managers. This conflict of interest arises from the belief that managers were maximizing their own utility. Similarly, shareholders desire to maximize their own profits. The conflict arises when decisions made by managers to maximize their own utility do not maximize shareholder wealth. For example, a manager may choose accounting alternatives that increase accounting earnings when a management compensation scheme is tied to those earnings.

Agency relationships involve costs to the principals. The costs of an agency relationship have been defined as the sum of (1) monitoring expenditures by the principal, (2) bonding expenditures by the agent, and (3) the residual loss.[10] Watts explains these concepts as follows.

> *Monitoring expenditures are expenditures by the principal to "control" the agent's behavior (e.g., costs of measuring and observing the agent's behaviour, costs of establishing compensation policies, etc.). The agent has incentives to make expenditures to guarantee that he will not take certain actions to harm the principal's interest or that he will compensate the principal if he does. These are bonding costs. Finally, even with monitoring and bonding expenditures, the actions taken by the agent will differ from the actions the principal would take himself. . . . the wealth effect of this divergence in actions [is defined] as "residual loss."*[11]

Since this theory holds that all individuals will act to maximize their own utility, managers and shareholders would be expected to incur bonding and

---

[10]M. Jensen and W. H. Meckling, "Theory of the Firm: Managerial Behavior, Agency Costs and Ownership Structures," *Journal of Financial Economics* (October 1976), p. 308.

[11]R. L. Watts, "Corporate Financial Statements, a Product of the Market and Political Processes," *Australian Journal of Management* (September 1977), p. 131.

monitoring costs as long as those costs were less than the reduction in the residual loss. For instance, a management compensation plan that ties management wealth to shareholder wealth would reduce the agency cost of equity, or a bond convenant that restricts dividend payments would reduce the agency costs of debt. Examples of this last type of costs were included in corporate charters as early as the 1600s. According to agency theory, in an unregulated economy, the preparation of financial statements will be determined by the effect of such statements on agency costs. That is, financial statements would tend to be presented more often by companies with many bond covenants (e.g., restrictions on dividends or relatively more outside debt). Similarly, the greater the value of a company's fixed assets, the more likely a charge for maintenance, repair, or depreciation will be included in the financial statements. The conclusion drawn by agency theory is that multiple methods of accounting for similar circumstances have developed from the desires of various individuals, such as managers, shareholders, and bondholders, to minimize agency costs.

Since private-sector regulations and federal legislation help to determine the items disclosed in financial statements, the effects of regulation and the political process must be added to the results of agency relationships. However, the regulation process is affected by external pressures. Groups of individuals may have incentives to band together to cause the government to transfer wealth, as in farm subsidies. The justification for these transfers is that they are ''in the public interest.'' Additionally, elected officials and special interest groups may use the so-called high profits of corporations to create crises, which are solved by wealth transfers ''in the public interest.'' A prime example is the ''windfall profits'' tax enacted at the time of the oil crisis.

The larger a corporation is, the more susceptible it is to political scrutiny and subsequent wealth transfers. Therefore, the larger a company is, the more likely it is to choose accounting alternatives that minimize net income. Conversely, small companies often have incentives to show greater net income in order to increase borrowing potential and available capital. Agency theory holds that these varying desires are a reason for the diversity of acceptable accounting practices.

Agency theory also attributes the preponderance of normative theories of accounting to impact on the political processes. When a crisis develops, elected officials base their positions on ''public interest'' arguments. These positions are frequently grounded in the notion that the problem is caused by an inefficiency in the market that can only be remedied by government intervention. Elected officials then seek justification of their position in the form of normative theories supporting that position. They also tend to look for theories prescribing accounting procedures that should be used to increase the information available to investors or make the market more efficient.

The advocates of agency theory maintain that it helps to explain financial statements and the absence of a comprehensive theory of accounting. However, the basic assumption that everyone acts to maximize his or her own expected utility causes this theory to be politically and socially unacceptable. Agency theory advocates maintain that this is true regardless of how logically sound the theory may be, or even how well it may stand up to empirical testing. For example, if an elected official supported a theory that explained her or his actions as those that maximize her or his own utility, rather than the public good, the official would not be maximizing her or his own utility.

Agency theory may help to explain the lack of existence of a comprehensive accounting theory. It implies that a framework of accounting theory cannot be developed because of the diverse interests involved in financial reporting. However, there is an even more basic reason why agency theory will have limited direct impact on financial accounting. Agency theory is a descriptive theory in that it helps to explain why a diversity of accounting practices exists. Therefore, even if subsequent testing supports this theory, it will *not* identify the correct accounting procedures to be used in various circumstances, and thus accounting practice will not be changed.

HUMAN INFORMATION PROCESSING

The annual reports of large corporations provide investors with vast amounts of information. These reports may include a balance sheet, an income statement, a statement of changes in financial position, numerous footnotes to the financial statements, a five-year summary of operations, a description of the various activities of the corporation, a message to the stockholders from the top management of the corporation, a discussion and analysis by management of the annual operations, and the report of the company's independent certified public accountant.

The disclosure of all of this information is intended to aid investors and potential investors in making buy-hold-sell decisions about the company's securities. Studies attempting to assess an individual's ability to utilize information have been entitled *human information processing* research. The disclosure issue addressed by these studies is, How do individuals utilize available information?

In general, this research has indicated that individuals have a very limited ability to process large amounts of information.[12] There are three main consequences of this finding.

---

[12]See, for example, R. Libby and B. Lewis, "Human Information Processing Research in Accounting: The State of the Art," *Accounting Organizations and Society,* Vol. 2, No. 3 (1977), pp. 245–268.

1. An individual's perception of information is quite selective. That is, since individuals are only capable of apprehending a small part of their environment, their anticipation of what they expect to perceive about a particular situation will determine to a large extent what they do perceive.
2. Since individuals make decisions on the basis of a small part of the total information available, they do not have the capacity to make optimal decisions.
3. Since individuals are incapable of integrating a great deal of information, they process information in a sequential fashion.

In summary, individuals use a selective, stepwise information processing system. This system has limited capacity and uncertainty is frequently ignored.[13]

These findings may have far-reaching disclosure implications for accountants. The current trend of the FASB and SEC is to require the disclosure of more and more information. But if the tentative conclusions of the human information processing research are correct, these additional disclosures may have an effect opposite to what was intended. That is, the goal of the FASB and SEC is to provide all relevant information so that individuals may make informed decisions about the company. However, the annual reports may already contain more information than can be adequately and efficiently processed by individuals.

Research is needed to determine the most relevant information to include in corporate annual reports. Once this goal has been accomplished, accountants will have taken a large step in determining what information to disclose about accounting entities.

SUMMARY

Full and fair disclosure has become increasingly important in financial reporting. The ethical and auditing standards of the AICPA, various pronouncements and reporting requirements of the SEC, and relevant research findings make it abundantly clear that the nature and format of disclosures are extremely important to the users of financial statements.

In the readings for this chapter, John M. Fedders and L. Glenn Perry take the position that the SEC's top priority should be policing financial disclosure fraud. And J. Edward Ketz and Arthur Wyatt explore the goals and objectives of the FASB in light of efficient market research.

---

[13]For a more thorough discussion, see R. M. Hogarth. "Process Tracing in Clinical Judgments," *Behavioral Science* (September 1974), pp. 298–313.

POLICING FINANCIAL DISCLOSING FRAUD: THE SEC'S TOP PRIORITY

JOHN M. FEDDERS

L. GLENN PERRY*

Central to the disclosure system are financial statements and the disclosure of financial information. No other aspect of the disclosure process has a greater impact on the judgment of investors. No other disclosure has a greater impact on market prices.

Financial information is of the utmost relevance in 1984. The United States is recovering from a recession, and business enterprises continue to experience economic uncertainties and difficulties. History tells us that periods of fiscal turmoil and economic difficulties spawn abuses and deceptions. During periods of economic stress and business stagnation, some managements have engaged in acts designed to create an appearance of financial stability and prosperity. The reasons are obvious—to maintain the market price of a company's stock; to create the appearance of profitability in order to obtain financing or to prevent a default on bank loans; or to satisfy management greed and ego.

There are substantial pressures on managements to minimize financial problems. This environment has led to the collective efforts of the Securities and Exchange

Commission's Divisions of Enforcement and Corporation Finance and the Office of the Chief Accountant to identify fiscal trends and related disclosure problems which require close surveillance and may lead to the need for enforcement actions.

THE ENFORCEMENT PROGRAM

No matter what the composition of the commission or who manages the various offices and divisions, the enforcement program against financial fraud will remain at the forefront. We are focusing our enforcement actions against financial fraud, including "cooking the books," accounting irregularities, reckless application of GAAP and GAAS, and improprieties arising from "shopping" for auditors' opinions. We have initiated a score of these cases, and a greater number are in investigation. The longest and most significant chapter in the enforcement legacy of John S. R. Shad, the current chairman of the commission, will be the financial fraud program—longer and more significant than the much publicized "insider trading" prosecutions chapter.

A principal focus when "prospecting" for financial fraud is management's discussion and analysis (MD&A) of financial condition and results of operations. Since the MD&A was first required in 1974, its importance has dramatically increased. It provides information to enhance an understanding of historical financial statements. Also, it provides information to improve an understanding of the enterprise itself, including its future prospects. For example, the MD&A requires a description of known trends or uncertainties that are reasonably expected to have a material favorable or unfavorable impact on future operations.

Although the financial disclosure fraud enforcement program is designed to include a broad variety of misconduct, several areas have been particularly emphasized. They are as follows:

1. Liquidity problems, such as (a) decreased inflow of collections from sales to customers, (b) the lack of availability of credit from suppliers, banks, and others, and (c) the inability to meet maturing obligations when they fall due. Corporate disclosure must not minimize or fail fully to explain liquidity problems.

2. Operating trends and factors affecting profits and losses, such as (a) curtailment of operations, (b) decline of orders, (c) increased competition, or (d) cost overruns on major contracts. Disclosure must include early notice of a significant reversal of previously reported sales trends. There must be an objective discussion of poor financial results.

Not only must material facts affecting a company's operations be reported, they must be reported promptly. Corporate releases which disclose favorable developments but do not describe material adverse developments do not serve investors' needs and may violate the antifraud provisions. In the case of an issuer making an offering or a continuous offering of its shares, the failure to disclose such material adverse developments also may violate the Securities Act of 1933 if there is not an appropriate updating of information.

Unless adequate and accurate information is publicly available, a company may not purchase its own securities or make acquisitions using its securities. Furthermore, insiders who trade in the securities of their companies in these circumstances violate the antifraud provisions of the Securities Exchange Act of 1934.

3. Material increases in problem loans must be reported by financial institutions. Increased financial pressure on certain industries has caused a sharp increase in uncollectible and nonperforming loans. Disclosure must be made when there is a material increase in (a) interest that has not been paid, (b) interest that is reduced or deferred, or (c) doubtful collections. When necessary, an increase in provisions for losses must be timely reported.

4. Corporations cannot avoid their disclosure obligations when they approach business decline or failure. Economists report that the business failure rate is the highest since the trough of the Depression in 1932.

The principal method of projecting seeming economic well-being in the face of business decline and possible failure is through deceptive and fraudulent accounting practices. In order to hide fiscal difficulties and to deceive investors, declining and failing companies have (a) prematurely recognized income, (b) improperly treated operating leases as sales, (c) inflated inventory by improper application of the LIFO inventory method, (d) included fictitious amounts in inventories, (e) failed to recognize losses through write-offs and allowances, (f) improperly capitalized or deferred costs and expenses, (g) included unusual gains in operating income, (h) overvalued marketable securities, (i) created "sham" year-end transactions to boost reported earnings, and (j) changed their accounting practices to increase earnings without disclosing the changes.

These are not the universe of the trends and disclosure areas we have under scrutiny. The commission staff is looking for emerging problems. Although our focus is not entirely on financial information, the crucial choices for America's future are economic. Consequently, accurate reporting of material financial information is essential.

PROSECUTORIAL DISCRETION

By prosecutorial discretion, the commission applies the available enforcement sanctions and remedies to the fraud or misconduct involved. Each fraud or misconduct does not require the most severe sanction. Although the commission's enforcement remedies are limited to (a) civil injunctions, (b) section 15(c)(4) and rule 2(e) administrative proceedings, and (c) section 21(a) reports of investigation, and do not include the ability to levy fines, the remedial purposes of the federal securities laws have been satisfied by the application of these remedies. Indeed, there are situations in which misconduct has occurred and prosecutorial discretion dictates that no enforcement action be initiated. Certain situations are best resolved by the company's voluntarily taking action such as a restatement of financial statements.

After the discovery of all facts regarding a financial fraud or an accounting irregularity, the difficult task is the application of prosecutorial discretion. The commission possesses wide discretion in ways that help the disclosure system function effectively. Because certain conduct violates the federal securities laws does not mean that the commission must file charges and seek to impose sanctions on the malefactor. The task is not merely action which places sanctions on the malefactors and deters potential wrongdoers, but has as its principal focus the protection of investors and the maintenance of the integrity of the U.S. securities markets.

A difficult aspect of prosecutorial discretion regarding financial disclosure fraud relates to whether directors, officers, or employees of the entity also should be charged and, if so, whether as (a) participants, (b) control persons, or (c) aiders and abettors. Our objective is to identify the corporate officials responsible and to impose sanctions on them for their misconduct.

There also is the question whether the underwriters, lawyers, and accountants participated in the fraud or misconduct and, if so, should be charged (a) in injunctive actions as participants or aiders and abettors or (b) in administrative proceedings. The commission has not shied away from charging professionals, including accountants, in rule 2(e) administrative proceedings.

If a professional's conduct amounts to a violation of, or aiding and abetting a violation of, the federal securities laws, the commission should as a general matter sue to enjoin the professional from repetition of such conduct—not bring a rule 2(e) adminstrative proceeding. However, even if there is a violation of law, in appropriate circumstances, prosecutorial discretion may lead to a decision that an injunction would be improper and an administrative proceeding under rule 2(e) would be appropriate.

Accounting firms are the major key to sustaining high-quality work by the accounting profession. In our view, it is therefore imperative that the commission maintain its ability to influence the activities of such firms through its enforcement-related programs, while at the same time striving to use its enforcement and regulatory tools fairly and carefully within the legal constraints which the courts and others have construed or are likely to construe.

The fact that an accounting firm permits its name to be attached to a report on, or certification of, financial statements is a factor, but in our view not itself a sufficient factor, to support the appropriateness of naming the firm, instead of or in addition to individual firm members, in any rule 2(e) proceeding that might be instituted because of deficiencies in the audit. In determining whether proceedings should be instituted against an accounting firm under rule 2(e), it is important to the commission's deliberations to have information regarding the relationship of the alleged audit deficiencies, violations of the federal securities laws, or improper professional conduct to (a) the adequacy of applicable firm audit engagement and review practices or procedures and the extent to which those procedures were adhered to in the audit under inquiry; (b) the selection, training, supervision, and conduct of members or employees of the accounting firm involved in the engagement; (c) the role played by top-level managers in the firm; and (d) the audit work performed on other engagements in which deficiencies have been uncovered.

THE SEC'S TRACK RECORD

Enough talk about policy and objectives. What has the commission done? The track record permits an evaluation of whether it has met its objectives.

The following is a description of 12 actions in this area.

1. In July 1982 the commission published a section 21(a) report of investigation regarding Fidelity Financial Corporation, a savings and loan holding company, and Fidelity Savings and Loan Association, its principal subsidiary. This report emphasizes the commission's concern with respect to the disclosure issues raised in connection with (a) offerings and sales of retail repurchase agreements and (b) a press release announcing fiscal year-end operational and financial results.

The commission alleged that Fidelity and the Association violated the antifraud provisions of the securities laws by (a) making false and misleading statements and omitting to state material facts concerning the security interest in the collateral backing the "retail repos," the existence of a trust, and the financial condition of its subsidiary and (b) failing to disclose material information concerning its financial condition in a 1981 year-end press release in January 1982.

The commission emphasized that issuers of retail repos should be mindful of the need to comply with the disclosure requirements of the securities laws as well as disclosure guidelines of other federal and state regulatory agencies. It also said it is incumbent on companies, when issuing press statements announcing year-end results prior to their release, to inform the public not only of the extent of losses suffered but also of the adverse impact that the continuation of losses may have on operations in the pending year if it is reasonably anticipated that such losses will continue.

2. In September 1982 the commission initiated an injunctive action against Saxon Industries and certain senior officers. The commission alleged that, from as early as 1968, Saxon and its officers knowingly and willfully falsified books and records to inflate earnings.

It was alleged that the scheme was carried out by the creation of nonexistent inventories on the records of various divisions of Saxon. This allegedly was done by (a) creating and maintaining false records, (b) Saxon's computer being programmed automatically to add false inventory, and (c) transferring nonexistent inventory from one division to another to avoid detection. By 1981 the nonexistent inventory was approximately $75 million.

3. In December 1982 the commission initiated an injunctive action against McCormick & Company, Incorporated, and the general manager of its Grocery Products Division. It was alleged that from at least 1976 the company engaged in a scheme to inflate earnings to meet profit objectives mandated by corporate management by improperly deferring certain promotional and advertising expenses and by prematurely recognizing revenues for goods that were not shipped until a later fiscal period.

In order to conceal these improper accounting practices from its independent accountants, it was alleged that McCormick personnel (a) intentionally made false statements to auditors, (b) maintained two sets of records, and (c) altered various documents, including shipping invoices and advertising bills.

4. In February 1983 a section 15(c)(4) administrative proceeding was initiated against Clabir Corporation. It used a method to price its marketable equity securities other than what is required by GAAP.

The commission concluded that the use of a price other than the quoted market price for determining the market value of marketable equity securities is provided for neither by GAAP nor by commission pronouncements.

5. In March 1983 an injunctive action was initiated against the president and vice-president for operations of Security America Corporation, a holding company whose sole operating subsidiary was a multiple-line casualty and property insurance company. It was alleged that Security America overstated its earnings by understating loss reserves both for assumed workers' compensation claims and for direct insurance business.

It was alleged that the defendants overstated the reserves by (a) using an outdated mortality table, (b) reducing estimated annual medical costs, (c) failing to factor in an inflation rate when estimating future claims, (d) failing to consider some unpaid claims in establishing reserves, and (e) arbitrarily reducing reserves. The commission also alleged deficiencies in disclosures of cash flow problems and false statements to the company's auditors.

6. In May 1983 the commission initiated an injunctive action against A.M. International, Inc. It was alleged that throughout its 1980 fiscal year and continuing in its 1981 fiscal year, A.M. misrepresented its financial condition and results of operations by (a) making improper adjustments to its allowance and accrual accounts and its gross profit, (b) attributing certain expenses and charges to periods other than those to which the expenses and charges belonged, and (c) inflating revenues and results of operations. Moreover, it was alleged that A.M. failed to record on its books and records material amounts of adjustments relating to its results of operations.

This investigation uncovered examples of extreme management pressure on subordinates to meet performance goals. In response to such pressure, various divisions of A.M. engaged in widespread and pervasive accounting irregularities in order to present results of operations which conformed to budgeted performance objectives.

7. In July 1983 the commission issued a section 21(a) report of investigation regarding Aetna Life and Casualty Company. In 1981 it began recognizing currently in its financial statements anticipated future tax benefits of net operating loss (NOL) carry-forwards. The commission's position was that Aetna did not meet the "assurance beyond any reasonable doubt" standard imposed by GAAP.

GAAP states that tax benefits of NOLs should not be recognized until they are actually realized, except in unusual circumstances in which realization is assured beyond any reasonable doubt at the time the loss carry-forwards arise. Without admitting or denying the validity of the commission's position, Aetna restated its 1982 year-end and quarterly financial statements.

8. In August 1983 the commission initiated the second of two cases against Ronson Corporation in less than a year. In a civil action for an order directing compliance with the commission's order issued in the first case, it was alleged that Ronson failed to describe in its MD&A and business description that its largest customer (a) had shut down its operations, (b) had suspended all purchases from Ronson, and (c) was unlikely to resume such purchases until some future period. It also was alleged that Ronson failed to state that when sales to its largest customer resumed, such sales would most likely be reduced by 30 percent to 50 percent below previous levels.

9. In October 1983 the commission initiated a section 15(c)(4) proceeding against Southeastern Savings & Loan Company and Scottish Savings and Loan Association. The commission alleged that losses on the sale of securities hedged by future contracts must be recognized at the time of sale unless the sale qualifies as a "wash sale." The SEC believed in this case that the sale of 15 percent and 16 percent "Ginnie Mae" certificates and the purchase of 8 percent through 12.5 percent Ginnie Mae certificates did not qualify as a wash sale because the certificates purchased and sold were not the same or substantially the same as contemplated by GAAP.

The commission ordered the two savings and loan associations to restate previously issued financial statements because they both improperly deferred net losses on these transactions when GAAP required the recognition of the losses in the period in which the transaction occurred.

10. In February 1984 the commission filed an injunctive action against United States Surgical Corporation and various senior corporate officials. It was alleged that from 1979 through 1981 they had engaged in various improper practices in which pretax earnings were overstated by more than $18 million. It was further alleged that certain of these practices continued during 1982 and 1983.

The commission alleged that these practices included (a) the falsification of corporate records, (b) the recording as sales of unordered products, (c) the improper capitalization of costs as fixed assets, (d) the improper capitalization of legal expenses, (e) the improper capitalization of various expenses as assets, and (f) the failure to write off assets which could not be located.

As part of its relief, the commission required that bonuses paid to certain officers which were based on the improperly reported earnings be repaid to the corporation.

11. In February 1984 the commission initiated an injunctive action against IntraWest Financial Corporation, a bank holding company, and two of its officers. The commission alleged that the allowance for possible loan and lease losses was understated for the first three-quarters of fiscal year 1982, causing IntraWest's reported income to be overstated materially.

The commission alleged that, despite material adverse information about their own loan portfolio, IntraWest's officers used an improper method to calculate the allowance for possible loan and lease losses that were based on average allowance percentages of a peer group.

12. In February 1984 the commission brought a section 15(c)(4) administrative proceeding against Utica Bankshares Corporation, a bank holding company. The commission alleged that UBC understated its allowance for possible loan losses for the third quarter of 1982 and, thus, materially overstated its reported income.

It was alleged that the former management of the bank, in establishing its allowance for possible loan losses, failed to give adequate consideration to the adverse impact on the quality of its loan portfolio of significant developments and trends, including a severe decline in the energy segment of the regional economy and the failure of a major bank in its operating area.

These are not the universe of the cases initiated in the past several years. They are representative of the types of financial disclosure investigations and enforcement actions on which the commission will continue to focus.

The commission will remain vigorous in the enforcement of the antifraud and reporting provisions of the federal securities laws. Whether investment decisions will be correct depends directly on the accuracy, quality, and timeliness of the financial information on which they are based. The commission will not temporize with financial disclosure fraud.

Public confidence in the commission is on the shoulders of its enforcement program. As custodian of this important responsibility, we are dedicated to protecting the interests of investors and the integrity of the capital markets.

THE FASB IN A WORLD WITH PARTIALLY EFFICIENT MARKETS

J. EDWARD KETZ
ARTHUR R. WYATT

During the past twenty years or so, accounting argumentation has increasingly dealt with the issue of stock market efficiency. Finance and accounting literature contains a plethora of articles on stock market efficiency, many of which indicate that the stock market is an efficient processor of information. Since the evidence for stock market efficiency seems abundant, some accountants have argued that controversial topics should be adjudicated in terms of efficient market theory.

While the evidence of stock market efficiency is quite convincing and while the concept can be helpful in standards-setting, it is doubtful that it can or should become

Reprinted with permission from *Journal of Accounting, Auditing & Finance,* Fall 1983 Vol. 7, No. 1, Copyright © 1983 Wanen, Gorham & Lamont, Inc., 210 South St. Boston MA 02111. All Rights Reserved.

the major vehicle for resolving accounting issues. Accounting theorists and accounting standards-setting bodies have always been concerned with more than just how financial markets obtain, interpret, assimilate, and use accounting information. Stock markets are important, but they are not the alpha and omega of accounting.

The purpose of this article is to explore the goals and the objectives of the Financial Accounting Standards Board (FASB) in a world characterized by partially efficient markets. The next section of the article reviews the concept of stock market efficiency and the FASB's objectives in a world of efficient markets. In the third section the focus is on institutions other than stock markets. We note that in the real world there are institutions other than stock markets, such as credit markets, labor markets, and government agencies, for which the concept of stock market efficiency is irrelevant. The fourth part of this article contains our arguments that in the real world stock markets are not completely efficient and that the objectives for the FASB will differ in a world of partially efficient markets from a world characterized by completely efficient markets. The fifth section examines some of the welfare implications of stock market efficiency. We conclude the article with a discussion of implications for the FASB.

STOCK MARKET EFFICIENCY

A stock market is said to be efficient if the stock market prices fully reflect the available information at any time. In other words, the investor is not playing a game of chance. Rather, stock market returns are a function of the underlying risk of the firm. In pricing assets, the market utilizes whatever information is available, including accounting information. Thus, investors cannot earn abnormally high returns because stock prices are reflective of the risk of the firm.

Fama depicts three levels of efficient markets.[1] The weak form of the efficient markets hypothesis states that the equilibrium expected prices fully reflect the sequence of historical prices. This means that historical price data and volume data for securities cannot be used to earn abnormal returns. For example, technical analysts and chartists can do no better than a simple buy and hold strategy. The semistrong form of the efficient markets hypothesis states that the equilibrium expected prices fully reflect all publicly available informa-

tion. This means that information about stock splits, stock dividends, secondary offerings of common stock, new issues of stocks, changes in interest rates, etc., cannot be used to earn abnormal information. The semistrong form of the hypothesis implies that information contained in annual reports also cannot be used to earn abnormal returns. The strong form of the efficient markets hypothesis states that the equilibrium expected prices fully reflect all information, public and private. In other words, no trading rule based on inside information can be used to earn abnormal returns.

The evidence is compelling that the stock market is indeed efficient in the weak form. Much evidence also supports the notion of efficient markets in the semistrong form, although a number of anomalies exist.[2] The strong form, however, may not be a realistic hypothesis since management insiders and exchange specialists appear able to earn excess returns.

Two aspects of the efficient markets hypothesis are important. First, capital asset prices adjust rapidly to new information. Second, capital asset prices adjust to new information in an unbiased manner. This means that capital markets will react to published accounting reports very quickly and quite accurately, assuming accounting reports convey relevant information for assessing share value.

What should be the FASB's objectives given an efficient stock market? Beaver has stated four implications for the FASB given an efficient stock market [1]. First, many reporting issues are trivial. Firms should report using one method and provide sufficient disclosure to permit adjustment to other methods. Second, the role of

[1] Eugene F. Fama, "Efficient Capital Markets: A Review of Theory and Empirical Work," *Journal of Finance*, May 1970, pp. 383–417. For a review and a refinement of Fama's definitions, see William H. Beaver, "Market Efficiency," *The Accounting Review*, Jan. 1981, pp. 23–37.

[2] For example, see Thomas R. Dyckman, David H. Downes, and Robert P. Magee, *Efficient Capital Markets: A Critical Analysis* (Prentice-Hall, 1975), Ch. 3.

financial reports is to prevent individuals from earning abnormal returns from inside information. All items should be disclosed if there are no additional costs. Third, naive investors can get hurt by presuming they can trade on published accounting data and earn abnormal returns. The FASB should discourage these beliefs. Fourth, the FASB should realize that accounting reports are not the only suppliers of information. Other sources of information may be more appropriate for disseminating firm information if they involve less cost.

The implications for FASB objectives detailed by Beaver are open to serious question for three reasons. First, stock market agents are not the only users of accounting information. Other consumers have financial information needs that should concern the FASB. Second, we feel that the efficient markets hypothesis is overstated. We present arguments against the efficient markets hypothesis and argue instead for what is termed the partially efficient markets hypothesis. Third, even if stock markets were completely efficient in the informational sense, various reasons suggest that stock markets are not efficient in the allocative sense. These reasons are explained below.

THE STOCK MARKET IS NOT THE UNIVERSE

Without a doubt, financial reporting is important for investors. Accounting reports are not the source of information leading to investment decisions; the data are obviously too old. But the discipline of the financial report has a controlling effect on other financial information, which makes the FASB decisions important. Buying and selling shares of stock is not, however, the only economic activity of concern to the FASB. The FASB has a broader mandate

than to provide technical guidance related to financial data of interest to stock market agents.

Numerous accounting theorists have based their propositions in part on users other than investors in equity securities, and standards setters have also recognized interests of others than investors in equity securities. The following discussion will demonstrate that often accountants are interested in broad economic effects of accounting, not just the effects in the stock market.

In developing their monograph on corporate accounting, Paton and Littleton do not ignore the effects of accounting numbers [2]. They state, "Investors are not the only parties at interest" [2:2]. Others include employees, customers, governments, and the general public. They also say, "Capital should flow into those industries which serve the public interest, and within an industry into those enterprises in which the management is capable of using capital effectively" [2:3].

Edwards and Bell also were very interested in allocational efficiency [3]. "The essential decision-making function of management is the allocation of resources" [3:3]. "Real realized profit would in many respects be useful as a basis for tax payment. It has the advantages of its money counterpart and also excludes fictional gains from the tax base" [3:128].

Bedford develops his theory on income determination in part because of the role of income in society. Using previous work of May and Alexander, Bedford points out that income may be used as a basis for fiscal policy, as an aid to government supervision, as a basis for price or rate regulation, and as a basis for taxation. Bedford goes on to assert that economists are interested in the concept of income because:

(1) The income objective tends to cause resources to be allocated to their most productive use, provided that competition is free; (2) Measured past income may be used either by itself or in combination with other factors as a basis for computing the return on investment to evaluate the effectiveness of management, assuming that income is the primary objective of management; (3) "Real" income may be used to evaluate the growth of a nation and the effectiveness, in an economic sense, of the political system under which the nation operates [4:14].

Chambers bases his theory on the importance of accounting, with respect to law, producers and consumers of goods, and taxes [5]. In Chapter 3, Chambers discusses ends, preferences, and valuations and continues by describing the interaction between income and production, consumption, and savings. In Chapter 14, Chambers argues that the role of accounting is related to the theory of economic behavior in organized systems and that accountants need a better understanding of these relationships.

In establishing a defense of historical cost accounting, Ijiri focuses in part on the potential controversy concerning performance measurement.

A conflict may arise between past and present shareholders after some shareholders sell their shares based on a poor earnings report. When there is a dispute over the maximum amount the corporation can distribute as dividends, the conflict may be between shareholders and creditors. Perhaps consumers will disagree with shareholders of a regulated corporation on a "fair" return on shareholders' investment, or the corporation may vie with the Internal Revenue Service over taxable income, or divisions may challenge headquarters about incentive compensations that managers are entitled to receive based on divisional profit [6:35].

These excerpts are only a few of those that could have been cited. They are not comprehensive, nor are they intended to be. They do, however, present mosaic that accountants are concerned about economic effects in addition to stock market effects. While these views do not address the efficient markets hypothesis, they support a contention that the focus of accounting is not solely on stock market agents.

Standards-setting bodies have also maintained a perspective on the economic effects of accounting that is broader than stock market effects. This perspective is demonstrated for the Accounting Principles Board (APB) and for the FASB.

The APB issued APB Statement No. 4 in 1970 [7]. While the primary purpose of the Statement is to delineate and explain the basic concepts and elements of financial accounting, it is interesting that the report begins with a discussion about the uses and users of accounting reports. Admittedly, the APB began with a description of financial information and owners and creditors. The APB extended this list of users to include taxing authorities, employees, customers, lawyers, regulatory or registration authorities, trade associations, and labor unions. These users might make the following decisions for which they would use financial accounting information:

- *Taxing authorities*—evaluate tax returns; assess taxes or penalties; make investigations and audits.
- *Employees*—negotiate wages; terminate employment; or, for prospective employees, apply for employment.

- *Customers*—anticipate price changes; seek alternative sources or broader bases of supply.
- *Lawyers*—determine whether covenants and contractual provisions are fulfilled; advise on legality of dividends and profit sharing and deferred compensation agreements; draft pension plan terms.
- *Regulatory or registration authorities*—assess reasonableness of rate of return; allow or require increases or decreases in prices or rates; require or recommend changes in accounting or disclosure practices; issue cease-and-desist or stock-trading-suspension orders.
- *Trade associations*—compile industry statistics and make comparisons; analyze industry results.
- *Labor unions*—formulate wage and contract demands; assess enterprise and industry prospects and strengths.

The APB also discussed the organization of economic activity in society. Societies typically engage in the following economic activities: production, income distribution, exchange, consumption, saving, and investment. Financial accounting may impact each of these economic activities. Indeed, generally accepted accounting principles can be evaluated by relating the financial accounting information to the economic activities impacted.

The FASB is also concerned about the economic effects of promulgated standards and has articulated such concern in Concepts Statement No. 1 on the objectives of accounting [8].

Financial reporting is not an end in itself but is intended to provide information that is useful in making business and economic decisions—for making reasoned choices among alternative uses of scarce resources in the conduct of business and economic activities. . . . Ac-

cordingly, the objectives in this Statement are affected by the economic' legal, political, and social environment in the United States [8:¶9].

Potential users identified by the FASB include owners, lenders, suppliers, potential investors and creditors, employees, management, directors, customers, financial analysts and advisers, brokers, underwriters, stock exchanges, lawyers, economists, taxing authorities, regulatory authorities, legislators, financial press and reporting agencies, labor unions, trade associations, business researchers, teachers and students, and the public. While the FASB is principally interested in owners and lenders, it is still very much concerned with other users.

The FASB naturally is concerned about information efficiency. This is seen, for example, in paragraph 34 of Concepts Statement No. 1: "Financial reporting should provide information that is useful to present and potential investors and creditors and other users in making rational investment, credit, and similar decisions." Yet the FASB's objectives are broader than information efficiency. Allocational efficiency is also an issue before the FASB.

To the extent that financial reporting provides information that helps identify relatively efficient and inefficient users of resources, aids in assessing relative returns and risks of investment opportunities, or otherwise assists in promoting efficient functioning of capital and other markets, it helps to create a favorable environment for capital formation decisions [8:¶33].

The scope of the FASB's standards-setting is broad. The FASB needs to investigate, ponder, and decide how accounting numbers induce or hinder or have no effect on the total economy and the actors and institutions thereof. Since the FASB's objectives are broader than those involving only information efficiency of stock markets, the FASB should not necessarily be constrained by implications of the efficient markets hypothesis.

A classic example of this issue is the savings and loan industry. The concept of efficient capital markets is essentially irrelevant for this industry because the vast majority of savings and loan associations are mutual corporations, not stock corporations. Mutual associations do not have common stock, so they obviously do not issue and reacquire shares of stock, nor do investors buy and sell shares of mutual savings associations. There simply is not a stock market price for mutual associations. How can the concept of stock market efficiency apply if a market does not exist?

Accounting issues are nevertheless important for the savings and loan industry. Not too long ago, the Federal Home Loan Bank Board proposed allowed associations to retire mortgage receivables and delay the reporting of the losses. This proposal was not adopted. Specifically, any loss on such a transaction would be set up as an asset account which would be amortized over ten years. The FASB has objected to such a convoluted rule, and we concur with the FASB. More important for our concern in this article, we agree with the FASB that it should get involved in this area. The FASB has a role to play: It needs to argue for improvement in financial reporting and protest any waywardness such as distorting the definition of an asset and covering up the fact that losses exist.

We also note with interest that the Federal Home Loan Bank Board is considering a proposal to change to current value accounting [9]. A preliminary report by a task force recommends that since high and fluctuating interest rates have grossly distorted financial reports of savings associations, current value reports should supplant conventional statements. We recommend that the FASB study this proposal and provide guidance to the Federal Home Loan Bank Board.

STOCK MARKETS ARE NOT COMPLETELY EFFICIENT

A second limitation on the value of applying stock market efficiency to policy issues in accounting is that the concept of stock market efficiency probably is not fairly descriptive of the real world.[3] Stock markets are not necessarily inefficient; stock markets are only partially efficient. The degree to which markets are efficient is a function of a variety of factors, including the costs of information, the costs of stock market transactions, the quality of information, and the degree of market completeness. We argue that these and other factors tend to impair market efficiency. For simplicity, we focus only on one factor: costs of information.

Stocks are an economic commodity. Ac-

[3]There is a rich literature primarily in the economics journals that has challenged the efficient markets hypothesis. See Sanford J. Grossman and Joseph E. Stiglitz, "Information and Competitive Price Systems," *American Economic Review*, May 1976, pp. 246–253; Steve Salop, "Information and Monopolistic Competition," *American Economic Review*, May 1976, pp. 240–245; Sanford Grossman, "On the Efficiency of Competitive Stock Markets Where Trades Have Diverse Information," *Journal of Finance*, May 1976, pp. 573–585; Sanford Grossman, "Further Results on the Informational Efficiency of Competitive Stock Markets," *Journal of Economic Theory*, June 1978, pp. 81–101; Sanford J. Grossman and Joseph E. Stiglitz, "On the Impossibility of Informationally Efficient Markets," *American Economic Review*, June 1980, pp. 393–408; Stephen Figlewski, "Information Diversity and Market Behavior," *Journal of Finance*, March 1982, pp. 85–102.

Figure 1 Stock prices in a world of costless information.

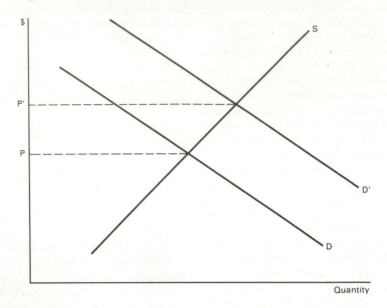

cordingly, equilibrium stock prices are de- termined by supply and demand. At equi- librium supply equals demand. The role of information in such an environment is to lead actors and institutions to change the supply and demand curves. New informa- tion leads to new equilibrium prices be- cause demand curves shift on the basis of the new information.

Suppose now that there are two classes of investors, those who are informed and those who are uninformed. Assume that the stock in question has supply S and demand D such that its equilibrium price is P. This relationship is depicted in Figure 1. As- sume that new information becomes avail- able such that the correct demand curve is D' and the correct price is P'.

Initially let us assume that information is costless. What happens? The informed in- vestors would immediately recognize that profits can be attained by purchasing the stock at P and selling at P'. They would

purchase the stock at P. But the increased demand for the security by the informed investors would drive up the price. As long as an informed investor can purchase the stock at a price below P', that individual would do so. But this would continually drive up the price. This process would con- tinue until the demand curve is shifted to the correct demand curve D' and the price would continually increase until it reached P', the correct price. This phenomenon is termed "arbitrage." Note that the capital asset prices would adjust very rapidly to the new information and that they would do so in an accurate manner.

When the adjustment is complete, the price of the security conveys the effects of all the information from the informed in- vestors to the uninformed investors. The uninformed individuals may not know the precise details of the new information, but they know the implications. In other words, when the uninformed investors observe the price of the security change from P to P', they know that new information has been generated and that the new information implies that the correct new equilibrium price is P'. This characterization is the essence of the efficient markets hypothesis; that is, markets are efficient if the price system conveys all of the information from the informed individuals to the uninformed.

Now assume a more realistic world where information is costly. Information costs include education costs, search costs, and costs of analysis. Education costs are the costs of learning and understanding what information is and what it means and how to search for and analyze information. Search costs are the costs for gathering information. These costs include time and effort expended as well as out-of-pocket costs to acquire the information. Costs of analysis are the costs of analyzing information about a security to make a decision about it. These costs are primarily the time and effort expended to process the data. The form of these costs may be transferred; for example, an individual might hire a financial analyst to perform the task rather than do it himself.

Costly information changes the model in a fundamental way. An individual who chooses to be informed and incurs costs to be informed will expect a reasonable return not only on the risky asset being invested in but also on the information costs. This is depicted in Figure 2. As before, we assume that the initial supply is S and the initial demand is D so that the equilibrium price is P. New information emanates such that it implies that the "correct" price is P'. Informed investors will buy the security at price P and the increased demand will again drive up the price. Unlike the previous example, though, the equilibrium price will never move to the "correct" price P'. In-

Figure 2   Stock prices in a world of costly information.

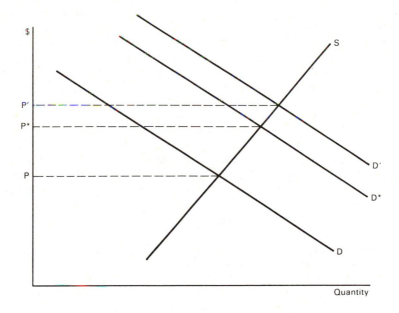

stead the price of the security will be driven up to some price, say P*. It will go no further because the informed investors would be unable to earn a return on their information costs. Indeed, if the price were to move to P', the informed individuals would earn less than the uninformed individuals because the informed investors pay the information costs while the uninformed do not. In this more realistic model, prices do not fully reflect the information. The price system conveys some but not all information. We refer to this concept as the "partially efficient markets hypothesis." This, it should be noted, is not the same thing as the semistrong form described earlier.

The role of the FASB is somewhat different in a world of partially efficient markets than it is in a world of completely efficient markets. Reporting issues might not be trivial. It is not necessarily sufficient to allow firms to choose one method and provide disclosure to permit adjustments to other methods. Adjustments involve costs: education costs in knowing when and how to adjust and costs of analyzing and interpreting the data. If these costs are significant, the related reporting issue is certainly not trivial. Second, the role of financial reports may be broader than simply preventing individuals from earning abnormal returns from inside information. The FASB might perceive that its role is to reduce the noise in accounting numbers so that the resulting capital asset prices are more informative than they otherwise might be. Another possibility is that the FASB might perceive that its role is to reduce or reallocate society's cost of information by requiring disclosure of items that are otherwise searched for and analyzed by some individuals at great cost. The point is that the FASB's role seems to be broader than if the markets were completely efficient.

INFORMATIONAL EFFICIENCY AND ALLOCATIONAL EFFICIENCY

Even if stock markets were completely efficient, another issue would have to be raised. The efficient markets hypothesis refers essentially to the results of informational efficiency. Even if stock markets are highly competitive, prices react quickly to new information, and prices accurately reflect new information, do these imply an efficient allocation of scarce resources in the U.S. economy? Unfortunately, the answer appears to be no.

It should be pointed out that economists define efficiency as an allocation of resources such that no alternative feasible allocation can make at least one person better off without making any person worse off. Economists call this Pareto optimality. Notice that the term "efficiency" in the finance and accounting literature means something very different from that in the economics literature. Stock market efficiency necessarily leads to Pareto optimality if complete risk markets exist. "Complete markets" means that markets exist for all commodities or claims. In such a case, market prices are observable for each commodity or claim. Such a requirement is obviously not met in the real world. Stiglitz has examined a variety of other scenarios, and in each one stock market efficiency does not lead to allocational efficiency.[4]

Stiglitz depicts three levels at which one may analyze the efficiency of the market: exchange efficiency; production efficiency; and information efficiency. Exchange efficiency is a market state where, given the

[4]The arguments of this section are based on Joseph E. Stiglitz, "Pareto Optimality and Competition," *Journal of Finance*, May 1981, pp. 235–251.

available assets and available information, in a trade or trades of assets no person can be made better off without making someone worse off. Production efficiency is a market wherein assets are produced at such a level that no person can be made better off without making someone worse off, given the available technology, resources, and information. Information efficiency is a market state where information is gathered and utilized so that no person can be made better off without making someone worse off, given the existing assets and beliefs of investors. Note that stock market efficiency examines only information efficiency; it says nothing about exchange or production efficiency.

That stock market efficiency does not in general lead to Pareto optimality is fundamentally important to accounting. If accounting numbers have an impact on the allocation of scarce resources in the United States, accounting theorists and accounting standards-setters should focus on that impact. The question of the relationships between accounting and efficient stock markets takes on a secondary position to the critical question of the impact of accounting on the allocational efficiency of the U.S. society. Many accounting theorists and accounting standards-setters have been interested in allocational efficiency at least in a general sense, but this issue has been obscured somewhat recently by those who apparently believe that informational efficiency implies allocational efficiency. Since it does not, accounting theorists and accounting standards-setters must address the problems facing the profession with a scope broader than the efficient markets viewpoint.

To cement the arguments made thus far, a specific accounting issue will be examined: inflation accounting. Basically, the stock market may not be affected either by the requirements to disclose inflation accounting numbers or by the numbers themselves. Such a state of affairs does not imply that inflation accounting is useless, for the numbers may have an impact on other users.

For the purposes of this article, let us suppose that empirical tests prove beyond a shadow of doubt that constant dollar accounting and current cost accounting do not enhance the decision-making processes of investors and creditors. Does this supposition lead us to the conclusion that inflation accounting is an exercise in futility? If we consider the needs of labor, the federal government, internal management, and others, then inflation accounting may not prove to be useless and irrelevant, but it may become a basis for providing better economic decisions in U.S. society [10].

One facet involving inflation accounting deals with labor-management. When labor discusses its percentage increase in wages, it almost always adjusts wages for the inflation rate so that it can report the increase or decrease in real wages. That is certainly a sound approach to follow. United States businesses, however, report profits that are not adjusted for changing prices. These firms are reporting money profits, not real profits. Given that money profits are inevitably greater than real profits during an inflationary period, labor might use the corporate entity's own reported earnings data to support the ability of the entity to raise wages. Rates of profit growth are asserted to exceed rates of wage growth. The fact that the growth rates lack comparability is often overlooked. Would not all interested parties be better served if comparisons such as these were based on data that were comparable?

A second aspect of inflation accounting lies in the tax implications when earnings provide the tax base. Taxes are based primarily on income reported under the historical cost model. Congress often makes some attempts, however, to adjust for inflation, to encourage economic growth, or to achieve some other economic goal. No basis exists, however, to evaluate whether adjustments made to counter inflation have achieved that objective. If earnings were adjusted for the effects of price changes, aggregate income taxes might be different from taxes generated even when inflation adjustments have been attempted. Even if aggregate income taxes were unchanged, taxing on the basis of inflation accounting would produce different effects upon different segments of the economy.

Inflation accounting is by no means the only accounting issue that demonstrates possible economic effects outside the stock markets. Other issues include:

- Does SFAS No. 2, "Accounting for Research and Development Costs," affect the level of research and development activity in the United States?
- Does SFAS No. 5, "Accounting for Contingencies," affect the exchange efficiency of risky assets?
- Does SFAS No. 7, "Accounting and Reporting by Development Stage Enterprises," affect the formation of new business in the United States?
- Does SFAS No. 13, "Accounting for Leases," affect debt covenants? Does it affect the exchange of capital assets?
- Does SFAS No. 15, "Accounting by Debtors and Creditors for Troubled Debt Restructurings," affect the regulation of the banking industry?
- Does SFAS No. 21, "Suspension of the Reporting of Earnings per Share and Segment Information," affect the small business segment of society?
- Does SFAS No. 30, "Disclosure of Information About Major Customers," affect other customers and suppliers?
- Does SFAS No. 34, "Capitalization of Interest Cost," affect the trading of capital assets?
- Do SFAS Nos. 35, "Accounting and Reporting by Defined Benefit Pension Plans," and 36, "Disclosure of Pension Information," affect employees and labor unions?
- Does SFAS No. 52, "Foreign Currency Translation," affect international trading?

These questions all deal with possible economic effects other than stock market effects. Researchers should not be limited to the efficient markets paradigm. Many other economic factors are at work and need to be explored. Accounting researchers are encouraged to expand their horizons and investigate all the economic implications of accounting.

IMPLICATIONS FOR THE FASB

One of the strengths of the FASB relative to its predecessors is extensive research before issuing a major statement of financial accounting standards. Much of the funded research has focused on stock market reactions to certain events. We caution the FASB not to place undue emphasis on these studies. First, a variety of institutions are affected by accounting rules in addition to the stock markets. The FASB should also examine the effects, real or alleged, on these other institutions. Second, the efficient markets hypothesis does not seem to be descriptive of the real world with costly information. We find it difficult to interpret some of the results of capital market research because of the unrealistic assumptions employed, and so we are not sure what policy implications they have. Third, markets might be efficient informationally but not in an allocational sense. The FASB's purpose should, in our opinion, relate to issues of allocational efficiency and not simply to informational efficiency. Essentially, we feel that the world is far more complex and far more diverse than is captured by the efficient markets paradigm. While the concept is helpful in some re-spects, it would definitely be a mistake to formulate accounting policy on the basis that we live in a world of efficient markets. The FASB is constrained to operate in the real world: It needs to formulate policy given the fact that partially efficient markets characterizes the real world.

REFERENCES

1. William H. Beaver, "What Should Be the FASB's Objectives?" *The Journal of Accountancy,* Aug. 1973, pp. 49–56.

2. W. A. Paton and A. C. Littleton, *An Introduction to Corporate Accounting Standards* (American Accounting Association, 1940).

3. Edgar O. Edwards and Philip W. Bell, *The Theory and Measurement of Business Income* (University of California Press, 1961).

4. Norton M. Bedford, *Income Determination Theory: An Accounting Framework* (Addison-Wesley, 1965).

5. Raymond J. Chambers, *Accounting, Evaluation and Economic Behavior* (Prentice-Hall, 1966).

6. Yuji Ijiri, *Theory of Accounting Measurement* (American Accounting Association, 1975).

7. APB Statement No. 4, "Basic Concepts and Accounting Principles Underlying Financial Statements of Business Enterprises" (1970), especially Ch. 3.

8. Statement of Financial Accounting Concepts No. 1, "Objectives of Financial Reporting by Business Enterprises" (FASB, Nov. 1978).

9. *Preliminary Report of the Interoffice Task Force on Market Value Accounting* (Federal Home Loan Bank Board, Aug. 27, 1982).

10. Daryl N. Winn, "The Potential Effect of Alternative Measures on Public Policy and Resource Allocation," in *Economic Consequences of Financial Accounting Standards* (FASB, 1978), pp. 3–37.

QUESTIONS

1. Footnotes to financial statements should not be used to
   a. Describe the nature and effect of a change in accounting principles
   b. Identify substantial differences between book and tax income
   c. Correct an improper financial statement presentation
   d. Indicate bases for valuing assets

2. Assuming that none of the following have been disclosed in the financial statements, the most appropriate item for footnote disclosure is the
   a. Collection of all receivables subsequent to year end
   b. Revision of employees' pension plan
   c. Retirement of president of company and election of new president
   d. Material decrease in the advertising budget for the coming year and its anticipated effect upon income
3. The primary responsibility for the adequacy of disclosure in the financial statements and footnotes rests with the
   a. Partner assigned to the engagement
   b. Auditor in charge of fieldwork
   c. Staffman who drafts the statements and footnotes
   d. Client
4. Which of the following situations would require adjustment to or disclosure in the financial statements?
   a. A merger discussion
   b. The application for a patent on a new production process
   c. Discussions with a customer that could lead to a 40 percent increase in the client's sales
   d. The bankruptcy of a customer who regularly purchased 30 percent of the company's output
5. With respect to disclosure, the unqualified short-form report
   a. States that disclosure is adequate in the financial statements including the footnotes thereto
   b. States that disclosure is sufficiently adequate to make the statements not misleading
   c. States that all material items are disclosed in conformity with the generally accepted accounting principles
   d. Implies that disclosure is adequate in the financial statements including the footnotes thereto
6. Which of the following should be disclosed in the Summary of Significant Accounting Policies?
   a. Composition of plant assets
   b. Pro forma effect of retroactive application of an accounting change
   c. Basis of consolidation
   d. Maturity dates of long-term debt
7. An Accounting Principles Board Opinion is concerned with disclosure of accounting policies. A singular feature of this particular opinion is that it
   a. Calls for disclosure of every accounting policy followed by a reporting entity
   b. Applies to immaterial items whereas most opinions are concerned solely with material items

c. Applies also to accounting policy disclosures by not-for-profit entities, whereas most opinions are concerned solely with accounting practices of profit-oriented entities

d. Prescribes a rigid format for the disclosure of policies to be reported upon

8. Significant accounting policies may not be

a. Selected on the basis of judgment

b. Selected from existing acceptable alternatives

c. Unusual or innovative in application

d. Omitted from financial statement disclosure on the basis of judgment

9. The stock of Gates, Inc., is widely held, and the company is under the jurisdiction of the Securities and Exchange Commission. In the annual report, information about the significant accounting policies adopted by Gates should be

a. Omitted because it tends to confuse users of the report

b. Included as an integral part of the financial statements

c. Presented as supplementary information

d. Omitted because all policies must comply with the regulations of the Securities and Exchange Commission

10. The basic purpose of the securities laws of the United States is to regulate the issue of investment securities by

a. Providing a regulatory framework in those states which do not have their own securities laws

b. Requiring disclosure of all relevant facts so that investors can make informed decisions

c. Prohibiting the issuance of securities which the Securities and Exchange Commission determines are not of investment grade.

d. Channeling investment funds into uses which are economically most important

e. Ensuring that all shareholders have the right to vote in the election of directors

11. The Securities and Exchange Commission (SEC) was established in 1934 to help regulate the U.S. securities market. Which of the following statements is true concerning the SEC?

a. The SEC prohibits the sale of speculative securities.

b. The SEC regulates only securities offered for public sale.

c. Registration with the SEC guarantees the accuracy of the registrant's prospectus.

d. The SEC's initial influence and authority has diminished in recent years as the stock exchanges have become more organized and better able to police themselves.

e. The SEC's powers are broad with respect to enforcement of its reporting requirements as established in the 1933 and 1934 acts, but narrow with respect to new reporting requirements because these require confirmation by the Congress.

12. One of the major purposes of federal security regulation is to
   a. Establish the qualifications for accountants who are members of the profession
   b. Eliminate incompetent attorneys and accountants who participate in the registration of securities to be offered to the public
   c. Provide a set of uniform standards and tests for accountants, attorneys, and others who practice before the Securities and Exchange Commission.
   d. Provide sufficient information to the investing public who purchases securities in the marketplace

13. Under the Securities Act of 1933, subject to some exceptions and limitations, it is unlawful to use the mails or instruments of interstate commerce to sell or offer to sell a security to the public unless
   a. A surety bond sufficient to cover potential liability to investors is obtained and filed with the Securities and Exchange Commission
   b. The offer is made through underwriters qualified to offer the securities on a nationwide basis
   c. A registration statement has been properly filed with the Securities and Exchange Commission, has been found to be acceptable, and is in effect
   d. The Securities and Exchange Commission approves of the financial merit of the offering

14. Major, Major & Sharpe, CPAs, are the auditors of MacLain industries. In connection with the public offering of $10 million of MacLain securities, Major expressed an unqualified opinion as to the financial statements. Subsequent to the offering, certain misstatements and omissions are revealed. Major has been sued by the purchasers of the stock offered pursuant to the registration statement, which included the financial statements audited by Major. In the ensuing lawsuit by the MacLain investors, Major will be able to avoid liability if
   a. The errors and omissions were caused primarily by MacLain
   b. It can be shown that at least some of the investors did not actually read the audited financial statements
   c. It can prove due diligence in the audit of the financial statements of MacLain
   d. MacLain had expressly assumed any liability in connection with the public offering.

15. A major impact of the Foreign Corrupt Practices Act of 1977 is that registrants subject to the Securities Exchange Act of 1934 are now required to
   a. Keep records which reflect the transactions and dispositions of assets and maintain a system of internal accounting controls

b. Provide access to records by authorized agencies of the federal government

c. Record all correspondence with foreign nations

d. Prepare financial statements in accordance with international accounting standards

e. Produce full, fair, and accurate periodic reports on foreign commerce and/or foreign political party affiliations

16. The Securities and Exchange Commission's fraud rule prohibits trading on the basis of inside information of a business corporation's stock by
   a. Officers
   b. Officers and directors
   c. All officers, directors, and stockholders
   d. Officers, directors, and beneficial holders of 10 percent of the corporations stock
   e. Anyone who bases their trading activities on the inside information

17. A CPA is subject to criminal liability if the CPA
   a. Refuses to turn over the working papers to the client
   b. Performs an audit in a negligent manner
   c. Willfully omits a material fact required to be stated in a registration statement
   d. Willfully breaches the contract with the client

18. The concept of adequate disclosure continues to be one of the most important issues facing accountants, and disclosure may take various forms.

   Required:
   a. Discuss the various forms of disclosure available in published financial statements.
   b. Discuss the disclosure issues addressed by each of the following sources.
      i. The AICPA's Code of Professional Ethics.
      ii. The Securities Act of 1933.
      iii. The Securities Exchange Act of 1934.
      iv. The Foreign Corrupt Practices Act of 1977.
      v. The efficient market hypothesis.
      vi. Agency theory.
      vii. Human information processing research.

19. The Securities Act of 1933 and the Securities Exchange Act of 1934 established guidelines for the disclosures necessary and the protection from fraud when securities are offered to the public for sale.

   Required:
   a. Discuss the terms *going public* and *being public* as they relate to these pieces of legislation.
   b. Regulation S-X requires management to discuss and analyze certain financial conditions and results of operations. What are these items?

20. During the course of a year-end audit the following matters are brought to your attention:

1. Your client is a defendant in a patent infringement suit involving a material amount; you have received from the client's counsel a statement that a loss is not at all likely, though it is possible.
2. At the beginning of the year the client entered into a 10-year nonrenewable lease agreement. Provisions in the lease will require the client to make substantial reconditioning and restoration expenditures at the termination of the lease.
3. The client expects to recover a substantial amount in connection with a pending refund claim for a prior year's taxes. Although the claim is being contested, counsel for the company has confirmed this expectation.
4. Due to a general increase in the number of labor disputes and strikes, both within and outside the industry, there is an increased likelihood that the client will suffer a costly strike in the near future.

For each of the preceding situations, describe the accounting treatment you would recommend for both the current year and until the condition terminates. (Include in your discussion equally acceptable alternatives, if any.) Justify your recommended treatment for each situation.

21. Lancaster Electronics produces electronic components for sale to manufacturers of radios, television sets, and phonographic systems. In connection with his examination of Lancaster's financial statements for the year ended December 31, 1982, Don Olds, CPA, completed fieldwork two weeks ago. Mr. Olds now is evaluating the significance of the following items prior to preparing his auditor's report. Except as noted, none of these items has been disclosed in the financial statements or footnotes.

Item 1. Recently Lancaster interrupted its policy of paying cash dividends quarterly to its stockholders. Dividends were paid regularly through 1981, discontinued for all of 1981 to finance equipment for the company's new plant, and resumed in the first quarter of 1983. In the annual report, dividend policy is to be discussed in the president's letter to stockholders.

Item 2. A 10-year loan agreement, which the company entered into 3 years ago, provides that dividend payments may not exceed net income earned after taxes subsequent to the date of the agreement. The balance of retained earnings at the date of the loan agreement was $298,000. From that date through December 31, 1982, net income after taxes has totaled $360,000 and cash dividends have totaled $130,000. Based on these data, the staff auditor assigned to this review concluded that there was no retained earnings restriction at December 31, 1982.

Item 3. The company's new manufacturing plant building, which cost $600,000 and has an estimated life of 25 years, is leased from the Sixth

National Bank at an annual rental of $100,000. The company is obligated to pay property taxes, insurance, and maintenance. At the conclusion of its 10-year noncancelable lease, the company has the option of purchasing the property for $1. In Lancaster's income statement the rental payment is reported on a separate line.

Item 4. A major electronics firm has introduced a line of products that will compete directly with Lancaster's primary line, now being produced in the specially designed new plant. Because of manufacturing innovations, a competitor's line will be of comparable quality but priced 50 percent below Lancaster's line. The competitor announced its new line during the week following completion of fieldwork. Mr. Olds read the announcement in the newspaper and discussed the situation by telephone with Lancaster executives. Lancaster will meet the lower prices that are high enough to cover variable manufacturing and selling expenses but will permit recovery of only a portion of fixed costs.

For each of the preceding items, discuss any additional disclosures in the financial statements and footnotes that the auditor should recommend to his client. (The cumulative effect of the four items should not be considered.)

22. You have completed your audit of Carter Corporation and its consolidated subsidiaries for the year ended December 31, 1982, and were satisfied with the results of your examination. You have examined the financial statements of Carter Corporation for the past three years. The corporation is now preparing its annual report to shareholders. The report will include the consolidated financial statements of Carter Corporation and its subsidiaries and your short-form auditor's report. During your audit the following matters came to your attention.

1. The Internal Revenue Service is currently examining the corporation's 1980 federal income tax return and is questioning the amount of a deduction claimed by the corporation's domestic subsidiary for a loss sustained in 1979. The examination is still in process and any additional tax liability is indeterminable at this time. The corporation's tax counsel believes that there will be no substantial additional tax liability.

2. A vice-president who is also a stockholder resigned on December 31, 1982, after an argument with the president. The vice-president is soliciting proxies from stockholders and expects to obtain sufficient proxies to gain control of the board of directors so that a new president will be appointed. The president plans to have a footnote prepared that would include information of the pending proxy fight, management's accomplishments over the years, and an appeal by management for the support of stockholders.

3. In 1982 the corporation changed its method of accounting for the invest-

ment credit. An investment credit of $121,000 deferred in prior years was credited to income and the full 1982 investment credit of $50,000 was recorded as a reduction of income after taxes for 1982 were increased by $45,000. You approved of this change as an acceptable alternative accounting treatment.

Required:

a. Prepare the footnotes, if any, that you would suggest for the foregoing listed items.

b. State your reasons for not making disclosure by footnote for each of the listed items for which you did not prepare a footnote.

BIBLIOGRAPHY

Abdel-Khalik, A. Rashad. "The Efficient Market Hypothesis and Accounting Data: A Point of View, *The Accounting Review* (October 1972), pp. 791–793.

Adelberg, Arthur H., and Richard A. Lewis. "Financial Reports Can Be Made More Understandable." *Journal of Accountancy* (June 1980), pp. 44–50.

American Accounting Association. "Report of the 1976–77 Committee on Human Information Processing." *Committee Reports,* Volume 1978–2 (August 1977).

Baker, H. Kent, and John A. Haslem. "Information Needs of Individual Investors." *Journal of Accountancy* (November 1973), pp. 64–69.

Beaver, William H. "The Behavior of Security Prices and Its Implications for Accounting Research (Methods)." In American Accounting Association, "Report of the Committee on Research Methodology in Accounting." *The Accounting Review.* Supplement to Vol. 47 (1972), pp. 407–437. Also in Robert R. Sterling, ed., *Research Methodology in Accounting.* Lawrence, Kansas: Scholars Book Co., 1972, pp. 9–37.

Beaver, William H. "Current Trends in Corporate Disclosure." *Journal of Accountancy* (January 1978), pp. 44–52.

Bedford, Norton M. *Extension in Accounting Disclosure.* Englewood Cliffs, N.J.: Prentice-Hall, Inc., 1973.

Benjamin, James J., and Keith G. Stanga. "Differences in Disclosure Needs of Major Users of Financial Statements." *Accounting and Business Research* (Summer 1977), pp. 187–192.

Benston, George J. "The Value of the SEC's Accounting Disclosure Requirements." *The Accounting Review,* (July 1969), pp. 515–532.

Benston, George J. "Evaluation of the Securities Exchange Act of 1934." *Financial Executive* (May 1974), pp. 28–36, 40–42.

Bierman, Harold, Jr. "The Implications to Accounting of Efficient Markets and the Capital Asset Pricing Model." *The Accounting Review* (July 1974), pp. 557–562.

Briloff, Abraham J. *Unaccountable Accounting*. New York: Harper & Row, 1972.

Briloff, Abraham J. *More Debits Than Credits*. New York: Harper & Row, 1976.

Brown, Frank A., and Philip L. Kintzele. "An Analysis of Current Disaggregate Reporting Requirements." *The Ohio CPA* (Spring 1978), pp. 47–51.

Brown, Victor H. "The Economic Impact Of Financial Accounting Standards." *Financial Executive* (September 1979), pp. 32–36, 38–39.

Burton, John C. "Ethics in Corporate Financial Disclosure." *Financial Analysts Journal* (January–February 1972), pp. 49–53.

Carmichael, D. R. *The Auditor's Reporting Obligation*. New York: American Institute of Certified Public Accountants, 1972.

Carmichael, D. R. "Standards for Financial Reporting." *Journal of Accountancy* (May 1979), pp. 76–84.

Chambers, Anne E., and Stephen H. Penman. "Timeliness of Reporting and the Stock Price Reaction to Earnings Announcements." *Journal of Accounting Research* (Spring 1984), pp. 21–47.

Chambers, R. J. "Stock Market Prices and Accounting Research." *Abacus* (June 1974), pp. 39–54.

Chandra, Gyan. "Study of the Consensus on Disclosure among Public Accountants and Security Analysis." *The Accounting Review* (October 1974), pp. 733–742.

Chazen, Charles, and Benjamin Benson. "Fitting GAAP to Smaller Businesses. *Journal of Accountancy* (February 1978), pp. 46–51.

Clark, John L., and Pieter Elgers. "Forecasted Income Statements: An Investor Perspective." *The Accounting Review* (October 1973), pp. 668–678.

Collins, Frank, and John A. Yeakel. "Range Estimates in Financial Statements: Help or Hindrance?" *Journal of Accountancy* (July 1979), pp. 73–78.

Downers, David, and Thomas R. Dyckman. "A Critical Look at the Efficient Market Empirical Research Literature as it Relates to Accounting Information." *The Accounting Review* (April 1973), pp. 300–317.

Duff and Phelps, Inc. *A Management Guide to Better Financial Reporting: Ideas for Strengthening Reports to Shareholders and the Financial Analysts's*

Perspective on Financial Reporting Practices. Chicago: Arthur Anderson & Co., 1976.

Dyckman, Thomas R., David H. Downes, and Robert P. Magee. *Efficient Capital Markets and Accounting: A Critical Analysis.* Englewood Cliffs, N.J.: Prentice-Hall, Inc., 1975.

Gibson, Charles H., and Patricia A. Boyer. "The Need for Disclosure of Uniform Financial Ratios." *Journal of Accountancy* (May 1980), pp. 78, 80, 82, 84.

Gonedes, Nicholas J. "Efficient Capital Markets and External Accounting." *The Accounting Review* (January 1972), pp. 11–21.

Groves, Ray J. "Corporate Disclosure in the 1980's." *Financial Executive* (June 1980), pp. 14–19.

Kripke, Homer. "A Search for a Meaningful Securities Disclosure Policy." *The Arthur Andersen Chronicle* (July 1976), pp. 14–32.

Libby, Robert, and Barry L. Lewis. "Human Information Processing Research in Accounting: The State of the Art." *Accounting, Organizations and Society,* Vol. 2, No. 3 (1977), pp. 246–268.

Mautz, R. K., and William G. May. *Financial Disclosure in a Competitive Economy.* New York: Financial Executives Research Foundation, 1978.

Mayer-Sommer, Alan P. "Understanding and Acceptance of the Efficient Markets Hypothesis and its Accounting Implications." *The Accounting Review* (January 1979), pp. 88–106.

Mueller, Willard F. "Corporate Disclosure: The Public's Right to Know." In Alfred Rappaport, ed., *Corporate Financial Reporting.* Chicago: Commerce Clearing House, Inc., 1971, pp. 67–93.

Pastena, Victor. "Some Evidence on the SEC's System of Continuous Disclosure." *The Accounting Review* (October 1979), pp. 776–783.

Pointer, Larry G., and Richard G. Schroeder. *An Introduction to the Securities and Exchange Commission.* Plano, Tex.: Business Publications, Inc., 1986.

Singhvi, Surendra S. "Corporate Management's Inclination to Disclose Financial Information." *Financial Analysts Journal* (July–August 1972), pp. 66–73.

Skekel, Ted D. "Management Reports of Financial Statements." *The CPA Journal* (July 1979), pp. 32–37.

Skousen, K. Fred. *An Introduction to the SEC,* 2nd ed. Cincinnati: South-Western Publishing Co., 1980.

Stanga, Keith G. "Disclosure in Published Annual Reports." *Financial Management* (Winter 1976), pp. 42–53.

Worthington, James S. "Footnotes: Readability or Liability?" *The CPA Journal* (May 1978), pp. 27–32.

Wyatt, Arthur R. "Efficient Market Theory: Its Impact on Accounting." *Journal of Accountancy* (February 1983), pp. 56–65.

Index